D1094139

Persuasive Prose

A READER

PRENTICE-HALL INTERNATIONAL, INC., *London*
PRENTICE-HALL OF AUSTRALIA, PTY., LTD., *Sydney*
PRENTICE-HALL OF CANADA, LTD., *Toronto*
PRENTICE-HALL FRANCE, S.A.R.L., *Paris*
PRENTICE-HALL OF INDIA (PRIVATE) LTD., *New Delhi*
PRENTICE-HALL OF JAPAN, INC., *Tokyo*
PRENTICE-HALL DE MEXICO, S.A., *Mexico City*

Persuasive Prose

A READER

edited by

RICHARD E. HUGHES *and* P. ALBERT DUHAMEL

Professors of English, Boston College

Prentice-Hall, Inc. Englewood Cliffs, New Jersey

Library of Congress Catalog Card No.: 64-17607
PRINTED IN THE UNITED STATES OF AMERICA
[66143-C]

Preface

To the Teacher

We will begin by acting on a sound rhetorical principle, and make our intentions clear.

First, as to the selections themselves: Because rhetoric is a *skill* and not a *subject matter,* we have included essays dealing with the natural sciences, the social sciences, the arts, and belles-lettres. Persuasiveness is not limited to any one field of writing, and the range of the selections is meant to make that point. Nor are the selections limited to any one time-span—selections from the fourteenth century to the present time are included here. But we have not chosen a selection such as Matthew Arnold's comments on culture because it is a classic or because it is "old." We have included it because Arnold has said it best. We have not chosen to include Wylie Sypher's analysis of mannerist art because it is novel or "new." We have included it because Sypher has said it best. We have chosen the best examples we could find of each phase of rhetoric.

Second, as to the editorial material which accompanies the selections: It is our experience that the imaginative teacher and the perceptive student both resent an overengineered text, with exhaustive introductions, questions which leave no room for discovery, and theme assignments which discourage initiative. We offer only as much editorial machinery as will introduce the reader to crucial rhetorical principles. Education is participation, not observation, and a classroom dialogue which develops out of basic principles and absorption of the selections themselves will discover better questions and more valuable writing assignments than can be provided by any amount of textual apparatus. This is the belief underlying our text on rhetoric (*Rhetoric: Principles and Usage,* Prentice-Hall, 1962), and we have found no reasons for abandoning that belief in preparing this reader.

Finally, we intend to admit our debt to Mr. Paul O'Connell and Mr. Richard Lambert, both of Prentice-Hall, who have recognized the value of rhetoric studies and have let us have our say on the subject. We would also like to thank Miss Mary Turnbull and Barry A. Jedrick whose insistence upon precision kept us from many inaccuracies. Those that remain are entirely our own.

To the Student

We intend, with this collection of readings, to accomplish the following:

First, to make the reader aware that a *persuasive* presentation of an idea is preferable to a simply *adequate* presentation of that same idea. We believe that all good writing ought to be based on an understanding of *rhetoric,* which we define as the use of all the available means of persuasion in all writing situations.

Second, to demonstrate that *persuasive* or *rhetorical* presentation is to be achieved through a strategic use of all the elements of composition: Organization, forms of argument, sentence style, and diction. The student must be concerned, at this stage of his university education, more with the expository than with the narrative or descriptive arts of composition; therefore the examples are primarily expositions (with a few relevant exceptions). These essays are arranged in an order of increasing specialization, climaxed by what must always be of central concern to the rhetorically minded writer: A consideration of the audience for whom the writing is intended, and an adaptation of all the devices of rhetoric to the aim of interesting, convincing, and persuading that audience.

This collection of readings moves, therefore, from a study of the major expository forms to a consideration of types of arguments, sentence styles, and range of diction, up to the final point where writer, subject, and audience may cooperate in such a way that *persuasion* may take place. The ideas involved in the examples are important, diversified, and challenging; these essays are meant to provoke not only an awareness of their own formal efficiency, but also a realization that rhetoric is a study essentially related to the effective presentation of issues and the educated response to those issues.

R. E. H.

P. A. D.

Contents

VI *Style and the Forms of Thought* 513

Persuasive Prose

A READER

I Focus

THESIS AS HYPOTHESIS AND THESIS AS CALL TO ACTION

Unless he composes solely for his own amusement or satisfaction, the writer is conscious of an audience and conscious that the audience is important to him. He wants *assent;* he hopes for acceptance; he wants his ideas to be considered. Important as all the mechanics of composition are, mere mechanical facility in writing will not win that assent, acceptance, or consideration. There must be a hard core of ideas, a focus around which all the separate parts of the composition will congregate in a unified, coherent, and emphatic way. Such a hard core is referred to in rhetoric as an *argument,* by which is meant the setting forth of a statement or theme or point of view. Whether he is narrating, describing, revealing, or debating, the writer has come to a conclusion on some issue. He writes so that his audience will recognize and perhaps subscribe to his conclusion. A writer wishes his audience to see something as he has seen it. He has designs on his reader's reason and imagination. He has an *argument* to present.

This argument, or focus, may take several shapes. It may be a simple assertion of fact or what the author thinks of as fact; the audience assent in this case would be recognition. It may be the author's opinion of a certain matter, a preference he holds; the assent he hopes to achieve is an admission by the audience that his opinion is worth considering. Finally, it may be a judgment, a thoughtful conclusion which the author has reached on a subject after careful consideration of evidence; here the assent he looks for is the audience's adopting *his* judgment as the *right* judgment. No matter what the focus may be—assertion, opinion, or judgment—the writer is making a claim on the reactions of his audience. He is trying to *persuade* them to perceive, to admit, or to agree. But if he has no focus, he will accomplish none of these.

This necessary focus we shall term the *thesis*. The focusing thesis will ordinarily be explicitly stated in the composition. When this happens, it is referred to as *the thesis sentence* and is recognized as the single point to which all details must be referred. The thesis may also be implicit, so clearly implied and strongly suggested that to openly state it would be redundant. Whether explicit or implicit, the thesis is the center of the composition; all other elements will exist as examples of, proofs for, or amplifications of that thesis.

The thesis will make one of two different demands of an audience. If it is an *active* thesis, it will call for an action or a decision. If it is a *hypothetical* or *cognitive* thesis, it will call for a consideration of an idea, but not an immediate action or final decision.

If the thesis is recognizable, the organization firm, and the supporting details effective, the writer will be well on his way to securing that assent which he wants the audience to give. But the most important element is focus, which is central to the purposes of persuasion.

Carl G. Jung

The psychological theories of Doctor Carl G. Jung (1875–1961) have become almost as well known as those of Sigmund Freud. Freud studied dreams and myths to come to a better understanding of the sex drives, which he considered fundamental in all human behavior. Jung analyzed the same material in an attempt to arrive at a better understanding of the collective unconscious, which he believed strongly influenced much of human behavior. The following essay, originally published in the Journal of St. Bartholomew's Hospital *(London) in 1936, was an early attempt on Jung's part to interest the British medical profession in his hypothesis. Within the last thirty years many psychiatrists have adopted Jung's concepts, finding in them a better explanation of some quirks of human behavior than Freud's. Jung's ideas have also been widely used by literary critics as a means of arriving at interpretations of poems and novels whose symbols had previously proved mystifying.*

The following essay is particularly interesting because of the straightforward manner in which Jung goes about defining his terms, stating his thesis as a hypothesis which he considers worthy of further exploration, and suggesting how he hopes to go about collecting evidence to prove or disprove it. The entire essay is a calm invitation to interested people to consider the hypothesis, to criticize it, and to help him prove or disprove it.

THE CONCEPT OF THE COLLECTIVE UNCONSCIOUS *

Probably none of my empirical concepts has met with so much misunderstanding as the idea of the collective unconscious. In what follows I shall try to give (1) a definition of the concept, (2) a description of what it means for psychology, (3) an explanation of the method of proof, and (4) an example.

1. DEFINITION

The collective unconscious is a part of the psyche which can be negatively distinguished from a personal unconscious by the fact that it does not, like the latter, owe its existence to personal experience and is consequently not a personal acquisition. While the personal unconscious is made up essentially of contents which have at one time been conscious but which have disappeared from consciousness through having been forgotten or repressed, the con-

* Reprinted with permission from The Bollingen Foundation.

tents of the collective unconscious have never been in consciousness, and therefore have never been individually acquired, but owe their existence exclusively to heredity. Whereas the personal unconscious consists for the most part of *complexes*, the content of the collective unconscious is made up essentially of *archetypes*.

The concept of the archetype, which is an indispensable correlate of the idea of the collective unconscious, indicates the existence of definite forms in the psyche which seem to be present always and everywhere. Mythological research calls them "motifs"; in the psychology of primitives they correspond to Lévy-Bruhl's concept of *représentations collectives*, and in the field of comparative religion they have been defined by Hubert and Mauss as "categories of the imagination." Adolf Bastian long ago called them "elementary" or "primordial thoughts." From these references it should be clear enough that my idea of the archetype—literally a pre-existent form—does not stand alone but is something that is recognized and named in other fields of knowledge.

My thesis, then, is as follows: In addition to our immediate consciousness, which is of a thoroughly personal nature and which we believe to be the only empirical psyche (even if we tack on the personal unconscious as an appendix), there exists a second psychic system of a collective, universal, and impersonal nature which is identical in all individuals. This collective unconscious does not develop individually but is inherited. It consists of pre-existent forms, the archetypes, which can only become conscious secondarily and which give definite form to certain psychic contents.

2. THE PSYCHOLOGICAL MEANING OF THE COLLECTIVE UNCONSCIOUS

Medical psychology, growing as it did out of professional practice, insists on the *personal* nature of the psyche. By this I mean the views of Freud and Adler. It is a *psychology of the person*, and its etiological or causal factors are regarded almost wholly as personal in nature. Nonetheless, even this psychology is based on certain general biological factors, for instance on the sexual instinct or on the urge of self-assertion, which are by no means merely personal peculiarities. It is forced to do this because it lays claim to being an explanatory science. Neither of these views would deny the existence of *a priori* instincts common to man and animals alike, or that they have a significant influence on personal psychology. Yet instincts are impersonal, universally distributed, hereditary factors of a dynamic of motivating character, which very often fail so completely to reach consciousness that modern psychotherapy is faced with the task of helping the patient to become conscious of them. Moreover, the instincts are not vague and indefinite by nature, but are specifically formed motive forces which, long before there is any consciousness, and in spite of any degree of consciousness later on, pursue their inherent goals. Consequently they form very close analogies to the archetypes, so close, in fact, that there is good reason for supposing that the archetypes are the unconscious images of the instincts themselves, in other words, that they are *patterns of instinctual behavior.*

The hypothesis of the collective unconscious is, therefore, no more daring than to assume there are instincts. One admits readily that human activity is influenced to a high degree by instincts, quite apart from the rational motivations of the conscious mind. So if the assertion is made that our imagination, perception, and thinking are likewise influenced by inborn and universally present formal elements, it seems to me that a normally functioning intelligence can discover in this idea just as much or just as little mysticism as in the theory of instincts. Although this reproach of mysticism has frequently been leveled at my concept, I must emphasize yet again that the concept of the collective unconscious is neither a speculative nor a philosophical but an empirical matter. The question is simply this: are there or are there not unconscious, universal forms of this kind? If they exist, then there is a region of the psyche which one can call the collective unconscious. It is true that the diagnosis of the collective unconscious is not always an easy task. It is not sufficient to point out the often obviously archetypal nature of unconscious products, for these can just as well be derived from acquisitions through language and education. Cryptomnesia should also be ruled out, which it is almost impossible to do in certain cases. In spite of all these difficulties, there remain enough individual instances showing the autochthonous revival of mythological motifs to put the matter beyond any reasonable doubt. But if such an unconscious exists at all, psychological explanation must take account of it and submit certain alleged personal etiologies to sharper criticism.

What I mean can perhaps best be made clear by a concrete example. You have probably read Freud's discussion of a certain picture by Leonardo da Vinci: St. Anne with the Virgin Mary and the Christ-child. Freud interprets this remarkable picture in terms of the fact that Leonardo himself had two mothers. This causality is personal. We shall not linger over the fact that this picture is far from unique, nor over the minor inaccuracy that St. Anne happens to be the grandmother of Christ and not, as required by Freud's interpretation, the mother, but shall simply point out that interwoven with the apparently personal psychology there is an impersonal motif well known to us from other fields. This is the motif of the *dual mother,* an archetype to be found in many variants in the field of mythology and comparative religion and forming the basis of numerous *représentations collectives.* I might mention, for instance, the motif of the *dual descent,* that is, descent from human and divine parents, as in the case of Heracles, who received immortality through being unwittingly adopted by Hera. What was a myth in Greece was actually a ritual in Egypt: Pharaoh was both human and divine by nature. In the birth chambers of the Egyptian temples Pharaoh's second (divine) conception and birth is depicted on the walls; he is "twice-born." It is an idea that underlies all rebirth mysteries, Christianity included. Christ himself is "twice-born": Through his baptism in the Jordan he was regenerated and reborn from water and spirit. Consequently, in the Roman liturgy the font is designated the *uterus ecclesiae,* and, as you can read in the Roman missal, it is called this even today, in the "benediction of the font" on Holy Saturday before Easter. Further, according to an early Christian-Gnostic idea, the spirit which appeared in the form of a dove was interpreted as Sophia-Sapientia—Wisdom and the Mother of Christ. Thanks to this motif of the dual birth, children today, instead of having good and evil fairies who magically "adopt" them at birth with blessings and curses, are given sponsors—a "godfather" and a "godmother."

The idea of a second birth is found at all times and in all places. In the earliest beginnings of medicine it was a magical means of healing; in many religions it is the central mystical experience; it is the key idea in medieval, occult philosophy; and last, but not least, it is an infantile fantasy occurring in numberless children, large and small, who believe that their parents are not their real parents but merely fosterparents to whom they were handed over. Benvenuto Cellini also had this idea, as he himself related in his autobiography.

Now it is absolutely out of the question that all individuals who believe in a dual descent have in reality always had two mothers, or conversely that those few who shared Leonardo's fate have infected the rest of humanity with their complex. Rather, one cannot avoid the assumption that the universal occurrence of the dual-birth motif, together with the fantasy of the two mothers, answers an omnipresent human need which is reflected in these motifs. If Leonardo da Vinci did in fact portray his two mothers in St. Anne and Mary—which I doubt—he nonetheless was only expressing something which countless millions of people before and after him have believed. The vulture symbol (which Freud also discusses in the work mentioned) makes this view all the more plausible. With some justification he quotes as the source of the symbol the *Hieroglyphica* of Horapollo, a book much in use in Leonardo's time. There you read that vultures are female only and symbolize the mother. They conceive through the wind (*pneuma*). This word took on the meaning of "spirit" chiefly under the influence of Christianity. Even in the account of the miracle of Pentecost the pneuma still has the double meaning of wind and spirit. This fact, in my opinion, points without doubt to Mary, who, a virgin by nature, conceived through the pneuma, like a vulture. Furthermore, according to Horapollo, the vulture also symbolizes Athene, who sprang unbegotten directly from the head of Zeus, was a virgin, and knew only spiritual motherhood. All this is really an allusion to Mary and the rebirth motif. There is not a shadow of evidence that Leonardo meant anything else by his picture. Even if it is correct to assume that he identified himself with the Christ-child, he was in all probability representing the mythological dual-mother motif and by no means his own personal prehistory. And what about all the other artists who had painted the same theme? Surely not all of them had two mothers?

Let us now transpose Leonardo's case to the field of the neuroses, and assume that a patient with a mother complex is suffering from the delusion that the cause of his neurosis lies in his having really had two mothers. The personal interpretation would have to admit that he is right—and yet it would be quite wrong. For in reality the cause of his neurosis would lie in the reactivation of the dual-mother archetype, quite regardless of whether he had one mother or two mothers, because, as we have seen, this archetype functions individually and historically without any reference to the relatively rare occurrence of dual motherhood.

In such a case, it is of course tempting to presuppose so simple and personal a cause, yet the hypothesis is not only inexact but totally false. It is admittedly difficult to understand how a dual-mother motif—unknown to a physician trained only in medicine—could have so great a determining power as to produce the effect of a traumatic condition. But if we consider the tremendous powers that lie hidden in the mythological and religious sphere in man, the etiological significance of the archetype appears less fantastic In numerous cases of neurosis the cause of the disturbance lies in the very fact that the psychic life of the patient lacks the co-operation of these motive forces. Nevertheless a purely personalistic psychology, by reducing everything to personal causes, tries its level best to deny the existence of archetypal motifs and even seeks to destroy them by personal analysis. I consider this rather a dangerous procedure which cannot be justified medically. Today you can judge better than you could twenty years ago the nature of the forces involved. Can we not see how a whole nation is reviving an archaic symbol, yes, even archaic religious forms, and how this mass emotion is influencing and revolutionizing the life of the individual in a catastrophic manner? The man of the past is alive in us today to a degree undreamt of before the war, and in the last analysis what is the fate of great nations but a summation of the psychic changes in individuals?

So far as a neurosis is really only a private affair having its roots exclusively in personal causes, archetypes play no role at all. But if it is a question of a general incompatibility or an otherwise injurious condition productive of neuroses in relatively large numbers of individuals, then we assume the presence of constellated archetypes. Since neuroses are in most cases not just private concerns, but *social* phenomena, we must assume that archetypes are constellated in these cases too. The archetype corresponding to the situation is activated, and as a result those explosive and dangerous forces hidden in the archetype come into action, frequently with unpredictable consequences. There is no lunacy people under the domination of an archetype will not fall a prey to. If thirty years ago anyone had dared to predict that our psychological development was tending towards a revival of the medieval persecutions of the Jews, that Europe would again tremble before the Roman fasces and the tramp of legions, that people would once more give the Roman salute, as two thousand years ago, and that instead of the Christian Cross an archaic swastika would lure onward millions of warriors ready for death—why, that man would have been hooted at as a mystical fool. And today? Surprising as it may seem, all this absurdity is a horrible reality. Private life, private etiologies, and private neuroses have become almost a fiction in the world of today. The man of the past who lived in a world of archaic *représentations collectives* has risen again into very visible and painfully real life, and this not only in a few unbalanced individuals but in many millions of people.

There are as many archetypes as there are typical situations in life. Endless repetition has engraved these experiences into our psychic constitution, not in the form of images filled with content, but at first only as *forms without content,* representing merely the possibility of a certain type of perception and action. When a situation occurs which corresponds to a given archetype, that archetype becomes activated and a compulsiveness appears, which, like an instinctual drive, gains its way against all reason and will, or else produces a conflict of pathological dimensions, that is to say, a neurosis.

3. METHOD OF PROOF

We must now turn to the question of how existence of archetypes can be proved. Since archetypes are supposed to produce certain psychic forms, we must discuss how and where one can get hold of the material demonstrating these forms. The main source, then, is *dreams,* which have the advantage of being involuntary, spontaneous products of the unconscious psyche, and are therefore pure products of nature, not falsified by any conscious purpose. By questioning the individual one can ascertain which of the motifs appearing in the dream are known to him. From those which are unknown to him we must naturally exclude all motifs which *might* be known to him, as for instance—to revert to the case of Leonardo—the vulture symbol. We are not sure whether Leonardo took this symbol from Horapollo or not, although it would have been perfectly possible for an educated person of that time, because in those days artists were distinguished for their wide knowledge of the humanities. Therefore, although the bird motif is an archetype par excellence, its existence in Leonardo's fantasy would still prove nothing. Consequently, we must look for motifs which could not possibly be known to the dreamer and yet behave functionally in his dream in such a manner as to coincide with the functioning of the archetype known from historical sources.

Another source for the material we need is to be found in "active imagination." By this I mean a sequence of fantasies produced by deliberate concentration. I have found that the existence of unrealized, unconscious fantasies increases the frequency and intensity of dreams, and that when these fantasies are made conscious the dreams change their character and become weaker and less frequent. From this I have drawn the conclusion that dreams often contain fantasies which "want" to become conscious. The sources of dreams are often repressed instincts which have a natural tendency to influence the conscious mind. In cases of this sort, the patient is simply given the task of contemplating any one fragment of fantasy that seems significant to him—a chance idea, perhaps, or something he has become conscious of in a dream—until its context becomes visible, that is to say, the relevant associative material in which it is embedded. It is not a question of the "free association" recommended by Freud for the purpose of dream-analysis, but of elaborating the fantasy by observing the further fantasy material that adds itself to the fragment in a natural manner.

This is not the place to enter upon a technical discussion of the method. Suffice it to say that the resultant sequence of fantasies relieves the unconscious and produces material rich in archetypal images and associations. Obviously, this is a method that can only be used in certain carefully selected cases. The method is not entirely without danger, because it may carry the patient too far away from reality. A warning against thoughtless application is therefore in place.

Finally, very interesting sources of archetypal material are to be found in the delusions of paranoiacs, the fantasies observed in trance states, and the dreams of early childhood, from the third to the fifth year. Such material is available in profusion, but it is valueless unless one can adduce convincing mythological parallels. It does not, of course, suffice simply to connect a dream about a snake with the mythological occurrence of snakes, for who is to guarantee that the functional meaning of the snake in the dream is the same as in the mythological setting? In order to draw a valid parallel, it is necessary to know the functional meaning of the individual symbol and then to find out whether the apparently parallel mythological symbol has a similar context and therefore the same functional meaning. Establishing such facts not only requires lengthy and wearisome researches, but is also an ungrateful subject for demonstration. As the symbols must not be torn out of their context, one has to launch forth into exhaustive descriptions, personal as well as symbological, and this is practically impossible in the framework of a lecture. I have repeatedly tried it at the risk of sending one half of my audience to sleep. . . .[1]

TOPICS FOR DISCUSSION AND WRITING

1. What sentence, in your opinion, provides the clearest definition of what Jung means by the collective unconscious? Why did you choose that particular sentence? Are there other sentences which also contain approximate definitions of the collective unconscious? Can you construct a definition which is clearer and more precise than any to be found in the essay?
2. What is the difference between the personal unconscious and the collective unconscious? How does Jung's conception of the unconscious

[1] The remainder of the essay is devoted to a detailed and clinical demonstration of how a particular dream can be explained only in terms of an archetypal memory.

differ from Freud's? What is the difference between a personal explanation and a collective explanation?

3. What does Jung mean by an archetypal form? Which of his illustrations of archetypal forms is the clearest for you? How many archetypal forms are there? Is it possible to give a definite number?
4. What happens when an individual encounters a situation corresponding to an archetypal form?
5. What is the relationship between instincts and archetypes? Why does Jung emphasize the similarities?
6. What is the thesis, or focus, of Jung's essay (what is his proposition)? What is he trying to prove? What is the subject term of his proposition? What is the predicate term? In other words, what is he writing about and what is he affirming about it?
7. How does Jung suggest he will go about seeking proof for the existence of the collective unconscious and of the various archetypes? What are some of the sources of proof that he seeks to explore?
8. Why must he look for specialized motifs to prove his thesis? What characteristics is he most anxious to find in the motifs or themes that he explores?

Henry David Thoreau

*Henry David Thoreau (1817–1862) disagreed with several aspects of his social environment: He deplored the growing specialization which decreed that a man should be proficient at one skill only; he would not accept a centralized government which ruled from above and was aloof from the individual; he refused to accept coercion in any form, legalized or not. Instead, Thoreau believed in the doctrine of self-reliance, whereby any man is sufficient unto himself; he insisted on the rights and freedoms of the individual; he preached a policy of passive resistance against any governmental interference in the life of the private person. His account of his two-year sojourn at Walden Pond, near Concord, Massachusetts (*Walden, *1854) demonstrated his own self-reliance. His essay* On the Duty of Civil Disobedience *(1849) is the statement of his belief in the necessary freedoms and the right to resist whatever authority interferes with those freedoms. Thoreau's principle of passive resistance has been resurrected in this century by the Indian leader Mohandas Gandhi (1869–1948) and more recently by the leaders of the integration movement in both North and South.*

Civil Disobedience

I heartily accept the motto, *That government is best which governs least,* and I should like to see it acted up to more rapidly and systematically. Carried out, it finally amounts to this, which also I believe, *That government is best which governs not at all,* and when men are prepared for it, that will be the kind of government which they will have. Government is at best but an expedient, but most governments are usually, and all governments are sometimes, inexpedient. The objections which have been brought against a standing army, and they are many and weighty, and deserve to prevail, may also at last be brought against a standing government. The standing army is only an arm of the standing government. The government itself, which is only the mode which the people have chosen to execute their will, is equally liable to be abused and perverted before the people can act through it. Witness the present Mexican war, the work of comparatively a few individuals using the standing government as their tool; for, in the outset, the people would not have consented to this measure.

This American government—what is it but a tradition, though a recent one, endeavoring to transmit itself unimpaired to posterity, but each instant losing some of its integrity? It has not the vitality and force of a single living man, for a single man can bend it to his will. It is a sort of wooden gun to the people themselves. But it is not the less necessary for this; for the people must have some complicated machinery or other, and hear its din, to satisfy that idea of government which they have. Governments show thus how successfully men can be imposed on, even impose on themselves, for their own advantage. It is excellent, we must all allow. Yet this government never of itself furthered any enterprise, but by the alacrity with which it got out of its way. *It* does not keep the country free. *It* does not settle the West. *It* does not educate. The character inherent in the American people has done all that has been accomplished; and it would have done somewhat more, if the government had not sometimes got in its way. For government is an expedient by which men would fain succeed in letting one another alone; and, as has been said, when it is most expedient, the governed are most let alone by it. Trade and commerce, if they were not made of indiarubber, would never manage to bounce over the obstacles which legislators are continually putting in their way; and, if one were to judge these men wholly by the effects of their actions and not partly by their intentions, they would deserve to be classed and punished with those mischievous persons who put obstructions on the railroads.

But, to speak practically and as a citizen, unlike those who call themselves no-government men, I ask for, not at once no government, but *at once* a better government. Let every man make known what kind of government would command his respect, and that will be one step toward obtaining it.

After all, the practical reason why, when the power is once in the hands of the people, a majority are permitted, and for a long period continue, to rule is not because they are most likely to be in the right, nor because this seems fairest to the minority, but because they are physically the strongest. But a government in which the majority rule in all cases cannot be based on justice, even as far as men understand it. Can there be a government in which majorities do not virtually decide right and wrong, but conscience?—in which majorities decide only those questions to which the rule of expediency is applicable? Must the citizen ever for a moment, or in the least degree, resign his conscience to the legislator? Why has every man a conscience, then? I think that we should be men first, and subjects afterward. It is not desirable to cultivate a respect for the law, so much as for the right. The only obligation which I have a right to assume is to do at any time what I think right. It is truly enough said that a corporation has no conscience, but a corporation of conscientious men is a corporation *with* a conscience. Law never made men a whit more just; and, by means of their respect for it, even the well-disposed are daily made the agents of injustice. A common and natural result of an undue respect for law is, that you may see a file of soldiers, colonel, captain, corporal, privates, powder-monkeys, and all, marching in admirable order over hill and dale to the wars, against their wills, ay, against their common sense and consciences, which makes it very steep marching indeed, and produces a palpitation of the heart. They have no doubt that it is a damnable business in which they are concerned; they are all peaceably inclined. Now, what are they? Men at all, or small movable forts and magazines, at the service of some unscrupulous man in power? Visit the navy yard, and behold a marine, such a man as an American government can make, or such as it can make a man with its black arts—a mere shadow and reminiscence of humanity, a man laid out alive and standing, and already, as one may say, buried under arms with funeral accompaniments, though it may be—

> Not a drum was heard, not a funeral note,
> As his corpse to the rampart we hurried;
> Not a soldier discharged his farewell shot
> O'er the grave where our hero we buried.

The mass of men serve the state thus, not as men mainly, but as machines, with their bodies. They are the standing army, and the militia, jailers, constables, *posse comitatus*, etc. In most cases there is no free exercise whatever of the judgment or of the moral sense, but they put themselves on a level with wood and earth and stones, and wooden men can perhaps be manufactured that will serve the purpose as well. Such command no more respect than men of straw or a lump of dirt. They have the same sort of worth only as horses and dogs. Yet such as these even are commonly esteemed good citizens. Others—as most legislators, politicians, lawyers, ministers, and officeholders—serve the state chiefly with their heads and, as they rarely make any moral distinctions, they are as likely to serve the devil, without *intending* it, as God. A very few—as heroes, patriots, martyrs, reformers in the great sense, and *men*—serve the state with their consciences also, and so necessarily resist it for the most part, and they are commonly treated as enemies by it. A wise man will only be useful as a man, and will not submit to be "clay," and "stop a hole to keep the wind away," but leave that office to his dust at least:

> I am too high-born to be propertied,
> To be a secondary at control,
> Or useful serving-man and instrument
> To any sovereign state throughout the world.

He who gives himself entirely to his fellow men appears to them useless and selffish, but he who gives himself partially to them is pronounced a benefactor and philanthropist.

Lovely
Lovely

How does it become a man to behave toward this American government today? I answer, that he cannot without disgrace be associated with it. I cannot for an instant recognize that political organization as *my* government which is the *slave's* government also.

All men recognize the right of revolution; that is, the right to refuse allegiance to, and to resist, the government, when its tyranny or its inefficiency are great and unendurable. But almost all say that such is not the case now. But such was the case, they think, in the revolution of '75. If one were to tell me that this was a bad government because it taxed certain foreign commodities brought to its ports, it is most probable that I should not make an ado about it, for I can do without them. All machines have their friction, and possibly this does enough good to counterbalance the evil. At any rate, it is a great evil to make a stir about it. But when the friction comes to have its machine, and oppression and robbery are organized, I say, let us not have such a machine any longer. In other words, when a sixth of the population of a nation which has undertaken to be the refuge of liberty are slaves, and a whole country is unjustly overrun and conquered by a foreign army, and subjected to military law, I think that it is not too soon for the honest men to rebel and revolutionize. What makes this duty the more urgent is the fact that the country so overrun is not our own, but ours is the invading army.

Paley, a common authority with many on moral questions, in his chapter on the "Duty of Submission to Civil Government," [1] resolves all civil obligation into expendiency, and he proceeds to say:

> . . . that so long as the interest of the whole society requires it, that is, so long as the established government cannot be resisted or changed without public inconveniency, it is the will of God . . . that the established government be obeyed, and no longer. This principle being admitted, the justice of every particular case of resistance is reduced to a computation of the quantity of the danger and grievance on the one side, and of the probability and expense of redressing it on the other.

Of this, he says, every man shall judge for himself. But Paley appears never to have contemplated those cases to which the rule

[1] William Paley, *Principles of Moral and Political Philosophy* (1785).

of expediency does not apply, in which a people, as well as an individual, must do justice, cost what it may. If I have unjustly wrested a plank from a drowning man, I must restore it to him though I drown myself. This, according to Paley, would be inconvenient. But he that would save his life, in such a case, shall lose it. This people must cease to hold slaves, and to make war on Mexico, though it cost them their existence as a people.

In their practice, nations agree with Paley, but does any one think that Massachusetts does exactly what is right at the present crisis?

> A drab of state, a cloth-o'-silver slut,
> To have her train borne up, and her soul trail
> in the dirt.

Practically speaking, the opponents to a reform in Massachusetts are not a hundred thousand politicians at the South, but a hundred thousand merchants and farmers here, who are more interested in commerce and agriculture than they are in humanity, and are not prepared to do justice to the slave and to Mexico, *cost what it may*. I quarrel not with far-off foes, but with those who, near at home, cooperate with, and do the bidding of, those far away, and without whom the latter would be harmless. We are accustomed to say that the mass of men are unprepared; but improvement is slow, because the few are not materially wiser or better than the many. It is not so important that many should be as good as you, as that there be some absolute goodness somewhere, for that will leaven the whole lump. There are thousands who are *in opinion* opposed to slavery and to the war, who yet in effect do nothing to put an end to them; who, esteeming themselves children of Washington and Franklin, sit down with their hands in their pockets and say that they know not what to do, and do nothing; who even postpone the question of freedom to the question of free trade, and quietly read the prices-current along with the latest advices from Mexico, after dinner, and, it may be, fall asleep over them both. What is the price-current of an honest man and patriot today? They hesitate, and they regret, and sometimes they petition, but they do nothing in earnest and with effect. They will wait, well disposed, for others to remedy the evil, that they may no longer have it to regret. At most, they give only a cheap vote and a feeble countenance and Godspeed, to the right, as it goes by them. There are nine hundred and ninety-nine patrons of virtue to one virtuous man. But it is easier to deal with the real possessor of a thing than with the temporary guardian of it.

All voting is a sort of gaming, like checkers or backgammon, with a slight moral tinge to it, a playing with right and wrong, with moral questions, and betting naturally accompanies it. The character of the voters is not staked. I cast my vote, perchance, as I think right, but I am not vitally concerned that that right should prevail. I am willing to leave it to the majority. Its obligation, therefore, never exceeds that of expediency. Even voting *for the right* is *doing* nothing for it. It is only expressing to men feebly your desire that it should prevail. A wise man will not leave the right to the mercy of chance, nor wish it to prevail through the power of the majority. There is but little virtue in the action of masses of men. When the majority shall at length vote for the abolition of slavery, it will be because they are indifferent to slavery, or because there is but little slavery left to be abolished by their vote. *They* will then be the only slaves. Only *his* vote can hasten the abolition of slavery who asserts his own freedom by his vote.

I hear of a convention to be held at Baltimore, or elsewhere, for the selection of a candidate for the presidency, made up chiefly of editors, and men who are politicians by profession; but I think, what is it to any independent, intelligent, and respectable man what decision they may come to? Shall we not have the advantage of his wisdom and honesty, nevertheless? Can we not count upon some independent votes? Are there not many individuals in the country who do not attend conventions? But no: I find that the respectable man, so called, has immediately drifted from his position, and despairs of his country, when his country has more reason to despair of him. He forthwith adopts one of the candidates thus selected as the only *available* one, thus proving that he is himself *available* for any purposes of the demagogue. His vote is of no more worth than that of any unprincipled foreigner or hireling native, who may have been bought. O for a man who is a *man*, and, as my neighbor says, has a bone in his back which you cannot pass your hand through! Our statistics are at fault; the population has been returned too large. How many *men* are there to a square thousand miles in this country? Hardly one. Does not America offer any inducement for men to settle here? The American has dwindled into an Odd Fellow, one who may be known by the development of his organ of gregariousness, and a manifest lack of intellect and cheerful self-reliance; whose first and chief concern, on coming into the world, is to see that the almshouses are in good repair; and, before yet he has lawfully donned the virile garb, to collect a fund for the support of the widows and orphans that may be; who, in short, ventures to live only by the aid of the mutual insurance company, which has promised to bury him decently.

It is not a man's duty, as a matter of course, to devote himself to the eradication of any, even the most enormous wrong; he may still properly have other concerns to engage him; but it is his duty, at least, to wash his hands of it, and, if he gives it no thought longer, not to give it practically his support. If I devote myself to other pursuits and contemplations, I must first see, at least, that I do not pursue them sitting upon another man's shoulders. I must get off him first, that he may pursue his contemplations too. See what gross inconsistency is tolerated. I have heard some of my townsmen say, "I should like to have them order me out to help put down an insurrection of the slaves, or to march to Mexico —see if I would go"; and yet these very men have each, directly by their allegiance, and so indirectly, at least, by their money, furnished a substitute. The soldier is applauded who refuses to serve in an unjust war by those who do not refuse to sustain the unjust government which makes the war; is applauded by those whose own act and authority he disregards and sets at naught; as if the state were penitent to that degree that it hired one to scourge it while it sinned, but not to that degree that it left off sinning for a moment. Thus, under the name of Order and Civil Government, we are all made at last to pay homage to and support our own meanness. After the first blush of sin comes its indifference; and from immoral it becomes, as it were, *un*moral, and not quite unnecessary to that life which we have made.

The broadest and most prevalent error requires the most disinterested virtue to sustain it. The slight reproach to which the virtue of patriotism is commonly liable, the noble are most likely to incur. Those who, while they disapprove of the character and measures of a government, yield to it their allegiance and support, are undoubtedly its most conscientious supporters, and so frequently the most serious obstacles to reform. Some are petitioning the State to dissolve the Union, to disregard the requisitions of the President. Why do they not dissolve it themselves—the union between themselves and the State—and refuse to pay their quota into its treasury? Do not they stand in the same relation to the State that the State does to the Union? And have not the same reasons prevented the State from resisting the Union which have prevented them from resisting the State?

How can a man be satisfied to entertain an opinion merely, and enjoy *it*? Is there any enjoyment in it, if his opinion is that he is aggrieved? If you are cheated out of a single dollar by your neighbor, you do not rest satisfied with knowing that you are cheated, or with saying that you are cheated, or even with petitioning him to pay you your due; but you take effectual steps at once to obtain the full amount, and see that you are never cheated again. Action from principle, the perception and the performance of right, changes things and relations; it is essentially revolutionary, and does not consist wholly with anything which was. It not only divides States and churches, it divides families; ay, it divides the *individual,* separating the diabolical in him from the divine.

Unjust laws exist: shall we be content to obey them, or shall we endeavor to amend them, and obey them until we have succeeded, or shall we transgress them at once? Men generally, under such a government as this, think that they ought to wait until they have persuaded the majority to alter them. They think that, if they should resist, the remedy would be worse than the evil. But it is the fault of the government itself that the remedy *is* worse than the evil. *It* makes it worse. Why is it not more apt to anticipate and provide for reform? Why does it not cherish its wise minority? Why does it cry and resist before it is hurt? Why does it not encourage its citizens to be on the alert to point out its faults, and *do* better than it would have them? Why does it always crucify Christ, and excommunicate Copernicus and Luther, and pronounce Washington and Franklin rebels?

One would think that a deliberate and practical denial of its authority was the only offense never contemplated by government; else, why has it not assigned its definite, its suitable and proportionate penalty? If a man who has no property refuses but once to earn nine shillings for the State, he is put in prison for a period unlimited by any law that I know, and determined only by the discretion of those who placed him there; but if he should steal ninety times nine shillings from the State, he is soon permitted to go at large again.

If the injustice is part of the necessary friction of the machine of government, let it go, let it go: perchance it will wear smooth—certainly the machine will wear out. If the injustice has a spring, or a pulley, or a rope, or a crank, exclusively for itself, then perhaps you may consider whether the remedy will not be worse than the evil; but if it is of such a nature that it requires you to be the agent of injustice to another, then, I say, break the law. Let your life be a counter friction to stop the machine. What I have to do is to see, at any rate, that I do not lend myself to the wrong which I condemn.

As for adopting the ways which the State has provided for remedying the evil, I know not of such ways. They take too much time, and a man's life will be gone. I have other affairs to attend to. I came into this world, not chiefly to make this a good place to live in, but to live in it, be it good or bad. A man has not everything to do, but something; and because he cannot do *everything*, it is not necessary that he should do *something* wrong. It is not my business to be petitioning the governor or the legislature any more than it is theirs to petition me; and if they should not hear my petition, what should I do then? But in this case the State has provided no way: its very Constitution is the evil. This may seem to be harsh and stubborn and unconciliatory, but it is to treat with the utmost kindness and consideration the only spirit that can appreciate or deserves it. So is all change for the better, like birth and death, which convulse the body.

I do not hesitate to say that those who call themselves Abolitionists should at once effectually withdraw their support, both in person and property, from the government of Massachusetts, and not wait till they constitute a majority of one, before they suffer the right to prevail through them. I think that it is enough if they have God on their side, without waiting for that other one. Moreover, any man more right than his neighbors constitutes a majority of one already.

I meet this American government, or its representative, the State government, directly, and face to face, once a year—no more—in the person of its taxgatherer; this is the only mode in which a man situated as I am necessarily meets it; and it then says distinctly, "Recognize me," and the simplest, the most effectual, and in the present posture of affairs, the indispensablest mode of treating with it on this head, of expressing your little satisfaction with and love for it, is to deny it then. My civil neighbor, the taxgatherer, is the very man I have to deal with—for it is, after all, with men and not with parchment that I quarrel—and he has voluntarily chosen to be an agent of the government. How shall he ever know well what he is and does as an officer of the government or as a man, until he is obliged to consider whether he shall treat me, his neighbor, for whom he has respect, as a neighbor and well-disposed man, or as a maniac and disturber of the peace, and see if he can get over this obstruction to his neighborliness without a ruder and more impetuous thought or speech corresponding with his action. I know this well, that if one thousand, if one hundred, if ten men whom I could name—if ten *honest* men only—ay, if *one* HONEST man, in this State of Massachusetts, *ceasing to hold slaves*, were actually to withdraw from this copartnership, and be locked up in the county jail therefor, it would be the abolition of slavery in America. For it matters not how small the beginning may seem to be: What is once well done is done forever. But we love better to talk about it: That we say is our mission. Reform keeps many scores of newspapers in its service, but not one man. If my esteemed neighbor, the State's ambassador, who will devote his days to the settlement of the question of human rights in the Council Chamber, instead of being threatened with the prisons of Carolina, were to sit down the prisoner of Massachusetts, that State which is so anxious to foist the sin of slavery upon her sister—though at present she can discover only an act of inhospitality to be the ground of a quarrel with her—the legislature would not wholly waive the subject the following winter.

Under a government which imprisons any unjustly, the true

place for a just man is also a prison. The proper place today, the only place which Massachusetts has provided for her freer and less desponding spirits, is in her prisons, to be put out and locked out of the State by her own act, as they have already put themselves out by their principles. It is there that the fugitive slave, and the Mexican prisoner on parole, and the Indian come to plead the wrongs of his race should find them; on that separate, but more free and honorable ground, where the State places those who are not *with* her, but *against* her—the only house in a slave State in which a free man can abide with honor. If any think that their influence would be lost there, and their voices no longer afflict the ear of the State, that they would not be as an enemy within its walls, they do not know by how much truth is stronger than error, nor how much more eloquently and effectively he can combat injustice who has experienced a little in his own person. Cast your whole vote, not a strip of paper merely, but your whole influence. A minority is powerless while it conforms to the majority; it is not even a minority then; but it is irresistible when it clogs by its whole weight. If the alternative is to keep all just men in prison, or give up war and slavery, the State will not hesitate which to choose. If a thousand men were not to pay their tax bills this year, that would not be as violent and bloody a measure as it would be to pay them and enable the State to commit violence and shed innocent blood. This is, in fact, the definition of a peaceable revolution, if any such is possible. If the taxgatherer, or any other public officer, asks me, as one has done, "But what shall I do?", my answer is, "If you really wish to do anything, resign your office." When the subject has refused allegiance, and the officer has resigned his office, then the revolution is accomplished. But even suppose blood should flow. Is there not a sort of blood shed when the conscience is wounded? Through this wound a man's real manhood and immortality flow out, and he bleeds to an everlasting death. I see this blood flowing now.

I have contemplated the imprisonment of the offender, rather than the seizure of his goods—though both will serve the same purpose—because they who assert the purest right, and consequently are most dangerous to a corrupt State, commonly have not spent much time in accumulating property. To such the State renders comparatively small service, and a slight tax is wont to appear exorbitant, particularly if they are obliged to earn it by special labor with their hands. If there were one who lived wholly without the use of money, the State itself would hesitate to demand it of him. But the rich man—not to make any invidious comparison—is always sold to the institution which makes him rich. Absolutely speaking, the more money, the less virtue; for money comes between a man and his objects, and obtains them for him; and it was certainly no great virtue to obtain it. It puts to rest many questions which he would otherwise be taxed to answer, while the only new question which it puts is the hard but superfluous one, how to spend it. Thus his moral ground is taken from under his feet. The opportunities of living are diminished in proportion as what are called the "means" are increased. The best thing a man can do for his culture when he is rich is to endeavor to carry out those schemes which he entertained when he was poor. Christ answered the Herodians according to their condition. "Show me the tribute-money," said he, and took one penny out of his pocket; if you use money which has the image of Caesar on it and which he has made current and valuable, that is, *if you are men of the State*, and gladly enjoy the advantages of Caesar's government, then pay him back some of his own when he demands it. "Render therefore to Caesar that which is Caesar's, and to God those things which are God's"—leaving them no wiser than before as to which was which; for they did not wish to know.

When I converse with the freest of my neighbors, I perceive that, whatever they may say about the magnitude and seriousness of the question, and their regard for the public tranquillity, the long and the short of the matter is, that they cannot spare the protection of the existing government, and they dread the consequences to their property and families of disobedience to it. For my own part, I should not like to think that I ever rely on the protection of the State. But, if I deny the authority of the State when it presents its tax-bill, it will soon take and waste all my property, and so harass me and my children without end. This is hard. This makes it impossible for a man to live honestly, and at the same time comfortably, in outward respects. It will not be worth the while to accumulate property; that would be sure to go again. You must hire or squat somewhere, and raise but a small crop, and eat that soon. You must live within yourself, and depend upon yourself always tucked up and ready for a start, and not have many affairs. A man may grow rich in Turkey even, if he will be in all respects a good subject of the Turkish government. Confucius said: "If a state is governed by the principles of reason, poverty and misery are subjects of shame; if a state is not governed by the principles of reason, riches and honors are the subjects of shame." No: until I want the protection of Massachusetts to be extended to me in some distant Southern port, where my liberty is endangered, or until I am bent solely on building up an estate at home by peaceful enterprise, I can afford to refuse allegiance to Massachusetts, and her right to my property and life. It costs me less in every sense to incur the penalty of disobedience to the State than it would to obey. I should feel as if I were worth less in that case.

Some years ago, the State met me in behalf of the Church, and commanded me to pay a certain sum toward the support of a clergyman whose preaching my father attended, but never I myself. "Pay," it said, "or be locked up in the jail." I declined to pay. But, unfortunately, another man saw fit to pay it. I did not see why the schoolmaster should be taxed to support the priest, and not the priest the schoolmaster; for I was not the State's schoolmaster, but I supported myself by voluntary subscription. I did not see why the lyceum should not present its tax bill, and have the State to back its demand, as well as the Church. However, at the request of the selectmen, I condescended to make some such statement as this in writing: "Know all men by these presents that I, Henry Thoreau, do not wish to be regarded as a member of any incorporated society which I have not joined." This I gave to the town clerk, and he has it. The State, having thus learned that I did not wish to be regarded as a member of that church, has never made a like demand on me since, though it said that it must adhere to its original presumption that time. If I had known how to name them, I should then have signed off in detail from all the societies which I never signed on to; but I did not know where to find a complete list.

I have paid no poll tax for six years. I was put into a jail once on this account, for one night; and, as I stood considering the walls of solid stone, two or three feet thick, the door of wood and iron, a foot thick, and the iron grating which strained the light, I could not help being struck with the foolishness of that institution which treated me as if I were mere flesh and blood and bones, to be locked up. I wondered that it should have concluded at length that this was the best use it could put me to, and had never thought to avail itself of my services in some way. I saw that, if there was a wall of stone between me and my townsmen, there was a still more difficult one to climb or break through before they could get to be as free as I was. I did not for a moment feel confined, and the walls seemed a great waste of stone and mortar. I felt as if I alone of all my townsmen had paid my tax. They plainly did not know how to treat me, but behaved like persons who are underbred. In every threat and in every compliment there was a blunder; for they thought that my chief desire was to stand the other side of that stone wall. I could not but smile to see how industriously they locked the door on my meditations, which followed them out again without let or hindrance, and *they* were really all that was dangerous. As they could not reach me, they had resolved to punish my body; just as boys, if they cannot come at some person against whom they have a spite, will abuse his dog. I saw that the State was half-witted, that it was timid as a lone woman with her silver spoons, and that it did not know its friends from its foes, and I lost all my remaining respect for it, and pitied it.

Thus the State never intentionally confronts a man's sense, intellectual or moral, but only his body, his senses. It is not armed with superior wit or honesty, but with superior physical strength. I was not born to be forced. I will breathe after my own fashion. Let us see who is the strongest. What force has a multitude? They only can force me who obey a higher law than I. They force me to become like themselves. I do not hear of *men* being *forced* to live this way or that by masses of men. What sort of life were that to live? When I meet a government which says to me, "Your money or your life," why should I be in haste to give it my money? It may be in a great strait, and not know what to do: I cannot help that. It must help itself; do as I do. It is not worth the while to snivel about it. I am not responsible for the successful working of the machinery of society. I am not the son of the engineer. I perceive that, when an acorn and a chestnut fall side by side, the one does not remain inert to make way for the other, but both obey their own laws, and spring and grow and flourish as best they can, till one, perchance, overshadows and destroys the other. If a plant cannot live according to its nature, it dies; and so a man.

The night in prison was novel and interesting enough. The prisoners in their shirtsleeves were enjoying a chat and the evening air in the doorway, when I entered. But the jailer said, "Come, boys, it is time to lock up"; and so they dispersed, and I heard the sound of their steps returning into the hollow apartments. My roommate was introduced to me by the jailer as "a first-rate fellow and a clever man." When the door was locked, he showed me where to hang my hat, and how he managed matters there. The rooms were whitewashed once a month; and this one, at least, was the whitest, most simply furnished, and most probably the neatest apartment in the town. He naturally wanted to know where I came from, and what brought me there; and when I had told him, I asked him in my turn how he came there; presuming him to be an honest man, of course, and, as the world goes, I believe he was. "Why," said he, "they accuse me of burning a barn; but I never did it." As near as I could discover, he had probably gone to bed in a barn when drunk, and smoked his pipe there, and so a barn was burnt. He had the reputation of being a clever man, had been there some three months waiting for his trial to come on, and would have to wait as much longer; but he was quite domesticated and contented, since he got his board for nothing, and thought that he was well treated.

He occupied one window, and I the other; and I saw that if one stayed there long, his principal business would be to look out the window. I had soon read all the tracts that were left there, and had examined where former prisoners had broken out, and where a grate had been sawed off, and heard the history of the various occupants of that room—for I found that even here there was a history and a gossip which never circulated beyond the walls of the jail. Probably this is the only house in the town where verses are composed, which are afterward printed in circular form, but not published. I was shown quite a long list of verses which were composed by some young men who had been detected in an attempt to escape, who avenged themselves by singing them.

I pumped my fellow prisoner as dry as I could, for fear I should never see him again; but at length he showed me which was my bed, and left me to blow out the lamp.

It was like traveling into a far country, such as I had never expected to behold, to lie there for one night. It seemed to me that I never had heard the town clock strike before, nor the evening sounds of the village; for we slept with the windows open, which were inside the grating. It was to see my native village in the light of the Middle Ages, and our Concord was turned into a Rhine stream, and visions of knights and castles passed before me. They were the voices of old burghers that I heard in the streets. I was an involuntary spectator and auditor of whatever was done and said in the kitchen of the adjacent village inn—a wholly new and rare experience to me. It was a closer view of my native town. I was fairly inside of it. I never had seen its institutions before. This is one of its peculiar institutions, for it is a shire town. I began to comprehend what its inhabitants were about.

In the morning, our breakfasts were put through the hole in the door, in small oblong-square tin pans, made to fit, and holding a pint of chocolate, with brown bread and an iron spoon. When they called for the vessels again, I was green enough to return what bread I had left, but my comrade seized it, and said that I should lay that up for lunch or dinner. Soon after he was let out to work at haying in a neighboring field, whither he went every day, and would not be back till noon; so he bade me good-day, saying that he doubted if he should see me again.

When I came out of prison—for some one interfered, and paid that tax—I did not perceive that great changes had taken place on the common, such as he observed who went in a youth and emerged a tottering and gray-headed man; and yet a change had to my eyes come over the scene—the town, and State, and country—greater than any that mere time could effect. I saw yet more distinctly the State in which I lived. I saw to what extent the people among whom I lived could be trusted as good neighbors and friends; that their friendship was for summer weather only; that they did not greatly propose to do right; that they were a distinct race from me by their prejudices and superstitions, as the Chinamen and Malays are; that in their sacrifices to humanity they ran no risks, not even to their property; that after all they were not so noble but they treated the thief as he had treated them, and hoped, by a certain outward observance and a few prayers, and by walking in a particular straight though useless path from time to time, to save their souls. This may be to judge my neighbors harshly, for I believe that many of them are not aware that they have such an institution as the jail in their village.

It was formerly the custom in our village, when a poor debtor came out of jail, for his acquaintances to salute him, looking through their fingers, which were crossed to represent the grating of a jail window, "How do ye do?" My neighbors did not thus salute me, but first looked at me, and then at one another, as if I had returned from a long journey. I was put into jail as I was going to the shoemaker's to get a shoe which was mended. When I was let out the next morning, I proceeded to finish my errand, and, having put on my mended shoe, joined a huckleberry party, who were impatient to put themselves under my conduct; and in half an hour—for the horse was soon tackled—was in the midst of a huckleberry field, on one of our highest hills, two miles off, and then the State was nowhere to be seen.

This is the whole history of "My Prisons."

I have never declined paying the highway tax, because I am as desirous of being a good neighbor as I am of being a bad subject; and as for supporting schools, I am doing my part to educate my fellow countrymen now. It is for no particular item in the tax bill that I refuse to pay it. I simply wish to refuse allegiance to the State, to withdraw and stand aloof from it effectually. I do not care to trace the course of my dollar, if I could, till it buys a man or a musket to shoot one with—the dollar is innocent—but I am concerned to trace the effects of my allegiance. In fact, I quietly declare war with the State, after my fashion, though I will still make what use and get what advantage of her I can, as is usual in such cases.

If others pay the tax which is demanded of me, from a sympathy with the State, they do but what they have already done in their own case, or rather they abet injustice to a greater extent than the State requires. If they pay the tax from a mistaken interest in the individual taxed, to save his property, or prevent his going to jail, it is because they have not considered wisely how far they let their private feelings interfere with the public good.

This, then, is my position at present. But one cannot be too much on his guard in such a case, lest his action be biased by obstinacy or an undue regard for the opinions of men. Let him see that he does only what belongs to himself and to the hour.

I think sometimes, "Why, this people mean well, they are only ignorant; they would do better if they knew how: why give your neighbors this pain to treat you as they are not inclined to?" But I think again, "This is no reason why I should do as they do, or permit others to suffer much greater pain of a different kind." Again, I sometimes say to myself, "When many millions of men, without heat, without ill will, without personal feeling of any kind, demand of you a few shillings only, without the possibility, such is their constitution, of retracing or altering their present demand, and without the possibility, on your side, of appeal to any other millions, why expose yourself to this overwhelming brute force? You do not resist cold and hunger, the winds and the waves, thus obstinately; you quietly submit to a thousand similar necessities. You do not put your head into the fire. But just in proportion as I regard this as not wholly a brute force, but partly a human force, and consider that I have relations to those millions as to so many millions of men, and not of mere brute or inanimate things, I see that appeal is possible, first and instantaneously, from them to the Maker of them, and, secondly, from them to themselves. But if I put my head deliberately into the fire, there is no appeal to fire or to the Maker of fire, and I have only myself to blame. If I could convince myself that I have any right to be satisfied with men as they are, and to treat them accordingly, and not according, in some respects, to my requisitions and expectations of what they and I ought to be, then, like a good Mussulman and fatalist, I should endeavor to be satisfied with things as they are, and say it is the will of God. And, above all, there is this difference between resisting this and a purely brute or natural force, that I can resist this with some effect, but I cannot expect, like Orpheus, to change the nature of the rocks and trees and beasts.

I do not wish to quarrel with any man or nation. I do not wish to split hairs, to make fine distinctions, or set myself up as better than my neighbors. I seek rather, I may say, even an excuse for conforming to the laws of the land. I am but too ready to conform to them. Indeed, I have reason to suspect myself on this head; and each year, as the taxgatherer comes around, I find myself disposed to review the acts and position of the general and State governments, and the spirit of the people, to discover a pretext for conformity.

> We must affect our country as our parents,
> And if at any time we alienate
> Our love or industry from doing it honor,
> We must respect effects and teach the soul
> Matter of conscience and religion,
> And not desire of rule or benefit.

I believe that the State will soon be able to take all my work of this sort out of my hands, and then I shall be no better a patriot than my fellow countrymen. Seen from a lower point of view, the Constitution, with all its faults, is very good; the law and the courts are very respectable; even this State and this American government are, in many respects, very admirable, and rare things, to be thankful for, such as a great many have described them; but seen from a point of view a little higher, they are what I have described them; seen from a higher still, and the highest, who shall say what they are, or that they are worth looking at or thinking of at all?

However, the government does not concern me much, and I shall bestow the fewest possible thoughts on it. It is not many moments that I live under a government, even in this world. If a man is thought-free, fancy-free, imagination-free, that which *is not* never for a long time appearing *to be* to him, unwise rulers or reformers cannot fatally interrupt him.

I know that most men think differently from myself, but those whose lives are by profession devoted to the study of these or kindred subjects content me as little as any. Statesmen and legislators, standing so completely within the institution, never distinctly and nakedly behold it. They speak of moving society but have no resting place without it. They may be men of a certain experience and discrimination, and have no doubt invented ingenious and even useful systems, for which we sincerely thank them, but all their wit and usefulness lie within certain not very wide limits. They are wont to forget that the world is not governed by policy and expediency. Webster [2] never goes behind government, and so cannot speak with authority about it. His words are wisdom to those legislators who contemplate no essential reform in the existing government; but for thinkers, and those who legislate for all time, he never once glances at the subject. I know of those whose serene and wise speculations on this theme would soon reveal the limits of his mind's range and hospitality. Yet, compared with the cheap professions of most reformers, and the still cheaper wisdom and eloquence of politicians in general, his are almost the only sensible and valuable words, and we thank Heaven for him. Comparatively, he is always strong, original, and above all, practical. Still, his quality is not wisdom, but prudence. The lawyer's truth is not Truth, but consistency or a consistent expediency. Truth is always in harmony with herself, and is not concerned chiefly to reveal the justice that may consist with wrongdoing. He well deserves to be called, as he has been called, "the Defender of the Constitution." There are really no blows to be given by him but defensive ones. He is not a leader, but a follower. His leaders are the men of '87. "I have never made an effort," he says, "and never propose to make an effort; I have never countenanced an effort, and never mean to countenance an effort, to disturb the arrangement as originally made, by which the various States came into the Union." Still thinking of the sanction which the Constitution gives to slavery, he says, "Because it was a part of the original compact—let it stand." Notwithstanding his political acuteness and ability, he is unable to take a fact out of its merely political relations, and behold it as it lies absolutely to be disposed of by the intellect—what, for instance, it behooves a man to do here in America today with regard to slavery—but ventures, or is driven, to make some such desperate answer as the following, while professing to speak absolutely, and

[2] Daniel Webster, 1782–1852, American statesman, diplomat, senator. Secretary of State under both President John Tyler and President Millard Filmore.

as a private man—from which what new and singular code of social duties might be inferred? "The manner," says he,

> in which the governments of those States where slavery exists are to regulate it is for their own consideration, under their responsibility to their constitutents, to the general laws of propriety, humanity, or any other cause, have nothing whatever to do with it. They have never received any encouragement from me, and they never will.

They who know of no purer sources of truth, who have traced up its stream no higher, stand, and wisely stand, by the Bible and the Constitution, and drink at it there with reverence and humility; but they who behold where it comes trickling into this lake or that pool, gird up their loins once more, and continue their pilgrimage toward its fountainhead.

No man with a genius for legislation has appeared in America. They are rare in the history of the world. There are orators, politicians, and eloquent men, by the thousand; but the speaker has not yet opened his mouth to speak who is capable of settling the much-vexed questions of the day. We love eloquence for its own sake, and not for any truth which it may utter, or any heroism it may inspire. Our legislators have not yet learned the comparative value of free trade and of freedom, of union, and of rectitude, to a nation. They have no genius or talent for comparatively humble questions of taxation and finance, commerce and manufactures and agriculture. If we were left solely to the wordy wit of legislators in Congress for our guidance, uncorrected by the seasonable experience and the effectual complaints of the people, America would not long retain her rank among the nations. For eighteen hundred years, though perchance I have no right to say it, the New Testament has been written; yet where is the legislator who has wisdom and practical talent enough to avail himself of the light which it sheds on the science of legislation?

The authority of government, even such as I am willing to submit to—for I will cheerfully obey those who know and can do better than I, and in many things even those who neither know nor can do so well—is still an impure one: to be strictly just, it must have the sanction and consent of the governed. It can have no pure right over my person and property but what I concede to it. The progress from an absolute to a limited monarchy, from a limited monarchy to a democracy, is a progress toward a true respect for the individual. Even the Chinese philosopher was wise enough to regard the individual as the basis of the empire. Is a democracy, such as we know it, the last improvement possible in government? Is it not possible to take a step further towards recognizing and organizing the rights of man? There will never be a really free and enlightened State until the State comes to recognize the individual as a higher and independent power, from which all its own power and authority are derived, and treats him accordingly. I please myself with imagining a State at last which can afford to be just to all men, and to treat the individual with respect as a neighbor; which even would not think it inconsistent with its own repose if a few were to live aloof from it, not meddling with it, nor embraced by it, who fulfilled all the duties of neighbors and fellow men. A State which bore this kind of fruit, and suffered it to drop off as fast as it ripened, would prepare the way for a still more perfect and glorious State, which also I have imagined, but not yet anywhere seen.

TOPICS FOR DISCUSSION AND WRITING

1. Thoreau's title adequately defines a conclusion he reached after having examined certain ideas about the nature of government. What is his central thesis concerning government? Is it explicit or implicit?
2. How does the strong personal note ("I cannot for an instant recognize that political organization as *my* government." "What I have to do is to see, at any rate, that I do not lend myself to the wrong which I condemn.") help to define the kind of thesis, active or hypothetical, which Thoreau is advancing?
3. What kind of audience acceptance is Thoreau seeking? Does he expect his readers to follow his example?
4. Do you think that Thoreau's thesis is more important or less important now than when his essay first appeared? Are there any conditions in society which make his thesis more dangerous or more acceptable than it was in 1849?
5. Write an essay comparing or contrasting Thoreau's attitude toward

society with that expressed in other selections which appear later in this collection, particularly those of John Locke, John Stuart Mill, William Whyte, or the *Federalist* paper by Hamilton. How would you distinguish the different attitude each of these men has toward the issue of the individual in a collective society?

Crane Brinton

Crane Brinton (1898–) has been associated with Harvard as student and teacher of history since 1915. The only two significant interruptions were his years at Oxford as a Rhodes scholar and his service during World War II as a special assistant in the Office of Strategic Services. He is the author of numerous historical works, including English Political Thought in the Nineteenth Century *and* Anatomy of Revolution.

The following essay originally appeared as the last chapter of his book From Many One *(1948), which was based on a series of lectures delivered the previous year at Pomona College, Claremont, California. This essay should prove exceptionally interesting to the student of argumentation and persuasive prose; instead of advancing a series of proofs in defense of one proposition or thesis, it examines and evaluates arguments which may be offered in support of several different theses or propositions.*

Professor Brinton begins as a historian and states several conclusions, in the form of propositions, which he thinks summarize some of what we have learned from a study of the past. He then continues, somewhat as a prophet, to consider some propositions which have been advanced in an attempt to outline the future. Thus the essay contains many propositions which the author asks his readers to consider.

The essay does *have a central focus, or over-all proposition, with which Professor Brinton hopes his readers will come to agree. This central proposition is not a call to action, but a moderate conclusion reached after considering the evidence on both sides. The essay tries to lead its reader to reach the same conclusion as its author by asking the reader to join in a reflective examination of several possible positions.*

The Chances for a World State *

Before I take on, modestly I hope, the role of prophet, I should like to review summarily and very broadly what can be quite solidly established as the experience of the past in the maintenance of peace by political integration.

First of all, it is certain that we of Western society have never, in our five thousand years of recorded history, kept peace for long within an area save by bringing that area within the authority of a single government. Leagues, alliances, ententes, the subtlest or the simplest forms of balance of power, the Truce of God, the Peace of God—by none of these have men kept peace for more than a generation. That generalization is as certain an induction from history as I know. In short, those proponents of a world-state who maintain that long-lasting peace is impossible among sovereign states would seem to be right.

Second, the authority of a single government has, in the past, been extended territorially in a variety of ways, which for purposes of analysis can be sorted into a polarity of force and consent, of imperialism and federalism. The federal solution has been far less common than the imperialist solution in the initial steps of political integration, but successfully integrated states have almost always proved in practice to rest on a mixture of force and consent, of imperialism and federalism.

Third, once the newly integrated state has become a going concern, it is possible to distinguish certain general characteristics which seem to be necessary characteristics of any international or supranational state in our own time. These general characteristics, these uniformities are: (a) a symbolic head of state, in the past of our Western society almost always an individual, but an individual made symbol by ceremonial pomp, ritual, etiquette, and if you like, by "propaganda"; (b) an elite, not always an aristocracy in the conventional European sense of the word, an elite commonly charged with responsibility for administration, for setting the tone of society and education, conditioned morally as well as intel-

* Reprinted by permission of the publishers from *From Many One—The Process of Political Integration, the Problem of World Government* by Crane Brinton (Cambridge, Mass.: Harvard University Press, 1948). Copyright 1948 by the President and Fellows of Harvard College.

lectually to the service of the integrated state, thoroughly cosmopolitan or international in outlook; (c) at least some loyalty on the part of the masses who live under its authority, though this loyalty would seem both more widespread and deeper in such examples of integration as the modern nation-state than it was in the really international Roman Empire; (d) some degree of local autonomy, especially where there is among the constituent units a tradition of self-rule; (e) an absence of groups, and especially of groups with a territorial basis, which feel that the existence of the integrated state is incompatible with their own existence. This last point is merely the negative aspect of the previous one about autonomy, and comes down in practice to this: No integrated political unit can afford to have its Irelands, its Polands, its *irredenta.*

Finally, in the past the process of political integration has almost invariably been a slow one, whether it came about imperialistically or federally. The Roman Empire, the great modern nation-states like France, Britain, Germany took centuries in the making, and no one specific historical act can be taken as in itself wholly a determinant in their making. Here as so often American experience is in a sense unique. Our Constitutional Convention at Philadelphia in 1787 does seem to have made the beginnings of a nation. Yet, just as we nowadays cannot quite think of the Constitution as "struck off by the mind of man" in one moment, so we cannot think historically of the building of the American nation without the preparatory work of the colonial period—and without the great test of the Civil War.

II

There is, then, in the past of our civilization little—indeed, no—precedent for the immediate success of the kind of effort well-meaning men and women are now making in the cause of world government and a sovereign world-state. Were the historian to desert his serious and dignified business and turn bookmaker, he would be obliged to say that the odds against the world federationists are prohibitive, astronomical. But perhaps the historian ought not to be consulted here at all? Perhaps these are *unprecedented* times in fact as so often in our rhetoric; perhaps there are new factors, new variables in our equation, which invalidate all past attempts at solution. It is time we investigated this possibility.

Most obvious of new factors, new certainly within the last century, is the decrease in the size of the earth. You have all seen some of these ingenious diagrams by which the size of the earth when men had to sail or ride horseback is compared with its size when men can go in jet planes. In this sense, the world today, thanks to the airplane, is smaller than the Hellas of Pericles. Thanks to the radio, communication around the globe can be instantaneous. True enough, there remain numerous isolated and backward regions, and the actualities of modern transport and communication are not always what they seem to be in essays on the miracles of modern science. There are pockets on earth where men travel much less than 600 miles per hour. Nonetheless, ours is physically one world.

This means that no such self-isolated political unit as the Roman Empire can now exist. It will not be sufficient, though it may be helpful, to organize regional federations, a United States of Europe, or a Danubian federation. It would not be possible for a European, an Asiatic, and an American superstate to live in virtual separateness and self-sufficiency, as did in the first centuries of our era the Roman and the Chinese Empires.[1] Any arrangements for lessening the chances of war, whether through a United Nations held together as hardly more than an alliance or through a genuine governmental unit with police and taxing powers, would in our world ultimately have to be world-wide.

This is a new factor. But I cannot believe that this new factor makes our problem simpler, makes political integration easier, quicker, more likely than it has been in the past. On the contrary, I believe it makes our problem harder. Necessity may be the mother of invention, but surely not of perfection. Massachusetts and Virginia were hard to bring together under a common government. France and Britain, despite the Entente, despite the famous offer of union Churchill made in 1940, will be hard to bring together under a common government. Think of bringing Chinese, Argentinians, Russians, and all the other seventy-odd "sovereign" peoples together in this way! What have these people in common? Not religion, not language, not tradition, not habits. They have in

[1] This separateness was not of course absolute. See F. J. Taggart's *Rome and China* (University of California Press, 1939).

common only the barest, undeveloped, and unfulfilled attributes of *homo sapiens.*

Perhaps even more obvious to some of you is another new factor, the atomic bomb. On this subject it is difficult, and perhaps immoral, even to try to take up an objective attitude. Nevertheless, I shall make the attempt. The first thing to be clear about is that we really do not know what effect the existence of the atomic bomb will have on the process of political integration in our world. Probably, as my friends among the physicists tell me, we can rule out the chance that the bomb in any prospective form will set off a chain-reaction among the staid, ordinary atoms that surround us, and thus actually blow this planet to bits, or at least destroy all living things on the planet. Yet we cannot rule out of our calculations the fact that a certain number of people believe this complete destruction possible, even likely, and fear it. We are dealing, not so much with a question of physics as with the question of human hopes and fears.

New books and lectures on the atomic bomb multiply daily. I cannot here pretend to take up the subject thoroughly, and were I to do so, I should distort this book. In broad lines, I think one can say that the main possibilities of the influence of the atomic bomb, as a fact and as a threat, on our contemporary problem of political integration are three. First, the bomb may in the hands of a very skilful and very lucky nation prove to be the weapon that permits that nation to unify the world by conquest, by the method of imperialism, to do what Napoleon and Hitler failed to do. Second, the bomb, especially as a threat, may so work on the fears of the many, may so inspire the crusading, intelligent few, that a successful world government will be set up federally, by the method of consent. Third, the bomb may be no more than the starting point for sermons, editorials, books, and pamphlets by prophets, crusaders, alarmists, editors, preachers, and professors, much as poison gas was last time, and have no really important effect as a variable in the equation of international politics, at least until the next world war.

Those who have followed me discerningly so far, whether in agreement or disagreement, will know that I consider this third possibility the most likely one. I incline to the belief that the atomic bomb will not greatly alter the basic problem of political integration, that it is *not* a new variable that invalidates the lessons of history. Yet I do not wish to be dogmatic. Both of the other possibilities I have mentioned seem to me to be real ones. We should all keep our minds open to new evidence in favor of either of them. Personally, I think that the bomb is more likely to promote the imperialist solution than the federal solution. Above all, if the bomb proves in the next few years to have had as its main psychological effect an increase in men's fears, then I think it clear that we shall be further than ever from the federal solution. For fear breeds distrust and aggression, not confidence and collaboration. The notion that if enough people fear they'll be blown to bits by an atomic bomb they will get together in a parliament of man is a singularly naive one. As an element in turning public opinion toward international cooperation, a reasonable fear of the consequences of atomic warfare is no doubt a factor that must be weighed in the total balance; but an obsessive fear, an overshadowing fear of the kind some of our wilder prophets apparently want to promote, seems to me one of the surest roads to war. We need not be Freudians to acknowledge the relation between anxiety and aggression.

A third new factor I see is a very real one. We can, I think, admit that some part of Marx's economic interpretation of history affords us valid uniformities about the behavior of men in society. Now it is quite true that the rise of a money economy was incompatible with the self-sufficient feudal manor, and helped very greatly to produce the nation-state of modern times. I think it quite likely that the growth of really large-scale industry, the industrial revolution of our own times, that of the internal combustion engine, oil, electricity, the assembly line, has made the nation-state, especially in Europe and in Latin America, a unit impossibly small for the kind of economic life that its inhabitants are trying to lead. The autarkic nation-state, unless it is a subcontinental state like Russia, Brazil, or the United States, is perhaps an economic anomaly in 1947, as the feudal lordship was in 1497.

But there is no reason why the devotees of world union *now* should take encouragement from this economic factor. In the first place, and subject always to the catastrophic potentialities of atomic warfare, the means of production under our modern neotechnical large industry needs for real efficiency either much freer international trade, or an autarkic political unit bigger than France or Peru; it does not in itself necessitate a world union. It could quite readily accommodate itself to a world of four or five independent superstates holding themselves in the kind of war-breeding balance of power we are thoroughly familiar with.

Second, we must realize that if economic necessity, or what seems to enough people to be economic necessity, is a powerful force in human affairs, this felt necessity does have to work through human beings imperfectly trained in the science of economics, and not at all likely to behave as the economist wants them to. In the long run, we human beings do perhaps adapt ourselves to material necessity. But it is a very long run, in the course of which, oddly enough, material necessity seems to get softened up, altered. If you will forgive another excursion into history, I should like to point out that the political transition from feudalism to the nation-state, though more rapid in England, say, than in Germany, everywhere took centuries, and was everywhere somewhat, and often a great deal, slower than economic change.

Third, if our sentiments and our habits cannot adapt themselves in time to the political and economic needs of large-scale industry, then it always remains possible that we shall have to abandon large-scale industry. This possibility is shocking to those brought up in the faith of the necessary progress toward bigger and better things; but it is in no way inconsonant with the record of the past.

Fourth, just as with the atomic bomb, this economic variable can be said to make the solution by imperialism at least as likely as that by federalism, perhaps more likely. We Americans are today the greatest masters of the new economic techniques. We have, perhaps, so great a comparative advantage in industrial capability over any likely combination of opponents that we might physically at least be able to conquer the world. If at any given moment a single state possesses a really great comparative advantage of this sort—and that state may not always be the USA—it may be sorely tempted to world conquest.

These three new factors, the shrinking of this earth to country size, the invention of the atomic bomb, and the development of the techniques of modern large-scale industry, do not seem to me to invalidate what we have learned from the past of political integration. They *are* new factors, and their existence should make us more than ever cautious and tentative in making generalizations. We cannot be quite sure how they will operate. The threat of the atomic bomb may actually smooth the way to world peace. I repeat, I think such a result very unlikely, but I would not entirely close my mind to its possibility.

No doubt we could discover a great many other novel factors in the present international situation. We might, for instance, consider the chances of a widespread spiritual revolution in mankind, the advent of a new, or reborn, world religion of gentleness and love which would make all men brothers, and end war. These are delicate matters into which the objectively inquiring mind is likely to blunder awkwardly. I cannot myself really conceive such a revolution in the hearts of men as would make them gentle. At any rate, it is clear that the despairing cry, "if only they'd *try* Christianity," is not very relevant here. The Christian must, I suppose, always hope that men will shortly try to behave like Christians—or Buddhists, or Mohammedans. Until they do so behave, we shall have to go by the precedents of their past actions.

III

We have constructed, as the economists are fond of saying, a sort of "model" of a political unit made from once independent units. This new unit has a symbolic head, an administrative system possessing what is commonly called "sovereignty," an elite loyal above all to the new unit, a general population at least mildly loyal to the new unit, and sufficiently autonomous to be free from chronic and ingrowing nationalism. We have seen that it is at least very unlikely that modern scientific achievement, the pressure of economic forces, or the sudden religious conversion of mankind will build this model, or something like it, quite quickly here on earth. We must assume that the process of political integration will in the near future be not altogether unlike that process in the past.

At this point, I must enter frankly on the way of the prophet. Our first general possibility is that the work of integration will be done predominantly by the means I have called imperialist. We have seen that it is by no means inconceivable that the atomic bomb and other wonders of science would permit the quick and easy conquest of the world by a small group of determined men based almost of necessity on some existing nation-state, and probably supported by the patriotic feelings of the great mass of the inhabitants of that state. Yet on the likelihood of so melodramatic an event I remain, if not from Missouri, at least from New England, which is not a very credulous region. I promised to go against professional ethics of historians, and try to prophesy; I did not promise to try to give you science-fiction. World unity may be achieved in circumstances suited to a Buck Rogers comic strip. I am constitutionally quite unable to key my imagination to depicting such a result. It seems to me more likely that men will fight with the new weapons not too unequally, that victory will be hard won, and that a world-empire will have to be built slowly, and by political as well as by military or magical skills. I do not say a new world-empire would have to be built as slowly as that of Rome, for much has been speeded up in our time; but I do not expect such an empire to be built by a single *coup de théâtre*.

If then, world union by force must be achieved not too rapidly, and by means of force wisely guided, and helped by tolerance, organizing skill, hard work, the devotion of a trained elite, intelligent but not too intellectual—in short, by methods familiar from Roman and British history—what signs do existing nation-states show of providing such resources and such skills? What China or India, or the *united* peoples of old Europe might achieve in another future one cannot sensibly guess. At the moment, I see for the near future only three potential imperialist world-organizers, the United States, Russia, and the British Commonwealth and Empire. Now, to come out bluntly, I do not think that any of the three has what it takes to do the job.

We Americans have many assets for the task, but I do not believe we could make a *pax Americana* for the globe. We have great energy, and we are today as ubiquitous in the farthest corners of the world as was once the Englishman. We have to the full the great Anglo-Saxon gift of identifying our desires with universal human obligations. We should never attempt, as Hitler did, to conquer crudely for our own avowed good; when we conquer people, or indeed have any dealings with them, we do so for their good. Please do not think I am being cynical, or even, as is quaintly said in authoritarian leftist circles in America, "liberal." What shallow rationalists call hypocrisy is apparently one of the essentials of an imperial people. One of the grave troubles with the Germans as an imperial people is their bluntness as to their aims. And, of course, we Americans have great wealth, a magnificent production plant, and still abundant natural resources. Some of us, however, are beginning to worry about these resources, and wondering if they cannot be supplemented abroad. Of course, this desire for other peoples' goods is initially one of the great spurs of imperialism.

Yet I doubt whether we should make good imperialists, good enough to carry the job through to world unity. To begin with, we are still in most ways a democracy, and democracies in the past have never proven to be good at building empires. They cannot, apparently, pursue for long enough a consistent policy toward other peoples; they cannot provide the right sort of imperial administrations. But these are abstract considerations. I think I get nearer the heart of the matter if I say that I just don't feel my countrymen have the stuff of imperialists. Our armies in this war, though they did well the job they had to do, were surely the most homesick of armies. The lad who went through Britain, France, Italy, or New Guinea bemoaning the absence of the corner drugstore seems to me no fit successor to the Roman legionary. Again, though as a people we have grave failures from the standpoint of any high ethical and aesthetic codes ever devised, though, for instance, many American boys overseas in this war treated the inhabitants of foreign countries with amused contempt, nonetheless there remains as a basis of the American character a willingness to live and let live, a pathetic desire for a world in which nobody is pushed about. Perhaps I am trying to say that there is a rather profound emotional sense in which Americans really are believers in democracy. At any rate, there has to be a deal of pushing about to found a world-empire, and I don't believe we'll do it.

As for the Russians, I shall have to confess that I have no inside information, and no really profound first-hand acquaintance with the Russian people. I have to struggle—though frankly I don't know why I should struggle—against a tendency to believe the truth to be the opposite, the antipodean opposite, of whatever appears in the

Hearst or the McCormick press. Since these vicious newspapers have for several years been telling me that the Russians intend to try to conquer the world, I naturally incline to believe that the Russians have no such intention. But I suppose it is conceivable that even such as Mr. Hearst and Colonel McCormick may occasionally be right. I have been trying awfully hard in this discussion to be open-minded and objective, so I suppose we can stretch a point, and envision truth in relation with Messrs. Hearst and McCormick.

Grant then to the Russians the *will* to try for world conquest. They have still a good deal of technological inferiority to overcome, and that is bound to take time. They have, however, a broad territorial base, rich in natural resources, a growing and active population, a national pride and energy greatly enhanced by their successful stand against the Germans. They are not handicapped for the imperialist struggle by the kind of habits and institutions we Americans associate with democracy. They have given proof of ability to organize in the unity of the Union of Socialist Soviet Republics a considerable number and variety of peoples and nationalities. In fact, the present USSR represents in itself a very considerable achievement in political integration.

Yet, again, I cannot see our world organized under a *pax Russica.* I do not really believe the Russian people are prepared to make the sacrifices, to acquire the conditioning, necessary for such an imperial achievement. The aggressiveness, even the megalomania, often shown by some of their leaders seem to me in part the inevitable or at any rate customary bluster of competitive international politics, in part, as any psychiatrist can tell you, a mask for anxiety and fear, fear above all of us and of our atomic bomb. But I prefer not to rest my case on a statement so controversial as that the Russians don't want to conquer the world, but do want to be secure. I should like to bring forward two more obviously valid reasons why I do not think the Russians will make successful world conquerors. The first is psychological. It is not so much a matter of the celebrated and inefficient Slavic soul—that I think contemporary Russians have pretty well lived down—but rather one of simple getting on with other peoples, or at least not rousing their hatreds. Here I see good signs that the Russians, like the Germans, are not only unable to make themselves loved by other peoples—as a matter of fact, one people probably never does love another people—but are unable to make themselves at all acceptable to other peoples. And remember that one thing is very clear from our historical record: mere force is not enough. A successful imperial people must be acceptable to those it rules. Second, I believe that the Russian commitment to a new religion, that of Communism, is on the whole a handicap to any Russian attempt to build a world-empire, or even a world-state under her own hegemony. Communism has already roused religious hatreds against itself, and these hatreds reinforce whatever opposition Russia as a political entity in the rivalry of international politics would naturally rouse. What therefore may seem to the hopes of the convert to Communism or to the fears of the worried conservative a source of strength in Russia, that is, the Russian espousal of the cause of the proletariat, seems to me a source of weakness. I think it clear by now that, however the unity of the world is to be achieved, it will not come because the proletarians of the world unite.

On the possibility that the already very great agglomeration of lands and peoples known as the British Commonwealth and Empire—it is roughly one quarter of the earth's land and people—might imperialistically absorb the rest of the world, I can be briefer. The British have displayed what can only be called at least a Roman aptitude for empire. But the core of their Empire, the British Isles, has been reduced by two world wars in close succession to a point where it can hardly support the strain of further expansion. I am not among those who believe the British are done for, but I do not think they are capable of bringing the whole world, including Russia and these United States, under a *pax Britannica.* Their great self-governing dominions are too widely scattered and too thinly populated to support the task of helping their motherland conquer the rest of the world, even if they wanted to do it. India, statistically the source of most of the imposing figures for the British agglomeration, is certainly no foundation stone of empire at the present moment. We need hardly pursue this matter further.

There remains the greatest threat, or if you prefer, the greatest promise. This is an Anglo-American combination to rule the world through a *pax Anglo-Americana.* I can conceive such a combination, if it were made effective, having quite the best stab at world domination in modern times, quite a bit better than those of Charles V, Louis XIV, Napoleon, and Hitler. I think, however, for reasons I shall come to shortly, that even this attempt would fail. But I do not think there is the slightest chance that it will be made. That there are a few British and a few Americans who have dreamed and still dream of a world benignly ruled by English-speaking peoples, clean, honest, and practically blond, it would be foolish to deny. Could the most effective possible Anglo-American imperial elite be formed, and could it work in harmony, it might well push the rest of us Americans and British into this more than Rhodesian attempt. But the great mass of Americans and British are in no mood for such adventures, and seem unlikely in the foreseeable future to attain such a mood. Specific union of some sort between the two countries, or the reduction of Great Britain to the status of Commonwealth in an *American* Commonwealth and Empire, would seem to be essential to any Anglo-American world rule. And while legislators still talk, and finally vote, on Capitol Hill and in Westminster, I think such union impossible. Finally, we must remember that the rest of the world would have a voice in the establishment of a *pax Anglo-Americana.* Quantitatively quite a voice, for even today only about one human being in ten is English-speaking.

This brings me to my firmest reason for not believing that the method of imperialism will be successful within a predictable future. In our modern past, in the five hundred years of the nation-state, no one power has ever got dominance for the simple reason that sooner or later the other powers, big, middle-sized, and little, all ganged up against the aggressor, and eventually defeated him. Sooner or later against the most powerful aggressor a coalition is formed, and in the long run this coalition is too strong for the aggressor.[2] Now, in spite of loose talk about there being only two real powers left on this earth, the USA and the USSR, it is clear that there are still seventy-odd nation-states. Should the United

[2] I cannot resist referring here to my attempt to apply this line of reasoning at the beginning of this last war: Crane Brinton, "Napoleon and Hitler," *Foreign Affairs* (January, 1942).

States, or the Russians, or the British attempt world conquest by force, I confidently expect that the other nations would line up with whichever powers seemed least aggressive, least a threat to their own independence. And, in this world, if not in Buck Rogers's, I should expect this coalition to beat the aggressive superpower. I know this is history, and I feel it is common sense.

IV

If there is little prospect of world unity by the method of imperialism, may there not be greater prospect of such unity by the method of federalism? I think there is a somewhat greater prospect of unity by this method, though I should be dishonest with myself were I to maintain here that I think world unity through federalism likely in our time.

A few months ago I was leading a discussion group among wounded veterans in a Massachusetts hospital. I was expressing my doubts as to the success in our time of the movement for world federation, when one of the men remarked, "Oh, yes, Mr. Brinton, I know people of your temperament. Had you been in Philadelphia in 1787 you would have said that of course the efforts of the Constitutional Convention were doomed in advance to failure." What that veteran said certainly bit into my conscience, but I still am unable to believe that the task facing world federations today and the task facing Franklin, Hamilton, Madison, and the others at Philadelphia in 1787 are really comparable. We Americans had in 1787 one language, one law, one cultural tradition, with no more than the sort of provincial differences that separated Boston, Philadelphia, and Charleston; we had worked together as a going concern, as a team, in spite of our quarrels, ever since the first Continental Congress. The nation-states of 1948 have no such common linguistic, legal, or cultural inheritance; they have just fought two major wars among themselves; and their brief and incomplete union in the League of Nations is hardly comparable to our Congress. The League was very little more than a form of the balance of power.

Moreover, praise though you may the skill and wisdom of the men who assembled at Philadelphia, weigh heavily if you will as a superb job of propaganda the famous *Federalist Papers*, you cannot really maintain that the current movement for world federation is in any part of the world in a position at all comparable to that of the proponents of our federal Constitution of 1787–1789. In this country, men like Mr. Justice Roberts, Mr. Clarence Streit, Mr. Grenville Clark, Mr. Robert Humber, Mr. Emery Reves, and Mr. Cord Meyer, able, inspired, and virtuous though they undoubtedly are, are simply not in a position to get things done as were Franklin, Jefferson, Washington, Hamilton, Madison, Jay, and the other Founding Fathers. Historically, real federal unions have been relatively few, hard to establish, and limited to groups which already possessed much, and that much positive, not a mere negative like fear, in common.

The American Constitution, moreover, was ultimately established by the active consent of the people of the thirteen states. It was indeed produced by an elite, and to a certain extent made acceptable to the people by the prestige and the political skill of this elite. No one of course supposes that the peoples of this earth, all the twenty-two thousand million, could assemble and will themselves a world-state. There will have to be leaders, an elite. But the ultimate decision *under the method of federalism* will have to be made by the peoples; and even if you rule out black Africans and Polynesians, you can hardly rule out Chinese, and Japanese, and East Indians. In other words, you will need not only the eventual allegiance of the masses to the world-state—as I noted in the first chapter, I think the Roman superstate did not really secure the allegiance of the masses—but you will have to have their initial and active acceptance of the world federation. You will have, in American, to sell them a constitution. Can you really imagine a new *Federalist* winning over the Chinese, the Arabs, the Russians, and the Americans? Can you really conceive such acceptance from the Americans who only twenty-odd years ago balked at Article 10 of the League Covenant? Can you see how the Russian people would go about accepting, supposing that they wanted to? Would you get the Jews and the Arabs to lie down together peacefully even in a parliament of man? Who will sign acceptance for Spain? for China? I give these horrendous concrete difficulties, not out of a spirit of contrariousness, but because these difficulties are there, now, in 1948.

If you think of the human passions, the human habits, all of what Mark Twain called the "damned human race," lying behind these concrete difficulties, I think you will not have the temerity to call them ephemeral difficulties. They, and their like, are in our times permanent difficulties. They, and their like, in our times make the attainment of a world-state by the method of federal union impossible. "Impossible," Napoleon is said to have said, "is not a French word." That is not, by the way, one of the remarks he made at St. Helena; he must have made it rather before the retreat from Moscow. Impossible is of course a most human word in every language. We use it of undignified matters, like gardening, and say quite readily that it is impossible to grow oranges outdoors in our time in New England. Why can we not use it of dignified matters, like morals and politics, and say that in our time a United States of the World is impossible?

V

Yet I should not like to close this book on so pessimistic a note. After all, if we cannot grow oranges in New England we can, no matter what New York City novelists may say, grow many things there. In many sorts of human activities, such as gardening, farming, perhaps most of the duller business of life, we are really conditioned to working with recalcitrant, complex, perverse materials that won't behave just as we want them to behave. One might even say that most of us as parents in relation to our children realize we are working with such materials. The materials out of which someday world peace may be made are at least as difficult, as complicated, as perverse as those with which we struggle in our daily problems. Because the questions of international order seem to us remote, abstract, grand, we ought not to think them more easily, more idealistically, solvable than our little ones, which we never quite solve, never quite expect to solve, and yet, while we keep out of the madhouse, never quite give up trying to solve.

I think the immediate future, then, will see no world-state established either by the method of imperialism or by the method of federalism. I should expect the present world-system of seventy-odd nation-states to continue in a precarious equilibrium, known historically as a balance of power, until some such aggression as the last two German ones broke the balance. Judging from the past of the system, I should not expect this new aggression to reach the active stage of provoking a new war on a world scale before thirty or forty years, and perhaps even longer. But concrete prediction here is very risky, as in the somewhat similar task of predicting the business cycle in a world of imperfect economic planning (and perhaps even in a world of perfect economic planning). The United Nations I regard as a possibly very effective palliative of war and as a means of lengthening the spells of actual peace; and though this may seem to the more enthusiastic faint praise indeed, I mean it to be very real praise. At any rate, the United Nations is like a spray which we've got to keep using; we may not even then get perfect fruit, indeed we shan't get perfect fruit, but we ought to get a crop.

In the long pull, I see certain encouraging signs. I have throughout this book endeavored to follow the dry light of science, and avoid those more generous speculations of the imaginative prophets of our day, the Toynbees, the Sorokins, the Spenglers, the Rosenstock-Huessys, and other philosophers of history. I have tried not to generalize beyond the evidence. You will then perhaps forgive me if I nibble just once in the green pastures of the imagination. It seems possible that what Arnold Toynbee calls "universal states" —that is, the end product of what I have called here the process of political integration—are, or at any rate have been, signs of death and disintegration of cultures. I cannot here go into this fascinating problem, and can only suggest that the Roman Empire, which I have here taken as an achievement in political integration, may be taken as a form of human and cultural disintegration. The wrangling Lilliputian states of fifth-century Hellas have seemed to many sensitive moderns alive in a sense that Rome was never alive. Our Victorian grandfathers, indeed, who had little direct experience of such competition in the form of war, tended to regard competition among independent political units, such as nation-states, as a source of life-giving evolutionary energy.

We cannot in 1948, it seems to me, consider the competitive nation-state system a desirable thing in itself. Some form of political integration transcending the sovereign nation-state seems to me personally an almost inevitable purpose for all who still cherish the generous hopes with which this country was founded. We may hope ultimately to do better than the Romans, if we can have the patience—and if the scientists and inventors will let us exercise the patience—to try to transcend the nation-state by the method of consent. For may not the answer to those who associate universal states with the decline of human energy and human culture be that universal states in the past have been put together initially by force, not by consent, and that they have never recovered from the wounds they received at their birth? Can we perhaps meet successfully the challenge men have rarely if ever met before, the challenge to make of many one without destroying the many?

There are certain indications that we human beings are slowly improving relations among nation-states. The progress is modest, so modest as to seem neglible to the confirmed idealist, and to all who habitually accept that deadliest of formulas: "either . . . or." But at the conclusion of almost every one of the recent world wars, in 1713, in 1815, in 1918, and in 1945, a more explicit, more concrete, more far-reaching, and in many senses more successful attempt to set up machinery for international consultation to maintain peace has been made. Only the settlement of 1763 is an apparent exception here. But from the Congresses of Cambrai and of Soissons, so bitterly ridiculed by Carlyle in his *Frederick the Great,* through Vienna and Versailles to the Conference of San Francisco there is evident most clearly what less disillusioned people than ourselves would have called simply "progress."

Again, there is the slow growth of international law. I know that some of the clear-minded, who are often also the simple-minded insist that where there is no authority to make law there is no law possible, and that since there is no international authority there is no international law. I shall not here pick a quarrel with these people. I shall merely say that it seems to me that law is at least as much a product of human desires and of human habits as of human commands, and that there has been some kind of international law ever since there were international relations. What has come out of Nuremberg seems to me again, in innocent language, progress in international law.

There is clearly, though again slowly, being formed an international elite. In one sense, modern Europe has never wholly lacked such an elite. In the early eighteenth century, and largely under French cultural influence, cosmopolitan administrators and intellectuals seemed almost on the point of restoring at least the kind of cultural unity Europe had in the Middle Ages. Their work was largely destroyed by the romantic nationalists of the next century. Nowadays, in the working bodies of the League of Nations and its successor the United Nations, in the churches, in the universities and the learned foundations, in the press, even in the more extreme pressure groups, such as the world federationists I have been faintly and ambiguously damning, yes, even in the chancelleries of professional diplomacy, even in departments of State, there is growing a group of men and women skilled in the ways of cooperation among varied peoples, trained and practiced persons, an international elite not entirely divorced from national allegiance, but on the whole devoted to the task of getting in practice beyond the sovereign nation-state. This elite has not yet all the characteristics we found in other international elites. Notably these people have not yet a common language—and, parenthetically, I cannot believe that language will be English, if only because the language will have to be spelled as well as spoken—and they have no such common faith as the Stoics had. They are perhaps too sharply divided into the hard-boiled and the soft-boiled, and there are not enough just properly set. The proportion of preachers and teachers among them may still be a bit excessive. They probably form too much of a coterie, if not a sect, who see too much of one another at meetings, conferences, congresses, and other places where the converted preach to the converted. But they exist, and to me their existence is a sign of progress.

They do not, as a matter of fact, wholly preach to the converted; they do make converts—subject, like all converts, to occasional backsliding. No one who remembers 1918 can doubt that there has been in this country a vast increase in public interest in foreign affairs. There are no doubt many reasons why, after refusing to join the League of Nations, we now find ourselves a charter member of the United Nations. But one of the chief reasons is surely that the American people are beginning to try to understand their place in the world, to try to implement their firm desire for peace.

In Britain and in France the story is the same. We have throughout the world the beginnings, perhaps only the faint beginnings, of the kind of mass interest and mass participation in the affairs of the world without which precedent would indicate no lasting world order is possible. I know you will not accuse me of innocent idealism. We have a very long way to go before we can get the participation of the common man in a common thing greater than the nation-state as we know it. Even in Britain, where the people are perhaps the most internationally minded of any, John Smith and Jack Jones are certainly more interested in the Football Cup, the Oaks, or the Ashes, than they are in international relations. But again, there is in public opinion all over the world a foundation, a beginning, something on which we can all get to work.

How far regional federations promote world peace is difficult to say. Four or five superstates could, and probably would, quarrel as badly as have the miscellaneous dozens of today, or hundreds of yesterday, or thousands of ancient times. Perhaps there is a certain naïveté in holding that the reduction of the states of South America or of Europe by federation would be a step toward world unity. Yet I incline to believe that some such federations are in fact a necessary step on the long road to world unity, that only by bringing together states closely allied by tradition (even if like that of France and England it is a tradition of hostility), by geographic and economic conditions, by a certain similarity of culture, can we test the capacity of the human race to unite. On the whole, we human beings usually in practice do quite strongly prefer to attempt the easier thing before the harder thing, even though such a choice may seem inglorious, and is not approved by our more idealistic spiritual leaders.

I need hardly add that science and technology can help build international peace, and that they can help destroy it. Rapid transportation and communications can help solve the problems they have so largely served to raise. But their use depends on the heads and hearts of the men who use them. There are no machines that can, by themselves, promote the process of political integration—nor, I believe, wholly and catastrophically destroy the possibility of such integration. Even the atomic bomb remains an instrument within the scope of human purpose; its force is the force of human will.

We have, then, seen signs that the goal of ending war among territorial units by the establishment of some sort of world government is, very distantly, to be glimpsed by the eye of faith. I cannot believe the goal so near that there will be no war between us and it. I cannot, therefore, believe that those extremists who go about insisting that there can and hence must never be another war, that we must have world government immediately or be blown to bits, are doing the least good. Indeed, I fear that to the extent that plain people take these extremists seriously, the world federationists are doing harm. But, finally, I do not think plain people do take the extremists, the idealists, the "either . . . or" folk, seriously. No one has yet called this last one the "war to end war." We human beings are perhaps rather silly animals, rather stupid ones, but we are also very tough ones; men, women and children of our great and supposedly effete European cities stood up under months of bombardment, though the Italian military prophet Guilio Douhet had before the war written confidently that no civilian population could stand forty-eight hours of air attacks. And we are very persistent animals; we go on spraying, oranges or apples, California or New England, year after year without a ray of hope that we can ever totally eliminate insect pests and fungi, and so not ever again have to spray. Some of our scientists may cherish such hopes, but they have not contaminated the workers in the field. Some of our social scientists may cherish the hope that they can find a way to prevent war ever again breaking out, but they clearly have not contaminated the workers in the field. I cannot really believe that even atomic war will finish so tough an organism as man.

TOPICS FOR DISCUSSION AND WRITING

1. What is the proposition in the second paragraph? Does the author offer any proof in its support? Do you consider the proof adequate?
2. What is the proposition in the third paragraph? Does the author supply any proof? Is it adequate?
3. What is the proposition in the fourth paragraph? Again, is it supported by proof? Is the proof adequate?
4. What is the proposition in the fifth paragraph? Again, is it supported by adequate proof?
5. Why do you think that Professor Brinton began this essay by asking his readers to consider these four propositions?

6. Is the entire essay merely concerned with reviewing the proof which may be advanced in support of various propositions, or does the essay have an overriding proposition of its own which it is trying to prove? Is the author merely interested in suggesting the weaknesses and strengths of various propositions, or is this evaluation a way of proving the author's own proposition? Can you state in a single sentence what you consider the unifying focus of this essay (the proposition which the author is interested in proving)?
7. What are some of the new factors which some people think have invalidated what could be learned from the past? If these new factors have invalidated past experience, does it follow that they have invalidated what we can learn from the study of history?
8. What is the proposition implied in the second paragraph of section III of this essay about the one way in which a world government may most likely be brought about? What three imperialist world organizers does he foresee as possibly organizing the world in a new world state, and what conclusions does he draw concerning each?
9. What are his proofs in support of his proposition that world unity will be not brought about through force? Are they adequate?
10. What part does he think regional federations may play in bringing about a world unity? Does he have any real hope that this unity can be brought about in the near future? Can you state in propositional or thesis form his position about the way in which world unity may be brought about?
11. How would you characterize the purpose of this essay? Is it a call to action? Is it merely to review various positions, their strengths and weaknesses? Would the essay achieve its purpose if all it did was to involve the reader in a review of arguments on both sides? Is it fair to say that the author was trying to involve his audience in a dialogue, and that he has achieved his purpose if he has led his audience to a greater understanding of the complexities in the way of world unity?
12. Read the essay by Herman Kahn *On Thermonuclear War.* Would Kahn agree with Brinton's statement that fear of the atom bomb will bring people together is a "naive one"?
13. Read ahead through Marx and Engels' *Communist Manifesto.* What is Brinton's thesis about the effects of large-scale industry on national states? Does his position on the effects of increasing industrialization agree with or contradict the position of the *Manifesto?* Does Brinton support his position?

William Shakespeare, Henry V

Henry V *is William Shakespeare's dramatic re-creation of some of the great moments in the life of the fifteenth-century English king whom Shakespeare and his contemporaries regarded as England's greatest king. For his audiences at the Globe theater, Shakespeare wove together fact and fiction to produce a picture of an "English Harry" who united the British and conquered the French. Reluctant to start a war which was sure to bring sufferings upon his people, Harry could not overlook the insults of the boastful French. Assured that he had a just claim on French lands and the French crown, he gathered an army, crossed the channel, and sacked Harfleur. As he pursued the French into the interior he saw his small army weakened by disease and short rations, while the French daily grew stronger in numbers and weaponry. The two armies finally met near the small village of Agincourt, in northern France, on October 25, 1415. The result was a triumph of the British spirit and the longbow over French disorganization and heavy armor.*

Shakespeare pictured Henry as delivering the following speech to his troops just before this battle, which took place on the feast day of the two third-century brother martyrs, Saints Crispinus and Crispianus, thus "Crispin Crispian's Day." The speech has been called by Winston Churchill "the most stirring expression of high courage in the English language," and is a remarkable illustration of a thesis calling for action. Henry urges his men to fight bravely—not wishing themselves safely home in England, but considering how others will envy them the honor which is to be theirs on this day.

from HENRY V (ACT IV, SCENE III)

If we are marked to die, we are enow
To do our country loss, and if to live,
The fewer men, the greater share of honor.
God's will! I pray thee wish not one man more.
By Jove, I am not covetous for gold,
Nor care I who doth feed upon my cost.
It yearns me not if men my garments wear,

Such outward things dwell not in my desires.
But if it be a sin to covet honor,
I am the most offending soul alive.
No, faith, my coz, wish not a man from England.
God's peace! I would not lose so great an honor
As one man more, methinks, would share from me
For the best hope I have. Oh, do not wish one more!
Rather proclaim it, Westmoreland, through my host,
That he which hath no stomach to this fight,
Let him depart. His passport shall be made
And crowns for convoy put into his purse.
We would not die in that man's company
That fears his fellowship to die with us.
This day is called the feast of Crispian.
He that outlives this day and comes safe home
Will stand a-tiptoe when this day is named
And rouse him at the name of Crispian.
He that shall live this day and see old age
Will yearly on the vigil feast his neighbors
And say, "Tomorrow is Saint Crispian."
Then will he strip his sleeve and show his scars,
And say "These wounds I had on Crispin's Day."
Old men forget, yet all shall be forgot,
But he'll remember with advantages
What feats he did that day. Then shall our names,
Familiar in his mouth as household words,
Harry the King, Bedford and Exeter,
Warwick and Talbot, Salisbury and Gloucester,
Be in their flowing cups freshly remembered.
This story shall the good man teach his son,
And Crispin Crispian shall ne'er go by,
From this day to the ending of the world,
But we in it shall be remembered.
We few, we happy few, we band of brothers.
For he today that sheds his blood with me
Shall be my brother. Be he ne'er so vile,
This day shall gentle his condition.
And gentlemen in England now abed
Shall think themselves accursed they were not here,
And hold their manhoods cheap whiles any speaks
That fought with us upon Saint Crispin's Day.

TOPICS FOR DISCUSSION AND WRITING

1. What is King Henry trying to prove? What is the subject of his thesis? What is he affirming about himself? about his men?
2. What action does he call for? What emotions does he play upon? Courage? Pride? Loyalty?
3. Why does he say that he does not care for gold or for what might happen to his armor? What is his only concern?
4. Why does the King say that he would not have one man more with him? Is he sincere, or is this mere bravado?
5. What is the strongest reason he gives his men for courage in battle?
6. What is the purpose of Henry's speech: to cheer up his men? to make them think about the implications of the battle? to make them want to follow him? to make them want to do their best?
7. How would you characterize the tone of this speech? Why?
8. Is the tone appropriate to the purpose of the speech? Are the arguments appropriate? Do you think the speech was effective because of its arguments or because of the example of leadership provided by the King himself? Is the quality of the speaker as important as the arguments he uses?

Franklin D. Roosevelt

The first inauguration of Franklin Delano Roosevelt took place against a background of national uncertainty and fear about the future. The American economy had been in decline since the crash of 1929. By Inauguration Day the banks were closed, business transactions had been suspended, and the national output had fallen to a very low level. Unemployment was widespread and the general feeling across the nation was one of utter helplessness.

In a note appended to the published version of this inaugural address, the President said: "I sought principally to banish, so far as possible, the fear of the present and of the future which held the American people and the American spirit in its grasp." Consequently, he did not call for any specific action or demand support for any particular program, but instead tried to bring about a change in the emotional climate, to create an atmosphere of willingness to believe in the future and a readiness to support the legislation which he would soon be recommending. On the very next day, he issued a call for an extraordinary session of Congress, and immediately thereafter he began to send to Congress the legislation he wanted the people to support.

This first inaugural address was, therefore, a critical point in the program of the Roosevelt administration. It had to dispel the atmosphere of defeatism and to generate an atmosphere of expectancy. Like King Henry before Agincourt, the main purpose was to stir to action, not to review the past or predict the future.

INAUGURAL ADDRESS (MARCH 4, 1933) *

I am certain that my fellow Americans expect that on my induction into the Presidency I will address them with a candor and a decision which the present situation of our nation impels. This is preeminently the time to speak the truth, the whole truth, frankly and boldly. Nor need we shrink from honestly facing conditions in our country today. This great nation will endure as it has endured, will revive and will prosper. So, first of all, let me assert my firm belief that the only thing we have to fear is fear itself —nameless, unreasoning, unjustified terror which paralyzes needed efforts to convert retreat into advance. In every dark hour of our national life a leadership of frankness and vigor has met with that understanding and support of the people themselves which is essential to victory. I am convinced that you will again give that support to leadership in these critical days.

In such a spirit on my part and on yours we face our common difficulties. They concern, thank God, only material things. Values have shrunken to fantastic levels; taxes have risen; our ability to pay has fallen; government of all kinds is faced by serious curtailment of income; the means of exchange are frozen in the currents of trade; the withered leaves of industrial enterprise lie on every side; farmers find no markets for their produce; the savings of many years in thousands of families are gone.

More important, a host of unemployed citizens face the grim problem of existence, and an equally great number toil with little return. Only a foolish optimist can deny the dark realities of the moment.

Yet our distress comes from no failure of substance. We are stricken by no plague of locusts. Compared with the perils which our forefathers conquered because they believed and were not afraid, we have still much to be thankful for. Nature still offers her bounty and human efforts have multiplied it. Plenty is at our door-

* From *The Public Papers and Addresses of Franklin D. Roosevelt, Vol. II.*

step, but a generous use of it languishes in the very sight of the supply. Primarily this is because rulers of the exchange of mankind's goods have failed through their own stubbornness and their own incompetence, have admitted their failure, and have abdicated. Practices of the unscrupulous money changers stand indicted in the court of public opinion, rejected by the hearts and minds of men.

True, they have tried, but their efforts have been cast in the pattern of an outworn tradition. Faced by failure of credit, they have proposed only the lending of more money. Stripped of the lure of profit by which to induce our people to follow their false leadership, they have resorted to exhortations, pleading tearfully for restored confidence. They know only the rules of a generation of self-seekers. They have no vision, and when there is no vision the people perish.

The money changers have fled from their high seats in the temple of our civilization. We may now restore that temple to the ancient truths. The measure of the restoration lies in the extent to which we apply social values more noble than mere monetary profit.

Happiness lies not in the mere possession of money, it lies in the joy of achievement, in the thrill of creative effort. The joy and moral stimulation of work no longer must be forgotten in the mad chase of evanescent profits. These dark days will be worth all they cost us if they teach us that our true destiny is not to be ministered unto, but to minister to ourselves and to our fellow men.

Recognition of the falsity of material wealth as the standard of success goes hand in hand with the abandonment of the false belief that public office and high political position are to be valued only by the standards of pride of place and personal profit; and there must be an end to a conduct in banking and in business which too often has given to a sacred trust the likeness of callous and selfish wrongdoing. Small wonder that confidence languishes, for it thrives only on honesty, on honor, on the sacredness of obligations, on faithful protection, on unselfish performance; without them it cannot live.

Restoration calls, however, not for changes in ethics alone. This nation asks for action, and action now.

Our greatest primary task is to put people to work. This is no unsolvable problem if we face it wisely and courageously. It can be accomplished in part by direct recruiting by the government itself, treating the task as we would treat the emergency of a war, but at the same time, through this employment, accomplishing greatly needed projects to stimulate and reorganize the use of our natural resources.

Hand in hand with this we must frankly recognize the overbalance of population in our industrial centers and, by engaging on a national scale in redistribution, endeavor to provide a better use of the land for those best fitted for the land. The task can be helped by definite efforts to raise the values of agricultural products, and with this the power to purchase the output of our cities. It can be helped by presenting realistically the tragedy of the growing loss through foreclosure of our small homes and our farms. It can be helped by insistence that the Federal, State, and local governments act forthwith on the demand that their cost be drastically reduced. It can be helped by the unifying of relief activities which today are often scattered, uneconomical, and unequal. It can be helped by national planning for and supervision of all forms of transportation and of communications and other utilities which have a definitely public character. There are many ways in which it can be helped, but it can never be helped merely by talking about it. We must act and act quickly.

Finally, in our progress toward a resumption of work we require two safeguards against a return of the evils of the old order: there must be a strict supervision of all banking and credits and investments, so that there will be an end to speculation with other people's money; and there must be provision for an adequate but sound currency.

These are the lines of attack. I shall presently urge upon a new Congress, in special session, detailed measures for their fulfillment, and I shall seek the immediate assistance of the several States.

Through this program of action we address ourselves to putting our own national house in order and making *income* balance *outgo*. Our international trade relations, though vastly important, are in point of time and necessity secondary to the establishment of a sound national economy. I favor as a practical policy the putting of first things first. I shall spare no effort to restore world trade by international economic readjustment, but the emergency at home cannot wait on that accomplishment.

The basic thought that guides these specific means of national recovery is not narrowly nationalistic. It is the insistence, as a first consideration, upon the interdependence of the various elements in and parts of the United States—a recognition of the old and permanently important manifestation of the American spirit of the pioneer. It is the way to recovery. It is the immediate way. It is the strongest assurance that the recovery will endure.

In the field of world policy I would dedicate the nation to the policy of the good neighbor—the neighbor who resolutely respects himself and, because he does so, respects the rights of others—the neighbor who respects his obligations and respects the sanctity of his agreements in and with a world of neighbors.

If I read the temper of our people correctly, we now realize as we have never realized before our interdependence on each other; that we cannot merely take but we must give as well; that if we are to go forward, we must move as a trained and loyal army willing to sacrifice for the good of a common discipline, because without such discipline no progress is made, no leadership becomes effective. We are, I know, ready and willing to submit our lives and property to such discipline, because it makes possible a leadership which aims at a larger good. This I propose to offer, pledging that the larger purposes will bind upon us all as a sacred obligation with a unity of duty hitherto evoked only in time of armed strife.

With this pledge taken, I assume unhesitatingly the leadership of this great army of our people dedicated to a disciplined attack upon our common problems.

Action in this image and to this end is feasible under the form of government which we have inherited from our ancestors. Our Constitution is so simple and practical that it is possible always to meet extraordinary needs by changes in emphasis and arrangement without loss of essential form. That is why our constitutional system has proved itself the most superbly enduring political mechanism the modern world has produced. It has met every stress of vast expansion of territory, of foreign wars, of bitter internal strife, of world relations.

It is to be hoped that the normal balance of executive and

legislative authority may be wholly adequate to meet the unprecedented task before us. But it may be that an unprecedented demand and need for undelayed action may call for temporary departure from that normal balance of public procedure.

I am prepared under my constitutional duty to recommend the measures that a stricken nation in the midst of a stricken world may require. These measures, or such other measures as the Congress may build out of its experience and wisdom, I shall seek, within my constitutional authority, to bring to speedy adoption.

But in the event that Congress shall fail to take one of these two courses, and in the event that the national emergency is still critical, I shall not evade the clear course of duty that will then confront me. I shall ask the Congress for the one remaining instrument to meet the crisis—broad executive power to wage a war against the emergency, as great as the power that would be given to me if we were in fact invaded by a foreign foe.

For the trust reposed in me I will return the courage and the devotion that befits the time. I can do no less.

We face the arduous days that lie before us in the warm courage of national unity; with the clear consciousness of seeking old and precious moral values; with the clean satisfaction that comes from the stern performance of duty by old and young alike. We aim at the assurance of a rounded and permanent national life.

We do not distrust the future of essential democracy. The people of the United States have not failed. In their need they have registered a mandate that they want direct, vigorous action. They have asked for discipline and direction under leadership. They have made me the present instrument of their wishes. In the spirit of the gift I take it.

In this dedication of a nation we humbly ask the blessing of God. May He protect each and every one of us. May He guide me in the days to come.

TOPICS FOR DISCUSSION AND WRITING

1. What is the subject of Roosevelt's first inaugural address? What does he affirm about it?
2. What is the state of the nation? Does he describe it in detail, or refer to it only in general terms? Why?

3. Does he give any explanation for the current state of affairs? Does he try to make a scapegoat responsible?
4. Does he give the people any real grounds for hope? Are his suggestions specific proposals or only indications of general lines of action which might be followed? What is the effect of indicating some steps which might be taken? What would have been the effect of his speech if he had not given any specific indications of steps to be taken or general courses of action to be pursued?
5. How would you characterize the tone of this speech? Does it propose a thesis for discussion? Does it try to bring people to action? How is it similar in tone to Henry V's speech before Agincourt? Would Henry's tone have been appropriate here?
6. What do you think was mainly responsible for the impact of this speech: the arguments? the tone of the speech as a whole? the personality of the speaker?
7. Does the speech give any indication of how Roosevelt viewed the presidency? How does the speech prepare the public for New Deal reforms?

Bertrand Russell

Bertrand Russell (1872–), holder of the Order of Merit of the British Empire, Fellow of the Royal Society, winner of the Nobel Prize for literature in 1950, author of such germinal studies as Principles of Mathematics *(1903),* Principia Mathematica *(with Alfred North Whitehead, 1910), and* Problems of Philosophy *(1911), has also written on economics, history, marriage, sociology, politics, and in 1953 published a collection of short stories,* Satan in the Suburbs. *A sceptic, relativist, and probabilist by his own admission, he has been most articulate about the problems posed by nuclear development in such works as* Common Sense and Nuclear Warfare *(1958),* Has Man a Future? *(1961), and a great number of periodical articles on the subject. One of the most controversial figures in one of the most controversial issues today, Bertrand Russell's position at least demands a hearing. The audience will decide whether he wins assent.*

CO-EXISTENCE OR NO EXISTENCE: THE CHOICE IS OURS *

The recent changes in the technique of war have produced a situation which is wholly unprecedented. War has existed ever

* Reprinted by permission from *The Nation,* CLXXX, No. 25 (June 18, 1955).

since there were organized states, that is to say, for some six thousand years. This ancient institution is now about to end. There are two ways in which the end may come about: The first is the extinction of the human race; the second is an agreement not to fight. I do not know which of these will be chosen.

Neither the general public nor the majority of powerful statesmen have as yet realized that war with modern weapons cannot serve the purposes of any government in the world. It is of the first importance that this should be realized by those who control policy both in the East and in the West. It is generally conceded by those who are in a position to speak with authority that no complete defense against an H-bomb attack is possible. We must, I think, consider it the most likely hypothesis that if a great war broke out tomorrow each side would be successful in attack and unsuccessful in defense. This means that in the first days of such a war all the great centers of population on each side would be obliterated. Those who survived this first disaster would perish slowly or quickly as a result of the fall-out from radioactive clouds. Destruction of life from this cause would not be confined to the belligerent countries. The winds would gradually spread death throughout the world. This, at least, is what is to be feared. It cannot be said that the worst outcome is certain, but it is sufficiently probable to deter any sane man from incurring the risk.

Apart from the totality of destruction, there is another new element in the situation. In old days, if you had a military advantage over your enemy, you might hope to win in time. But now, if each side has enough H-bombs to wipe out the other, there is no longer any advantage in having twice as many as your adversary.

Both in the United States and in Great Britain there has been much talk of civil defense. Russian military journals contain talk of the same kind. All such plans, I am convinced, show either ignorance or hypocrisy in those who advocate them. Deep shelters would enable a portion of the population to survive the first explosion, but sooner or later these people would have to emerge from their shelters into a radioactive world.

Although the H-bomb is the center of public attention at the moment, it is only one of the possibilities of destruction which science has put in the hands of irresponsible politicians. Chemical and bacteriological warfare are studied by all powerful states and may have consequences at least as horrifying as those of the H-bomb. There is no visible end to the methods of inflicting death that may be invented. Even if a portion of the human race were to survive a great war now, it cannot be doubted that the next war, if scientific technique survives, would complete what its predecessor had left unfinished.

There is therefore no escape from the choice that lies before us: Shall we renounce war, or shall we bring our species to an end?

ESCAPE FROM REALITY

If men realized that these are the only alternatives, no one can doubt that they would choose peace. But there are various ways in which people escape the realization of unpleasant facts. I have seen statements by Russians and Chinese that a thermonuclear war would of course destroy the rotten capitalistic civilization of the West but would not vitally injure the sturdy Communist nations of the East. I have also seen statements by American authorities claiming that the West would be victorious. Both seemed to me, if genuinely believed, to be mere fantasies of wish-fulfillment and, if not genuinely believed, to be part of the silly game of bluff which great nations have been allowing themselves. I hope that this is beginning to be understood. Recently there have been hopeful signs that neither side is willing to push issues to the point of war. And with every month that passes there is a better chance that statesmen both in the East and in the West will become aware of some of the important facts by which their policy ought to be guided.

Another widespread delusion is that perhaps in a great war H-bombs would not be employed. People point to the fact that gas was not employed in the Second World War. They forget that gas had not proved a decisive weapon even in the First World War and that in the meantime gas-masks had been provided which were a complete protection. Any analogy is therefore entirely misleading.

It is thought by many that the first step forward should be an international agreement not to use H-bombs in the event of war, and this is generally coupled with the suggestion that both sides should destroy their existing stock of these weapons. This suggestion has certain merits but also certain drawbacks. Its chief merit is that if the destruction of existing stocks were honestly carried out, the danger of a sudden attack in the style of Pearl Harbor would be lessened. Against this we must set the fact that no system of inspection can now make sure that bombs are not being manufactured. This is a new fact. At the time of the Baruch proposal it was still possible for an inspectorate to gain control of the raw materials, but this is so no longer. Each side would therefore suspect that the other side was manufacturing bombs surreptitiously, and this might make relations worse than if no agreement had been concluded. What is even more important is that, if war did break out, neither side would consider itself bound by the agreement, and after a certain number of months H-bomb warfare would be in full swing. Only by not making war can the danger be avoided. We must therefore turn our thoughts away from war to the methods by which peace can be made secure.

PEACE BY STAGES

The transition from the cold war to a condition of secure peace cannot be made in a day. But it can be made, and it must be made. It will have to be made by stages. The first stage will consist in persuading all powerful governments of the world that their aims, whatever they may be, cannot be achieved by war. In this first stage, scientists—not only nuclear physicists but also physiologists, geneticists, and bacteriologists—have a very important part to play. Their discoveries have created the dangers, and it is their obvious duty to arouse the public and the governments to a sense of the risks they are running. They may, in performing this duty, be compelled to take action of which their governments disapprove, but loyalty to mankind should be for them the paramount consideration. I am convinced that it is within their power to persuade the governments both of the East and of the West to look to negotiation rather than war for a solution of their problems.

The next stage must be to create temporary machinery to negotiate settlements of all the questions at present causing conflict between East and West. It will be necessary to refer such questions to a body of negotiators in which East and West have equal representation and the balance of power is in the hands of the neutrals. I do not venture to suggest what solution should be reached on any of the vexed questions of the present. I think that a body constituted as I have suggested would avoid gross unfairness to either side, and subject to this condition almost any settlement would be preferable to a continuation of the present state of tension. A very important part of any settlement should of course be a drastic reduction of armaments. It is hardly to be supposed that the very delicate negotiations which will be required can be conducted successfully in the atmosphere of strained hostility that has existed during recent years. Each side will have to abandon perpetual abuse of the other and learn to practice that degree of toleration which after centuries of warfare was at last achieved between Christians and Moslems and between Catholics and Protestsants. We cannot now wait for the slow operation of reason through the discouragements of long indecisive wars. We must learn in advance a manner of thinking and feeling which in the past has been learned slowly and through bitter experience. I will not pretend that this is easy. But if men can be made to realize the dreadful alternative I do not think it will prove impossible.

THE THIRD STEP

If the immediate problems that now divide East and West were settled in some such way, we could reach the third stage of progress toward secure peace. The international problems of our day are not the last that will ever arise. There will be new problems, perhaps dividing the world quite differently from the way in which it is now divided between communist and anti-communist blocs. So long as there is not an established international authority capable of enforcing peace, the risk of war will remain, and with every advance in science the risk will become more terrible. The international anarchy resulting from a multitude of states with unrestricted sovereignty must be brought to an end. The international authority which is to end it will have to be federal and endowed with only such powers as are necessary for preserving the peace of the world. The most important of these powers, and also the most difficult to secure, will be an obvious preponderance of armed forces over those of any national state or alliance of states. The anarchic liberty at present enjoyed by sovereign states is dear to most people and will not be surrendered easily, but it will have to be surrendered if the human species is to survive. The process required is a continuation of that which occurred in the fifteenth and sixteenth centuries. Before that time powerful barons in their castles could defy national governments, and there was the same sort of anarchy within a nation as now exists between nations. Gunpowder and artillery put an end to internal anarchy in France, Spain, and England. The hydrogen bomb has the same part to play in ending international anarchy. The loss of liberty, though it may be distasteful, is precisely of the same kind as that which private individuals suffer by being forbidden to commit murder, for after all it is the right to murder which hitherto sovereign states will be asked to surrender.

LEGITIMATE HOPES

I have been speaking of dangers and how to avoid them, but there is another thing which is just as important to emphasize, for while fears are at present unavoidable, hopes are equally legitimate. If we take the measures needed to end our fears, we shall thereby create a world capable of such well-being as has never been known and scarcely even imagined. Throughout the long ages since civilization began, the bulk of mankind have lived lives of misery and toil and bondage. All the long burden of misery that has darkened the slow progress of mankind has now become unnecessary. If we can learn to tolerate each other and to live in amity, poverty can be abolished everywhere more completely than it is now abolished in the most fortunate nations. Fear can be so much diminished that a new buoyancy and a new joy will brighten the daily lives of all. The work of science, which while war survives is largely evil, will become wholly beneficent. Nothing stands in the way but the darkness of atavistic evil passions. New technical possibilities of well-being exist, but the wisdom to make use of them has hitherto been lacking. Shall we collectively continue to turn our back upon the things that each one of us individually desires? We can make a world of light, or we can banish life from our planet. One or other we must do, and do soon. A great duty rests upon those who realize these alternatives, for it is they who must persuade mankind to make the better choice.

TOPICS FOR DISCUSSION AND WRITING

1. Is there a third alternative, beyond the two which Russell presents in his opening statement? If there is, what effect would it have upon his essay?
2. How does Russell's statement of alternatives, specifically known as a dichotomy, influence the structure of his essay?
3. What is Russell's thesis? How is his thesis both like and unlike Henry V's in the speech on the battlefield of Agincourt (p. 57)?
4. Write an essay showing how events since 1955 (when this essay was first published) have re-enforced or weakened the validity of Russell's position.
5. Write an essay showing how Russell's position tends to find support in Thoreau's essay on *Civil Disobedience* (p. 13). What would Thoreau's position have been if he had had to face the issues presented in Russell's essay?
6. How is Russell's position strengthened or weakened by some of Brinton's (p. 35) examples derived from history? Do any of the lessons which Brinton claims we have learned from history confirm or weaken Russell's attitudes?
7. Compare Russell's position to that taken by Herman Kahn in his essay *On Thermonuclear War.*

II Defending a Thesis

INDUCTIVE ARGUMENT

A fact, an opinion, or a judgment is not something which simply happens. We need to have observed, to have experienced, and to have considered before we can produce any of the three. Before we can formulate a thesis, we must go through a preliminary process in which we have examined and thought about a subject. Only after such preliminaries do we have the right to say "this is a fact," "this is my opinion," "this is my considered judgment." If there is no evidence of such preliminary investigation, or insufficient evidence, any audience would have the right to dismiss our thesis.

Assuming that the prerequisite observation, experience, and consideration have resulted in our being able to present a thesis, how are we to convince an audience that our thesis is worth consideration, deserving of assent? One way is *induction,* which is the selective recapitulation of the same process we went through before we formed the thesis. Convinced that our own preliminary study has been thorough enough and convincing enough to have resulted in a thesis, we invite the audience to retrace that process and to arrive at the same conclusion (the thesis) as we did.

This retracing will ordinarily be selective. Any investigation of a new subject will be, at first, disorderly; there will be dead ends, reversals, anticlimaxes in the course of the investigation itself. Eventually there will come a point where the meaning of the evidence becomes clear, and the thesis begins to emerge.

But before that happens, there will be unruly, disorderly accumulation of information which we hope will result in a thesis but for which we can give no guarantees. It would be fruitless, in most cases, to make our audience retrace that whole necessary drudgery. Instead, we rearrange the investigating experience, omitting the irrelevant, emphasizing development and showing that at the end of the investigation comes a thesis. This controlled survey of the single facts or single experiences which finally resulted in the discovery of a thesis is the inductive form of argument.

As an example of induction, consider this: you have been given an assignment in history in which you are asked to write on the causes of the American Civil War. You will examine the economic, the sociological, the geographic factors as they affect both the North and the South. Eventually the separate pieces of evidence which you examine will become coherent. You will recognize certain recurring themes, certain cooperating elements, general characteristics which individual items of evidence will have in common. When you have been able to infer a general conclusion from the series of individual facts, you will have completed an induction. There will always be the possibility that your conclusion may have to be changed, should some further evidence later present itself. You will not be able to argue that any future complex of economy, sociology, and geography will inevitably result in a second Civil War. But you will be able to pass a reasonable, probable judgment on the causes of the Civil War; and if your research and enumeration of evidence have been thorough enough, you will be in a position to persuade a reader that your judgment is a correct one.

If the investigating process has been full enough in itself; if the evidence that has been examined is unambiguous, relevant, and complete as possible; if the reconstruction of the process is effectively done; then the thesis which stands at the end of the process may win assent.

John Rader Platt

John Rader Platt is the author of numerous technical papers on physics as well as many essays interpreting recent scientific achievements for the general reader. He studied under Enrico Fermi at the University of Chicago and stayed on as a member of the staff to conduct research in the chemical and physical properties of the infrared and ultraviolet regions of the spectrum. Of late, he has become more and more interested in new areas of study, such as biophysics. He is a working scientist, abreast of developments in his own field, but he is also a student of the history of science, interested in the ways in which changing scientific methods have influenced scientific discovery.

The following essay is interesting to students of effective writing because it illustrates the use of induction while discussing induction as a scientific method. Professor Platt's thesis is that all scientists have their own style in scientific investigation. To demonstrate his thesis, he has to examine several individual examples. In the process of considering how different scientists have tried to demonstrate their hypotheses in different ways, he is led into a discussion of induction and deduction and the differences between them. His own essay thereby becomes an illustration of one of the methods he is discussing.

STYLE IN SCIENCE *

All scientists are not alike. Look at any laboratory or university science department. Professor Able is the kind of man who seizes an idea as a dog seizes a stick, all at once. As he talks you can see him stop short, with the chalk in his fingers, and then almost jump with excitement as the insight grips him. His colleague, Baker, on the other hand, is a man who comes to understand an idea as a worm might understand the same stick, digesting it a little at a time, drawing his conclusions cautiously, and tunneling slowly through it from end to end and back again.

Which of these methods is likely to make the greater contribution to science? There are drawbacks to both. Able is volatile. He may drop his idea as rapidly as he acquired it. In a short time he can race through a forest of ideas and leave all his colleagues breathless behind, including Baker. Baker is scornful of such a procedure, perhaps a little envious. He can never try so many ideas, though in the end each one he tries becomes part of him, each one tested in every aspect.

Or consider another pair of scientific minds, whose contrasted inner workings are revealed by their contrasted footnote habits.

Charlson is the one who discovers everything for himself. He dislikes reading other men's efforts because they stale the fresh springs of his thought. Though he is famous to the world, his scientific enemies are numbered by the dozens because he never bothered to look up their prior parallelisms and dim anticipations. So he left out all the references that would have been their tendril grasps on fame. Rumors of plagiarism are heard at the Society meetings.

Doctor Doggett, instead, is footnote-happy. No historical cranny is safe. He pries out the foreshadowings, the counterarguments, and the misprints. If he makes a creative contribution himself it is lost among the references, for there are more lines of footnotes than there are of text. Yet he gathers a thousand strands together and may find distant connections which pass unnoticed by other men.

Will it be Doggett or Charlson who makes the great discovery?

This is a question we could pursue through the whole academic alphabet, contrasting the syndromes and merits of the types of scientific personality. Simply as writers, one man is dull, one witty; one verbose, another terse. This man's equations lie like boulders on the page, that man's like a fog. It is amusing to see how the differences show through the attempted impersonality of scientific verbiage.

But we soon realize that the question of relative merit hinges on a more fundamental question: Is personality significant for science? We often hear the arguments for scientific determinism, which is the belief that scientific discoveries are somewhat like the measles, breaking out everywhere at once when the time is ripe. If this is so, is not one man in a given field as likely as another to make an important discovery? Does it make any difference to knowledge who invents a thing first, or what kind of mind and style he has?

If we look at some examples from the history of science with this problem in mind, I think we will see that personality does indeed make a difference. The two aspects interpenetrate. To a remarkable extent the discovery ripe to be born selects one discoverer from among the contestants, picking out the master of a line of thought and method essential to its birth. But equally remarkable is the extent to which the undetermined and peculiar stamp of his parenthood is embedded forever in the body of pure knowledge.

The evidence for scientific determinism—with its lesser emphasis on personality—is the familiar catalogue of the instances of multiple discovery. The great cases of this kind were the simultaneous and independent discovery of the calculus by Newton and Leibnitz three centuries ago, and the simultaneous Darwin and Wallace discoveries of natural selection in the last century. Hundreds of lesser examples could be listed. Each idea, with variations, is found and found again. Patent lawyers make their living from such competition.

Independent discoveries are sometimes only months or weeks apart, especially today in the fields crowded with first-rate competitors. In physics, for example, the synchrocyclotron was invented simultaneously in the United States and in Russia. Independent communications from this country and from Germany announced the current theoretical "shell model" of atomic nuclei in the very same issue of the *Physical Review*. The race for priority hinges on days, and the Saturday afternoon Letter-to-the-Editor becomes a regular event.

Such examples make scientific developments appear almost inevitable, maturing like dandelions on both sides of company fences and national ones, to the despair of Congressmen and drug houses. The reason for this is that discoveries have preconditions that must be met. Once these are met, even a nongenius may make a discovery if he is playing with the right apparatus and tries everything. To a certain extent, science is successful because it is a code of rules that enables ordinary brains with ordinary motivations to set up, one step at a time, the necessary preconditions.

Some are mechanical. Take the discoveries of electrons and of X-rays, which occurred within two years of each other in the 1890's. Both required the application of a high voltage to a good vacuum.

This in turn required the knowledge of direct current electricity, a good cheap high-voltage generator, and a good cheap vacuum pump, with an electronic motor drive for convenience. All these are late nineteenth-century items. The incandescent lamp, not a discovery but an invention, had similar preconditions; but it could be made with a lower voltage and a poorer vacuum, and so was invented a few years earlier.

This is not to say that these discoveries could have been predicted. No one foresaw that such phenomena existed. But if anything were there to be found with that apparatus, it must have been found *then*. The discoveries were made by highly competent experimenters; yet within a few years almost any intelligent student might have made them independently, while experimenters ten times as competent could scarcely have set the dates of discovery earlier by as much as two decades. In present times, the antiproton could be predicted, and planned for at Berkeley, years in advance; and then discovered almost as soon as the apparatus was designed, finished, and turned on. We can see why one celebrated physicist said that half of his success consisted in knowing what to order and where to order it.

There are also intellectual conditions that must be met before a discovery can be made or appreciated or understood. The brilliant idea requires intellectual groundwork and, what is equally important, a scientific community ready for the novelty. It is just as sure a recipe for failure to have the right idea fifty years too soon as five years too late. William James might have been advising young men in any science when he said "Decide what important thing will be done in the next twenty years, then do it."

Occasionally, untimely ideas do get preserved to be marveled at. In mathematics, Fermat's Last Theorem still tantalizes us; and Hamilton's Quaternions, which were thought by his contemporaries to indicate mild insanity, were simply premature by two or three generations.

Abbé Mendel, father of genetics, actually bred his sweet peas decades too soon. His contribution was finally disinterred at the time when it could be understood. Roentgen made the discovery of X-rays in a momentary lapse from a lifelong study of crystals, which was no doubt equally painstaking and inspired but is almost unremembered because it was fifty years too early. Sometimes even a short time makes a great difference in the response to a new idea. Stories persist that the equations of quantum mechanics were derived by this man or that but were rejected by editors only a year or two before Schrödinger got his version accepted and won a Nobel prize.

We may speculate on how many good scientists may have died mute, inglorious, and bitter because their work was too advanced to be understood. This is the standard defense of the ill-prepared and the crackpot. Yet the failure to recognize a brilliant man is only partly due to the stupidity or stubbornness of the scientific community; it is also partly his own fault.

For brilliance has an obligation not only to create but also to communicate. A scientist can not really go "voyaging through strange seas of thought alone." The more penetrating eye will see him to be surrounded by a cloud of witnesses. He takes from others; he gives to others. He must address the problems of his time. He must translate his thoughts into the language of his contemporaries. He must scatter them abroad for interaction. A thought which has not penetrated to other minds will die unfruitful.

As a result, the scientist can hardly be recognized posthumously, like the artist or poet. He is much less independent, much more bound to the current needs and purposes of the scientific community. His achievement of thought needs to be at the same time an achievement of communication and leadership which must be acknowledged by the group—by at least one editor!—before its intellectual viability fades away.

It is a perishable achievement. Not many of us know who first cut the trees or cleared the land beside our houses. The scientific explorer, like the wilderness explorer, exists to be superseded. Wandering at random, he finds a first, clumsy way to the new goal. The more important the goal, the greater the speed with which his path is bypassed by short-cuts, ridden over by electronic computing machines, and obliterated by the marching masses of Ph.D.'s. His hesitations, his sextant readings, the art and intuition by which he avoided this pitfall or that rabbit track—these make dull hard reading after a few years, for they apply to a world of difficulties which, because of his very efforts, has vanished and can scarcely be reconstructed. But such a man is properly contemptuous of the incoherent genius whose ravishing discoveries are too strange and vague to be communicable.

Determinism also plays a more intimate role. Not only is the time of a discovery approximately determined, it seems that the personality of the discoverer may to some extent be determined. To find America, we must have a fifteenth-century Western sea captain, uncommercial, convinced, dogged, persuasive, with delusions of grandeur—whether his name is Columbus or something else.

To see this principle in science, we must concentrate on two components of personality which I shall call method and style. By method, I mean the type of a scientist's intuition, his normally preferred method of attack. One man loves most to design and build apparatus, a glorified instrument maker. Another is a human measuring engine who can turn out more data or more precise data than anyone else. Some like to improve on other men's experiments in familiar fields, others prefer wild and novel experiments of their own at the limit of the possible. In these differences, one major axis of variation ought to be especially emphasized. It is the difference between the generally inductive and the generally deductive types of mind.

In an inductive mind, the internal monologue might go somewhat as follows: "Now here's a funny result. It doesn't fit in at all with Smollengoble's theorem! Yes, the apparatus is okay. Didn't I see last month where someone else had trouble with that theorem? But he had lower pressure. If we increased the pressure, would it go farther in the same direction?"

The general from the particular. This is the man who covers his laboratory walls with graphs of his data and squints at them every morning before he turns on his power supply, wondering if those deviations are experimental error or a real effect. There is something of this turn of mind in all of us. A talented few, like the master organic chemists, develop it until they can play their residues and hunches as a virtuoso plays the violin.

The deductive genius may be tone deaf to such music. His passion is not for the uncertain new order but for elegance and clarity in the old. At his highest pinnacle, he is the Euclid or Maxwell who stands and looks back after a period of growth and sees that a few simple postulates will unite a whole body of separate rules into a symmetrical system.

Like the inductive mind, he sees patterns, but in a different medium. Perhaps when he closes his eyes by the fire he stares into a magnificent void where the luminous theorems move and intersect and enclose each other and he leaps up shouting, "I have it! I have it!" However jumbled his desk may be, there is some distant region of the spirit where his files are clearly labeled and his papers have been written in a neat hand on one side only and are stapled into bundles with their edges straight—the great plan encompassing every particular in every pigeonhole. There is something of this, too, in all of us.

One of these minds anticipates, the other reconstructs. Inductive steps must come before deductive ones. So in each subject area there is a time when one method is most appropriate. Then it exhausts its material, at least for the moment, and recedes as the important discoveries begin to fall to another kind of mental machine. A field of knowledge has a curve of growth and a morphology, branches and stem—a beginning, a middle, and an end. Different talents are needed in the gardeners at different times. Those with a green thumb must plant, while others with a sure balance climb ladders later for the fruit.

Take the discovery of the law of gravitation. First there is visual observation and instrumentation, from the ancients to Tycho Brahe's quadrant and his tables of years of nights of measurement. Then there are the rule-makers, from the Ptolemaic astronomers to Kepler, who asked how all this would look from the nearest star and searched Tycho's tables for regularities, boiling the regularities down to his three laws of planetary motion.

Wandering in and out of the procession are the speculators—Lucretius, Copernicus—who animate the mixture with their lively controversies. At one side are the auxiliaries: Archimedes on conic sections; the navigators, defining the shape and size of the earth; Galileo, hurling balls and abstracting from them that ingenious invention, the ideal free body.

What a preparation for Newton! It might be compared to some Biblical prophecy in its visions and connections and anticipations across the milleniums. These are the shoulders of giants, with linked arms—not merely a human pyramid, but the braced and giant framework of knowledge itself.

The main line of development in scientific theory follows this sequence of work methods: observation, rule of thumb, speculation, synthesis. Naturally the methods of work are not perfectly separated in time nor even in the individual scientists. Every research man must be capable of performing all the functions in some degree—especially the speculative function—if he is to be worth his scientific salt. He may even have several highly developed talents, like Newton. This should not blind us to the big difference in the different mental processes, even such as that between the maker of the important little first syntheses—frequently an experimenter—and the maker of final grand syntheses who often shows a native distaste for the raw and original datum.

To see the historical necessity that selects these types, let us try a thought experiment on history. Consider what would have happened if the minds of Newton and Kepler had been interchanged. The slightest acquaintance with the work of either man will show that Newton's mind was not the one to unravel Tycho's data, and Kepler's was not the one to do Newton's necessary preliminary work of discovering the calculus. Not that it would have been absolutely impossible; only that it would have been slow and burdensome for either mind to try to use intuition methods like the other, and that they would have turned aside soon and wisely to more congenial discoveries.

A mature research worker needs to seek out tasks which he can undertake best with his mental gifts at his moment of history. A Maxwell in the eighteenth century could not have united electricity and magnetism but would have had to work on, let us say, astronomy, while the Franklins did the groundwork of electricity. Maxwell in the nineteenth century could and did perfect electricity but would have been lost in atomic spectra, where a Kepler kind of mind was needed. A Maxwell today might find chemistry or field-theory almost ripe for his talents, but would probably be foolish to go back to the well-plowed area of electricity unless he proposed to make a still larger synthesis, or a synthesis from a completely new point of view.

The time sequence of work methods is never perfectly clear-cut, however; in a single field the different types of talent co-exist and make simultaneous contributions. For the different types of talent need each other. Inductive and deductive, intuitive and classical, are the two halves of a pair of scissors and cut only when they are opposed. Each work method produces its own peculiar excesses which must be seen from another viewpoint before their deformity can be recognized.

The inductive mind often goes too far. Not having the advantage of the grand synthesis, it does not know where to stop. Searching for important relations, it finds unimportant ones. Experimental error may be turned into law, or clear disproof dismissed as experimental error.

Pythagoras' useful relation between the sides of triangles seems to have been associated in his own enthusiasm with the lengths of musically harmonious strings, and so with the harmonies of the universe and the music of the spheres. This goes too far, but it is not all nonsense: the lengths of harmonious strings do indeed have simple numerical ratios.

The first regularity of planets which Kepler thought he found was that they moved on spheres circumscribed and inscribed in five vast regular polyhedrons in the heavens. This is not all nonsense: the regular spacing of the orbits is a main feature of several recent cosmologies.

Such jumps "beyond Reason" need to be continuously criticized by the deductive and classical mind. Yet the inductive mind is like a sentry who must be forgiven for firing at an occasional shadow provided he always fires toward the enemy.

The sin of the deductive mind is that it derides and suppresses those inductive jumps that later prove to be right about as harshly as those that prove to be wrong. Newton rejected Huygens' and Hooke's wave theory of light which swept out Newton's own ideas a hundred years later. An esteemed critic showed that Balmer's formula, the first real regularity found in atomic spectra, must be a mathematical accident. De Broglie's paper, which contained the first germ of quantum mechanics, was widely regarded as nonsense.

Still, this conservatism has a good result. The success of an innovator is meted out in proportion to his scientific persuasiveness, his patience in amassing crucial observations, like Darwin, to show that the old faith is unjustified. It is not the moment of insight but the moment of acceptance that marks a firm step forward. Scientific growth is by conflict. The truth is found only in the heat of controversy as each man is forced to defend his thesis: the classicist his sufficiency, the innovator his necessity.

The historical counterpoint between the inductive and deductive mind is useful even in its subtler manifestations. It provides an unspectacular tension which is a major force is keeping science balanced. Each creative worker lives in a steady stream of deductive criticism—normally, in fact, self-criticism—curbing and channeling his intuitive impulses.

It is not so much that his little daily jumps and inferences must not violate "reason" as that they must satisfy more delicate canons of scientific good taste. How many readings or decimal places to take; what precautions; how ignorant or speculative to show oneself at various stages of scientific friendship; how soon to publish; and so on. A large part of the training of science students is really devoted to instilling this code of scientific manners.

The code is a balance of opposites. A man may acquire deductive good manners at the expense of some of his inductive hope, faith, and fire; fanning the fire may soften in turn the rigor of his self-criticism. Some individuals and groups try to solve the problem by separating the two processes, starting with an idea stage in which the imagination runs wild and free, followed by an analytical stage in which the ideas are critically selected and combined. The genius is the one who can maximize both elements and maintain at the time the fiercest productivity and the most exacting standards.

Likewise for a successful scientific group, the curbing of inductive jumps by the canons of taste must be neither too rigid nor too loose. The scissors will not cut if the blades are locked or if they are wobbly. The rigor of editors is needed to restrict the wilder flights as much as the zeal of speculators is needed to keep knowledge alive. Science cannot be fruitful where publishers indulge unready authors, wild fancies, and incompetent techniques; nor where hoary academic despots hold the seats of power and press the young men to a mold two generations old. But neither side can afford to be dogmatic, for it is only in the light of the syntheses of a succeeding generation that we can look back and be certain what was excess of speculation and what was excess of repression.

These remarks have perhaps conveyed some idea of the depth to which scientific determinism goes. A social necessity fixes not only the timing of a discovery but the work methods of the discoverer; it affects the heat of the controversies engendered, and where science is successful it sets the canons of taste which determine whether the discovery is accepted or rejected at a given stage of proof.

Nevertheless, all is not fixed. If we move about inside this framework we can now begin to see the ornaments and gargoyles added, unnecessarily and delightfully and sometimes unexpectedly, by exuberant craftsmen, shaped by personality above and beyond strict scientific need.

For one thing, each person has his own combination of fields of interest. A scientist trained in one subject often makes spectacular contributions when his novel outlook and work methods are turned into another field. Think of the special approach of Helmholtz, the physiologist turned physicist; or of Pasteur, the chemist, among the diseases.

Personality also enters through language, with its hidden assumptions. Without Newton himself, we might never have had "force" or "mass" in the equations of motion; or they might have had very different definitions and emphases. Philosophers have pulled and hauled at them for centuries; the difficulties were ineradicable, because these symbols were written from the beginning in the Newtonian equations that worked. The Father of Physics has imprinted "force" and "mass," like intellectual genes, into every cell of the physical sciences today.

Kepler, on the other hand, seems to have eschewed, largely on aesthetic grounds, the anthropomorphic concept of "force" between heavenly bodies. In this question of taste, he anticipates Einstein. If history had put the Kepler mind in the Newton body, it might have delayed the discovery of universal gravitation, which would have been difficult for Kepler—but it might have accelerated the discovery of general relativity.

Terminology is often chained to such initial biases. Franklin's choice of the arithmetic terms "positive" and "negative" to designate the two supplementary types of electricity still plagues our thinking and may have delayed who knows what happier synthesis.

The idiosyncrasies of taste and choice, of abilities and workmanship, embellish and modify a discovery. The work method is determined; the style is not. Any physical law is exhibited in many places and forms and may be found by single experiments on hundreds of compounds or by hundreds of experiments on a grain of sand. And the discoverer may be an exhibitionist or a conservative, an equation maker or a model maker; he may want priority, or certainty. He may succeed by testing everything to destruction, at unusual temperatures and pressures, or by exploring his materials with nothing but a beam of light. He may be guided by shrewd and almost superstitious hunches, that only fluorocarbons will give him clear-cut answers, or density-matrix methods, or Drosophila, or sweet peas.

Sometimes the effects of such variations are profound indeed. There is one instance where a vast intellectual development has been hung on the deficiencies of a single piece of apparatus. We might not believe that electrons are in atoms except for some equipment assembled in 1898 by Zeeman in Holland, with which he found that the spectrum lines of atoms were broadened and polarized by a magnetic field. This "Zeeman effect" was explained by Lorentz on the assumption that the atoms contained the newly discovered corpuscles called electrons. Later, Bohr continued to assume this in his atomic theory; and whole-electrons-in-atoms passed on into the quantum mechanics that we now use.

But meanwhile, what of the Zeeman effect? If Zeeman had had a better spectrograph or had improved his apparatus before publishing his first results, he would have reported what a college senior can discover now; that each of his broadened spectrum lines is really a complex array of many lines, with every array different. Neither Lorentz nor anyone else would then have believed that there were intact electrons, all alike, inside the atom; perhaps fractional ones would have been assumed. The Bohr atom would have been different, or impossible. Quantum mechanics as we know it might never have appeared. No doubt some other theoretical system would have been produced in its place, but by now, after fifty years, its practitioners would speak a language incomprehensible or perhaps unbelievable to our best physicists. (The scientists will not find it any easier to talk to scientists they meet from another planet than laymen will.)

If a piece of apparatus can shape a field of knowledge, a brilliant scientist may also have a great personal effect. Many of the peculiarities of modern physics seem to have this individual stamp. Bohr, de Broglie, Schrödinger, Heisenberg, Dirac—each is responsible for some aspects of the synthesis of atomic structure which is quantum mechanics. Yet their approaches are very different: Bohr with his electron-orbits in space; de Broglie with his almost mystical waves; Heisenberg with his matrices and strict operationalism; Dirac with his formalism. If we had lost one of these, it would not have affected our ability to predict experimental results, which is often said to be the aim of science, but it would have been a great loss indeed to our understanding.

And a great change. Without Bohr himself, would the earlier ideas of an atom as a vibrating jelly have been strangely modified by some other young pseudo-Bohr in the 1910's to explain the spectra and win the day? Without the particular style of a particular man, Dirac, we might have had formalism of a sort, but probably not the chaste, terse, awful elegance that now strikes fear and admiration into the graduate students.

The work of Willard Gibbs in chemical thermodynamics may be the most individual tour de force of all. Somewhat cut off in late nineteenth-century America from the larger body of European theoretical physicists and chemists, he evolved an unusual kind of thinking; perhaps as an island population evolves aberrant species when cut off from the mainland. His equations show no trace of the mechanical particles bombarding the walls of a box which still dominated the thought of European scientists. He produced a theory without "forces" and without imaginary models of what was happening in the box, using simply relations among the things observed on the outside, such as temperature, pressure, and volume. And he combined these with a logical absolute, a naked and apparently vulnerable assertion about entropy.

True, this was not completely alien to contemporary style.

Differential equations like his were the admired mathematical form in other areas. There had been some interest in the physical power of syllogisms; and Mach and Einstein were shortly to remove "force" from motion and from gravitation and to assert other logical absolutes. But taken together and applied to chemistry, what a change! Small wonder that nobody noticed him but Maxwell. Small wonder that the best science students still go blank and dumb, and the little philosophy major at the back of the room suddenly begins to get the right answers, when they come to this part of the course. It hurts a three-dimensional man to see temperature computed from a syllogism.

It seems probable to me that if Gibbs had lived in England or Germany this fusion of ideas might not have occurred until at least a generation later. By that time chemical thinking would have been set in another mold, and chemistry today would be a different thing.

There are many lessons, for our culture, for our teachers, and for our scientists, to be learned from examining closely the interplay of the Great Man aspect of history with the Determinist aspect. It is exhibited in the microcosm of the scientific world in a relatively simple form in which the causal intellectual strands are rather easy to trace. The general cultural or political historian might find this limited but precisely known area a good testing ground for theories of history.

I think he would conclude, as I have here, that the nature of the achievements of a large competing scientific group is determined by the group and its history, and depends little on the behavior of individual discoverers. We can almost write down equations for the speed and scope of advance in some departments of knowledge. But the pressure of scientific determinism becomes weak and random as we approach the great unitary syntheses. For they are not only discoveries. They are also artistic creations, shaped by the taste and style of a single hand.

TOPICS FOR DISCUSSION AND WRITING

1. What are some of the ways in which scientists differ in their approaches to problems?

2. What is scientific determinism? How, as a theory, does it explain scientific discoveries? What theory opposes it, and how does *this* theory explain scientific discoveries?
3. Why have many of the more recent scientific discoveries been made almost simultaneously by two or more researchers?
4. What are some of the intellectual conditions which must be met before a scientific discovery can be made or understood?
5. What is the subject matter of Platt's essay? What is he affirming about his subject? In your opinion, what sentence comes closest to stating his thesis most clearly? Paraphrase it in your own words.
6. What does he mean by a scientist's method? A scientist's style? How do they differ? Does he make clear what he means by *style?*
7. How does a scientist using the inductive method proceed? A scientist using the deductive method?
8. Are both inductive and deductive methods equally useful in solving any particular problem? How do the methods differ? What determines which method will be used?
9. What is scientific method? Is it merely inductive, merely deductive, or a combination of the two?
10. How does Platt proceed to demonstrate his thesis in this essay (inductively or deductively)? What is his *style?*
11. What part does a scientist's style play in the making of scientific discoveries? Could any scientist have made any discovery if he had been in the right place at the right time?
12. Which of the essays in the first section of this text attempt to prove their thesis by induction?

Barbara Ward

Barbara Ward, Lady Robert Jackson (1914–   ) was educated in England, France, and Germany, and holds degrees in philosophy, political history, and economics. An economist of international reputation, she has been a lecturer at Oxford and Harvard universities and holds honorary degrees from Fordham, Smith, Columbia, Kenyon, Brandeis, and other universities. She is the author of several books, including The West at Bay *(1948),* Interplay of East and West *(1957),* India and the West *(1961), and* The Rich and the Poor Nations *(1962). In her lectures and in her writings, Lady Jackson has insisted on a policy of cooperation among nations, combined with firmness and decisiveness on the part of the noncommunist nations. Her insistence that we must act rather than temporize in the face of crisis lends to her statements an especially urgent quality and helps to define her as an* active *rhetorician. Her point of view may be profitably compared with that of Bertrand Russell. The following essay is a distillation of both her sense of urgency and one of her recurring arguments.*

In Time of Trial *

"These are the times that try men's souls." Nearly two centuries have passed since Tom Paine wrote these words, but they are as relevant to our own day as to his. Now, as then, we face the most profound trial that can test the courage of man. Such trials are not created by the surface play of politics—the ins and outs of government, civil discussions, even wars which occur within a reasonably stable order of society. The real test comes in times of radical change in the foundations of the social order. During Tom Paine's lifetime the Americans were engaged in such a revolution. They were attacking not simply the colonial link with Britain, but the principle of imperialism itself. They proclaimed republicanism in a system of monarchies, the rights of man in an aristocratic world, and federalism in the dawning age of nation-states. In short, they were engaged in a fundamental redrawing of the social and political map of humanity.

Such crises of change strike straight to the soul. Faced with a drastic reordering of the very bases of social life, men can hardly remain indifferent. They must react. But they may do so in opposite ways, with fear and rejection, or with steadfastness and hope. It is very easy to be afraid. Thousands of American settlers denounced the Revolution as treason and subversion, fought it, retreated to Canada or took ship to England, leaving behind the men of faith, who went on to build a continent. Before the French Revolution, all of France was in the grip of that strange phenomenon which came to be known as *La Grande Peur*. Fifty years later, the Manchus reacted to the incoming West with hatred and rejection and a backward-looking fear. The collapse of Europe's interwar economy combined with communist pressure produced, in the Nazi party, the greatest organized movement of hate, fear, and reaction the world has ever seen.

Today the crisis of change is so much more profound than any that has gone before that we must expect the reactions to be more violent. What is left that is stable? Science has abolished distance, established instant communication, and placed us on the brink of planetary space. The world order based on Western dominance has collapsed in a single decade. The interdependence of economies has become such that a small percentage increase in one nation's interest rates can undermine the gold reserves of another. Above all, the world has become a single neighborhood of potential atomic destruction. These facts of upheaval and interdependence are inescapable. They spring from a century of growing scientific and technological sophistication—in short, from the most far-reaching technical revolution to overcome humanity since the advent of agriculture and the wheel. But they are exploited, too, by Communism—the first postindustrial world philosophy, and one which claims to work with and not against the grain of a world caught in revolutionary change.

We need not, therefore, be surprised to see the reactions of fear and rejection and hate reappear. They are apparent in certain aspects of General de Gaulle's foreign policy, and in Dr. Adenauer's. They come to the surface in the negative defeatism of some of Britain's nuclear disarmers. And perhaps the most radical expressions of the mood are beginning to reappear in the United States. The hate is there. All the crises and upheavals of our current world are attributed to "the Communist conspiracy." Without the machinations of these evil men, so goes the argument, the old order could continue in blissful stability—despite, apparently, such stubborn facts as supersonic flight, sputniks, and atomic power.

The refusal to face change is there, in the tendency to look with nostalgia to a golden past in which America was free of Communists and allies and taxes and unions and "big government," in the exaltation of purely nationalistic interests, in economic isolationism and the growth of the protectionist spirit.

Above all, fear is there. Only fear could paint the picture of a vast, successful Communist conspiracy, advancing irresistably on every front to extinguish freedom. It is fear, as General Eisenhower has reminded us, that paints our adversaries "eight feet tall." And only a fearful collapse of confidence in the democratic system could suppose that a majority of its leaders are "soft on Communism" and dupes of a nation-wide system of subversion. Fear breeds more fear until reality is left behind for a world of paranoiac obsession in which every neighbor is a potential subversive and, as in Hitler's Germany, extremists of the Right destroy freedom in the name of defending it.

This loss of nerve is all the more tragic in that its picture of craven retreat by the West before the triumphant advance of Communism is a perversion of the facts. The greatest single development in the postwar world has been the West's extraordinary recovery of political creativeness and initiative. In the 1930's, it was indeed possible to think of the West as in a process of retreat and disintegration. The Fascists spoke contemptuously of "pluto-democratic decadence," and there was more than a little truth in their analysis of a society in which large-scale poverty and unemployment coexisted with great wealth in essentially stagnant economies, in which nationalist rivalries choked all efforts at recovery and the vast colonial world drifted on in a mixture of political malaise and economic decline.

Since the end of the war, all this has changed. The old stagnant economies of western Europe now regard an annual growth rate of anything less than 5 per cent as near recession. Brave new techniques of economic cooperation, starting with the magnificent gesture of the Marshall Plan, have built the Common Market in Europe and introduced the idea as a new and hopeful expedient to Latin America and Africa. The old dependent world is largely independent, and in economic assistance the West has discovered a new tool of world-wide solidarity, which it is learning by experience to use better.

As a result, any communist hope of conquering by subversion the heartland of the West has vanished in the newfound prosperity. The wall across Berlin is the symbol of the fact that, on the contrary, the pressures now work the other way. In Asia two major societies, Japan and India, are increasing their economic elbowroom, one precipitately, the other steadily, within the frame of freedom. And even where pressure is greatest—on the Asian fringes, in the unstable new lands of Africa, or amid the feudal poverty of

Latin America—only in Southeast Asia have the Communists made, by brutal military intervention, an important breakthrough. Elsewhere, there has been no gadarene rush to Communism. The "contested lands" can still be contested; and this situation, in view of their poverty, their pride, and their colonial or semicolonial experience, is no negligible setback to the Communists' confident prophecies of rapid victory.

It follows that in these days, when once again history is forcing on the souls of free men a time of trial, those who work and look forward in hope and confidence can confront the heavier tasks that lie ahead by drawing on an existing capital of achievement. The precise nature of the trial we face is that each of our new Western initiatives has now to be carried further, and into new fields of difficulty. The prospect can exhilarate us or daunt us. But the difficulty is not in doubt.

• • •

In the Western world, two economies have lagged behind the others in vigor, competitiveness, inventiveness, and growth. Since 1953, Britain and the United States have shown growth rates which are only half of those of western Europe and not an eighth of Japan's. In America, the sluggishness is further manifest in something like a hard core of unemployment. Britain, in the wake of the sixth or seventh exchange crisis since the war, has started to reconsider its future radically. By adopting a version of France's Monnet Plan, it hopes to use government stimulus to expand and modernize private industry. By seeking to join Europe's Common Market, it expects to bring into the more conservative sectors of the British economy that enlargement of both markets and competition which has changed the face of Europe since 1958.

These are tough steps for traditional Britain. But the larger challenge for the West lies in the question of whether the United States will accept the same logic of events. Will it be ready for a judicious use of the powers of government to stimulate and modernize the whole economy, or will cries against "planning" and "inflation" keep it jogging along at the old inadequate 2 per cent rate of growth? Will it be ready to seek creative association with an enlarged European Common Market and, in Christian Herter's vivid phrase, "take a giant step" toward the building of a cooperative, free-trading, expansive Atlantic commonwealth? Or will it shrink back before the rigors of the choice? The whole momentum of the West depends upon a bold response.

The first task before the Atlantic powers is to consolidate their base. The next is to secure, inside and outside the Atlantic community, the widest possible extension of the benefits gained. The shape and extent of economic assistance in this context will be decisive for the future. On the one hand lies the choice of minimal appropriations granted grudgingly for the negative purpose of stopping Communism. On the other lies a united effort on the part of all the Atlantic nations to commit a given amount of their resources to a sustained effort of modernization on the developing world, with the ultimate objective of making lively, progressive common markets in Asia, in Africa, in Latin America partners in a cooperative ordering of the world economy. Here, too, the time of decision is at hand, for under the old negative aim of anti-Communism, the aid program is losing hope, drive, and popular support. Only with new efficiency, and as an Atlantic community policy, can long-term assistance recover its proper place in the West's world wide vision of a good society.

At this point, critics may be inclined to dismiss these prospects as at best irrelevant and at worst injurious in the West's crisis of survival. Why talk of growth rates, of economic assistance, of Atlantic cooperation, when the stark issue turns on war, on hydrogen bombs, on the outcome of Berlin, on potential total nuclear destruction? "Do not let us divert our attention from the real challenge," they argue. "Survival is at stake, not Pollyanna illusions of a reordered world. Even to talk of such hopes deflects men from the stern task of resistance. We are soldiers, not prophets. Give us discipline. Do not give us dreams."

In fact, however, every one of these wider issues is relevant to the immediate needs of defense. If an arms race lies ahead, how can the West better sustain it than by more rapid industrial advance and the provision of a larger base for the whole economy? If the battle is engaged with communist subversion throughout the developing world, what other, better instrument has the West at its disposal than economic aid, which can attack the poverty, the hopelessness, the hunger of millions—conditions from which Communists derive so much of their support?

What is more relevant to survival than a strong, unified Atlantic world? If power alone deters Khrushchev, the closer Western unity, the greater its strength. If, on the contrary, a genuine fear of German military revival underlies his pressure on Berlin, a completely united Atlantic community can more safely negotiate special concessions on its fringe—say, a nonnuclear zone in central Europe—than a divided alliance which the least abrasion might cause to fly apart.

Above all, there is no evidence in history that men who face challenges in fear and reaction survive to win great rewards. Nineteenth-century China lost its autonomy to the West by looking backward; Japan, at the same time, maintained itself by strenuous, forward-looking reform. Europe in the twenties and thirties destroyed itself by trying to restore 1914. Learning nothing and forgetting nothing, it contrived, almost with a sleepwalker's automatism, to walk twice into the same war.

Nor should we be surprised that the historical record gives us this verdict. In its roots and aspirations, Western civilization is turned toward the future, not the past; toward experiment, not the status quo; toward creation; toward "a new heaven and a new earth," not a safe and static world. It is precisely this quality of inventiveness, of vision, of the courage to dream that has made Western society, for good and evil, the catalyst and prime mover in a world of magnificent but somnolent civilizations. If that quality were lost today, if no vision of the future informed its policies, no lift of hope encouraged its efforts, no faith to go further and do better inspired its aims, then the hulk of its greatness might survive. But the spirit would be dead. The trial of soul we face today is to outdream the communist visionaries, outwork the communist fanatics, and outdare the voices of defeatism and discouragement within our own society. And this is precisely the challenge which Western man, again and again in his millennial record, has met and measured and triumphantly overcome.

TOPICS FOR DISCUSSION AND WRITING

1. What are the alternatives to a time of crisis, as Lady Jackson envisages them? What examples does she offer of the first kind of reactions? Can

these examples be considered the inductive prelude to her generalization?

2. The author states that today's crisis is more profound than any previous crisis. What reasons does she suggest for such a difference? Could you supply further evidence to support her statement?
3. What proof does the author present to justify her belief that the violent reactions of hate and fear are now in the ascendancy? Do you see any resemblance between her picture of today's society and Franklin Delano Roosevelt's comment on society in his Inaugural Address (p. 60)?
4. What alternative to hate and fear does Lady Jackson propose? What arguments does she offer to persuade us to accept her proposals? Why is her argument to be defined as an induction?
5. Compare Lady Jackson's position with Bertrand Russell's (p. 65). Summarize the main argument of each. Which author is the more persuasive? Why?
6. Write an essay in which you either defend or attack the validity of Lady Jackson's inductive argument, showing either how her conclusions must inevitably follow from her facts or how still another conclusion might result from the same induction.
7. Write an essay in which you comment on the possible significance of both Lady Jackson and Bertrand Russell viewing the world situation in terms of inescapable alternatives.

Ernst Cassirer

Ernst Cassirer (1874–1945) was one of the few authoritative scholars who encouraged his own contemporaries to restudy the ancient myths, and he was one of the few responsible for our understanding of the meaning and significance of myth. Cassirer argued, in such works as Language and Myth *(1946),* The Problem of Knowledge *(1950), and* The Myth of the State *(1946)—the latter two published posthumously—that myth was not an idle fairy tale, but an expression of the "desire of human nature to come to terms with reality, to live in an ordered universe, and to overcome the chaotic state in which things and thoughts have not yet assumed a definite shape and structure." Man fears instability and disorder, and myth is a symbolic ordering of that disorder into a wished-for coherence. Myth is a natural and innate habit of mankind which has, unfortunately, been abused by some political myth-makers, as when, through propaganda and the appeal to emotions, a "myth of the state" is foisted upon a populace (Nazi Germany, for example). Cassirer's book*

The Myth of the State *is an inductive examination of several "mythical states"; the last chapter, part of which is reprinted below, is an inductive examination of modern political myths and Cassirer's statement of the thesis which emerges from his induction.*

THE TECHNIQUE OF THE MODERN POLITICAL MYTHS *

If we try to resolve our contemporary political myths into their elements we find that they contain no entirely new feature. All the elements were already well known. Carlyle's theory of hero worship and Gobineau's thesis of the fundamental moral and intellectual diversity of races had been discussed over and over again. But all these discussions remained in a sense merely academic. To change the old ideas into strong and powerful political weapons something more was needed. They had to be accommodated to the understanding of a different audience. For this purpose a fresh instrument was required—not only an instrument of thought but also of action. A new technique had to be developed. This was the last decisive factor. To put it into scientific terminology we may say that this technique had a catalytical effect. It accelerated all reactions and gave them their full effect. While the soil for the Myth of the Twentieth Century had been prepared long before, it could not have borne its fruit without the skilful use of the new technical tool.

The general conditions which favored this development and contributed to its final victory appeared in the period after the First World War. At this time all the nations which had been engaged in the war encountered the same fundamental difficulties. They began to realize that, even for the victorious nations, the war had, in no field, brought a real solution. On all sides new questions arose. The international, the social, and the human conflicts became more and more intense. They were felt everywhere. But in England, France, and North America there remained always some prospect of solving these conflicts by ordinary and normal means. In Germany, however, the case was different. From one day to the next

* From *The Myth of the State* by Ernst Cassirer. Reprinted by permission of Yale University Press.

the problem became more acute and more complicated. The leaders of the Weimar Republic had done their best to cope with these problems by diplomatic transactions or legislative measures. But all their efforts seemed to have been made in vain. In the times of inflation and unemployment Germany's whole social and economic system was threatened with a complete collapse. The normal resources seemed to have been exhausted. This was the natural soil upon which the political myths could grow up and in which they found ample nourishment.

Even in primitive societies where myth pervades and governs the whole of man's social feeling and social life it is not always operative in the same way nor does it always appear with the same strength. It reaches its full force when man has to face an unusual and dangerous situation. Malinowski, who lived for many years among the natives of the Trobriand Islands and who has given us a searching analysis of their mythical conceptions and their magic rites, has repeatedly insisted upon this point. As he points out, even in primitive societies the use of magic is restricted to a special field of activities. In all those cases that can be dealt with by comparatively simple technical means man does not have recourse to magic. It appears only if man is confronted with a task that seems to be far beyond his natural powers. There remains, however, always a certain sphere which is not affected by magic or mythology, and which, therefore, may be described as the secular sphere. Here man relies on his own skill instead of the power of magic rites and formulae. "When the native has to produce an implement," says Malinowski in *The Foundations of Faith and Morals,*

> he does not refer to magic. He is strictly empirical, that is, scientific, in the choice of his material, in the manner in which he strikes, cuts and polishes the blade. He relies completely on his skill, on his reason and his endurance. There is no exaggeration in saying that in all matters where knowledge is sufficient the native relies on it exclusively. . . . The Central Australian possesses genuine science or knowledge, that is, tradition completely controlled by experience and reason, and completely unaffected by any mystical elements.
>
> . . .
>
> There is a body of rules, handed from one generation to another, which refers to the manner in which people live in their little shelters, make their fire by friction, collect their food and cook it, make

> love to each other, and quarrel. . . . That this secular tradition is plastic, selective, and intelligent, and also well founded, can be seen from the fact that the native always adopts any new and suitable material.[1]

In all those tasks that need no particular and exceptional efforts, no special courage or endurance, we find no magic and no mythology. But a highly developed magic and connected with it a mythology always occurs if a pursuit is dangerous and its issues uncertain.

This description of the role of magic and mythology in primitive society applies equally well to highly advanced stages of man's political life. In desperate situations man will always have recourse to desperate means—and our present-day political myths have been such desperate means. If reason has failed us, there remains always the *ultima ratio*, the power of the miraculous and mysterious. Primitive societies are not ruled by written laws, statutes, institutions or constitutions, bills of right or political charters. Nevertheless, even the most primitive forms of social life show us a very clear and a very strict organization. The members of these societies are by no means living in a state of anarchy or confusion. Perhaps the most primitive societies we know of are those totemistic societies that we find among the American aboriginal tribes and among the native tribes of northern and central Australia, that have been carefully studied and described in the works of Spencer and Gillen. In these totemistic societies we find no complex and elaborate mythology, comparable to Greek, Indian, or Egyptian mythologies; we find no worship of personal gods and no personification of the great powers of nature. But they are held together by another, and even stronger, force; by a definite ritual based upon mythical conceptions—their beliefs in the animal ancestors. Every member of the group belongs to a special totemistic clan; and thereby he is bound in the chain of fixed tradition. He has to abstain from certain kinds of food; he has to observe very strict rules of exogamy or endogamy; and he has to perform, at certain times, in regular intervals and in a rigid and unchangeable order the same rituals which are a dramatic representation of the life of the totemistic ancestors. All this is imposed upon the members of the tribe not by force but by

[1] B. Malinowski, *The Foundations of Faith and Morals* (London: Oxford University Press, 1936), pp. 32f.

their fundamental and mythical conceptions, and the binding power of these conceptions is irresistible; it is never called into question.

Later on there appear other political and social forces. The mythical organization of society seems to be superseded by a rational organization. In quiet and peaceful times, in periods of relative stability and security, this rational organization is easily maintained. It seems to be safe against all attacks. But in politics the equipoise is never completely established. What we find here is a labile rather than a state equilibrium. In politics we are always living on volcanic soil. We must be prepared for abrupt convulsions and eruptions. In all critical moments of man's social life, the rational forces that resist the rise of the old mythical conceptions are no longer sure of themselves. In these moments the time for myth has come again. For myth has not been really vanquished and subjugated. It is always there, lurking in the dark and waiting for its hour and opportunity. This hour comes as soon as the other binding forces of man's social life, for one reason or another, lose their strength and are no longer able to combat the demonic mythical powers.

A French scholar, E. Doutté, has written a very interesting book, *Magie et religion dans l'Afrique du Nord*. In this book he tries to give a concise and clear-cut definition of myth. According to Doutté the gods and demons that we find in primitive societies are nothing but the personifications of collective wishes. Myth, say Doutté, is "le désir collectif personifié"—the collective desire personified. This definition was given about thirty-five years ago. Of course the author did not know and did not think of our current political problems. He spoke as an anthropologist who was engaged in a study of the religious ceremonies and the magic rites of some savage tribes in North Africa. On the other hand, this formula of Doutté could be used as the most laconic and trenchant expression of the modern idea of leadership or dictatorship. The call for leadership only appears when a collective desire has reached an overwhelming strength and when, on the other hand, all hopes of fulfilling this desire in an ordinary and normal way have failed. At these times the desire is not only keenly felt but also personified. It stands before the eyes of man in a concrete, plastic, and individual shape. The intensity of the collective wish is embodied in the leader. The former social bonds—law, justice, and constitutions—are declared to be without any value. What alone remains is the mystical power and authority of the leader, and the leader's will is supreme law.

It is, however, clear that the personification of a collective wish cannot be satisfied in the same way by a great civilized nation as by a savage tribe. Civilized man is, of course, subject to the most violent passions, and when these passions reach their culminating point he is liable to yield to the most irrational impulses. Yet even in this case he cannot entirely forget or deny the demand of rationality. In order to believe he must find some "reasons" for his belief; he must form a "theory" to justify his creeds. And this theory, at least, is not primitive; it is, on the contrary, highly sophisticated.

We easily understand the assumption in savage life that all human powers and all natural powers can be condensed and concentrated in an individual man. The sorcerer, if he is the right man, if he knows the magic spells, and if he understands how to use them at the right time and in the right order, is the master of everything. He can avert all evils, he can defeat every enemy; he commands all natural forces. All this is so far removed from the modern mind that it seems to be quite unintelligible. Yet, if modern man no longer believes in a natural magic, he has by no means given up the belief in a sort of "social magic." If a collective wish is felt in its whole strength and intensity, people can easily be persuaded that it only needs the right man to satisfy it. At this point Carlyle's theory of hero worship made its influence felt. This theory promised a rational justification for certain conceptions that, in their origin and tendency, were anything but rational. Carlyle had emphasized that hero worship is a necessary element in human history. It cannot cease till man himself ceases. "In all epochs of the world's history, we shall find the Great Man to have been the indispensable saviour of his epoch; the lightning, without which the fuel never would have burnt." [2] The word of the great man is the wise healing word which all can believe in.

But Carlyle did not understand his theory as a definite political program. His was a romantic conception of heroism—far different from that of our modern political "realists." The modern politicians

[2] Thomas Carlyle, *On Heroes, Hero-Worship and the Heroic in History* (1840).

have had to use much more drastic means. They had to solve a problem that in many respects resembles squaring the circle. The historians of human civilization have told us that mankind in its development had to pass through two different phases. Man began as *homo magus*; but from the age of magic he passed to the age of technics. The homo magus of former times and of primitive civilization became a *homo faber*, a craftsman and artisan. If we admit such an historical distinction our modern political myths appear indeed as a very strange and paradoxical thing. For what we find in them is the blending of two activities that seem to exclude each other. The modern politician has had to combine in himself two entirely different and even incompatible functions. He has to act, at the same time, as both a homo magus and a homo faber. He is the priest of a new, entirely irrational and mysterious religion. But when he has to defend and propagate this religion he proceeds very methodically. Nothing is left to chance; every step is well prepared and premeditated. It is this strange combination that is one of the most striking features of our political myths.

Myth has always been described as the result of an unconscious activity and as a free product of imagination. But here we find myth made according to plan. The new political myths do not grow up freely; they are not wild fruits of an exuberant imagination. They are artificial things fabricated by very skilful and cunning artisans. It has been reserved for the twentieth century, our own great technical age, to develop a new technique of myth. Henceforth myths can be manufactured in the same sense and according to the same methods as any other modern weapon—as machine guns or airplanes. That is a new thing—and a thing of crucial importance. It has changed the whole form of our social life. It was in 1933 that the political world began to worry somewhat about Germany's rearmament and its possible international repercussions. As a matter of fact this rearmament had begun many years before but had passed almost unnoticed. The real rearmament began with the origin and rise of the political myths. The later military rearmament was only an accessory after the fact. The fact was an accomplished fact long before; the military rearmament was only the necessary consequence of the mental rearmament brought about by the political myths.

The first step that had to be taken was a change in the function of language. If we study the development of human speech we find that in the history of civilization the word fulfils two entirely different functions. To put it briefly we may term these functions the semantic and the magical use of the word. Even among the so-called primitive languages the semantic function of the word is never missing; without it there could be no human speech. But in primitive societies the magic word has a predominant and overwhelming influence. It does not describe things or relations of things; it tries to produce effects and to change the course of nature. This cannot be done without an elaborate magical art. The magician, or sorcerer is alone able to govern the magic word. But in his hands it becomes a most powerful weapon. Nothing can resist its force. *Carmina vel coelo possunt deducere lunam,* says the sorceress Medea in Ovid's *Metamorphoses*—by magic songs and incantations even the moon can be dragged down from the heavens.

Curiously enough all this recurs in our modern world. If we study our modern political myths and the use that has been made of them we find in them, to our great surprise, not only a transvaluation of all our ethical values but also a transformation of human speech. The magic word takes precedence of the semantic word. If nowadays I happen to read a German book, published in these last ten years, not a political but a theoretical book, a work dealing with philosophical, historical, or economic problems—I find to my amazement that I no longer understand the German language. New words have been coined; and even the old ones are used in a new sense; they have undergone a deep change of meaning. This change of meaning depends upon the fact that those words which formerly were used in a descriptive, logical, or semantic sense, are now used as magic words that are destined to produce certain effects and to stir up certain emotions. Our ordinary words are charged with meanings; but these new-fangled words are charged with feelings and violent passions.

Not long ago there was published a very interesting little book, *Nazi-Deutsch, A Glossary of Contemporary German Usage.* Its authors are Heinz Paechter, Bertha Hellman, Hedwig Paechter, and Karl O. Paetel. In this book all those new terms which were produced by the Nazi regime were carefully listed, and it is a tremendous list. There seem to be only a few words which have survived the general destruction. The authors made an attempt to translate the new terms into English, but in this regard they were, to my mind, unsuccessful. They were able to give only circumlocutions of the German words and phrases instead of real translations. For unfortunately, or perhaps fortunately, it was impossible to render these words adequately in English. What characterizes them is not so much their content and their objective meaning as the emotional atmosphere which surrounds and envelops them. This atmosphere must be felt; it cannot be translated nor can it be transferred from one climate of opinion to an entirely different one. To illustrate this point I content myself with one striking example chosen at random. I understand from the *Glossary* that in recent German usage there was a sharp difference between the two terms *Siegfriede* and *Siegerfriede*. Even for a German ear it will not be easy to grasp this difference. The two words sound exactly alike, and seem to denote the same thing. *Sieg* means victory, *Friede* means peace; how can the combination of the two words produce entirely different meanings? Nevertheless we are told that, in modern German usage, there is all the difference in the world between the two terms. For a Siegfriede is a peace through German victory; whereas a Siegerfriede means the very opposite; it is used to denote a peace which would be dictated by the allied conquerers. It is the same with other terms. The men who coined these terms were masters of their art of political propaganda. They attained their end, the stirring up of violent political passions, by the simplest means. A word, or even the change of a syllable in a word, was often good enough to serve this purpose. If we hear these new words we feel in them the whole gamut of human emotions—of hatred, anger, fury, haughtiness, contempt, arrogance, and disdain.

But the skilful use of the magic word is not all. If the word is to have its full effect it has to be supplemented by the introduction of new rites. In this respect, too, the political leaders proceeded very thoroughly, methodically, and successfully. Every political action has its special ritual. And since, in the totalitarian state, there is no private sphere, independent of political life, the whole life of man is suddenly inundated by a high tide of new rituals. They are as regular, as rigorous and inexorable as those rituals that we find in primitive societies. Every class, every sex, and every age has a rite of its own. No one could walk in the street, nobody could greet his neighbor or friend without performing a political ritual. And just as in primitive societies the neglect of one of the prescribed rites has meant misery and death. Even in young children this is not regarded as a mere sin of omission. It becomes a crime against the majesty of the leader and the totalitarian state.

The effect of these new rites is obvious. Nothing is more likely to lull asleep all our active forces, our power of judgment and critical discernment, and to take away our feeling of personality and individual responsibility than the steady, uniform, and monotonous performance of the same rites. As a matter of fact, in all primitive societies ruled and governed by rites, individual responsibility is an unknown thing. What we find here is only a collective responsibility. Not the individuals but the group is the real "moral subject." The clan, the family, and the whole tribe are responsible for the actions of all the members. If a crime is committed it is not imputed to an individual. By a sort of miasma or social contagion, the crime spreads over the whole group. Nobody can escape the infection. Revenge and punishment too are always directed to the group as a whole. In those societies in which the blood feud is one of the highest obligations it is by no means necessary to take revenge upon the murderer himself. It is enough to kill a member of his family or his tribe. In some cases, as for instance in New Guinea or among the African Somalis, it is the eldest brother rather than the offender himself who is killed.

In the last two hundred years our conceptions of the character of savage life, when compared to the life of civilized men, have completely changed. In the eighteenth century Rousseau gave his famous description of savage life and the state of nature. He saw in it a real paradise of simplicity, innocence, and happiness. The savage lived alone in the freshness of his native forest, following his instincts and satisfying his simple desires. He enjoyed the highest good, the good of absolute independence. Unfortunately the progress of anthropological research made during the nineteenth century has completely destroyed this philosophical idyll. Rousseau's description was turned into its very opposite. "The savage," says E. Sidney Hartland in his book, *Primitive Law*,

> is far from being the free and unfettered creature of Rousseau's imagination. On the contrary, he is hemmed in on every side by the customs of his people; he is bound in the chains of immemorial tradition. . . . These fetters are accepted by him as a matter of course; he never seeks to break forth. . . . To the civilized man the same observations may very often apply; but the civilized man is too restless, too desirous of change, too eager to question his environment, to remain long in the attitude of acquiescence.[3]

These words were written twenty years ago; but in the meantime we have learned a new lesson, a lesson that is very humiliating to our human pride. We have learned that modern man, in spite of his restlessness, and perhaps precisely because of his restlessness, has not really surmounted the condition of savage life. When exposed to the same forces, he can easily be thrown back to a state of complete acquiescence. He no longer questions his environment; he accepts it as a matter of course.

Of all the sad experiences of these last twelve years this is perhaps the most dreadful one. It may be compared to the experience of Odysseus on the island of Circe. But it is even worse. Circe had transformed the friends and companions of Odysseus into various animal shapes. But here are men, men of education and intelligence, honest and upright men who suddenly give up the highest human privilege. They have ceased to be free and personal agents. Performing the same prescribed rites they begin to feel, to think, and to speak in the same way. Their gestures are lively and violent; yet this is but an artificial, a sham life. In fact they are moved by an external force. They act like marionettes in a puppet show—and they do not even know that the strings of this show and of man's whole individual and social life are henceforward pulled by the political leaders.

For the understanding of our problem this is a point of crucial importance. Methods of compulsion and suppression have ever been used in political life. But in most cases these methods aimed at material results. Even the most fearful systems of despotism contented themselves with forcing upon men certain laws of action. They were not concerned with the feelings, judgments, and thoughts of men. It is true that in the great religious struggles the most

[3] E. Sidney Hartland, *Primitive Law* (London: Methuen & Co., 1924), p. 138.

violent efforts were made not only to rule the actions of men but also their consciousness. But these attempts were bound to fail; they only strengthened the feeling for religious liberty. Now the modern political myths proceeded in quite a different manner. They did not begin with demanding or prohibiting certain actions. They undertook to change the men, in order to be able to regulate and control their deeds. The political myths acted in the same way as a serpent that tries to paralyze its victims before attacking them. Men fell victims to them without any serious resistance. They were vanquished and subdued before they had realized what actually happened.

The usual means of political oppression would not have sufficed to produce this effect. Even under the hardest political pressure men have not ceased living their own lives. There has always remained a sphere of personal freedom resistant to this pressure. The classical ethical ideas of antiquity maintained and strengthened their force amidst the chaos and the political decay of the ancient world. Seneca lived in the times and at the court of Nero. But this did not prevent him from giving, in his treatises and moral letters, an epitome of the loftiest ideas of Stoic philosophy, ideas of the autonomy of the will and the independence of the wise man. Our modern political myths destroy all these ideas and ideals before they begin their work. They do not have to fear any opposition from this quarter. In our analysis of Gobineau's book we have studied the methods by which this opposition was broken down. The myth of the race worked like a strong corrosive and succeeded in dissolving and disintegrating all other values.

To understand this process it is necessary to begin with an analysis of the term *freedom*. Freedom is one of the most obscure and ambiguous terms not only of philosophical but also of political language. As soon as we begin to speculate about the freedom of the will we find ourselves involved into an inextricable labyrinth of metaphysical questions and antinomies. As to political freedom all of us know that it is one of the most used and abused slogans. All political parties have assured us that they are ever the true representatives and guardians of freedom. But they have always defined the term in their own sense and used it for their particular interests. Ethical freedom is, at bottom, a much simpler thing. It is free from those ambiguities that seem to be unavoidable both in metaphysics and in politics. Men act as free agents not because they possess a *liberum arbitrium indifferentiae.* It is not the absence of a motive but the character of the motives that marks a free action. In the ethical sense a man is a free agent if these motives depend upon his own judgment and own conviction of what moral duty is. According to Kant freedom is equivalent to autonomy. It does not mean "indeterminism," it rather means a special kind of determination. It means that the law which we obey in our actions is not imposed from without but that the moral subject gives this law to itself.

In the exposition of his own theory Kant always warns us against a fundamental misunderstanding. Ethical freedom, he declares, is not a fact but a postulate. It is not *gegeben* but *aufgegeben*; it is not a gift with which human nature is endowed; it is rather a task, and the most arduous task that man can set himself. It is no datum, but a demand; an ethical imperative. To fulfill this demand becomes especially hard in times of a severe and dangerous social crisis when the breakdown of the whole public life seems to be imminent. At these times the individual begins to feel a deep mistrust in his own powers. Freedom is not a natural inheritance of man. In order to possess it we have to create it. If man were simply to follow his natural instincts he would not strive for freedom; he would rather choose dependence. Obviously it is much easier to depend upon others than to think, to judge, and to decide for himself. That accounts for the fact that both in individual and in political life freedom is so often regarded much more as a burden than a privilege. Under extremely difficult conditions man tries to cast off this burden. Here the totalitarian state and the political myths step in. The new political parties promise, at least, an escape from the dilemma. They suppress and destroy the very sense of freedom; but, at the same time, they relieve men from all personal responsibility.[4]

[4] "To a German grocer, not unwilling to explain things to an American visitor," relates Stephen Raushenbush, "I spoke of our feeling that something invaluable had been given up when freedom was surrendered. He replied: 'But you don't understand at all. Before this we had to worry about elections, and parties, and voting. We had responsibilities. But now we don't have any of that. Now we're free.'" See Stephen Raushenbush, *The March of Fascism* (New Haven, Conn.: Yale University Press, 1939), p. 40.

That leads us to another aspect of our problem. In our description of the modern political myths one feature is still missing. As we pointed out, in the totalitarian states the political leaders have had to take charge of all those functions that, in primitive societies, were performed by the magician. They were the absolute rulers; they were the medicine men who promised to cure all social evils. But that was not enough. In a savage tribe the sorcerer has still another important task. The *homo magus* is, at the same time, the *homo divinans*. He reveals the will of the gods and foretells the future. The soothsayer has his firm place and his indispensable role in primitive social life. Even in highly developed stages of political culture he is still in full possession of his old rights and privileges. In Rome, for instance, no important political decision was ever made, no difficult enterprise was undertaken, no battle was fought without the advice of the augurs and haruspices. When a Roman army was sent out it was always accompanied by its haruspices; they were an integral part of the military staff.

Even in this respect our modern political life has abruptly returned to forms which seemed to have been entirely forgotten. To be sure, we no longer have the primitive kind of sortilege, the divination by lot; we no longer observe the flight of birds nor do we inspect the entrails of slain animals. We have developed a much more refined and elaborate method of divination—a method that claims to be scientific and philosophical. But if our methods have changed the thing itself has by no means vanished. Our modern politicians know very well that great masses are much more easily moved by the force of imagination than by sheer physical force. And they have made ample use of this knowledge. The politician becomes a sort of public fortuneteller. Prophecy is an essential element in the new technique of rulership. The most improbable or even impossible promises are made; the millennium is predicted over and over again.

Curiously enough this new art of divination first made its appearance not in German politics but in German philosophy. In 1918 there appeared Oswald Spengler's *Decline of the West*. Perhaps never before had a philosophical book such a sensational success. It was translated into almost every language and read by all sorts of readers—philosophers and scientists, historians and politicians, students and scholars, tradesmen and the man in the street. What was the reason for this unprecedented success, what was the magic spell that this book exerted over its readers? It seems to be a paradox, but to my mind the cause of Spengler's success is to be sought rather in the title of his book than in its contents. The title *Der Untergang des Abendlandes* was an electric spark that set the imagination of Spengler's readers aflame. The book was published in July, 1918, at the end of the First World War. At this time many, if not most of us, had realized that something was rotten in the state of our highly praised Western civilization. Spengler's book expressed, in a sharp and trenchant way, this general uneasiness. It was not at all a scientific book. Spengler despised and openly challenged all methods of science. "Nature," he declared, "is to be handled scientifically, history poetically." Yet even this is not the real meaning of Spengler's work. A poet lives in the world of his imagination; and a great religious poet, like Dante or Milton, also lives in a world of prophetic vision. But he does not take these visions for realities; nor does he make of them a philosophy of history. This, however, was precisely the case of Spengler. He boasted of having found a new method by which historical and cultural events could be predicted in the same way and with the same exactness as an astronomer predicts an eclipse of the sun or the moon.

> In this book is attempted for the first time the venture of predetermining history, of following the still unraveled stages in the destiny of a culture, and specifically of the only culture of our times and our planet which is actually in the phase of fulfillment—the West European-American.

These words give us a clue to Spengler's book and its enormous influence. If it be possible not only to relate the story of human civilization but to predetermine its future course, a great step in advance has, indeed, been made. Obviously the man who spoke in this way was no mere scientist, nor was he a historian or philosopher. According to Spengler the rise, decline, and fall of civilizations do not depend upon the so-called laws of nature. They are determined by a higher power, the power of destiny. Destiny, not causality, is the moving force in human history. The birth of a cultural world, says Spengler, is always a mystical act, a decree of destiny. Such acts are entirely impenetrable to our poor, abstract, scientific, or philosophical concepts.

> A culture is born in the moment when a great soul awakens out of the protospirituality of ever-childish humanity, and detaches itself, a form from the formless, a bounded and mortal thing from the boundless and enduring. . . . It dies when this soul has actualized the full sum of its possibilities, in the shape of peoples, languages, dogmas, arts, states, sciences, and reverts into the protosoul.[5]

Here, too, we find the rebirth of one of the oldest mythical motives. In almost all mythologies of the world we meet with the idea of an inevitable, inexorable, irrevocable destiny. Fatalism seems to be inseparable from mythical thought. In the Homeric poems even the gods have to submit to Fate: Fate (Moira) acts independently of Zeus. In the tenth book of his *Republic* Plato gave his famous description of the "distaff of Necessity" on which the revolutions of all the heavenly bodies turn. The spindle turns on the knees of Necessity while the Fates, daughters of Necessity, Lachesis, Clotho, and Atropos, sit on thrones, Lachesis singing of the past, Clotho of the present, Atropos of the future.[6] This is a Platonic myth, and Plato always makes a sharp distinction between mythical and philosophical thought. But in some of our modern philosophers this distinction seems to be completely effaced. They give us a metaphysics of history that shows all the characteristic features of myth. When I first read Spengler's *Untergang des Abendlandes* I happened to be engrossed in studies of the philosophy of the Italian Renaissance. What struck me most at this time was the close analogy between Spengler's book and some astrological treatises that I had quite recently read. Of course Spengler made no attempt to read the future of civilizations in the stars. But his prognostics are of exactly the same type as the astrological prognostics. The astrologers of the Renaissance did not content themselves with exploring the destiny of individual men. They applied their method also to the great historical and cultural phenomena. One of these astrologers was condemned by the Church and burnt

[5] Oswald Spengler, *Der Untergang des Abendlandes* (München: Beck, 1918), English trans. by Charles F. Atkinson, *The Decline of the West* (London: G. Allen & Unwin, 1926), p. 106. See the whole of chap. IV, "The Destiny-Idea and the Causality-Principle."

[6] Plato, *The Republic,* pp. 616f.

at the stake because he had cast the horoscope of Christ and from Christ's nativity had predicted the near fall of Christian religion. Spengler's book was, as a matter of fact, an astrology of history—the work of a diviner who unfolded his somber apocalyptic visions.

But can we really connect the work of Spengler with the political prophecies of later times? Can we put the two phenomena on the same level? At first sight such a parallel seems to be highly questionable. Spengler was a prophet of evil; the new political leaders wished to rouse in their adherents the most extravagant hopes. Spengler spoke of the decline of the West; the others spoke of the conquest of the world by the German race. Obviously these are not the same things. Nor was Spengler personally an adherent of the Nazi movement. He was a conservative, an admirer and eulogist of the old Prussian ideals; but the program of the new men made no appeal to him. Nevertheless the work of Spengler became one of the pioneer works of National Socialism. For what was the conclusion that Spengler drew from his general thesis? He vehemently protested when his philosophy was termed a philosophy of pessimism. He declared himself to be no pessimist. It is true that our Western civilization is doomed once for all. But it is no use lamenting this obvious and inevitable fact. If our culture is lost there still remain many other things to the present generation, and perhaps much better things.

> Of great painting or great music there can no longer be, for Western people, any question. . . . Only *extensive* possibilities are left to them. Yet, for a sound and vigorous generation that is filled with unlimited hopes, I fail to see that it is any disadvantage to discover betimes that some of these hopes must come to nothing. . . . It is true that the issue may be a tragic one for some individuals who in their decisive years are overpowered by the conviction that in the spheres of architecture, drama, painting, there is nothing left for *them* to conquer. What matter if they do go under! . . . Now at last the work of centuries enables the West-European to view the disposition of his own life in relation to the general culture-scheme and to test his own powers and purposes. And I can only hope that men of the new generation may be moved by this book to devote themselves to technics instead of lyrics, the sea instead of the paint-brush, and politics instead of epistemology. Better they could not do.[7]

[7] Spengler, *The Decline of the West,* pp. 40f.

Technic instead of lyrics, politics instead of epistemology, this advice of a philosopher of human culture could easily be understood. The new men were convinced that they fulfilled Spengler's prophecy. They interpreted him in their own sense. If our culture —science, philosophy, poetry, and art—is dead, let us make a fresh start. Let us try our vast possibilities, let us create a new world and become the rulers of this world.

The same trend of thought appears in the work of a modern German philosopher who, at first sight, seems to have very little in common with Spengler and who developed his theories quite independently of him. In 1927 Martin Heidegger published the first volume of his book *Sein und Zeit*. Heidegger was a pupil of Husserl and was reckoned among the outstanding representatives of the German phenomenological school. His book appeared in Husserl's *Jahrbüchen für Philosophie und phänomenologische Forschung*.[8] But the attitude of the book was diametrically opposed to the spirit of Husserl's philosophy. Husserl had started from an analysis of the principles of logical thought. His whole philosophy depends on the results of this analysis. His highest aim was to make philosophy an "exact science," to found it upon unshakable facts and indubitable principles. Such a tendency is entirely alien to Heidegger. He does not admit that there is something like "eternal" truth, a Platonic "realm of ideas," or a strict logical method of philosophic thought. All this is declared to be elusive. In vain we try to build up a logical philosophy; we can only give an *Existenzialphilosophie*. Such an existential philosophy does not claim to give us an objective and universally valid truth. No thinker can give more than the truth of his own existence; and this existence has a historical character. It is bound up with the special conditions under which the individual lives. To change these conditions is impossible. In order to express his thought Heidegger had to coin a new term. He spoke of the *Geworfenheit* of man (the being-thrown). To be thrown into the stream of time is a fundamental and inalterable feature of our human situation. We cannot emerge from this stream and we cannot change its course. We have to accept the historical conditions of our existence.

[8] Vol. VIII, Second edition (Halle, Germany: Niemeyer, 1929).

We can try to understand and to interpret them; but we cannot change them.

I do not mean to say that these philosophical doctrines had a direct bearing on the development of political ideas in Germany. Most of these ideas arose from quite different sources. They had a very "realistic" not a "speculative" purport. But the new philosophy did enfeeble and slowly undermine the forces that could have resisted the modern political myths. A philosophy of history that consists in somber predictions of the decline and the inevitable destruction of our civilization and a theory that sees in the Geworfenheit of man one of his principal characteristics have given up all hopes of an active share in the construction and reconstruction of man's cultural life. Such philosophy renounces its own fundamental theoretical and ethical ideals. It can be used, then, as a pliable instrument in the hands of the political leaders.

The return of fatalism in our modern world leads us to another general question. We are proud of our natural science, but we should not forget that natural science is a very late achievement of the human mind. Even in the seventeenth century, in the great century of Galileo and Kepler, of Descartes and Newton, it was by no means firmly established. It had still to struggle for its place in the sun. During the Renaissance the so-called occult sciences, magic, alchemy, and astrology were still predominant, they even had a new flourishing period. Kepler was the first great empirical astronomer who was able to describe the movements of the planets in exact mathematical terms. Yet it was extremely difficult to take this decisive step. For Kepler not only had to struggle against his times but also against himself. Astronomy and astrology were still inseparable. Kepler himself was appointed as an astrologer at the Imperial Court of Prague, and at the end of his life he became the astrologer of Wallenstein. The way in which he finally freed himself is one of the most important and fascinating chapters in the history of modern science. He never broke away entirely from astrological conceptions. He declared astronomy to be the daughter of astrology and he said that it would not be becoming for the daughter to neglect or despise her mother. Prior to the seventeenth and eighteen centuries of our modern era, it is impossible to draw a line between empirical and mystical thought. A scientific chemistry in the modern sense of this term did not exist until the time of Robert Boyle and Lavoisier.

How could this state of affairs be changed? How did natural science, after innumerable vain efforts, finally break the magic spell? The principle of this great intellectual revolution can best be described in the words of Bacon, one of the pioneers of modern empirical thought, "Natura non vincitur nisi parendo"—the victory over nature can only be won by obedience. But his mastery must be understood in the right way. Man cannot subjugate or enslave nature. In order to rule her he must respect her; he must obey her fundamental rules. Man must begin by freeing himself; he must get rid of his fallacies and illusions, his human idiosyncrasies and fancies. In the first book of his *Novum organon* Bacon tried to give a systematic survey of these illusions. He described the different kinds of idols, the *idola tribus,* the *idola specus,* the *idola fori,* and the *idola theatri,* and he tried to show how to overcome them in order to clear the way that will lead to a true empirical science.

In politics we have not yet found this way. Of all human idols the political idols, the idola fori, are the most dangerous and enduring. Since the times of Plato all great thinkers have made the greatest efforts to find a rational theory of politics. The nineteenth century was convinced that it had at last found the right path. In 1830 Auguste Comte published the first volume of his *Cours de philosophie positive.* He began with analyzing the structure of natural science; he went from astronomy to physics, from physics to chemistry, from chemistry to biology. But according to Comte natural science is only a first step. His real aim and highest ambition was to become the founder of a new social science and to introduce into this science the same exact way of reasoning, the same inductive and deductive method as we find in physics or chemistry.

The sudden rise of the political myths in the twentieth century has shown us that these hopes of Comte and of his pupils and adherents were premature. Politics is still far from being a positive science, let alone an exact science. I have no doubt that later generations will look back at many of our political systems with the same feeling as a modern astronomer studies an astrological book or a modern chemist an alchemistic treatise. In politics we have not yet found firm and reliable ground. Here there seems to be no clearly established cosmic order; we are always threatened with a sudden relapse into the old chaos. We are building high and proud edifices; but we forget to make their foundations secure. The belief that man by the skilful use of magic formulae and rites can change the course of nature has prevailed for hundreds and thousands of years in human history. In spite of all the inevitable frustrations and disappointments mankind still clung stubbornly, forcibly, and desperately to this belief. It is, therefore, not to be wondered at that in our political actions and our political thoughts magic still holds its ground. Yet when small groups do try to enforce their wishes and their fantastic ideas upon great nations and the whole body politic, they may succeed for a short time, and they may even achieve great triumphs, but these must remain ephemeral. For there is, after all, a logic of the social world just as there is a logic of the physical world. There are certain laws that cannot be violated with impunity. Even in this sphere we have to follow Bacon's advice. We must learn how to obey the laws of the social world before we can undertake to rule it.

What can philosophy do to help us in this struggle against the political myths? Our modern philosophers seem long ago to have given up all hope of influencing the course of political and social events. Hegel had the highest opinion of the worth and dignity of philosophy. Nevertheless it was Hegel himself who declared that philosophy comes always too late for the reform of the world. It is therefore just as foolish to fancy that any philosophy can transcend its present time as that an individual can leap out of his own time. "When philosophy paints its grey in grey one form of life has become old and by means of grey it cannot be rejuvenated, but only known. The owl of Minerva takes its flight only when the shades of night are gathering." [9] If this dictum of Hegel were true, philosophy would be condemned to an absolute quietism; an entirely passive attitude toward man's historical life. It has simply to accept and to explain the given historical situation and to bow down before it. In this case philosophy would be nothing but a sort of speculative idleness. I think, however, that this is in contradic-

[9] Georg Wilhelm Friedrich Hegel, *Grundlinien der philosophie des rechts* [*Philosophy of Right*] (1821).

tion both to the general character and to the history of philosophy. The classical example of Plato alone would be enough to refute this view. The great thinkers of the past were not only "their own times apprehended in thought." Very often they had to think beyond and against their times. Without this intellectual and moral courage, philosophy could not fulfil its task in man's cultural and social life.

It is beyond the power of philosophy to destroy the political myths. A myth is in a sense invulnerable. It is impervious to rational arguments; it cannot be refuted by syllogisms. But philosophy can do us another important service. It can make us understand the adversary. In order to fight an enemy you must know him. That is one of the first principles of a sound strategy. To know him means not only to know his defects and weaknesses; it means to know his strength. All of us have been liable to underrate this strength. When we first heard of the political myths we found them so absurd and incongruous, so fantastic and ludicrous that we could hardly be prevailed upon to take them seriously. By now it has become clear to all of us that this was a great mistake. We should not commit the same error a second time. We should carefully study the origin, the structure, the methods, and the technique of the political myths. We should see the adversary face to face in order to know how to combat him.

TOPICS FOR DISCUSSION AND WRITING

1. When, according to Cassirer, are myths likely to have a particularly strong appeal and to hold man's imagination? What evidence does he examine which permits him to state such a thesis?
2. How is a political myth different from a primitive myth? What features do they share?
3. What does Cassirer mean by "the magical use of the word" and "political ritual"? What evidence does he offer to support his definitions? Might Roosevelt's inaugural address (p. 60) be thought of as "political ritual"?
4. What thesis does Cassirer advance in regard to the nature of the modern state? What does he mean when he says that "Prophecy is an essential element in the new technique of rulership"? What are the common elements he discovers in the writings of Spengler, Heidegger, Bacon, and Comte which allow him to state the thesis: "When small

groups do try to enforce their wishes and their fantastic ideas upon great nations and the whole body politic, they may succeed for a short time, and they may even achieve great triumphs, but these must remain ephemeral"? Why is his procedure in argument to be considered an induction?

5. What are some of the political myths which are in force today? How might Cassirer's last paragraph be applied to a consideration of any of the present-day myths?
6. Write an essay explaining how the success of a political myth as defined by Cassirer can be explained in terms of Jung's conception of the archetypal form and the collective unconscious. What are the elements in a successful myth? To what archetypal form do they appeal? Does Jung's psychology provide an explanation for Cassirer's myths?

DEDUCTIVE ARGUMENT

Induction is first of all the *mental* process we must go through in order to create a thesis. Induction is also a *written* process when we describe, in an ordered and selective way, the steps we took to arrive at our thesis. Only in rare cases will either the written or mental induction be total; it is unlikely that every piece of evidence on any given subject would come under the scrutiny of the investigator, no matter how conscientious he might be. Some new evidence, some particle of information that had gone unnoticed, will come to light on most subjects, no matter how painstaking the original induction had been.

When that happens, one of two things will occur. Either the new evidence will discredit the thesis that had been formed earlier, in which case a new induction will have to take place; and this new induction will have to take into account what had been overlooked; or the new evidence will in no way contradict the original thesis, and will be explainable in terms of the original thesis. This act of explaining an item which had not been in the original inductive series, in terms of the original thesis, is called *deduction.* Induction is the discovery of a generalization through a related series of individual terms; deduction is the explanation of a single item by means of a prior generalization.

In the practical order of thought, induction must precede deduction. As a way of organizing argument, deduction may provide the pattern, the general blueprint of the composition. As a writer may rehearse a series of items leading to the statement of a thesis, so too he may begin with the statement of his thesis and continue through an explanation of how that thesis is applicable to a case in point. If the thesis itself has evident validity, and if its application is credible, the writer will be able to produce a new assertion, opinion, or judgment—he will have produced a new thesis. If we advanced the judgment that

"Student government is a useful part of university training," we should be able to defend that thesis by pointing out the prior inductive process which led to that judgment. If we advanced the judgment that "Our college should admit student government," we could defend that judgment by the deduction based on the first thesis; student government is a useful part of university training; our college is anxious to fulfill university standards; therefore our college should admit student government.

The typical and basic form of the deductive argument is the syllogism. The parts of the syllogism are three: *major premise, minor premise,* and *conclusion.* The major premise is the previously accepted generalization; the minor premise is the new item under discussion; and the conclusion is the result of considering the minor in terms of the major. Thus, in the example already cited, *Student government is a useful part of university training* is the MAJOR PREMISE. *Our college is anxious to fulfill university standards* is the MINOR PREMISE. *Therefore our college should admit student government* is the CONCLUSION.

Proof by deduction arrives at its thesis not by the accumulation of individual items, but by the relevant application of an earlier validated thesis to a new subject. Such application may both support an argument and provide a pattern of organization in writing.

John Milton

John Milton (1608–1674) is best known today for his epic poem Paradise Lost. *In his own day, Milton was well known for his many prose works. There was little that happened in England during the middle years of the seventeenth century about which Milton did not have an opinion. He wrote in opposition to episcopacy and in favor of divorce. He attacked the rights of kings to unqualified tenure and defended the rights of the commonwealth form of government. In the year 1644 he published two essays, a tract on education and the* Areopagitica, *which are still relevant discussions of their subjects.*

Areopagitica *is a defense of the freedom of the press. It was written in an attempt to persuade Parliament to reconsider its action and to revoke an act of June 14, 1643 which required all books to be licensed by an official censor before they could be printed. An increasingly severe Presbyterian Parliament was anxious to silence opposition and to insure uniformity of religious practice. Milton considered the preservation of diversity of opinion essential to the preservation of freedom of conscience as well as to the intellectual vitality of the nation.*

Milton's thesis in the Areopagitica *is that the act of censorship ought to be revoked. His arguments can be classified, according to their sources, into four large groups. The first group, based upon a comparison of the controversial act with other forms of censorship in the past, is intended to show that the censors of the past were people with whom the present Parliamentarians would not want to be associated. The second group is derived from an analysis of the nature of reading and of the way in which good and evil are inevitably linked in nature. The third group is a consideration of whether or not this censorship act can really accomplish its purpose. The fourth group of arguments is based upon a consideration of what can be expected as effects of this censorship which, Milton thought, would "be primely to the discouragement of all learning, and the stop of truth, not only by disexercising and blunting our abilities, in what we know already, but by hindering and cropping the discovery that might be yet further made, both in religious and civil wisdom."*

The following excerpt is taken from the second group of arguments. Milton assumes that his readers will agree with him that good and evil are so closely bound together that it is almost impossible to isolate one from the other, then goes on to show that they can hardly be separated by an act of Parliament. His argument proceeds from a general assumption about the nature of the involvement of good with evil, through a minor premise which says, in effect, that Parliament has attempted to do the impossible, and concludes with a restatement of Milton's thesis that the act of censorship ought to be revoked.

from Areopagitica

Good and evil we know in the field of this world grow up together almost inseparably; and the knowledge of good is so involved and interwoven with the knowledge of evil, and in so many cunning resemblances hardly to be discerned, that those confused seeds which were imposed upon Psyche as an incessant labor to cull out, and sort asunder, were not more intermixed. It was from out the rind of one apple tasted, that the knowledge of good and evil, as two twins cleaving together, leaped forth into the world. And perhaps this is that doom which Adam fell into of knowing good and evil; that is to say, of knowing good by evil.

As therefore the state of man now is; what wisdom can there be to choose, what continence to forbear, without the knowledge of evil? He that can apprehend and consider vice with all her baits and seeming pleasures, and yet abstain, and yet distinguish, and yet prefer that which is truly better, he is the true warfaring Christian. I cannot praise a fugitive and cloistered virtue unexercised and unbreathed, that never sallies out and sees her adversary, but slinks out of the race, where that immortal garland is to be run for, not without dust and heat. Assuredly we bring not innocence into the world, we bring impurity much rather; that which purifies us is trial, and trial is by what is contrary. That virtue, therefore, which is but a youngling in the contemplation of evil, and knows not the utmost that vice promises to her followers, and rejects it, is but a blank virtue, not a pure; her whiteness is but an excremental whiteness; which was the reason why our sage and serious poet Spenser (whom I dare be known to think a better teacher than Scotus or Aquinas) describing true temperance under the person of Guion, brings him in with his palmer through the cave of Mammon, and the bower of earthly bliss, that he might see and know, and yet abstain.

Since therefore the knowledge and survey of vice is in this world so necessary to the constituting of human virtue, and the scanning of error to the confirmation of truth, how can we more safely, and with less danger, scout into the regions of sin and falsity, than by reading all manner of tractates, and hearing all manner of reason? And this is the benefit which may be had of books promiscuously read.

TOPICS FOR DISCUSSION AND WRITING

1. Reread John Rader Platt's essay on *Style in Science* to review his definition of a deductive argument. How does the deductive method differ

from the inductive? State Milton's argument as succinctly as you can. Does it conform to Platt's definition of a deductive argument?

2. What, in your own words, is Milton's conception of the relationship between good and evil? Does he prove that his conception is right? Would everyone be likely to agree with him?
3. What is the state of man's knowledge of good and evil? Can man avoid coming to a knowledge of evil?
4. How can he come to know good from evil? How can reading help? Can a man who has never resisted the temptation of evil be considered a virtuous man?
5. Does the following argument, which is the statement of a thesis and its supporting reason, adequately summarize Milton's argument in this section?

   Man must be permitted to read promiscuously
   because he must learn to distinguish good from evil.

6. Does the following syllogism summarize the argument adequately?

   MAJOR PREMISE: Whatever is necessary to enable man to distinguish good from evil must be permitted to man.

   MINOR PREMISE: Promiscuous reading enables man to distinguish between good and evil.

   CONCLUSION: Therefore, promiscuous reading must be permitted; and, conversely, censorship must be revoked.

7. Which is the weakest step in the argument? Which is the strongest?
8. Would Milton's argument be applicable to recent censorship cases such as those involving the publication of Joyce's *Ulysses,* Miller's *Tropic of Cancer,* Lawrence's *Lady Chatterley's Lover,* and Cleland's *Fanny Hill?* Do you think Milton's argument was intended to apply to such works?

John Locke

John Locke (1632–1704) wrote two essays on the theory of government in an attempt to justify the Revolution of 1688 which had resulted in the expulsion of James II, legitimate Stuart (but Catholic) heir to the throne, and the accession of the Protestants, William and Mary. In the First Treatise *Locke, who is undoubtedly the most representative thinker in the whole Anglo-American political tradition, argued against a patriarchal theory which maintained that all kings had inherited their right to rule because they were direct descendants of Adam. The* Second Treatise, *from which the following section has been taken, was intended as a refutation of the absolutism of Thomas Hobbes'* Leviathan. *Hobbes had maintained that men were by nature bellicose and entered into civil societies only as a protection against the eventual domination of the weak by the strong. According to Hobbes, only an absolutist state could control the vicious tendencies in human nature.*

In this selection, which is the complete, crucial ninth chapter of the Second Treatise, *Locke argues that all men enter into a compact to form a society "for the mutual preservation of their lives, liberties, and estates." Once he has defined his conception of the purpose of civil society, he then goes on to deduce from this purpose the kinds of laws which are necessary if society is to achieve this end.*

The method of argument throughout the Second Treatise *is, as here, deductive. Locke first establishes, by assumption or definition, some abstract principle. From this principle, he then goes on to derive some of the necessary characteristics of a just society. Basic to the entire* Second Treatise *is his conception of human nature. Once he has made clear his position on this subject, he proceeds to derive from it a complete conception of a law of nature. From this law of nature, he infers a whole series of consequent obligations. These in turn furnish the bases of the laws of all just societies, and all men are, by nature, obliged to obey them. This and not an inherited right of kings is the true source of civil society.*

Of the Ends of Political Society and Government *

If man in the state of nature be so free, as has been said, if he be absolute lord of his own person and possessions, equal to the greatest, and subject to nobody, why will he part with his freedom, why will he give up his empire and subject himself to the dominion and control of any other power? To which it is obvious to answer that though in the state of nature he has such a right, yet the enjoyment of it is very uncertain and constantly exposed to the invasion of others; for all being kings as much as he, every man his equal, and the greater part no strict observers of equity and justice, the enjoyment of the property he has in this state is very unsafe, very unsecure. This makes him willing to quit a condition which, however free, is full of fears and continual dangers; and it is not without reason that he seeks out and is willing to join in society with others who are already united, or have a mind to unite, for the mutual preservation of their lives,

* From *The Second Treatise of Government* (1690).

liberties, and estates, which I call by the general name "property."

The great and chief end, therefore, of men's uniting into commonwealths and putting themselves under government is the preservation of their property. To which in the state of nature there are many things wanting:

First, there wants an established, settled, known law, received and allowed by common consent to be the standard of right and wrong and the common measure to decide all controversies between them; for though the law of nature be plain and intelligible to all rational creatures, yet men, being biased by their interest as well as ignorant for want of studying it, are not apt to allow of it as a law binding to them in the application of it to their particular cases.

Secondly, in the state of nature there wants a known and indifferent judge with authority to determine all differences according to the established law; for every one in that state being both judge and executioner of the law of nature, men being partial to themselves, passion and revenge is very apt to carry them too far and with too much heat in their own cases, as well as negligence and unconcernedness to make them too remiss in other men's.

Thirdly, in the state of nature there often wants power to back and support the sentence when right, and to give it due execution. They who by any injustice offend will seldom fail, where they are able, by force, to make good their injustice; such resistance many times makes the punishment dangerous and frequently destructive to those who attempt it.

Thus mankind, notwithstanding all the privileges of the state of nature, being in an ill condition while they remain in it, are quickly driven into society. Hence it comes to pass that we seldom find any number of men live any time together in this state. The inconveniences that they are therein exposed to by the irregular and uncertain exercise of the power every man has of punishing the transgressions of others make them take sanctuary under the established laws of government and therein seek the preservation of their property. It is this makes them so willingly give up every one his single power of punishing, to be exercised by such alone as shall be appointed to it amongst them; and by such rules as the community, or those authorized by them to that purpose, shall agree on. And in this we have the original right of both the legislative and executive power, as well as of the governments and societies themselves.

For in the state of nature, to omit the liberty he has of innocent delights, a man has two powers:

The first is to do whatsoever he thinks fit for the preservation of himself and others within the permission of the law of nature, by which law, common to them all, he and all the rest of mankind are one community, make up one society, distinct from all other creatures. And, were it not for the corruption and viciousness of degenerate men, there would be no need of any other, no necessity that men should separate from this great and natural community and by positive agreements combine into smaller and divided associations.

The other power a man has in the state of nature is the power to punish the crimes committed against the law. Both these he gives up when he joins in a private, if I may so call it, or particular politic society and incorporates into any commonwealth separate from the rest of mankind.

The first power, viz., of doing whatsoever he thought fit for the preservation of himself and the rest of mankind, he gives up to be regulated by laws made by the society, so far forth as the preservation of himself and the rest of that society shall require; which laws of the society in many things confine the liberty he had by the law of nature.

Secondly, the power of punishing he wholly gives up, and engages his natural force—which he might before employ in the execution of the law of nature by his own single authority, as he thought fit—to assist the executive power of the society, as the law thereof shall require; for being now in a new state, wherein he is to enjoy many conveniences from the labor, assistance, and society of others in the same community as well as protection from its whole strength, he is to part also with as much of his natural liberty, in providing for himself, as the good, prosperity, and safety of the society shall require, which is not only necessary, but just, since the other members of the society do the like.

But though men when they enter into society give up the equality, liberty, and executive power they had in the state of nature into the hands of the society, to be so far disposed of by the legislative as the good of the society shall require, yet it being only with an intention in every one the better to preserve himself, his liberty and property—for no rational creature can be supposed to change his condition with an intention to be worse—the power of the society, or legislative constituted by them, can never be supposed to extend farther than the common good, but is obliged to secure every one's property by providing against those three defects above-mentioned that made the state of nature so unsafe and uneasy. And so whoever has the legislative or supreme power of any commonwealth is bound to govern by established standing laws, promulgated and known to the people, and not by extemporary decrees; by indifferent and upright judges who are to decide controversies by those laws; and to employ the force of the community at home only in the execution of such laws, or abroad to prevent or redress foreign injuries, and secure the community from inroads and invasion. And all this to be directed to no other end but the peace, safety, and public good of the people.

TOPICS FOR DISCUSSION AND WRITING

1. What is the difference between the privileges enjoyed by man in the state of nature and man in the state of society? Is man freer in the state of nature than he is in the state of society?
2. Why does man abandon the state of nature to join a civil society? What is the purpose of society?
3. What is wanting to man in the state of nature? What inconveniences to the enjoyment of property does he experience?
4. What powers and privileges does man enjoy in the state of nature? Does he retain all these powers in the state of society?
5. What obligations does the legislative or supreme power of a society incur as a result of the reason why men enter into a society?
6. What is Locke's thesis in this chapter? What is its subject? How does he support his thesis?
7. Does the following enthymeme summarize, adequately, the thesis of this selection?

   Whoever has supreme power in a commonwealth must govern justly because of the reasons why people enter into civil society.
8. Is there any sentence in the text which, in your opinion, comes close to stating Locke's thesis and a summary of the supporting reasons?

9. Does Locke's conclusion follow if one agrees with his conception of human nature, the state of society, and the reasons why men join a civil society? Does his conclusion follow if one disagrees with any of his concepts?
10. Write an essay showing how Locke's arguments are opposed to the position taken by Thoreau in *Civil Disobedience*. Can a member of society, according to Locke's definition, behave as independently as Thoreau did?

Alexander Hamilton, Federalist No. 27

The Federalist Papers *were a series of eighty-five essays written by Alexander Hamilton, James Madison, and John Jay. These articles were published in various New York newspapers between October 1787 and April 1788. They were intended to persuade the people of New York to favor the adoption of the proposed Constitution of the United States. Though the* Federalist Papers *do not seem to have been the most important factor influencing the New York Convention to favor ratification in June 1788, they still remain some of the best commentaries ever written on our Constitution.*

About two-thirds of the Federalist Papers *were written by Alexander Hamilton. His papers are characterized by a frequent use of arguments based on theoretical considerations of the nature of man and the nature of government. In* Federalist No. 27 *he is arguing in favor of the general thesis of all the* Federalist Papers, *that the proposed Constitution should be adopted. His specific thesis in this particular paper is that the proposed Constitution would exercise a control over the daily affairs of men in such a fashion that it would be obeyed. His reason for believing that the people would obey without the use of force stems from his concept of human nature—that man is a creature of habit.*

The structure of the argument of Federalist No. 27, *as well as its relation to the* Federalist Papers *as a whole, can be represented in the following fashion:*

General thesis of *Federalist Papers:*	The proposed Constitution should be adopted—
Specific thesis of *Federalist No. 27:*	it will be obeyed
Specific reason proving thesis:	because man is a creature of habit.

The argument of Federalist No. 27 *can also be represented in syllogistic fashion as follows:*

Any political system which is based on a sound conception of human nature will be obeyed.
The proposed Constitution is based on a sound conception of human nature.
The proposed Constitution will be obeyed.

The Federalist No. 27 *

To the People of the State of New York:

It has been urged, in different shapes, that a Constitution of the kind proposed by the convention cannot operate without the aid of a military force to execute its laws. This, however, like most other things that have been alleged on that side, rests on mere general assertion, unsupported by any precise or intelligible designation of the reasons upon which it is founded. As far as I have been able to divine the latent meaning of the objectors, it seems to originate in a presupposition that the people will be disinclined to the exercise of federal authority in any matter of an internal nature. Waiving any exception that might be taken to the inaccuracy or inexplicitness of the distinction between internal and external, let us inquire what ground there is to presuppose that disinclination in the people. Unless we presume at the same time that the powers of the general government will be worse administered than those of the State government, there seems to be no room for the presumption of ill will, disaffection, or opposition in the people. I believe it may be laid down as a general rule that their confidence in and obedience to a government will commonly be proportioned to the goodness or badness of its administration. It must be admitted that there are exceptions to this rule; but these exceptions depend so entirely on accidental causes, that they cannot be considered as having any relation to the intrinsic merits or demerits of a constitution. These can only be judged of by general principles and maxims.

Various reasons have been suggested, in the course of these papers, to induce a probability that the general government will be better administered than the particular governments: the prin-

* From the *New York Packet* (Tuesday, December 25, 1787).

cipal of which reasons are that the extension of the spheres of election will present a greater option, or latitude of choice, to the people; that through the medium of the State legislatures—which are select bodies of men, and which are to appoint the members of the national Senate—there is reason to expect that this branch will generally be composed with peculiar care and judgment; that these circumstances promise greater knowledge and more extensive information in the national councils, and that they will be less apt to be tainted by the spirit of faction, and more out of the reach of those occasional ill humors, or temporary prejudices and propensities, which, in smaller societies, frequently contaminate the public councils, beget injustice and oppression of a part of the community, and engender schemes which, though they gratify a momentary inclination or desire, terminate in general distress, dissatisfaction, and disgust. Several additional reasons of considerable force, to fortify that probability, will occur when we come to survey, with a more critical eye, the interior structure of the edifice which we are invited to erect. It will be sufficient here to remark, that until satisfactory reasons can be assigned to justify an opinion, that the federal government is likely to be administered in such a manner as to render it odious or contemptible to the people, there can be no reasonable foundation for the supposition that the laws of the Union will meet with any greater obstruction from them, or will stand in need of any other methods to enforce their execution, than the laws of the particular members.

The hope of impunity is a strong incitement to sedition; the dread of punishment, a proportionably strong discouragement to it. Will not the government of the Union, which, if possessed of a due degree of power, can call to its aid the collective resources of the whole Confederacy, be more likely to repress the *former* sentiment and to inspire the *latter,* than that of a single State, which can only command the resources within itself? A turbulent faction in a State may easily suppose itself able to contend with the friends to the government in that State; but it can hardly be so infatuated as to imagine itself a match for the combined efforts of the Union. If this reflection be just, there is less danger of resistance from irregular combinations of individuals to the authority of the Confederacy than to that of a single member.

I will, in this place, hazard an observation, which will not be the less just because to some it may appear new; which is, that the more the operations of the national authority are intermingled in the ordinary exercise of government, the more the citizens are accustomed to meet with it in the common occurrences of their political life, the more it is familiarized to their sight and to their feelings, the further it enters into those objects which touch the most sensible chords and put in motion the most active springs of the human heart, the greater will be the probability that it will conciliate the respect and attachment of the community. Man is very much a creature of habit. A thing that rarely strikes his senses will generally have but little influence upon his mind. A government continually at a distance and out of sight can hardly be expected to interest the sensations of the people. The inference is, that the authority of the Union, and the affections of the citizens towards it, will be strengthened, rather than weakened, by its extension to what are called matters of internal concern; and will have less occasion to recur to force, in proportion to the familiarity and comprehensiveness of its agency. The more it circulates through those channels and currents in which the passions of mankind naturally flow, the less will it require the aid of the violent and perilous expedients of compulsion.

One thing, at all events, must be evident, that a government like the one proposed would bid much fairer to avoid the necessity of using force, than that species of league contended for by most of its opponents; the authority of which should only operate upon the States in their political or collective capacities. It has been shown that in such a Confederacy there can be no sanction for the laws but force; that frequent delinquencies in the members are the natural offspring of the very frame of the government; and that as often as these happen, they can only be redressed, if at all, by war and violence.

The plan reported by the convention, by extending the authority of the federal head to the individual citizens of the several States, will enable the government to employ the ordinary magistracy of each, in the execution of its laws. It is easy to perceive that this will tend to destroy, in the common apprehension, all distinction between the sources from which they might proceed; and will give the federal government the same advantage for securing a due obedience to its authority which is enjoyed by the government of each State, in addition to the influence on public opinion which will result from the important consideration of its having power to call to its assistance and support the resources of the whole Union. It merits particular attention in this place, that the laws of the Confederacy, as to the *enumerated* and *legitimate* objects of its jurisdiction, will become the SUPREME LAW of the land; to the observance of which all officers, legislative, executive, and judicial, in each State, will be bound by the sanctity of an oath. Thus the legislatures, courts, and magistrates, of the respective members, will be incorporated into the operations of the national government *as far as its just and constitutional authority extends;* and will be rendered auxiliary to the enforcement of its laws. Any man who will pursue, by his own reflections, the consequences of this situation, will perceive that there is good ground to calculate upon a regular and peaceable execution of the laws of the Union, if its powers are administered with a common share of prudence. If we will arbitrarily suppose the contrary, we may deduce any inferences we please from the supposition; for it is certainly possible, by an injudicious exercise of the authorities of the best government that ever was, or ever can be instituted, to provoke and precipitate the people into the wildest excesses. But though the adversaries of the proposed Constitution should presume that the national rulers would be insensible to the motives of public good, or to the obligations of duty, I would still ask them how the interests of ambition, or the views of encroachment, can be promoted by such a conduct?

PUBLIUS

TOPICS FOR DISCUSSION AND WRITING

1. What is the thesis which Hamilton sets out to refute? What reasons, if any, have been offered in support of this thesis to which Hamilton is opposed? Can a thesis which has been gratuitously asserted (i.e., proposed without any supporting reasons) be gratuitously denied (i.e., rejected without giving any reasons)?
2. What does Hamilton believe determines whether or not people obey a government?
3. Why does he believe that the general government will be better obeyed than the particular or state governments?

4. Does the following syllogism adequately summarize the argument of the first two paragraphs of the essay?

   MAJOR: The better administered a government is, the better it will be obeyed.

   MINOR: The national government will be better administered than the state governments.

   CONCLUSION: The national government, therefore, will be better obeyed than the state governments.

5. Is this a deductive argument? Why? What is its weakest point?
6. What, in Hamilton's opinion, determines whether factions obey a government or plot sedition?
7. Why does Hamilton believe that a national government which will be involved in the daily affairs of its citizens will be obeyed? Contrast Hamilton's view of human nature with Locke's.
8. Does the following enthymeme summarize the argument of the third and fourth paragraphs?

   The more the authority of the national government is felt in the daily affairs of men, the more it is likely to win respect and obedience because man is a creature of habit.

   Is there any sentence in these paragraphs which comes close to stating the thesis and its supporting reason?
9. Write an essay showing how Hamilton's arguments in favor of the American Constitution could be used in favor of a world state. Do any of these arguments suggest ways in which the world state of Crane Brinton could be brought to realization more rapidly?
10. Write an essay contrasting Hamilton's with Locke's views of the nature and purpose of governments.

John Stuart Mill

John Stuart Mill (1806–1873) was as devoted to the cause of social reform as were his contemporaries John Ruskin and Matthew Arnold (who are represented elsewhere in this collection) but his ideas moved in a different direction. Whereas Ruskin and Arnold sought a version of "The Great Man" for social improvement (and by implication looked forward to the corporate, homogeneous, hierarchical society that is prevalent today), Mill insisted on the unique rights of the individual, even at the expense of a weakness in the social structure. His essay On Liberty *(1859) appeared in the same year as Darwin's* Origin of Species, *and it would be difficult to say which has had the greater impact on man's understanding of himself. Like*

Milton's Areopagitica *and Thoreau's* Civil Disobedience *(with which it should be compared),* On Liberty *is an eloquent argument for the rights of man in a society which has grown too large and too complex to deal with him as an individual.*

from On Liberty

The principles asserted in these pages must be more generally admitted as the basis for discussion of details, before a consistent application of them to all the various departments of government and morals can be attempted with any prospect of advantage. The few observations I propose to make on questions of detail, are designed to illustrate the principles, rather than to follow them out to their consequences. I offer, not so much applications, as specimens of application; which may serve to bring into greater clearness the meaning and limits of the two maxims which together form the entire doctrine of this essay, and to assist the judgment in holding the balance between them, in the cases where it appears doubtful which of them is applicable to the case.

The maxims are, first, that the individual is not accountable to society for his actions, in so far as these concern the interests of no person but himself. Advice, instruction, persuasion, and avoidance by other people, if thought necessary by them for their own good, are the only measures by which society can justifiably express its dislike or disapprobation of his conduct. Secondly, that for such actions as are prejudicial to the interests of others, the individual is accountable, and may be subjected either to social or to legal punishment, if society is of opinion that the one or the other is requisite for its protection.

In the first place, it must by no means be supposed, because damage, or probability of damage, to the interests of others, can alone justify the interference of society, that therefore it always does justify such interference. In many cases, an individual, in pursuing a legitimate object, necessarily and therefore legitimately causes pain or loss to others, or intercepts a good which they had a reasonable hope of obtaining. Such oppositions of interest between individuals often arise from bad social institutions, but are unavoidable while those institutions last; and some would be unavoidable under any institutions. Whoever succeeds in an over-crowded profession, or in a competitive examination; whoever is preferred to another in any contest for an object which both desire, reaps benefit from the loss of others, from their wasted exertion and their disappointment. But it is, by common admission, better for the general interest of mankind, that persons should pursue their objects undeterred by this sort of consequences. In other words, society admits no right, either legal or moral, in the disappointed competitors, to immunity from this kind of suffering; and feels called on to interfere, only when means of success have been employed which it is contrary to the general interest to permit—namely, fraud or treachery, and force.

Again, trade is a social act. Whoever undertakes to sell any description of goods to the public, does what affects the interest of other persons, and of society in general; and thus his conduct, in principle, comes within the jurisdiction of society: accordingly, it was once held to be the duty of governments, in all cases which were considered of importance, to fix prices, and regulate the processes of manufacture. But it is now recognized, though not till after a long struggle, that both the cheapness and the good quality of commodities are most effectually provided for by leaving the producers and sellers perfectly free, under the sole check of equal freedom to the buyers for supplying themselves elsewhere. This is the so-called doctrine of Free Trade, which rests on grounds different from though equally solid with, the principle of individual liberty asserted in this essay. Restrictions on trade, or on production for purposes of trade, are indeed restraints; and all restraint, *qua* restraint, is an evil: but the restraints in question affect only that part of conduct which society is competent to restrain, and are wrong solely because they do not really produce the results which it is desired to produce by them. As the principle of individual liberty is not involved in the doctrine of Free Trade, so neither is it in most of the questions which arise respecting the limits of the doctrine; as, for example, what amount of public control is admissible for the prevention of fraud by adulteration; how far sanitary precautions, or arrangements to protect work-people employed in dangerous occupations, should be enforced on employers. Such questions involve considerations of liberty, only in so far as leaving people to themselves is always better, *caeteris paribus,* than controlling them: but that they may be legitimately controlled for these ends, is in principle undeniable. On the other hand, there are questions relating to interference with trade, which are essentially questions of liberty; such as the Maine Law [prohibition of the manufacture and sale of intoxicants, 1851], already touched upon; the prohibition of the importation of opium into China; the restriction of the sale of poisons; all cases, in short, where the object of the interference is to make it impossible or difficult to obtain a particular commodity. These interferences are objectionable, not as infringements on the liberty of the producer or seller, but on that of the buyer.

One of these examples, that of the sale of poisons, opens a new question; the proper limits of what may be called the functions of police; how far liberty may legitimately be invaded for the prevention of crime, or of accident. It is one of the undisputed functions of government to take precautions against crime before it has been committed, as well as to detect and punish it afterwards. The preventive function of government, however, is far more liable to be abused, to the prejudice of liberty, than the punitory function; for there is hardly any part of the legitimate freedom of action of a human being which would not admit of being represented, and fairly too, as increasing the facilities for some form or other of delinquency. Nevertheless, if a public authority, or even a private person, sees any one evidently preparing to commit a crime, they are not bound to look on inactive until the crime is committed, but may interfere to prevent it. If poisons were never bought or used for any purpose except the commission of murder, it would be right to prohibit their manufacture and sale. They may, however, be wanted not only for innocent but for useful purposes, and restrictions cannot be imposed in the one case without operating in the other. Again, it is a proper office of public authority to guard against accidents. If either a public officer or any one else saw a person attempting to cross a bridge which had been ascertained to be unsafe, and there were no time to warn him of his danger, they might seize him and turn him back, without any real infringement of his liberty; for liberty consists in doing what one desires, and he does not desire to fall into the river. Nevertheless, when there is not a certainty, but only a danger of mischief, no one but the person himself can judge of the sufficiency of the motive which may prompt him to incur the risk: in this case, therefore (unless he is a child, or delirious, or in some state of excitement or absorption incompatible with the full use of the reflecting faculty), he ought, I conceive, to be only warned of the danger; not forcibly prevented from exposing himself to it. Similar considerations, applied to such a question as the sale of poisons, may enable us to decide which among the possible modes of regulation are or are not contrary to principle. Such a precaution, for example, as that of labeling the drug with some word expressive of its dangerous character, may be enforced without violation of liberty: the buyer cannot wish not to know that the thing he possesses has poisonous qualities. But to require in all cases the certificate of a medical practitioner would make it sometimes impossible, always expensive, to obtain the article for legitimate uses. The only mode apparent to me, in which difficulties may be thrown in the way of crime committed through this means, without any infringement, worth taking into account, upon the liberty of those who desire the poisonous substance for other purposes, consists in providing what, in the apt language of Bentham, is called "preappointed evidence." This provision is familiar to everyone in the case of contracts. It is usual and right that the law, when a contract is entered into, should require as the condition of its enforcing performance, that certain formalities should be observed, such as signatures, attestation of witnesses, and the like, in order that in case of subsequent dispute, there may be evidence to prove that the contract was really entered into, and that there was nothing in the circumstances to render it legally invalid: the effect being to throw great obstacles in the way of fictitious contracts, or contracts made in circumstances which, if known, would destroy their validity. Precautions of a similar nature might be enforced in the sale of articles adapted to be instruments of crime. The seller, for example, might be required to enter in a register the exact time of the transaction, the name and address of the buyer, the precise quality and quantity sold; to ask the purpose for which it was wanted, and record the answer he received. When there was no medical prescription, the presence of some third person might be required to bring home the fact to the purchaser, in case there should afterwards be reason to believe that the article had been applied to criminal purposes. Such regulations would in general be no material impediment to obtaining the article, but a very considerable one to making an improper use of it without detection.

The right inherent in society, to ward off crimes against itself by antecedent precautions, suggests the obvious limitations to the maxim, that purely self-regarding misconduct cannot properly be meddled with in the way of prevention or punishment. Drunkenness, for example, in ordinary cases, is not a fit subject for legislative interference; but I should deem it perfectly legitimate that a person, who had once been convicted of any act of violence to others under the influence of drink, should be placed under a special legal restriction, personal to himself; that if he were afterwards found drunk, he should be liable to a penalty, and that if when in that state he committed another offence, the punishment to which he would be liable for that other offence should be increased in severity. The making himself drunk, in a person whom drunkenness excites to do harm to others, is a crime against others. So, again, idleness, except in a person receiving support from the public, or except when it constitutes a breach of contract, cannot without tyranny be made a subject of legal punishment; but if, either from idleness or from any other avoidable cause, a man fails to perform his legal duties to others, as for instance to support his children, it is no tyranny to force him to fulfill that obligation, by compulsory labour, if no other means are available.

Again, there are many acts which, being directly injurious only to the agents themselves, ought not to be legally interdicted, but which, if done publicly, are a violation of good manners, and coming thus within the category of offences against others, may rightfully be prohibited. Of this kind are offences against decency; on which it is unnecessary to dwell, the rather as they are only connected indirectly with our subject, the objection to publicity being equally strong in the case of many actions not in themselves condemnable, nor supposed to be so.

There is another question to which an answer must be found, consistent with the principles which have been laid down. In cases of personal conduct supposed to be blameable, but which respect for liberty precludes society from preventing or punishing, because the evil directly resulting falls wholly on the agent; what the agent is free to do, ought other persons to be equally free to counsel or instigate? This question is not free from difficulty. The case of a person who solicits another to do an act is not strictly a case of self-regarding conduct. To give advice or offer inducements to any one is a social act, and may, therefore, like actions in general which affect others, be supposed amenable to social control. But a little reflection corrects the first impression, by showing that if the case is not strictly within the definition of individual liberty, yet the reason on which the principle of individual liberty is grounded is applicable to it. If people must be allowed, in whatever concerns only themselves, to act as seems best to themselves at their own peril, they must equally be free to consult with one another about what is fit to be so done; to exchange opinions, and give and receive suggestions. Whatever is permitted to do, it must be permitted to advise to do. The question is doubtful, only when the instigator derives a personal benefit from his advice; when hc makes it his occupation, for subsistence or pecuniary gain, to promote what society and the State consider to be an evil. Then, indeed, a new element of complication is introduced; namely, the existence of classes of persons with an interest opposed to what is considered as the public weal, and whose mode of living is grounded on the counteraction of it. Ought this to be interfered with, or not? Fornication, for example, must be tolerated, and so must gambling; but should a person be free to be a pimp, or to keep a gambling house? The case is one of those which lie on the exact boundary line between two principles, and it is not at once apparent to which of the two it properly belongs. There are arguments on both sides. On the side of toleration it may be said, that the fact of following anything as an occupation, and living or profiting by the practice of it, cannot make that criminal which would otherwise be admissible; that the act should either be consistently permitted or consistently prohibited; that if the principles which we have hitherto defended are true, society has no business, *as* society, to decide anything to be wrong which concerns the individual; that it cannot go beyond dissuasion, and that one person should be as free to persuade, as another to dissuade. In opposition to this it may be contended, that although the public, or the State, are not warranted in authoritatively deciding, for purposes of repression or punishment, that such or such conduct affecting only the interests of the individual is good or bad, they are fully justified in assuming, if they regard it as bad, that its being so or not is at least a disputable question: That, this being supposed, they cannot be acting wrongly in endeavouring to exclude the influence of solicitations which are not disinterested, of instigators who cannot possibly be impartial—who have a direct personal interest on one side, and that side the one which the State believes to be wrong, and who confessedly promote it for personal objects only. There can surely, it may be urged, be nothing lost, no sacrifice of good, by so ordering matters that persons shall make their election, either wisely or foolishly, on their own prompting, as free as possible from the arts of persons, who stimulate their inclinations for interested purposes of their own. Thus (it may be said) though the statutes respecting unlawful games are utterly indefensible—though all persons should be free to gamble in their own or each other's houses, or in any place of meeting established by their own subscriptions, and open only to the members and their visitors—yet public gambling-houses should not be permitted. It is true that the prohibition is never effectual, and that, whatever amount of tyrannical power may be given to the police, gambling-houses can always be maintained under other pretences; but they may be compelled to conduct their operations with a certain degree of secrecy and mystery, so that nobody knows about them but those who seek them; and more than this, society ought not to aim at. There is considerable force in these arguments. I will not venture to decide whether they are sufficient to justify the moral anomaly of punishing the accessory, when the principal is (and must be) allowed to go free; of fining or imprisoning the procurer, but not the fornicator, the gambling-house keeper, but not the gambler. Still less ought the common operations of buying and selling to be interfered with on analogous grounds. Almost every article which is bought and sold may be used in excess, and the sellers have a pecuniary interest in encouraging that excess; but no argument can be founded on this, in favour, for instance, of the Maine law; because the class of dealers in strong drink, though interested in their abuse, are indispensably required for the sake of their legitimate use. The interest, however, of these dealers in promoting intemperance is a real evil, and justifies the State in imposing restrictions and requiring guarantees which, but for that justification, would be infringements of legitimate liberty.

A further question is, whether the State, while it permits, should nevertheless indirectly discourage conduct which it deems contrary to the best interests of the agent; whether, for example, it should take measures to render the means of drunkenness more costly, or add to the difficulty of procuring them by limiting the number of the places of sale. On this as on most other practical questions, many distinctions require to be made. To tax stimulants for the sole purpose of making them more difficult to be obtained is a measure differing only in degree from their entire prohibition, and would be justifiable only if that were justifiable. Every increase of cost is a prohibition, to those whose means do not come up to the augmented price; and to those who do, it is a penalty laid on them for gratifying a particular taste. Their choice of pleasures, and their mode of expending their income, after satisfying their legal and moral obligations to the State and to individuals, are their own concern, and must rest with their own judgment. These considerations may seem at first sight to condemn the selection of stimulants as special subjects of taxation for purposes of revenue. But it must be remembered that taxation for fiscal purposes is absolutely inevitable; that in most countries it is necessary that a considerable part of that taxation should be indirect; that the State, therefore, cannot help imposing penalties, which to some persons may be prohibitory, on the use of some articles of consumption. It is hence the duty of the State to consider, in the imposition of taxes, what commodities the consumers can best spare; and *a fortiori,* to select in preference those of which it deems the use, beyond a very moderate quantity, to be positively injurious. Taxation, therefore, of stimulants, up to the point which produces the largest amount of revenue (supposing that the State needs all the revenue which it yields) is not only admissible, but to be approved of.

The question of making the sale of these commodities a more

or less exclusive privilege, must be answered differently, according to the purposes to which the restriction is intended to be subservient. All places of public resort require the restraint of a police, and places of this kind peculiarly, because offences against society are especially apt to originate there. It is, therefore, fit to confine the power of selling these commodities (at least for consumption on the spot) to persons of known or vouched-for respectability of conduct; to make such regulations respecting hours of opening and closing as may be requisite for public surveillance, and to withdraw the license if breaches of the peace repeatedly take place through the connivance or incapacity of the keeper of the house, or if it becomes a rendezvous for concocting and preparing offences against the law. Any further restriction I do not conceive to be, in principle, justifiable. The limitation in number, for instance, of beer and spirit houses, for the express purpose of rendering them more difficult of access, and diminishing the occasions of temptation, not only exposes all to an inconvenience because there are some by whom the facility would be abused, but is suited only to a state of society in which the labouring classes are avowedly treated as children or savages, and placed under an education of restraint, to fit them for future admission to the privileges of freedom. This is not the principle on which the labouring classes are professedly governed in any free country; and no person who sets due value on freedom will give his adhesion to their being so governed, unless after all efforts have been exhausted to educate them for freemen, and it has been definitely proved that they can only be governed as children. The bare statement of the alternative shows the absurdity of supposing that such efforts have been made in any case which needs be considered here. It is only because the institutions of this country are a mass of inconsistencies, that things find admittance into our practice which belong to the system of despotic, or what is called paternal, government, while the general freedom of our institutions precludes the exercise of the amount of control necessary to render the restraint of any real efficacy as a moral education. . . . A government cannot have too much of the kind of activity which does not impede, but aids and stimulates, individual exertion and development. The mischief begins when, instead of calling forth the activity and powers of individuals and bodies, it substitutes its own activity for theirs; when, instead of informing, advising, and, upon occasion, denouncing, it makes them work in fetters, or bids them stand aside and does their work instead of them. The worth of a State, in the long run, is the worth of the individuals composing it; and a State which postpones the interests of *their* mental expansion and elevation, to a little more of administrative skill, or of that semblance of it which practice gives, in the details of business; a State which dwarfs its men, in order that they may be more docile instruments in its hands even for beneficial purposes—will find that with small men no great thing can really be accomplished; and that the perfection of machinery to which it has sacrificed everything, will in the end avail it nothing, for want of the vital power which, in order that the machine might work more smoothly, it has preferred to banish.

TOPICS FOR DISCUSSION AND WRITING

1. The earlier sections of *On Liberty* were composed of an induction which ultimately led to a statement of principles. In this section, Mill deductively applies these principles to specific problems. What are these principles?
2. Does Mill make his deduction credible by raising only those specific problems which are easily solved? Would his principles have been admitted if he had chosen less complicated problems?
3. How does Mill provide that the liberty of persons shall not become anarchy, a complete absence of government and control? In his provision, is he consistent to his principles?
4. It is a simple thing to agree with Mill in *principle;* do you agree with the implications and consequences of those principles?
5. What would probably be Mill's reaction to the society which Riesman describes (p. 243) or which Lippmann describes (p. 160)?
6. Would Mill's conception of the bases of liberty support the attitude taken by Thoreau in his essay *Civil Disobedience?* Write an essay on this topic.
7. Write an essay showing how Mill's conception of the bases of liberty agrees or disagrees with Locke's conception of the purposes of civil society.
8. Compare Mill's conception of liberty with Hamilton's conception of the nature of government in *Federalist #27.*

III Derivation of Arguments

The critical reader is constantly on the alert, testing the validity of the arguments which are being presented. Therefore the writer, anxious to convince others of the correctness of his point of view, is always anxious to use all the best arguments which could be offered in support of his thesis. To help the reader evaluate what he is reading and to aid the writer in discovering all the best available arguments, classical rhetoricians developed a system for classifying arguments according to their sources. The reader who is familiar with this system can identify various arguments according to sources from which they were drawn and thereby determine whether they are strong or weak arguments. The writer who is familiar with this system can review what he has written to see if he has exploited all possible sources of arguments.

Classified according to the sources from which they can be derived, all arguments fall into two large categories: intrinsic arguments and extrinsic arguments. Intrinsic arguments are arguments implied in the terms of the thesis itself. Intrinsic arguments are of three kinds: (1) arguments derived from analogical relationships existing between the situation defined or implied in the thesis and some other situations, as, for example, when we predict the outcome of a presidential election because of some similarities existing between the current candidates and past candidates; (2) arguments derived from antecedents or consequences of the situation defined or implied in the thesis, as when we urge the election of some candidate because of the benefits which will result from the inauguration of his programs; (3) arguments derived from the nature of the subject or predicate terms of the thesis, as when we urge the election of a particular candidate because of his ability, experience, and character. Extrinsic arguments can be considered as constituting a fourth type. These arguments are called extrinsic because their content is not implicit within the terms of the thesis or the situation implied in the thesis. Extrinsic arguments are all based on the testimony and opinions of witnesses who are supposedly authorities on the point at issue.

Classical rhetoricians called these sources of arguments *the topics,* from the Greek word *topos* meaning place or location. The topics with which we will be concerned can be represented schematically as follows:

Sources of Arguments

Topics	Intrinsic	(1) from analogical relation
		(2) from antecedents and consequences
		(3) from the nature of the subject
	Extrinsic	(4) from testimony

Some classical rhetoricians recognize many more topics or sources of arguments than these four. Cicero, for example, distinguishes some twelve or thirteen by breaking down each of four groups into two or more subgroups. Aristotle employs a classification system with more than twenty topics. These more complicated systems of topical classification tend to divert a reader or writer's attention from the main point (the discovery and evaluation of arguments) to specialized and scholarly questions (whether a particular argument is derived from the topic of "conjugates" or "correlates." Working with the simpler scheme described above, the student may readily make his own subgroups whenever they seem appropriate.

TESTIMONY

An argument from testimony is a statement made by someone who is supposedly an authority on the subject. Every advertisement which urges its readers to buy a product because of the endorsement of some famous personage is in effect an argument from testimony because it is giving the statement of some person as a reason for purchasing the product. The person whose testimony is being used to endorse the product is supposedly an authoritative witness whose opinion should influence the reader's decision in favor of the product.

The argument from testimony is also familiar to anyone who has ever attended a court trial, witnessed a re-enactment on television, or read a mystery story. Defense counsels are commonly portrayed as using witnesses to testify to the moral character of the accused or to provide them with an alibi. The testimony of these witnesses is considered to be an argument in favor of the defendant's character. Arguments from testimony are effective only to the extent that the witnesses are considered authoritative and reliable. Prosecuting attorneys, therefore, may attempt to impugn the authority and reliability of witnesses who testify in behalf of the accused. The prosecutor asks questions intended to raise doubts whether the witness is really an authority on the facts to which he is testifying. Many of the questions are intended to ascertain whether or not the witness could have known the facts at issue. Other questions are asked to determine whether the witness has any reason for not telling the truth. If the prosecution cannot cast doubts on the witness' ability to know the facts, or on his reasons for testifying, the witness can be presumed to be telling the truth.

Though the average student can hardly be expected to evaluate the validity of courtroom testimony, every time he uses a footnote, whether it is to show that someone else is of the same opinion or to provide corroborating statistics, he is using an argument from testimony, and the same principles used to test the authority and reliability of a courtroom witness should be used to test the validity of a footnote reference. A footnote is a citation of an authority as a reason in favor of the thesis which a student is defending. Every student, therefore, should make sure, before citing a particular reference in a footnote, that the scholar being cited is considered authoritative. In similar fashion, the student who is critical of what he is reading should be constantly examining the authority and reliability of those persons whose opinions he is being asked to accept as confirming the truth of the author's thesis.

The argument from testimony is the only kind of argument which can be considered an extrinsic argument, because it alone consists of material drawn from outside the terms of the thesis. The existence of an expert witness, as, for example, a witness to a crime, is accidental. There may or may not be a witnesses to a crime; there may or may not be anyone who is available as an authority on a particular subject. If there is an authority, his existence may or may not be known to the person writing on the question. Therefore, whether one knows of the existence of an authority and whether an authority can be brought to bear on an issue depends on the possession of knowledge which is not implicit in the thesis.

Arguments derived even from the testimony of expert witnesses are not the strongest of arguments, because there is always the possibility that the witness may have been mistaken or that he may have had a reason for distorting what he thought to be the truth. Few arguments from testimony are compelling because few authorities are unquestionable.

Among the selections which have been chosen as examples of the use of arguments derived from testimony, the selection from Geoffrey Chaucer's *Canterbury Tales* illustrates the everlasting quarrel between the appeal to experience and the appeal to authority and testimony. William Temple's *Gardens of*

Epicurus shows how classical authors can be cited to testify to the correctness of the "true definition" of Epicurean philosophy. In the passage taken from Walter Lippmann's *The Public Philosophy,* contemporary witnesses as well as later scholars testify to the decline of a belief in a public philosophy. Barbara Ward's essay, *In Time of Trial,* which demonstrates inductive argumentation in a previous section, is also an illustration of the use of arguments derived from testimony, but in a fashion similar to the way in which such arguments are commonly used in term papers and other scholarly essays. In every instance, the author's thesis is confirmed or weakened by the authority and reliability of the witnesses he has summoned to testify on its behalf.

Geoffrey Chaucer's Wife of Bath

One of the great comic creations in literature is the Wife of Bath, a garrulous and outspoken pilgrim of The Canterbury Tales *by Geoffrey Chaucer (1343?–1400). The framework of Chaucer's famous work is familiar: A group of travelers, assembled for the common purpose of visiting the shrine of Thomas à Becket, agree to tell tales along the way to help pass the time. The descriptions of each of the storytellers, together with their stories, constitute one of the most enduring monuments of English literature, and the enduring fame of* The Canterbury Tales *owes no small measure to the character of the famous five-times-married wife from the city of Bath. An arch-feminist, the good lady regales the whole troupe of pilgrims with accounts of each of her five husbands, over all of whom she has exerted "sovereignty" or dominance. Her last husband, however, was most troublesome. A learned man, he was able to keep his wife in awe and subjection by his impressive citation of authorities and testimony dealing with the subject of conjugal duty and obligation. Only when she fell back on the ultimate female weapon, tears, was the Wife of Bath able to "refute" her husband's arguments. This selection from the Prologue to the Wife of Bath's Tale is a classic instance of Chaucer's use of rhetoric for poetic and dramatic effect. (A note on the text: We have preferred to keep as close as possible to the Middle English of Chaucer's poem instead of using a modern translation. However, we have modernized the spelling, even at the cost of occasionally harming the meter of the poetic lines so that the student should not experience any difficulty in reading the text.)*

from Prologue to the Wife of Bath's Tale

Experience, though no authority
Were in this world, is right enough for me
To speak of woe that is in marriage;
For, lordings, since I twelve years was of age,
Thanked be God that is eternally in life,
Husbands at church door I have had five—
If I so often might have wedded been—
And all were worthy men in their degree.
But me was told, certain, not long ago is,
That since that Christ went never but once
To wedding, in the Caana of Galilee,
That by the same example taught he me
That I should wedded be but once.
Hark ye, lo, which a sharp word for the nonce,
Beside a well, Jesus, God and man,
Spake in reproof of the Samaritan:
"Thou hast had five husbands," quoth he,
"And that ilk man that now hath thee
Is not thine husband," thus said he certain.
What that he meant thereby, I can not say;
But then I ask, why that the fifth man
Was no husband to the Samaritan?
How many might she have in marriage?
Yet heard I never tell in mine age
Upon this number definition.
Men may divine and gloss, up and down,
But well I wot, express, without lie,
God bad us for to wax and multiply;
That gentle text I can well understand.
Eke well I wot, he said my husband
Should leave father and mother, and take to me.
But of no number mention made he,
Of bigamy, or of octogamy;
Why should men then speak of it villainy?
Lo, here the wise king, don Solomon;

I trow he had wives more than one.
As would God it were lawful unto me
To be refreshed half so oft as he!
Which gift of God had he for all his wives!
No man hath such that in this world alive is.
God wot, this noble king, as to my wit
The first night had many a merry fit
With each of them, so well was he alive.
Blessed be God that I have wedded five!
Welcome the sixth, when that ever he shall.
For sooth, I will not keep me chaste in all.
When my husband is from the world gone,
Some Christian man shall wed me anon.

[After this opening statement of her philosophy of marriage, the Wife of Bath gives an account of her life with her first four husbands, all of whom were properly domesticated under her rule. Her fifth husband, however, a young scholar by the name of Jankyn, was cast in a different mould. Immediately after marriage, Jankyn forbade his wife to gossip, to spend her time visiting friends, and in general challenged her usual mode of conduct. The Wife continues with her woeful tale:]

Now will I say you sooth, by Saint Thomas,
Why that I rent out of his book a leaf,
For which he smote me so that I was deaf.
He had a book that gladly, night and day,
For his disport he would read always;
He called it Valerie [1] and Theofraste,[2]
At which book he laughed always full fast.
And eke there was sometime a clerk at Rome,
A cardinal, that was named Saint Jerome,[3]
That made a book against Jovinian;
In which book there was Tertullan,[4]
Crisippus,[5] Trotula,[6] and Helowys,[7]

1 A reference to an anti-feminist tract by Walter Map.
2 Theophrastus, who wrote a book on matrimonial obligations.
3 St. Jerome's polemic against women, *Epistola Adversus Jovinianum.*
4 Tertullian, who had written on chastity and monogamy.
5 Probably a reference to a Stoic philosopher by that name.
6 A female doctor who had written treatises on women's diseases.
7 Heloise, wife of the philosopher Abelard: a traditional instance of a woman who destroyed a man's career.

That was abbess not far from Paris;
And eke the Parables of Solomon,[8]
Ovid's Art,[9] and books many a one,
And all these were bound in one volume.
And every night and day was his custom,
When he had leisure and vacation
From other worldly occupation,
To read on this book of wicked wives,
He knew of them more legends and lives
Than be of good wives in the Bible.
For trusteth well, it is impossible
That any clerk will speak good of wives,
But if it be of holy saints' lives,
But of no other women never the more.
Who painted the lion, tell me who?
By God! if women had written stories,
As clerks have within their oratories,
They would have written of men more wickedness
Than all the mark of Adam may redress. . . .
  Of Livia told he me, and of Lucy: [10]
They both made their husbands for to die;
That one for love, that other was for hate.
Livia her husband, on an evening late,
Empoisoned hath, for that she was his foe;
Lucia, lecherous, loved her husband so
That, for he should always upon her think,
She gave him such a manner love-drink
That he was dead ere it were by the morrow;
And thus always husbands have sorrow.
  Then told he me how one Latumyus
Complained unto his fellow Arrius
That in his garden grew such a tree
On which he said how that his wives three
Hanged themselves for heart's despite.
"O dear brother," quoth this Arrius,

[8] The book of the Old Testament which lays stress on the allegiance the wife owes the husband.

[9] Ovid's *Ars Amatoris,* which is in great part a satire against the excesses of love.

[10] The following episodes and parables are taken from the "wicked book" that Jankyn is forever reading.

"Give me a plant of this blessed tree,
And in my garden planted shall it be."
  Of latter date, of wives hath he read
That some have slain their husbands in their bed,
And let their lovers remain all the night
When that the corpse lay on the floor upright.
And some have driven nails in their brain,
While that they slept, and thus they have them slain.
Some have them given poison in their drink.
He spoke more harm than heart may bethink;
And therewithal he knew of more proverbs
Than in this world there grows grass or herbs.
"Better is," quoth he, "thy habitation
Be with a lion or a foul dragon,
Than with a woman accustomed to chide.
"Better is," quoth he, "high in the roof abide,
Than with an angry wife down in the house;
They be so wicked and contrarious,
They hate that their husband love at all."
He said, a "woman cast her shame away,
When she cast off her smock"; and furthermore,
"A fair woman, but she be chaste also,
Is like a gold ring in a sow's nose."
Who would ween, or who would suppose,
The woe that in my heart was, and pain?
  And when I saw he would never cease
To read on this cursed book all night,
All suddenly three leaves have I plucked
Out of his book, right as he read, and eke
I with my fist so took him on the cheek
That in our fire he fell backward a-down.
And he up started as doth a wood lion,
And with his fist he smote me on the head,
That on the floor I lay as I were dead.
And when he saw how still that I lay,
He was aghast, and would have fled his way,
Till at last out of my swoon I brayed.
"O! hast thou slain me, false thief?" I said,
"And for my land thus hast thou murdered me?
Ere I be dead, yet will I kiss thee."
  And near he came, and knelt fair a-down,
And said, "Dear sister Alisoun,

As help me God! I shall thee never smite.
That I have done, it is thyself to blame.
Forgive it me, and that I thee beseech!"
And yet eftsoons I hit him on the cheek,
And said, "Thief, thus much am I wroth;
Now will I die, I may no longer speak."
But at last, with much care and woe,
We reached agreement by ourselves two.
He gave me all the bridle in my hand,
To have the governance of house and land,
And of his tongue, and of his hand also;
And made him burn his book anon right so.
And when that I had gotten unto me,
By mastery, all the sovereignty,
And that he said, "My own true wife,
Do as thou list the term of all thy life;
Keep thine honor, and keep eke my estate"—
After that day we had never debate.

TOPICS FOR DISCUSSION AND WRITING

1. There is an implied antagonism throughout this prologue between the appeal to experience and the appeal to authority and testimony. Does this seem to you to be a natural antagonism, or does Chaucer contrive such a debate only for the sake of the comedy?
2. Is the Wife of Bath's final victory a valid "refutation" of her husband's appeal to testimony?
3. The Wife of Bath, in the opening lines of the prologue, appeals to a few testimonials herself. How does she make use of the "arguments" in the various Bible stories? Would you say that her logic is valid?
4. Is there anything basically comic in the extreme use of the argument from testimony? Can you cite any examples from current journalism or advertising that would call attention to the ludicrousness of such an argument when it is carried too far?
5. Chaucer is not developing a thesis in this prologue, but it is possible to to read the prologue as an *example* of experience triumphing over testimony. Must testimony always surrender to experience? Write an essay in which you defend your answer to this question.

Sir William Temple

Sir William Temple (1628–1699) was for a great part of his life an impressive, perhaps brilliant, diplomat. As ambassador to Holland, Temple effected the Triple Alliance, a confederation of England, Holland, and Sweden, to stand as a united front against France, whose policy of French domination of Europe was a constant source of worry in the seventeenth century. But Temple was betrayed by his own government, and a secret treaty between the English and the French was negotiated. Temple retired from public office in protest. As the diplomatic winds shifted and an English alliance with Holland was again deemed valuable to national interests, Temple once more entered public life. He remained at his post until 1681, at which time, disturbed by the lack of moderation and bitter partisanship of national politics and embittered by his failure to convince his masters of the need for unity and restraint, he retired to his country estate. Several visits by heads of state, tempting him with offers of the Secretaryship of State, were rejected by Temple, who had elected a life of contemplation and the cultivation of his own taste—this he saw as the only antidote to a frantic and self-deluded society, and his essay Upon the Gardens of Epicurus *(1685) is primarily an argument for the value of a life of retirement, of intellectual sanity, and of a poised detachment from the foibles of mankind.*

from Upon the Gardens of Epicurus

The same faculty of reason, which gives mankind the great advantage and prerogative over the rest of the creation, seems to make the greatest default of human nature; and subjects it to more troubles, miseries, or at least disquiets of life than any of its fellow creatures: 'tis this furnishes us with such variety of passions, and consequently of wants and desires, that none other feels; and these followed by infinite designs and endless pursuits, and improved by that restlessness of thought, which is natural to most men, give him a condition of life suitable to that of his birth; so that as he alone is born crying, he lives complaining, and dies disappointed.

Since we cannot escape the pursuit of passions, and perplexity of thoughts, which our reason furnishes us, there is no way left, but to endeavour all we can, either to subdue or to divert them. This last is the common business of common men, who seek it by all sorts of sports, pleasures, play, or business. But because the two first are of short continuance, soon ending with weariness, or decay of vigour and appetite, the return whereof must be attended, before the others can be renewed; and because play grows dull, if it be not enlivened with the hopes of gain, the general diversion of mankind seems to be business, or the pursuit of riches in one kind or other, which is an amusement, that has this one advantage above all others, that it lasts those men who engage in it, to the very ends of their lives; none ever growing too old for the thoughts and desires of increasing his wealth and fortune, either for himself, his friends, or his posterity.

In the first and most simple ages of each country, the conditions and lives of men seem to have been very near of kin with the rest of the creatures; they lived by the hour, or by the day, and satisfied their appetite with what they could get, from the herbs, the fruits, the springs they met with when they were hungry or dry; then, with what fish, fowl, or beasts they could kill, by swiftness of strength, by craft or contrivance, by their hands or such instruments as wit helped, or necessity forced them to invent. When a man had got enough for the day, he laid up the rest for the morrow, and spent one day in labour, that he might pass the other at ease; and lured on by the pleasure of this bait, when he was in vigour, and his game fortunate, he would provide for as many days as he could, both for himself and his children, that were too young to seek out for themselves. Then he cast about, how by sowing of grain, and by pasture of the tamer cattle, to provide for the whole year. After this, dividing the lands necessary for these uses, first among children, and then among servants, he reserved to himself a proportion of their gain, either in the native stock, or something equivalent, which brought in the use of money; and where this once came in, none was to be satisfied, without having enough for himself and his family, and all his and their posterity forever; so that I know a certain lord who professes to value no lease, though for an hundred or a thousand years, nor any estate or possession of land that is not for ever and ever.

From such small beginnings have grown such vast and extravagant designs of poor mortal men: yet none could ever answer the naked Indian, why one man should take pains, and run hazards by sea and land all his life, that his children might be safe and lazy all theirs: and the precept of taking no care for the morrow, though never minded as impracticable in the world, seems but to reduce mankind to their natural and original condition of life. However by these ways and degrees the endless increase of riches seems to be grown the perpetual and general amusement or business of mankind.

Some few in each country make those higher flights after honour and power, and to these ends sacrifice their riches, their labour, their thought, and their lives; and nothing diverts nor busies men more than these pursuits, which are usually covered with the pretences, of serving a man's country, and of public good. But the true service of the public is a business of so much labour and so much care, that though a good and wise man may not refuse it, if he be called to it by his prince or his country, and thinks he can be of more than vulgar use, yet he will seldom or never seek it, but leaves it commonly to men, who under the disguise of public good, pursue their own designs of wealth, power, and such bastard honours as usually attend them, not that which is the true and only true reward of virtue.

The pursuits of ambition, though not so general, are yet as endless as those of riches, and as extravagant; since none ever yet thought he had power of empire enough: and what prince soever seems to be so great, as to live and reign without any further desires or fears, falls into the life of a private man, and enjoys but those pleasures and entertainments, which a great many several degrees of private fortune will allow, and as much as human nature is capable of enjoying.

The pleasures of the senses grow a little more choice and refined; those of imagination are turned upon embellishing the scenes he chooses to live in; ease, conveniency, elegancy, magnificence are sought in building first, and then in furnishing houses or palaces: the admirable imitations of nature are introduced by pictures, statues, tapestry, and other such achievements of arts. And the most exquisite delights of sense are pursued, in the contrivance and plantation of gardens, which, with fruits, flowers, shades, fountains, and the music of birds that frequent such happy places, seem to furnish all the pleasures of the several senses, and with the greatest, or at least the most natural perfections.

Thus the first race of Assyrian kings, after the conquests of Ninus and Semiramis, passed their lives, till their empire fell to the Medes. Thus the Caliphs of Egypt, till deposed by their Mamalukes. Thus passed the latter parts of those great lives of Scipio, Lucullus, Augustus, Diocletian. Thus turned the great thoughts of Henry the Second of France, after the end of his wars with Spain. Thus the present King of Morocco, after having subdued all his competitors, passes his life in a country villa, gives audience in a grove of orange trees planted among purling streams. And thus the King of France, after all the successes of his councils or arms, and in the mighty elevation of his present greatness and power, when he gives himself leisure from such designs or pursuits, passes the softer and easier parts of his time in country houses and gardens, in building, planting or adorning the scenes, or in the common sports and entertainments of such kind of lives. And those mighty emperors, who contented not themselves with these pleasures of common humanity, fell into the frantic or the extravagant; they pretended to be gods, or turned to be devils, as Caligula and Nero, and too many others known enough in story. . . .

For this reason Epicurus passed his life wholly in his garden; there he studied, there he exercised, there he taught his philosophy; and indeed, no other sort of abode seems to contribute so much, to both the tranquillity of mind, and indolence of body, which he made his chief ends. The sweetness of air, the pleasantness of smells, the verdure of plants, the cleanness and lightness of food, the exercises of working or walking, but above all, the exemption from cares and solicitude, seem equally to favour and improve, both contemplation and health, the enjoyment of sense and imagination, and thereby the quiet and ease both of the body and mind.

TOPICS FOR DISCUSSION AND WRITING

1. What is Temple's view of human life? Would you define his view as cynical?
2. How are his comments on the cultivation of the senses and the intellect conditioned by his attitude toward life in general?
3. What conclusions does Temple reach as regards man's proper place in society? What would you say is his central thesis? Is his thesis hypothetical or active?

4. What part does his citation of such figures as Scipio, Augustus, and Epicurus play in his argument? Are they merely part of an historical survey, or are they intended to persuade us of something? Could his citations be considered as both argument from examples and argument from testimony?
5. What does the garden represent?
6. Write an essay comparing and contrasting Temple's view of a man's responsibility toward the society of which he is a part with Russell's (p. 65).
7. Write an essay explaining why you agree or disagree with Temple's solution of the problem of what an individual ought to do when a civilization presses in upon him. Is Temple's solution possible today? Is Temple's solution a form of escapism?

Walter Lippmann

Walter Lippmann (1889–   ), author of some twenty-odd books and a newspaper column ("Today and Tomorrow") which is read by some thirty-eight million people, is one of the most widely respected analysts of contemporary political problems. His first book, A Preface to Morals *(1929), was a penetrating analysis of the problems of the Thirties which generated widespread discussion at home and abroad. His most recent book,* The Public Philosophy *(1955), is an attempt to prove the thesis that "liberal democracy is not an intelligible form of government and cannot be made to work except by men who possess the philosophy in which liberal democracy was conceived and founded."*

Though Lippmann recognizes many attempts to formulate this public philosophy, he thinks one of the earliest, that of the Roman orator philosopher Cicero, is still worthy of consideration. For Cicero

> . . . law was the bond of civil society, and . . . all men, governors and the governed, are always under, are never above, laws. These laws can be developed and refined by rational discussion, and the highest laws are those upon which all rational men of good will, when fully informed, tend to agree.

The selection which follows—one of the most critical parts of Lippmann's argument—attempts to demonstrate the passing of a belief in a public philosophy similar to that of Cicero. To prove his thesis, he summons authoritative witnesses to testify that a former widespread belief in the existence and efficacy of a natural law no longer exists. Whether or not people still believe in a public philosophy cannot be determined by analyzing that philosophy. It can only be determined by summoning people to testify whether they do or do not believe. Consequently, Lippmann was constrained at this point in his argument to use an extrinsic argument, to go outside the terms of his thesis and invoke the testimony of qualified witnesses.

The Neglect of the Public Philosophy *

We come, then, to a crucial question. If the discussion of public philosophy has been, so to speak, tabled in the liberal democracies, can we assume that, though it is not being discussed, there is a public philosophy? Is there a body of positive principles and precepts which a good citizen cannot deny or ignore? I am writing this book in the conviction that there is. It is a conviction which I have acquired gradually, not so much from a theoretical education, but rather from the practical experience of seeing how hard it is for our generation to make democracy work. I believe there is a public philosophy. Indeed there is such a thing as the public philosophy of civility. It does not have to be discovered or invented. It is known. But it does have to be revived and renewed.

The public philosophy is known as *natural law,* a name which, alas, causes great semantic confusion.[1] This philosophy is the premise of the institutions of the Western society, and they are, I believe, unworkable in communities that do not adhere to it. Except on the premises of this philosophy, it is impossible to reach intelligible and workable conceptions of popular election, majority rule, representative assemblies, free speech, loyalty, property, corporations and voluntary associations. The founders of these institutions, which the recently enfranchised democracies have inherited, were all of them adherents of some one of the various schools of natural law.

[1] Cf. Mortimer Adler, "The Doctrine of Natural Law in Philosophy," *University of Notre Dame Natural Law Institute Proceedings,* I, 65–84.

In our time the institutions built upon the foundations of the public philosophy still stand. But they are used by a public who are not being taught, and no longer adhere to, the philosophy. Increasingly, the people are alienated from the inner principles of their institutions. The question is whether and how this alienation can be overcome, and the rupture of the traditions of civility repaired.

Needless to say I am not about to argue that the rupture can be repaired by a neoclassical or neomedieval restoration, or by some kind of romantic return to feudalism, folkdancing, and handicrafts. We cannot rub out the modern age, we cannot roll back the history that has made us what we are. We cannot start again as if there had been no advance of science, no spread of rationalism and secularism, no industrial revolution, no dissolution of the old habitual order of things, no sudden increase in the population. The poignant question is whether, and, if so, how modern men could make vital contact with the lost traditions of civility.

The appearance of things is quite obviously unpromising. There is radical novelty in our modern ways of life. The climate of feeling and the style of thought have changed radically. Modern men will first need to be convinced that the traditions of civility were not abandoned because they became antiquated. This is one of the roots of their unbelief and there is no denying its depth. Since the public philosophy preceded the advance of modern science and the industrial revolution, how can it be expected to provide a positive doctrine which is directly and practically relevant to the age we live in?

It does, one must admit, look like that, and quite evidently the original principles and precepts do not now provide the specific rules and patterns of a way of life in the circumstances of this age. A rereading of the political classics from Aristotle to Burke will not give the answers to the immediate and concrete questions: to the burning issues of diplomacy, military defense, trade, taxes, prices, and wages. Nor have the classical books anything to say about repairing automobiles, treating poliomyelitis, or proceeding with nuclear fission. As handbooks for the busy man, wanting to know how to do this or that, they are now lamentably out of date. The language is archaic, the idiom is strange, the images are unfamiliar, the practical precepts are addressed to forgotten issues.

But this irrelevance and remoteness might be the dust which has settled during the long time when philosophers and scholars and popular educators have relegated the public philosophy to the attic, when they have treated it as no longer usable by modern and progressive men. It is a neglected philosophy. For several generations it has been exceptional and indeed eccentric to use this philosophy in the practical discussion of public policies.

Neglect might well explain its dilapidated condition. If this were the explanation, it would encourage us to explore the question of a renascence. Could modern men again make vital contact with the traditions of civility? At least once before something of the sort did happen. The traditions were articulated in the Graeco-Roman world, and submerged in the West by the decline and the fall of the Western empire. Later on they were revived and renovated and remade in a great flowering of discovery and enterprise and creativity. The revival of learning did not provide maps for Columbus to use in discovering America. But it did produce much human wisdom which helped Columbus and his contemporaries to discover themselves and their possibilities.

The ancient world, we may remind ourselves, was not destroyed because the traditions were false. They were submerged, neglected, lost. For the men adhering to them had become a dwindling minority who were overthrown and displaced by men who were alien to the traditions, having never been initiated and adopted into them. May it not be that while the historical circumstances are obviously so different, something like that is happening again?

For over two thousand years, says Barker, European thought has been acted upon by the idea that the rational faculties of men can produce a common conception of law and order which possesses a universal validity. This conception was first formulated as a theory by Zeno and the Stoics. It was absorbed by the Roman lawyers, was adopted by the Christian fathers, was re-established and re-worked by Saint Thomas Aquinas, and in a new formulation, after the Renaissance and Reformation, it provided the philosophy of the English Revolution of 1688 and of the American Revolution of 1776. The long life of this idea and, above all, the recurring revival of the idea in all ages, would seem to indicate that it reflects a wide and recurring human need—that it is involved with practical questions of policy in the face of recurring political problems.

That the idea is not mere moonshine and cobwebs is attested by history. Barker tells us that in 330 B.C. Alexander was planning the empire in which he would be equally lord of the Greeks and the Persians, in which both Greeks and Persians would be equally bound to perform military service, and would be encouraged to intermarry. This was a revolutionary idea. Aristotle, who was then teaching at the Lyceum, advised Alexander against a policy which would bring the two worlds—the Greek and the barbarian—into the same political system. Aristotle advised Alexander to deal with the Greeks as a leader and with the Persians as a master.

But Alexander rejected the advice, certainly for practical reasons, and perhaps also for idealistic reasons. He

> acted in the spirit of the policy afterwards enunciated by Eratosthenes [an Alexandrian scholar of the next century] who, "refusing to agree with men who divided mankind into Greeks and barbarians . . . declared that it was better to divide men simply into the good and bad." [2]

In adopting this policy, Alexander anticipated in action what Zeno and the Stoics were soon to be teaching—that, as Plutarch wrote long afterwards,

> men should not live their lives in so many civic republics, separated from one another by different systems of justice; they should reckon *all* as their fellow citizens, and there should be one life and one order *(cosmos),* as it were of one flock on a common pasture, feeding in common under one joint law.[3]

We must here dwell specially on the fact that Alexander anticipated in action what Zeno and the Stoics were soon to be teaching. This shows that the idea of a rational order is not only an attractive and a sublime conception but that it is a necessary assumption in the government of large and heterogeneous states. Alexander

[2] Ernest Baker, Introduction to his translation of *Aristotle's Politics,* p. lix (New York: Oxford University Press, 1946).

[3] *Ibid.,* pp. lix-lx. Cf. Saint Paul on the One Church, which was "neither Greek nor Jew . . . Barbarian, Scythian, bond nor free."

came to it in spite of Aristotle's teaching to the contrary. His practical experience compelled him to see that in an empire which included the Persians as well as the Greeks there had to be a common law which was valid for both. To be valid for both the Greeks and the Persians, the law had in some significant degree to have their consent. The Persians could not be commanded and coerced.

As in fact the laws were promulgated to the Persians by Alexander, who was a Greek, it was necessary to convince the Persians that Alexander's laws reflected something that was higher than the will and the intentions of the Greeks, something that was binding on both the Greeks and the Persians. That something was the faculty of distinguishing by reason the good and the bad. For this faculty was not peculiar to the Greeks but was common to both Persians and Greeks.

Alexander had discovered empirically what Zeno was to formulate theoretically—that a large plural society cannot be governed without recognizing that, transcending its plural interests, there is a rational order with a superior common law. This common law is "natural" in the sense that it can be discovered by any rational mind, that it is not the willful and arbitrary positive command of the sovereign power.[4] This is the necessary assumption, without which it is impossible for different peoples with their competing interests to live together in peace and freedom within one community.

The Roman lawyers worked out what Alexander had anticipated and what the Stoics taught. By the time of Cicero there were, says Barker, three different bodies and conceptions of law.[5] The first, called *ius civile,* was applicable only to Roman citizens. The second was a body of commercial laws, known as the *ius gentium,* that were enforced by the Roman courts in all commercial cases: "a common law of contract throughout the empire." [6]

The *ius gentium* was meant to contain what was common and

[4] Cf. Otto von Gierke, *Natural Law and the Theory of Society,* translated with an Introduction by Ernest Barker (Cambridge, Mass.: Harvard University Press, 1934), I, 224–25.

[5] *Ibid.,* p. xxxvi.

[6] F. de Zulueta, "The Science of Law," in *The Legacy of Rome,* edited by Cyril Bailey (Oxford: Clarendon Press, 1928), p. 202.

universal, separated from what was peculiar and local, in the laws of all states. And beyond this practical common law for commercial intercourse, the Roman jurists recognized that in theory there was also natural law, the *ius naturale,* which is "the law imposed on mankind by common human nature, that, by reason in response to human needs and instincts." [7] This is not, says Barker,

> a body of actual law, which can be enforced in actual courts . . . [but] a way of looking at things—a spirit of "humane interpretation" in the mind of the judge and the jurist—which may, and does, affect the law which is actually enforced, but does so without being actual law itself.

The idea of a universal rational order became substantial and effective in the Roman law. This was the law of a great society which did in fact bring peace and order to the Western world. The remembrance of the Roman peace is stamped indelibly on the consciousness of Western men. After the fall of the Roman Empire, the Roman law, which was practiced in some degree almost everywhere, and was taught everywhere, was recognized as "the law of an international civilization and relatively universal." [8]

With the beginning of the new age, after 1500, Roman law, as codified and digested in the *Corpus Juris* of Justinian, was regarded as the concrete expression of universal human reason. When the question came to be asked, says Barker, "What does this conception of natural law actually contain or include?" the answer tends to be, during the Middle Ages generally and down to the rise of a new school of natural law after 1500, "It contains or includes the *whole* of Roman law, which is, *as a whole,* both supremely reasonable and universally diffused, and is therefore natural." [9]

The new school of natural law, which flourished from about 1500 to 1800, was a response to the pluralism of the modern age, to the rise of national states, to the schism of the Church, to the explorations and to the expansion of world commerce, to the advance of science and of secularism, to the progressive division

[7] *Ibid.,* p. 204.
[8] *Ibid.,* p. 181.
[9] Gierke, *Natural Law and the Theory of Society,* p. xxxix.

and specialization of labor. As the diversity of belief, opinion and interest became greater, the need for a common criterion and for common laws became more acute.

The new school of natural law was able to meet this need until the end of the eighteenth century. That was long enough to preside over the founding of the British and the American constitutional orders, and of those which derive from them. But the school of natural law has not been able to cope with the pluralism of the later modern age—with the pluralism which has resulted from the industrial revolution and from the enfranchisement and the emancipation of the masses of the people.

In the simple and relatively homogeneous society of the eighteenth century, natural law provided the principles of a free state. But then the mode of such thinking went out of fashion. In the nineteenth century little was done to remint the old ideas. They were regarded as obsolete and false, as hostile to the rise of democracy, and they were abandoned to the reactionaries. The great frame of reference to the rational order was missing. No body of specific principles and precepts was worked out in order to regulate international relations, nor to cope with the problems raised by the industrial revolution and the advance of science and technology.

Yet, in this pluralized and fragmenting society a public philosophy with common and binding principles was more necessary than it had ever been. The proof of the need is in the impulse to escape from freedom, which Erich Fromm has described so well.[10] It has been growing stronger as the emancipation of the masses of the people from authority has brought the dissolution of public, general, objective criteria of the true and the false, the right and the wrong. "I can assure you," wrote André Gide in 1928, "that the feeling of *freedom* can plunge the soul into a sort of anguish." [11]

"We know it from within, by a sort of immediate and personal experience," says Gilson, who was writing between the wars, that "Western culture was steadily following its process of dissolution." [12] Similarly, Spengler's famous book on *The Decline*

[10] Erich Fromm, *Escape from Freedom.*

[11] *The Journals of André Gide,* trans. Justin O'Brien (New York: Alfred A. Knopf, Inc., 1947–51) III, 26.

[12] Etienne Gilson, *The Unity of Philosophical Experience* (New York: Charles Scribner's Sons, 1937), p. 271.

of the West was first published in 1918 but it was written before the outbreak of the war.

But until the historic disasters of our own time, the loneliness and anxiety of modern men had been private, without public and overt political effect. As long as the public order still provided external security, their inner insecurity was still a personal and private and inward affair. Since the breakdown of public order during the First World War, there has been no security for multitudes and no ease of mind for anyone.

Observing the public disorder in which he himself had always lived, and knowing how the inner disorder provoked the impulse to escape from it, Hitler conceived his doctrine. He had the insight of genius into human weakness, and he wrote in *Mein Kampf* that the masses are

> like a woman . . . who will submit to the strong man rather than dominate the weakling . . . the masses love the ruler rather than the suppliant, and inwardly they are far more satisfied by a doctrine which tolerates no rival than by the grant of liberal freedom; they often feel at a loss what to do with it, and even easily feel themselves deserted.[13]

The masses that Hitler was planning to dominate are the modern men who find in freedom from the constraints of the ancestral order an intolerable loss of guidance and of support. With Gide they are finding that the burden of freedom is too great an anxiety. The older structures of society are dissolving and they must make their way through a time of troubles. They have been taught to expect a steady progress towards a higher standard of life, and they have not been prepared to withstand the frustrations of a prolonged crisis in the outer world and the loneliness of their self-centered isolation.

They are the men who rise up against freedom, unable to cope with its insoluble difficulties and unable to endure the denial of communion in public and common truths. They have found no answer to their need and no remedy for their anguish in the principles and practice of freedom as they have known them in the liberal democracies of this century. There is a profound disorientation in their experience, a radical disconnection between

[13] Adolf Hitler, *Mein Kampf* (Boston: Houghton Mifflin Company, 1939), p. 56.

the notions of their minds and the needs of their souls. They have become the "lonely crowd" [14] that Riesman has described. They are Durkheim's anomic mass.[15] They are Toynbee's proletarians who are "of" but not "in" the community they live in; for they have "no 'stake' in that community beyond the fact of its physical existence." Their "true hallmark . . . is neither poverty nor humble birth but is the consciousness—and the resentment that this consciousness inspires—of being disinherited." [16] They are, as Karl Jaspers says, men dissolved into "an anonymous mass" because they are "without an authentic world, without provenance or roots," [17] without, that is to say, belief and faith that they can live by.

[14] David Riesman, *The Lonely Crowd.*

[15] Emile Durkheim, *Suicide.*

[16] Arnold Toynbee, *A Study of History* (London: Oxford University Press, 1951), I, 41; V, 63.

[17] Karl Jaspers, *The Origin and Goal of History,* translated from the German edition of 1949 by Michael Bullock (London: Routledge and Kegan Paul, Ltd., 1953), pp. 127–128.

TOPICS FOR DISCUSSION AND WRITING

1. What is another term for what Lippmann calls the "public philosophy"? How important does he think a "public philosophy" is to the existence of free institutions?
2. Where was the conception first formulated that the rational faculties of man can produce a common conception of law and order which possesses a universal validity?
3. How does Lippmann seek to prove that there was a commonly accepted public philosophy during the classical period?
4. How does Lippmann prove that by the time of Cicero there were three different conceptions of law? How did these three conceptions differ?
5. What was the validity of Roman law? How does Lippmann prove his conception?
6. How does Lippmann attempt to show that Western culture was undergoing a dissolution in the late nineteenth and early twentieth centuries?
7. How does Lippmann attempt to show that modern man is an "anonymous mass," a "lonely crowd," an "anomic mass"? Does he really demonstrate that these are appropriate designations for modern society or does he just borrow these terms? Is there any difference between

the way in which he cites authorities for these terms and the ways in which he cites authorities to substantiate his other assertions?

8. Are the authorities he cites good ones? How would you go about determining whether or not his authorities were reliable?
9. Is every citation of authorities an attempt to use testimony to prove the same kind of thesis? Does he use authority to establish a fact? to establish an opinion? to substantiate a phrase? Is there any difference in the use of authoritative testimony to establish any of these three different things?
10. Write an essay showing why common agreement on a public philosophy will be a necessary prelude to the creation of world government as suggested by Brinton (p. 36). If Lippmann is right about the necessity of a belief in a public philosophy to the existence of a national democracy, does it not follow that there would have to be a worldwide belief in a similar philosophy to provide a basis for a world government?

ANALOGICAL RELATIONSHIPS

An analogical relationship is any relation of similarity which exists between two things. Arguments derived from analogical relationships are arguments which point to similarities or dissimilarities believed to exist between two different ideas, situations, or proposals. We frequently use analogical relationships to explain an idea or to argue on behalf of some thesis. Every time we note that some situation which we are now experiencing reminds us of some other situation which we have previously experienced, we are calling attention to some analogical relationship between the two experiences. Every time we use a simile (for example, when we say that his face turned white as a sheet) we are calling attention to an analogical relationship, this time between the whiteness of a sheet and the color of his face. Analogical arguments can take a variety of forms.

One form of this occurs when a writer is urging some course of action. He tries to prove his thesis by calling attention to the similarities existing between the course of action he is proposing and some previous actions which he believes his audience admires. The writer can also urge the omission of an action, as Milton does in the selection from the *Areopagitica* included in this section, because its performance would identify the doers with people of whom they must disapprove. Milton argues that the British Parliament should not pass a law requiring the censorship of books because censorship is a practice of tyrannical governments of which Parliament certainly can not approve.

The argument derived from analogical relationships can take another form wherein the writer argues that a present course of action is bound to have unhappy results because similar courses of actions in the past always preceded undesirable consequences. In the selections by Amaury de Riencourt and

Oswald Spengler included in this section, we have two illustrations of this form of the argument, for both writers argue that a present state of a society is to be followed by a decline because of the similarities they notice between the current situation and past situations which preceded a disaster.

Perhaps the most common form of the argument from analogical relationships is to be found in essays which maintain comparative proportions, i.e., maintain that one thing is better than another. A common way of attempting to demonstrate that x is better than y, where both x and y can stand for any idea, situation, or product, is to point to a number of similarities existing between x and y, and then to point to a dissimilarity. It is this dissimilarity (to be found in x and not in y) which is supposed to constitute the main reason why x is better than y. Thus much of product advertising either explicitly or implicitly maintains that product x is better than product y because, though x has everything that y has to offer, x has something else not to be found in y.

Logicians are constantly reminding us that every analogy limps. Consequently, once a reader has decided that he is dealing with an argument derived from analogical relationships, he must also remind himself that it cannot be a logically compelling argument. Every analogy limps because no two things are ever quite identical. Every situation is unique. Though there may be many similarities between two terms, and an imaginative writer can discover many analogies, the dissimilarities may be more important. Though product x may contain some quality not found in y which an advertiser is proud to call to attention, there may be some other dissimilarities which are being glossed over and which may be even more important.

Though analogical arguments may not be logically compelling, they can be emotionally telling. A vivid comparison of the detailed similarities supposedly existing between two situations may not persuade the critical reader who keeps his attention focused on the logical structure of an argument, but it can be very effective with audiences who can be diverted from paying attention to logic. It is also important to recall that there have been long periods of history, such as the Middle Ages and the Renaissance, wherein the discovery of an analogy between an existing problematic situation and some other previous situation constituted the strongest possible reason in favor of a course of action. The strongest arguments in Shakespeare's plays are dependent upon analogical relationships. Even today's scientists, though they may remain sceptical about the actual configuration of atomic structure, use models which they continue to trust as analogues [1] of reality as long as these models suggest fruitful courses of experimentation. Finally, students frequently ask for examples to help them come to a better understanding of difficult material. What are these examples but analogues of the general principles they are trying to grasp? Analogies are tricky. They can be so weak that they prove nothing. Yet without analogies we would be hard pressed to understand much of the world about us.

John Milton

We have already considered a brief section of Milton's Areopagitica *as an illustration of deductive argument. In the introduction to that section (p. 121) it was pointed out that Milton relied upon four groups of arguments to demonstrate his thesis. The following selection is taken from the opening section of the* Areopagitica, *and it contains the first group of arguments (those derived from an examination of the previous acts of censorship to which the existing act is considered analogous). This section also contains Milton's statement of his thesis as well as his own indication of the four different kinds of arguments he is going to use.*

It is worth noting that though the over-all structure of the argument in this selection is that of an argument based upon analogy, Milton must use the testimony of classical authors to estab-

[1] An analogy is a *relation* of likeness; an analogue is a *thing* which is like another thing.

lish the existence and characteristics of previous censorships. Thus, within the larger structure of one kind of argument, an argument based on analogy, Milton uses another kind of argument, an argument based on testimony. Most effective writing uses a combination of arguments, and the skill of the combination is a reflection of the imagination and resourcefulness of the writer.

from AREOPAGITICA

They, who to states and governors of the commonwealth direct their speech, high court of parliament! or wanting such access in a private condition, write that which they foresee may advance the public good; I suppose them, as at the beginning of no mean endeavor, not a little altered and moved inwardly in their minds; some with doubt of what will be the success, others with fear of what will be the censure; some with hope, others with confidence of what they have to speak. And me perhaps each of these dispositions, as the subject was whereon I entered, may have at other times variously affected; and likely might in these foremost expressions now also disclose which of them swayed most, but that the very attempt of this address thus made, and the thought of whom it hath recourse to, hath got the power within me to a passion, far more welcome than incidental to a preface.

Which I stay not to confess ere any ask, I shall be blameless, if it be no other than the joy and gratulation which it brings to all who wish and promote their country's liberty; whereof this whole discourse proposed will be a certain testimony, if not a trophy.[1] For this is not the liberty which we can hope, that no grievance ever should arise in the commonwealth: that let no man in this world expect; but when complaints are freely heard, deeply considered, and speedily reformed, then is the utmost bound of civil liberty attained that wise men look for. To which if I now manifest, by the very sound of this which I shall utter, that we are already in good part arrived, and yet from such a steep disadvantage of tyranny and superstition grounded into our principles, as was beyond the manhood of a Roman recovery, it will be

[1] A memorial of a victory raised on the field of battle.

attributed first, as is most due, to the strong assistance of God, our deliverer; next, to your faithful guidance and undaunted wisdom, lords and commons of England! Neither is it in God's esteem, the diminution of his glory, when honorable things are spoken of good men, and worthy magistrates; which if I now first should begin to do, after so fair a progress of your laudable deeds, and such a long obligement upon the whole realm to your indefatigable virtues, I might be justly reckoned among the tardiest and the unwillingest of them that praise ye.

Nevertheless there being three principal things, without which all praising is but courtship and flattery; first, when that only is praised which is solidly worth praise; next, when greatest likelihoods are brought, that such things are truly and really in those persons to whom they are ascribed; the other, when he who praises, by showing that such his actual persuasion is of whom he writes, can demonstrate that he flatters not; the former two of these I have heretofore endeavored, rescuing the employment from him who went about to impair your merits with a trivial and malignant encomium; the latter as belonging chiefly to mine own acquital, that whom I so extolled I did not flatter, hath been reserved opportunely to this occasion. For he who freely magnifies what hath been noble done, and fears not to declare as freely what might be done better, gives ye the best covenant of his fidelity; and that his loyalest affection and his hope waits on your proceedings. His highest praising is not flattery, and his plainest advice is a kind of praising; for though I should affirm and hold by argument, that it would fare better with truth, with learning, and the commonwealth, if one of your published orders, which I should name, were called in. Yet at the same time it could not but much redound to the lustre of your mild and equal government, whenas private persons are hereby animated to think ye better pleased with public advice than other statists have been delighted heretofore with public flattery. And men will then see what difference there is between the magnanimity of a triennial parliament, and that jealous haughtiness of prelates and cabin counsellors that usurped of late, whenas they shall observe ye in the midst of your victories and successes more gently brooking written exceptions against a voted order, than other courts, which had produced nothing worth memory but the weak ostentation of wealth, would have endured the least signified dislike at any sudden proclamation.

If I should thus far presume upon the meek demeanor of your civil and gentle greatness, lords and commons! as what your published order hath directly said, that to gainsay, I might defend myself with ease, if any should accuse me of being new or insolent, did they but know how much better I find ye esteem it to imitate the old and elegant humanity of Greece, than the barbaric pride of a Hunnish and Norwegian stateliness. And out of those ages, to whose polite wisdom and letters we owe that we are not yet Goths and Jutlanders, I could name him who from his private house wrote that discourse to the parliament of Athens, that persuades them to change the form of democracy which was then established. Such honor was done in those days to men who professed the study of wisdom and eloquence, not only in their own country, but in other lands, that cities and signiories [2] heard them gladly, and with great respect, if they had aught in public to admonish the state. Thus did Dion Prusaeus, a stranger and a private orator, counsel the Rhodians against a former edict; and I abound with other like examples, which to set here would be superfluous. But if from the industry of a life wholly dedicated to studious labors, and those natural endowments haply not the worst for two and fifty degrees of northern latitude, so much must be derogated, as to count me not equal to any of those who had this privilege, I would obtain to be thought not so inferior, as yourselves are superior to the most of them who received their counsel; and how far you excel them, be assured, lords and commons! there can be no greater testimony appear, than when your prudent spirit acknowledges and obeys the voice of reason, from what quarter soever it be heard speaking; and renders ye as willing to repeal any act of your own setting forth, as any set forth by your predecessors.

If ye be thus resolved, as it were injury to think ye were not, I know not what should withhold me from presenting ye with a fit instance wherein to show both that love of truth which ye eminently profess, and that uprightness of your judgment which is not wont to be partial to yourselves; by judging over again that

[2] Older plural form of *seigneury,* the territory over which a lord holds jurisdiction.

order which ye have ordained "to regulate printing: that no book, pamphlet, or paper shall be henceforth printed, unless the same be first approved and licensed by such, or at least one of such, as shall be thereto appointed." For that part which preserves justly everyman's copy to himself, or provides for the poor, I touch not; only wish they be not made pretences to abuse and persecute honest and painful men, who offend not in either of these particulars. But that other cause of licensing books, which we thought had died with his brother quadragesimal and matrimonial when the prelates expired, I shall not attend with such a homily, as shall lay before ye, first, the inventors of it to be those whom ye will be loath to own; next, what is to be thought in general of reading, whatever sort the books be; and that this order avails nothing to the suppressing of scandalous, seditious, and libelous books, which were mainly intended to be suppressed. Last, that it will be primely to the discouragement of all learning, and the stop of truth, not only by disexercising and blunting our abilities, in what we know already, but by hindering and cropping the discovery that might be yet further made, both in religious and civil wisdom.

I deny not, but that it is of greatest concernment in the church and commonwealth, to have a vigilant eye how books demean themselves, as well as men; and thereafter to confine, imprison, and do sharpest justice on them as malefactors; for books are not absolutely dead things, but do contain a potency of life in them to be as active as that soul whose progeny they are; nay, they do preserve as in a vial the purest efficacy and extraction of that living intellect that bred them. I know they are as lively, and as vigorously productive, as those fabulous dragon's teeth: and being sown up and down, may chance to spring up armed men. And yet, on the other hand, unless wariness be used, as good almost kill a man as kill a good book: who kills a man kills a reasonable creature, God's image; but he who destroys a good book, kills reason itself, kills the image of God, as it were, in the eye. Many a man lives a burden to the earth; but a good book is the precious lifeblood of a master spirit, embalmed and treasured up on purpose to a life beyond life. 'Tis true, no age can restore a life, whereof, perhaps, there is no great loss; and revolutions of ages do not oft recover the loss of a rejected truth, for the want of which whole nations fare the worse. We should be wary, therefore, what persecution we raise against the living labors of public men, how we spill that seasoned life of man, preserved and stored up in books; since we see a kind of homicide may be thus committed, sometimes a martyrdom; and if it extend to the whole impression, a kind of massacre, whereof the execution ends not in the slaying of an elemental life, but strikes at that ethereal and fifth essence, the breath of reason itself; slays an immortality rather than a life. But lest I should be condemned of introducing license, when I oppose licensing, I refuse not the pains to be so much historical, as will serve to show what hath been done by ancient and famous commonwealths, against this disorder, till the very time that this project of licensing crept out of the inquisition, was catched up by our prelates, and hath caught some of our presbyters.

In Athens, where books and wits were ever busier than in any other part of Greece, I find but only two sorts of writings which the magistrate cared to take notice of; those either blasphemous and atheistical, or libelous. Thus the books of Protagoras were by the judges of Areopagus, commanded to be burnt, and himself banished the territory for a discourse, begun with his confessing not to know "whether there were gods, or whether not." And against defaming, it was decreed that none should be traduced by name, as was the manner of Vetus Comoedia, whereby we may guess how they censured libeling; and this course was quick enough, as Cicero writes, to quell both the desperate wits of other atheists, and the open way of defaming, as the event showed. Of other sects and opinions, though tending to voluptuousness, and the denying of divine Providence, they took no heed. Therefore we do not read that either Epicurus, or that libertine school of Cyrene, or what the Cynic impudence uttered, was ever questioned by the laws. Neither is it recorded that the writings of those old comedians were suppressed, though the acting of them were forbid; and that Plato commended the reading of Aristophanes, the loosest of them all, to his royal scholar, Dionysius, is commonly known, and may be excused, if holy Chrysostom, as is reported, nightly studied so much the same author, and had the art to cleanse a scurrilous vehemence into the style of a rousing sermon.

That other leading city of Greece, Lacedaemon, considering that

Lycurgus their lawgiver was so addicted to elegant learning, as to have been the first that brought out of Ionia the scattered works of Homer, and sent the poet Thales from Crete, to prepare and mollify the Spartan surliness with his smooth songs and odes, the better to plant among them law and civility; it is to be wondered how museless and unbookish they were, minding nought but the feats of war. There needed no licensing of books among them, for they disliked all but their own laconic apophthegms, and took a slight occasion to chase Archilochus out of their city, perhaps for composing in a higher strain than their own soldiery ballads and roundels could reach to; or if it were for his broad verses, they were not therein so cautious, but they were as dissolute in their promiscuous conversing; whence Euripedes affirms, in Andromache, that their women were all unchaste.

Thus much may give us light after what sort of books were prohibited among the Greeks. The Romans also for many ages trained up only to a military roughness, resembling most the Lacedaemonian guise, knew of learning little but what their twelve tables and the pontific college with their augurs and flamens taught them in religion and law; so unacquainted with other learning that when Carneades and Critolaus, with the stoic Diogenes, coming ambassadors to Rome, took thereby occasion to give the city a taste of their philosophy, they were suspected for seducers by no less a man than Cato the Censor, who moved it in the senate to dismiss them speedily, and to banish all such Attic babblers out of Italy. But Scipio and others of the noblest senators withstood him and his old Sabine austerity; honored and admired the men; and the censor himself at last, in his old age, fell to the study of that whereof before he was so scrupulous. And yet, at the same time, Naevius and Plautus, the first Latin comedians, had filled the city with all the borrowed scenes of Menander and Philemon. Then, began to be considered there also what was to be done to libelous books and authors; for Naevius was quickly cast into prison for his unbridled pen, and released by the tribunes upon his recantation; we read also that libels were burnt, and the makers punished, by Augustus.

The like severity, no doubt, was used, if aught were impiously written against their esteemed gods. Except in these two points, how the world went in books, the magistrate kept no reckoning.

And therefore Lucretius, without impeachment, versifies his Epicurism to Memmius, and had the honor to be set forth the second time by Cicero, so great a father of the commonwealth; although himself disputes against that opinion in his own writings. Nor was the satirical sharpness or naked plainness of Lucilius, or Catullus, or Flaccus, by any order prohibited. And for matters of state, the story of Titus Livius, though it extolled that part which Pompey held, was not therefore suppressed by Octavius Caesar, of the other faction. But that Naso was by him banished in his old age, for the wanton poems of his youth, was but a mere covert of state over some secret cause; and besides, the books were neither banished nor called in. From hence we shall meet with little else but tyranny in the Roman empire, that we may not marvel, if not so often bad as good books were silenced. I shall therefore deem to have been large enough, in producing what among the ancients was punishable to write, save only which, all other arguments were free to treat on.

By this time the emperors were become Christians, whose discipline in this point I do not find to have been more severe than what was formerly in practice. The books of those whom they took to be grand heretics were examined, refuted, and condemned in the general councils; and not till then were prohibited or burnt, by authority of the emperor. As for the writings of heathen authors, unless they were plain invectives against Christianity, as those of Porphyrius and Proclus, they met with no interdict that can be cited, till about the year 400, in a Carthaginian council, wherein bishops themselves were forbid to read the books of Gentiles, but heresies they might read; while others long before them, on the contrary, scrupled more the books of heretics, than of Gentiles. And that the primitive councils and bishops were wont only to declare what books were not commendable, passing no further, but leaving it to each one's conscience to read or to lay by, till after the year 800, is observed already by Padre Paolo, the great unmasker of the Trentine council. After which time the popes of Rome, engrossing what they pleased of political rule into their own hands, extended their dominion over men's eyes, as they had before over their judgments, burning and prohibiting to be read what they fancied not; yet sparing in their censures, and the books not many which they so dealt with; till Martin the Fifth, by his bull, not only prohibited, but was the first that excommunicated the reading of heretical books; for about that time Wickliff and Husse growing terrible, were they who first drove the papal court to a stricter policy of prohibiting. Which course Leo the Tenth and his successors followed, until the Council of Trent and the Spanish Inquisition, engendering together, brought forth or perfected those catalogues and expurging indexes, that rake through the entrails of many an old good author with a violation worse than any could be offered to his tomb.

Nor did they stay in matters heretical, but any subject that was not to their palate, they either condemned in a prohibition, or had it straight into the new purgatory of an index. To fill up the measure of encroachment, their last invention was to ordain that no book, pamphlet, or paper should be printed (as if St. Peter had bequeathed them the keys of the press also out of Paradise) unless it were approved and licensed under the hands of two or three glutton friars. For example:

> Let the chancellor Cini be pleased to see if in this present work be contained aught that may withstand the printing,
>
> —Vincent Rabbata, Vicar of Florence.
>
> I have seen this present work, and find nothing athwart the Catholic faith, and good manners; in witness whereof I have given, &c.
>
> —Nicolo Cini, Chancellor of Florence.
>
> Attending the precedent relation, it is allowed that this present work of Davanzati may be printed.
>
> —Vincent Rabbata. &c.
>
> It may be printed, July 15.
>
> —Friar Simon Mompei d'Amelia, Chancellor of the Holy Office in Florence.

Sure they have a conceit, if he of the bottomless pit had not long since broke prison, that this quadruple exorcism would bar him down. I fear their next design will be to get into their custody the licensing of that which they say Claudius intended, but went not through with. Vouchsafe to see another of their forms, the Roman stamp:

Imprimatur, if it seems good to the reverend
master of the Holy Palace,
—Belcastro, Vicegerent.

Imprimatur,
—Friar Nicholo Rodolphi, Master of the
Holy Palace.

Sometimes five imprimaturs are seen together, dialogue wise, in the piazza of one title page, complimenting and ducking each to other with their shaven reverences, whether the author, who stands by in perplexity at the foot of his epistle, shall to the press or to the sponge. These are the pretty responsories, these are the dear antiphonies, that so bewitched of late our prelates and their chaplains, with the goodly echo they made; and besotted us to the gay imitation of a lordly imprimatur, one from Lambeth-house, another from the west end of Paul's; so apishly Romanizing, that the word of command still was set down in Latin; as if the learned grammatical pen that wrote it would cast no ink without Latin; or perhaps, as they thought, because no vulgar tongue was worthy to express the pure conceit of an imprimatur; but rather, as I hope, for that our English, the language of men ever famous and foremost in the achievements of liberty, will not easily find servile letters enow to spell such a dictatory presumption English.

And thus ye have the inventors and the original of book licensing ripped up and drawn as lineally as any pedigree. We have it not, that can be heard of, from any ancient state, or polity, or church, nor by any statute left us by our ancestors elder or later; nor from the modern custom of any reformed city or church abroad; but from the most anti-Christian council, and the most tyrannous inquisition that ever inquired. Till then books were ever as freely admitted into the world as any other birth; the issue of the brain was no more stifled than the issue of the womb: no envious Juno sat crosslegged over the nativity of any man's intellectual offspring; but if it proved a monster, who denies but that it was justly burnt, or sunk into the sea? But that a book, in worse condition than a peccant soul, should be to stand before a jury ere it be born to the world, and undergo yet in darkness the judgment of Radamanth and his colleagues, ere it can pass the ferry backward into light, was never heard before, till that mysterious iniquity, provoked and troubled at the first entrance of reformation, sought out new limboes and new hells wherein they might include our books also within the number of their damned. And this was the rare morsel so officiously snatched up, and so ill-favoredly imitated by our inquisiturient bishops, and the attendant minorities, their chaplains. That ye like not now these most certain authors of this licensing order, and that all sinister intention was far distant from your thoughts, when ye were importuned the passing it, all men who knew the integrity of your actions, and how ye honor truth, will clear ye readily. . . .

TOPICS FOR DISCUSSION AND WRITING

1. What tone does Milton attempt to establish in his first paragraph? Why does he suggest that some people will be writing half in hope and half in fear?
2. Why, in the second paragraph, does he distinguish between a false conception of liberty which hopes that no grievance against the government should ever arise and the utmost in civil liberty which occurs when complaints are freely heard?
3. What distinguishes true praise from flattery? Why does Milton make this distinction?
4. How does Milton approach the statement of his thesis, gradually or directly? Why? Why does he call attention to similarities between Parliament and the eloquent humanity of Greece? Why does he call attention to the dissimilarities between Parliament and the barbaric pride of the Huns and the Goths?
5. How does Milton finally come to a statement of his thesis? Is there any sentence which you think comes close to stating the thesis of the entire *Areopagitica* as well as the main supporting reasons?
6. Does he believe that Parliament is completely wrong in showing concern for the possible effects of bad books? Does he think that every kind of censorship is wrong?
7. Under what conditions were books banned in Greece? In Rome?
8. What, in Milton's opinion, was the first clear act of censorship which he thinks comparable to the act of censorship passed by Parliament?
9. Does Milton prove that censorship existed in the form in which he claims it existed, or does he merely state that censorship in this form existed? Does he prove the statements he makes about the history of censorship?
10. What sentence summarizes Milton's argument in this section? What is the conclusion he wants the members of Parliament to draw from his argument?

11. Do you think Milton has proven his thesis? Would Milton's argument be as effective today? Why do you think he decided to use an argument based on comparison as his opening argument?
12. Where does Milton make use of irony? Is it effective?

Oswald Spengler

Oswald Spengler (1880–1936), at one time a professor of mathematics and history (two fields of study which are intricately related in his writings), gave up his professorial post in 1911 to begin work on what became his massive Decline of the West, *the first volume of which appeared in 1918, the second volume in 1922. The view of history presented in these volumes is not the linear, forward-moving view; rather, Spengler saw all history as a series of cycles, ever repeating, analogous to the yearly cycle of spring, summer, autumn, and winter. Each "culture" in history (the Greek, the Egyptian, the Western) possessed its own "form" or organic quality, and passed through its own kind of springtime, summer, harvest, and death. There are, therefore, analogies existing between cultures, regardless of their chronological order. The springtime of a culture that flourished 1000 years ago has resemblances to a contemporary culture in its early, or springtime, phase. Perceiving these resemblances, we may be able to draw conclusions and make predictions. A poet and philosopher rather than a historian, Spengler's insights have been rejected by most historians but applauded by poets and philosophers as possessing* symbolic *(if not* literal*) significance. A German philosopher whose works were banned in Nazi Germany, a self-styled prophet without honor amongst those whom he tried to reach, Spengler has nevertheless had a tremendous impact upon the minds of his readers.*

from THE DECLINE OF THE WEST *

In this book is attempted for the first time the venture of predetermining history, of following the still untraveled stages

* Reprinted from *The Decline of the West* by Oswald Spengler, by permission of Alfred A. Knopf, Inc. Trans. by Charles Francis Atkinson. Copyright 1926 by Alfred A. Knopf, Inc.

in the destiny of a culture, and specifically of the only culture of our time and on our planet which is actually in the phase of fulfillment—the West European-American.

Is there a logic of history? Is there, beyond all the causal and incalculable elements of the separate events, something that we may call a metaphysical structure of historic humanity, something that is essentially independent of the outward forms—social, spiritual and political—which we see so clearly? Are not these actualities indeed secondary or derived from that something? Does world-history present to the seeing eye certain grand traits, again and again, with sufficient constancy to justify certain conclusions? And if so, what are the limits to which reasoning from such premises may be pushed?

Is it possible to find in life itself—for human history is the sum of mighty life-courses which already have had to be endowed with ego and personality, in customary thought and expression, by predicating entities of a higher order like "the Classical" or "the Chinese culture," "Modern Civilization,"—a series of stages which must be traversed, and traversed moreover in an ordered and obligatory sequence? For everything organic the notions of birth, death, youth, age, lifetime, are fundamentals—may not these notions, in this sphere also, possess a rigorous meaning which no one has as yet extracted? In short, is all history founded upon general biographic archetypes?

The decline of the West, which at first sight may appear, like the corresponding decline of the Classical culture, a phenomenon limited in time and space, we now perceive to be a philosophical problem that, when comprehended in all its gravity, includes within itself every great question of Being.

If therefore we are to discover in what form the destiny of the Western culture will be accomplished, we must first be clear as to what culture *is*, what its relations are to visible history, to life, to soul, to nature, to intellect, what the forms of its manifestation are and how far these forms—peoples, tongues and epochs, battles and ideas, states and gods, arts and craft works, sciences, laws, economic types and world ideas, great men and great events—may be accepted and pointed to as symbols.

The means whereby to identify dead forms is Mathematical

Law. The means whereby to understand living forms is Analogy. By these means we are enabled to distinguish polarity and periodicity in the world.

It is, and has always been, a matter of knowledge that the expression-forms of world history are limited in number, and that eras, epochs, situations, persons are ever repeating themselves true to type. Napoleon has hardly ever been discussed without a side glance at Caesar and Alexander—analogies of which, as we shall see, the first is morphologically quite inacceptable and the second is correct. Frederick the Great, in his political writings—such as his *Considérations* (1738)—moves among analogies with perfect assurance. Thus he compares the French to the Macedonians under Philip and the Germans to the Greeks. "Even now," he says, "the Thermopylae of Germany, Alsace and Lorraine, are in the hands of Philip," therein exactly characterizing the policy of Cardinal Fleury. We find him drawing parallels also between the policies of the Houses of Habsburg and Bourbon and the proscriptions of Antony and of Octavius.

Still, all this was only fragmentary and arbitrary, and usually implied rather a momentary inclination to poetical or ingenious expressions than a really deep sense of historical forms. In this region no one hitherto has set himself to work out a *method,* nor has had the slightest inkling that there is here a root, in fact the only root, from which can come a broad solution of the problems of history. Analogies, insofar as they laid bare the organic structure of history, might be a blessing to historical thought. Their technique, developing under the influence of a comprehensive idea, would surely eventuate in inevitable conclusions and logical mastery. But as hitherto understood and practised, they have been a curse, for they have enabled the historians to follow their own tastes, instead of soberly realizing that their first and hardest task was concerned with the symbolism of history and its analogies.

Thus our theme, which originally comprised only the limited problem of present-day civilization, broadens itself into a new philosophy—*the* philosophy of the future, so far as the metaphysically exhausted soil of the West can bear such, and in any case the only philosophy which is within the *possibilities* of the West European mind in its next stages. It expands into the conception of a *morphology of world history*, of the world-as-history in contrast to the morphology of the world-as-nature that hitherto has been almost the only theme of philosophy. And it reviews once again the forms and movements of the world in their depths and final significance, but this time according to an entirely different ordering, which groups them, not in an ensemble picture inclusive of everything known, but in a picture of *life*, and presents them not as things-become, but as things-becoming.

The *world-as-history*, conceived, viewed and given form out of its opposite, the *world-as-nature*—here is a new aspect of human existence on this earth. And yet, in spite of its immense significance, both practical and theoretical, this aspect has not been realized, still less presented. Some obscure inkling of it there may have been, a distant momentary glimpse there has often been, but no one had deliberately faced it and taken it in with all its implications. We have before us two possible ways in which man may inwardly possess and experience the world around him. With all rigour I distinguish (as to form, not substance) the organic from the mechanical world impression, the content of images from that of laws, the picture and the symbol from the formula and the system, the instantly actual from the constantly possible, the intents and purposes of imagination ordering according to plan from the intents and purposes of experience dissecting according to scheme; and—to mention even thus early an opposition that has never yet been noted, in spite of its significance—the domain of *chronological* from that of *mathematical number*.

Consequently, in a research such as that lying before us, there can be no question of taking spiritual-political events, as they become visible day by day on the surface, at their face value, and arranging them on a scheme of "causes" or "effects" and following them up in the obvious and intellectually easy directions. Such a "pragmatic" handling of history would be nothing but a piece of "natural science" in disguise, and for their part, the supporters of the materialistic idea of history make no secret about it—it is their adversaries who largely fail to see the similarity of the two methods. What concerns us is not what the historical facts which appear at this or that time *are*, per se, but what they signify, what they point to, *by appearing*. I have not hitherto found one who has carefully considered the *morphological relationship* that inwardly binds together the expression-forms of *all* branches of a culture. Yet, viewed from this morphological standpoint, even the humdrum facts of politics assume a symbolic and even a metaphysical character, and—what has perhaps been impossible hitherto—things such as the Egyptian administrative system, the Classical coinage, analytical geometry, the cheque, the Suez Canal, the book printing of the Chinese, the Prussian army, and the Roman road-engineering, can, as symbols, be made *uniformly* understandable and appreciable.

But at once the fact presents itself that as yet there exists no theory-enlightened art of historical treatment. What passes as such draws its methods almost exclusively from the domain of that science which alone has completely disciplined the methods of cognition, viz., physics, and thus we imagine ourselves to be carrying on historical research when we are really following out objective connections of cause and effect. Judged by the standards of the physicist and the mathematician, the historian becomes *careless* as soon as he has assembled and ordered his material and passes on to interpretation. That there is, besides a necessity of cause and effect—which I may call the *logic of space*—another necessity, an organic necessity in life, that of Destiny—the *logic of time*—is a fact of the deepest inward certainty, a fact which suffuses the whole of mythological religions and artistic thought and constitutes the essence and kernel of all history (in contradistinction to nature) but is unapproachable through the cognition-forms which the *Critique of Pure Reason* [1] investigates. This fact still awaits its theoretical formulation.

Mathematics and the principle of casuality leads to a naturalistic chronology and the idea of Destiny to a historical ordering of the phenomenal world. Both orderings, each on its own account, cover the *whole* world. The difference is only in the eyes by which and through which this world is realized.

[1] By Immanuel Kant (1724–1804), German philosopher.

TOPICS FOR DISCUSSION AND WRITING

1. What does Spengler mean by "biographic archetypes"? What is the analogy which he draws?

2. Why does he distinguish between Mathematical Law and Analogy? What is the difference between "world-as-history" and "world-as-nature"?
3. If we admit Spengler's analogy, what arguments could result from such analogy?
4. What are the dangers inherent in such analogical argument? What are the values which might result from the discovery of analogies between different cultures and civilizations?
5. What are the similarities which exist between Spengler's argument and Amaury de Riencourt's (p. 189)?
6. Do you think it a fair judgment to say "Demonstration, but not prediction, can result from analogy"?
7. Write an essay contrasting the ways in which Carl Jung (p. 3) defines archetypes with Oswald Spengler's use of the term in this essay. Do they both use the term in the same sense? Do they both prove the validity of the concept? After reading both essays, which use of the concept of the archetype seems most valid?

Amaury de Riencourt

Amaury de Riencourt (1918–   ) received his A.B. from the Sorbonne and his M.A. from the University of Algiers. Since that time he has lived in many parts of the world: Asia, Africa, Europe, the Balkans, and North America. He has written and lectured on many subjects. His most recent book The Coming Caesars *(1960), of which the following selection is the last chapter, is the first in a projected series of many volumes wherein he intends to develop a comprehensive philosophy of history.*

The thesis of The Coming Caesars *is that the Western world is on the verge of returning to a form of government which ruled the Mediterranean world under the Roman Caesars. De Riencourt argues that Caesarism does not come about overnight through political revolution but results from the gradual erosion of personal liberties. He points to a number of symptoms in the contemporary scene which he considers similar to conditions which characterized the classical world just before the Caesars took over. He maintains that all of the crises—military, political, and economic—which the Western world has experienced since the First World War have resulted in a strengthening of the power and prestige of the American presidency, so that all conditions necessary for the creation of an imperialism similar to that of the Caesars are now present. His study of history has convinced him that, given the currently existing antecedent symptoms, the consequences (Caesarism) are bound to follow.*

from THE COMING CAESARS *

The legitimacy of all institutions rests on one factor: *time.* Those that endure over a long period of time are legitimate. Those that happen to seem logical at the immediate moment are not necessarily legitimate. This is the cardinal difference between Caesarism and tyrannies or dictatorships. Legitimacy involves a slow buildup over a period of generations, not a sudden seizure of power. Aristotle had already observed, from Greek experience, that tyrannies are short-lived. Not so Caesarism, which is a slow, organic growth within a society tending toward democratic equality.

Western society today, and especially American society, presents the spectacle of an immense multitude of equal and similar men and women who think alike, work alike, and enjoy the same standardized pleasures. The more uniform the level, the less the inequality and greater the compact emotional power of the multitude of like-minded men. But this power has to be concentrated and personalized by one man who acts as its articulate spokesman. Who can this man be, today, except the incumbent of the most powerful office in the most powerful state in the world—the President of the United States?

The United States Congress has repeatedly expressed its fear, especially since the New Deal and World War II, that the Constitution and the separation of powers is being steadily undermined —and so it is. Under present conditions, democratic equality ends inevitably in Caesarism. No system of checks and balances can hold out against this profound evolution, a psychological alteration that bypasses specific institutions. The thirst for equality and distrust of any form of hierarchy have ever weakened Congress itself through its seniority rule. Dislike for aristocratic distinctions eventually ends by eliminating that most indispensable of all elites—

the aristocracy of talent. This is the elite that in Britain, substituting for the former aristocracy of birth and wealth, makes the parliamentary system workable. Since most of the work of the U. S. Congress is done in committees, there is little occasion for great debates on the floor of either House or Senate comparable with the dramatic debates of European parliaments. The need of Americans to personalize and dramatize all issues can be satisfied only by concentrating attention on the President—thereby giving him increasing power. Because he can now communicate over the head of Congress with the nation, he can always dominate legislative proceedings. He can dramatize, Congress cannot—or if it does, as in the case of Senator Joseph McCarthy, it is largely because of presidential failure or unwillingness to use the immense potentialities vested in the White House.

Long ago, James Bryce discounted the usual fears of Americans and Europeans who thought that some ambitious President might attempt to seize absolute power through a brutal *coup d'etat.* But he added this warning: "If there be any danger, it would seem to lie in another direction. The larger a community becomes, the less does it seem to respect an assembly, the more it is attracted by an individual man." The reason for this is plain: the larger the masses, the more they display *feminine* traits by emphasizing emotional reactions rather than rational judgment. They instinctively tend to look for masculine leadership as a compensation—the leadership they can find in a strong man but never in an assembly, which is after all only a reproduction in miniature of their own faults and weaknesses. Instinct always prevails in the end. The great predominance of women in contemporary America can only bolster this trend.

Alongside this internal evolution, another trend asserts itself unmistakably: the development of imperial expansion, military might, and foreign commitments continues to increase the power of the American Executive. This trend was still concealed a century ago when Alexis de Tocqueville wrote:

> The President of the United States, it is true, is the Commander in Chief of the army, but the army is composed of only six thousand men; he commands the fleet, but the fleet reckons but few sail; he conducts the foreign relations of the Union, but the United States is

> a nation without neighbors. Separated from the rest of the world by the ocean, and too weak as yet to aim at the dominion of the seas, it has no enemies and its interests rarely comes into contact with those of any other nations on the globe.

Now, compare this picture with the present: armies of millions of men, the most powerful fleets in the world, commitments all over the globe, and vast nuclear power.

The President's role as Commander in Chief has now become preponderant in an age of world-wide wars and tensions. His role as director of American foreign policy has grown correspondingly. He can take many steps that are beyond recall or repair. He can start a war according to his own judgment. Singlehanded, he can influence decisively the political situation in scores of foreign nations. President Truman sent American troops into the Korean fray without waiting for Congressional approval, in spite of Senator Taft's vehement protests. But there can be no collective initiative, no collective action, and no collective responsibility.

President Truman's formula "the buck stops here" sums up the immense responsibility of the one man who heads the American government. His cabinet is entirely his own tool because he alone decides on policy and is not bound to consult its members as a prime minister in a parliamentary regime. New emergencies after World War II led to the creation of the National Security Council in 1947, a body independent of both the cabinet and Congress. And to what extent can Congress control the actual working of the Atomic Energy Commission? The President's already considerable veto power has been reinforced by the new possibility of applying it to single items of the appropriation bills. The veto becomes more sensitive and discriminating. From being largely negative, the President's legislative power becomes increasingly positive. . . . His power has been increasingly emphasized in the annual legislative program submitted in the "State of the Union" message, and if he controls his party, through his overriding influence in pushing it through.

In truth, no mental effort is required to understand that the President of the United States is the most powerful single human being in the world today. Future crises will inevitably transform him into a full-fledged Caesar, if we do not beware. Today he wears ten hats—as Head of State, Chief Executive, Minister of Foreign Affairs, Chief Legislator, Head of Party, Tribune of the People, Ultimate Arbitrator of Social Justice, Guardian of Economic Prosperity, and World Leader of Western Civilization. Slowly and unobtrusively, these hats are becoming crowns and this pyramid of hats is slowly metamorphosing itself into a tiara, the tiara of one man's world imperium.

Wars are the main harbingers of Caesarism. The Punic and Macedonian wars proved to Rome that great undertakings in an increasingly equalitarian society can be the responsibility of one man only, never of a democratic assembly. In grave emergencies, leadership can never be collective, and we are now living in an age of permanent emergency. Presidential power in America has grown as American power and expansion have grown, one developing within the other. This fact has not remained unnoticed in America since the passing of Franklin Roosevelt, and a great deal of the postwar developments in American politics can be written down as Congressional reaction against the power of the White House.

Although by no means a weak President, Harry Truman did not have the authority of his predecessor, and Congress raised its head once more. And when the Republicans came back to power in 1952, a deliberate effort was made by President Eisenhower to restore to Congress that dignity and prestige which had been so damaged during the New Deal and World War II. A similar reaction took place in Rome when Sulla attempted to undo some of the worst features of Marius' New Deal and eliminate all possibilty of another such concentration of supreme power in the hands of one man.

After World War II, the American Congress voted a Constitutional amendment forbidding future Presidents more than two terms of office. But the precedent has been set and in America historical precedents have an overwhelming influence. Such belated moves can no more halt the trend toward Caesarism than those of Sulla limiting all offices to a one-year tenure, specifying that no one could ever be, as Marius had been, both Commander in Chief and supreme magistrate, and handing back military authority to the Roman Senate.

Sulla, the victorious foe of Mithridates, was a determined conservative. He came back from his campaigns in the Hellenistic East after having destroyed the power of the redoubtable "Hitler" of the Classical world. Although endowed with absolute power, he had regularly consulted the Assembly and the Senate before carrying out any reform. He did not have to be murdered or thrown out of office by force. He resigned of his own free will in 79 B.C. hoping that his reforms would endure, and that Rome would never again have to bow to a one-man rule. This conservative reaction was doomed, not because of any shady ambition lurking in the breasts of would-be dictators but because it was far too late to sidetrack an historical evolution. A volatile and emotional public opinion looked increasingly for the one-man Executive, for the inspiring leadership of one responsible human being. Sulla's reforms, like those of our modern republicans, were noble-minded but unworkable in the long run because of the profound social and political evolution. They merely skimmed the surface by legislating instead of working in depth to correct the psychological and social trends. Sulla struck down Rome's most powerful office, the Tribunate, but it bounced back to power after his death. Then as now, the problem was not so much constitutional as psychological. It is a human problem, and only human will can preserve liberty. More honest and more perceptive than many of our contemporaries, Cicero, without the benefit of our historical perspective, pointed it out clearly: "It is due to our own moral failure and not to any accident of chance that, while retaining the name, we have lost the reality of a republic."

New emergencies and the ceaseless trend toward democratic equality brushed aside Rome's conservative reaction. There was no more ruling class and there was urgent need for a strong, farsighted ruler. We today, who stand roughly in a "Sullan" period, can now see this clearly. The gradual convergence of historical trends joins ever closer together the unconscious longing for Caesarism and the external emergencies that bring it about. We stand on the threshold of a mysterious future and try to discern its broad outline. But let us once more look at the past, the remote past that was once the present, long before our Western history was born. Before facing the future, let us once again project the full meaning of

Rome's most dramatic epoch: the coming of the imperial Caesars.

Time and again, before and after Sulla, the Romans tried not to interfere in the East for fear of being dragged into the infinite spaces of the Orient and lost among the multitude of hostile Asians —just as no sane Westerner today would contemplate with equanimity the prospect of invading the vastness of Russia, China, and Central Asia. The Romans even retreated for a time, refusing to accept Egypt, bequeathed to Rome by her ruler in 81 B.C. The Romans were patient and long suffering, sluggish and often unable to make up their collective mind. Circumstances made it up for them, and war started again, because this time the Romans had decided to accept a new legacy willed to them by the King of Bithynia.

The irresponsible agitation of political parties in Rome and the disasters in the Orient finally smashed what was left of Rome's republican institutions. The decadent Senate was totally unable to cope with the situation and Rome drifted again into a new one-man rule, that of Pompeius. In 67 B.C. the popular Assembly, panic-stricken, transferred the administration of the state from the Senate to Pompeius. The elaborate safeguards of Sulla were swiftly brushed aside. It was then that desperate, high-minded Romans began to see the hated specter of monarchy take shape on the horizon.

Public opinion was by and large still in favor of the old constitution of the republic, but without being willing to make the necessary sacrifices to uphold it. Everywhere, it was a sentimental attachment to constitutional forms rather than to the substance of freedom. All that could now be done was support one strong man against another and, eventually, throw Pompeius against Julius Caesar, who had become the leader of the democratic *Populares* party, standing on a platform of "people and democratic progress." The struggle was on between two strong men, not between an unavoidable Caesarism and a doomed republic. The conservative *Optimates,* who believed that they could control strong men like Pompeius and restore the republican institutions, were only fooling themselves. As usual, it was only when the democrats rose to power in 67 B.C. that real imperialism started again and that Roman power was restored throughout the Mediterranean basin. But democracy is an expansive state of mind, not a system whereby an extensive empire can be ruled. The Romans had to choose a leader.

Democracy endures only so long as it expands, and the seeds of Caesarism lay in its very expansion. Crassus, the millionaire, joined the democratic party and showed it the road to a further rise in the people's standard of living through the annexation of Egypt and the appropriation of her corn harvest. The moral scruples of the conservative Senate were brushed aside when Crassus appealed over its head to Rome's imperialistic masses. When Caesar moved on to the conquest of Gaul, he was the acknowledged leader of Rome's democratic party. He did not embark on a deliberately imperialistic conquest but on a war conducted in self-defense against the incursions of Germanic hordes—thus proving to Rome, in Guglielmo Ferrero's words "that only the democrats could defend her against the northern barbarians." He helped the Gauls against their hereditary enemy, but ended up by conquering and absorbing them.

Julius Caesar was a bold democrat whose "notion was to found at Rome a democracy similar to the democracies of Greece, which dispensed with a Senate and governed their empires single-handed through the deliberative assembly of the people." The conservatives, traditionally isolationist, did not want the conquest of Gaul but they were unable to stem the imperialistic tide. This, however, was a new form of imperialism, generous and world-wide. Julius Caesar was, in fact, a great internationalist who attempted to carry out the dream of many generations: the unification of the world, the foundation of an Italo-Hellenic empire in which all worthy men would be citizens with equal rights. He made every effort to internationalize the Classical world, destroy the remnants of vicious nationalisms and narrow-minded chauvinism. He used the powerful but scattered Jewish communities as "effective leaven of cosmopolitanism and of national decomposition."

The fact that Julius Caesar was elected Tribune for life in 48 B.C. did not subtract anything from his sincerity when he claimed that he came "not to destroy liberty but to fulfill it." He most likely believed it. But the plain truth was that his power was far greater than that of the old kings because now there was no civic-minded upper class to check it, no complex network of traditions and social inequalities to cramp his style. There was nothing but a vast multitude of anonymous, conformist men thirsting for peace and security.

Faced with creeping Caesarism, there are some who are blind and imitate freedom-loving Cato, who committed suicide at Utica. There may be others, however—reflective men like Cicero—who understand the new requirements of new historical times. Cicero was no blind admirer of Caesar's, but he knew that the old order had passed away, that the old republic was dead in all but name. Leadership was required and would spring up whether the old traditionalists liked it or not. Cicero, the typical representative of the new middle class, looked for a powerful executive, not a tyrant, an enlightened ruler who would look upon himself as an Aristotelian leader: *esse parem ceteris, principem dignitate*—to be the first citizen in a republic of citizens with equal rights. Neither Caesar nor Cicero could force the masses to be responsible citizens rather than slavish subjects. That was entirely beyond their power. Cicero wanted a strong president, not an absolute monarch of the Asiatic type, and it was Octavian, his vindictive foe, who was eventually to embody this type of leadership under the name of Augustus.

In Cicero, also, we have the first man of a new age, the man who stands on the threshold of civilization and world empire even as he looks back on an epoch of frightful wars and revolutions. He saw the greatest curse of his time in the increasing division of labor and the extreme specialization that had deprived leading men of the encyclopedic outlook which belongs to the well-balanced, comprehensively cultured man. The talents of lawyers, orators, military commanders, businessmen, farmers, statesmen had in the past been fused within the vigorous personalities of the ruling class; they were now dispersed among multitudes of men who could not rise above their narrow specialization. Of course, the situation rings true to us now, because this is exactly what we are suffering from today, in America perhaps more than elsewhere. Overspecialization and the atomization of intellectual knowledge account for the inconsistencies of Western statesmanship and leaves us wide open to some form of absolute autocracy that will seek to reunite the disconnected fragments.

The real founder of Rome's Caesarism was Octavian, not Caesar. When Brutus and his die-hard conservative associates murdered Julius Caesar, they failed to understand the full meaning of historical requirements. The past was dead and done for. There was no hope of resuscitating a republic that had actually died generations before, of inspiring the amorphous citizens of Rome with a desire for true political freedom when they had long ago bartered it away for equality and security. Murdering Caesar solved nothing and chaos was the result, leading directly to the bloody Proscriptions of the Triumvirate and the gory massacre of upper classes and capitalists. Exterminated by the Proscriptions in Rome, the last remaining forces of the republicans were hopelessly crushed at Philippi. Their futile attempt to stem the tide of history only made it certain that the Caesarism of the future would degenerate into an Oriental despotism in spite of the efforts of the coming Caesars themselves. Brutus destroyed with his own hands the pitiful remains of what he wanted to save, instead of associating it in a constructive manner with the unavoidable Caesarism—and therefore curbing it. Compromise is the essence of enduring institutions and discarding compromise only makes it certain that the institutions one is out to save will eventually perish altogether.

Once more, it should be emphasized that enduring Caesarism, just like enduring imperialism, is an involuntary development, not the result of any one man's ambition. It is of prime importance to recall Suetonius' words—"Octavian wanted to abandon power after Actium and restore the republic." If he became Augustus, invested with the full "imperial" dignity inherited from his adoptive father, it was because public opinion wanted it so, not because of his own personal ambition. Caesars no more seize and hold supreme power against the wishes of public opinion than enduring empires build themselves up on oppressed and unwilling populations. Both are called into being by voids begging to be filled. Octavian was prudent, cold, and cautious, saturated with wealth and glory. Physically weak, plagued by poor health, he dreamed of retiring like Sulla rather than attempting to reshape the world like Caesar.

Having reluctantly accepted the responsibility of rebuilding a shattered world, Octavian had to make a fundamental choice. Should he continue to develop the cosmopolitan bureaucratic state on the Hellenistic pattern that Sextus Pompeius and Julius Caesar had started, or should he revert to the constitutional traditions of Rome and enhance the elective system? Deciding in favor of the latter, he moved to bolster the authority of the Senate. In vain. The Senators refused to assume any responsibility.

Long before the advent of Augustus, an insidious belief had taken hold of the Roman world. This was the belief in the "indispensable man," a feeling that becomes so potent at that stage of history that it finally results in canceling the short tenure of office and tends to prolong supreme power almost indefinitely in the hands of the same man. Continuity in office becomes essential. What is more, a world power no longer belongs exclusively to the citizens who promoted it. A world power belongs to the world that it dominates and its government is as much responsible to the noncitizens as to its electors. The power and prestige of its Executive in other lands requires that he adapt himself to satisfy many vastly different psychological tempers.

One of the chief reasons that forced Augustus to give up his idea of resigning in 28 B.C. was that he had become, in fact, King of Egypt, a land of proud people devoted to the monarchical principle who could never be ruled by the proconsul of an alien republic. President of the Roman republic for life, Augustus could remain an Oriental monarch in the eyes of the Egyptians—but only so long as he remained the supreme magistrate of the Roman state. He became a Janus-like ruler, the republican side turned toward Italy, the monarchical toward the East. And since Egypt's food supplies were of paramount importance to Rome, there was nothing to do but humor both Egyptians and Romans, and alter the Roman constitution. Is it any different in our contemporary world? When the Emperor of Japan had to divest himself of his divinity in 1946 it became obvious that General MacArthur retrieved the fallen dignity without too much reluctance.

But, to return to Rome, there was no complete break with the former constitution, although Octavian was both consul and proconsul, two offices that were deemed incompatible in the old days. What it amounted to, in fact, was that Octavian "agreed to accept an appointment for ten years as sole President of the Latin republic, with supreme military command and wide but constitutional powers, rather resembling those of the federal President in America than of an Asiatic monarch." He became *princeps,* the first citizen of the republic, as visualized by his unfortunate enemy Cicero, and finally brought to maturity all the potentialities of the Tribuneship. In the words of a British historian, "the Principate was not a dictatorship or a kingship or a more potent consulship, but a magnified Tribuneship. It definitely linked the Princeps with the popular traditions of the Gracchi and of Julius, and set him before the world as pre-eminently the guardian of the plain man's interests." And the *res gestae,* Augustus' "Memoirs," proves that he understood it as such and placed the highest of all values in this office.

Psychologically, it is easy to understand why the republican ideal had survived all those wars and upheavals. "The Roman republic, far from falling beneath the yoke of foreign monarchs, had destroyed every monarchy founded by Alexander. Thus it was inconceivable that a system of government which had enjoyed such vast successes should be abolished at any moment by the act of one man or of a small party." It also explains why the Caesars themselves attempted time and again to bolster those failing institutions that had raised Rome above all other nations, and also why they could not find the men to do so. It was not the republican institutions as such but a high-minded ruling class that had raised Rome above all other nations, and this class no longer existed.

For forty-one years after the restoration in 27 B.C., Augustus attempted to reform the Roman state along the lines laid down by Cicero in his *de officiis.* His policy was conservative whereas that of Julius Caesar had been frankly revolutionary. Caesar was a bold, imaginative, aristocratic revolutionary, endowed with immense charm and generosity. Augustus, the grandson of a usurer of the city of Velitrae, was the prudent, pragmatic, calculating representative of the now dominant middle class that had gradually become reconciled to Caesarism for fear of republican chaos—and eventually became Caesarism's mainstay. The middle class populations of the entire Classical world refused to look far into the future, were determined to move slowly and cautiously, and to make the preservation of world peace their paramount task. As their representative, Augustus tried strenuously to inculcate a respect for the constitution and revive the "rule of law" that the exaggerated adulation of the Roman masses and the Oriental populations for his person made difficult. He was forced by the popular will to become the absolute monarch he did not want to be. It was the long-term change in psychological climate, not the formal breaches of the constitution, that destroyed the republic.

Time and again, Augustus absented himself from Rome so as to accustom the Senate and Assembly to think and act for themselves instead of always coming to him for advice and command. But it was useless. The Senate remained lethargic. There were not even enough candidates for the public offices: the twenty Quaestorships in 25 B.C. could not be filled. Formerly, in a more aristocratic Rome, magistrates were content with the prestige of an unpaid office and the satisfaction of fulfilling a duty. But the long predominance of Big Business and the mercantile worship of money, linked with the rising taste for democratic equality, had destroyed the old prestige of social distinctions. Augustus was now forced to pay them salaries, transform elective offices into administrative appointments, transform elected magistrates into government officials, and lay the foundations of a bureaucratic state which gradually superseded the elective one of the old days. From Julius Caesar's foundation of an imperial secretariat under Oppius and Albus to the full-edged establishment of a salaried civil service under Claudius, the growth of the imperial bureaucracy was uninterrupted, dwarfing and eventually eliminating Senate and Assembly altogether.

On the other hand, all of Augustus' initiatives were approved without opposition. He attempted to revive the Senate by a massive infusion of new members, but to no avail. When in 27 B.C. physical illness made him wish to resign and retire to private life, consternation and panic swept Rome. Begged to remain in power, Augustus took the opportunity to revise the constitution, relieving himself of the burdens imposed by the Caesarian tradition of cumulative offices, retaining merely the proconsular dignity and the Tribuneeship. He attempted to induce the Senate to resume its former responsibilities in the conduct of foreign affairs. But the Senate referred everything back to him, thus abandoning forever its former prerogatives by transferring full authority, of its own free will, into the hands of one man. And when, almost simultaneously, famine made its appearance in Rome, the people rioted in the streets, threatened to burn down the Senate, and proclaimed Augustus dictator. Not yet convinced, Augustus attempted in 18 B.C. to divide the executive office by splitting it up between two Princeps nominated for a five-year term.

Augustus was wise enough to know that it was the decadence of the ruling class and the trend toward democratic equality that had led directly to Caesarism. He knew that liberty thrives only on a certain amount of inequality and nonconformity. But there was no more ruling class, only an *owning* class of new rich, the spineless *novi homines* who could substitute socially, but never politically, for the fallen aristocracy. Augustus could not stem the tide of history, although he was not the last one to try. Austere, stern, and unbending, Tiberius tried to instill self-reliance into the Senate, refused to allow it to take an oath to support all his decisions and, in exasperation at the contemptible fawning of which he was the object, exclaimed in despair: "O men, ready for slavery!"

Growing public indifference to politics was already deplored in Caesar's days, lamented by Augustus, and bitterly resented by Tiberius. But it was too late. With Caesarism and civilization, the great struggles between political parties are no longer concerned with principles, programs, and ideologies, but with *men*. Marius, Sulla, Cato, Brutus still fought for principles. But now, everything became personalized. Under Augustus, parties still existed, but there were no more *Optimates* or *Populares,* no more conservatives or democrats. Men campaigned for or against Tiberius or Drusus or Caius Caesar. No one believed any more in the efficacy of ideas, political panaceas, doctrines, or systems, just as the Greeks had given up building great philosophic systems generations before. Abstractions, ideas, and philosophies were rejected to the periphery of their lives and of the empire, to the East where Jews, Gnostics, Christians, and Mithraists attempted to conquer the world of souls and minds while the Caesars ruled their material existence.

Caesars were not crowned monarchs, since monarchy had become as meaningless a symbol then as it has largely become today. They remained powerful lifetime Presidents of what was still technically the Roman Republic. From Augustus to Trajan they observed the old constitutional forms and stately traditions of the republic. Trajan himself, upon his inauguration, "swore before the consul's tribunal that he would observe the law." As Gibbon pointed out, the emperors remained mere citizens:

> In all the offices of life they affected to confound themselves with their subjects and maintained with them an equal intercourse of visits and entertainments. Their habit, their palace, their table was suited only to the rank of an opulent senator. . . . Augustus or Trajan would have blushed at employing the meanest of the Romans in those menial offices, which in the household and bedchamber of a limited monarch, are so eagerly solicited by the proudest nobles of Britain.

The rise of Caesarism in America is considerably eased by a number of American features. In the first place, democratic equality, with its concomitant conformism and psychological socialization, is more fully deveoped in the United States than it has ever been anywhere, at any time. There are no social barriers, such as existed in Rome's remnants of aristocratic tradition, because Britain's ruling class played that part on behalf of America. Whatever tensions there were within the Roman state are partly transmuted in our modern world into international tensions between Britain and America.

The next most important feature is that Caesarism can come to America constitutionally, without having to alter or break down any existing institution. The White House is already the seat of the most powerful tribunician authority ever known to history. All it needs is amplification and extension. Caesarism in America does not have to challenge the Constitution as in Rome or engage in civil warfare and cross any fateful Rubicon. It can slip in quite naturally, discreetly, through constitutional channels.

The psychological climate is almost ripe. What irked the Romans of the stamp of Brutus was not so much Julius Caesar's effective power as the ostentation with which he displayed it. Republican institutions can long be dead and still survive as a sacred ideal in the minds of men. Most Romans were ready to admit the reality of Caesarism but not the symbol of a hated monarchy. It is not too different today. Ideology, the realities of geography, and insularity have made of the Americans tamers of nature rather than subduers of men. Americans have always tended to be repelled by open display of authority over men as much as they enjoy power over "things." So far, they have been nonmilitaristic out of circumstances rather than conviction. Individually, they are far from disliking violence. Their nonmilitaristic disposition does not spring from dislike of effective power—hero worship and bossism are marked American features—nor from dislike for military discipline, since they are more disciplined, group-minded, and eager for leadership than most Europeans. It comes simply from their instinct for equality, which makes them dislike the inevitable hierarchy of military organization. They frown on any form of hierarchy whatsoever. They have no feeling of awe or reverence for other human beings and would, if circumstances warranted it, behave as did the Romans who hurled insults and mocked the victorious generals during their "triumph" in order to deflate their swelling vanity and thus compensate for the supreme honors decreed to them. Americans have no appreciation for the majestitc symbolism that moves Englishmen when they face their powerless Crown. They enjoy calling their President Tom, Dick, or Harry, even though he is probably the most powerful human being in the world.

Americans will accept immense, almost autocratic power over them so long as they do not have to see in it a transcendant authority, and they will always attempt to "humanize" such authority with the help of humor or incongruity. What they will always seek to cut down is not effective power but its awe-inspiring character. Through the gap thus opened between appearance and reality, the coming Caesars will march in if left free to do so. We shall legislate against them and rave against them. But there they will be, towering over us, far above such petty attacks, symbols of a mortal disease within our Western civilization. And, like a Shakespearean Brutus, all that will be left to us will be to cry in despair:

O Julius Caesar, thou art mighty yet!
Thy spirit walks abroad, and turns our swords
in our own proper entrails.

TOPICS FOR DISCUSSION AND WRITING

1. What sentence comes closest to an explicit statement of de Reincourt's thesis?
2. What are some of his reasons for believing that democratic equality is doomed?
3. What are some of the factors which he thinks have contributed to an increase in the power of the American executive?
4. How does he attempt to prove that "wars are the main harbingers of Caesarism"?
5. What, if anything, does he prove by his references to Sulla's attempts to bring about reforms at Rome?
6. Is he justified in concluding that, because Sulla's reforms were unavailing in classical Rome, all attempts to halt what he considers a current trend toward Caesarism must also fail?
7. Does he point up any similarities between the Roman world in 68 B.C. and the Western world of today, or does he merely refer to similarities, expecting his readers to supply them?
8. Does he make any analogies between Julius Caesar's rise to power and current trends?
9. Does he demonstrate that there are a great number of similarities between the Roman world as Cicero saw it and the current scene? Does he expect that his reader will immediately agree with him? Is he begging the question?
10. Does he demonstrate similarities between the way in which Octavian came to power and the way in which a contemporary Caesar will appear?
11. Are the analogies to which he calls attention essential or only accidental? Are there a sufficient number of similarities between the course of events in the two periods of history to validate his thesis?
12. Does his lengthy explanation of how Octavius Caesar attempted to reinforce the power of the Roman Senate cast any light on the contemporary scene?
13. What is the weakest part of his argument? The strongest? Has he proven his thesis or only called attention to interesting analogies?
14. Both Spengler and de Riencourt attempt to suggest the future by comparison with the past. Is one more convincing than the other? Why?
15. Write an essay contrasting Spengler's and De Riencourt's conceptions of history with Crane Brinton's (p. 36). Assuming that both De Riencourt and Spengler look upon the study of history as a means of

suggesting the course of the future, is this conception of the use of history shared by Brinton? When Brinton speaks of himself as playing the prophet, is he doing the same thing that Spengler does? Does Brinton make any use of induction in arriving at his lessons from the past? Do Spengler and de Riencourt use induction?

16. What part do general statements such as "Democracy endures only so long as it expands" (p. 195) and "liberty thrives on inequality" (p. 201) play in his argument? Does he prove these statements?

Wylie Sypher

Wylie Sypher (1905–), after receiving his doctorate from Harvard University, taught at Tufts College, the University of Wisconsin, and the University of Minnesota. He is now professor of English at Simmons College. In his book Four Stages of Renaissance Style *(1955), Wylie Sypher argues that the several arts of a given generation take their form and substance from the age itself; and that art reflects its cultural environment not only in the artists' choice of subjects, but in the subtle areas of mood, feeling, and impressions. In the following essay from his book, Wylie Sypher shows how analogies exist among several of the arts, analogies which demonstrate his basic thesis.*

from Four Stages of Renaissance Style *

For the renaissance artist beauty was exact proportion, clear outline, stable relations. Ghiberti said, "Only proportion makes beauty." Alberti repeats that beauty is a harmony, congruity, and consent of all the parts. Spenser believed that God framed the world in a comely Pattern. Then a spasm broke open this goodly Pattern, and religious schisms cleft a world charged with the new forces of the Protestant era—forces that played through politics and commerce as well as faith, and diverted the course of history on two continents. Luther burned the Papal bull in 1520. Rome itself was sacked in 1527 by the army of Emperor Charles V. The harmony between microcosm and macrocosm was untuned; "the circle was broken" when Tycho Brahe, Galileo, Kepler found the motions of the universe to be eccentric and elliptical.

A typical "renaissance" structure in poetry is Sidney's sonnet "Heart Exchange" with its clear units, its harmonious and uncomplicated parallels, its "closed" form and decisive coda:

> My true love hath my heart and I have his,
> By just exchange, one for the other given;
> I hold his dear, and mine he cannot miss;
> There never was a better bargain driven.
> His heart in me keeps me and him in one,
> My heart in him his thoughts and senses guides;
> He loves my heart, for once it was his own;
> I cherish his because in me it bides.
> His heart his wound received from my sight;
> My heart was wounded with his wounded heart,
> For as from me on him his hurt did light,
> So still methought in me his hurt did smart;
> Both equal hurt, in this change sought our bliss:
> My true love hath my heart and I have his.

Then, by contrast, there is the loose, devious zigzag development of that spasmodic mannerist poem "To His Coy Mistress" by Andrew Marvell, which shifts in theme and tone through three powerful dissonant passages. Under the attack of the sophisticated mannerist writer, the renaissance harmony, clarity, and unity are "disturbed." As if echoing Donne's mockery of love, the poem opens with a condescending extravagant praise of Marvell's mistress, whose eyes, forehead, and breasts deserve centuries of adoration. *But* (and the poem swivels abruptly to a sardonic perspective on himself and this coy mistress of his) her Honor and his Lyric will not be found in the grave—that fine and private place. Then Marvell, abandoning both trifling and sardonic tones, is shaken by his own sense of panic: he and this delicate, knowing mistress with her enchanting flesh must tear their pleasures, like birds of prey, from the iron gates of the tomb. The poem ends with a frantic—and suspended—jest, which betrays Marvell's own urgency to love:

> Thus, though we cannot make our Sun
> Stand still, yet we will make him run.

Marvell's sharp but unsustained attack—brilliant, sensitive, private—is like the loose and surprising adjustment and counter-adjustment of figure to figure in Parmigianino's paintings, with their evidence of subjective stress. Parmigianino relies upon an involved energy, not a closed design, and his equilibriums are always momentary and undependable.

Formal as Donne's language may be, his logic is as spasmodic as Marvell's. Eliot has remarked that Donne brings to every experience "an awareness of the apparent irrelevance and unrelatedness of things"; he has an appetite for opposite responses; he develops his poems with "hardly any attempt at organization," if we mean by organization coherent progress; he extracts every minim of emotion from each isolated situation, and in so doing wrenches the accent of his verse. Yet it is wrong to think that Donne, or the Jacobean playwright either, makes hardly any attempt at organization; for the poets and dramatists of this era have a logic of their own, a rhetorical and dramatic logic that does not operate by transition and sequence but by circulating through extremes, opposites, and divergencies, digesting every sort of experience by putting sudden stress on language and gesture. It seems fair to say that Donne employs a great many logical devices but is entirely careless of the *direction* in which his logic leads him. Consequently Donne, like the Jacobean dramatists, seems as ready to defend sophistry as truth, and in describing his art we need to have in mind a kind of logic or structure essentially different from the logic or structure of both renaissance and baroque art—the logic and structure of mannerism, devious, contradictory, shuttling, perverse, and always dramatic in an immediate intense way. Francis Bacon wrote as a mannerist when he said, "There is no excellent beauty that hath not some strangeness in the proportion."

Mannerist painters and poets alike defy rules of proportion and perspective to satisfy the needs of their subjective view of reality. One of the reasons it is difficult to define the mannerist style is that each painting, statue, façade, each poem and play is a special case, a personal manipulation of design, material, situation, language, response. Metaphysical poetry is not original exactly in the way Eliot and other critics once suppose—that is, in "toughness" and "unified sensibility." The real originality of Donne, whose wit resembles Jonson's and the Cavaliers', is his being an essentially private poet, giving each verse a personal note; thus in reading Donne we must always attend first to the tone, the inner vibration that makes each poem sound like a personal intrigue even if it is not. Webster's is a drama of obscure exploration, suggesting the private imbalance of a Hamlet. Donne, Webster, and Tourneur, Cellini, Tintoretto, and El Greco approach everything from hidden and inward angles, and their readings are in one or another way ambiguous. It is hard for us to "read" Donne's "Extasie" or Middleton and Rowley's *The Changeling*; it is hard to "read" the façade of the Palazzo Massimi alle Colonne in Rome (Peruzzi, 1535).

Mannerism means experimental response, tentative commitment, learned but personal research, overcleverness in handling conventional forms and elements. Its style and its temperament are variable and diverse. Montaigne, in fact, speaks with the unofficial philosophic voice of mannerism: *"Que sçay je?"* he asks—What do I know? In his "Apology of Raymond Sebond" all absolute judgments come under his gentle but scathing regard, and he thinks of himself as willing to exist in the element of uncertainty—"the uncertainty that every man feels in himself" when he is wise at his own cost:

> How variously we judge of things! How often we change our opinions! What I hold and believe today I hold and believe with my whole belief; with all my tools and all my strength I grasp that opinion; and they guarantee it with all the power at their command. . . . But has it not happened, not once, but a hundred, nay a thousand times, and every day, that, with those same implements and under the same conditions, I have embraced something else, which I have since concluded to be false?

Montaigne moves freely over the whole philosophic terrain between passion and detachment. The senses, he knows, are full of uncertainty and cannot guarantee any truth; thus we must have recourse to reason. But every reason is built upon the quaking foundation of a preceding reason: "so here we are retreating backwards to all eternity." Montaigne, too, has a "subjective" relation to his world, since our senses give us only the impressions of outside objects, and impressions and objects "are different things." Thus we must live amid appearances; and he is brought to question with Hamlet whether our mere thinking does not make it so. "There is," Montaigne placidly continues, "no permanent existence, either of our being or of that of the objects." We, our opinions, our mortal selves, "incessantly go flowing and rolling on." Meanwhile we live convinced that "truth ought to have one face, always and everywhere the same." Surely Montaigne did not have Hamlet's bad dreams, and he seems less damaged than Hamlet by his own curiosity. But he has a great deal of Hamlet's sense of insecurity brought about by living in a world without a known order; and, like Hamlet or Donne, he has glimpses of man's life as a passionate comedy:

> Is it possible to imagine anything more ridiculous than that this miserable and puny creature, who is not so much as master of himself, exposed to shocks on all sides, should call himself Master and Emperor of the universe, of which it is not in his power to know the smallest part, much less to command it? . . . Who has sealed him this privilege? Let him show us his letters-patent for this great and noble charge.

Significantly, tragicomedy is a particularly mannerist form of drama. Plays like *The Changeling* are inscrutable because the pathos and the laughter are both pressed as far as they can be in opposite directions without any attempt to reconcile, compromise, or accept the logic of either. Donne, Webster and Tourneur do not seem to conquer their disillusions, and not being able to mediate between irreconcilables, leave us with a sense of disrelationship, ambiguity, and in general what Woelfflin calls in painting a "complexity of direction." It is symptomatic that the many prose passages in Jacobean drama gradually encroach upon verse, implying in the author a frame of mind with a minimum of formal articulation.

Donne's false and verbal (perhaps false? perhaps verbal?) resolutions—his incapacity to commit himself wholly to any one world or view—appear in his extraordinary poem on his own death, "Hymn to God the Father," resigning his soul to his Redeemer, asking whether He can forgive the sins which he has *done*, and which, he says, he deplores—although we have strongly the sense that the poet is only too convinced of the profit of each sin as a means of fulfilling his adventurous experience of life:

> When thou hast done, thou hast not done,
>   For I have more.
> I have a sinne of feare that when I have spunne

My last thred, I shall perish on the shore;
Sweare by thy selfe that at my death thy sonne
Shall shine as he shines now, and heretofore;
And, having done that, Thou hast done,
I feare no more.

This calling his Judge to account, this demand for reassurance from God, this trifling in puns with his sins in the flesh and spirit and his fear of hell is either extreme devotion or extreme insolence; and we cannot clearly tell which. The resolution is gained, if at all, only rhetorically by a logic of the pun, not reason. But there is no doubt of Donne's fear for his soul. So in Donne's last and most cavalier pun there is the tension of mannerist techniques. In *The Duchess of Malfi* and other plays by Webster we find the same high tension of the moment together with a blurring of total meaning—glaring flashes of perception along with brutal acts and unexplained contradictions.

The unresolved tensions and contradictions in mannerist art appear early in Michaelangelo's designs for the Laurentian Library anteroom and the Medici Chapel (1526–34). Michaelangelo never seems to have decided whether architecture is, or is not, simply a background for sculpture, an uncertainty revealed fully in the Medici Chapel, where his architectural plan seems to be a framework for some shocking feats in sculpture and for niches some of which, by a breakdown of logic, are left vacant. Burckhardt thought the Laurentian anteroom to be "an incomprehensible joke," just as, we might add, the literary historians before Grierson thought Donne's poetry a joke, and a bad joke at that. In fact, Michaelangelo was the first to turn architecture into a medium for individual expression, and both the Chapel and the anteroom show us a world of frustration where all the forces seem active, yet frozen or paralyzed by a highly artificial, severe, and uncomfortable system.

As if Michaelangelo had intended to parody architectural logic, the Laurentian anteroom, with its restless narrow proportions, its complex black moldings, columns, and pediments crowded and broken, leaves the observer everywhere in doubt about structure and function. The relations of column to wall are reversed, since the columns, being set within niches, stand not before, but *within* or even *behind*, the wall. Ungainly brackets on the *surface* of the wall "support" the *inset* doubled columns, whose weight does not bear directly on these absurd brackets, which nevertheless receive full plastic emphasis. Thus *the logic of the structure does not coincide with the structural elements.* The moldings and the frames of the door and niches are broken, or not held in one plane; the triangular pediment over the harsh narrow door is twice broken, and so heavy that it seems to press unbearably down upon the frame of the doorway. The empty niches beside the door are crowned with semicircular pediments, rasping against the pediment above the door and also against the engaged pilasters framing the niches. These pilasters taper toward the bottom—another *reductio ad absurdum* of normal support for weight. The molding is broken inward precisely above the outward-moving capitals of the inset columns, and the ugly little black tablets set below the frames of the niches only emphasize that these frames are not supported by the molding beneath them. The mass of the steps is heavy, sluggish, inert, a lumpy flow "as of lava," and while the side flights go straight upward, the central flight, rounded in the middle, then again rounded as it clashes against the balusters, lacks any convincing rhythm, volume, or weight. There is an insoluble conflict between logic and appearance, horizontal and vertical movement, motion and rest, energy and paralysis.

In mannerist façades there is a frank display of illogicality in the frequent *double functioning of members,* particularly where there appears a kind of architectural pun, a single member having a duplex use—a molding, for example, used as a sill. There is also a "principle of inversion" in mannerist façades, for the customary relation of orders is reversed by "permutations" of elements, conflicting directions, shifts in scale, or other overingenious devices that are learned but irresponsible. Often the closed units are not really bounded but placed in doubtful adjustment to the open units.

One of the decisively mannerist façades is that of the Palazzo Massimi alle Colonne in Rome (1535) which, being slightly curved, obscures the harmonious clear logic of the renaissance surface, and dramatizes the "poignant contrast between the deep darkness of the ground-floor loggia and the papery thinness and flatness of the upper parts." The façade of the Chigi Palace in the Piazza Colonna,

Rome (begun in 1562 by Giacomo della Porta?), also shows the mannerist inversions and the tendency to mask the logic of the structure. At the corners the coigns are far too bulky for the flimsy-looking walls; so also is the heavy cornice casting melodramatic shadow over the plane surface beneath. This surface is kept in a restless, "interesting" movement by four stories (five, if we count the windows *above* the cornice) completely out of proportion, making us wonder what the interior structure could be. Over the thick casings of the lowest windows, shadowed by giant canopies, runs a thin string course touching the sills of the next rank of windows and serving, like a pun again, a double function as string course and continuous sill. Above the upper shallow casings are huge pediments, alternately triangular and semicircular, that are supported "wittily" by massive brackets. Immediately above these pediments runs a series of tiny absurd "horizontal" windows, over which are corresponding "vertical" windows of larger size. The whole effect is one of melodrama and levity—or demented ingenuity.

In designing both churches and palaces mannerist architects broke up the renaissance a-b-a-b symmetry in open and closed bays of naves, or in alternating triangular and semicircular pediments. On the façade of the Palazzo Bevilacqua, Verona (1530), the pediments were planned irregularly (a-B-B-a-a-B); and in such palaces the portals may not be symmetrically placed. The width of bays, the handling of columns, the treatment of orders and other elements, may also be whimsical. The eye *jumps* across a mannerist façade since there is little repose or balance; or else the balances are false. In the Redentore, Venice (1576–92), Palladio's interpenetrating giant and minor orders make the façade difficult and surprising to "read." Even Inigo Jones' Banqueting House in Whitehall has certain mannerist features, for the front does not keep the plane, the cornices are broken, the accents "move" somewhat because the central axis is so strong, and although the interior is one large room, the exterior uses three levels.

The architectural symmetries wavered and broke up as soon as the balanced, "centralized" renaissance church was replaced by the mannerist church having a strong medial axis because of its long nave, surmounted by a dome at the crossing, where the high altar stands in a flare of sunlight. Except for this, the mannerist church is dim, the chapels along the aisles serving as nooks for private devotion, each chapel having its painting, lighted by candles. The heightened devotional atmosphere of the mannerist church, together with its irregular architectural features and dramatic austerity, seems to betoken the "bad conscience" also expressed in the somewhat chill yet agitated mannerist art which "contracts its material" yet gains an effect of spirituality from its strong verticality and constraint. Certainly that typical mannerist façade of the Gesù Church in Rome (1569–80), with its unnatural withering of rich materials, has a false austerity, a thwarted and puny upward motion. Deprived of respose by Vignola's and Della Porta's plans, the central unit is of painfully narrow proportions; the small side doors are huddled up against the central door, and the double engaged pilasters move inward away from the receding wings of this façade; these wings support the shrunken awkward brackets intended to make a transition between the superior orders and the orders of the ground floor. The coherence is uncertain. The disharmony of the triangular-within-semicircular pediments over the main door is probably not due to Vignola, who is, however, responsible for the conflict between the engaged pilasters on the ground story and the columns set about the rectangular window in the upper story.

Thus the mannerist churches have a repressed elegance, an ascetic refusal to achieve baroque splendor; in this architecture there is a sign of struggle, but no fulfillment, no conquest—except for a *"tendency to excess within rigid boundaries."* The mannerist energy suddenly expends itself in surprising, illogical places. But the uncertain proportions, the wavering accents, do not reduce the mannerist tensions; neither the vertical motion nor the awkward masses give any sense of release or exuberance. The mannerist architect uses weighty volumes only with reluctance or indecision; at least the appearance of weight is denied by broken rhythms. The play of forces is checked, dissonant, perplexed. The major plastic accents do not coincide with the major structural accents. Consequently in mannerist art *the psychological effect diverges from the structural logic.* The style is "atectonic." It seems to be a response to the temper of Europe between 1520 and 1620, one of tormenting doubt and rigorous obedience to ardently felt but incoherent dogmatic principles. Mannerism is full of contradictions: rigid formality and obvious "disturbance," bareness and overelegance, mysticism and pornography, El Greco and Parmigianino.

During the mannerist era prose writers broke up the classic ("tectonic") rhythms of the Ciceronian style, which in slow and orderly cadence progressed to a clear emphasis and closed the period harmoniously. One reaction against this "grand" Ciceronian style was the "curt" period with a lack of syntactical relation between members, a deliberate asymmetry of phrase, and many shifts from concrete to abstract language, alternating the "planes" of the vocabulary, so to speak. The accents in this new prose "hover" and sometimes are determined by emotive stress instead of any logic of syntax. The "loose" style of the age is even more subjective, with emergent meanings, sharply phrased statements budding off into new members at will, unfolding toward an *O Altitudo*. Though the loose style willfully violates coherence, it uses many connectives; yet these connectives are of doubtful logic since the period develops by a series of dangling members introduced by a *which*, a *wherein*, a *whereto*—or by some absolute construction amounting to a *non sequitur*, a breakdown in symmetry. With their erratic tempo both kinds of style are "exploratory." In one or another way Montaigne, Bacon, Browne, and Burton all brought to bear, in curt or loose manner, a strain on their sentences beyond the capacities of syntax; one sign is their abuse of interpolation and parenthesis. Burton's language, so variable as to be freakish, with its whimsical lardings of Latin, has the "broken" eccentric, unsustained mannerist energy. In verse Donne does not "keep the accent" either, as Ben Jonson complained, for he wrenched his meter by every sort of dissonant stress, making the ear jump just as the eye jumps across a mannerist façade. The new seventeenth-century prose is called "baroque"; but it is, properly, mannerist in its explosive accent, its experimental and indecisive "hovering" order of statement.

The hovering is partly psychological. In Donne, too, the psychological effect is not coordinated with the structural effect; often the metaphor does not coincide with the mood of devotion, for there is an interplay between John Donne, very insolent and neat, and Dr. Donne, the Dean of Saint Paul's who dreads to be damned eternally, eternally, eternally, and dropped into the flaming pit—

unless he can jest his God out of His righteous anger. Donne writes of the Church in terms one usually applies to an adulteress or whore: "Show me, deare Christ, thy Spouse so bright and cleare," he begins; and then urges:

> Betray kind husband thy spouse to our sights,
> And let myne amorus soule court thy mild Dove,
> Who is most trew, and pleasing to thee, then
> When she's embrac'd, and *open to most men.*

This is witty; this has a lively stress; this shows a capacity for every range of response, an ability to assimilate opposite and diverse appetites and experiences. But it is strained, and the resolution is equivocal. If it is true that pornography is a sign of sensuousness with a bad conscience, Donne comes near betraying a bad conscience. In the same way subject and image—devotion and rhetoric—diverge in Góngora's witty religious poems. In a sense, mannerism is a reaction, after the renaissance optimism, to medieval faith; but a gulf is fixed between the two eras. The tendency of all the cinquecento art and thought is to be "rich in directions," and we must associate Donne's ability to digest heterogeneous experiences with the mannerist instability and tension in architecture, its inversion of orders, its permutations and double functions, its impulse toward austerity and the vertical—the verticality of the Gesù façade, more troubled, complex, jarring, self-conscious, and frigid than any gothic verticality. If mannerism shares some of the gothic religious spirit, it oversophisticates and overintellectualizes the Gothic line. Its rationalism has lost direction.

The quasi-austerity, the wavering aspiration, are both in Donne's "Divine Poems," which use a double functioning of members, since the so-called *catena* group of sonnets interlocks the opening and closing verses of successive sonnets, although the meaning of the verse shifts constantly in tone and direction from piety to wit to hysteria to resignation to query, and every excess within artificial boundaries. A more subtle complexity is the sixth Holy Sonnet, showing the mannerist tension, dissonance, and perversion. Purportedly the verses claim that Donne does not fear death; yet the argument only conceals Donne's horror of the grave. The strain on the logic is very great, and the resolution occurs by a leap or ellipsis due to faith—or fright:

> This is my playes last scene, here heavens appoint
> My pilgrimages last mile; and my race
> Idly, yet quickly runne, hath this last pace,
> My spans last inch, my minutes latest point,
> And gluttonous death, will instantly unjoynt
> My body, and soule, and I shall sleepe a space,
> But my'ever-waking part shall see that face,
> Whose feare already shakes my every joynt:
> Then, as my soule, to'heaven her first seate, takes flight,
> And earth-born body, in the earth shall dwell,
> So, fall my sinnes, that all may have their right,
> To where they'are bred, and would presse me, to hell.
> Impute me righteous, thus purg'd of evill,
> For thus I leave the world, the flesh, the devill.

The clash between the psychological and rhetorical directions is audible in the wavering caesura, the sliding meter, the wrenched accents. The renaissance sonnet did not try to accommodate these strains, which suggest the curious torment in mannerist faith—and mannerist doubt.

TOPICS FOR DISCUSSION AND WRITING

1. What is the distinction which Sypher makes between *renaissance* and *mannerist?* How do the poems of Sidney (p. 206) and Donne (p. 209) exemplify the two?
2. Why does Sypher make reference to Luther, the sack of Rome, Tycho Brahe, Galileo, and Kepler in defining *mannerist?* Is there any similarity here to John Ruskin's method of analysis of the works of Turner and Scott (p. 282)?
3. What is the unifying link which Sypher discovers between Donne and Marvell? Between the poets and the painters?
4. Do you see any resemblance between the style of the quoted Montaigne passage (paragraph 6) and the selection from Browne's *Religio Medici* (p. 539)? How does Sypher account for such a style?
5. How does Sypher's description of the Laurentian Library anteroom support his argument? What is his analogy? How, according to Sypher, will an awareness of architectural forms help us to understand mannerist literature?
6. Could you, by discovering analogies among the various arts of today, assemble a definition of this modern age? Would you say that we today are mannerist or renaissance?

7. Does Sypher use analogies in the same way as Spengler? Does he use similarities between two periods in history to suggest anything about a third?

Harold H. Watts

Harold H. Watts (1911–) is the author of several books and critical essays. The following essay, which stimulated thoughtful discussion when it originally appeared in Cross Currents *in 1955, is interesting both for its subject matter and its method.*

Its main purpose is to formulate a satisfactory definition of tragedy. As the opening paragraphs of the essay point out, the problem of defining tragedy has been one of the recurring topics of contemporary criticism. Many critics have expressed reservations about the adequacy of the traditional definition to be found in Aristotle's Poetics, *and have attempted to formulate more satisfactory definitions by adapting some of the conceptions of modern psychologists like Carl Jung. A review of Jung's conception of the collective unconscious and of archetypal mythic patterns as discussed in the first essay in this text will enable you to read the following essay with a deeper appreciation of the implications of its definitions.*

The author's method of proof is in keeping with his subject matter. Defending the thesis that artistic expression is analogous to religious expression, he calls attention to analogical similarities which he believes have never been adequately understood—similarities between comedy and tragedy, between drama and ritual, between literature and myth. His purpose is not to blur distinctions between the various forms of expression, but to clarify these relationships. Those who agree with Jung's psychological assumptions and attach great significance to analogical relationships will find Watt's arguments more cogent than those who adhere to a more traditional psychology. In classical psychology an analogy can never constitute a satisfactory proof, though it may serve to explain and illuminate.

Myth and Drama *

Every century—perhaps every decade—has its topics. In one sense, the effort to state the essence of tragedy and of comedy is one

* From *Cross Currents,* V (1955), 154–70. Reprinted by permission of the author and the editors.

of our topics. This, unlike other topics that obsess us, is certainly not ours alone. Very nearly as long as men have possessed comedies and tragedies, they have labored to explain to each other what it was they possessed; it has never seemed "good enough" simply to luxuriate in the immediate pleasure which either tragedy or comedy affords. Thus, speculation on the natures of comedy and tragedy is a permanent as well as a twentieth-century topic. But our accent, as we discuss these problems, is not the accent of other centuries. We are not very deeply impressed by the useful distinctions between the mechanics of the two forms; nor does the insight that one form moves us to tears and the other stirs us to laughter seem to take us to the heart of the question.

That the insights of earlier men into tragedy and comedy do not satisfy us may be an oblique reflection of a parlous condition; so be it. We have not the soundness and health to rest satisfied with the perceptions of difference that other men have found clarifying. With us, the tragedy-comedy difference has become not a question of dramaturgy or of surface-level psychology. It has become closely entwined with the religious question as it too is debated among us. Indeed, one of our recurrent suspicions is that the tragedy-comedy question is in fact the religious question. (This suspicion, I shall show, is part-right, part-wrong.) Such a suspicion once would have been termed sacrilegious since it mingles sacred and profane. It is a suspicion that now is inacceptable to some parties to the tragedy-comedy discussion for very different reasons; for it hints that there persists, for man, an area apart, an area of the sacred, on which tragedy and comedy impinge.

It is strange but true that to say that drama is closely allied with the sacred stirs, in our times, resistance not from the clergy, who now draw freely on terms proper to dramatic discussion to cast light on religious mysteries; the resistance comes from hard-headed students of the drama who want to peg the discussion at a level that reflects Aristotle or that records "actual practice" or that traces the better-known and more obvious human responses to both tragedy and comedy. But these hard-headed efforts but prolong the confidence that drama is an utterly secular activity, one that has no tangential relations with religion—one that, in consequence, will be in no way illuminated by an association with religion, with myth and cult. This resistance, as it persists among us, is chiefly useful as astringent to all sorts of discussion of drama that hints or announces that the play and the theatre constitute one of the few sacred activities left to us. Criticism that refuses to trace analogies between drama and myth is certainly limiting, but it is certainly less misleading than an interpretation of the drama that finds it a valid surrogate for all that used to go under the name of religion.

Our relation to the drama, the drama's possible goods for us in this century, are described correctly by neither of the extremes just mentioned. A fair account of the situation of nineteenth- and twentieth-century man in relation to the drama is this: By the unfolding "logic" of Western intellectual growth, the forms of the sacred that seemed real and compulsive in many centuries—that indeed enabled earlier men to treat drama and other forms of art as manifestly secular—lost their power to stir the majority of cultivated minds. Thus, the present sense of many persons that drama, at least, is sacred and is in clear opposition to the emptiness of modern life is a sense which records an interesting shift in the meaning of the words *sacred* and *secular. Sacred* once referred to the portion of human life in which revealed truth, offered us by a church, made specific demands on us and gave us specific aids, and the secular was just that portion of life that seemed free of those demands and not dependent on those aids. This traditional division—once drama had reached the inn-yard or princely halls—definitely regarded both comedy and tragedy as secular creations. The drama was an amusement, a distraction, an activity on which the church did not "move in" except when stirred by excess of indecency or atheism. To us, this assignment of the drama to a secular realm seems less obvious. We partake of a general intellectual atmosphere in which the sacred (to put the matter mildly) is not hedged securely against the secular; the secular so occupies our waking thoughts that we may even regard the realm of the sacred as a pious fiction rather than as a going reality. And some of us find that the real sacred (if indeed it does exist) flourishes in an activity that men used confidently to regard as secular; we find the sacred in music or art or—as here—the drama with its power to light up our existence, to criticize or transform our secular boredom.

Those who find that drama is, for modern man, a locus of the sacred are a rather mixed company. Skeptics, workers in depth psychology, liturgists, ordinarily devout persons—these unlikely companions share what I have called a twentieth-century topical debate, the degree of sacredness in drama, and find they respond to the effects of drama—effects that they find peculiar and haunting. The traditional sacred is gone or—we suspect with varying emotions—is on the point of leaving us. We discover with relief that what we are about to lose is "really" available to us elsewhere—in the drama, for example.

Before we accept this discovery as fact, we ought to ask whether the relation between drama and religion, drama and myth, is one of essential identity or one of similarity. It is my feeling that the relation is one of similarity: a similarity that must be studied since it is deep, persistent, and illuminating to both drama and religion. Drama is no surrogate for myth and cult, but what it offers us finds partial explanation in what myth and cult have offered men.

So long as drama had, for its undoubted locus, the region of the secular, questions about tragedy and comedy, about their common root and their differences, were debated in what one must now regard as a dry, bright atmosphere. There is something cold as well as competent, insensitive as well as clear, in the treatment Aristotle and others accorded the tragedy they knew. It is plain that many modern persons, skeptics as well as believers, find a more tremendous, more "sacred" import in tragedy than Aristotle found. (By extension, we find the same sort of import in comedy.) Rightly or wrongly, we are drawn by the dark uncertainties which drama embodies; and if this is our taste, we will experience no satisfaction when we read critics who wrote in other centuries and could reduce both tragedy and comedy to bright certainties, who looked to the playhouse for mechanically clever vehicles that enforced the moral platitudes of an era. Yet if both comedy and tragedy indeed do more, if they constantly draw us back toward their two Western sources of origin—the church chancel or the sacred grove—this covert filiation is a source of irritation to students who are willing to concede that drama is powerful and yet maintain that drama's "real" climate is certainly the climate of secular life: life untouched in any way by the sacred. Persons who feel that the "real" locus of drama has always been the sacred—or, the contention here, displays a close similarity to the sacred—turn from matters of construction, turn from the rise and fall of fashion in dramatic form, to the *effects* of viewed drama that pass beyond amusement and such superficial categories of criticism as realism, naturalism, and romanticism.

Yet is not this latter interest in drama, if uncritically followed, but a pursuit of surrogates for the conventional forms of the sacred: the church, its ritual, its body of organized dogma? Doubtless. We would not be impelled to isolate the sacred in drama did we not have some qualms about the conventional locus of the sacred. If we are devout, our study of drama is probably an attempt to win intellectual confirmation for truths that we still believe but which we find no longer self-confirming. And if we are skeptical, our study of drama proceeds with more passion still; drama does not just explain and validate the sacred—a religion that we persist in believing. Instead, drama *is* the sacred.

Both these approaches to the sacred—or, as I believe, the *resemblance* to the sacred—in the drama are partisan approaches. What is the sacred if we define it (as we now try to) not in terms of a church of a lapsed tradition? One ought to be able to define the sacred in terms of human action, or at least attempt to. The sacred is "created"—exists for us and probably becomes available to other persons who are in any way like us—by any gesture or word which makes a total assertion. Any word or gesture which offers, to our own awareness and the awareness that we are able to reach, some insight about what existence collectively *is*—this is a sacred word or announcement rather than a secular one. In contrast, a secular utterance concerns itself with some smaller portion of experience; neither actually nor by implication does it describe some aspect of the total act of existing. It is concerned with conveying facts, practical procedures under certain explicit circumstances, or—at its most ambitious—short-range predictions.

This distinction between what is sacred and what is secular does not rest on the authority of a particular revelation or the encrusted, polychrome prestige of a religious tradition. Rather do all churches and traditions rest on such a distinction; and all revolts against church and tradition are in essence (whatever they are accidentally, as *specific* protests) denials that the distinction between sacred and secular, between total assertion and what we may call partial assertion is a valid one. (The revolts usually express an understandable bitterness with some of the applications of the sacred, of total assertions; they do not usually envisage their own result: a denial that any total assertion whatever is valid. Yet this is the uneasy course that, in part, has created our present question.)

The peculiar twentieth-century attitude toward drama, whether it is developed in a skeptic or a believer, is testimony that the distinction between total assertion, the sacred, and partial assertion, the secular, is one that, at least, haunts us. It is felt that one sort of gesture and assertion—here, drama—has an impact and validity different from another kind of gesture and assertion—say, a radio commercial praising a dentifrice.

So viewed, the contrast between the sacred and the secular makes little reference to church and tradition; the contrast rests on a juxtaposition of two sorts of direct experience. A sacred assertion—whether it be couched in myth, performed in rite, codified in dogma or (as some of us seem to suspect) enacted in significant drama—is a total assertion. It asserts what man's life is, and it cannot be demonstrated as true; it can be only accepted or rejected as true. A secular assertion is an observation of fact. It is a reference to a physical fact that can readily be checked; it makes—less clearly, we will admit if we are at all reflective—some observation about comparatively small phases of society, and offers us ways of seeming to manage "small" areas of human social and moral relations. When we are secularized, when we congratulate ourselves (if that is our mood) that the sacred has been driven from our lives, we believe that we are freed of the burden and the nonsense of making total assertions or of listening to discourses based on the total assertions that men "like us" have made in the past.

There are many reasons why such freedom is to be desired. For many decades, secular evangelists, working in the spirit of Lucretius, have impellingly pled with us to give up a frustrating taste for total assertion; man can (the evangel runs) live better by partial assertions. We can always check partial assertions, whether they be scientific laws or the little useful rules of thumb by which "actually" we conduct our societies and personal affairs. Yet we should never cease to observe—and this is what drives us back to drama or art or music as possible loci of the sacred—that secular evangelists offer us at least one total assertion, at least one *sacred* statement: that man *ought* to be willing to live by partial or secular assertions. Whether this one unavoidable, irreducible total assertion—the assertion that makes possible the cancellation of the sacred—is true, right, and correct we cannot say; faced with it, we are in as much doubt as we are when we face any of the other total, sacred assertions about man and his destiny. Perhaps we do well when we hesitate to accept it as bindingly true. At least, the current plunge into the depths harbored by comedy and tragedy may indicate that the sacred resembles proverbial truth: crushed to earth at a particular point, it rises vigorously elsewhere. But what would St. Augustine and other foes of secular spectacle think if they were to learn that a quasi-sacred light shines behind the theatrical proscenium?

Despite resemblances, it is stupid—it is, I believe, indefensible—to maintain that drama proffers to man *all* the effects of the sacred. Likewise, it is misleading to press too far the analogy between full religious activity, "pegged" to a myth, and the public performance of a play. Church-harbored rite and theatre-harbored drama have their rich similarities, similarities which I shall explore. But it is useless to wring final drops from perceived similarities that, say, draw *Oedipus Rex* and a religious rite toward each other. Music and art and drama *and* church-harbored rite may be akin since, in our terms, they all make inclusive rather than partial statements about life. But not all inclusive statements are the same statement. These various "statements," moreover, exist within unlike media, which make possible effects that are different although they may supplement each other intimately. Beethoven's Ninth may give us a feeling of transcendence (indeed, it does); it may give us the feeling that our ears have now listened to the music of the spheres and that our minds, for once, encompass the universe. But all this encompassing is not the precise encompassing that religious rite makes possible, when at a gesture from the priest we come forward to drink from a cup rather than—in response to Beethoven's invitation as celebrant—to immerse ourselves in a wonderful sea of harmony. Likewise, a retablo in a well-lighted art gallery is not a retablo in the Cathedral at Seville. A changed context has altered a powerful religious object into a powerful work of art; on the gallery wall, it has become something new, for, cut off from the gestures of the priest, the imprecision of cathedral light, and the mélange of cathedral odors pleasant and nauseous, the retablo addresses us in a different way. The way is still sacred since the effect the art-object, the retablo, creates is an inclusive one; it makes a total assertion. But it is not the inclusive effect to which it once contributed an essential note in a Spanish chapel.

The retablo's history can be our clue to the limitations we ought to impose on any discussion of the sacred in drama. Drama, let us concede, abounds in the sacred as here defined; it is indeed a sacred that can be studied in relation to the sacred of rite and myth. Modern criticism of drama abounds in overassertions on this point; and these overassertions but testify to a slightly frantic desire to offset religious *accidie*. No less than the Ninth Symphony and the Spanish retablo on the gallery wall does drama make total assertions. But they can never be identical with the assertions mediated to man by the complex of myth, rite, and dogma that makes up any "church." Consider the retablo on the gallery wall. It does not cease to make some of the total assertions it made in a chapel. But its assertions become involved in a different context of effect. The new context, let me insist, is not an unworthy one. (What is more essential to a full, even a sacred, existence than comprehension of the nuances and the mergings of styles of visual assertion that the skillfully displayed retablo offers us?) But it is not the same context. Vision is the "faculty" that the retablo always appealed to and always will appeal to. But a changed context—museum rather than chapel—has certainly altered the assertion that is mediated. In the chapel we "saw" this assertion: Existence finds its sum and center in a figure extended on several pieces of wood. In the gallery we "see" something like this: Existence finds its meaning in the competence of a creative and ingenious mind that is able to fuse—completely and for eternity—shades of color, given "real" objects (a body and a cross), and the lines that reproduce on a flat surface the colors and shapes of nature. This is not a contemptible fusion; it is, in my sense, sacred. But it is not the still more complex fusion that once took place in the Spanish chapel.

The analogy provided by the two states of the retablo is clear.

Drama has great power, like the retablo in the museum, to remind us of what was, for many centuries, regarded as the sole locus of the sacred: the church, the temple-cave, the sacred grove. Drama rests on narrative, just as religious ceremonial rests on narrative (or myth). But we are too quick to say that drama gives to us—because of this and other resemblances—the essential of what has been, for "historical reasons," lost to us: the assertions that came to man in church or cave or grove. To insist on this perception of difference is not to attempt to discredit drama; it is the first step toward a precise definition of what drama does indeed make available to us.

If drama gives the sacred, it does not give the complete sacred assertion if our standard is (as it should be) the experience of the religious person rather than (as it often is), the experience of the person who feels religious while he is in the theatre. When this is the emphasis, it is drama that is teaching us (if we are interested) what religion is. Nor does it do this badly if we do not posit an identity between the two, if we do not suppose that one of the two (here religion) is expendable. (This is Cromwell's heresy toward drama in reverse.) At the present stage of our scrutiny of the topic (What is drama? What are the relations between tragedy and comedy?), there may be profit in sending drama to school to religion instead of religion to school to drama. (It is this latter relation that is set up when we say that the viable elements of religion "live on" in drama. It is the thesis of this essay that, whatever the resemblances, neither activity can hope to "live on" in the other.)

What do these two vehicles of total assertion have in common? Most strikingly, gesture and costume. Gesture and costume alike set the priest apart from his congregation and the personages of a drama from *their* congregations. Also in common, the two vehicles have a story. But the differences are at once apparent. How soon costume and gesture become inalterable in a "church," and how quickly the abundance of story that human fancy can supply becomes only one or two stories! And in drama—whatever its roots in old rite—how comparatively free is the range of costume and gesture, and how endlessly abundant—though this lies only on the surface—is the combination of represented event!

There are, however, differences just as immediate and striking. Religion "aspires" toward a state of fixity; drama exists—survives even—only by displaying a *superficial* ferment of change and innovation. How can we say that drama and religion are the same? A drama that does not produce new formulas dies, and a religion that lives in an unceasing ferment of innovation is (we usually judge) on its way to death. Let these differences be acknowledged then. For it is an acknowledgment that should make us quite humble about theories that "explain" the origin of the drama in religion; how could that which had to be conservative to survive (religion) "beget" that which has to be innovating to survive (drama)? Is not the history of Greek drama, conservative though it be by our standards, a series of innovations? Is not the failure of Greek religion, its tendency to respond to novel modes of thought, a negative testimony to the root-fixity of that sacred which we call religion?

But over and above this difference and beyond the similarity of gesture and costume that does not take our understanding very far, there is this resemblance that, first, casts a light on drama in general and, second, casts a most startling light on what has always been a key question: the difference between comedy and tragedy. The resemblance is this: *Religion and drama both rest on narrative.*

What narrative is in drama we presume we know. That we may presume too much—that we may be too sure that we know what narrative "does" in a play—will not be clear to us until we make an attempt to be more precise about its religious analogue, myth. A myth is simply a narrative that a cult *happens* to employ for the purpose of making an over-all assertion about man's experience of existing. Further, religion makes not one but two distinct uses of narrative material, uses that we will presently be explicit about. These two distinct uses are a sure clue to the two distinct sorts of drama, tragedy and comedy. This correspondence once perceived, we are far on our way to answering two questions: How are we to explain the coexistence of tragedy and comedy? (Answer: The coexistence is explained *by analogy* to the two uses made of narrative by cult.) How are we to explain the effects—often contradictory—of tragedy and comedy on us? How—to rephrase this second question—may we state, in some approximation to rational assertion, the permanently moving power of the logically contradictory allover assertions that drama provides us with?

It is plain that in answering the question about the coexistence of comedy and tragedy we shall be explaining an effect in terms of its origin (an origin resembling if not identical with the two sorts of use of myth by religion that we shall identify). It is also plain that an explanation of the permanently moving power of the logical opposites, tragedy and comedy, must be a psychological explanation, an explanation that draws on one's insight into human reactions *now*. Yet the two answers are finally identical if one assumes—as I do—that there has been no great change in man himself—that the men whose expectations in a sense "created" the two forms, tragedy and comedy, are not altogether unlike the men who, in this century, continue to "demand" (if only in debased forms) both the laughable and the frightening.

Let us, as lovers of drama or as esteemers of the *effects* of drama, seek to be instructed by the two uses of myth that we can observe in developed religions. For in these two uses are both the roots of comedy and tragedy and the rationale of their persisting appeal.

If religion has any distinguishing mark, it is this: it is an allover assertion about the existence in which man is involved. (Magic is no such allover assertion. It is not so much science before science as pragmatics before pragmatics.) Logically, one would expect that there would be, in religion, only one allover assertion. But logic is a minor though not utterly absent element in religion and in drama; whatever their differences, both religion and drama must be faithful to existence first and only secondarily faithful to a pursuit of order. Thus, from the point of view of logic, a religious statement about the complete nature of reality, a statement made in terms of myth and cherished by cult, "ought" to make other statements of a similar nature impossible of assertion. Logic would suggest this question: if existence "at its heart" is thus and so, is it likely that the very same existence is "at its heart" something quite different? Yet developed religions make two such assertions, not one—assertions logically opposed to each other and cancelling.

One must, however, insist that religion does not proliferate uselessly contradictory statements about what is the total existence (its nature, its place for man) which we experience. But most developed religions find place for the following two (and contradictory) statements about existence. Logic would cancel one or the other, and we indeed find that systematizers of religion and secular systematizers of insights that have a religious origin if not at present a religious context struggle to cancel one of the two allover statements as a false or as an obscure form of the other statement. But these efforts overlook this truth: that both religion and drama are primarily records of man existing rather than of man trying to put his existence into comprehensible order. Religion and drama share this function; they enable man to *endure* existing, whereas philosophy and (in an often delusive way) science offer man the prospect of *comprehending* existence. Religion and drama are not interchangeable, despite certain present hopes. But one of the signs that they address themselves to the same task is that both are involved in advancing, at the same time, contradictory assertions about man and his existence. (That is, portions of a religious ritual make assertions that later portions cancel, logically. Comedy makes assertions about existence which tragedy always casts doubt on.)

Religion rests on a narrative. From the narrative may be drawn doctrines exceedingly abstract and indeed opposed to an esteem for narrative, for time-contained event, as the primary means of revelation (e.g., Buddhism). But what religion latterly becomes (and not all developed religions become the same thing) is not our interest here. Our interest must concern itself with how religion "began"—at least, "began" when it reached a point at which it supplemented its direct perceptions of numen—the wonderful, the pervasively compulsive—with narrative. The contrast between Greek religion, which richly supplemented its perceptions of the numinous with narrative and Latin religion which simply preserved, for several historical centuries, the perception of numen suggests that man did—at some unrecorded time in some civilizations—build into the structure of religion key-narratives that came to bear the great weight of religious superstructure—the weight of cult, rite, and dogma.

What were the two uses to which narrative was put at this point in the growth of religion—a point early, real, but mostly unrecoverable? They are sharply contrasting uses. They are uses that record two logically opposed insights which man came to have about his position in the world. Both insights are valid and real; they may be incompatible with each other, but they are not, by that circumstance, either to be disregarded or discredited. Man created and used mythological narrative for these two purposes: he asserted that existence, in its root organization, was *cyclic*; he asserted that existence—and this was an unconscious criticism of his cyclic assertion—was not what he had at first thought it but was, instead, *linear*.

We shall presently define and distinguish these two assertions. Let us grant at once the logical contradiction—indeed, to many, the puerility—involved in entertaining these two assertions simultaneously. It is plain that once the opposition between these two assertions is clearly perceived, many persons will judge that they have one more reason to dismiss the authority of religious experience. One may concede that such persons move in intellectual regions that are less demanding on the sympathetic imagination—regions that have their own sort of profit. But such persons are cut off from the profit that is the gift to man of religion and myth, and they are also in a poor position to measure the conflicting endowments, to man, of tragedy and comedy. These persons are not likely to see the significance of the likewise perplexing fact that tragedy and comedy are also logical incompatibles that coexist and that are intimately related in ways that vex and elude. Both tragedy and comedy are representations of experience; both mediate comprehension of experience. Are these two acts of comprehension so opposed to each other as to coexist only senselessly, as do random acts? Or do they have a supplementing function as they present their opposed visions of the universe? One form gives us the universe as a place suffused with laughter (*sustained* by laughter, we shall see); the other gives us the universe as a place falling in pieces, all props awry, "all coherence gone." Tragedy and comedy—the preliminary answer must be—constitute an uneasy unity: drama. But their coexistence *is* a unity and not an accident, not "random" coexistence, as above. And we can best understand the supplementary functions of these humanly contrived narratives—narratives that constantly vary on the surface—by seeking the analogy that links them with the two *uses* of myth that we discover in many developed religions.

As noted, what we present is an analogy only. Yet it is an analogy that (I believe) puts our ideas about comedy and tragedy in better order. Yet it is an analogy valid at only one point; it concerns only the two contrasting *uses* to which myth is put in religion and the two contrasting trains of reaction, of sensibility and induced comment, which the two forms of drama can stir in man. To make no mystery: comedy has its religious analogue in the *cyclic* assertions that myth enables religion to make, and tragedy finds its analogue in the noncyclic, *linear* assertions that myth sometimes supports. I would deny utterly the truth or usefulness of the analogy were it pushed beyond this point—were it argued that the myth that "asserts cycle" is comic *in substance* and that the myth that asserts the linear perception tragic in substance. There is no comedy-tragedy contrast by which one can divide the abundance of myth. The *story* of Osiris and the *story* of Jesus—it has often been observed—resemble each other. Certainly the story of Osiris, a story that is the vehicle of a cyclic assertion, is not comic; it is quite as grim as the story of Jesus which, I judge, mediates a linear assertion. The story of Osiris "happened" to be "captured" by a religion which, at a particular time, needed to "assert cycle"; and the story of Jesus happened to be put to use as a narrative support to a linear, noncyclic insight about existence. (The bulk of myth—of narrative that exists and functions to some degree in a religious context—asserts cycle. But the normal is not a binding norm; there is nothing abnormal about a story that a religion uses to express a linear insight about man's life. To my mind, the story of the "white god" Quetzalcoatl—the god who abandons his people *once* and promises a single return—asserts the linear almost as forcefully as does the narrative about Jesus.)

Deeper in drama, then—if the analogy I am drawing has real power to cast light—than the contrast between the laughable and the "weepable" is this one: comedy is a representation of life that asserts cycle (as does the bulk of myth), and tragedy is that representation of life that asserts the linear, the noncyclic. The laughter that, rightly, we associate with comedy is important but surface testimony to the fact that we have cause to rejoice when we contemplate the totality of existence as cycle; the tears that we shed for tragedy, the qualm that tragedy is said to stir, is a natural by-product of the perception that total existence is not cyclic at all—at least, not cyclic when it concerns us most intimately.

Comedy and tragedy, then, are secular purveyors—I mean no

disrespect by the word—of two allover assertions about the root-nature of existence as man must experience it. (In *one* of these two ways he must experience it; he has no further choice.) The *materials* of comedy and tragedy do often differ much more than do the narrative materials that constitute the two sorts of myth. But, as often observed, what really distinguishes comedy from tragedy is the treatment accorded the materials that come to hand. It would not be impossible to alter *Oedipus Rex* into a knock-about farce, nor would it be difficult to transform Malvolio into a figure of devastating import, particularly were one writing a naturalistic or sociological tragedy. The imperfect religious analogue to all this is what we have already noted: that the narrative that becomes myth does not automatically proclaim whether it will be cyclic or linear; *that* is determined by the kind of existence it takes on in a specific religious context.

What are the distinguishing marks of these two allover assertions, the cyclic and the linear?

Let us begin their precise definition thus. When we say that myth asserts two allover insights into existence, we are concerned with existence collectively perceived and *not* discriminated. "Early man" had many of the powers of discriminatory judgment that we have; that is, he could look sensibly at *portions* of existence. Aspects of his arts, the bulk of his "civil law" and the conduct of his economy are sufficient records of this. But he—no more than can we—could not escape making a collective or allover assertion about the world in which he was immersed. Nor is the "advance of human thought" —as modern drama, for one, obliquely testifies—from collective assertions to assertions that are more modest, more discriminated. Indeed, without a collective assertion of some kind, discrimination itself ceases; and this is just as true in a secular context as in a religious one. What we regard as the "advance of human thought" is simply a substitution of a later and more logically defensible collective assertion for an earlier one. The later assertion may be more valid, more soundly based. But that is not the point here. What we must perceive is that our "advance" has not freed our thought from the task of making total assertions not completely unlike the early religious cyclic and linear assertions.

Respect for them established, one may attempt a genetic explanation of the two mythological assertions that (I believe) casts great light on the way tragedy and comedy still function for us. A genetic explanation is not exhaustive; and, in this instance, it involves this bold hypothesis: that we can reproduce the intellectual and emotional growth of early man. What we say firmly on such a topic, we should also say modestly. But we need not abandon the effort; it is no more bold than the genetic efforts of literary scholars who speak of the formative attention of "Shakespear's audience"—it is no more risky than the discourses on medieval pity that "explain" certain beautiful tensions at Chartres.

Man was first aware—and to this ancient scriptures are witness—of that which bore in on him from outside. He was aware of the great forces of nature as he saw them in wind and wave and weather; he was aware of his terrible dependence on the fertility of grassland and arable field. And he was just as deeply impressed by the social forces that weighed on him: his family, his tribe, his tribal enemies. To assume as early man did that these outside forces—nature and the collective groups—made up each man's existence is to assume truly; it is also to assume incompletely, as religion after religion discovered at some point in its course.

Yet this incomplete assumption—that man's existence is composed of the awful natural and social forces that toss man about—"created" as its corollary an assertion made in terms of myth rather than, as here, in terms of abstract concept. Man employed myth for this reason: man must be more than the victim of the forces that are outside him; he must be their *imaginative* master. It is not enough to discriminate these external forces and come to a competent control of *some* of them. The nascent arts of agriculture did not free man from the need of myths about the forces of growth; the early and perhaps relatively satisfactory codes of law did not obviate the preservation of myths about the "origin" of law; and successful magic and medicine was never a threat to the inclusive assertions of religion. In short, all the practical control and knowledge of what bore in on man had to be supplemented by assertions that provided man *imaginative* allover control. This control was provided by myths that, whatever their variety, were put to one task, the task of asserting cycle; they were man's warrant over and above his own observation for the recurrence of season and crop and for the persistence (despite the aging of all men and the death of leaders) of a given and experienced social form. It was myth and rite that could assure men that what man could not control was, in the long run, as much to be depended on as what he could control; natural and social phenomena would be exactly what man already knew them to be. Nature and society, myth testified, would always come full circle, would offer apprehensive man familiarity and not novelty. Man used, for example, the myth of Osiris to give himself this cyclic assurance. Osiris, we know, dies not once but many times; his scattered members are gathered by Isis in a basket again and again—in fact, year after year, so long as the society that uses the myth of Osiris persists. Mr. Joseph Campbell, in *The Hero with a Thousand Faces,* has revealed to us the impressive and yet monotonous use to which certain narrative materials were once put; the "thousand faces" are really the face of one hero. Beneath surface variety, the hero offers man the assurance of a *recurrent* salvation, of security in nature and in society that can never be really threatened by natural catastrophe or military invasion. The myth always repeats itself and is *cyclic.* If Osiris eternally dies and eternally is brought back to life, each man can feel secure: his plot of land will bear again, and the tribe or society to which he belongs will survive any temporary perils. Thanks to the myth, man is in calm imaginative control of what actually is beyond his just-nascent science and his nonexistent sociology.

Is Christ Osiris? Is he too a vegetation god, a supporter of cycle? Not to those who cherished his story. Yet the bold outlines of his story are similar to the Osiris narrative; for this, some persons call him the last and most triumphant of the Asia Minor vegetation deities. On the basis of narrative materials, there is no utterly conclusive way of repudiating the similarity. But what one may deny—concerning Christ, concerning Quetzacoatl as well—is that the Christ-story was put to the use the Osiris story was put to. A central Christian phrase refers to Christ as "our sacrifice once offered"; whatever the contradictory implications of certain Christian rituals, a sense that Christ did indeed die only once and rise only once remains at the heart of the Christian assertion and is opposed to the sense that lies at the heart of the Osiris mystery and similar mysteries.

Genetically speaking, what "begot" the Christian assertion? It was a second total perception of what existence was. After he had gained imaginative control of what lay outside him, man became aware of himself. He could express this awareness of himself only by uttering—with the aid of some myth—a total assertion that, logically, but not actually, cancelled the cyclic assertion. (There are few developed religions in which the two assertions do not persist as peers.) When man turns to himself, he "knows" that what myth and cult have, to that point, told him either is not true or is very incompletely true. Nature and society are eternally dying and eternally reborn: let that stand. But man himself—man apart from the great processes that very nearly have him at their utter mercy—man is eternally dying and he never will be reborn.

What is this second total assertion which the story of Christ, as well as other stories, implements? The assertion that man's existence is in time, historical. The assertion that to man *as man* (as opposed to man when he is plainly the creature of natural and social forces) the same event, the same choice, never comes round again. Man as man makes a choice among a series of events that follow each other in a nonrepeating sequence; he has only one chance to make a certain choice since the time for a certain choice comes only once. As man, his experience is basically linear however much he may be, as an object, subject to the effects of natural and social cycle. As a cyclically oriented creature, man plants a crop at a certain time of the year and rethatches his house against the monsoons, and also prepares himself for the public fasts and the public rejoicings peculiar to his society. These come round again and again. But man comes to see that such preparations are not *all* his destiny or even a finally distinguishing part. He is, at the center of his nature, a creature of time, of *line*; and he and his forebears were, at the least, misled when they found the clue to human nature in what, in some sense, lay outside each separate man: in nature and the social group. The essential lies inside each man, in his experience of choice, of sequence; hence, the second total assertion, the one we have called the *linear* one.

The essential—we should observe when we watch *Hamlet* or *Oedipus* as well as when we savor the impact of the Christ-story—lies inside each man; it lies in man's experience of a horrid, sheerly linear necessity which no man, once he is aware of it, is ever able to evade. This is the necessity of choice; it is a necessity that gets no comforting "moral support" from the phases of the moon or the return of a season. Each human choice, at a certain time in a nonrepetitive sequence of events, projects into future time only a certain portion of the past; each choice denies to the future significant developments of other portions of the past. This is human choice; it is also existence conceived in a linear fashion.

This allover perception sought—and, of course, found—an august warrant. Not just the Jesus-myth itself but the whole body of what used to be called "sacred history" constituted a widely embracing myth that detached itself from the bulk of ancient myth and its cyclic assertions. The bulk of story that we may call the Christian myth—as well as groups of story that have some resemblance to it—braced man for the assertion that is just as essential to his health as is the earlier assertion of cycle. The linear assertion is, I believe, a record of a later, a more subtle, and certainly a more intimate reading of man's position in the world since it sees that man as a person, an individual, has an "economy" for which there are very few clues and models outside man. Why was this insight comparatively late in coming? Because what was outside man first rushed in on human awareness promising inclusive instruction. (And the cyclic instruction is one that man has never been able to dispense with.) But insofar as man has discovered individuality and personality, he has involved himself in myths that limit if they do not cancel the assurances of cyclic legend. A god that dies only once "answers" to man's more subtle analysis of the conditions of human action (as opposed to the conditions of natural event to which man was first eager to assimilate human action.) A god that dies only once, a god that does not enjoy the easy luxury of dying again and again, a god that traces the arc of choice only once—that god is a human god. His myth is a warrant for our most painful perceptions about what it is to be a human being rather than a tide that rushes up the shore or a society that persists even though its members unimportantly perish.

The point of the analogy between cyclic and linear myth on the one hand and comedy and tragedy on the other now shapes up. Comedy, on a nonreligious level, offers man the assurance that he can bank on the universe and its laws and, more importantly, on society and its structure. As does the myth that asserts cycle, comedy offers the individual the illusion that he exists and moves in a universe he can count on. This illusion, when it is effectively held, is a cause for rejoicing; it is a cause for *laughter*. It was in this sense that Dante wrote a *Comedy*; his poem was, at the last, an assurance of order—to be sure, an order of a complex kind. Even more ordinary comedy makes available to man some of the comforts that early man drew from religiously "asserting cycle." The comic narrative—in materials gulfs apart from the Osiris legend but in effect quite close to it—must, like *all* narratives, embody an upset, a threat to our sense of certainty. Farce or high comedy—the effect is the same. What is the archetypical plot? A shift of forces, a social realignment, threatens the security of the chief persons on the stage—threatens *our* security. Comedy, it appears, has its qualms as well as tragedy. But the qualm is allayed by a combination of strategies that disassociates comedy from tragedy. For it is soon clear that the threat is neither serious nor permanently effective. It is a trivial threat, no more, to the status quo—to what we would call in religious terms the continuance of cycle. And it is also soon clear that the persons involved are not full, real persons like ourselves. They are "comic"; in religious language, they have only that degree of reality that marks a cyclic interpretation of man's experience—they are not sufficiently alive to qualify or even shatter that view. Since the characters in a comedy are incomplete, they easily loom before us as quasi-ritual figures who march through the events of the comic play as unconcernedly as did the King of Egypt when he performed his yearly role of Osiris in the New Year festivals.

What is all that comedy offers us? It is certainly not a contemptible "all." It is simply an "all" that is inferior to the "all" that tragedy offers us, just as the "all" of Egyptian religion is at once valid and yet distinctly inferior to the gifts of a religion that has strong linear marks. In fact, all that comedy offers us is a *sense of regain*. The comic "qualm"—the "situation," the misunderstanding, the threat of someone's security—threatens the status quo in a way that is sometimes playful and sometimes serious. But very few comedies leave us with anything but a sense that the status quo has been essentially re-established. The happy ending reasserts the security of the important characters; much more important, their individual security amounts to a promise that well-known social forms will persist. The effect of cycle, put slightly in doubt, has, with the descent of the last curtain, been established more firmly than ever.

And as audience we have *regained* the security, personal and social, that the initial dramatic situation playfully threatened. We are, as characters, where we were at the commencement of the play, or where we deserved to be. The society to which we, as audience, imaginatively belong has been "established" more firmly than ever. In a popular farce, it is the most obvious sort of conventional standards which have been threatened by (say) adultery or sharp business practice and which are, in the last insincere minutes of the play, refounded; in a play of Shaw's like *Candida* it is the society of the Shavian elect. The differences are there, but they do not, in our connection, count. *Parlor, Bedroom, and Bath* and *Candida* function for their different audiences in exactly the same way. They mediate—in an obscure secular way, I admit—a counterpart of the cyclic religious assurance. They tell us that there is a secure, predictable, and even recurrent place provided for man in the universe. Further, they tell us that man can exercise imaginative control over this universe. The threats to this control—the situation that troubles Act I—always turn out to be delusive; and the comic drama always terminates with man more in imaginative command of his universe than before.

Not so tragedy. Tragedy, like the linear total assertion which it resembles, is no play for imaginative control of the world; it is a confession, sometimes noble and sometimes desponding, that man's "game"—the "game" utterly proper to him—lies somewhere else. It is a perception that, for man, imaginative control of the world that is distinctly external to him is beside the point. And when we regard comedy from the vantage-point of tragedy, we see that what it offers man is not so much a sense of regain as an *illusion* of regain. Comedy keeps man domiciled—and fairly securely domiciled—in a world that he does not live in properly unless he wills to live in a contradictory world at the same time. Comedy offers man an illusory paradise: the paradise of imaginative control of what is outside man. But man is driven from this paradise by his dismaying discovery that he does not entirely belong there. He is driven out not by any flaming sword but by his own nature whose destiny it is to exercise choice and thus deny or qualify all cyclically based perceptions. For the reassuring continuum of cycle external to man, tragedy puts before us a discontinuity: man that chooses not to repeat, man that by his choice wills the unknown. Such a being is, from the cyclic point of view, a *lusus naturae,* one that taints and distorts the secure universe for which both Osiris and comedy stand. Were we to pair phrases, we might say that tragedy offers us a gift as permanent and pervasive as the comic sense of regain; it is a sense of loss, an awareness that man, in his most intimate activities, follows a line that leads only to darkness and an enigma—a line that will never curve back upon itself and so in the future confirm what it has been. The characteristic human act—that of choice—is closely allied with loss, even though we seem to choose to win something, to gain something. Choice, the specific linear activity, the activity that we see brought to sharp focus in Gethsemane and in the palace at Elsinore, always has for its ground-bass the note of loss. We turn our back on the joys we are certain of and might like to repeat, and we put ourselves in the trust of the future: a moment or an hour that we do not know but yet must count on—and we have willed to lose, if we must, the profit that can come to us from past moments: moments we have savored and could—did not choice intervene with its crucial break—still count on. Agony and death at some future time are but incidental marks of tragedy. The real agony, the real death, come at the moment when we choose; when, willing loss, we trust ourselves to an enigma; when we abandon the comic vein and cease counting on limited certainties. Not only is the crucifixion "a sacrifice once offered"; each crucial choice that marks a tragic drama is such a sacrifice, for it is loss of the world that the cyclic temper would preserve as man's great comfort and support. Whatever the upshot of tragic choice, whatever temporary palliatives and patent compensations may move toward us, the fact persists: we have given up or, at least, qualified a very useful insight into man's experience, the comic insight, the insight that we have compared with the cyclic assertions certain myths have made. In comedy the world we inhabit is but playfully threatened; by the end of the play, it is refounded more firmly than before. But in tragedy, as if in accord with its linear, nonreversible nature, choice threatens the world, the status quo, in deadly earnest. In choice, we do not know with much confidence what it is we shall create; we know with grim certainty what it is that we destroy: our happiness, our security—in short, our confidence in a future that follows—or seems to follow—cyclic laws.

Both tragic insight and the religious assertion that we call linear are not easy to endure, whether we arrogate to them exclusive truth or confess sadly that the comic or the cyclic insights are true also. Christians have permitted themselves the alleviation of encrusting their linear faith with recurrent ritual that prolongs, throughout the "Christian year," a necessary minimum of cyclic illusion. And, when we draw back from the blank that is choice and act in time, in linear succession, we may turn back to comedy which, in its way, represents our human lot if not our essential human lot. One way to endure tragedy, on the stage and off, is to listen to some of the things that comedy tells us when it speaks of "fundamental decency" and the recurrence of events and their correspondence to an understandable, definable order.

It is plain that there is nothing "wrong" with a penchant for comedy; tragedy is "truer" than comedy (it is a more penetrating comment on our lot) but it is less endurable. This relation between the truth of the two dramatic forms also gains light from the comparable religious tension. There is nothing "wrong" about the persistence of cyclic insights in a religion basically linear (e.g., the Christian). A perception that, at the centers of our being, we exist linearwise can never cancel the truth that in relation to external forces we live under a cyclic dispensation. What is perhaps "wrong" is a reworking of the two religious insights that deprives either of its proper authority. This is the chief heresy that Western eyes find in Buddhism: the denial that both recurrence and unique event have high significance in man's life.

Finally, all that tragedy offers us in the audience is loss or deprivation: the possibility of becoming something that we have not yet been. If tragedy offers us a gain, it is a gain that is, unlike the comic gain, incalculable. If the tragedy we watch is real tragedy and not deterministic tragedy, which has the *events* of tragedy but the *certainty* of comedy, we live for a while lives from which the cyclic effects have fallen away or have received into the background.

Comedy occurs at any moment (it has the effect, if not the actuality, of being repeatable); tragedy occurs at only one moment: a moment that has come *this time* and that will never come again. It presents us with the spectacle of ourselves urged by the logic inherent in once-occurring events to make a choice. We cannot escape choice and responsibility for the choice which we make. Yet we make the choice without a full knowledge of the consequences. How can we, in a universe conceived in a linear way, have such knowledge? It is only in a cyclically conceived universe that we seem to have such knowledge. It is a knowledge which the other sort of drama strips from us.

For this reason, the tragic qualm—however purgation be explained—is never really purged. When we watch the acts of Oedipus and Hamlet and the results of those acts, the only comfort we draw is analogous to that which we get from a myth aligned with linear perceptions. Christ on the cross or Quetzalcoatl on his raft of serpents wrenches our eyes from a flattering and comforting view of our destinies as men. As men, we are apart from mountain and stream, we are apart from society collectively considered; we are—in all conventional or comic sense—apart from each other. We can find union only in the insight given to us by linear myth or by its analogue in tragic drama: that every moment is a crucifixion if we face it seriously. To do this we are most of the time incompetent. We would like to deny that we are Prince Hamlet. We would rather, along with Eliot's Prufrock, go to swell a crowd and there take refuge in sententious and (in our sense) "comic" remarks.

If we are correct, if the similarities between drama and religion are indeed striking, are we correct to oppose those who, directly or covertly, treat drama as a full surrogate for religious assertion? I think we are. The basic dissimilarity persists although it is not our duty here to study it. The religious context provides fixity and hence authority as the companions of the opposed total assertions, and drama provides a context of constant variety and change. This latter context will seem the correct and perhaps the only one to those who doubt that even the most sensitive and analytical attention to experience can win to binding answers. Such doubt is not hampering provided the doubter does not take the final step and observe that religion is really about the same thing as that which drama treats in two logically opposed ways. Religion, we should repeat, is "about" that which is sensed as permanently true; drama handles the permanently uncertain in what we see and recollect. All that the similarities we have traced here support is this observation: there are two sovereign ways of naming the impermanent and the fixed. Since these ways belong to both religion and drama, we are tempted to identify religion and drama. This we must refuse to do, for when we say "the same" we offer up, in the name of system and simplicity, discriminations rich, suggestive, and illogical that are a large part of the treasure that has been put into our hands.

TOPICS FOR DISCUSSION AND WRITING

1. What is the main thesis? What is the subject with which he is particularly concerned—the definition of myth, the definition of drama, the definition of comedy and tragedy? What does he affirm about this subject? Is there any sentence in the essay which expressly states his thesis?
2. How does Watts view the relationship between drama and myth? Does he approve of criticism that refuses to trace analogies between drama and myth? Does he approve of an interpretation of drama that finds it a valid substitute for religion?
3. What are some differences between sacred and secular assertions? Between religious and dramatic statements? What do religion and drama have in common?
4. How does he prove that differences exist between sacred and secular statements? Does he have a strong argument?
5. How does the use of narrative differ in tragedy and comedy?
6. How does he prove that his distinction between tragedy and comedy is valid—inductively, deductively, or some other way?
7. What does Watts consider to be the validity of myth? Would he agree with Carl Jung, in the first essay studied in this text, that myths are archetypal patterns? Would a reader who subscribed to Jung's theories consider the analogies underscored in this essay stronger arguments than someone who did not?
8. Write an essay comparing Watts' definition of tragedy as a linear progression and comedy as a cyclic progression with Spengler's view of history (p. 183). Do both Watts and Spengler mean the same when they use the idea of linear progression? Is there any evidence that Watts could have been influenced by Spengler? Would it be fair to apply Watts' definition of comedy to Spengler's conception of history? Does Spengler, in Watts' terms, see history as a comedy?

David Riesman

In 1948 David Riesman (1909–) began his research on the problem of defining the American character. He brought to bear a background which included a legal education, experience as a business executive, study of psychiatry, and some years of lecturing as a Professor of Sociology at the University of Chicago. When the results of his research were published in The Lonely Crowd *(1950), it immediately became a best seller. Ever since, its insights have been repeatedly used as a key to the understanding of problems in contemporary American civilization.*

One of the basic points of departure for the entire book was a distinction among three different kinds of civilizations and the kinds of character which tend to predominate in them. The first type of civilization was one wherein there is a high birth rate and a high death rate. Since there is doom for all, each person tends to follow in the footsteps of his predecessors, and the prevailing character type is guided by tradition (tradition-directed).

The second type of civilization is characterized by a high birth rate and a low death rate. Here there are more people than there are places in society to provide for them, so every individual has to try to find his own niche. The prevailing character type tends to be inner-directed, *to look within for guides to proper behavior in hitherto uncharted situations.*

The third type of civilization more common in Europe and the United States in the period preceding World War II, is characterized by a declining birth rate and a low death rate. In this advanced type of civilization, which is now to be found in some European countries, successful existence depends upon cooperation among the members of society. Consequently, the dominant character type tends to be other-directed. *He is a person who looks to his contemporaries for cues on how he should behave.*

In the following selection, Riesman tries to suggest by the use of analogies that the American character is other directed. The contemporary American scene, taken as a whole, would have presented too many complexities and possible diversions for the author to prove his point to a general audience. By using analogical situations which are simpler and easier to define, he can avoid the possible distractions of unessential details and focus on the essentials. His reduction of the American scene to three possible typological situa-

tions raises other problems, however, and the careful reader may want to ask himself about the accuracy and adequacy of the proposed analogies.

from THE LONELY CROWD *

The image of power in contemporary America presented in the preceding chapters will possibly not be easily recognized by the reader. Current discussions of power in America are usually based on a search for a ruling class (for instance, Burnham's discovery of the "managers," Mills's of the labor leaders and others), and Americans themselves, rather than being the mild and cooperative people we have portrayed, are, to many observers and to themselves, power-obsessed or money-mad or concerned with conspicuous display. Or, as in the parable I shall use to illustrate my argument, Americans are felt, and feel themselves, to be more like rivalrous Kwakiutl Indian chiefs and their followers, than like peaceable, cooperative Pueblo agriculturists. Perhaps by further pursuing these images of power and personality we may be able to clarify the discrepancies between political fact and political ideology dwelt on in preceding chapters.

Ruth Benedict's book, *Patterns of Culture,* describes in vivid detail three primitive societies: the Pueblo Indians of the southwest, the people of the Island of Dobu in the Pacific, and the Kwakiutl Indians of the northwest coast of America.[1]

The Pueblo Indians are pictured as a peaceable, cooperative society, in which no one wishes to be thought a great man and everyone wishes to be thought a good fellow. Sexual relations are taken with little jealousy or other violent response; infidelity is not severely punished. Death, too, is taken in stride, with little violent emotion; indeed, emotion is, in general, subdued. While there are considerable variations in economic status, there is little display of economic power and even less of political power; there is a spirit of cooperation with family and community.

[1] *Patterns of Culture* (Boston: Houghton Mifflin, 1934; reprinted New York: Pelican Books, 1946).

The Dobu, by contrast, are portrayed as virtually a society of paranoids in which each man's hand is against his neighbor's in sorcery, theft and abuse; in which husband and wife alternate as captives of the spouse's kin; and in which infidelity is deeply resented. Dobuan economic life is built on sharp practice in interisland trading, on an intense feeling for property rights, and on a hope of getting something for nothing through theft, magic, and fraud. Except for nearby Alor, few pictures as grim as this are to be found in anthropological literature.

The third society, the Kwakiutl, is also intensely rivalrous. But the rivalry consists primarily in conspicuous consumption, typified by feasts called "potlatches," at which chiefs outdo each other in providing food and in burning up the blankets and sheets of copper which are the main counters of wealth in the society; sometimes even a house or a canoe is sent up in flames in a final bid for glory. Indeed, the society is a caricature of Veblen's conspicuous consumption; certainly, the potlatches of the Kwakiutl chiefs serve "as the legitimate channel by which the community's surplus product has been drained off and consumed, to the greater spiritual comfort of all parties concerned." Veblen was, in fact, familiar with these northwest-coast "coming out parties."

I have asked students who have read Ruth Benedict's book which of these three cultures in their opinion most closely resembles the obviously more complex culture of the United States. The great majority see Americans as Kwakiutls. They emphasize American business rivalry, sex and status jealousy, and power drive. They see Americans as individualists, primarily interested in the display of wealth and station.

A minority of students, usually the more politically radical, say that America is more like Dobu. They emphasize the sharp practice of American business life, point to great jealousy and bitterness in family relations, and in terms of aggression see American politics, domestic and international, as existing almost in Hobbes' state of nature.

No students have argued that there are significant resemblances between the culture of the Hopi and Zuñi Pueblos and American culture—they wish that there were.

Yet when we turn then to examine the culture patterns of these very students, we see little evidence either of Dobu or Kwakiutl ways. The wealthy students go to great lengths not to be conspicuous—things are very different from the coon-coated days of the '20's. The proper uniform is one of purposeful shabbiness. In fact, none among the students except a very rare Lucullus dares to be thought uppity. Just as no modern Vanderbilt says "the public be damned," so no modern parents would say: "Where Vanderbilt sits, there is the head of the table. I teach my son to be rich." [2]

It is, moreover, not only in the virtual disappearance of conspicuous consumption that the students have abandoned Kwakiutl-like modes of life. Other displays of gifts, native or acquired, have also become more subdued. A leading college swimming star told me: "I get sore at the guys I'm competing against. Something's wrong with me. I wish I could be like *X* who really cooperates with the other fellows. He doesn't care so much about winning."

There seems to be a discrepancy between the America that students personally meet and make for themselves as students and the America they think they will move into when they leave the campus. Their image of the latter is based to a large extent on legends about America that are preserved in our literature. For example, many of our novelists and critics still believe that America, as compared with other cultures, is a materialistic nation of would-be Kwakiutl chiefs. There may have been some truth in this picture in the Gilded Age, though Henry James saw how ambiguous the issue was between America and Europe even then.

The materialism of these older cultures has been hidden by their status systems and by the fact that they had inherited many values from the era dependent on tradition-direction. The European masses simply have not had the money and leisure, until recent years, to duplicate American consumership patterns; when they do, they are, if anything, sometimes more vulgar, more materialistic.

The Europeans, nevertheless, have been only too glad to tell Americans that they were materialistic; and the Americans, feeling themselves *nouveaux riches* during the last century, paid to be told. They still pay: it is not only my students who fail to see that it is

[2] The remark is quoted by Justice Oliver Wendell Holmes, Jr., in "The Soldier's Faith," 1895, reprinted in *Speeches* (Boston: Little Brown & Co., 1934), p. 56. I am indebted to Carl Withers for discerning observations concerning changing campus mores.

the turn of the rest of the world to be *nouveaux riches,* to be excited over the gadgets of an industrial age, while millions of Americans have turned away in boredom from attaching much emotional significance to the consumer-goods frontier.[3]

When, however, I try to point these things out to students who compare Americans with Kwakiutls, they answer that the advertisements show how much emotion is attached to goods consumption. But, when I ask them if they believe the ads themselves, they say scornfully that they do not. And when I ask if they know people who do, they find it hard to give examples, at least in the middle class. (If the advertisements powerfully affected people in the impoverished lower class who had small hope of mobility, there would surely be a revolution!) Yet the advertisements must be reaching somebody, the students insist. Why, I ask, why isn't it possible that advertising as a whole is a fantastic fraud, presenting an image of America taken seriously by no one, least of all by the advertising people who create it? Just as the mass media persuade people that other people think politics is important, so they persuade people that everyone else cannot wait for his new refrigerator or car or suit of clothes. In neither case can people believe that "others" are as apathetic as they feel themselves to be. And, while in the case of politics their indifference may make people feel on the defensive, in the case of advertising their indifferences may allow them to feel superior.

In fact, I think that a study of American advertising during the last quarter century would clearly show that the advertising men themselves realize the consumer's loss of emotional enthusiasm. Where once car and refrigerator advertisements showed the housewife or husband exulting in the new possessions, today it is often only children in the ads who exult over the new Nash their father has just bought. In many contemporary ads the possession itself recedes into the background or is handled abstractly, even surrealistically; it no longer throws off sparks or exclamation points; and copy itself has become subtler or more matter of fact. Of course many old-fashioned enthusiasts of consumption remain in America who have not yet been affected by the spread of other-directed

[3] Mary McCarthy's fine article, "America the Beautiful," *Commentary,* IV (1947), 201, takes much the same attitude as the text.

consumer sophistication and repression of emotional response. A wonderful example is the small-town Irish mother in the movie, *A Letter to Three Wives,* whose greatest pride and joy in her dingy railroad-side home is the big, shiny, new, not yet paid-for refrigerator. And it may be argued that even middle-class Americans have only covered their materialism with a veneer of "good taste," without altering their fundamental drives. Nevertheless, the other-directed person, oriented as he is toward people, is simply unable to be as materialistic as many inner-directeds were. For genuine inner-directed materialism—real acquisitive attachment to things—one must go to the Dutch bourgeois or French peasant or others for whom older ways endure.

It is the other-directedness of Americans that has prevented their realizing this; between the advertisers on the one hand and the novelists and intellectuals on the other, they have assumed that *other* Americans were materialistic, while not giving sufficient credence to their *own* feelings. Indeed, the paradoxical situation in a stratum which is other-oriented is that people constantly make grave misjudgments as to what others, at least those with whom they are not in peer-group contact, but often also those with whom they spend much time, feel, and think.

To be sure, the businessmen themselves often try to act as if it were still possible to be a Kwakiutl chief in the United States. When they write articles or make speeches, they like to talk about free enterprise, about tough competition, about risk taking. These businessmen, of course, are like World War I legionnaires, talking about the glorious days of yore. Students and many others believe what the businessmen say on these occasions, but then have little opportunity to watch what they do. Perhaps the businessmen themselves are as much the victims of their own chants and rituals as the Kwakiutls are.

Those few students who urge that America resembles Dobu can find little in student life to sustain their view, except perhaps a bit of cheating in love or on examinations. It is rather that they see the "capitalistic system" as a jungle of sharp practice, as if nothing had changed since the days of Mark Twain, Jack London, and Frank Norris. America is to them a land of lynchings, gangsterism, and deception by little foxes and big foxes. Yet, today, only small businessmen (car dealers or furnace repairmen, for instance) have many opportunities for the "wabu-wabu" trading, that is, the sharply manipulative property-pyramiding of the Dobuan canoeists.

If, however, these students turn to social science for their images of power in America, they will very frequently find their own view confirmed. The scattered remarks on the United States in *Patterns of Culture* are themselves an illustration. My students also read Robert Lynd's chapter on "The Pattern of American Culture" in *Knowledge for What?* [4] While noting contradictory exhortations to amity and brotherhoods, Lynd emphasizes business as highly individualistic and politically ruthless; elsewhere he stresses the masterful ambition and conspicuous consumption typified by the older generation of the "X family" of Middletown—though this sedate group would hardly be equated by him with Kwaiutl chiefs. Ironically, the outlook of these and other sociological critics of business is confirmed and reflected by those neoclassical economists who construct models for the rational conduct of the firm—wittingly or unwittingly presenting businessmen as dismally "economic men."

Partly as a result of this image of the businessman, many students at privately endowed universities have become reluctant to consider business careers, and, as more and more young people are drawn into the colleges, the attitudes become increasingly widespread. The abler ones want something "higher" and look down their noses at the boys at Wharton or even at the Harvard Business School. Business is thought to be both dull and disagreeable as well as morally suspect, and the genuine moral problem involved in career choice—namely, how best to develop one's potentialities for a full existence—is obfuscated by the false choice of making money (and losing one's soul) in business versus penury (and saving one's soul) in government service or teaching. The notion that business today, especially big business, presents challenging intellectual problems and opportunities and is no more noticeably engaged in Dobuan sharp practice and Kwakiutl rivalry than any other career, seems not to exist even in the minds of students whose fathers are (perhaps woefully inarticulate) businessmen.

It is likely, then, that the students' image of business, and of

[4] Robert S. Lynd, *Knowledge for What?* (Princeton: Princeton University Press, 1939), pp. 54–113.

American life generally, will have some self-confirming effects. Business will be forced to recruit from the less gifted and sensitive, who will muff their opportunities. People who expect to meet hostility and calculation in others will justify an anticipatory hostility and calculation in themselves.

To be sure, there are plenty of unlovely, vicious, and mean Americans, in and out of business life; plenty of frightening southern mobs, northern hoodlums, dead-end kids with and without tuxedoes. There are many cultural islands in the United States where Dobu ways abound, just as there are survivals of late nineteenth-century Kwakiutl patterns. But these islands and survivals do not make a system of power, nor are they linked by any conspiracy, fascist or otherwise.

Now, of course, to show that Americans are neither like Kwakiutls nor Dobuans does not prove they are like Zuñi and Hopi Indians. Obviously, in any case, the comparisons must be very rough; from the standpoint of my character types all three tribes, as long as they are in the phase of high population growth potential, would be more or less dependent on tradition-direction. My purpose is to present a parable, not a description. There is evidence, though it is perhaps somewhat understressed by Ruth Benedict, that the Pueblo Indians are actually not so bland and amiable as they seem, that they are, to a degree, antagonistic cooperators, with a good deal of repressed hostility and envy that crops up in dreams and malicious gossip. But this only strengthens the analogy with the middle-class Americans, whose other-directed cooperativeness is also not completely mild but contains repressed antagonistic elements.

Indeed, the whole emotional tone of life in the Pueblos reminds me strongly of the American peer-group, with its insulting "You think you're big." While the Kwakiutls pride themselves on their passions that lead them to commit murder, arson, and suicide, the Pueblos frown on any violent emotion.[5] Ruth Benedict writes:

> A good man has . . . "a pleasing address, a yielding disposition, and a generous heart." . . . He should "talk lots, as they say—that is, he should always set people at their ease—and he should without fail

[5] B. L. Whorf, "The Relation of Habitual Thought and Behavior to Language," *Language, Culture, and Personality,* ed. L. Spier, *et al.* (Menasha, Wisconsin: Sapir Memorial Publication Fund, 1941), pp. 75–93.

cooperate easily with others either in the field or in ritual, never betraying a suspicion of arrogance or a strong emotion."

The quotation brings to mind the young Vermont new style political indifferents whom we discussed in Chapter IX. It also is illustrative of one of the most striking findings from our interviews with young people. When we ask them their best trait they are hard pressed for an answer, though they sometimes mention an ability to "get along well with everybody." When we ask them, "What is your worst trait?" the most frequent single answer is "temper." And when we go on to ask, "Is your temper, then, so bad?" it usually turns out that the interviewee has not got much of a temper. If we ask whether his temper has gotten him into much trouble, he can cite little evidence that it has. What do these answers—of course no proper sample—mean? Perhaps the interviewee is boasting—he wishes he *did* have a temper. But on the whole, my impression is that temper is considered the worst trait in the society of the glad hand. It is felt as an internal menace to one's cooperative attitudes. Moreover, as business enterprise eliminates the men of lean and hungry look, so the peer-group regards temper as faintly riduculous: one must be able to take it with a smile or be charged with something even worse than temper, something so terrible that no one will accuse himself of it even in an interview—lack of a sense of humor. The inner-directed man may also worry about temper, for instance, if he is religious, but his conscience-stricken inhibitions and reaction formations leave the emotion still alive, volcanolike, within him—often ready to erupt in political indignation—whereas the other-directed man allows or compels his emotions to heal, though not without leaving scars, in an atmosphere of enforced good fellowship and tolerance.

Many young people today also set themselves an ideal in their sex lives not too different from the Zuñi norm. They feel they ought to take sex with little interpersonal emotion and certainly without jealousy. The word of the wise to the young—"Don't get involved"—has changed its meaning in a generation. Once it meant: don't get, or get someone, pregnant; don't run afoul of the law; don't get in the newspapers. Today the injunction seeks to control the personal experiencing of emotion that might disrupt the camaraderie of the peer-group.

The chief worry of the Pueblo Indians is directed not to each other's behavior but to the weather, and their religious ceremonies are primarily directed toward rain-making. To quiet their anxiety the Indians go through rituals that must be letter perfect. American young people have no such single ritual to assure personal or tribal success. However, one can see a similarity in the tendency to create rituals of a sort in all spheres of life. I have found, for example, than when I ask students why they come to class so regularly day after day, why they do not take two weeks off to go somewhere or do something on their own (as they are technically free to do), I receive answers that are mainly rationalizations. For instance, I am told that they must come to class or else they will flunk. But when we examine this allegation, it turns out to be contrary to the evidence; students often get ahead just when they break through the not yet completely bureaucratized routines of university life. It is just this prospect that is frightening. The students feel safer when they are assured of a course of approval from their peers, their antagonistic cooperators, as well as from the adult authorities. They feel safer when they can engage in a common ritual of attendance. Likewise, people make a ritual out of work, out of having fun, out of political participation as inside-dopesters or as indignants, as well as out of countless private compulsions. But the rituals, whether private or public, have usually to be rationalized as necessary; and since this is not self-evident and since the sign of success is not so explicit as a downpour of rain, the American young people can hardly get as much comfort from their rituals as the Pueblo Indians do from theirs.

What does all this mean as an indicator of the way in which a group of young people sizes up the distribution of power and power practices in America? The young people have begun to pass out of the adolescent peer-groups; they have not yet taken their places in the adult patterning of American life. What will be the effect of the discrepancy in their seeing the United States as a place led by Kwakiutl chiefs, leading Kwakiutl-style followers, when they themselves have set their feet along the "Hopi Way"? Will they seek to bring about changes, through social and political action, that will make America more comfortable for the tolerant, other-directed types? Or will they seek to adopt more ruthless, Kwakiutl-like behavior as supposedly more compatible with real life? Or, perchance, will they admit that *they*, too, are Americans, after all not so unique, which might require a revision of their images of power, their images of what Americans in general are like?

Doubtless, all these things can occur, and many more. But there is perhaps one additional factor which will shape both changing ideology and changing character. The students, aware of their own repressed competitiveness and envy, think that others may try to do to them what they themselves would not dare to do to others. The society feels to them like Kwakiutl or even Dobu, not only because that is the ideology about America they have learned but also because their own cooperativeness is tinged with an antagonism they have not yet completely silenced. And perhaps this gives us another answer to our puzzle about tolerance in the previous chapters, when we asked why, if the other-directed person is tolerant, he is himself so afraid of getting out of line? It may be that he feels his own tolerance precarious, his dreadful temper ready to let fly when given permission; if he feels so irritable himself, no matter how mild his behavior, he must fear the others, no matter how amiable they, too, may appear.

This may be simply a way of saying that the transition from inner-direction to other-direction is not complete—possibly, can never be complete.

Perhaps neither my students nor the authorities they read are representative. Perhaps the "Zuñification" of America is more widely recognized than I think. In any event it is significant that these students would prefer to live in the Pueblo culture, if they had to choose among the three described by Ruth Benedict. And, while this choice is in itself not to be quarreled with, the important fact is that they do not know that they already are living in such a culture. They want social security, not great achievements. They want approval, not fame. They are not eager for talents that might bring them into conflict; whereas the inner-directed young person tended to push himself to the limit of his talents and beyond. Few of them suffer, like youth in the earlier age, because they are "twenty, and so little accomplished." Whereas the inner-directed middle-class boy often had to learn after twenty to adjust, to surrender his adolescent dreams and accept a burgher's modest lot, the other-directed boy never had such dreams. In a profound sense he never experiences adolescence, moving as he does uninterruptedly with the peer-group, from the nursery years on. He learns to conform to the group almost as soon as he learns anything. He does not face, at adolescence, the need to choose between his family's world and that of his own generation or between his dreams and a world he never made.

Since, moreover, his adjustment to this group reality begins earlier, it becomes more a matter of conforming character and less a matter of conforming behavior. The popular song, "I don't want to set the world on fire," expresses a typical theme. The Kwakiutl wanted to do just that, literally to set the world on fire. The other-directed person prefers "love" to "glory." As Tocqueville saw, or foresaw: "He willingly takes up with low desires without daring to embark on lofty enterprises, of which he scarcely dreams."

There is a connection between the feeling these students and other young people have about their own fates and the contemporary notions of who runs the country. We have seen that the students feel themselves to be powerless, safe only when performing a ritual in approving company. Though they may seek to preserve a factitious emotional independence by not getting involved, this requirement is itself a peer-group mandate. How, then, as they look about them in America, do they explain their powerlessness? Somebody must have what they have not got: their powerlessness must be matched by power somewhere else. They see America as composed of Kwakiutls, not only because of their own residual and repressed Kwakiutl tendencies but even more because of their coerced cooperativeness. Some big chiefs must be doing this to them, they feel. They do not see that, to a great extent, it is they themselves who are doing it, through their own character.

The chiefs have lost the power, but the followers have not gained it. The savage believes that he will secure more power by drinking the blood or shrinking the head of his enemy. But the other-directed person, far from gaining, only becomes weaker from the weakness of his fellows.

TOPICS FOR DISCUSSION AND WRITING

1. Why, according to the first paragraph of this essay, does Riesman use a parable (i.e., some analogical situations) to attempt to clarify the nature of motivation in contemporary American society?
2. What are the characteristics of Hopi or Zuñi Pueblo society?
3. What are the characteristics of Dobu society?
4. What are the characteristics of Kwakiutl society?
5. Why do many students come to different conclusions as to which of these cultures American culture most closely resembles? Do the errors made by students in relating American culture to Kwakiutl or Dobuan culture suggest any of the dangers to be on guard against in the use of any comparisons? Why do some students consider American culture similar to Dobuan culture? Are the similarities between Kwatiutl culture and American culture sufficient proof for analogical purposes? If not, why not?
6. What is the evidence that American culture differs from Kwakiutl culture? Why do students tend to exaggerate the similarities? Do Americans tend to be more inner-directed, or more other-directed than Dutch bourgeois? French peasants?
7. What is the evidence which differentiates American culture from Dobuan culture? Why do some students exaggerate the similarities?
8. What is the evidence that tends to show that American culture tends to resemble Hopi or Zuñi Pueblo culture?
9. What is Riesman's thesis? Has he proven it? What is the weak point of his argument? The strong point? Are his analogies adequate? Does his use of analogies clarify or confuse the issue?
10. On what grounds is an analogy classed as adequate or inadequate?
11. Does Riesman use the Hopi, Dobu, and Kwakiutl civilizations as archetypes or merely as illustrations of different culture patterns with which American culture can be compared? Does he anywhere imply a belief in archetypes? Does he anywhere suggest that the future of American culture can be predicted from a comparison with other cultures? Would he agree with the use Spengler makes of historical analogies?
12. Reread Thoreau on *Civil Disobedience.* Write an essay explaining why you think Thoreau would have looked upon American civilization as either Hopi, Dobu, or Kwakiutl.
13. Reread Russell's essay on *Co-Existence or No Existence.* Write an essay explaining why you think American culture must tend to become more Hopi or Kwakiutl if Russell's goal is to be achieved.

ANTECEDENTS AND CONSEQUENCES

Many essays are written to persuade an audience to adopt a particular course of action. Much of daily speech is intended to persuade others to do something with us or for us. In both cases, the argument most commonly used in these circumstances consists of pointing to the desirable consequences which will follow if the proposed course of action is adopted. We try to persuade a roommate to accompany us to a movie by pointing to the pleasant consequences (an enjoyable evening) and glossing over the unpleasant consequences (being unprepared for tomorrow's exam). Congressmen argue for an increase in foreign aid by pointing to the many benefits this would bring to undeveloped countries and to the increase in prestige for the United States. Any argument which calls attention to something preceding or following an action as a reason for adopting that course of action is an argument derived from antecedents or consequences.

Arguments proceeding from cause to effect or effect to cause are species of arguments derived from antecedents and consequences. The argument from cause to effect is illustrated in T. B. Macaulay's *Letter to H. S. Randall.* Macaulay argues that democracy is sure to fail because the multiplication of sources of authority (a cause) always results in the loss of liberty (an effect).

The argument from effects to cause is illustrated in the selection from Herman Kahn's influential book, *On Thermonuclear War.* Kahn is arguing that the strength and strategy of our armed forces is to be determined by the effect we hope to achieve. If the nation desires a certain effect—lasting peace or unquestionable military superiority—the nation must be prepared to support the force necessary to bring about this effect.

Another version of the argument derived from antecedents

and consequences is illustrated by the *Communist Manifesto.* Marx and Engels argue that capitalism is doomed to be replaced by the rule of the proletariat. Their chief reason for this thesis is that the measures which had to be taken to bring about the domination of the capitalist system in the world (the antecedents) must be followed by other measures (the consequences) which are sure to result in its destruction. This kind of antecedents-consequences argument usually takes the form of isolating a chain of events and of pointing to the interrelationship of these events as a necessary relationship. Accordingly, if the antecedents have taken place, the consequences are certain to follow.

Arguments from antecedents or consequences can be logically very compelling. Ultimately these arguments are based on the principle of causality; if the writer or speaker can clearly establish that something is the cause or effect of something else, the argument is on certain ground. If the argument involves physical objects and physical laws, it is a certain argument. An argument involving individuals or groups of individuals is not as certain, for though people may have always acted consistently in the past, they can choose to act differently in the future. The form of argument based on the inevitability of a series of antecedents and consequences can be as strong or weak as the basis of the series. When, in a famous oration entitled *Second Spring,* Cardinal Newman argues that the return of spring is as certain as the sequence of the seasons, his argument is as certain as the physical laws which guarantee the sequence of the seasons. But when a writer argues that there will always be wars because, as he sees it, a certain sequence of events has always led to wars, the basis of the pattern is different. Here there is room for the human element. People can choose to avoid wars, and where there is the possibility of choice, there is also the possibility of a change in the pattern.

Thomas Babington Macaulay

Thomas Babington Macaulay (1800–1859) is an outstanding figure in Victorian literature. His History of England *and other historical essays were widely admired in his own day because he had succeeded in his intention of making history read like a romance. Though his works are still read today, they are admired for the music and color of his style rather than for the reliability of his historical interpretations.*

In addition to writing, Macaulay was also active in Victorian politics and was elected to Parliament three times. First a member of the Whig party, he later became a Liberal, and, in 1839, was appointed Secretary of War of the Melbourne cabinet. Though he espoused many minority causes (sections of his History of England *reflect a sympathy for popular movements), he was never convinced of the eventual survival of democratic governments. Like many of Macaulay's contemporaries, H. S. Randall, to whom Macaulay is replying in the letter which follows, supposed that Macaulay must be an admirer of Jefferson and Jeffersonian theories. Macaulay's letter is a succinct résumé of the reasons why he believed that all popular democracies were eventually doomed to failure.*

His reasons for disbelieving in the eventual survival of democracy are ultimately based upon his conception of the nature of man and the nature of society. The unavoidable consequences of popular government to which he calls attention in his letter can be considered unavoidable only if one assumes that men will always be motivated by immediate self-interest and that a democratic society can never subscribe to a code of values. If one disagrees with these assumptions, the consequences of the establishment of a democratic form of government which Macaulay foresees with such complete conviction may not seem so unavoidable.

Letter to H. S. Randall, Esq.

Holly Lodge, Kensington
London, May 23, 1857

Dear Sir,

The four volumes of the *Colonial History of New York* reached me safely. I assure you that I shall value them highly. They contain much to interest an English as well as an American reader.

Pray accept my thanks, and convey them to the Regents of the University.

You are surprised to learn that I have not a high opinion of Mr. Jefferson, and I am surprised at your surprise. I am certain that I never wrote a line, and that I never, in Parliament, in conversation, or even on the hustings—a place where it is the fashion to court the populace—uttered a word indicating an opinion that the supreme authority in a state ought to be intrusted to the majority of citizens told by the head; in other words, to the poorest and most ignorant part of society. I have long been convinced that institutions purely democratic must, sooner or later, destroy liberty or civilization, or both.

In Europe, where the population is dense, the effect of such institutions would be almost instantaneous. What happened in France is an example. In 1848 a pure democracy was established there. During a short time there was reason to expect a general spoliation, a national bankruptcy, a new partition of the soil, a maximum of prices, a ruinous load of taxation laid on the rich for the purpose of supporting the poor in idleness. Such a system would, in twenty years, have made France as poor and barbarous as the France of the Carlovingians. Happily the danger was averted; and now there is a despotism, a silent tribune, an enslaved press. Liberty is gone, but civilization has been saved. I have not the smallest doubt that, if we had a purely democratic government here, the effect would be the same. Either the poor would plunder the rich, or civilization would be saved by a strong military government, and liberty would perish.

You may think that your country enjoys an exemption from these evils. I will frankly own to you that I am of a very different opinion. Your fate I believe to be certain, though it is deferred by a physical cause. As long as you have a boundless extent of fertile and unoccupied land, your laboring population will be far more at ease than the laboring population of the Old World, and, while that is the case, the Jefferson policies may continue to exist without causing any fatal calamity. But the time will come when New England will be as thickly peopled as old England. Wages will be as low, and will fluctuate as much with you as with us. You will have your

Manchesters and Birminghams, and in those Manchesters and Birminghams hundred of thousands of artisans will assuredly be sometimes out of work. Then your institutions will be fairly brought to the test.

Distress everywhere makes the laborer mutinous and discontented, and inclines him to listen with eagerness to agitators who tell him that it is a monstrous iniquity that one man should have a million while another cannot get a full meal. In bad years there is plenty of grumbling here, and sometimes a little rioting. But it matters little. For here the sufferers are not the rulers. The supreme power is in the hands of a class, numerous indeed, but select; of an educated class; of a class which is, and knows itself to be, deeply interested in the security of property and the maintenance of order. Accordingly, the malcontents are firmly yet gently restrained. The bad time is got over without robbing the wealthy to relieve the indigent. The springs of national prosperity soon begin to flow again: work is plentiful, wages rises, and all is tranquillity and cheerfulness. I have seen England pass three or four times through such critical seasons as I have described.

Through such seasons the United States will have to pass in the course of the next century, if not of this. How will you pass through them? I heartily wish you a good deliverance. But my reason and my wishes are at war, and I cannot help foreboding the words. It is quite plain that your government will never be able to restrain a distressed and discontented majority. For with you the majority is the government, and has the rich, who are always a minority, absolutely at its mercy.

The day will come when in the State of New York a multitude of people, none of whom has had more than half a breakfast, or expects to have more than half a dinner, will choose a Legislature. Is it possible to doubt what sort of a Legislature will be chosen? On one side is a statesman preaching patience, respect for vested rights, strict observance of public faith. On the other is a demagogue ranting about the tyranny of capitalists and usurers, and asking why any body should be permitted to drink champagne and to ride in a carriage while thousands of honest folks are in want of necessaries. Which of the two candidates is likely to be preferred by a working-man who hears his children cry for more bread? I seriously apprehend that you will, in some such season of adversity as I have described, do things which will prevent prosperity from returning; that you will act like people who should in a year of scarcity devour all the seedcorn, and thus make the next a year not of scarcity, but of absolute famine.

There will be, I fear, spoliation. The spoliation will increase the distress. The distress will produce fresh spoliation. There is nothing to stop you. Your Constitution is all sail and no anchor. As I said before, when a society has entered on this downward progress, either civilization or liberty must perish. Either some Caesar or Napoleon will seize the reigns of government with a strong hand, or your republic will be as fearfully plundered and laid waste by barbarians in the twentieth century as the Roman Empire was in the fifth, with this difference, that the Huns and Vandals who ravaged thc Roman Empire came from without, and that your Huns and Vandals will have been engendered within your own country by your own institutions.

Thinking thus, of course, I cannot reckon Jefferson among the benefactors of mankind. I readily admit that his intentions were good and his abilities considerable. Odious stories have been circulated about his private life; but I do not know on what evidence those stories rest, and I think it probable that they are false or monstrously exaggerated. I have no doubt that I shall derive both pleasure and information from your account of him.

I have the honor to be, dear Sir, your faithful servant,

T. B. Macaulay

H. S. Randall, Esq., etc.

TOPICS FOR DISCUSSION AND WRITING

1. What is Macaulay's thesis? Does he affirm something only about a particular democratic government, or about all democratic governments?
2. What are some of the reasons he offers in support of his thesis? Are his reasons for believing in his thesis based upon testimony of others, upon a comparison between the course of democratic government in two or more instances, or upon what he believes must always follow the establishment of a democratic government? What are some of the effects which he believes must always follow the establishment of popular democracy?

3. What will delay the eventual fate of popular government in the New World?
4. What will eventually guarantee the failure of popular democracy? Is it something in the circumstances surrounding the establishment of democracy itself?
5. Why does he believe so firmly that the consequences which he foresees must come about?
6. Do you think he has proven his thesis? What do you think is the strongest part of his argument? The weakest part? Under what conditions would you be willing to accept an argument based upon consequences as a certain argument? What conditions do you think must be fulfilled before effects supposed to follow upon a cause can be certainly known?
7. Do you agree with Macaulay's assumptions? How would you go about refuting them if you disagree with them? How would you explain his belief in these assumptions? Do his assumptions agree with Roosevelt's? De Riencourt's?
8. Write an essay showing how Macaulay's predictions have, or have not, been borne out by recent events. Does Riesman's analysis of our culture tend to confirm or refute Macaulay?

Karl Marx and Friederich Engels

At a congress of the Communist League held in London in November of 1847, Karl Marx and Friederich Engels were asked to draw up a program of action for the Party. The Communist Manifesto *was the result. In a preface to a later edition of the* Manifesto, *published in London in 1888, Friederich Engels explained its thesis and purpose in this fashion:*

> The "manifesto" being our (i.e., Marx's and Engel's) joint production, I consider myself bound to state that the fundamental proposition which forms its nucleus belongs to Marx. The proposition is: that in every historical epoch the prevailing mode of economic production and exchange, and the social organization necessarily following from it, form the basis upon which is built up, and from which alone can be explained, the political and intellectual history of that epoch; that consequently the whole history of mankind (since the dissolution of primitive tribal society, holding land in common ownership) has been a history of class struggles, contests between exploiting and exploited, ruling and oppressed classes; that the history of these class struggles

> forms a series of evolution in which, nowadays, a stage has been reached where the exploited and oppressed classes (the proletariat) cannot attain its emancipation from the sway of the exploiting and ruling class (the bourgeois) without, at the same time, and once and for all, emancipating society at large from all exploitations, oppression, class distinction and class struggles.

Marx and Engels wanted to suggest a plan of action and also to give the members of the Communist League, who had witnessed the failure of many recent attempts to establish popular fronts all over Europe, some hope of eventual success. To do this, they review the sequence of events which have led to the development and supremacy of the bourgeois or capitalist class. They then proceed to show how these developments will have consequences which must eventually result in the overthrow of the bourgeois class. The climax of their argument occurs in the following two sentences:

> The weapons with which the bourgeoisie felled feudalism to the ground are now turned against the bourgeoisie itself.
>
> But not only has the bourgeoisie forged the weapons that bring death to itself; it has also called into existence the men who are to wield those weapons—the modern working class—the proletarians.

The advent of the consequences of bourgeois greed—as seen by Marx and Engels—is part of the inexorable march of history. Whether or not one agrees with the Manifesto's *view of history depends in part on whether or not one believes in economic determinism. Whether or not one concedes any argument based upon a supposedly inexorable sequence of events depends on what one believes to be the nature of the relationship between this series of events. Is the basis of the nexus between events in the series a natural law or mere custom? Natural laws never fail to operate; customs are always subject to change and emendation.*

from THE COMMUNIST MANIFESTO *

The history of all hitherto existing society is the history of class struggles.

Freeman and slave, patrician and plebeian, lord and serf, guild

* *The Communist Manifesto and Other Writings* by Karl Marx. Reprinted by permission of Random House, Inc.

master and journeyman, in a word, oppressor and oppressed, stood in constant opposition to one another, carried on uninterrupted, now hidden, now open fight, a fight that each time ended, either in a revolutionary re-constitution of society at large, or in the common ruin of the contending classes.

In the earlier epochs of history we find almost everywhere a complicated arrangement of society into various orders, a manifold gradation of social rank. In ancient Rome we have patricians, knights, plebeians, slaves; in the Middle Ages, feudal lords, vassals, guild masters, journeymen, apprentices, serfs; in almost all of these classes, again, subordinate gradations.

The modern bourgeois society that has sprouted from the ruins of feudal society, has not done away with class antagonisms. It has but established new classes, new conditions of oppression, new forms of struggle in place of the old ones.

Our epoch, the epoch of the bourgeoisie, possesses, however, this distinctive feature; it has simplified the class antagonisms. Society as a whole is more and more splitting up into two great hostile camps, into two great classes directly facing each other: Bourgeoisie and Proletariat.

From the serfs of the Middle Ages sprang the chartered burghers of the earliest towns. From these burgesses the first elements of the bourgeoisie were developed.

The discovery of America, the rounding of the Cape, opened up fresh ground for the rising bourgeoisie. The East Indian and Chinese markets, the colonization of America, trade with the colonies, the increase in the means of exchange and in commodities generally, gave to commerce, to navigation, to industry, an impulse never before known, and thereby, to the revolutionary element in the tottering feudal society, a rapid development.

The feudal system of industry, under which industrial production was monopolized by closed guilds, now no longer sufficed for the growing wants of the new market. The manufacturing system took its place. The guild masters were pushed on one side by the manufacturing middle class: division of labor between the different corporate guilds vanished in the face of division of labor in each single workshop.

Meantime the markets kept ever growing, the demand ever

rising. Even manufacture no longer sufficed. Thereupon, steam and machinery revolutionized industrial production. The place of manufacture was taken by the giant, Modern Industry, the place of the industrial middle class, by industrial millionaires, the leaders of whole industrial armies, the modern bourgeois.

Modern Industry has established the world market, for which the discovery of America paved the way. This market has given an immense development to commerce, to navigation, to communication by land. This development has, in its turn, reacted on the extension of industry; and in proportion as industry, commerce, navigation, railways extended, in the same proportion the bourgeoisie developed, increased its capital, and pushed into the background every class handed down from the Middle Ages.

We see, therefore, how the modern bourgeoisie is itself the product of a long course of development, of a series of revolutions in the modes of production and of exchange.

Each step in the development of the bourgeoisie was accompanied by a corresponding political advance of that class. An oppressed class under the sway of the feudal nobility, an armed and self-governing association in the mediaeval commune, here independent urban republic (as in Italy and Germany), there taxable "third estate" of the monarchy (as in France), afterwards, in the period of manufacture proper, serving either the semi-feudal or the absolute monarchy as a counterpoise against nobility, and, in fact, corner stone of the great monarchies in general, the bourgeoisie has at last, since the establishment of Modern Industry and of the world market, conquered for itself, in the modern representative State, exclusive political sway. The executive of the modern State is but a committee for managing the common affairs of the whole bourgeoisie.

The bourgeoisie, historically, has played a most revolutionary part.

The bourgeoisie, wherever it has got the upper hand, has put an end to all feudal, patriarchal, idyllic relations. It has pitilessly torn asunder the motley feudal ties that bound man to his "natural superiors," and has left no other nexus between man and man than naked self-interest, than callous "cash payment." It has drowned the most heavenly ecstasies of religious fervor, of chivalrous enthusiasm, of Philistine sentimentalism, in the icy water of egotistical calculation. It has resolved personal worth into exchange value, and in place of the numberless indefeasible chartered freedoms, has set up that single, unconscionable freedom—Free Trade. In one word, for exploitation, veiled by religious and political illusions, it has substituted naked, shameless, direct, brutal exploitation.

The bourgeoisie has stripped of its halo every occupation hitherto honored and looked up to with reverent awe. It has converted the physician, the lawyer, the priest, the poet, the man of science, into its paid wage laborers.

The bourgeoisie has torn away from the family its sentimental veil, and has reduced the family relation to a mere money relation.

The bourgeoisie has disclosed how it came to pass that the brutal display of vigor in the Middle Ages, which reactionists so much admire, found its fitting complement in the most slothful indolence. It has been the first to show what man's activity can bring about. It has accomplished wonders far surpassing Egyptian pyramids, Roman aqueducts, and Gothic cathedrals; it has conducted expeditions that put in the shade all former exoduses of nations and crusades.

The bourgeoisie cannot exist without constantly revolutionizing the instruments of production, and thereby the relations of production, and with them the whole relations of society. Conservation of the old modes of production in unaltered form was, on the contrary, the first condition of existence for all earlier industrial classes. Constant revolutionizing of production, uninterrupted disturbance of all social conditions, everlasting uncertainty and agitation distinguish the bourgeois epoch from all earlier ones. All fixed, fast frozen relations, with their train of ancient and venerable prejudices and opinions, are swept away, all new formed ones become antiquated before they can ossify. All that is solid melts into the air, all that is holy is profaned, and man is at last compelled to face with sober senses, his real conditions of life, and his relations with his kind.

The need of a constantly expanding market for its products chases the bourgeoisie over the whole surface of the globe. It must nestle everywhere, settle everywhere, establish connections everywhere.

The bourgeoisie has through its exploitation of the world market given a cosmopolitan character to production and consumption in every country. To the great chagrin of reactionists, it has drawn from under the feet of industry the national ground on which it stood. All old established national industries have been destroyed or are daily being destroyed. They are dislodged by new industries, whose introduction becomes a life and death question for all civilized nations, by industries that no longer work up indigenous raw material, but raw material drawn from the remotest zones; industries whose products are consumed, not only at home, but in every quarter of the globe. In place of the old wants, satisfied by the productions of the country, we find new wants, requiring for their satisfaction the products of distant lands and climes. In place of the old local and national seclusion and self-sufficiency, we have intercourse in every direction, universal interdependence of nations. And as in material, so also in intellectual production. The intellectual creations of individual nations become common property. National onesidedness and narrowmindedness become more and more impossible, and from the numerous national and local literatures there arises a world literature.

The bourgeoisie, by the rapid improvement of all instruments of production, by the immensely facilitated means of communication, draws all, even the most barbarian nations, into civilization. The cheap prices of its commodities are the heavy artillery with which it batters down all Chinese walls, with which it forces the barbarians' intensely obstinate hatred of foreigners to capitulate. It compels all nations, on pain of extinction, to adopt the bourgeois mode of production; it compels them to introduce what it calls civilization into their midst, *i.e.,* to become bourgeois themselves. In a word, it creates a world after its own image.

The bourgeoisie has subjected the country to the rule of the towns. It has created enormous cities, has greatly increased the urban population as compared with the rural, and has thus rescued a considerable part of the population from the idiocy of rural life. Just as it has made the country dependent on the towns, so it has made barbarian and semibarbarian countries dependent on civilized ones, nations of peasants on nations of bourgeois, the East on the West.

The bourgeoisie keeps more and more doing away with the scattered state of the population, of the means of production, and of property. It has agglomerated population, centralized means of production, and has concentrated property in a few hands. The necessary consequence of this was political centralization. Independent, or but loosely connected provinces, with separate interests, laws, governments, and systems of taxation, became lumped together in one nation, with one government, one code of laws, one national class interest, one frontier, and one customs tariff.

The bourgeoisie, during its rule of scarce one hundred years, has created more massive and more colossal productive forces than have all preceding generations together. Subjection of Nature's forces to man, machinery, application of chemistry to industry and agriculture, steam navigation, railways, electric telegraphs, clearing of whole continents for cultivation, canalization of rivers, whole populations conjured out of the ground—what earlier century had even a presentiment that such productive forces slumbered in the lap of social labor?

We see then: the means of production and of exchange on whose foundation the bourgeoisie built itself up, were generated in feudal society. At a certain stage in the development of these means of production and of exchange, the conditions under which feudal society produced and exchanged, the feudal organization of agriculture and manufacturing industry, in one word, the feudal relations of property became no longer compatible with the already developed productive forces; they became so many fetters. They had to burst asunder; they were burst asunder.

Into their places stepped free competition, accompanied by social and political constitution adapted to it, and by economical and political sway of the bourgeois class.

A similar movement is going on before our own eyes. Modern bourgeois society with its relations of production, of exchange and of property, a society that has conjured up such gigantic means of production and of exchange, is like the sorcerer who is no longer able to control the powers of the nether world whom he has called up by his spells. For many a decade past, the history of industry and commerce is but the history of the revolt of modern productive forces against modern conditions of production, against the property relations that are the conditions for the existence of the bourgeoisie and of its rule. It is enough to mention the commercial crises that by their periodical return put on its trial, each time more threateningly, the existence of the entire bourgeois society. In these crises a great part not only of the existing products, but also of the previously created productive forces, are periodically destroyed. In these crises there breaks out an epidemic that, in all earlier epochs, would have seemed an absurdity–the epidemic of overproduction. Society suddenly finds itself put back into a state of momentary barbarism; it appears as if a famine, a universal war of devastation, had cut off the supply of every means of subsistence; industry and commerce seem to be destroyed; and why? Because there is too much civilization, too much means of subsistence, too much industry, too much commerce. The productive forces at the disposal of society no longer tend to further the development of the conditions of the bourgeois property; on the contrary, they have become too powerful for these conditions by which they are fettered, and as soon as they overcome these fetters they bring disorder into the whole of bourgeois society, endanger the existence of bourgeois property. The conditions of bourgeois society are too narrow to comprise the wealth created by them. And how does the bourgeoisie get over these crises? On the one hand by enforced destruction of a mass of productive forces; on the other, by the conquest of new markets, and by the more thorough exploitation of the old ones. That is to say, by paving the way for more extensive and more destructive crises, and by diminishing the means whereby crises are prevented.

The weapons with which the bourgeoisie felled feudalism to the ground are now turned against the bourgeoisie itself.

But not only has the bourgeoisie forged the weapons that bring death to itself; it has also called into existence the men who are to wield those weapons–the modern working class–the proletarians.

In proportion as the bourgeoisie, *i.e.,* capital, is developed, in the same proportion is the proletariat, the modern working class, developed, a class of laborers who live only so long as they find work, and who find work only so long as their labor increases capital. These laborers, who must sell themselves piecemeal, are a commodity, like every other article of commerce, and are consequently exposed to all the vicissitudes of competition, to all the fluctuations of the market.

Owing to the extensive use of machinery and to division of labor, the work of the proletarians has lost all individual character, and, consequently, all charm for the workman. He becomes an appendage of the machine, and it is only the most simple, most monotonous, and most easily acquired knack that is required of him. Hence, the cost of production of a workman is restricted almost entirely to the means of subsistence that he requires for his maintenance, and for the propagation of his race. But the price of a commodity, and also of labor, is equal to its cost of production. In proportion, therefore, as the repulsiveness of the work increases, the wage decreases. Nay more, in proportion as the use of machinery and division of labor increases, in the same proportion the burden of toil increases, whether by prolongation of the working hours, by increase of the work enacted in a given time, or by increased speed of the machinery, etc.

Modern industry has converted the little workshop of the patriarchal master into the great factory of the industrial capitalist. Masses of laborers, crowded into factories, are organized like soldiers. As privates of the industrial army they are placed under the command of a perfect hierarchy of officers and sergeants. Not only are they the slaves of the bourgeois class and of the bourgeois state, they are daily and hourly enslaved by the machine, by the overlooker, and, above all, by the individual bourgeois manufacturer himself. The more openly this despotism proclaims gain to be its end and aim, the more petty, the more hateful, and the more embittering it is.

The less the skill and exertion or strength implied in manual labor, in other words, the more modern industry becomes developed, the more is the labor of men superseded by that of women. Differences of age and sex have no longer any distinctive social validity for the working class. All are instruments of labor, more or less expensive to use, according to their age and sex.

No sooner is the exploitation of the laborer by the manufacturer, so far at an end, that he receives his wages in cash, than he is set upon by the other portions of the bourgeoisie, the landlord, the shopkeeper, the pawnbroker, etc.

The lower strata of the middle class—the small tradespeople, shopkeepers and retired tradesmen generally, the handicraftsmen and peasants—all these sink gradually into the proletariat, partly because their diminutive capital does not suffice for the scale on which modern industry is carried on, and is swamped in the competition with the large capitalists, partly because their specialized skill is rendered worthless by new methods of production. Thus the proletariat is recruited from all classes of the population.

The proletariat goes through various stages of development. With its birth begins its struggle with the bourgeoisie. At first the contest is carried on by individual laborers, then by the work-people of a factory, then by the operatives of one trade, in one locality, against the individual bourgeois who directly exploits them. They direct their attacks not against the bourgeois conditions of production, but against the instruments of production themselves; they destroy imported wares that compete with their labor, they smash to pieces machinery, they set factories ablaze, they seek to restore by force the vanished status of the workman of the Middle Ages.

At this stage the laborers still form an incoherent mass scattered over the whole country, and broken up by their mutual competition. If anywhere they unite to form more compact bodies, this is not yet the consequence of their own active union, but of the union of the bourgeoisie, which class, in order to attain its own political ends, is compelled to set the whole proletariat in motion, and is moreover yet, for a time, able to do so. At this stage, therefore, the proletarians do not fight their enemies, but the enemies of their enemies, the remnants of absolute monarchy, the landowners, the nonindustrial bourgeois, the petty bourgeoisie. Thus the whole historical movement is concentrated in the hands of the bourgeoisie, every victory so obtained is a victory for the bourgeoisie.

But with the development of industry the proletariat not only increases in number; it becomes concentrated in greater masses, its strength grows and it feels that strength more. The various interests and conditions of life within the ranks of the proletariat are more and more equalized, in proportion as machinery obliterates all distinctions of labor, and nearly everywhere reduces wages to the same low level. The growing competition among the bourgeois, and the resulting commercial crisis, make the wages of the workers even more fluctuating. The unceasing improvement of machinery, ever more rapidly developing, makes their livelihood more and more precarious; the collisions between individual workmen and individual bourgeois take more and more the character of collisions between two classes. Thereupon the workers begin to form combinations (Trades' Unions) against the bourgeois; they club together in order to keep up the rate of wages; they found permanent associations in order to make provision beforehand for these occasional revolts. Here and there the contest breaks out into riots.

Now and then the workers are victorious, but only for a time. The real fruit of their battle lies not in the immediate result but in the ever-expanding union of workers. This union is helped on by the improved means of communication that are created by modern industry, and that places the workers of different localities in contact with one another. It was just this contact that was needed to centralize the numerous local struggles, all of the same character, into one national struggle between classes. But every class struggle is a political struggle. And that union, to attain which the burghers of the Middle Ages with their miserable highways, required centuries, the modern proletarians, thanks to railways, achieve in a few years.

This organization of the proletarians into a class, and consequently into a political party, is continually being upset again by the competition between the workers themselves. But it ever rises up again, stronger, firmer, mightier. It compels legislative recognition of particular interests of the workers by taking advantage of the divisions among the bourgeoisie itself. Thus the ten hours' bill in England was carried.

Altogether collisions between the classes of the old society further, in many ways, the course, of development of the proletariat. The bourgeoisie finds itself involved in a constant battle. At first with the aristocracy; later on, with those portions of the bourgeoisie itself whose interests have become antagonistic to the progress of industry; at all times, with the bourgeoisie of foreign countries. In all these battles it sees itself compelled to appeal to the proletariat, to ask for its help, and thus, to drag it into the political arena. The bourgeoisie itself, therefore, supplies the proletariat with its own elements of political and general education; in other words, it furnishes the proletariat with weapons for fighting the bourgeoisie.

Further, as we have already seen, entire sections of the ruling classes are, by the advance of industry, precipitated into the proletariat, or are at least threatened in their own conditions of existence. These also supply the proletariat with fresh elements of enlightenment and progress.

Finally, in times when the class struggle nears the decisive hour, the process of dissolution going on within the ruling class—in fact, within the whole range of an old society—assumes such a violent, glaring character that a small section of the ruling class cuts itself adrift and joins the revolutionary class, the class that holds the future in its hands. Just as, therefore, at an earlier period, a section of the nobility went over to the bourgeoisie, so now a portion of their bourgeoisie goes over to the proletariat, and in particular, a portion of the bourgeois ideologists, who have raised themselves to the level of comprehending theoretically the historical movements as a whole.

Of all the classes that stand face to face with the bourgeoisie today the proletariat alone is a really revolutionary class. The other classes decay and finally disappear in the face of modern industry; the proletariat is its special and essential product.

The lower middle class, the small manufacturer, the shopkeeper, the artisan, the peasant, all these fight against the bourgeoisie, to save from extinction their existence as fractions of the middle class. They are therefore not revolutionary, but conservative. Nay, more; they are reactionary, for they try to roll back the wheel of history. If by chance they are revolutionary, they are so only in view of their impending transfer into the proletariat; they thus defend not their present, but their future interests; they desert their own standpoint to place themselves at that of the proletariat.

The "dangerous class," the social scum, that passively rotting mass thrown off by the lowest layers of old society, may, here and there, be swept into the movement by a proletarian revolution; its conditions of life, however, prepare it far more for the part of a bribed tool of reactionary intrigue.

In the conditions of the proletariat, those of the old society at large are already virtually swamped. The proletarian is without property; his relation to his wife and children has no longer anything in common with the bourgeois family relations; modern industrial labor, modern subjection to capital, the same in England as in France, in America as in Germany, has stripped him of every trace of national character. Law, morality, religion, are to him so many bourgeois prejudices, behind which lurk in ambush just as many bourgeois interests.

All the preceding classes that got the upper hand sought to fortify their already acquired status by subjecting society at large to their conditions of appropriation. The proletarians cannot become masters of the productive forces of society, except by abolishing their own previous mode of appropriation, and thereby also every other previous mode of appropriation. They have nothing of their own to secure and to fortify; their mission is to destroy all previous securities for and insurances of individual property.

All previous historical movements were movements of minorities, or in the interest of minorities. The proletarian movement is the self-conscious, independent movement of the immense majority. The proletariat, the lowest stratum of our present society, cannot stir, cannot raise itself up without the whole superincumbent strata of official society being sprung into the air.

Thought not in substance, yet in form, the struggle of the proletariat with the bourgeoisie is at first a national struggle. The proletariat of each country must, of course, first of all settle matters with its own bourgeoisie.

In depicting the most general phases of the development of the proletariat, we traced the more or less veiled civil war, raging within existing society, up to the point where that war breaks out into open revolution, and where the violent overthrow of the bourgeoisie lays the foundations for the sway of the proletariat.

Hitherto every form of society has been based, as we have already seen, on the antagonism of oppressing and oppressed classes. But in order to oppress a class, certain conditions must be assured to it under which it can, at least, continue its slavish existence. The serf, in the period of serfdom, raised himself to membership in the commune, just as the petty bourgeois, under the yoke of feudal absolutism, managed to develop into a bourgeois.

The modern laborer, on the contrary, instead of rising with the progress of industry, sinks deeper and deeper below the conditions of existence of his own class. He becomes a pauper, and pauperism develops more rapidly than population and wealth. And here it becomes evident that the bourgeoisie is unfit any longer to be the ruling class in society, and to impose its conditions of existence upon society as an overriding law. It is unfit to rule, because it is incompetent to assure an existence to its slave within his slavery, because it cannot help letting him sink into such a state that it has to feed him, instead of being fed by him. Society can no longer live under this bourgeoisie; in other words, its existence is no longer compatible with society.

The essential condition for the existence and for the sway of the bourgeois class is the formation and augmentation of capital; the condition for capital is wage labor. Wage labor rests exclusively on competition between the laborers. The advance of industry, whose involuntary promoter is the bourgeoisie, replaces the isolation of the laborers, due to competition, by their involuntary combination, due to association. The development of Modern Industry, therefore, cuts from under its feet the very foundation on which the bourgeoisie produces and appropriates products. What the bourgeoisie therefore produces, above all, are its own grave diggers. Its fall and the victory of the proletariat are equally inevitable.

TOPICS FOR DISCUSSION AND WRITING

1. What, in the opinion of Marx and Engels, has been the cause of all historical change? Do they prove their generalization? How?
2. What is the difference between the "epoch of the bourgeoisie" and other epochs?
3. What is the meaning of the term "bourgeoisie" as employed in this essay?
4. How did the bourgeoisie class come into existence?
5. What have been some of the consequences of the rise of the bourgoisie as the dominant economic and political class? How does bourgeois society come to create a world after its own image?
6. Can the progress of history be stopped? Are there some consequences which must inevitably follow upon the establishment of the bourgeois

class? Are there certain conditions which must be ever present if the bourgeoisie are to survive as a class? What must be some of the consequences of these conditions?

7. Why is modern bourgeois society "like the sorcerer who is no longer able to control the powers of the nether world whom he has called up by his spells" Why do "the productive forces at the disposal of society no longer tend to further the development of the conditions of the bourgeois property"?
8. What are the weapons which will bring an end to bourgeois society? Who are the men who will wield these weapons?
9. What are some of the consequences of modern industrialization? Are these consequences inevitable? Were they the result of choice on the part of a few individual capitalists, or were they the inevitable result of the evolution of history?
10. How have modern industrial methods contributed to the expansion of the proletariat? What has led to the uniting of hitherto incoherent masses of laborers?
11. Do Marx and Engels believe that the more the bourgeoisie do to insure their survival as a class, the more they insure their destruction? Is there a weak link in their chain of antecedents and consequences?
12. By the time you reach the last sentence, do you agree with it? If not, why not? Where does their argument fail?

John Henry Cardinal Newman

John Henry Cardinal Newman (1801–1890), a well-known English prose stylist, was a Cardinal of the Roman Catholic Church. As an undergraduate (and later as a tutor) at Oxford University, he was deeply involved in writing and speaking on behalf of various movements in defense of the Anglican Church. In the process of writing various tracts in defense of Anglicanism, he was led to examine the tenability of all Catholic doctrines and, in 1845, he became a convert to Roman Catholicism. As a Catholic he continued to write and speak on various educational and religious subjects. His lectures on his Idea of a University *(1852) are perhaps his best known work.*

The Tamworth Reading Room *is a collection of discourses which were orginally published in 1841 as a series of letters addressed to the editor of* The Times *of London. These letters were occasioned by an address delivered by Sir Robert Peel (1788–1850), Tory Prime Minister in 1841, upon the opening of a library at Tamworth, a market town in Staffordshire. According to Newman's first letter,*

Sir Robert Peel gave expression to the theory that unassisted human nature becomes sensual and degraded. He was of the opinion that "Education is the cultivation of the intellect and the heart, and useful knowledge is the great instrument of education. It is the parent of virtue, the nurse of religion; it exalts man to his highest perfection and is the sufficient scope of his most earnest exertions." All of this was directly contrary to Newman's belief that in Christianity alone can man find a goal and a way to the perfection of his nature.

The selection which follows (from the third letter) is the crucial nexus in the entire Tamworth Reading Room *series. It is here that Newman attempts to demonstrate the superiority of Christianity to all other beliefs as means to human realization.*

from The Tamworth Reading Room

SECULAR KNOWLEDGE NOT A DIRECT MEANS OF MORAL IMPROVEMENT

Now, independent of all other considerations, the great difference, in a practical light, between the object of Christianity and of heathen belief, is this—that glory, science, knowledge, and whatever other fine names we use, never healed a wounded heart, nor changed a sinful one; but the Divine Word is with power. The ideas which Christianity brings before us are in themselves full of influence, and they are attended with a supernatural gift over and above themselves, in order to meet the special exigencies of our nature. Knowledge is not "power," nor is glory "the first and only fair"; but "Grace," or the "Word," by whichever name we call it, has been from the first a quickening, renovating, organizing principle. It has new created the individual, and transferred and knit him into a social body, composed of members each similarly created. It has cleansed man of his moral diseases, raised him to hope and energy, given him to propagate a brotherhood among his fellows, and to found a family or rather a kingdom of saints all over the earth; it introduced a new force into the world, and the impulse which it gave continues in its original vigour down to this day. Each one of us has lit his lamp from his neighbour, or received it from his fathers, and the lights thus transmitted are at this time as strong and as clear as if 1800 years had not passed since the kindling of the sacred flame. What has glory or knowledge been able to do like this? Can it raise the dead? Can it create a polity? Can it do more than testify man's need and typify God's remedy?

And yet, in spite of this, when we have an instrument given us, capable of changing the whole man, great orators and statesmen are busy, forsooth, with their heathen charms and nostrums, their sedatives, correctives, or restoratives; as preposterously as if we were to build our men-of-war, or conduct our ironworks, on the principles approved in Cicero's day. The utmost that Lord Brougham [1] seems to propose to himself in the education of the mind is to keep out bad thoughts by means of good—a great object, doubtless, but not so great in philosophical conception, as is the destruction of the bad in Christian fact. "If it can be a pleasure," he says, in his *Discourse Upon the Objects and Advantages of Science,*

> if it can be a *pleasure to gratify curiosity,* to know what we were ignorant of, to have our *feelings of wonder* called forth, *how pure a delight of this very kind* does natural science hold out to its students! How wonderful are the laws that regulate the notions of fluids! Is there anything in all the idle books of tales and horrors, more truly astonishing than the fact, that a few pounds of water may, by mere pressure, without any machinery, by merely being placed in one particular way, produce very irresistible force? What can be more strange, than that an ounce weight should balance hundreds of pounds by the intervention of a few bars of thin iron? Can anything surprise us more than to find that the colour white is a mixture of all others? That water should be chiefly composed of an inflammable substance? Akin to this pleasure of contemplating new and extraordinary truths is the *gratification of a more learned curiosity,* by tracing resemblances and relations between things which to common apprehension seem widely different, etc., etc.

And in the same way Sir Robert [2] tells us even of a *devout* curiosity. In all cases *curiosity* is the means, *diversion* of mind the highest end; and though of course I will not assert that Lord Brougham, and certainly not that Sir Robert Peel, denies any higher kind of morality, yet when the former rises above Ben-

[1] Henry Peter Baron Brougham and Vaux (1778–1868) was a prominent Whig who founded the Society for the Diffusion of Useful Knowledge.

[2] Sir Robert Peel (1788–1850), Tory statesman and Prime Minister in 1841.

thamism, in which he often indulges, into what may be called *Broughamism proper,* he commonly grasps at nothing more real and substantial than these Ciceronian ethics.

In morals, as in physics, the stream cannot rise higher than its source. Christianity raises men from earth, for it comes from heaven; but human morality creeps, struts, or frets upon the earth's level, without wings to rise. The Knowledge School does not contemplate raising man above himself; it merely aims at disposing of his existing powers and tastes, as is most convenient or is practicable under circumstances. It finds him, like the victims of the French tyrant, doubled up in a cage in which he can neither lie, stand, sit, nor kneel, and its highest desire is to find an attitude in which his unrest may be least. Or it finds him like some musical instrument, of great power and compass, but imperfect; from its very structure some keys must ever be out of tune, and its object, when ambition is highest, is to throw the *fault* of its nature where least it will be observed. It leaves man where it found him—man, and not an angel—a sinner, not a saint; but it tries to make him look as much like what he is not as ever it can. The poor indulge in low pleasures; they use bad language, swear loudly and recklessly, laugh at coarse jests, and are rude and boorish. Sir Robert would open on them a wider range of thought and more intellectual objects, by teaching them science; but what warrant will he give us that, if his object could be achieved, what they would gain in decency they would not lose in natural humility and faith? If so, he has exchanged a gross fault for a more subtle one. "Temperance topics" stop drinking; let us suppose it; but will much be gained, if those who give up spirits take to opium? *Naturam expellas furcâ, tamen usque recurret,*[3] is at least a heathen truth, and universities and libraries which recur to heathenism may reclaim it from the heathen for their motto.

Nay, everywhere, so far as human nature remains hardly or partially Christianized, the heathen law remains in force; as is felt in a measure even in the most religious places and societies. Even there, where Christianity has power, the venom of the old Adam is not subdued. Those who have to do with our colleges

3 "Drive out nature with a spear, nevertheless she will persist in returning."—Horace.

give us their experience, that in the case of the young committed to their care, external discipline may change the fashionable excess, but cannot allay the principle of sinning. Stop cigars, they will take to drinking parties; stop drinking, they gamble; stop gambling, and a worse license follows. You do not get rid of vice by human expedients; you can but use them according to circumstances, and in their place, as making the best of a bad matter. You must go to a higher source for renovation of the heart and of the will. You do but play a sort of "hunt the slipper" with the fault of our nature, till you go to Christianity.

I say, you must use human methods *in their place,* and there they are useful; but they are worse than useless out of their place. I have no fanatical wish to deny to any whatever subject of thought or method of reason a place altogether, if it chooses to claim it, in the cultivation of the mind. . . . The great and true maxim is to sacrifice none—to combine, and therefore to adjust, all. All cannot be first, and therefore each has its place, and the problem is to make what is secondary first, than to leave it out altogether. . . . Christianity, and nothing short of it, must be made the element and principle of all education. Where it has been laid as the first stone, and acknowledged as the governing spirit, it will take up into itself, assimilate, and give a character to literature and science. Where revealed truth has given the aim and direction to knowledge, knowledge of all kinds will minister to revealed truth. The evidences of religion, natural theology, metaphysics—or, again, poetry, history, and the classics—or physics and mathematics, may all be grafted into the mind of a Christian, and give and take by the grafting. But if in education we begin with nature before grace, with evidences before faith, with science before conscience, with poetry before practice, we shall be doing much the same as if we were to indulge the appetites and passions, and turn a deaf ear to the reason. In each case we misplace what in its place is a divine gift. If we attempt to effect a moral improvement by means of poetry, we shall but mature into a mawkish, frivolous, and fastidious sentimentalism; if by means of argument, into a dry, unamiable longheadedness; if by good society, into a polished outside, with hollowness within, in which vice has lost its grossness, and perhaps increased its malignity; if by experimental science, into an uppish, supercilious temper, much inclined to scepticism. But reverse the order of things: put Faith first and Knowledge second; let the university minister to the church, and then classical poetry becomes the type of Gospel truth, and physical science a comment on Genesis or Job. . . .

Far from recognizing this principle, the teachers of the Knowledge School would educate from natural theology up to Christianity, and would amend the heart through literature and philosophy. Lord Brougham, as if faith came from science, gives out that "henceforth nothing shall prevail over us to praise or to blame any one for his belief, which he can no more change than he can the hue of his skin, or the height of his stature." And Sir Robert, whose profession and life give the lie to his philosophy, founds a library into which "no works of controversial divinity shall enter," that is, no Christian doctrine at all; and he tells us that "an increased sagacity will make men not merely believe in the cold doctrines of natural religion, but that it will *so prepare and temper the spirit* and understanding that they will be better *qualified to comprehend the great scheme of human redemption*." And again, Lord Brougham considers that "the pleasure of science tends not only to make our lives more agreeable, but better"; and Sir Robert responds that he entertains the hope that there will be the means afforded of useful occupation and rational recreation; that men will prefer the pleasure of knowledge above the indulgence of sensual appetite, and that there is a prospect of contributing to the intellectual and moral improvement of the neighbourhood.

Can the nineteenth century produce no more robust and creative philosophy than this?

TOPICS FOR DISCUSSION AND WRITING

1. What are some of the goals which, in Newman's opinion, motivated heathen behavior? What are some of the goals which Christianity holds out to men as ideals of motivation?
2. What does Newman assert is the difference between the aims of Christianity and the aims of secular knowledge? What is the specific thesis of this essay?

3. What does he point to in his first paragraph as proof of his thesis? Are these results the effects of Christian belief and motivation?
4. What does he consider the goals or objects of Lord Brougham's philosophy? Why is he opposed these goals?
5. What does Newman maintain must be the consequences of such a limited goal?
6. What does he conclude must be the effect of any system of morals limited to heathen or secular conceptions?
7. Does he prove his thesis? Has he demonstrated that Christianity has the effects he claims for it, or that secular knowledge can never achieve any but inferior effects?
8. What is the strongest part of his argument? The weakest? Under what conditions would you accept an argument from consequences as a certain argument?
9. What is Newman's view of human nature? Compare it to that of Locke. Is Newman overly pessimistic?

John Ruskin

John Ruskin (1819–1900) was both an art critic and a social reformer, but he would never have allowed that the two occupations were separate. He envisioned the artist as being subtly influenced by the society in which he lived, and at the same time capable of directing and guiding that society. He denied that a good society should be based only on laws of economics or laissez-faire *principles of trade, and insisted that morality, compassion, and good taste were essential if any society was to be healthy. He proposed that society should begin by cultivating its taste, for "good taste" would inevitably develop into "morality." "Taste is not only a part and an index of morality," he wrote, "it is the* only *morality." Only if a person is exposed to the best in art, in literature, and in architecture could he hope to develop his taste, his morality, and his society along sound and beneficial lines. The artist thus becomes a most important figure in society, because it is through the work of the great artist that society may learn morality. But Ruskin points out a dilemma, a circular difficulty: without the great artist, there can be no healthy society; but if the artist is influenced by his society, he will merely reflect its principles. Only if contemporary society will begin its own reform can there be a great art in which the good society is reflected. His belief that society is an antecedent to art, and that art is what it is because of that antecedent, is one of Ruskin's major arguments in* Modern Painters *(1843–1860), from which the following selection is taken.*

Of Modern Landscape

We turn our eyes . . . as boldly and as quickly as may be, from these serene fields and skies of mediaeval art, to the most characteristic examples of modern landscape. And, I believe, the first thing that will strike us, or that ought to strike us, is their *cloudiness.*

Out of perfect light and motionless air, we find ourselves on a sudden brought under somber skies, and into drifting wind; and, with fickle sunbeams flashing in our face, or utterly drenched with sweep of rain, we are reduced to track the changes of the shadows on the grass, or watch the rents of twilight through angry cloud. And we find that whereas all the pleasure of the mediaeval was in *stability, definiteness,* and *luminousness,* we are expected to rejoice in darkness, and triumph in mutability; to lay the foundation of happiness in things which momentarily change or fade; and to expect the utmost satisfaction and instruction from what is impossible to arrest, and difficult to comprehend.

We find, however, together with this general delight in breeze and darkness, much attention to the real form of the clouds, and careful drawing effects of mist; so that the appearance of objects, as seen through it, becomes a subject of science with us; and the faithful representation of that appearance is made of primal importance, under the name of aërial perspective. The aspects of sunset and sunrise, with all their attendant phenomena of cloud and mist, are watchfully delineated; and in ordinary daylight landscape, the sky is considered of so much importance, that a principal mass of foliage, or a whole foreground, is unhesitatingly thrown into shade merely to bring out the form of a white cloud. So that, if a general and characteristic name were needed for modern landscape art, none better could be invented than "the service of clouds."

And this name would, unfortunately, be characteristic of our art in more ways than one. In the last chapter, I said that all the

Greeks spoke kindly about the clouds, except Aristophanes; and he, I am sorry to say (since his report is so unfavourable) is the only Greek who had studied them attentively. He tells us, first, that they are "great goddesses to idle men"; then, that they are "mistresses of disputings, and logic, and monstrosities, and noisy chattering"; declares that whoso believes in their divinity must first disbelieve in Jupiter and place supreme power in the hands of an unknown god, "Whirlwind"; and, finally, he displays their influence over the mind of one of their disciples, in his sudden desire "to speak ingeniously concerning smoke."

There is, I fear, an infinite truth in this Aristophanic judgment applied to our modern cloud-worship. Assuredly, much of the love of mystery in our romances, our poetry, our art, and, above all, in our metaphysics, must come under that definition so long ago given by the great Greek, "speaking ingeniously concerning smoke." And much of the instinct, which, partially developed in painting, may be now seen throughout every mode of exertion of mind—the easily encouraged doubt, easily excited curiosity, habitual agitation, and delight in the changing and the marvellous, as opposed to the old quiet serenity of social custom and religious faith—is again deeply defined in those few words, the "dethroning of Jupiter," the "coronation of the whirlwind."

Nor of whirlwind merely, but also of darkness or ignorance respecting all stable facts. That darkening of the foreground to bring out the white cloud, is, in one aspect of it, a type of the subjection of all plain and positive fact, to what is uncertain and unintelligible. And as we examine farther into the matter, we shall be struck by another great difference between the old and the modern landscape, namely, that in the old no one ever thought of drawing anything but as well *as he could.* That might not be *well,* as we have seen in the case of rocks; but it was as well as he *could,* and always distinctly. Leaf, or stone, or animal, or man, it was equally drawn with care and clearness, and its essential characters shown. If it was an oak tree, the acorns were drawn; if a flint pebble, its veins were drawn; if an arm of the sea, its fish were drawn; if a group of figures, their faces and dresses were drawn—to the very last subtlety of expression and the end of thread that could be got into the space, far off or near.

But now our ingenuity is all "concerning smoke." Nothing is truly drawn but that; all else is vague, slight, imperfect, got with as little pains as possible. You examine your closest foreground, and find no leaves; your largest oak, and find no acorns; your human figure, and find a spot of red paint instead of a face; and in all this, again and again, the Aristophanic words come true, and the clouds seem to be "great goddesses to idle men."

The next thing that will strike us, after this love of clouds, is the love of liberty. Whereas the mediaeval was always shutting himself into castles, and behind fosses, and drawing brickwork neatly, and beds of flowers primly, our painters delight in getting to the open fields and moors; abhor all hedges and moats; never paint anything but free-growing trees, and rivers gliding "at their own sweet will"; eschew formality down to the smallest detail; break and displace the brickwork which the mediaeval would have carefully cemented; leave unpruned the thickets he would have deliberately trimmed; and, carrying the love of liberty even to license, and the love of wildness even to ruin, take pleasure at last in every aspect of age and desolation which emancipates the objects of nature from the government of men—on the castle wall displacing its tapestry with ivy, and spreading, through the garden, the bramble for the rose.

Connected with this love of liberty we find a singular manifestation of love of mountains, and see our painters traversing the wildest places of the globe in order to obtain subjects with craggy foregrounds and purple distances. Some few of them remain content with pollards and flat land; but these are always men of third-rate order; and the leading masters, while they do not reject the beauty of the low grounds, reserve their highest powers to paint Alpine peaks or Italian promontories. And it is eminently noticeable, also, that this pleasure in the mountains is never mingled with fear, or tempered by a spirit of meditation, as with the mediaeval; but it is always free and fearless, brightly exhilarating, and wholly unreflective: so that the painter feels that his mountain foreground may be more consistently animated by a sportsman than a hermit; and our modern society in general goes to the mountains, not to fast, but to feast, and leaves their glaciers covered with chicken bones and egg-shells.

Connected with this want of any sense of solemnity in mountain scenery, is a general profanity of temper in regarding all the rest of nature; that is to say, a total absence of faith in the presence of any deity therein. Whereas the mediaeval never painted a cloud but with the purpose of placing an angel in it, and a Greek never entered a wood without expecting to meet a god in it, *we* should think the appearance of an angel in the cloud wholly unnatural, and should be seriously surprised by meeting a god anywhere. Our chief ideas about the wood are connected with poaching. We have no belief that the clouds contain more than so many inches of rain or hail, and from our ponds and ditches expect nothing more divine than ducks and watercresses.

Finally: connected with this profanity of temper is a strong tendency to deny the sacred element of colour, and make our boast in blackness. For though occasionally glaring or violent, modern colour is on the whole eminently somber, tending continually to grey or brown, and by many of our best painters consistently falsified, with a confessed pride in what they call chaste or subdued tints; so that, whereas a mediaeval paints his sky bright blue, and his foreground bright green, gilds the towers of his castles, and clothes his figures with purple and white, we paint our sky grey, our foreground black, and our foliage brown, and think that enough is sacrificed to the sun in admitting the dangerous brightness of a scarlet cloak or a blue jacket.

These, I believe, are the principal points which would strike us instantly, if we were to be brought suddenly into an exhibition of modern landscapes out of a room filled with mediaeval work. It is evident that there are both evil and good in this change; but how much evil, or how much good, we can only estimate by considering, as in the former divisions of our inquiry, what are the real roots of the habits of mind which have caused them.

And first, it is evident that the title "Dark Ages," given to the mediaeval centuries, is, respecting art, wholly inapplicable. They were, on the contrary, the bright ages; ours are the dark ones. I do not mean metaphysically, but literally. They were the ages of gold; ours are the ages of umber.

This is partly mere mistake in us; we build brown brick walls, and wear brown coats, because we have been blunderingly taught to do so, and go on doing so mechanically. There is, however, also some cause for the change in our own tempers. On the whole, these are much *sadder* ages than the early ones; not sadder in a noble and deep way, but in a dim, wearied way—the way of ennui, and jaded intellect, and uncomfortableness of soul and body. The Middle Ages had their wars and agonies, but also intense delights. Their gold was dashed with blood, but ours is sprinkled with dust. Their life was inwoven with white and purple; ours is one seamless stuff of brown. Not that we are without apparent festivity, but festivity more or less forced, mistaken, embittered, incomplete —not of the heart. How wonderfully, since Shakespeare's time, have we lost the power of laughing at bad jests! The very finish of our wit belies our gaiety.

The profoundest reason of this darkness of heart is, I believe, our want of faith. There never yet was a generation of men (savage or civilized) who, taken as a body, so woefully fulfilled the words, "having no hope, and without God in the world," as the present civilized European race. A Red Indian or a Tahitian savage has more sense of a divine existence round him, or government over him, than the plurality of refined Londoners and Parisians, and those among us who may be in some sense said to believe, are divided almost without exception into two broad classes, Romanist and Puritan; who, but for the interference of the unbelieving portions of society, would, either of them, reduce the other sect as speedily as possible to ashes; the Romanist having always done so whenever he could, from the beginning of their separation, and the Puritan at this time holding himself in complacent expectation of the destruction of Rome by volcanic fire. Such division as this between persons nominally of one religion, that is to say, believing in the same God, and the same revelation, cannot but become a stumbling-block of the gravest kind to all thoughtful and far-sighted men—a stumbling-block which they can only surmount under the most favourable circumstances of early education. Hence, nearly all our powerful men in this age of the world are unbelievers; the best of them in doubt and misery; the worst in reckless defiance; the plurality, in plodding hesitation, doing, as well as they can, what practical work lies ready to their hands. Most of our scientific men are in this last class; our popular authors either set themselves definitely against all religious form, pleading for simple truth and benevolence (Thackeray, Dickens), or give themselves up to bitter and fruitless statement of facts (Balzac), or surface-painting (Scott), or careless blasphemy, sad or smiling (Byron, Béranger). Our earnest poets, and deepest thinkers, are doubtful and indignant (Tennyson, Carlyle); one or two, anchored, indeed, but anxious or weeping (Wordsworth, Mrs. Browning), and of these two, the first is not so sure of his anchor, but that now and then it drags with him, even to make him cry out—

> Great God, I had rather be
> A Pagan suckled in some creed outworn;
> So might I, standing on this pleasant lea,
> Have glimpses that would make me less forlorn.

In politics, religion is now a name; in art, a hypocrisy, or affectation. Over German religious pictures the inscription, "See how Pious I am," can be read at a glance by any clear-sighted person. Over French and English religious pictures the inscription, "See how Impious I am," is equally legible. All sincere and modest art is, among us, profane.

This faithlessness operates among us according to our tempers, producing either sadness or levity, and being the ultimate root alike of our discontents and of our wantonnesses. It is marvellous how full of contradiction it makes us: we are first dull, and seek for wild and lonely places because we have no heart for the garden; presently we recover our spirits, and build an assembly room among the mountains, because we have no reverence for the desert.

* * *

I do not think Scott's supremacy among those who remain will any more be doubtful; nor would it, perhaps, have been doubtful before, had it not been encumbered by innumerable faults and weaknesses. But it is pre-eminently in these faults and weaknesses that Scott is representative of the mind of his age: and because he is the greatest man born amongst us, and intended for the enduring type of us, all our principal faults must be laid on his shoulders, and he must bear down the dark marks to the latest ages; while the smaller men, who have some special work to do, perhaps not so much belonging to this age as leading out of it to the next, are often kept providentially quit of the encumbrances which they had not strength to sustain, and are much smoother and pleasanter to look at, in their way; only that is a smaller way.

Thus, the most startling fault of the age being its faithlessness, it is necessary that its greatest man should be faithless. Nothing is more notable or sorrowful in Scott's mind than its incapacity of steady belief in anything. He cannot even resolve hardily to believe in a ghost, or a water spirit; always explains them away in an apologetic manner, not believing, all the while, even in his own explanation. He never can clearly ascertain whether there is anything behind the arras but rats; never draws his sword, and thrusts at it for life or death; but goes on looking at it timidly, and saying, "it must be the wind." He is educated a Presbyterian, and remains one, because it is the most sensible thing he can do if he is to live in Edinburgh; but he thinks Romanism more picturesque, and profaneness more gentlemanly: does not see that anything affects human life but love, courage, and destiny, which are, indeed, not matters of faith at all, but of sight. Any gods but those are very misty in outline to him; and when the love is laid ghastly in poor Charlotte's [his wife's] coffin; and the courage is no more of use, the pen having fallen from between the fingers; and destiny is sealing the scroll—the God-light is dim in the tears that fall on it.

He is in all this the epitome of his epoch.

TOPICS FOR DISCUSSION AND WRITING

1. What are the characteristics of Victorian art, as Ruskin defines them? How does he account for these characteristics?
2. Why does Ruskin single out Scott as the best representative of his age?
3. At what point do you become aware that Ruskin is moving from an analysis of art to an appeal for social reform?
4. Is Ruskin's essay entirely an argument from antecedents, or is it also an argument from possible consequences? Explain.
5. Could Ruskin's approach (defining a work of art in terms of its social and cultural antecedents) be applied to today's art? If so, can you defend your position by a practical demonstration?
6. Write an essay contrasting the ways in which Ruskin and Sypher (p. 205) relate art to its cultural background. Are they interested in the way in which art manifests the same aspects of a culture?

Aaron Copland

Aaron Copland (1900–), one of the most distinguished of contemporary composers, has accumulated an impressive catalogue of awards for his creative work, among which are numbered the New York Music Critics Circle Award in 1945, the Pulitzer Prize in the same year (both honors accorded him for his composition Appalachian Spring), *a Hollywood Oscar in 1950, and the Gold Medal for Music by the American Academy of Arts and Letters in 1956. He has composed concertos, ballet, operas, musical adaptations, sonatas and program music, and in addition has proved himself one of the most articulate commentators on the problems of the artist and his work in the present age. The essay printed here is one of his most incisive comments on the subject.*

The Composer in Industrial America *

Is it sheer chance, I sometimes wonder, that no one has ever published an adequate critical summary of the whole field of American serious composition? There are, of course, several compendiums containing mostly biographical data and lists of works, but no one has yet attempted to summarize what our composers have accomplished, nor to say what it feels like to be a composer in industrial America. What sort of creative life the composer leads, what his relation to the community is or should be—these and many other interesting facets of the composer's life have hardly been explored.

My colleague, the American composer Elliott Carter, once said to me that in his opinion only an imaginative mind could possibly conceive itself a composer of serious music in an industrial community like the United States. Actually it seems to me that we Americans who compose alternate between states of mind that make composition appear to be the most natural and ordinary pursuit and other moods when it seems completely extraneous to the primary interests

* Reprinted by permission of the publishers from *Music and Imagination* by Aaron Copland. Cambridge, Mass.: Harvard University Press. Copyright 1952 by The President and Fellows of Harvard College.

of our industrial environment. By temperament I lean to the side that considers composing in our community as a natural force—something to be taken for granted—rather than the freakish occupation of a very small minority of our citizens. And yet, judging the situation dispassionately, I can see that we ought not to take it for granted. We must examine the place of the artist and composer in our kind of society, partly to take account of its effect on the artist and also as a commentary on our society itself. The fact is that an industrial society must prove itself capable of producing creative artists of stature, for its inability to do so would be a serious indictment of the fundamental tenets of that society.

From the moment that one doesn't take composing for granted in our country, a dozen questions come to mind. What *is* the composer's life in America? Does it differ so very much from that of the European or even the Latin American composer of today? Or from the life of United States composers in other periods? Are our objectives and purposes the same as they always have been? These questions and many related ones are continually being written about by the literary critic, but they are infrequently dealt with in the musical world. I can best consider them by relating them to my own experence as a creative artist in America. Generalizing from that experience it may be possible to arrive at certain conclusions. This engenders an autobiographical mood, but it is impossible to avoid it if I am to use myself as guinea pig.

My own experience I think of as typical because I grew up in an urban community (in my case, New York City) and lived in an environment that had little or no connection with serious music. My discovery of music was rather like coming upon an unsuspected city—like discovering Paris or Rome if you had never before heard of their existence. The excitement of discovery was enhanced because I came upon only a few streets at a time, but before long I began to suspect the full extent of this city. The instinctual drive toward the world of sound must have been very strong in my case, since it triumphed over a commercially minded environment that, so far as I could tell, had never given a thought to art or to art expression as a way of life.

Scenes come back to me from my early high school years. I see myself digging out scores from the dusty upstairs shelves of the old Brooklyn Public Library on Montague Street; here were riches of which my immediate neighbors were completely unaware. Those were the impressionable years of exploration. I recall nights at home alone singing to myself the songs of Hugo Wolf—living on a plane which had no parallel in the rest of my daily life. Or explaining to a school friend, after hearing one of my first orchestral concerts in the Brooklyn Academy of Music, in the days before radio and recorded symphonies, what a large orchestra sounded like. I've forgotten my exact description except for the punch line: "And then, and then," I said, after outlining how the instrumental forces were gradually marshaled little by little, "and then—the whole ORchestra came in." This was musical glory manifesting itself. Most of all I remember the first time I openly admitted to another human being that I intended to become a composer of music. To set oneself up as a rival of the masters: what a daring and unheard-of project for a Brooklyn youth! It was summer time and I was fifteen years old—and the friend who heard this startling confession might have laughed at me. Fortunately, he didn't.

The curious thing, in retrospect, is the extent to which I was undisturbed by the ordinariness of the workaday world about me. It didn't occur to me to revolt against its crassness, for in the last analysis it was the only world I knew, and I simply accepted it for what it was. Music for me was not a refuge or a consolation; it merely gave meaning to my own existence, where the world outside had little or none. I couldn't help feeling a little sorry for those to whom music and art in general meant nothing, but that was their own concern. As for myself, I could not imagine my own life without it.

It seems to me now, some thirty-five years later, that music and the life about me did not touch. Music was like the inside of a great building that shut out the street noises. They were the noises natural to a street; but it was good to have the quiet of the great building available, not as a haven or a hiding place, but as a different and more meaningful place.

Here at the start, I imagine, is a first difference from the European musician, whose contacts with serious music, even when delayed, must seem entirely natural, since "classical music" is German,

English, French, Italian, and so forth—has roots, in other words, in the young composer's own background. In my America, "classical" music was a foreign importation. But the foreignness of serious music did not trouble me at all in those days: my early preoccupations were with technique and expressivity. I found that I derived profound satisfaction from exteriorizing inner feelings —at times, surprisingly concrete ones—and giving them shape. The scale on which I worked at first was small—two- or three-page piano pieces or songs—but the intensity of feeling was real. It must have been the reality of this inner intensity I speak of which produced the conviction that I was capable of some day writing a longer, and perhaps, significant work. There is no other way of explaining a young artist's self-assurance. It is not founded on faith alone (and of course there can be no certainty about it), but some real kernel there must be, from which the later work will grow.

My years in Europe from the age of twenty to twenty-three made me acutely conscious of the origins of the music I loved. Most of the time I spent in France, where the characteristics of French culture are evident at every turn. The relation of French music to the life around me became increasingly manifest. Gradually, the idea that my personal expression in music ought somehow to be related to my own back-home environment took hold of me. The conviction grew inside me that the two things that seemed always to have been so separate in America—music and the life about me—must be made to touch. This desire to make the music I wanted to write come out of the life I had lived in America became a preoccupation of mine in the twenties. It was not so very different from the experience of other young American artists, in other fields, who had gone abroad to study in that period; in greater or lesser degree, all of us discovered America in Europe.

In music our problem was a special one: it really began when we started to search for what Van Wyck Brooks calls a usable past. In those days the example of our American elders in music was not readily at hand. Their music was not often played, except perhaps locally. Their scores were seldom published, and even when published, were expensive and not easily available to the inquiring student. We knew, of course, that they too had been to Europe as students, absorbing musical culture, principally in Teutonic centers of learning. Like us, they came home full of admiration for the treasures of European musical art, with the self-appointed mission of expounding these glories to their countrymen.

But when I think of these older men, and especially of the most important among them—John Knowles Paine, George Chadwick, Arthur Foote, Horatio Parker—who made up the Boston school of composers at the turn of the century, I am aware of a fundamental difference between their attitude and our own. Their attitude was founded upon an admiration for the European art work and an identification with it that made the seeking out of any other art formula a kind of sacrilege. The challenge of the Continental art work was not: "Can we do better" or "Can we also do something truly our own," but merely, "Can we do as well." But of course one never does "as well." Meeting Brahms or Wagner on his own terms one is certain to come off second best. They loved the masterworks of Europe's mature culture not like creative personalities but like the schoolmasters that many of them became. They accepted an artistic authority that came from abroad, and seemed intent on conforming to that authority.

I do not mean to underestimate what they accomplished for the beginnings of serious American musical composition. Quite the contrary. Within the framework of the German musical tradition in which most of them had been trained, they composed industriously, they set up professional standards of workmanship, and encouraged a seriousness of purpose in their students that long outlasted their own activities. But judged purely on their merits as composers, estimable though their symphonies and operas and chamber works are, they were essentially practitioners in the conventional idiom of their own day, and therefore had little to offer us of a younger generation. No doubt it is trite to say so, but it is none the less true, I think, that a genteel aura hangs about them. There were no Dostoevskis, no Rimbauds among them; no one expired in the gutter like Edgar Allan Poe. It may not be gracious to say so, but I fear that the New England group of composers of that time were in all their instincts overgentlemanly, too well mannered, and their culture reflected a certain museum-like propriety and bourgeois solidity.

In some strange way Edward MacDowell, a contemporary of

theirs, managed to escape some of the pitfalls of the New Englanders. Perhaps the fact that he had been trained from an early age in the shadow of the *Conservatoire* at Paris and had spent many subsequent years abroad gave him a familiarity in the presence of Europe's great works that the others never acquired. This is pure surmise on my part; but it is fairly obvious that, speaking generally, his music shows more independence of spirit, and certainly more personality than was true of his colleagues around 1900. It was the music of MacDowell, among Americans, that we knew best, even in 1925. I cannot honestly say that we dealt kindly with his work at that period; his central position as "foremost composer of his generation" made him especially apt as a target for our impatience with the weaknesses and orthodoxies of an older generation. Nowadays, although his music is played less often than it once was, one can appreciate more justly what MacDowell had: a sensitive and individual poetic gift, and a special turn of harmony of his own. He is most successful when he is least pretentious. It seems likely that for a long time MacDowell's name will be secure in the annals of American music, even though his direct influence as a composer can hardly be found in present-day American music.

The search for a usable past, for musical ancestors, led us to examine most closely, as was natural, the music of the men who immediately preceded our own time—the generation that was active after the death of MacDowell in 1908. It was not until about that period that some of our composers were able to shake off the all-pervasive German influence in American music. With Debussy and Ravel, France had reappeared as a world figure on the international musical scene, and French impressionism became the new influence. Composers like Charles Martin Loeffler and Charles T. Griffes were the radicals of their day. But we see now that if the earlier Boston composers were prone to take refuge in the sure values of the academic world, these newer men were in danger of escaping to a kind of artistic ivory tower. As composers, they seemed quite content to avoid contact with the world they lived in. Unlike the poetry of Sandburg or the novels of Dreiser or Frank Norris, so conscious of the crude realities of industrial America, you will find no picture of the times in the music of Loeffler or Griffes. The danger was that their music would become a mere adjunct to the grim realities of everyday life, a mere exercise in polite living. They loved the picturesque, the poetic, the exotic—medievalisms, Hinduisms, Gregorian chants, *chinoiseries*. Even their early critics stressed the "decadent" note in their music.

Despite this *fin-de-siècle* tendency, Charles Griffes is a name that deserves to be remembered. He represents a new type of composer as contrasted with the men of Boston. Griffes was just an ordinary small-town boy from Elmira, New York. He never knew the important musical people of his time and he never managed to get a better job than that of music teacher in a private school for boys, outside Tarrytown, New York. And yet there are pages in his music where we recognize the presence of the truly inspired moment. His was the work of a sentient human being, forward-looking, for its period, with a definite relationship to the impressionists and to Scriabin. No one can say how far Griffes might have developed if his career had not been cut short by death in his thirty-sixth year, in 1920. What he gave those of us who came after him was a sense of the adventurous in composition, of being thoroughly alive to the newest trends in world music and to the stimulus that might be derived from such contact.

Looking backward for first signs of the native composer with an interest in the American scene one comes upon the sympathetic figure of Henry F. Gilbert. His special concern was the use of Negro material as a basis for serious composition. This idea had been given great impetus by the arrival in America in 1892 of the Bohemian composer. Antonin Dvorák. His writing of the New World Symphony in the new world, using melodic material strongly suggestive of Negro spirituals, awakened a desire on the part of several of the younger Americans of that era to write music of local color, characteristic of one part, at least, of the American scene. Henry Gilbert was a Boston musician, but he had little in common with his fellow New Englanders, for it was his firm conviction that it was better to write a music in one's own way, no matter how modest and restricted its style might be, than to compose large works after a foreign model. Gilbert thought he had solved the problem of an indigenous expression by quoting Negro or Creole themes in his overtures and ballets. What he did was suggestive on a primitive and pioneering level, but the fact is that he lacked the technique and musicianship for expressing his ideals in a significant way.

What, after all, does it mean to make use of a hymn tune or a cowboy tune in a serious musical composition? There is nothing inherently pure in a melody of folk source that cannot be effectively spoiled by a poor setting. The use of such materials ought never to be a mechanical process. They can be successfully handled only by a composer who is able to identify himself with, and re-express in his own terms, the underlying emotional connotation of the material. A hymn tune represents a certain order of feeling: simplicity, plainness, sincerity, directness. It is the reflection of those qualities in a stylistically appropriate setting, imaginative and unconventional and not mere quotation, that gives the use of folk tunes reality and importance. In the same way, to transcribe the cowboy tune so that its essential quality is preserved is a task for the imaginative composer with a professional grasp of the problem.

In any event, we in the twenties were little influenced by the efforts of Henry Gilbert, for the truth is that we were after bigger game. Our concern was not with the quotable hymn or spiritual: we wanted to find a music that would speak of universal things in a vernacular of American speech rhythms. We wanted to write music on a level that left popular music far behind—music with a largeness of utterance wholly representative of the country that Whitman had envisaged.

Through a curious quirk of musical history the man who was writing such a music—a music that came close to approximating our needs—was entirely unknown to us. I sometimes wonder whether the story of American music might have been different if Charles Ives and his work had been played at the time he was composing most of it—roughly the twenty years from 1900 to 1920. Perhaps not; perhaps he was too far in advance of his own generation. As it turned out, it was not until the thirties that he was discovered by the younger composers. As time goes on, Ives takes on a more and more legendary character, for his career as composer is surely unique not only in America but in musical history anywhere.

In the preceding chapter I mentioned the abundance of imagination in the music of Ives, its largeness of vision, its experimental side, and the composer's inability to be self-critical. Here I want to be more specific and stress not so much the mystical and transcendental side of his nature—the side that makes him most nearly akin to men like Thoreau and Emerson—but rather the element in his musical speech that accounts for his acceptance of the vernacular as an integral part of that speech. That acceptance, it seems to me, was a highly significant moment in our musical development.

Ives had an abiding interest in the American scene as lived in the region with which he was familiar. He grew up in Danbury, Connecticut, but completed his schooling at Yale University, where he graduated in 1898. Later he moved on to New York, where he spent many years as a successful man of business. Throughout his life one gets the impression that he was deeply immersed in his American roots. He was fascinated by typical features of New England small-town life: the village church choir, the Fourth of July celebration, the firemen's band, a barn dance, a village election, George Washington's Birthday. References to all these things and many similar ones can be found in his sonatas and symphonies. Ives treated this subject matter imaginatively rather than literally. Don't think for an instant that he was a mere provincial, with a happy knack for incorporating indigenous material into his many scores. No, Ives was an intellectual, and what is most impressive is not his evocation of a local landscape but the over-all range and comprehensiveness of his musical mind.

Nevertheless Ives had a major problem in attempting to achieve formal coherence in the midst of so varied a musical material. He did not by any means entirely succeed in this difficult assignment. At its worst his music is amorphous, disheveled, haphazard—like the music of a man who is incapable of organizing his many different thoughts. Simultaneity of impression was an idea that intrigued Ives all his life. As a boy he never got over the excitement of hearing three village bands play on different street corners at the same time. Ives tried a part solution for reproducing this simultaneity of effect which was subsequently dubbed "musical perspective" by one music critic. He composed a work which is a good example of this device. It is called "Central Park in the Dark," dates from 1907, and, like many of Ives' works, is based on a poetic transcription of a realistic scene. The composer thought up a simple but ingenious method for picturing this scene, thereby enhancing what was in reality a purely musical intention. Behind a velvet curtain he placed a muted string orchestra to represent the sounds of the night, and before the curtain he placed a woodwind ensemble which made city noises. Together they evoke Central Park in the dark. The effect is almost that of musical cubism, since the music seems to exist independently on different planes. This so-called musical perspective makes use of musical realism in order to create an impressionistic effect.

The full stature of Ives as a composer will not be known until we have an opportunity to judge his output as a whole. Up to now, only a part of his work has been deciphered and published. But whatever the total impression may turn out to be, his example in the twenties helped us not at all, for our knowledge of his work was sketchy—so little of it had been played.

Gradually, by the late twenties, our search for musical ancestors had been abandoned or forgotten, partly, I suppose, because we became convinced that there were none—that we had none. We were on our own, and something of the exhilaration that goes with being on one's own accompanied our every action. This self-reliant attitude was intensified by the open resistance to new music that was typical in the period after the First World War. Some of the opposition came from our elders—conservative composers who undoubtedly thought of us as noisy upstarts, carriers of dangerous ideas. The fun of the fight against the musical philistines, the sorties and strategies, the converts won, and the hot arguments with dull-witted critics partly explain the particular excitements of that period. Concerts of new music were a gamble: who could say whether Acario Catapos of Chile, or Josef Hauer of Vienna, or Kaikhosru Sorabji of England was the coming man of the future? It was an adventuresome time—a time when fresh resources had come to music and were being tested by a host of new composers with energy and ebullient spirits.

Sometimes it seems to me that it was the composers who were the very last to take cognizance of a marked change that came over the musical scene after the stimulating decade of the twenties. The change was brought about, of course, by the introduction for the first time of the mass media of distribution in the field of music. First came the phonograph, then radio, then the sound film, then the tape recorder, and now television. Composers were slow to realize that they were being faced with revolutionary changes: they were no longer merely writing their music within an industrial framework; industrialization itself had entered the framework of what had previously been our comparatively restricted musical life. One of the crucial questions of our times was injected: how are we to make contact with this enormously enlarged potential audience, without sacrificing in any way the highest musical standards?

Jacques Barzun recently called this question the problem of numbers. "A huge increase in the number of people, in the number of activities, and possibilities, of desires and satisfactions, is the great new fact." Composers are free to ignore this "great new fact" if they choose; no one is forcing them to take the large new public into account. But it would be foolish to side-step what is essentially a new situation in music: foolish because musical history teaches that when the audience changes, music changes. Our present condition is very analogous to that in the field of books. Readers are generally quick to distinguish between the book that is a best seller by type and the book that is meant for the restricted audience of intellectuals. In between there is a considerable body of literature that appeals to the intelligent reader with broad interests. Isn't a similar situation likely to develop in music? Aren't you able even now to name a few "best seller" compositions of recent vintage? Certainly the complex piece—the piece that is "born difficult"—is an entirely familiar musical manifestation. But it is the intelligent listener with broad interests who has tastes at the present time which are difficult to define. Composers may have to relinquish old thinking habits and become more conciously aware of the new audience for whom they are writing.

In the past, when I have proffered similar gratuitous advice on this subject, I have often been misinterpreted. Composers of abstruse music thought they were under attack, and claimed that complexities were natural to them—"born that way," a contention that I never meant to dispute. I was simply pointing out that certain modes of expression may not need the full gamut of post-tonal implications, and that certain expressive purposes can be appropriately carried out only by a simple texture in a basically tonal scheme. As I see it, music that is born complex is not inherently better or worse than music that is born simple.

Others took my meaning to be a justification for the watering down of their ideas for the purpose of making their works acceptable for mass consumption. Still others have used my own compositions to prove that I make a sharp distinction between those written in a "severe" and those in a "simple" style. The inference is sometimes drawn that I have consciously abandoned my earlier dissonant manner in order to popularize my style—and this notion is applauded enthusiastically, while those of a different persuasion are convinced that only my so-called "severe" style is really serious.

In my own mind there never was so sharp a dichotomy between the various works I have written. Different purposes produce different kinds of work, that is all. The new mechanization of music's media has emphasized functional requirements, very often in terms of a large audience. That need would naturally induce works in a simpler, more direct style than was customary for concert works of absolute music. But it did not by any means lessen my interest in composing works in an idiom that might be accessible only to cultivated listeners. As I look back, it seems to me that what I was trying for in the simpler works was only partly the writing of compositions that might speak to a broader audience. More than that they gave me an opportunity to try for a more homespun musical idiom, not so different in intention from what attracted me in more hectic fashion in my jazz-influenced works of the twenties. In other words, it was not only musical functionalism that was in question, but also musical language.

This desire of mine to find a musical vernacular, which, as language, would cause no difficulties to my listeners, was perhaps nothing more than a recrudescence of my old interest in making a connection between music and the life about me. Our serious composers have not been signally successful at making that kind of connection. Oblivious to their surroundings, they live in constant communion with great works, which in turn seems to make it *de rigueur* for them to attempt to emulate the great works by writing one of their own on an equivalent plane. Do not misunderstand me. I entirely approve of the big gesture for those who can carry it off. What seems to me a waste of time is the self-deceiving "major" effort on the part of many composers who might better serve the community by the writing of a good piece for a high school band. Young composers are especially prone to overreaching themselves—to making the grand gesture by the writing of ambitious works, often in a crabbed style, that have no future whatever. It is unrealistic and a useless aping, generally of foreign models. I have no illusion, of course, that this good advice will be heeded by anyone. But I like to think that in my own work I have, by example, encouraged the notion that a composer writes for different purposes and from different viewpoints. It is a satisfaction to know that in the composing of a ballet like *Billy the Kid* or in a film score like *Our Town*, and perhaps in the *Lincoln Portrait*, I have touched off for myself and others a kind of musical naturalness that we have badly needed along with "great" works.

An honest appraisal of the position of the American composer in our society today would find much to be proud of, and also much to complain about. The worst feature of the composer's life is the fact that he does not feel himself an integral part of the musical community. There is no deep need for his activities as composer, no passionate concern in each separate work as it is written. (I speak now not of my own personal experience, but of my observation of the general scene.) When a composer is played he is usually surrounded by an air of mild approval; when he is not played no one demands to hear him. Performances in any case are rare events, with the result that very few composers can hope to earn a livelihood from the music they write. The music-teaching profession has therefore been their principal resource, and the composing of music an activity reserved for their spare time. These are familiar complaints, I know, perhaps immemorial ones; but they show little sign of abatement, and in the aggregate they make composers as a group an unhappy lot, with the outward signs of unhappiness ranging from open resentment to inner frustration.

On the brighter side of the ledger there is the cheering fact that numerically there are many more active composers than there once were. There is private encouragement on the part of certain foundations and individuals, and prizes and commissions are much more frequently given. An occasional radio station or recording company will indicate a spurt of interest. The publishers have shown signs of gratifying awakening, by a willingness to invest in the future of unknowns. The music critics are, generally speaking, more open-minded in their attitude, more ready to applaud than they were a quarter of a century ago. And best of all, there appears to be a continual welling up of new talents from all parts of America that augurs well for our composing future.

In the final analysis the composer must look for keenest satisfaction in the work that he does—in the creative act itself. In many important respects creation in an industrial community is little different from what it has always been in any community. What, after all, do I put down when I put down notes? I put down a reflection of emotional states: feelings, perceptions, imaginings, intuitions. An emotional state, as I use the term, is compounded of everything we are: our background, our environment, our convictions. Art particularizes and makes actual these fluent emotional states. Because it particularizes and because it makes actual, it gives meaning to *la condition humaine*. If it gives meaning it necessarily has purpose. I would even add that it has moral purpose.

One of the primary problems for the composer in an industrial society like that of America is to achieve integration, so find justification for the life of art in the life about him. I must believe in the ultimate good of the world and of life as I live it in order to create a work of art. Negative emotions cannot produce art; positive emotions bespeak an emotion about something. I cannot imagine an art work without implied convictions; and that is true also for music, the most abstract of the arts.

It is this need for a positive philosophy which is a little frightening in the world as we know it. You cannot make art out of fear and suspicion; you can make it only out of affirmative beliefs. This sense of affirmation can be had only in part from one's inner being; for the rest it must be continually reactivated by a creative and yea-saying atmosphere in the life about one. The artist should feel himself affirmed and buoyed up by his community. In other words, art and the life of art must mean something, in the deepest sense, to the everyday citizen. When that happens, America will have achieved a maturity to which every sincere artist will have contributed.

TOPICS FOR DISCUSSION AND WRITING

1. Is Copland's basic assumption concerning the relationship between environment and artist any different from John Ruskin's assumption in his analysis of modern landscape?
2. What, precisely, are the questions which confront the modern American composer? How well does Copland answer some of those questions?
3. Copland speaks of the need for a native idiom, a sense of the national past—what might be called a myth. Read the essays by Ernst Cassirer (p. 97) and Harold Watts (p. 217). Do you perceive any connection that might be made between their ideas and Copland's?
4. Copland refers to several of his own compositions. If recordings of these are available to you, listen to the performances. Do they demonstrate the thesis of his essay?
5. Could Copland's views on the musical composer be applied as well to the painter, the sculptor, the poet, the architect?
6. How would you define the relationship between environment and artist: cause and effect, or consequence and antecedent? What is the difference?

Herman Kahn

Herman Kahn attended the University of California at Los Angeles and later studied at the California Institute of Technology. In 1948 he was a member of the RAND group which had been commissioned by the Department of Defense to conduct some studies on problems involved in atomic warfare. When many influential people in the nation were convinced that the possibility of thermonuclear war was unthinkable, the RAND group set about analyzing such unpleasant possibilities as how much radioactive contamination we might be willing to absorb for defense purposes. The analysis of this and many other related problems required the application of mathematical methods in areas where they had never been used before. The results were communicated to high military and civil defense officials in briefings which became famous for their precision and insight. When the book On Thermonuclear War *appeared in 1960 it contained a lot of material which had originally been included in these secret briefings but which had since been declassified. The book was the object of heated discussion on book review and editorial pages all over the country, and many of its concepts have become part of national policy.*

The following selection, which is substantially the first chapter of the book, begins by assuming that national policy is oriented toward "avoiding disaster and buying time," not covert preparation for aggressive war. Accepting this as the end or effect to be achieved, the first question to be asked is: What are some of the means or causes likely to achieve this effect? The book then goes on to list and examine several national strategies which have been proposed as alternative means of achieving the national goal.

Kahn's argument in this first chapter is intended to show that not all of these proposed strategies could possibly have the desired effect. The essay thus demonstrates the application of criteria which should always be brought to bear in testing the validity of arguments which proceed from cause to effect. Kahn keeps before his reader questions which reveal that proposed causes will not necessarily have the effects which their proponents suppose. Will this cause have this effect or another effect? Does this cause always produce this effect? Only occasionally? Under what conditions does it operate? Under what conditions does it fail to operate? If it fails to operate, we cannot be sure. If we cannot be sure, how can we entrust the success of national policy to this strategy?

from ON THERMONUCLEAR WAR *

On July 16, 1960, the world entered the sixteenth year of the nuclear era. Yet we are increasingly aware that after living with nuclear bombs for fifteen years we still have a great deal to learn about the possible effects of a nuclear war. We have even more to learn about conducting international relations in a world in which force tends to be both increasingly more available and increasingly more dangerous to use, and therefore, in practice increasingly unusable. As a result of this continuous secular change in the basic structure of the international situation, foreign and defense policies formulated early in the nuclear era badly need review and reformulation.

In considering these basic foreign and defense policies it is desirable to distinguish many different military postures and the corresponding possible strategies for both the United States and the Soviet Union. This treatment of thermonuclear warfare will mostly concern itself with four typical possible postures, which I will call Finite Deterrence, Counterforce as Insurance, Preattack Mobilization Base, and Credible First Strike Capability, respectively. I will discuss the possibilities and implications of these postures from the point of view of the Soviet Union and the United States. While there is no reason why the two most powerful nations should have similar views, I will not initially dwell on possible asymmetries, deferring discussion of the separate national problems. A number of typical basic postures (important concepts italicized for emphasis) are listed in Table 1, roughly in order of increasing ability to wage general war.

Probably the most valuable thing that the Executive Office could do to improve over-all defense planning would be to select one of these postures and the corresponding strategies, or possibly some clearly defined alternative not on the list, and let the office of Civil and Defense Mobilization, the Department of Defense, and the Department of State know its decision. The decision could then be debated at the proper level, and it would not be necessary to conduct a philosophical debate at the staff level, on what business the Department of Defense should be in every time somebody brought up a technical question on Air Defense, Command and Control, and so on. National debates should be conducted at the national level where feasibility, desirability, and possible consequences can be discussed responsibly and from proper points of view. It is not possible to do this even at the level of a senior but technical advisory group attached to Departments or even to the Executive Office,

TABLE 1

ALTERNATIVE NATIONAL POSTURES

1. Internal Police Force plus "World Government"
2. *Minimum Deterrence* plus *Limited War* plus *Arms Control*
3. Add insurance to the *Minimum Deterrent:*
    (a) for reliability (*Finite Deterrence*)
    (b) against unreliability (*Counterforce as Insurance*)
    (c) against a change in policy (*Preattack Mobilization Base*)
4. Add *Credible First Strike Capability*
5. "Splendid" First Strike and no Limited War Capability
6. Dreams

much less at lower staff levels. Advisory groups and agency and departmental staffs should be mainly concerned with implementing the general policy and reporting back to their superiors on cost, performance, and feasibility. In actual practice the great national debate on what business the Department of Defense should be in often occurs at the advisory group or relatively low staff levels, and important projects whose approval or disapproval may set crucial constraints on over-all policy are approved or rejected on the basis of some very narrow and parochial views of what this over-all national policy ought to be; sometimes the effects on over-all national policy are not even examined. All this could be eliminated if the big decisions were consciously formulated, debated, and then decided at the proper level rather than treated as a number of fragmented issues to be treated on an ad hoc basis.

In this first chapter I will consider the postures in Table 1 from an over-all point of view, deferring details to later chapters. In this discussion I will define certain widely used terms in a manner that disagrees with some (but not all) usage. In general, I feel it is better to do this than to invent some completely new word or term, and I will normally continue this practice throughout the book. One of the most important things that could be done to facilitate discussion of defense problems would be to create a vocabulary that is both small enough and simple enough to be learned, precise enough to communicate, and large enough so that all of the important ideas that are contending can be comfortably and easily described. One of my major objectives in writing this book is to facilitate the creation of such a vocabulary.

1. INTERNAL POLICE FORCE PLUS "WORLD GOVERNMENT"

There seems to be little point in discussing the view that finds a solution in a totally disarmed world. Neither our own emotional desires nor the fact that there are many earnest proponents for this policy should sway us toward a position that ignores some of the basic realities. It has probably always been impractical to imagine a completely disarmed world, and the introduction of the thermonuclear bomb has added a special dimension to this impracticality. Given the large nuclear stockpiles in the Soviet Union, the United

States, and the British Isles, it would be child's play for one of these nations to hide completely hundreds of these bombs. Even if some caches were found, one could not be sure that these were not decoys to allay suspicions, and yet there would be a great loathness to cancel the agreement just because "a few malcontents had conspired against the peace." The violator would then have an incredible advantage if the agreement ever broke down and the arms race started again. This surely means that even if all nations should one day agree to total nuclear disarmament, we must presume that there would be the hiding of some nuclear weapons or components as a hedge against the other side doing so. An international arrangement for banishing war through disarmament will not call for total disarmament but will undoubtedly include provisions for enforcement that cannot be successfully overturned by a small, hidden force. Otherwise, it would be hopelessly unstable. Even if the problem of what we may call the "clandestine cache" were solvable, the writer is still of the belief that one could not disarm the world totally and expect it to remain disarmed. But the problem of the clandestine nuclear cache in itself makes total disarmament especially infeasible.

While total disarmament can be ruled out as an immediate possibility, one can conceive of some sort of international authority which might have a monopoly of war-making capability. Such a postulated international authority would have to have enough power to be able to overwhelm any nation that had reserved hidden destructive potential. An international agency with a near-monopoly of force might come from any of the following possibilities (listed in order of apparent probability rather than desirability): (1) a Soviet or U.S. dominated world arising most likely out of war; (2) some other kind of postwar organization; (3) an S.U.-U.S. combination which is in effect a world government, thought it may not openly be called that; (4) some of the NATO nations and China added to the above combination as influential, if not equal partners; (5) the Haves against the Have Nots, most likely without exploitation, but with stringent arms control in which authority and responsibility are roughly proportioned to military and economic development and, perhaps, with aid to underdeveloped nations; (6) a sort of World Federal state where power is proportioned to sovereignty and population as in the U.S. Congress. However, it is most doubtful in the absence of a crisis or war that a world government can be set up in the next decade. There are to date no serious proposals along such lines. Certainly the official suggestions occasionally put out by the Soviet and U.S. governments are not to be taken seriously as possible solutions.

While it may seem high time to spell out practical proposals for world government, no such attempt will be made in this book. While I believe that even a poor world government might be preferable to an uncontrolled arms race, I also believe that the practical difficulties are so large that it is a digression to dwell on such possibilities as a possible solution for the problems of the sixties. And the problems of the sixties are important! About the only way "world government" and other long-run considerations affect the kind of analysis done here is the avoidance of otherwise desirable short-term measures that might seriously hinder or foreclose desirable long-term possibilities. Even this modest ambition toward shaping the seventies is difficult to realize because there are controversies over where we want to be, as well as how to get there. However, there seems to be some consensus on what we are trying to avoid even if we cannot agree on what we are for. This book will concentrate on the problem of avoiding disaster and buying time, without specifying the use of this time. This seeming unconcern for long-term objectives will distress some readers, but some of our immediate problems must be understood more clearly than in the past if we are to control the direction in which we are going. It is the hallmark of the amateur and dilettante that he has almost no interest in how to get to his particular utopia. Perhaps this is because the practical job of finding a path may be more difficult than the job of designing the goal. Let us consider, then, some of the practical military alternatives that we face in the 1960–1975 time period.

2. MINIMUM DETERRENCE PLUS LIMITED WAR ARMS CONTROL

This view, or the modest variant of it called Finite Deterrence, is probably the most widely held view in the West of what is a desirable and feasible strategic posture. Among the adherents to this position can be found most intellectuals interested in military affairs, staff people in the federal government, civilians who seek to qualify as "military experts" (including scientists and technicians), many military planners in the three services, and the vast majority of foreign and domestic analysts. What, then, is meant by Minimum Deterrence?

The notion is dramatic: It is that no nation whose decision makers are sane would attack another nation which was armed with a sufficiently large number of thermonuclear bombs. Thus all a nation that is so armed has to worry about is insanity, irresponsibility, accident, and miscalculation. Even such a sober expert as General Maxwell Taylor expressed this view as follows:

> The avoidance of deliberate general atomic war should not be too difficult since its unremunerative character must be clear to the potential adversaries. Although actual stockpile sizes are closely guarded secrets, a nation need only feel reasonably sure that an opponent has some high-yield weapons no matter how indefinite their exact number to be impressed with the possible consequences of attacking him.

The above was written in 1956 but is quoted in a book he published in 1959. It is only fair to add that General Taylor's views have changed and, as expressed in the book, now show much more concern with the problem of deterring general war than this quotation would indicate. He also mentions that it was very difficult for him to change his views and take the problem of deterrence seriously. It is even more difficult for laymen who do not have access to the same information to achieve this feat.

In general, the believers in Minimum Deterrence seem to view the deterrence of a rational enemy as almost a simple philosophical consequence of the *existence* of thermonuclear bombs. They argue that the decision to initiate thermonuclear war is such a momentous one—the risks are so great—that it is unlikely that such a decision will be affected by the relatively minor details of each side's military posture. One is tempted to call this "the layman's view," since people holding it show only the slightest interest in such matters as the status of the alert forces, holes in the warning networks, the range of the bombers, reliability of missiles, the degree of protection offered by current arrangements for hardening, dispersal, and concealment, and the multitude of other questions that bother sober students of the problems of retaliation. Nevertheless, the Minimum Deterrence view is held by such a surprisingly large number of experts that it may be gratuitously insulting to call it a layman's view.

An extreme form of the Minimum Deterrence theory is the view that the current strategic forces of the United States and the Soviet Union, if used, will automatically result in world annihilation or at least mutual homicide. In 1955, fifty-two Nobel laureates signed a statement (the Mainau Declaration) which included the following: "*All* nations must come to the decision to renounce force as a final resort of policy. If they are not prepared to do this they will *cease to exist.*" There is a beautiful simplicity about this statement. It does not differentiate between attacker and defender, belligerent and neutral, Northern and Southern Hemisphere, but simply says *all* nations. It does not talk about degree of damage but simply says *cease to exist.*

Everybody recognizes that statements such as the above are sometimes no more than rhetoric. If this were all there is to it one would not worry. But belief follows language as much as the other way round. Contemporary phrases, used by both experts and laymen in describing war, expressions like "balance of terror," "thermonuclear stalemate," "suicidal war," "mutual annihilation," "inescapable end of civilization," "destruction of all life," "end of history," "live together or die together," and "nobody wins a suicide pact," indicate a widespread inclination to believe that thermonuclear war would eventuate in mutual annihilation as the result of almost any plausible turn of military events. The view of the phrasemakers is reinforced by the use of deterrence analogies, such as two people on a single keg of dynamite—each with a button—two scorpions in a bottle, two heads on a single chopping block, or the bee that dies when it stings.

Why do reasonably sober and knowledgeable people hold some version of this view of automatic mutual annihilation? In this first lecture, I will try to describe some of the data and calculations that have given rise to these cataclysmic expectations and explain why the situation is not, at least for the immediate future, as they describe it.

A thermonuclear war is quite likely to be an *unprecedented catastrophe* for the defender. Depending on the military course of events, it may or may not be an unprecedented catastrophe for the attacker, and for some neutrals as well. But an "unprecedented" catastrophe can be a far cry from an "unlimited" one. Most important of all, sober study shows that *the limits on the magnitude of the catastrophe seem to be closely dependent on what kinds of preparations have been made, and on how the war is started and fought.*

While the notions in the above paragraph may strike some readers as being obvious, I must repeat that they are by no means so. The very existence of the irreconcilable group predicting total catastrophe is proof. One can divide military thinkers into two classes: those who believe that any war would result in no less than mutual annihilation, and those who feel that this is not necessarily so or even that it is in all likelihood wrong. The latter group is probably correct, at least for the military capabilities that are likely to be available in the next decade or so. Yet on the whole they have not done very much "homework" to prove their point. The total disaster group has done a great deal of homework. This could mean that the first group is likely for a time to win many an argument of this question.

This concept of mutual homicide, sure and certain, has in many ways been peculiarly comforting to those holding it. It makes plausible the conviction that when governments are informed of the terrible consequences of a nuclear war they will realize there could be no victors. There would be no sense to such a war. Would a sane leader ever start such a cataclysm? Of course not. The expected violence of war would deter him. Those who hold this comforting concept may even get angry at anyone who ventures to assay estimates of the precise degree of risk which a "successful" attacker might actually face.

The mutual homicide theory yields other comforts. If one grants that each side will utterly destroy the other, one must also grant that expensive preparations to reduce casualties, lessen damage, and facilitate postwar recuperation are useless. Can we not spare ourselves the financial burden of such preparations? The "logic" has sometimes been carried further, some arguing that modern weapons are so enormously destructive that only a few are needed to deter the enemy. Therefore, the argument goes, war can be deterred with much smaller forces than in the past; in any case we certainly do not need more.

The view from this plateau is attractive to many groups who are determined on disarmament and certain types of arms control. For them, the Minimum Deterrence notion implies a certain kind of automatic stability which makes it safe to be casual about both agreements and possible violations. One must concede that the very concept of Minimum Deterrence implies that the two nations involved have in effect signed a reliable nonagression treaty with their populations as hostages to insure adherence to this treaty; the only strategic problem that seems to be left is an accidental or unauthorized violation of this nonagression "treaty." It is such possibilities that are the subject of arms control negotiations.

The mutual annihilation view is also comforting to many idealistic individuals, particularly to those who have an intrinsic abhorrence of any use of force. The bizarreness of a war in which both sides expect to get annihilated confirms their intuition that this whole business of military preparations is silly; a stupid and dangerous game which we ought to discourage nations—our own country, at least—from playing. At the same time these idealists can afford to scoff at attempts to reduce casualties from, say, 100 million to 50 million Americans, reflecting that the situation is hopeless anyway and that the only respectable cause is the total elimination of war. They regard programs other than their own as foolish or sinister and designed to cause people discomfort by making it sound plausible that there really is a national security problem toward the relief of which considerable amounts of money, energy, and intelligence need to be allocated.

Among those who take the view that Minimum Deterrence is a desirable, feasible, or the only possible strategic goal are many who nevertheless seek to add a Limited War capability. They recognize that *even if the United States and the Soviet Union cannot wage all out war against each other this does not mean that the role of force will be entirely eliminated.* There may still be many disputes between the two nations—disputes which may tempt one side to use force on a small scale. If the only counter the other nation has is to commit suicide by starting a thermonuclear war, that nation most likely will not act. Therefore, one needs Limited War capabilities to meet limited provocations. Those who adhere to the Minimum Deterrence theory often feel that the "nonaggression treaty" of mutual deterrence is so binding and so stable it is impossible to provoke the other side to violate it by anything less than an all-out attack. Seen in this perspective, cannot one safely use the most extreme forms of violence in a limited war?

We must expand on this point. Some of those who feel strongly that it is easy to make deterrence reliable suggest using the threat of limited or controlled nuclear retaliation to "regulate" Soviet behavior. An extreme form of this notion might go as follows: If the Soviets threaten to take over Berlin, the U.S. could threaten to blow up a major Soviet city in retaliation, perhaps after warning the inhabitants to evacuate it. In their anger and distress the Soviets would then blow up one U.S. city in exchange. We would be enraged in turn, but because we would want to stop the tit-for-tat exchange, we would call a halt after warning the Soviets that any similar aggressions in the future would also result in a city exchange. However angry both of us would be, we would not start an all-out war, according to this argument, because suicide is not a rational way of expressing one's anger. It would be in the interests of both to stop the exchange at this point. By then, from the Soviet point of view, the taking of Berlin would seem unprofitable, since the loss of the Soviet city would appear more costly than the value of Berlin plus the destruction of a U.S. city. We have gained through making it clear to the Soviets that similar future actions would be equally unprofitable. On the other hand, by destroying a U.S. city, the Soviets have made it clear that we should not lightly use controlled thermonuclear retaliation as a tactic. While the whole idea sounds bizarre, concepts like this are bound to be a logical consequence of a world in which all-out war has been made to seem *rationally infeasible,* but one in which we feel it necessary to punish or limit the other side's provocations. The timid *or sober* may feel that Minimum Deterrence might be strained to the breaking point by such acts; for theme there must be caution on the types and levels of violence to accompany limited war or limited provocations.

3. THREE KINDS OF INSURANCE

The next view of what could result in a satisfactory strategic capability adds several kinds of "insurance" to the simple Minimum Deterrence position. There are at least three kinds of insurance which a survival-conscious person might wish to add, the first being *Insurance for Reliability*. We will label the view that *worries about the details* of obtaining a "punishing" retaliation, but does not want any more strategic capability than this, the *Finite Deterrence* strategy. In many ways, and with some inconsistencies, this is the official U.S. view. The believers in Finite Deterrence do not quite accept the idea that reliable deterrence can be obtained simply by stocking thermonuclear bombs and having a weapons system which could deliver these bombs in peacetime. They notice that when the problem of retaliation is studied, rather than asserted, it is difficult to retaliate effectively, since the enemy can do many things to prevent, hinder, or negate retaliation. Evaluation of the effectiveness of retaliation must bear in mind that the Russians can strike *at a time and with tactics of their choosing*. We will strike back, no doubt, but with *a damaged and not fully coordinated force* which must conduct its operations in the *postattack environment*. The Soviets may use *blackmail threats to intimidate our postattack* tactics. Under these conditions, the Russian defense system is likely be *alerted*. Indeed, if the strike has been preceded by a tense period, their active defense forces would long since have been *augmented*, and their cities may be at least partially *evacuated*.

Any of the considerations referred to by the italicized words can change the effectiveness of a retaliatory strike by an order of magnitude. Yet almost all of them are ignored in most discussions of the effectiveness of our deterrent force. Sometimes they are even relegated to the position of unimportant "technical details." They are far more than this. The possibilities indicated by the italicized words will be discussed at some length in Lecture II. I only want to mention here that the believer in Finite Deterrence is somewhat aware of these problems; he wants to have ready more than the bare minimum force that *might* be able to retaliate effectively (the Minimum Deterrence position). The advocate of the Finite Deterrence wants enough forces to cover *all* contingencies. He may even want mixed forces, considering that it may be possible for a clever enemy to discover an unexpected countermeasure against a single kind of force no matter how large. Thus he may well want different types of missiles, bombers, strategic submarines, aircraft carriers, and so forth. In addition, sober advocates of Finite Deterrence wish to have the various weapons systems so deployed and operated that they will have a guaranteed capability, even in a crisis in which the enemy has taken extraordinary measures to negate the capability. They want these forces dispersed, protected, and alert; the arrangements for command, control, and communications must be able to withstand degradation by both peacetime and wartime tactics of the enemy. These sober believers in Finite Deterrence tend to insist on an objective capability as opposed to one that is only "psychological." And even those believers in Finite Deterrence who would be satisfied with a façade yearn for an impressive-looking façade. One might characterize the Finite Deterrence position as an expert version of the Minimum Deterrence position, held by an expert who wants to look good to other experts.

The notion of Finite Deterrence is therefore not as dramatic as the notion of Minimum Deterrence. The believer in Finite Deterrence is willing to concede that it takes some effort to guarantee Mutual Homicide, that it is not automatic. However, the notion of Finite Deterrence is still dramatic, since most followers of this doctrine believe that *the advent of thermonuclear bombs has changed the character of an all-out war in such a way that if both opponents are prepared, the old-fashioned distinctions between victory, stalemate, and defeat no longer have much meaning.* It was once believed that if one country had forces twice as large as those of another country, the first country was the stronger. Those who believe in Finite Deterrence challenge this view. Sometimes they rest their case on this idea; the only purpose of strategic forces is to deter rather than to fight; once one has the ability to damage seriously, say, ten to twenty enemy cities, this is enough force to deter, and therefore enough force. More often, backers of Finite Deterrence take a more extreme position. They argue that you can do no more than kill somebody once; to overkill by a factor of ten is no more desirable than overkilling by a factor of two—it is simply a waste of effort. They also usually argue that with some thought it should be easy to design strategic systems that can overkill, even in retaliation. Once we procure the limited (i.e. finite) forces required to do this job we have enough strategic forces and do not need any more—no matter what the enemy does.

A surprisingly large number of official military experts and planners seem to hold views, at least unconsciously, which are really a variation of the Finite Deterrence view that the only purpose of the strategic forces is to deter. This is illustrated by the following apocryphal quotation:

TABLE 2

ONE PROFESSIONAL'S VIEW OF HIS PROFESSION

"If these buttons are ever pressed, they have *completely failed* in their purpose! The equipment is useful only if it is not used."

—General Aphorism

Even though the above statement may be intended to be rhetoric rather than policy, it is far from innocuous. If one were to deduce the beliefs of some policy makers from the decisions they make, he would find that in a rather high percentage of cases the planners seem to care less about what happens after the buttons are pressed than they do about looking "presentable" before the event. They show slight interest in maintaining an appreciable operational capability on the second day of the war; if deterrence should fail, they, as well as many scientists, could not be less interested in the details of what happens—so long as the retaliatory strike is launched.

It is my contention that failure to launch an effective retaliatory attack is only the first of many possible failures. Even if one retaliates successfully, there can ensue significant and meaningful failures. These will occur one after another if the attitude exemplified in the above quotation becomes too universal in either the making or execution of policy. And even Deterrence-Only advocates should realize that there are subtle but important differences between a posture which is to be a façade to impress the enemy and one which is supposed to have an objective capability.

Insurance Against Unreliability. Some of the proponents of Finite Deterrence do not have an antipathy toward all forms of counterforce. They are willing to insure against unreliability. That is, even though deterrence has been made as reliable as they think it can be made, they realize that it may still fail; for example, from accident, human irrationality, miscalculation, or unauthorized behavior. Given this nonzero probability of a war, they find it difficult not to go through the motions of doing "something" to mitigate its effects. Even totally convinced "mutual annihilation" decision makers may be unwilling to admit openly that there are no preparations to alleviate the consequences of a war. It is difficult for any government to look at its people and say in effect, "We can no longer protect you in a war. We have no answer to blackmail except a counter-blackmail threat, and we have no preparations to deal with accidental war except trying to make it so dreadful that everybody will be careful in advance."

A façade of being able to alleviate may also be useful in international relations. It reassures one's allies about one's resolve and induces uncertainty and (hopefully) fear in the enemy. Even if it were true that both sides in the cold war conflict were unwilling to risk a thermonuclear war over any issue that could arise between them, it would weaken their diplomatic strength to admit this openly since the admitting power would be conceding that the other power could always get its way by staking a little more.

Some decision makers who accept the Finite Deterrence view are willing to pay for Insurance against Unreliability for more than political or psychological reasons. Even those who hold that war means mutual annihilation are sometimes willing for us to act beyond their beliefs—or fears. While this is inconsistent, it is not necessarily irrational. They understand that paper calculations can be wrong and are willing to hedge against this possibility. Sometimes these decision makers are making a distinction that (rather surprisingly) is not usually made. They may distinguish, for example, between 100 million dead and 50 million dead, and argue that the latter state is better than the former. They may distinguish between war damage which sets the economy of a country back fifty years or only ten years. *Actually when one examines the possible effects of thermonuclear war carefully, one notices that there are indeed many postwar states that should be distinguished.* If most people do not or cannot distinguish among these states it is because the gradations occur as a result of a totally bizarre circumstance—a thermonuclear war. The mind recoils from thinking hard about that; one prefers to believe it will never happen. If asked, "How does a country look on the day of the war?" the only answer a reasonable person can give is "awful." It takes an act of iron will or an unpleasant degree of detachment or callousness to go about the task of distinguishing among the possible degrees of awfulness.

But surely one can ask a more specific question. For example, *"How does a country look five or ten years after the close of war, as a function of three variables: (1) the preparations made before the war, (2) the way the war started, and (3) the course of military events?"* Both very sensitive and very callous individuals should be able to distinguish (and choose, perhaps) between a country which survives a war with, say, 150 million people and a gross national product (GNP) of $300 billion a year, and a nation which emerges with only 50 million people and a GNP of $10 billion. The former would be the richest and the fourth largest nation in the world, and one which would be able to restore a reasonable facsimile of the prewar society; the latter would be a pitiful remnant that would contain few traces of the prewar way of life. When one asks this kind of question and examines the circumstances and possible outcomes of a future war in some detail, it appears that it is useful and necessary to make any distinctions among the results of thermonuclear war. The figures in Table 3 illustrate some simple distinctions which one may wish to make at the outset of his deliberations in this field.

TABLE 3

TRAGIC BUT DISTINGUISHABLE POSTWAR STATES

Dead	*Economic Recuperation*
2,000,000	1 year
5,000,000	2 years
10,000,000	5 years
20,000,000	10 years
40,000,000	20 years
80,000,000	50 years
160,000,000	100 years

Will the survivors envy the dead?

Here I have tried to make the point that if we have a posture which might result in 40 million dead in a general war, and as a result of poor planning, apathy, or other causes, our posture deteriorates and a war occurs with 80 million dead, we have suffered an additional disaster, an *unnecessary* additional disaster that is almost as bad as the original disaster. If on the contrary, by spending a few billion dollars, or by being more competent or lucky, we can cut the number of dead from 40 to 20 million, we have done something vastly worth doing! The survivors will not dance in the streets or congratulate each other if there have been 20 million men, women, and children killed; yet it would have been a worthwhile achievement to limit casualties to this number. It is very difficult to get this point across to laymen or experts with enough intensity to move them to action. The average citizen has a dour attitude toward planners who say that if we do thus and so it will not be 40 million dead—it will be 20 million dead. Somehow the impression is left that the planner said that there will be *only* 20 million dead. To him is often attributed the idea that this will be a tolerable or even, astonishingly enough, a desirable state!

The rate of economic recuperation, like the number of lives saved, is also of extreme importance. Very few Americans can get interested in spending money or energy on preparations which, even if they worked, would result in preindustrial living standards for the survivors of a war. As will be explained later, our analysis indicates that if a country is moderately well prepared to use the assets which survive there is unlikely to be a critical level of damage to production. A properly prepared country is not "killed" by the destruction of even a major fraction of its wealth; it is more likely to be set back a given number of years in its economic growth. While recuperation times may range all the way from one to a hundred years, even the latter is far different from the "end of history."

Perhaps the most important item on the table of distinguishable states is not the numbers of dead or the number of years it takes for economic recuperation; rather, it is the question at the bottom: "Will the survivors envy the dead?" It is in some sense true that one may never recuperate from a thermonuclear war. The world may be permanently (i.e., for perhaps 10,000 years) more hostile to human life as a result of such a war. Therefore, if the question, "Can we restore the prewar conditions of life?" is asked, the answer must be "No!" But there are other relevant questions to be asked. For example: "How much more hostile will the environment be? Will it be so hostile that we or our descendants would prefer being dead than alive?" Perhaps even more pertinent is this question, "How happy or normal a life can the survivors and their descendants hope to have?" *Despite a widespread belief to the contrary, objective studies indicate that even though the amount of human tragedy would be greatly increased in the postwar world, the increase would not preclude normal and happy lives for the majority of survivors and their descendants.*

My colleagues and I came to this conclusion reluctantly; not because we did not *want* to believe it, but because it is so *hard* to believe. Thermonuclear bombs are so destructive, and destructive in so many ways, that it is difficult to imagine that there would be anything left after their large-scale use. One of my tasks with The RAND Corporation was to serve as project leader for a study of the possibilities for alleviating the consequences of a thermonuclear war. That study was made as quantitatively and objectively as we could make it with the resources, information, and intellectual tools available to us. *We concluded that for at least the next decade or so, any picture of total world annihilation appears to be wrong, irrespective of the military course of events.* Equally important, the picture of total disaster is likely to be wrong even for the two antagonists. Barring an extraordinary course for the war, or that most of the technical uncertainties turn out to lie at the disastrous end of the spectrum, one, and maybe both of the antagonists should be able to restore a reasonable semblance of prewar conditions quite rapidly. Typical estimates run between one and ten years for a reasonably successful and well-prepared attacker and somewhat longer for the defender, depending mainly on the tactics of the attacker and the preparations of the defender. In the RAND study we tried to avoid using optimistic assumptions. With the exceptions to be noted, we used what were in our judgment the best values available, or we used slightly pessimistic ones. We believe that the situation is likely to be better than we indicate, rather than worse, though the latter possibility cannot be ruled out.

Exactly what is it that one must believe if he is to be convinced that it is worth while to buy Counterforce as Insurance? Listed below are eight phases of a thermonuclear war. If our decision makers are to justify the expense (and possible risk of strategic destabilization) that would be incurred in trying to acquire a capability for alleviating the consequences of a war, they must believe they can successfully negotiate each and every one of these phases, or that there is a reasonable chance that they can negotiate each of these phases.

TABLE 4

A COMPLETE DESCRIPTION OF A THERMONUCLEAR WAR

Includes the Analysis of:

1. Various time-phased programs for deterrence and defense and their possible impact on us, our allies, and others.
2. Wartime performance with different preattack and attack conditions.
3. Acute fallout problems.
4. Survival and patch-up.
5. Maintenance of economic momentum.
6. Long-term recuperation.
7. Postwar medical problems.
8. Genetic problems.

I repeat: To survive a war it is necessary to negotiate *all eight* stages. If there is a catastrophic failure in any one of them, there will be little value in being able to cope with the other seven. Differences among exponents of the different strategic views can often be traced to the different estimates they make on the difficulty of negotiating one or more of these eight stages. While all of them present difficulties, most civilian military experts seem to consider the *last six* the critical ones. Nevertheless, most discussions among "classical" military experts concentrate on the *first two*. To get a sober and balanced view of the problem, one must examine all *eight*.

4. CREDIBLE FIRST STRIKE CAPABILITY

The next position on Table 1, that there are circumstances in which a nation may wish to have a Credible First Strike Capability, may seem to many Americans like a possibility for the Soviets—but not for us. One sees many statements to the effect that "We will never strike first." In the context in which the remark is usually made (a "dastardly" surprise attack out of the blue against an unprepared enemy), this position is undoubtedly correct. Such a capability would not be worth much to the U.S. However, we have many treaties and other obligations. There is the obligation to come to the aid of NATO nations if they are attacked. It is generally supposed that this aid includes the use of our SAC against the Soviet heartland, even if the Soviets attack Europe *but not the United States.* From a technical point of view this means that in this instance *we* would strike *first!* The agonizing decision to start an all-out thermonuclear war would be ours. Surely there is a serious question whether we would live up to our treaty obligations under such circumstances.

That this doubt is plausible can be seen in the response of Christian Herter to a question by Senator Morse on the occasion of the hearings on his nomination: "I cannot conceive of any President involving us in an all-out nuclear war unless the facts showed clearly we are in danger of all-out devastation ourselves, *or that actual moves have been made toward devastating ourselves.*"

A thermonuclear balance of terror is equivalent to the signing of a nonaggression treaty which states that neither the Soviets nor the Americans will initiate an all-out attack, no matter how provoking the other side may become. Sometimes people do not understand the full implications of this figurative nonaggression treaty. Let me illustrate what it can mean if we accept absolutely the notion that there is no provocation that would cause us to strike the Soviets other than an immediately impending or an actual Soviet attack on the United States. Imagine that the Soviets have taken a very drastic action against our allies in Europe. Let the action be as extreme or shocking as the reader's imagination permits. Suppose, for example, that the Soviets have dropped bombs on London, Berlin, Rome, Paris, and Bonn *but have made no detectable preparations for attacking the United States, and our retaliatory force looks good enough to deter them from such an attack.* As far as we can tell they have done this horrible deed simply to demonstrate their strength and resolve. Suppose also that there is a device which restrains the President of the United States from acting for about twenty-four hours. It is probably true that if the President were not restrained he would order an attack on the S.U. (even if he had previously bought either the Minimum Deterrence or Finite Deterrence positions that no sane decision maker initiates a thermonuclear war against an enemy who can retaliate). However, we have assumed the existence of a twenty-four-hour device which forces him to stop and think and make his decision in cold blood. The President would presumably call together his advisors during this time. Most of the advisors would probably urge strongly that the U.S. fulfill its obligations by striking the Soviet Union. Now let us further suppose that the President is also told by his advisors that even though we will kill almost every Russian *civilian,* we will not be able to destroy all of the Soviet strategic forces, and that these surviving Soviet forces will (by radiation or Strontium-90 or something else) kill every American in their retaliatory blow—all 180 million of us.

Is it not difficult to believe that under these hypothetical circumstances any President of the United States would initiate a thermonuclear war by all-out retaliation against the Soviets with the Strategic Air Command? Few would contend that there is any plausible public policy which would justify ending life for everyone. It should be clear that our retaliation would not restore Europe; we could only succeed in further destroying it either as a by-product of our actions or because the surviving Soviet forces would subsequently destroy Europe as well as the United States. I am not saying that the United States would stand idly by. We would clearly declare war on the Soviets. We would make all kinds of limited military moves. We would go into a crash mobilization on at least the hundred-billion-dollars-a-year level. But there is one thing that we almost certainly would not do: We would not launch an all-out attack on Soviet cities.

It should now be clear what I mean by a Credible First Strike Capability. Credibility does not involve the question "Do we or the Soviets have the capability to hurt the other side on a first strike?" It is well known that this capability exists and in all likelihood will continue to exist. Credibility depends on being willing to accept the other side's retaliatory blow. It depends on the harm *he* can do, not on the harm *we* can do. It depends as much on *air defense* and *civil defense* as on *air offense*. It depends on *will* as well as *capability*. It depends on the *provocation* and on the *state of our mind* when the provocation occurs. One should also note that being able to use a Credible First Strike Capability to influence Soviet or European behavior depends not only on our will, but also on Soviet and European estimate of our will. Serious problems may be created for us if either of them does not believe in our willingness to attack under certain kinds of provocation.

Let us consider some European estimates first. I have discussed with many Europeans the question of how many casualties as American decision maker or planner would be willing to envisage and still be willing to see this country live up to its obligations. Their estimates, perhaps not surprisingly, range much lower than the estimates of Americans, that is, roughly 2 to 20 million (clustering toward the lower numbers). In fact, one distinguished European expert thought that the U.S. would be deterred from retaliating with SAC against a major Soviet aggression in Europe by a Soviet threat to destroy five or ten empty U.S. cities.

Will the Soviets find the threat of U.S. retaliation credible? I have not asked any Soviet citizens, so I lack the advantage of any introspection by Russians. But we do know that their formal writings emphasize that decision makers should be able to control their emotions. The Soviets do not believe in cutting off their noses to spite their faces; they write and seem to believe that one should not be provoked into self-destructive behavior. They probably assume that we do likewise. One would not think that the Soviets could believe that the U.S. would willingly commit suicide. In fact, I would conjecture that they would feel fairly certain about this matter. They could readily underestimate our *resolve*. We might easily be irrationally determined to resist the Soviets. We have no tradition in the United States of controlling our emotions. We have tended to emphasize the opposite notion (e.g., "Give me liberty or give me death!"). A Soviet underestimation of U.S. resolve could create the worst of all situations—one in which we had not made preparations for the failure of deterrence because we knew we had enough resolve, but the Soviets did not believe it so they went ahead and provoked us and we were forced to initiate a war in retaliation, a war in which we were not prepared to do anything more than kill Russians. But it seems likely that unless we initiate remedial measures, the Soviets may estimate that we will be deterred, and they will be right in their estimate. It should be realized that a very low additional probability of war might not deter the Soviets. It is not as if there were no probability at all of war and their action had created this probability. It would be much more reasonable to say that just the existence of the U.S.-S.U. rivalry means that somehow there is always a probability of war, of say, one in fifty every year, and that if the Soviet action increased this by, in any one year, fifty per cent—from the assumed .02 to .03—that this might not be, for many reasons, as deterring as raising the probability from .00 to .01. As the engineer would put it, the increased probability of war must dominate "the noise level" to be deterring. This is particularly true if the Soviets believe that their action would either decrease the long-run probability of war or increase markedly their chance of coming out of such a war very much better than if they had not improved their position. In addition, if the Soviets were not to risk all by a single attempt but tested our resolve more gradually by instigating a series of crises, then without running excessive risks they could probably find out experimentally a great deal about our reactions to extreme provocations. No matter what our *declared policy* might be, our *actual policy* could be probed. Most important of all, it is difficult to believe, in the absence of adequate measures for air defense and civil defense, that the Europeans will have faith in our declared policy when it is strained. The Soviets may be able to make their gains more easily by working on the will and resolve of the Europeans than by working on ours. We must convince the Europeans as well as the Russians of our resolve if we are to present appeasement or an undue degree of accommodation.

Here again is a summary of the situation:

TABLE 3

TRAGIC BUT DISTINGUISHABLE POSTWAR STATES

Dead	*Economic Recuperation*
2,000,000	1 year
5,000,000	2 years
10,000,000	5 years
20,000,000	10 years
40,000,000	20 years
80,000,000	50 years
160,000,000	100 years

Will the survivors envy the dead?

The first three lines in this table indicate circumstances under which *some* Europeans still believe in U.S. "retaliation." The next two lines show circumstances in which *most* Americans seem to believe in it, and the last two lines indicate states in which *neither* Europeans nor Americans (nor presumably the Soviets) would believe that the use of our Strategic Air Command against the Soviet Union is credible—no matter what the Soviets did in Europe—providing they gave U.S. decision makers time to ponder seriously on the consequences of a war.

Unclassified published estimates of the casualties that the United States would suffer in a nuclear war generally run around 50 to 80 million. If these estimates are relevant (which is doubtful since they generally assume a Soviet surprise attack on an unalert United States), we are already deterred from living up to our alliance obligations. If these casualty estimates are not relevant, then we ought to make relevant estimates for now and the future.

The critical point is whether the Soviets and the Europeans believe that we can keep our casualties to a level we would find acceptable, whatever that level may be. In such an eventuality the Soviets would be deterred from such provocative acts as a ground attack on Europe, Hitler-type blackmail threats, or evacuation of their cities and presentation to us of an ultimatum. But if they do not believe that we can keep casualties to a level we would find acceptable, the Soviets may feel safe in undertaking these extremely provocative adventures; or at least the Europeans may believe that the Soviets will feel safe, and this in itself creates an extremely dangerous negotiating situation—one in which the possibility of extreme pressure and blackmail will always be in the background, if not the foreground.

The situation is actually worse than the mere estimate of the casualties or economic damage is likely to indicate. The most crucial and difficult question is the one asked at the bottom of the table: "Will the survivors envy the dead?" Unless the President believes that the postwar world will be worth living in, he will in all likelihood be deterred from living up to our alliance obligations. . . .

As has already been explained, one does not have to be trying to achieve a Credible First Strike Capability to be interested in trying to cope with the eight phases of a thermonuclear war. Even if one believes in mutual annihilation, he may still be willing to endorse Counterforce as Insurance Capability (the insurance against unreliability discussed in the previous section). This is because a reasonable person generally knows that his beliefs can be wrong. Many will agree, therefore, that some portion of the defense budget should be allocated to Counterforce as Insurance and to other measures designed to alleviate the consequence of a war. Because paper calculations can be misleading, it is rational to have even an inconsistent program which hedges against this possibility.

There is, however, a difference between Counterforce as Insurance and Credible First Strike Capabilities. In the case of the latter we do not say that there is a *modest* probability that the mutual annihilation theory is wrong; instead, we require that there be a *very high* probability that it is wrong. In short, *the time has come when we must believe that our programs are very likely to be successful under wartime and postwar conditions.*

When this has been said, it is still important to know (abstractly, we hope) that a war in which the U.S. made the first strike would result in more favorable conditions for us than would the wars that are generally considered. And even here we are more interested in *deterrence* than in *striking first!* We are more deeply interested in what the Soviets will conclude when they ask themselves, "If we try this very provoking act, will the United States strike us?" than in speculating on what could happen to us if we should actually strike them. It is quite possible that the Soviets may conclude when contemplating action that their risks are too high (even though the fact may be that we have already concluded that we would not actually dare to initiate the war). It is for such reasons that even a façade may be invaluable. Everyone knows that there is an enormous difference between a probability and a certainty.

5. SPLENDID FIRST STRIKE AND NO LIMITED WAR CAPABILITY

It is difficult for most people to believe that any nation would initiate a thermonuclear war against an opponent capable of retaliation no matter what capabilities it had and no matter how much it was provoked; nevertheless, there are many military planners who oppose having limited war capabilities to handle modest provocations. They say this is a diversion of our resources from more important and essential central war capabilities. They seem to feel that our strategic force can be so effective in Soviet eyes that they would not dare to provoke us in even a minor way. They also believe that if the Soviets did provoke us we should then hit them at "a time and place of our choosing," thereby punishing the Soviets for their provocation. This is, roughly speaking, the massive retaliation theory as enunciated by former Secretary of State John Foster Dulles. While a Credible First Strike Capability to correct or avenge a limited but major aggression also involves massive retaliation, the distinction is that it is massive retaliation over *major* issues, not minor ones. It should also be clear that if the terror in the "balance of terror" intensifies, the line between major and minor issues will shift so that the level of provocation we will accept without triggering SAC will increase.

Anyone who studies even superficially the likely effects of thermonuclear war will inevitably reach certain conclusions. Chief among these is the idea that *even if one could launch a very successful first strike, the net damage, if only from the blacklash (i.e., the fallout on the U.S. and the world from the bombs dropped on Russia, not to speak of the Russian people who would be killed) would make it unreasonable to make such a strike on a minor issue.* Is it not true that if we were to launch such a war it would not be over the minor issue bothering us but really because we had decided to engage in a form of preventive war? In the real world we would have to worry about far more than just the backlash from our blow; we would have to worry about Soviet retaliatory action. For such *practical* reasons alone, not to speak of vitally important moral and political ones, the notion of having a "Splendid" First Strike Capability seems fanciful.

6. DREAMS

If a Splendid First Strike Capability seems in the light of facts and reason to be fanciful, it is no less strange than many of the ideas which make the rounds in Washington or in European capitals. In such places one finds consideration given to very implausible notions. One of these is a conflict in which a thermonuclear blow is followed by a three-year war of production accompanied by the kind of mobilization we had in World War II. Another is the notion that the enemy can go ahead and strike us first, but that our defenses would keep us essentially untouched, and that we in turn can strike back and then survey the situation. There is the fervid belief in the possibility of a "leakproof" active defense system. There is the concept of a long, drawn-out conflict, a "broken backed war," waged with conventional weapons because both sides have simultaneously used up all their nuclear weapons. There is the claim that in a thermonuclear war it is important to keep the sea lanes open. And there is the quaint idea that the main purpose of civil defense is to support a thermonuclear war effort with men and materials. Or the equally quaint notion that after a massive interchange of thermonuclear bombs the major objective of the U.S. Army forces in the United States will not be civilian recuperation but to move to a (destroyed) port of embarkation for the movement overseas. While all of these views are most implausible, they can be found in various types of official and semiofficial statements.

Where do such ideas come from? They generally result, it can be assumed, from doctrinal lags or from position papers which primarily reflect a very narrow departmental interest or which are the result of log-rolling compromises between several partisan departments of government. We are fortunate that on the whole these views are no longer taken seriously even by many of the decision makers who sign the papers. Unfortunately, this does not prevent the papers themselves from influencing public opinion and policy to an important extent.

It should be noted that those who are convinced of the efficacy of Minimum or Finite Deterrence tend to believe that the Counterforce as Insurance, the Credible First Strike Capability, and the Splendid First Strike Capability views are as fanciful as the dream capabilities mentioned above. If anything, they find them more dangerously fanciful because so many people take them seriously. In this book only the following strategic positions will be considered seriously: Finite Deterrence, Counterforce as Insurance, Preattack Mobilization Base, and Credible First Strike Capability—*all* with varying degrees of Arms Control and Limited War Capability. The burden of my discussion will be on the nature, feasibility, and problems associated with each of these strategies, with the purpose of suggesting which one should be the basis of national policy. Our national policy at this writing seems to be drifting (mostly as a result of decisions evaded or decided for relatively minor technical reasons) toward accepting a strategy between Finite Deterrence and Counterforce as Insurance. *It is one of my main arguments that at least for the immediate future we should be somewhere between the Preattack Mobilization Base and the Credible First Strike Capability.* This posture would have, at least, enough capability to launch a first strike in the kind of tense situation that would result from an outrageous Soviet provocation, so as to induce uncertainty in the enemy as to whether it would not be safer to attack us directly rather than provoke us. The posture should have enough of a retaliatory capability to make this direct attack unattractive. It should have enough of a Preattack Mobilization Base to enable us to increase our first strike and retaliatory capabilities rapidly enough so that, if international relations deteriorate seriously, we will be able to acquire sufficient power in time to control or influence events. There should be enough Counterforce as Insurance so that if a war occurs anyway—perhaps as a result of accident or miscalculations—the nation will continue and unnecessary death and destruction will not occur. And lastly, the posture should include enough Arms Control and Limited War Capability to deter and correct "minor" conflicts and to make the day-to-day course of international relations livable until more permanent and stable arrangements are set up.

TOPICS FOR DISCUSSION AND WRITING

1. Does the author assume that all agree on the goal of national policy? Why does he state the goal in the way he does? Can you think of some other words which might have been used? Why does he avoid them? Why does he urge that one of the alternative national strategies which he will be discussing be selected as national policy on the highest level and not be discussed on lower levels?
2. If the goal of national policy is considered as an effect to be achieved or brought about, what are some of the alternative means which can be considered as causes which might bring about the hoped for effect?

How many of these alternative strategies have been proposed? Does he believe that his enumeration is complete? Does he entertain the possibility that someone else might be able to suggest other means of bringing about the desired effect?

3. After reading through the entire essay, which of these alternative strategies does the writer believe ought to be adopted as national policy? What, in other words, is his thesis? Why does he begin by refuting alternatives to his own policy?
4. Why does he think that a policy of placing trust in an internal police force plus world government is inadequate? What is his fundamental reason? Does he believe that this policy could ever work?
5. Why does he consider a policy of Minimum Deterrence plus Limited War Capability plus Arms Control inadequate? Why do so many professionals seem to maintain this as the desired policy?
6. Why does the author insist upon distinguishing between several possible postwar states? How would a difference between expected postwar states affect national policy? What happens when people fail to distinguish several possibilities?
7. Discuss the concept of First Strike Capability. Why would this concept seem unthinkable to many people?
8. Assuming that the proposed alternative strategies are all considered as causes which might bring about a desired effect, what kind of relationship would the proponent of one of these causes have to demonstrate between his cause and its proposed effect?
9. How does Kahn prove that some of the proposed causes would never achieve their intended effect? What is the difference in reliability between a cause-effect relationship which involves the consent of people and a cause-effect relationship which is entirely dependent upon the operation of physical forces? What conditions might influence our action in emergencies?
10. Write an essay showing how Kahn's arguments tend to strengthen or weaken the arguments advanced by Bertrand Russell in his essay *Co-Existence or No-Existence* (p. 65).
11. Write an essay using some of Kahn's arguments to strengthen or weaken either of the two attitudes regarding the establishment of a world government as explained by Crane Brinton (p. 36).
12. Are Kahn's arguments verifiable? Are they ultimately arguments from testimony—his own opinions bolstered only by his theories? If they are only hypotheses, is his authority questionable?

THE NATURE OF THE SUBJECT

Anyone who has studied mathematics, especially geometry or calculus, is familiar with arguments based upon the nature of the concepts involved in a thesis. A mathematical thesis, or proposition, is an affirmation of a relationship between a subject term and a predicate term. The proof that this relationship exists frequently depends upon an examination of what is implied in the subject and predicate terms. All mathematical proofs based on the *definition* of the concepts involved are proofs based upon the *nature* of the concepts, for definitions are statements of the nature of concepts or objects. Arguments or proofs from definition maintain that something is so because of the nature of the subject or predicate terms or because of the relationship existing between them.

Arguments derived from the nature of the concepts or objects involved in the thesis are deductive arguments and involve some use of classification. Classes (or sets, as the mathematicians call them) are collections of objects. The individual objects are elements of the set. If a set has a finite number of elements, it is known as a finite set. All other sets are infinite sets. The set of numbers from one to ten is a finite set because it contains a limited number of elements, namely ten elements. The set of all the numbers on the other hand is an infinite set because there is no limit to the amount of possible numbers.

One of the first theses to be demonstrated about sets is that a set A is a subset of a set B if each element of A is also an element of B. The only way this thesis can be proved is by a reflective consideration of the definition of set, subset, set A, and set B. Diagrams can be used to help clarify the relationship, but they will not make the relationship any more or less certain. A large circle can be used to represent set B and a smaller circle, completely circumscribed by the larger circle, to represent set

A. The diagram shows that set A is completely contained within set B. Therefore set A can be considered a subset of set B. Verbal illustrations can also be used to clarify an argument based upon the nature of concepts involved in a thesis. For example, the thesis that set A is a subset of set B if every element of A is also an element of B can be illustrated by using redheaded girls as an example of set A and girls as an example of set B. Since all redheaded girls (set A) are also girls (set B), every element of A is also an element of B.

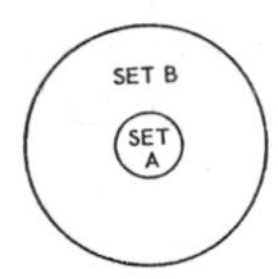

Arguments derived from the nature of ideas or objects under discussion tend to be very abstract. They are often more logically satisfying than rhetorically effective. Though they can be certain arguments, and may appeal to the careful reader who is more interested in the strength or weakness of an argument than in being entertained, they are difficult for readers who are not accustomed to critical reading or abstract demonstrations. Consequently, arguments derived from the nature of the subject are commonly found in writing which is more concerned with theory than practice and which is addressed to an informed, reflective audience.

Among the selections included in this section of the book is the first chapter of Zbigniew Brzezinski's book *The Permanent Purge*. The thesis of this book, implied in its title, is that a periodic purge of the upper administration echelons is essential to the survival of Stalinist Communism. The proof of the thesis consists, in part, of an analysis of the nature of Stalinist Communism. Once readers have had an opportunity to reflect on the implications of the concepts "permanent purge" and "Stalinist Communism," it is hoped that they will agree that there is a necessary connection between the two.

The section also includes a selection by K. E. Boulding on *The Religious Foundations of Economic Progress,* which argues that modern capitalism is the result of the theoretical support provided by Protestantism. The arguments in support of the thesis consist of analyzing the natures of contemporary capitalism and Protestantism to show how the theology provided a support for the economics. In similar fashion, Matthew Arnold and Sigmund Freud defend their respective theses by defining and analyzing the ideas with which they are concerned and by pointing to the interrelationships existing between these ideas.

Arguments derived from the nature of the subject tend to be very sound arguments. Weaknesses in arguments of this type can only result from an incorrect definition or incomplete analysis of the subject. If the definition is correct, whatever relations may be said to follow from it must be conceded. Consequently the critical reader who is interested in evaluating an argument derived from the nature of the subject should concentrate on determining whether or not the writer has correctly analyzed his terms. The writer anxious to discover all arguments which can be offered in support of his position might well begin by analyzing the nature of his terms to determine whether there are relationships existing between terms (either explicit or implicit) which would compel assent to his thesis. The more thorough the writer's initial analysis, the more familiar he will be with his thesis and the more likely he is to discover relationships in similar situations which will also help to prove his thesis. Therefore it is perhaps best for a writer to begin his argument with a thorough analysis of the ideas in his thesis, their implications, and the relationships which this analysis suggests.

Matthew Arnold

Matthew Arnold (1822–1888) was an essayist, poet, translator, literary and social critic, and one of the most eloquent defenders of tradition and the classics in an age when progress, science, and industry were exerting the strongest claims on men's attentions. Arnold's beliefs were revealed most clearly in a debate between himself and Thomas Henry Huxley, one of the champions of the scientific and progressivist school. In 1880, at the opening of a new college of science, Huxley delivered an address entitled Science and Culture, *in which he argued that*

> . . . neither the discipline nor the subject matter of classical education is of such direct value to the student of physical science as to justify the expenditure of valuable time upon either . . . (and) that for the purpose of attaining real culture, an exclusively scientific education is at least as effectual as an exclusively literary education.

Huxley's argument was primarily from consequence: The results of a scientific education are superior to a literary education; therefore let science be the chief object of study. Arnold answered Huxley in his essay Literature and Science, *first given at the University of Cambridge and later delivered in lectures on an American tour in 1883–1884. Arnold's argument is partly from consequence—the effects of literary study are valuable, therefore worthwhile—but it is chiefly an argument from nature: What do we mean by literature, and what can we learn from literature properly defined? A classic in its own right, Arnold's essay (we offer here his American version) is a landmark in the defense of the classics.*

Literature and Science

Practical people talk with a smile of Plato and of his absolute ideas; and it is impossible to deny that Plato's ideas do often seem unpractical and impracticable, and especially when one views them in connexion with the life of a great work-a-day world like the United States. The necessary staple of the life of such a world Plato regards with disdain; handicraft and trade and the working professions he regards with disdain; but what becomes of the life of an industrial modern community if you take handicraft and trade and the working professions out of it? The base mechanic arts and handicrafts, says Plato, bring about a natural weakness in the principle of excellence in a man, so that he cannot govern the ignoble growths in him, but nurses them, and cannot understand fostering any other. Those who exercise such arts and trades, as they have their bodies, he says, marred by their vulgar businesses, so they have their souls, too, bowed and broken by them. And if one of these uncomely people has a mind to seek self-culture and philosophy, Plato compares him to a bald little tinker, who has scraped together money, and has got his release from service, and has had a bath, and bought a new coat, and is rigged out like a bridegroom about to marry the daughter of his master who has fallen into poor and helpless estate.

Nor do the working professions fare any better than trade at the hands of Plato. He draws for us an inimitable picture of the working lawyer, and of his life of bondage; he shows this bondage from his youth up has stunted and warped him, and made him small and crooked of soul, encompassing him with difficulties which he is not man enough to rely on justice and truth as means to encounter, but has recourse, for help out of them, to falsehood and wrong. And so, says Plato, this poor creature is bent and broken, and grows up from boy to man without a particle of soundness in him, although exceedingly smart and clever in his own esteem.

One cannot refuse to admire the artist who draws these pictures. But we say to ourselves that his ideas show the influence of a primitive and obsolete order of things, when the warrior caste and the priestly caste were alone in honour, and the humble work of the world was done by slaves. We have now changed all that; the modern majority consists in work, as Emerson declares; and in work, we may add, principally of such plain and dusty kind as the work of cultivators of the ground, handicraftsmen, men of trade and business, men of the working professions. Above all is this true in a great industrious community such as that of the United States.

Now education, many people go on to say, is still mainly governed by the ideas of men like Plato, who lived when the warrior caste and the priestly or philosophical class were alone in honour, and the really useful part of the community were slaves. It is an education fitted for persons of leisure in such a community. This education passed from Greece to Rome to the feudal communities of Europe, where also the warrior caste and the priestly caste were alone held in honour, and where the really useful and working part of the community, though not nominally slaves as in the pagan world, were practically not much better off than slaves, and not more seriously regarded. And how absurd it is, people end by saying, to inflict this education upon an industrious modern community, where very few indeed are persons of leisure, and the mass to be considered has not leisure, but is bound, for its own great good, and for the great good of the world at large, to plain labour and to industrial pursuits, and the education in question tends necessarily to make men dissatisfied with these pursuits and unfitted for them!

That is what is said. So far I must defend Plato, as to plead that his view of education and studies is in the general, as it seems to me, sound enough, and fitted for all sorts and conditions of men, whatever their pursuits may be. "An intelligent man," says Plato, "will prize those studies which result in his soul getting soberness, righteousness, and wisdom, and will less value the others." I cannot consider *that* a bad description of the aim of education, and of the motives which should govern us in the choice of studies, whether we are preparing ourselves for a hereditary seat in the English House of Lords or for the pork trade in Chicago.

Still I admit that Plato's world was not ours, that his scorn of trade and handicraft is fantastic, that he had no conception of a great industrial community such as that of the United States, and that such a community must and will shape its education to suit its own needs. If the usual education handed down to it from the past does not suit it, it will certainly before long drop this and try another. The usual education in the past has been mainly literary. The question is whether the studies which were long supposed to be the best for all of us are practically the best now; whether others are not better. The tyranny of the past, many think, weighs on us injuriously in the predominance given to letters in education. The question is raised whether, to meet the needs of our modern life, the predominance ought not now to pass from letters to science; and naturally the question is nowhere raised with more energy than here in the United States. The design of abasing what is called "mere literary instruction and education," and of exalting what is called "sound, extensive, and practical scientific knowledge," is, in this intensely modern world of the United States, even more perhaps than in Europe, a very popular design, and makes great and rapid progress.

I am going to ask whether the present movement for ousting letters from their old predominance in education, and for transferring the predominance in education to the natural sciences, whether this brisk and flourishing movement ought to prevail, and whether it is likely that in the end it really will prevail. An objection might be raised which I will anticipate. My own studies have been almost wholly in letters, and my visits to the field of natural sciences have been very slight and inadequate, although those sciences have always strongly moved my curiosity. A man of letters, it will perhaps be said, is not competent to discuss the comparative merits of letters and natural science as means of education. To this objection I reply, first of all, that his incompetence, if he attempts the discussion but is really incompetent for it, will be abundantly visible; nobody will be taken in; he will have plenty of sharp observers and critics to save mankind from that danger. But the line I am going to follow is, as you will soon discover, so extremely simple, that perhaps it may be followed without failure even by one who for a more ambitious line of discussion would be quite incompetent.

Some of you may possibly remember a phrase of mine which has been the object of a good deal of comment; an observation to the effect that in our culture, the aim being *to know ourselves and the world,* we have, as the means to this end, *to know the best which has been thought and said in the world.* A man of science, who is also an excellent writer and the very prince of debaters, Professor Huxley, in a discourse at the opening of Sir Josiah Mason's college at Birmingham,[1] laying hold of this phrase, expanded it by quoting some more words of mine, which are these:

> The civilised world is to be regarded as now being, for intellectual and spiritual purposes, one great confederation, bound to a joint action and working to a common result; and whose members have for their proper outfit a knowledge of Greek, Roman, and Eastern antiquity, and of one another. Special local and temporary advantages being put out of account, that modern nation will in the intellectual and spiritual sphere make most progress which most thoroughly carries out this programme.

Now on my phrase, thus enlarged, Professor Huxley remarks that when I speak of the above-mentioned knowledge as enabling

[1] A reference to a college of applied science established in Birmingham, England, on October 1, 1880.

us to know ourselves and the world, I assert *literature* to contain the materials which suffice for thus making us know ourselves and the world. But it is not by any means clear, says he, that after having learnt all which ancient and modern literatures have to tell us, we have laid a sufficiently broad and deep foundation for that criticism of life, that knowledge of ourselves and the world, which constitutes culture. On the contrary, Professor Huxley declares that he finds himself "wholly unable to admit that either nations or individuals will really advance, if their outfit draws nothing from the stores of physical science. An army without weapons of precision, and with no particular base of operations, might more hopefully enter upon a campaign on the Rhine, than a man, devoid of knowledge of what physical science has done in the last century, upon a criticism of life."

This shows how needful it is for those who are to discuss any matter together, to have a common understanding as to the sense of the terms they employ—how needful, and how difficult. What Professor Huxley says implies just the reproach which is so often brought against the study of *belles lettres,* as they are called: that the study is an excellent one, but slight and ineffectual; a smattering of Greek and Latin and other ornamental things, of little use for any one whose object is to get at truth and to be a practical man. So, too, M. Renan [2] talks of the "superficial humanism" of a school course which treats us as if we were all going to be poets, writers, preachers, orators, and he opposes this humanism to positive science, or the critical search after truth. And there is always a tendency in those who are remonstrating against the predominance of letters in education, to understand by letters *belles lettres,* and by *belles lettres* a superficial humanism, the opposite of science or true knowledge.

But when we talk of knowing Greek and Roman antiquity, for instance, which is the knowledge people have called the humanities, I for my part mean a knowledge which is something more than a superficial humanism, mainly decorative. "I call all teaching scientific," says Wolf, the critic of Homer, "which is systematically laid out and followed up to its original sources. For example: a

[2] Ernest Renan, author of the philosophic essay *Questions Contemporaines* in which the question of "What is meant by a superior education?" was treated.

knowledge of classical antiquity is scientific when the remains of classical antiquity are correctly studied in the original languages." There can be no doubt that Wolf is perfectly right; that all learning is scientific which is systematically laid out and followed up to its original sources, and that a genuine humanism is scientific.

When I speak of knowing Greek and Roman antiquity, therefore, as a help to knowing ourselves and the world, I mean more than a knowledge of so much vocabulary, so much grammar, so many portions of authors in the Greek and Latin languages, I mean knowing the Greeks and Romans, and their life and genius, and what they were and did in the world; what we get from them, and what is its value. That, at least, is the ideal; and when we talk of endeavouring to know Greek and Roman antiquity, as a help to knowing ourselves and the world, we mean endeavouring so to know them as to satisfy this ideal, however much we may still fall short of it.

The same also as to knowing our own and other modern nations, with the like aim of getting to understand ourselves and the world. To know the best that has been thought and said by the modern nations, is to know, says Professor Huxley, "only what modern *literatures* have to tell us; it is the criticism of life contained in modern literature." And yet "the distinctive character of our times," he urges, "lies in the vast and constantly increasing part which is played by natural knowledge." And how, therefore, can a man, devoid of knowledge of what physical science has done in the last century, enter hopefully upon a criticism of modern life?

Let us, I say, be agreed about the meaning of the terms we are using. I talk of knowing the best which has been thought and uttered in the world: Professor Huxley says this means knowing *literature.* Literature is a large word; it may mean everything written with letters or printed in a book. Euclid's *Elements* and Newton's *Principia* are thus literature. All knowledge that reaches us through books is literature. But by literature Professor Huxley means *belles lettres.* He means to make me say, that knowing the best which has been thought and said by the modern nations is knowing their *belles lettres* and no more. And this is no sufficient equipment, he argues, for a criticism of modern life. But as I do not mean, by knowing ancient Rome, knowing merely more or less of

Latin *belles lettres,* and taking no account of Rome's military and political and legal and administrative work in the world; and as, by knowing ancient Greece, I understand knowing her as the giver of Greek art, and the guide to a free and right use of reason and to scientific method, and the founder of our mathematics and physics and astronomy and biology—I understand knowing her as all this, and not merely knowing certain Greek poems and histories and treatises and speeches—so as to the knowledge of modern nations also. By knowing modern nations, I mean not merely knowing their *belles lettres,* but knowing also what has been done by such men as Copernicus, Galileo, Newton, Darwin. "Our ancestors learned," says Professor Huxley, "that the earth is the centre of the visible universe, and that man is the cynosure of things terrestrial; and more especially was it inculcated that the course of nature had no fixed order, but that it could be, and constantly was, altered." But for us now, continues Professor Huxley, "the notions of the beginning and the end of the world entertained by our forefathers are no longer credible. It is very certain that the earth is not the chief body in the material universe, and that the world is not subordinated to man's use. It is even more certain that nature is the expression of a definite order, with which nothing interferes." "And yet," he cries, "the purely classical education advocated by the representatives of the humanists in our day gives no inkling of all this!"

In due place and time I will just touch upon that vexed question of classical education; but at present the question is as to what is meant by knowing the best which modern nations have thought and said. It is not knowing their *belles lettres* merely which is meant. To known Italian *belles lettres* is not to know Italy, and to known English *belles lettres* is not to know England. Into knowing Italy and England there comes a great deal more, Galileo and Newton amongst it. The reproach of being a superficial humanism, a tincture of *belles lettres,* may attach rightly enough to some other disciplines; but to the particular discipline recommended when I proposed knowing the best that has been thought and said in the world, it does not apply. In that best I certainly include what in modern times has been thought and said by the great observers and knowers of nature.

There is, therefore, really no question between Professor Huxley and me as to whether knowing the great results of the modern scientific study of nature is not required as a part of our culture, as well as knowing the products of literature and art. But to follow the processes by which those results are reached, ought, say the friends of physical science, to be made the staple education for the bulk of mankind. And here there does arise a question between those whom Professor Huxley calls with playful sarcasm "the Levites of culture," and those whom the poor humanist is sometimes apt to regard as its Nebuchadnezzars.[3]

The great results of the scientific investigation of nature we are agreed upon knowing, but how much of our study are we bound to give to the processes by which those results are reached? The results have their visible bearing on human life. But all the processes, too, all the items of fact, by which those results are reached and established, are interesting. All knowledge is interesting to a wise man, and the knowledge of nature is interesting to all men. It is very interesting to know, that, from the albuminous white of the egg, the chick in the egg gets the materials for its flesh, bones, blood and feathers; while, from the fatty yolk of the egg, it gets the heat and energy which enable it at length to break its shell and begin the world. It is less interesting, perhaps, but still it is interesting, to know that when a taper burns, the wax is converted into carbonic acid and water. Moreover, it is quite true that the habit of dealing with facts, which is given by the study of nature, is, as the friends of physical science praise it for being, an excellent discipline. The appeal, in the study of nature, is constantly to observation and experiment; not only is it said that the thing is so, but we can be made to see that it is so. Not only does a man tell us that when a taper burns the wax is converted into carbonic acid and water, as a man may tell us, if he likes, that Charon is punting his ferryboat on the river Styx, or that Victor Hugo is a sublime poet, or Mr. Gladstone the most admirable of statesmen; but we are made to see that the conversion into carbonic acid and water does actually happen. This reality of natural knowledge it is, which makes the

[3] The Levites were the guardians of the traditions and ceremonies of the Hebrew faith; Nebuchadnezzar was the Babylonian ruler who captured Jerusalem in the sixth century B.C. The contrast is being made between the traditionalist and the innovator.

friends of physical science contrast it, as a knowledge of things, with the humanist's knowledge, which is, say they, a knowledge of words. And hence Professor Huxley is moved to lay it down that, "for the purpose of attaining real culture, an exclusively scientific education is at least as effectual as an exclusively literary education." And a certain President of the Section for Mechanical Science in the British Association is, in Scripture phrase, "very bold," and declares that if a man, in his mental training, "has substituted literature and history for natural science, he has chosen the less useful alternative." But whether we go these lengths or not, we must all admit that in natural science the habit gained of dealing with facts is a most valuable discipline, and that every one should have some experience of it.

More than this, however, is demanded by the reformers. It is proposed to make the training in natural science the main part of education, for the great majority of mankind at any rate. And here, I confess, I part company with the friends of physical science, with whom up to this point I have been agreeing. In differing from them, however, I wish to proceed with the utmost caution and diffidence. The smallness of my own acquaintance with the disciplines of natural science is ever before my mind, and I am fearful of doing these disciplines an injustice. The ability and pugnacity of the partisans of natural science make them formidable persons to contradict. The tone of tentative inquiry, which befits a being of dim faculties and bounded knowledge, is the tone I would wish to take and not to depart from. At present it seems to me, that those who are for giving to natural knowledge, as they call it, the chief place in the education of the majority of mankind, leave one important thing out of their account: the constitution of human nature. But I put this forward on the strength of some facts not at all recondite, very far from it; facts capable of being stated in the simplest possible fashion, and to which, if I so state them, the man of science will, I am sure, be willing to allow their due weight.

Deny the facts altogether, I think, he hardly can. He can hardly deny that when we set ourselves to enumerate the powers which go to the building up of human life, and say that they are the power of conduct, the power of intellect and knowledge, the power of beauty, and the power of social life and manners—he can hardly deny that this scheme, though drawn in rough and plain lines enough, and not pretending to scientific exactness, does yet give a fairly true representation of the matter. Human nature is built up by these powers; we have the need for them all. When we have rightly met and adjusted the claims of them all, we shall then be in a fair way for getting soberness and righteousness, with wisdom. This is evident enough, and the friends of physical science would admit it.

But perhaps they may not have sufficiently observed another thing: namely, that the several powers just mentioned are not isolated, but there is, in the generality of mankind, a perpetual tendency to relate them one to another in diverse ways. With one such way of relating them I am particularly concerned now. Following our instinct for intellect and knowledge, we acquire pieces of knowledge; and presently, in the generality of men, there arises the desire to relate these pieces of knowledge to our sense for conduct, to our sense for beauty—and there is weariness and dissatisfaction if the desire is baulked. Now in this desire lies, I think, the strength of that hold which letters have upon us.

All knowledge is, as I said just now, interesting; and even items of knowledge which from the nature of the case cannot well be related, but must stand isolated in our thoughts, have their interest. Even lists of exceptions have their interest. If we are studying Greek accents, it is interesting to know that *pais* and *pas*, and some other monosyllables of the same form of declension, do not take the circumflex upon the last syllable of the genitive plural, but vary, in this respect, from the common rule. If we are studying physiology, it is interesting to know that the pulmonary artery carries dark blood and the pulmonary vein carries bright blood, departing in their respect from the common rule for the division of labour between the veins and the arteries. But every one knows how we seek naturally to combine the pieces of our knowledge together, to bring them under general rules, to relate them to principles; and how unsatisfactory and tiresome it would be to go on for ever learning lists of exceptions, or accumulating items of fact which must stand isolated.

Well, that same need of relating our knowledge, which operates here within the sphere of our knowledge itself, we shall find operating, also, outside that sphere. We experience, as we go on learning and knowing—the vast majority of us experience—the need of relating what we have learnt and known to the sense which we have in us for conduct, to the sense which we have in us for beauty.

A certain Greek prophetess of Mantineia in Arcadia, Diotima by name, once explained to the philosopher Socrates that love, and impulse, and bent of all kinds, is, in fact, nothing else but the desire in men that good should for ever be present to them. This desire for good, Diotima assured Socrates, is our fundamental desire, of which fundamental desire every impulse in us is only some one particular form. And therefore this fundamental desire it is, I suppose—this desire in men that good should be forever present to them—which acts in us when we feel the impulse for relating our knowledge to our sense for conduct and to our sense for beauty. At any rate, with men in general the instinct exists. Such is human nature. And the instinct, it will be admitted, is innocent, and human nature is preserved by our following the lead of its innocent instincts. Therefore, in seeking to gratify this instinct in question, we are following the instinct of self-preservation in humanity.

But, no doubt, some kinds of knowledge cannot be made to directly serve the instinct in question, cannot be directly related to the sense for beauty, to the sense for conduct. These are instrument-knowledges; they lead on to other knowledges which can. A man who passes his life in instrument-knowledges is a specialist. They may be invaluable as instruments to something beyond, for those who have the gift thus to employ them; and they may be disciplines in themselves wherein it is useful for every one to have some schooling. But it is inconceivable that the generality of men should pass all their mental life with Greek accents or with formal logic. My friend Professor Sylvester, who is one of the first mathematicians in the world, holds transcendental doctrines as to the virtue of mathematics, but those doctrines are not for common men. In the very Senate House and heart of our English Cambridge I once ventured, though not without an apology for my profaneness, to hazard the opinion that for the majority of mankind a little of mathematics, even, goes a long way. Of course this is quite consistent with their being of immense importance as an instrument to something else; but it is the few who have the aptitude for thus using them, not the bulk of mankind.

The natural sciences do not, however, stand on the same footing with these instrument-knowledges. Experience shows us that the generality of men will find more interest in learning that, when a taper burns, the wax is converted into carbonic acid and water, or in learning the explanation of the phenomenon of dew, or in learning how the circulation of the blood is carried on, than they find in learning that the genitive plural of *pais* and *pas* does not take the circumflex on the termination. And one piece of natural knowledge is added to another, and others are added to that, and at last we come to propositions so interesting as Mr. Darwin's famous proposition that "our ancestor was a hairy quadruped furnished with a tail and pointed ears, probably arboreal in his habits." Or we come to propositions of such reach and magnitude as those which Professor Huxley delivers, when he says that the notions of our forefathers about the beginning and the end of the world were all wrong, and that nature is the expression of a definite order with which nothing interferes.

Interesting, indeed, these results of science are, important they are, and we should all of us be acquainted with them. But what I now wish you to mark is, that we are still, when they are propounded to us and we receive them, we are still in the sphere of intellect and knowledge. And for the generality of men there will be found, I say, to arise, when they have duly taken in the proposition that their ancestor was "a hairy quadruped furnished with a tail and pointed ears, probably arboreal in his habits," there will be found to arise an invincible desire to relate this proposition to the sense in us for conduct, and to the sense in us for beauty. But this the men of science will not do for us, and will hardly even profess to do. They will give us other pieces of knowledge, other facts, about other animals and their ancestors, or about plants, or about stones, or about stars; and they may finally bring us to those great "general conceptions of the universe, which are forced upon us all," says Professor Huxley, "by the progress of physical science." But still it will be *knowledge* only which they give us; knowledge not put for us into relation with our sense for conduct, our sense for beauty, and touched with emotion by being so put; not thus put for us, and therefore, to the majority of mankind, after a certain while, unsatisfying, wearying.

Not to the born naturalist, I admit. But what do we mean by a born naturalist? We mean a man in whom the zeal for observing nature is so uncommonly strong and eminent, that it marks him off from the bulk of mankind. Such a man will pass his life happily in collecting natural knowledge and reasoning upon it, and will ask for nothing, or hardly anything, more. I have heard it said that the sagacious and admirable naturalist whom we lost not very long ago, Mr. Darwin, once owned to a friend that for his part he did not experience the necessity for two things which most men find so necessary to them—religion and poetry; science and the domestic affections, he thought, were enough. To a born naturalist, I can well understand that this should seem so. So absorbing is his occupation with nature, so strong his love for his occupation, that he goes on acquiring natural knowledge and reasoning upon it, and has little time or inclination for thinking about getting it related to the desire in man for conduct, the desire in man for beauty. He relates it to them for himself as he goes along, so far as he feels the need; and he draws from the domestic affections all the additional solace necessary. But then Darwins are extremely rare. Another great and admirable master of natural knowledge, Faraday, was a Sandemanian. That is to say, he related his knowledge to his instinct for conduct and to his instinct for beauty, by the aid of that respectable Scottish sectary, Robert Sandeman. And so strong, in general, is the demand of religion and poetry to have their share in a man, to associate themselves with his knowing, and to relieve and rejoice it, that, probably, for one man amongst us with the disposition to do as Darwin did in this respect, there are at least fifty with the disposition to do as Faraday.

Education lays hold upon us, in fact, by satisfying this demand. Professor Huxley holds up to scorn mediaeval education, with its neglect of the knowledge of nature, its poverty even of literary studies, its formal logic devoted to "showing how and why that which the Church said was true must be true." But the great mediaeval universities were not brought into being, we may be sure, by the zeal for giving a jejune and contemptible education. Kings have been their nursing fathers, and queens have been their nursing mothers, but not for this. The mediaeval universities came into being because the supposed knowledge, delivered by Scripture and the Church, so deeply engaged men's hearts, by so simply, easily, and powerfully relating itself to their desire for conduct, their desire for beauty. All other knowledge was dominated by this supposed knowledge and was subordinated to it, because of the surpassing strength of the hold which it gained upon the affections of men, by allying itself profoundly with their sense for conduct, their sense for beauty.

But now, says Professor Huxley, conceptions of the universe fatal to the notions held by our forefathers have been forced upon us by physical science. Grant to him that they are thus fatal, that the new conceptions must and will soon become current everywhere, and that everyone will finally perceive them to be fatal to the beliefs of our forefathers. The need of humane letters, as they are truly called, because they serve the paramount desire in men that good should be forever present to them—the need of humane letters, to establish a relation between the new conceptions, and our instinct for beauty, our instinct for conduct, is only the more visible. The Middle Age could do without humane letters, as it could do without the study of nature, because its supposed knowledge was made to engage its emotions so powerfully. Grant that the supposed knowledge disappears, its power of being made to engage the emotions will of course disappear along with it—but the emotions themselves, and their claim to be engaged and satisfied, will remain. Now if we find by experience that humane letters have an undeniable power of engaging the emotions, the importance of humane letters in a man's training becomes not less, but greater, in proportion to the success of modern science in extirpating what it calls "mediaeval thinking."

Have humane letters, then, have poetry and eloquence, the power here attributed to them of engaging the emotions, and do they exercise it? And if they have it and exercise it, *how* do they exercise it, so as to exert an influence upon man's sense for conduct, his sense for beauty? Finally, even if they both can and do exert an influence upon the senses in question, how are they to relate to them the results—the modern results—of natural science? All these questions may be asked. First, have poetry and eloquence the power of calling out the emotions? The appeal is to experience. Experience shows that for the vast majority of men, for mankind in general, they have the power. Next, do they exercise it? They do. But then, *how* do they exercise it so as to affect man's sense for conduct, his sense for beauty? And this is perhaps a case for applying the Preacher's words: "Though a man labour to seek it out, yet he shall not find it; yea, farther, though a wise man think to know it, yet shall he not be able to find it." Why should it be one thing, in its effect upon the emotions, to say, "Patience is a virtue," and quite another thing, in its effect upon the emotions, to say with Homer . . . "for an enduring heart have the destinies appointed to the children of men"? Why should it be one thing, in its effect upon the emotions, to say with the philosopher Spinoza, *Felicitas in eo consistit quod homo suum esse conservare potest*—"Man's happiness consists in his being able to preserve his own essence," and quite another thing, in its effort upon the emotions, to say with the Gospel, "What is a man advantaged, if he gain the whole world, and lose himself, forfeit himself?" How does this difference of effect arise? I cannot tell, and I am not much concerned to know; the important thing is that it does arise, and that we can profit by it. But how, finally, are poetry and eloquence to exercise the power of relating the modern results of natural science to man's instinct for conduct, his instinct for beauty? And here again I answer that I do not know *how* they will exercise it, but that they can and will exercise it I am sure. I do not mean that modern philosophical poets and modern philosophical moralists are to come and relate for us, in express terms, the results of modern scientific research to our instinct for conduct, our instinct for beauty. But I mean that we shall find, as a matter of experience, if we know the best that has been thought and uttered in the world, we shall find that the art and poetry and eloquence of men who lived, perhaps long ago, who had the most limited natural knowledge, who had the most erroneous conceptions about many important matters, we shall find that this art, and poetry, and eloquence, have in fact not only the power of refreshing and delighting us, they have also the power—such is the strength and worth, in essentials, of their authors' criticism of life—they have a fortifying and elevating and quickening and suggestive power, capable of wonderfully helping us to relate the results of modern science to our need for conduct, our need for beauty. Homer's conceptions of the physical universe were, I imagine, grotesque; but really, under the shock of hearing from modern science that "the world is not subordinated to man's use, and that man is not the cynosure of things terrestrial," I could, for my own part, desire no better comfort than Homer's line which I quoted just now . . . "for an enduring heart have the destinies appointed to the children of men!"

And the more that men's minds are cleared, the more that the results of science are frankly accepted, the more that poetry and eloquence come to be received and studied as what in truth they really are—the criticism of life by gifted men, alive and active with extraordinary power at an unusual number of points—so much the more will the value of humane letters, and of art also, which is an utterance having a like kind of power with theirs, be felt and acknowledged, and their place in education be secured.

Let us therefore, all of us, avoid indeed as much as possible any invidious comparison between the merits of humane letters, as means of education, and the merits of the natural sciences. But when some President of a Section for Mechanical Science insists on making the comparison, and tells us that "he who in his training has substituted literature and history for natural science has chosen the less useful alternative," let us make answer to him that the student of humane letters only, will, at least, know also the great general conceptions brought in by modern physical science; for science, as Professor Huxley says, forces them upon us all. But the student of the natural sciences only, will, by our very hypothesis, know nothing of humane letters; not to mention that in setting himself to be perpetually accumulating natural knowledge, he sets himself to do what only specialists have in general the gift for doing genially. And so he will probably be unsatisfied, or at any rate incomplete, and even more incomplete than the student of humane letters only.

I once mentioned, in a school report, how a young man in one of our English training-colleges having to paraphrase the passage in *Macbeth* beginning, "Can'st thou not minister to a mind diseased?" turned this line into, "Can you not wait upon the lunatic?"

And I remarked what a curious state of things it would be, if every pupil of our national schools knew, let us say, that the moon is two thousand one hundred and sixty miles in diameter, and thought at the same time that a good paraphrase for "Can'st thou not minister to a mind diseased?" was, "Can you not wait upon the lunatic?" If one is driven to choose, I think I would rather have a young person ignorant about the moon's diameter, but aware that "Can you not wait upon the lunatic?" is bad, than a young person whose education had been such as to manage things the other way.

Or to go higher than the pupils of our national schools, I have in my mind's eye a member of our British Parliament who comes to travel here in America, who afterwards relates his travels, and who shows a really masterly knowledge of the geology of this great country and of its mining capabilities, but who ends by gravely suggesting that the United States should borrow a prince from our Royal Family, and should make him their king, and should create a House of Lords of great landed proprietors after the pattern of ours; and then America, he thinks, would have her future happily and perfectly secured. Surely, in this case, the President of the Section for Mechanical Science would himself hardly say that our member of Parliament, by concentrating himself upon geology and mineralogy, and so on, and not attending to literature and history, had "chosen the more useful alternative."

If then there is to be separation and option between humane letters on the one hand, and the natural sciences on the other, the great majority of mankind, all who have not exceptional and overpowering aptitudes for the study of nature, would do well, I cannot but think, to choose to be educated in humane letters rather than in the natural sciences. Letters will call out their being at more points, will make them live more.

I said before I ended I would just touch on the question of classical education, and I will keep my word. Even if literature is to retain a large place in our educaton, yet Latin and Greek, say the friends of progress, will certainly have to go. Greek is the grand offender in the eyes of these gentlemen. The attackers of the established course of study think that against Greek, at any rate, they have irresistible arguments. Literature may perhaps be needed in education, they say; but why on earth should it be Greek literature? Why not French or German? Nay, "has not an Englishman models in his own literature of every kind of excellence?" As before, it is not on any weak pleadings of my own that I rely for convincing the gainsayers; it is on the constitution of human nature itself, and on the instinct of self-preservation in humanity. The instinct for beauty is set in human nature, as surely as the instinct for knowledge is set there, or the instinct for conduct. If the instinct for beauty is served by Greek literature and art as it is served by no other literature and art, we may trust to the instinct of self-preservation in humanity for keeping Greek as part of our culture. We may trust to it for even making the study of Greek more prevalent than it is now. Greek will come, I hope, some day to be studied more rationally than at present; but it will be increasingly studied as men increasingly feel the need in them for beauty, and how powerfully Greek art and Greek literature can serve this need. Women will again study Greek, as Lady Jane Grey did; I believe that in that chain of forts, with which the fair host of the Amazons are now engirdling our English universities, I find that here in America, in colleges like Smith College in Massachusetts, and Vassar College in the state of New York, and in the happy families of the mixed universities out West, they are studying it already.

Defuit una mihi symmetria prisca—"The antique symmetry was the one thing wanting to me," said Leonardo da Vinci, and he was an Italian. I will not presume to speak for the Americans, but I am sure that, in the Englishman, the want of this admirable symmetry of the Greeks is a thousand times more great and crying than in any Italian. The results of the want show themselves most glaringly, perhaps, in our architecture, but they show themselves, also, in all our art. *Fit details strictly combined, in view of a large general result nobly conceived;* that is just the beautiful *symmetria prisca* of the Greeks, and it is just where we English fail, where all our art fails. Striking ideas we have, and well-executed details we have; but that high symmetry which with satisfying and delightful effect combines them, we seldom or never have. The glorious beauty of the Acropolis at Athens did not come from single fine things stuck about on that hill, a statue here, a gateway there—no, it arose from all things being perfectly combined for a supreme total effect. What must not an Englishman feel about our deficiencies in this respect, as the sense for beauty, whereof this symmetry is an essential element, awakens and strengthens within him! What will not one day be his respect and desire for Greece and its *symmetria prisca,* when the scales drop from his eyes as he walks the London streets, and he sees such a lesson in meanness as the Strand, for instance, in its true deformity! But here we are coming to our friend Mr. Ruskin's province, and I will not intrude upon it, for he is its very sufficient guardian.

And so we at last find, it seems, we find flowing in favour of the humanities the natural and necessary stream of things, which seemed against them when we started. The "hairy quadruped furnished with a tail and pointed ears, probably arboreal in his habits," this good fellow carried hidden in his nature, apparently, something destined to develop into a necessity for humane letters. Nay, more; we seem finally to be even led to the further conclusion that our hairy ancestor carried in his nature, also, a necessity for Greek.

And therefore, to say the truth, I cannot really think that humane letters are in much actual danger of being thrust out from their leading place in education, in spite of the array of authorities against them at this moment. So long as human nature is what it is, their attractions will remain irresistible. As with Greek, so with letters generally: they will some day come, we may hope, to be studied more rationally, but they will not lose their place. What will happen will rather be that there will be crowded into education other matters besides, far too many; there will be, perhaps, a period of unsettlement and confusion and false tendency; but letters will not in the end lose their leading place. If they lose it for a time, they will get it back again. We shall be brought back to them by our wants and aspirations. And a poor humanist may possess his soul in patience, neither strive nor cry, admit the energy and brilliancy of the partisans of physical science, and their present favour with the public, to be far greater than his own, and still have a happy faith that the nature of things works silently on behalf of the studies which he loves, and that, while we shall all have to acquaint ourselves with the great results reached by modern science, and to give ourselves as much training in its disciplines as we can conveniently carry, yet the majority of men will always require humane letters; and so much the more, as they have the more and the greater results of science to relate to the need in man for conduct, and to the need in him for beauty.

TOPICS FOR DISCUSSION AND WRITING

1. What care does Arnold take, in the opening of his essay, not to antagonize his audience, most of whom probably sympathize with Huxley's point of view?
2. How does Arnold define literature? Is it the same definition as Huxley's? Is it a valid definition?
3. Why does Arnold undertake a definition of human nature? What does this have to do with his argument on behalf of literature?
4. What reason does Arnold have for rejecting the argument from effect and consequence? What is the *symmetria prisca* which Arnold puts in the place of *practical effects?* How does his example of the misinterpretation of the line from *Macbeth* illustrate his thesis?
5. Does Arnold's essay seem to you at all relevant to any of today's educational issues? If he were writing today, would he have to revise any of his opinions and judgments? Compare Arnold's position with Robert Oppenheimer's in the essay *Prospects in the Arts and Sciences* (p. 498). Is there any similarity?
6. Write an essay using Arnold's arguments to defend the importance of the study of literature against the demands for more and more science in today's curriculum. Or, if you disagree with Arnold, write an essay refuting his arguments. Isn't it more important to land a man on the moon than to waste valuable curriculum time on the study of Homer or Shakespeare?
7. Write an essay in which you discuss what you understand by "the humanistic definition of man" and "the scientific definition of man."

Sigmund Freud

Sigmund Freud (1856–1939), founder of psychoanalysis, began his professional career as a medical man; his first writings dealt with diseases of the nervous system, and he held a post as professor of neuropathology at the University of Vienna from 1902 until he fled the Nazi anti-Jewish pogrom in 1938. But it was in psychology and psychoanalysis that he made his greatest contribution to modern thought. Dissatisfied with the traditional explanations of the human mind and emotions, Freud redefined the human personality in terms which have now become part of our contemporary vocabularly. Professing to have discovered many of his ideas in the works of the great poets, Freud has repaid his debt to them by making available to artists and interpreters of art a challenging theory of how the mind and the imagination operate. His essay printed below is a definition of his major terms, and one of his attempts to re-examine and re-evaluate the human personality.

The Anatomy of the Mental Personality *

Ladies and gentlemen—I am sure you all recognise in your dealings, whether with persons or things, the importance of your starting point. It was the same with psychoanalysis: the course of development through which it has passed, and the reception which it has met with have not been unaffected by the fact that what it began working upon was the symptom, a thing which is more foreign to the ego than anything else in the mind. The symptom has its origin in the repressed, it is as it were the representative of the repressed in relation to the ego; the repressed is a foreign territory to the ego, an internal foreign territory, just as reality is—you must excuse the unusual expression—an external foreign territory. From the symptom the path of psychoanalysis led to the unconscious, to the life of the instincts, to sexuality, and it was then that psychoanalysis was met by illuminating criticisms to the effect that man is not merely a sexual being but has nobler and higher feelings. It might have been added that, supported by the consciousness of those higher feelings, he often allowed himself the right to think nonsense and to overlook facts.

You know better than that. From the very beginning our view was that men fall ill owing to the conflict between the demands of their instincts and the internal resistance which is set up against them; not for a moment did we forget this resisting, rejecting, and repressing factor, which we believed to be furnished with its own special forces, the ego-instincts, and which corresponds to the ego

* From *New Introductory Lectures in Psychoanalysis* by Sigmund Freud, by permission of W. W. Norton & Company, Inc. Translated by W. J. H. Sprott.

of popular psychology. The difficulty was that, since the progress of all scientific work is necessarily laborious, psychoanalysis could not study every part of the field at once or make a pronouncement on every problem in one breath. At last we had got so far that we could turn our attention from the repressed to the repressing forces, and we came face to face with the ego, which seemed to need so little explanation, with the certain expectation that there, too, we should find things for which we could not have been prepared; but it was not easy to find a first method of approach. That is what I am going to talk to you about today.

Before I start, I may tell you that I have a suspicion that my account of the psychology of the ego will affect you differently than the introduction into the psychological underworld that preceded it. Why that should be the case, I cannot say for certain. My original explanation was that you would feel that, whereas hitherto I have been telling you in the main about facts, however strange and odd they might appear, this time you would be listening chiefly to theories, that is to say, speculations. But that is not quite true; when I weighed the matter more carefully I was obliged to conclude that the part played by intellectual manipulation of the facts is not much greater in our ego-psychology than it was in the psychology of the neuroses. Other explanations turned out to be equally untenable, and I now think that the character of the material itself is responsible, and the fact that we are not accustomed to dealing with it. Anyhow I shall not be surprised if you are more hesitant and careful in your judgment than you have been hitherto.

The situation in which we find ourselves at the beginning of our investigation will itself suggest the path we have to follow. We wish to make the ego the object of our study, our own ego. But how can we do that? The ego is the subject *par excellence,* how can it become the object? There is no doubt, however, that it can. The ego can take itself as object, it can treat itself like any other object, observe itself, criticise itself, and do heaven knows what besides with itself. In such a case one part of the ego stands over against the other. The ego can, then, be split; it splits when it performs many of its functions, at least for the time being. The parts can afterwards join up again. After all that is saying nothing new; perhaps it is only underlining more than usual something that every one knows already. But on the other hand we are familiar with the view that pathology, with its magnification and exaggeration, can make us aware of normal phenomena which we should otherwise have missed. Where pathology displays a breach or a cleft, under normal conditions there may well be a link. If we throw a crystal to the ground, it breaks, but it does not break haphazard; in accordance with the lines of cleavage it falls into fragments, whose limits were already determined by the structure of the crystal, although they were invisible. Psychotics are fissured and splintered structures such as these. We cannot deny them a measure of that awe with which madmen were regarded by the peoples of ancient times. They have turned away from external reality, but for that very reason they know more of internal psychic reality and can tell us much that would otherwise be inaccessible to us. One group of them suffer what we call delusions of observation. They complain to us that they suffer continually, and in their most intimate actions, from the observation of unknown powers or persons, and they have hallucinations in which they hear these persons announcing the results of their observations: "now he is going to say this, now he is dressing himself to go out," and so on. Such observation is not the same thing as persecution, but it is not far removed from it. It implies that these persons distrust the patient, and expect to catch him doing something that is forbidden and for which he will be punished. How would it be if these mad people were right, if we all of us had an observing function in our egos threatening us with punishment, which, in their case, had merely become sharply separated from the ego and had been mistakenly projected into external reality?

I do not know whether it will appeal to you in the same way as it appeals to me. Under the strong impression of this clinical picture, I formed the idea that the separating off of an observing function from the rest of the ego might be a normal feature of the ego's structure; this idea has never left me, and I was driven to investigate the further characteristics and relations of the function which had been separated off in this way. The next step is soon taken. The actual content of the delusion of observation makes it probable that the observation is only a first step towards conviction and punishment, so that we may guess that another activity of this function must be what we call conscience. There is hardly anything that we separate off from our ego so regularly as our conscience and so easily set over against it. I feel a temptation to do something which promises to bring me pleasure, but I refrain from doing it on the ground that "my conscience will not allow it." Or I allow myself to be persuaded by the greatness of the expectation of pleasure into doing something against which the voice of my conscience has protested, and after I have done it my conscience punishes me with painful reproaches, and makes me feel remorse for it. I might say simply that the function which I am beginning to distinguish within the ego is the conscience; but it is more prudent to keep that function as a separate entity and assume that conscience is one of its activities, and that the self-observation which is necessary as a preliminary to the judicial aspect of conscience is another. And since the process of recognizing a thing as a separate entity involves giving it a name of its own, I will henceforward call this function in the ego the "super-ego."

At this point I am quite prepared for you to ask scornfully whether our ego-psychology amounts to no more than taking everyday abstractions literally, magnifying them, and turning them from concepts into things—which would not be of much assistance. My answer to that is, that in ego-psychology it will be difficult to avoid what is already familiar, and that it is more a question of arriving at new ways of looking at things and new groupings of the facts than of making new discoveries. I will not ask you, therefore, to abandon your critical attitude but merely to await further developments. The facts of pathology give our efforts a background for which you will look in vain in popular psychology. I will proceed. No sooner have we got used to the idea of this super-ego as something which enjoys a certain independence, pursues its own ends, and is independent of the ego as regards the energy at its disposal, than we are faced with a clinical picture which throws into strong relief the severity, and even cruelty, of this function, and the vicissitudes through which its relations with the ego may pass. I refer to the condition of melancholia, or more accurately the melancholic attack, of which you must have heard often enough, even if you are not psychiatrists. In this disease, about whose causes and mechanism we know far too little, the most remarkable characteristic is the way in which the super-ego—you may call it, but in a whisper, the conscience—treats the ego. The melancholiac during periods of health can, like any one else, be more or less severe towards himself; but when he has a melancholic attack, his super-ego becomes over-severe, abuses, humiliates, and ill-treats his unfortunate ego, threatens it with the severest punishments, reproaches it for long forgotten actions which were at the time regarded quite lightly, and behaves as though it had spent the whole interval in amassing complaints and was only waiting for its present increase in strength to bring them forward, and to condemn the ego on their account. The super-ego has the ego at its mercy and applies the most severe moral standards to it; indeed it represents the whole demands of morality, and we see all at once that our moral sense of guilt is the expression of the tension between the ego and the super-ego. It is a very remarkable experience to observe morality, which was ostensibly conferred on us by God and planted deep in our hearts, functioning as a periodical phenomenon. For after a certain number of months the whole moral fuss is at an end, the critical voice of the super-ego is silent, the ego is reinstated, and enjoys once more all the rights of man until the next attack. Indeed in many forms of the malady something exactly the reverse takes place during the intervals; the ego finds itself in an ecstatic state of exaltation, it triumphs, as though the super-ego had lost all its power or had become merged with the ego, and this liberated, maniac ego gives itself up in a really uninhibited fashion, to the satisfaction of all its desires. Happenings rich in unsolved riddles!

You will expect me to do more than give a mere example in support of my statement that we have learnt a great deal about the formation of the super-ego, that is, of the origin of conscience. The philosopher Kant once declared that nothing proved to him the greatness of God more convincingly than the starry heavens and the moral conscience within us. The stars are unquestionably superb, but where conscience is concerned God has been guilty of an uneven and careless piece of work, for a great many men have only a limited share of it or scarcely enough to be worth mentioning. This does not mean, however, that we are overlooking the fragment of psychological truth which is contained in the assertion that conscience is of divine origin! But the assertion needs interpretation. Conscience is no doubt something within us, but it has not been there from the beginning. In this sense it is the opposite of sexuality, which is certainly present from the very beginning of life, and is not a thing that only comes in later. But small children are notoriously amoral. They have no internal inhibitions against their pleasure-seeking impulses. The rôle, which the super-ego undertakes later in life, is at first played by an external power, by parental authority. The influence of the parents dominates the child by granting proofs of affection and by threats of punishment, which, to the child, mean loss of love, and which must also be feared on their own account. This objective anxiety is the forerunner of the later moral anxiety; so long as the former is dominant one need not speak of super-ego or of conscience. It is only later that the secondary situation arises, which we are far too ready to regard as the normal state of affairs; the external restrictions are introjected, so that the super-ego takes the place of the parental function, and thenceforward observes, guides and threatens the ego in just the same way as the parents acted to the child before.

The super-ego, which in this way has taken over the power, the aims and even the methods of the parental function, is, however, not merely the legatee of parental authority, it is actually the heir of its body. It proceeds directly from it, and we shall soon learn in what way this comes about. First, however, we must pause to consider a point in which they differ. The super-ego seems to have made a one-sided selection, and to have chosen only the harshness and severity of the parents, their preventive and punitive functions, while their loving care is not taken up and continued by it. If the parents have really ruled with a rod of iron, we can easily understand the child developing a severe super-ego, but, contrary to our expectations, experience shows that the super-ego may reflect the same relentless harshness even when the upbringing has been gentle and kind, and avoided threats and punishment as far as possible. We shall return to this contradiction later, when we are dealing with the transmutation of instincts in the formation of the super-ego.

I cannot tell you as much as I could wish about the change from the parental function to the super-ego, partly because that process is so complicated that a description of it does not fit into the framework of a set of introductory lectures such as these, and partly because we ourselves do not feel that we have fully understood it. You will have to be satisfied, therefore, with the following indications. The basis of the process is what we call an identification, that is to say, that one ego becomes like another, one which results in the first ego behaving itself in certain respects in the same way as the second: it imitates it, and as it were takes it into itself. This identification has been not inappropriately compared with the oral cannibalistic incorporation of another person. Identification is a very important kind of relationship with another person, probably the most primitive, and is not to be confused with object-choice. One can express the difference between them in this way: when a boy identifies himself with his father, he wants to *be like* his father; when he makes him the object of his choice, he wants to *have* him, to possess him; in the first case his ego is altered on the model of his father, in the second case that is not necessary. Identification and object-choice are broadly speaking independent of each other; but one can identify oneself with a person, and alter one's ego accordingly, and take the same person as one's sexual object. It is said that this influencing of the ego by the sexual object takes place very often with women, and is characteristic of femininity. With regard to what is by far the most instructive relation between identification and object-choice, I must have given you some information in my previous lectures. It can be as easily observed in children as in adults, in normal as in sick persons. If one has lost a love-object or has had to give it up, one often compensates oneself by identifying oneself with it; one sets it up again inside one's ego, so that in this case object-choice regresses, as it were, to identification.

I am myself not at all satisfied with this account of identification, but it will suffice if you will grant that the establishment of the super-ego can be described as a successful instance of identification with the parental function. The fact which is decisively in favour of this point of view is that this new creation of a superior function within the ego is extremely closely bound up with the fate of the Oedipus complex, so that the super-ego appears as the heir of that emotional tie, which is of such importance for childhood. When the Oedipus complex passes away the child must give up the intense object-cathexes which it has formed towards its parents, and to compensate for this loss of object, its identifications with its parents, which have probably long been present, become greatly intensified. Identifications of this kind, which may be looked on as precipitates of abandoned object-cathexes, will recur often enough in the later life of the child; but it is in keeping with the emotional importance of this first instance of such a transformation that its product should occupy a special position in the ego. Further investigation also reveals that the super-ego does not attain to full strength and development if the overcoming of the Oedipus complex has not been completely successful. During the course of its growth, the super-ego also takes over the influence of those persons who have taken the place of the parents, that is to say of persons who have been concerned in the child's upbringing, and whom it has regarded as ideal models. Normally the super-ego is constantly becoming more and more remote from the original parents, becoming, as it were, more impersonal. Another thing that we must not forget is that the child values its parents differently at different periods of its life. At the time at which the Oedipus complex makes way for the super-ego, they seem to be splendid figures, but later on they lose a good deal of their prestige. Identifications take place with these later editions of the parents as well, and regularly provide important contributions to the formation of character; but these only affect the ego, they have no influence on the super-ego, which has been determined by the earliest parental imagos.

I hope you will by now feel that in postulating the existence of a super-ego I have been describing a genuine structural entity, and have not been merely personifying an abstraction, such as conscience. We have now to mention another important activity which is to be ascribed to the super-ego. It is also the vehicle of the ego ideal, by which the ego measures itself, towards which it strives, and whose demands for ever increasing perfection it is always striving to fulfill. No doubt this ego ideal is a precipitation of the old idea of the parents, an expression of the admiration which the child felt for the perfection which it at that time ascribed to them. I know you have heard a great deal about the sense of inferiority which is said to distinguish the neurotic subject. It crops up especially in the pages of works that have literary pretensions. A writer who brings in the expression "inferiority complex" thinks he has satisfied all the demands of psychoanalysis and raised his work on to a higher psychological plane. As a matter of fact the phrase "inferiority complex" is hardly ever used in psychoanalysis. It does not refer to anything which we regard as simple, let alone elementary. To trace it back to the perception in oneself of some organic disability or other, as the school of so-called Individual Psychologists like to do, seems to us a shortsighted error. The sense of inferiority has a strong erotic basis. The child feels itself inferior when it perceives that it is not loved, and so does the adult as well. The only organ that is really regarded as inferior is the stunted penis—the girl's clitoris. But the major part of the sense of inferiority springs from the relationship of the ego to its super-ego, and, like the sense of guilt, it is an expression of the tension between them. The sense of inferiority and the sense of guilt are exceedingly difficult to distinguish. Perhaps we should do better if we regarded the former as the erotic complement to the sense of moral inferiority. We have paid but little attention to such questions of conceptual differentiation in psychoanalysis.

Seeing that the inferiority complex has become so popular, I shall venture to treat you to a short digression. A historical personage of our time, who is still living but who for the present has retired into the background, suffers from the maldevelopment of a limb caused by an injury at birth. A very well-known contemporary writer who has a predilection for writing the biographies of famous persons, has dealt with the life of the man to whom I am referring. Now if one is writing a biography, it is naturally very difficult to suppress the urge for psychological understanding. The author has therefore made an attempt to build up the whole development of his hero's character on the basis of a sense of inferiority, which was caused by his physical defect. While doing this he has overlooked a small but not unimportant fact. It is usual for mothers to whom fate has given a sickly or otherwise defective child to try to compensate for this unfair handicap with an extra amount of love. In the case we are speaking of, the proud mother behaved quite differently; she withdrew her love from the child on account of his disability. When the child grew up into a man of great power, he proved beyond all doubt by his behaviour that he had never forgiven his mother. If you will bear in mind the importance of mother-love for the mental life of the child, you will be able to make the necessary corrections in the inferiority theory of the biographer.

But let us get back to the super-ego. We have allocated to it the activities of self-observation, conscience, and the holding up of ideals. It follows from our account of its origin that it is based upon an overwhelmingly important biological fact no less than upon a momentous psychological fact, namely the lengthy dependence of the human child on its parents and the Oedipus complex; these two facts, moreover, are closely bound up with each other. For us the super-ego is the representative of all moral restrictions, the advocate of the impulse towards perfection, in short it is as much as we have been able to apprehend psychologically of what people call the "higher" things in human life. Since it itself can be traced back to the influence of parents, teachers, and so on, we shall learn more of its significance if we turn our attention to these sources. In general, parents and similar authorities follow the dictates of their own super-egos in the upbringing of children. Whatever terms their ego may be on with their super-ego, in the education of the child they are severe and exacting. They have forgotten the difficulties of their own childhood, and are glad to be able to identify themselves fully at last with their own parents, who in their day subjected them to such severe restraints. The result is that the super-ego of the child is not really built up on the model of the parents, but on that of the parents' super-ego; it takes over the same content, it becomes the vehicle of tradition and of all the age-long values which have been handed down in this way from generation to generation. You may easily guess what great help is afforded by the recognition of the super-ego in understanding the social behaviour of man, in grasping the problem of delinquency, for example, and perhaps, too, in providing us with some practical hints upon education. It is probable that the so-called materialistic conceptions of history err in that they underestimate this factor. They brush it aside with the remark that the "ideologies" of mankind are nothing more than resultants of their economic situation at any given moment or superstructures built upon it. That is the truth, but very probably it is not the whole truth. Mankind never lives completely in the present; the ideologies of the super-ego perpetuate the past, the traditions of the race and the people, which yield but slowly to the influence of the present and to new developments, and, so long as they work through the super-ego, play an important part in man's life, quite independently of economic conditions.

In 1921 I tried to apply the distinction between the ego and the super-ego to the study of group psychology. I reached a formula, which ran like this: A psychological group is a collection of individuals, who have introduced the same person into their super-ego, and on the basis of this common factor have identified themselves with one another in their ego. This naturally only holds for groups who have a leader. If we could find more applications of this kind, the hypothesis of the super-ego would lose all its strangeness for us, and we should be entirely relieved of the embarrassment which we cannot help feeling when, used as we are to the atmosphere of the underworld, we make excursions into the more superficial and higher planes of the mental apparatus. Of course we do not for a moment think that the last word on ego psychology has been spoken with the demarcation of the super-ego. It is rather the beginning of the subject, but in this case it is not only the first step that is difficult.

But now another task awaits us, as it were, at the opposite end of the ego. This question is raised by an observation which is made during analytic work, an observation which is, indeed, an old one. As so often happens, it has taken a long time for its true value to be appreciated. As you are aware, the whole of psychoanalytic theory is in fact built up on the perception of the resistance exerted by the patient when we try to make him conscious of his unconscious. The objective indication of resistance is that his associations stop short or wander far away from the theme that is being discussed. He may also become subjectively aware of the resistance by experiencing painful feelings when he approaches the theme. But this last indication may be absent. In such a case we say to the patient that we conclude from his behaviour that he is in a state of resistance, and he replies that he knows nothing about it and is only aware of a difficulty in associating. Experience shows that we were right, but if so, his resistance too must have been unconscious, just as unconscious as the repressed material which we were trying to bring to the surface. Long ago we should have asked from which part of the mind such an unconscious resistance could operate. The beginner in psychoanalysis will be ready at once with the answer that it must be the resistance of the unconscious. An ambiguous and useless answer! If it means that the resistance operates from the repressed, then we must say: "Certainly not!" To the repressed we must rather ascribe a strong upward-driving force, an impulsion to get through to consciousness. The resistance can only be a manifestation of the ego, which carried through the repression at one time or other and is now endeavouring to keep it up. And that too was our earlier view. Now that we have posited a special function within the ego to represent demand for restriction and rejection, *i.e.*, the super-ego, we can say that repression is the work of the super-ego,—either that it does its work on its own account or else that the ego does it in obedience to its orders. If now we are faced with the case where the patient under analysis is not conscious of his resistance, then it must be either that the super-ego and the ego can operate unconsciously in quite important situations, or, which would be far more significant, that parts of both ego and super-ego themselves are unconscious. In both cases we should have to take account of the disturbing view that the ego (including the super-ego) does not by any means completely coincide with the conscious, nor the repressed with the unconscious.

Ladies and Gentlemen—I feel I must have a little breathing space, which I expect you will welcome with relief, and before I go on I must make an apology. Here am I giving you a supplement to the introduction to psychoanalysis which I started fifteen years ago, and I am behaving as though you yourselves had been doing nothing but psychoanalysis all that time. I know it is a monstrous supposition, but I am helpless, I have no alternative. The reason is that it is exceedingly difficult to give an insight into psychoanalysis to any one who is not himself a psychoanalyst. I assure you that we do not like to give the effect of being members of a secret society carrying on a secret science. And yet we have been obliged to recognise and state as our considered opinion that no one has a right to a say in psychoanalysis unless he has been through certain experiences which he can only have by being analysed himself. When I delivered my lectures to you fifteen years ago I tried to let you off certain speculative parts of our theory, but it is with those very parts that are connected the new discoveries which I am going to speak of today.

Now let me return to my theme. With regard to the two alternatives—that the ego and the super-ego may themselves be unconscious, or that they may merely give rise to unconscious effects—we have for good reasons decided in favour of the former. Certainly, large portions of the ego and super-ego can remain unconscious, are, in fact, normally unconscious. That means to say that the individual knows nothing of their contents and that it requires an expenditure of effort to make him conscious of them. It is true, then, that ego and conscious, repressed and unconscious do not coincide. We are forced fundamentally to revise our attitude towards the problem of conscious and unconscious. At first we might be inclined to think very much less of the importance of conciousness as a criterion, since it has proved so untrustworthy. But if we did so, we should be wrong. It is the same with life: it is not worth much, but it is all that we have. Without the light shed by the quality of consciousness we should be lost in the darkness of depth-psychology. Nevertheless we must try to orientate ourselves anew.

What is meant by "conscious" we need not discuss; it is beyond all doubt. The oldest and best meaning of the word "unconscious" is the descriptive one; we call "unconscious" any mental process the existence of which we are obliged to assume—because, for instance, we infer it in some way from its effects—but of which we are not directly aware. We have the same relation to that mental process as we have to a mental process in another person, except that it belongs to ourselves. If we want to be more accurate, we should modify the statement by saying that we call a process "unconcious" when we have to assume that it was active *at a certain time,* although *at that time* we knew nothing about it. This restriction reminds us that most conscious processes are conscious only for a short period; quite soon they become *latent,* though they can easily become conscious again. We could also say that they had become unconscious, if we were certain that they were still something mental when they were in the latent condition. So far we should have learnt nothing, and not even have earned the right to introduce the notion of the unconscious into psychology. But now we come across a new fact which we can already observe in the case of errors. We find that, in order to explain a slip of the tongue, for instance, we are obliged to assume that an intention to say some particular thing had formed itself in the mind of the person who made the slip. We can infer it with certainty from the occurrence of the speech disturbance, but it was not able to obtain expression; it was, that is to say, unconscious. If we subsequently bring the intention to the speaker's notice, he may recognise it as a familiar one, in which case it was only temporarily unconscious, or he may repudiate it as foreign to him, in which case it was permanently unconscious. Such an observation as this justifies us in also regarding what we have called "latent" as something "unconscious." The consideration of these dynamic relations puts us in a position to distinguish two kinds of unconscious: one which is transformed into conscious material easily and under conditions which frequently arise, and another in the case of which such a transformations is difficult, can only come about with a considerable expenditure of energy, or may never occur at all. In order to avoid any ambiguity as to whether we are referring to the one or the other unconscious, whether we are using the word in the descriptive or dynamic sense, we make use of a legitimate and simple expedient. We call the unconscious which is only latent, and so can easily become conscious, the "preconscious," and keep the name "unconscious" for the other. We have now three terms, "conscious," "preconscious," and "unconscious," to serve our purposes in describing mental phenomena. Once again, from a purely descriptive point of view, the "preconscious" is also unconscious, but we do not give it that name, except when we are speaking loosely, or when we have to defend in general the existence of unconscious processes in mental life.

You will, I hope, grant that so far things are not so bad and that the scheme is a convenient one. That is all very well; unfortunately our psychoanalytic work has compelled us to use the word "unconscious" in yet another, third, sense; and this may very well have given rise to confusion. Psychoanalysis has impressed us very strongly with the new idea that large and important regions of the mind are normally removed from the knowledge of the ego, so that the processes which occur in them must be recognized as unconscious in the true dynamic sense of the term. We have consequently also attributed to the word "unconscious" a topographical or systematic meaning; we have talked of *systems* of the preconscious and of the unconscious, and of a conflict between the ego and the Ucs. (unconscious) system; so that the word "unconscious" has more and more been made to mean a mental province rather than a quality which mental things have. At this point, the discovery, inconvenient at first sight, that parts of the ego and super-ego, too, are unconscious in the dynamic sense, has a facilitating effect and enables us to remove a complication. We evidently have no right to call that region of the mind which is neither ego nor super-ego the Ucs. system, since the character of unconsciousness is not exclusive to it. Very well; we will no longer use the word "unconscious" in the sense of a system, and to what we have hitherto called by that name we will give a better one, which will not give rise to misunderstandings. Borrowing, at G. Groddeck's suggestion, a term used by Nietzsche, we will call it henceforward the "id." This impersonal pronoun seems particularly suited to express the essential character of this province of the mind—the character of being foreign to the ego. Super-ego, ego, and id, then, are the three realms, regions, or provinces into which we divide the mental apparatus of the individual; and it is their mutual relations with which we shall be concerned in what follows.

But before we go on I must make a short digression. I have no doubt that you are dissatisfied with the fact that the three qualities of the mind in respect to consciousness and the three regions of the mental apparatus do not fall together into three harmonious pairs, and that you feel that the clarity of our conclusions is consequently impaired. My own view is that we ought not to deplore this fact but that we should say to ourselves that we had no right to expect any such neat arrangement. Let me give you an analogy; analogies prove nothing, that is quite true, but they can make one feel more at home. Let us picture a country with a great variety of geographical configurations, hills, plains, and chains of lakes, and with mixed nationalities living in it, Germans, Magyars, and Slovaks, who, moreover, are engaged upon a number of different occupations. Now the distribution might be such that the Germans lived in the hills and kept cattle, the Magyars on the plains and grew corn and vines, while the Slovaks lived by the lakes and caught fish and plaited reeds. If this distribution were neat and exact it would no doubt give great satisfaction to a President Wilson; it would also be convenient for giving a geography lesson. It is probable, however, that you would find a less orderly state of affairs if you visited the region. Germans, Magyars and Slovaks would be living everywhere mixed up together, and there would be cornfields too in the hills, and cattle would be kept on the plains as well. One or two things would be as you expected, for one cannot catch fish on the mountains, and wine does not grow in water. The picture of the region which you had brought with you might on the whole fit the facts, but in details you would have to put up with departures from it.

You must not expect me to tell you much that is new about the id, except its name. It is the obscure inaccessible part of our personality; the little we know about it we have learnt from the study of dream-work and the formation of neurotic symptoms, and most of that is of a negative character, and can only be described as being all that the ego is not. We can come nearer to the id with images, and call it a chaos, a cauldron of seething excitement. We suppose that it is somewhere in direct contact with somatic processes, and takes over from them instinctual needs and gives them mental expression, but we cannot say in what substratum this contact is made. These instincts fill it with energy, but it has no organisation and no unified will, only an impulsion to obtain satisfaction for the instinctual needs, in accordance with the pleasure principle. The laws of logic—above all, the law of contradiction—do not hold for processes in the id. Contradictory impulses exist side by side without neutralising each other or drawing apart; at most they combine in compromise formations under the overpowering economic pressure towards discharging their energy. There is nothing in the id which can be compared to negation, and we are astonished to find in it an exception to the philosophers' assertion that space and time are necessary forms of our mental acts. In the id there is nothing corresponding to the idea of time, no recognition of the passage of time, and (a thing which is very remarkable and awaits adequate attention in philosophic thought) no alteration of mental processes by the passage of time. Conative impulses which have never got beyond the id, and even impressions which have been pushed down into the id by repression, are virtually immortal and are preserved for whole decades as though they had only recently occurred. They can only be recognised as belonging to the past, deprived of their significance, and robbed of their charge of energy, after they have been made conscious by the work of analysis, and no small part of the therapeutic effort of analytic treatment rests upon this fact.

It is constantly being borne in upon me that we have made far too little use of our theory of the indubitable fact that the repressed remains unaltered by the passage of time. This seems to offer us the possibility of an approach to some really profound truths. But I myself have made no further progress here.

Naturally, the id knows no values, no good and evil, no morality. The economic, or, if you prefer, the quantitative factor, which is so closely bound up with the pleasure principle, dominates all its processes. Instinctual cathexes seeking discharge—that, in our view, is all that the id contains. It seems, indeed, as if the energy of these instinctual impulses is in a different condition from that in which it is found in the other regions of the mind. It must be far more fluid and more capable of being discharged, for otherwise we should not have those displacements and condensations, which are so characteristic of the id and which are so completely independent of the qualities of what is cathected. (In the ego we shall call it an idea.) What would one not give to understand these things better? You observe, in any case, that we can attribute to the id other characteristics than that of being unconscious, and you are aware of the possibility that parts of the ego and super-ego are unconscious without possessing the same primitive and irrational quality. As regards a characterisation of the ego, in so far as it is to be distinguished from the id and the super-ego, we shall get on better if we turn our attention to the relation between it and the most superficial portion of the mental apparatus; which we call the Pcpt-cs. (perceptual-conscious) system. This system is directed on to the external world, it mediates perceptions of it, and in it is generated, while it is functioning, the phenomenon of consciousness. It is the sense organ of the whole apparatus, receptive, moreover, not only of excitations from without but also of such as proceed from the interior of the mind. One can hardly go wrong in regarding the ego as that part of the id which has been modified by its proximity to the external world and the influence that the latter has had on it, and which serves the purpose of receiving stimuli and protecting the organism from them, like the cortical layer with which a particle of living substance surrounds itself. This relation to the external world is decisive for the ego. The ego has taken over the task of representing the external world for the id, and so of saving it; for the id, blindly striving to gratify its instincts in complete disregard of the superior strength of outside forces, could not otherwise escape annihilation. In the fulfilment of this function, the ego has to observe the external world and preserve a true picture of it in the memory traces left by its perceptions, and, by means of the reality test, it has to eliminate any element in this picture of the external world which is a contribution from internal sources of excitation. On behalf of the id, the ego controls the path of access to motility, but it interpolates between desire and action the procrastinating factor of thought, during which it makes use of the residues of experience stored up in memory. In this way it dethrones the pleasure principle, which exerts undisputed sway over the processes in the id, and substitutes for it the reality principle, which promises greater security and greater success.

The relation to time, too, which is so hard to describe, is communicated to the ego by the perceptual system; indeed it can hardly be doubted that the mode in which this system works is the source of the idea of time. What, however, especially marks the ego out in contradistinction to the id, is a tendency to synthesise its contents, to bring together and unify its mental processes which is entirely absent from the id. When we come to deal presently with the instincts in mental life, I hope we shall succeed in tracing this fundamental characteristic of the ego to its source. It is this alone that produces that high degree of organisation which the ego needs for its highest achievements. The ego advances from the function of perceiving instincts to that of controlling them, but the latter is only achieved through the mental representative of the instinct becoming subordinated to a larger organisation, and finding its place in a coherent unity. In popular language, we may say that the ego stands for reason and circumspection, while the id stands for the untamed passions.

So far we have allowed ourselves to dwell on the enumeration of the merits and capabilities of the ego; it is time now to look at the other side of the picture. The ego is after all only a part of the id, a part purposively modified by its proximity to the dangers of reality. From a dynamic point of view it is weak; it borrows its energy from the id, and we are not entirely ignorant of the methods —one might almost call them "tricks"—by means of which it draws further amounts of energy from the id. Such a method, for example, is the process of identification, whether the object is retained or given up. The object-cathexes proceed from the instinctual demands of the id. The first business of the ego is to take note of them. But by identifying itself with the object, it recommends itself to the id in the place of the object and seeks to attract the libido of the id on to itself. We have already seen that, in the course of a person's life, the ego takes into itself a large number of such precipitates of former object-cathexes. On the whole the ego has to carry out the intentions of the id; it fulfils its duty if it succeeds in creating the conditions under which these intentions can best be fulfilled. One might compare the relation of the ego to the id with that between a rider and his horse. The horse provides the locomotive energy, and the rider has the prerogative of determining the goal and of guiding the movements of his powerful mount towards it. But all too often in the relations between the ego and the id we find a picture of the less ideal situation in which the rider is obliged to guide his horse in the direction in which it itself wants to go.

The ego has separated itself off from one part of the id by means of repression resistances. But the barrier of repression does not extend into the id; so that the repressed material merges into the rest of the id.

The proverb tells us that one cannot serve two masters at once. The poor ego has a still harder time of it; it has to serve three harsh masters, and has to do its best to reconcile the claims and demands of all three. These demands are always divergent and often seem quite incompatible; no wonder that the ego so frequently gives way under its task. The three tyrants are the external world, the super-ego, and the id. When one watches the efforts of the ego to satisfy them all, or rather, to obey them all simultaneously, one cannot regret having personified the ego, and established it as a separate being. It feels itself hemmed in on three sides and threatened by three kinds of danger, towards which it reacts by developing anxiety when it is too hard pressed. Having originated in the experiences of the perceptual system, it is designed to represent the demands of the external world, but it also wishes to be a loyal servant of the id, to remain upon good terms with the id, to recommend itself to the id as an object, and to draw the id's libido on to itself. In its attempt to mediate between the id and reality, it is often forced to clothe the Ucs. commands of the id with its own Pcs. rationalisations, to gloss over the conflicts between the id and reality, and with diplomatic dishonesty to display a pretended regard for reality, even when the id persists in being stubborn and uncompromising. On the other hand, its every movement is watched by the severe super-ego, which holds up certain norms of behaviour, without regard to any difficulties coming from the id and the external world; and if these norms are not acted up to, it punishes the ego with the feelings of tension which manifest themselves as a sense of inferiority and guilt. In this way, goaded on by the id, hemmed in by the super-ego, and rebuffed by reality, the ego struggles to cope with its economic task of reducing the forces and influences which work in it and upon it to some kind of harmony; and we may well understand how it is that we so often cannot repress the cry: "Life is not easy." When the ego is forced to acknowledge its weakness, it breaks out into anxiety: reality anxiety in face of the external world, normal anxiety in face of the super-ego, and neurotic anxiety in the face of the strength of the passions in the id.

I have represented the structural relations within the mental personality, as I have explained them to you, in a simple diagram, which I here reproduce.

You will observe how the super-ego goes down into the id; as the heir to the Oedipus complex it has, after all, intimate connections with the id. It lies further from the perceptual system than the ego. The id only deals with the external world through the medium of the ego, at least in this diagram. It is certainly still too early to say how far the drawing is correct; in one respect I know it is not. The space taken up by the unconscious id ought to be incomparably greater than that given to the ego or to the preconscious. You must, if you please, correct that in your imagination.

And now, in concluding this certainly rather exhausting and perhaps not very illuminating account, I must add a warning. When you think of this dividing up of the personality into ego, super-ego, and id, you must not imagine sharp dividing lines such as are artificially drawn in the field of political geography. We cannot do justice to the characteristics of the mind by means of linear contours, such as occur in a drawing or in a primitive painting, but we need rather the areas of colour shading off into one another that are to be found in modern pictures. After we have made our separations, we must allow what we have separated to merge again. Do not judge too harshly of a first attempt at picturing a thing so elusive as the human mind. It is very probable that the extent of these differentiations varies very greatly from person to person; it is possible that their function itself may vary, and that they may at times undergo a process of involution. This seems to be particularly true of the most insecure and, from the phylogenetic point of view, the most recent of them, the differentiation between the ego and the super-ego. It is also incontestable that the same thing can come about as a result of mental disease. It can easily be imagined, too, that certain practices of mystics may succeed in upsetting the normal relations between the different regions of the mind, so that, for example, the perceptual system becomes able to grasp relations in the deeper layers of the ego and in the id which would otherwise be inaccessible to it. Whether such a procedure can put one in possession of ultimate truths, from which all good will flow, may be safely doubted. All the same, we must admit that the therapeutic efforts of psychoanalysis have chosen much the same method of approach. For their object is to strengthen the ego, to make it more independent of the super-ego, to widen its field of vision, and so to extend its organization that it can take over new portions of the id. Where it was, there shall ego be.

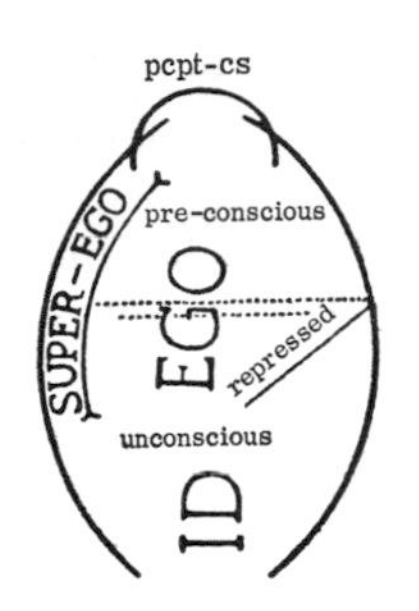

It is reclamation work, like the draining of the Zuyder Zee.

TOPICS FOR DISCUSSION AND WRITING

1. Freud's definition of human behavior has irritated or angered many people: his comments on the higher feelings resulting in nonsensical thinking (paragraph 1), his suggestion that the "mad" have something to teach the "sane" (paragraph 4), his ridicule of conscience (paragraph 6) are not likely to endear him to all readers. He realizes, however, that to consistently antagonize his audience would serve no purpose, and takes care to identify himself with his audience. Thus the first sentence of his lecture; the first sentence of the fourth paragraph; the anticipation of objections in paragraphs five, six, and seven—what is the strategy underlying all these examples of direct address?
2. Freud suggests (paragraph 3) that the audience reaction to his analysis of the human personality will be hesitant. Is that your reaction to his essay? Why?
3. This essay is primarily a definition of terms, and the test of any definition is its comprehensibility. Can you, after studying this essay, give a succinct account in your own terms of *ego, super-ego, repression, id,* and *pre-conscious?*
4. "Oedipus complex" has become a *cliché* and, like most clichés, it is not understood by those who use it. What does it mean? How is the complex to be understood in relation to Freud's several definitions?
5. Why does Freud's subject demand such extended definition? Are you persuaded to accept his definitions? What are some of the implications of this acceptance?
6. What does Freud mean when he says "Where id was, there shall ego be"? Is there any resemblance between this hoped-for result of psychoanalysis and Cassirer's expectations as he outlines them in the conclusion of his essay on *The Myth of the State* (p. 97)?
7. Write an essay contrasting Freud's way of explaining human behavior with Jung's (p. 3). Use some illustrations to show how Freud would seek to explain problematic behavior in "personal" terms whereas Jung might attempt to explain the same behavior in "collective" terms. If you think one theory is clearly better than the other, you might attempt to prove this.

Zbigniew K. Brzezinski

Zbigniew K. Brzezinski (1928–   ) is the author of many studies on Soviet history and political theory. Now teaching at Columbia, he was for several years a Research Fellow at the Russian Center at

Harvard where he had access to the Trotsky Archives, émigré memoirs, and many interviews with Soviet citizens who had defected. It was from this material that he fashioned The Permanent Purge *(1956) of which the following selection is the first chapter.*

The book maintains that the purge is a vital and continuing technique of the totalitarian state. Under Soviet totalitarianism the purge of some segment of the Party structure is not an unusual method reluctantly employed but part of a cyclic process which is inherent in the power structure. A purge does not signal the collapse of totalitarianism or indicate a death struggle between factions behind Kremlin walls; it is only a necessary readjustment of the Party machinery.

In his first chapter he argues that the purge is an essential part of the totalitarian system by first defining a totalitarian system and then showing that it is the nature of such a system to develop certain characteristics which are completely at variance with constitutional forms of government. Constitutional forms of government are elastic and in close touch with the electorate. Totalitarian systems are rigid and isolated. In the context of totalitarian systems pressures develop which can be relieved only by purges.

THE PURGE AND THE TOTALITARIAN SYSTEM *

The totalitarian purge is a new phenomenon in the field of politics. It is a product of the totalitarian system, and is continually fed by it. The purge is a complex and dynamic instrument of power, as different from the old methods of absolute rule as modern totalitarianism is from the old benevolent despotisms. Any analysis of the purge must, therefore, acknowledge the fact that the purge itself is influenced by the setting in which it operates. Such an analysis must recognize that any political system involves different ways of channeling such struggles, and that the institutional arrangements of the several systems have very much affected the nature of the political struggles within them. The dynamics and the motivations of the totalitarian purge are consequently closely related to the institutions of the totalitarian system, and are directly affected by the problems which the totalitarian system itself generates.

* Reprinted by permission of the publishers from Zbigniew K. Brzezinski, *The Permanent Purge, Politics in Soviet Totalitarianism* (Cambridge, Mass.: Harvard University Press). Copyright 1956 by the President and Fellows of Harvard College.

Let us approach the subject by making a cursory analysis of the manner in which constitutional societies resolve their internal political struggles. Constitutionalism is admittedly the most complex and delicate form of government. It attempts to combine a system of restraints on the power of the government, operating under the rule of law, with mechanisms designed to encourage change and mobility in government. This form of limited government grants the greatest possible freedom to the individual for the sake of his own personal development, consonant with his moral dignity and individual worth. The principles of Christianity have in particular made an outstanding contribution to the enshrining of the individual as an end in himself. With these principles providing the philosophical fiber, constitutionalism seeks to establish a form of government combining stability with elasticity. The fundamental assumption being that man should participate in governing himself, the structure of government is so designed as to encourage the greatest possible participation in it. This participation in self-government extends to all levels of society, through the channels of the various organizations which compete for the allegiance of the individual. The pluralistic form of social organization channels the individual's ambitions, and disruptive forces are cushioned by a hierarchy of groups, each with a claim on the loyalty of some individual citizens. The necessity for compromise as a substitute for the supremacy of one group or interest is obvious in such a situation, though compromise is not easily attained. The multiplicity of outlets absorbs the strains and tensions of conflicting tendencies.

The electoral system, built around the party system, further enhances the elasticity of the constitutional structure. The provisions for change and for direct participation in the government constantly enforce public accountability and ensure the influx of new people into responsible positions. Admittedly, the growth of the bureaucratic apparatus has somewhat divorced public supervision from the execution of policy, but over-all responsibility is still maintained by the removability of the political heads of the bureaucratic machine. We thus see, with obvious modifications depending on the given party system and the given electoral procedures, a steady movement of the "outs" becoming the "ins," and the "ins" becoming the "outs."

This process is furthered by the fact that the political leadership needs to keep in close touch with the prevailing currents of public opinion. A great deal of policy is actually formulated on the basis of anticipation of popular reaction; hence there is a very close interaction between those who are supposedly leading and those who are supposedly led. The role of the press, the radio and lately television in molding public opinion is frequently emphasized. But equally important is their role in keeping the political heads of the state close to reality, in preventing them from falling into the isolation which is frequently the fate of absolute rulers. Also not to be neglected is the role of such major intrastate organizations as the churches, which command a moral judgment which few governments can afford to entirely ignore.

The preceding discussion is designed to show how constitutional government, through compromise and adjustment, sets up a structure which lends itself uniquely to change and internal mobility. The dictum that "power tends to corrupt, and absolute power corrupts absolutely" has less chance to operate in a constitutional society. For here power is restrained and limited, and no one wields it for too long a time. Forces out of power operate openly on the surface in order to obtain power. Actions of the government are open to scrutiny and surveillance. Criticism eliminates the loafers, the laggards, the deadwood. The party in power is particularly anxious to rid itself of any potential sources of criticism. Its leaders realize that power remains theirs as long as their administration is efficient, active, and responsive. And, paradoxically, they are assisted in these endeavors by their opponents, who, through criticism and attack, point out the weaknesses and shortcomings in governmental policies. The government is thus kept constantly informed by its own foes about where the weak spots can be located, where the most acute problems are developing, and what measures to ameliorate the situation should be adopted. Constitutional leadership accordingly remains close to the facts of life; it is not faced with the necessity of accepting unreality as truth and then convincing its own population that the unreal is real.

With totalitarian leadership, on the other hand, the more totalitarian it becomes, the more isolated it finds itself to be. The very absoluteness of its power, the very scope of its coercion, the magnitude of its propaganda and agitation tend to have a paradoxical effect on its position vis-à-vis the masses which it controls. Instead of remaining in close contact with them, totalitarian leadership eventually finds itself very much alone, very much out of touch. Having imposed upon the masses the official conception of reality, totalitarian leadership begins to see nothing but the reflection of that "official" reality. This, in some ways, is a rather convenient situation. It permits the leadership to engage in various detours without once appearing to be straying from the official ideology. The masses are often in no position to distinguish reality from unreality, and all courses of action may seem on the surface to be in keeping with the orthodox foundations of the system. And those members of the totalitarian society who are unable to adjust themselves with sufficient rapidity to the zigzags of the official policy, all of which are always said to be dogma, are cast off as deviants and traitors. A supple backbone is a necessary piece of equipment for a totalitarian citizen.

This position of isolation, however, has some serious shortcomings for totalitarian leadership. It induces a simple but extremely serious defect: lack of adequate information. Totalitarian leadership, particularly one oriented on deep underlying philosophical assumptions, demands that all its subjects accept the official viewpoint, the official interpretations. Thus unavoidably almost all the information which it obtains either is as unreal as the totalitarian picture of reality, or else is easily suspect in the eyes of the leader. Those who supply the information have no choice but to comply with the ideological standard. The correspondence between the former Communist Polish military attaché in Washington, General Modelski, and his Soviet superiors in Warsaw is a particularly illuminating example. A number of his reports on the situation in the United States were criticized or even rejected by his superiors, on the grounds that he had become influenced by his "bourgeois environment" and had failed to draw his analysis in the proper perspective of the iron laws of Marxism. The famous Varga [1] debate in the USSR is another case in point. It is relatively safe to assume that

[1] Eugene Varga (1879–), an early Hungarian communist economic theorist whose postwar book argued that capitalism had changed and accommodation was possible.

similar pressures exist internally. Undoubtedly measures are taken to combat them. Totalitarian leadership, particularly the Soviet one, is doubtless fully aware of the problem and strives to cope with it by establishing alternate channels of communication and intelligence for purposes of cross-checking. But all of these channels are unavoidably subject to the inherent pressure of the entire system: one simply must conform in order to survive. It is surely safer to report what the regime wishes to hear than what one manages to see through the shadows of totalitarian unreality, thus risking accusations of deviationism or treason. All this results in totaliarian leadership's attempting desperately to grasp reality, or failing that, to make certain that its own conception of reality becomes accepted as fact.

This situation provokes two general consequences, each subject to many local variables. First, totalitarian leadership tends to overestimate the basis of its strength and to be misled by the *appearances* of universal support which it requires from all the citizens as their normal everyday standard of behavior. Thus it may fail to realize that its real support is dwindling away, until the very structure of the system begins to crumble and crash. It then reacts wildly and in desperation: Hitler's bloody and sadistic revenge following the unsuccessful *coup d'etat* of July 1944 was not only the last gasp of a mad tyrant but also the frantic reaction of a totalitarian leader to the realization of his isolation amidst seething hatred. This disappointment was only exceeded a year later when Hitler had to face the fact that his own organization, the thing he valued and trusted most, had betrayed him.

The second characteristic consequence of the isolation of totalitarian leadership is constant suspicion, hence, constant endeavors to eliminate causes of suspicion. A certain type of totalitarian leader, shrewdly realizing the coercive aspects of the apparently unanimous support which his regime enjoys, seeks out the real, imagined, or even potential foes of his organization and proceeds to eliminate them. The history of the Soviet Union, for example, is a singular collection of allegations of plots, conspiracies, and treasons, culminating in the celebrated purges of 1936–1938. Such a totalitarian leader cannot avoid a sense of panic—for to him the real is frequently the unknown, and the unknown is feared. Surrounded by sycophants, enshrined in mass adulation, this type of leader realizes that opposition may still lurk, that foes may still plot. The fact that all visible resistance has been successfully disposed of offers no relief. Treason may easily develop in the ranks of his own Party. Some lieutenants may become overambitious; others may merely be disappointed. Careerists and office seekers, whose motivating force is not personal loyalty to the leader and deep philosophical acceptance of the system, may succeed in entering the Party. The leader cannot forget that "traitors and capitulators penetrate the combat staff and the Party, the main stronghold of the proletariat. It is well known that citadels are most easily taken from within." [2]

This paranoia produced by the isolation of the leadership also penetrates to the lower levels of the totalitarian hierarchy, as well as to all the members of the community. Fear and suspicion result in a tendency to self-isolation and to the avoidance of all sincere contacts, although the superficial veneer of enthusiasm for the system is maintained. The Nazi wartime policy of executing "defeatists," i.e., those who recognized reality, was a manifestation of this phenomenon of totalitarian artificiality. Totalitarian isolation by necessity leads to a situation in which even the most minute deviation from the enforced norm is considered a threat to the regime, which must be dealt with in the severest fashion.

There thus develops an overwhelming pressure to eliminate all foes—first of all, those who have been defeated but are still in existence (the logic being clear: they are obviously plotting to seize the power they once shared and enjoyed), then all their former or present allies, then all potential foes. The slightest indication of opposition is feared and decried: "Even a mere shadow of opposing oneself to the Party signifies the political death of a fighter for socialism, his going over into the camp of the foreposts of counter-revolution." [3] Totalitarian leadership in this manner finds itself in a somewhat dichotomous situation: enjoying absolute power, it is forced to use it because of the very fact that it has it. Having power makes it isolated; isolation breeds insecurity; insecurity breeds suspicion and fear; suspicion and fear breed violence. For this rea-

[2] *Bolshevik #17* (Sept. 15, 1948).
[3] Karl Radik, addressing the XVII Party Congress (Moscow, 1934).

son totalitarianism has been characterized by many political scientists as a system of terror—it has to terrorize by reason of its inherent nature.

Totalitarian isolation is closely linked with the leadership's apprehension lest its Party, or even the entire monolithic apparatus of the state, become stagnant and corrupt. The relative isolation of the leadership does little to relieve such fears, which are usually well founded. The totalitarian party in its early revolutionary period is usually composed of power-motivated but frequently also ideologically minded leaders, of their idealistic supporters, and last, but not least, of brutal and politically ignorant thugs. These elements unite in their desire to seize power and are willing, for various reasons depending on their categorization, to take risks and make sacrifices.

The situation, however, changes drastically once power, to quote Mussolini, "has been picked off the floor." Many of the original followers, particularly the mass following, now desire to taste the fruits of victory and to partake of the spoils. But the totalitarian leadership cannot conceivably tolerate this. There are first of all power considerations—the revolution must go on so that the leadership's own position remains justified. But second and equally important is the ideology which has motivated the leaders—the ideology which points to the ultimate goals of the revolution and hence demands continued efforts for their achievement. A gap accordingly develops between the leadership and many of its followers.

As the regime becomes more stable the old supporters are joined by hordes of opportunists eager to get to the trough. In the absence of external institutions of control such as are found in constitutional societies, totalitarian leadership must proceed in its own way to ensure both loyalty and dynamism. To the suspicions bred by isolation is added the realization that "all revolutionary parties which have hitherto perished did so because they grew conceited, failed to see where there strength lay, and feared to speak of their own weaknesses." [4] The leadership of the totalitarian state, therefore, must be extremely intolerant of all failures. It must see in them indications of complacency, inefficiency, and, worst of all,

[4] J. V. Stalin, *Problems of Leninism* (Moscow, 1940), p. 347.

hostility towards itself. Nonfulfillment of quotas, for instance, very easily brings in charges of sabotage and wrecking. Failure in any sort of endeavor is a clear indication that personnel has become lazy or disloyal. Corrective measures, even of a drastic nature, must hence be applied. For this reason, the elite and somewhat visionary leadership must purge many of its weary followers and replace them with new ones. And as the latter begin to taste and enjoy the fruits of their new status, the need may again arise for their replacement by fresh and more vigorous cadres.

For unlike the traditional, reactionary dictatorship, the totalitarian system must emphasize a constant progress towards the ultimate good. The former cannot afford to introduce major programmatic changes into its realms, for any such changes are bound to affect its power adversely. Its appeal is based on the *status quo,* and in many cases even on the *status quo ante.* Study of the traditional dictatorship indicates that its power lies in its ability to prevent history from keeping in step with time. When it fails to do so, it itself becomes history.

Totalitarianism must, on the contrary, attempt to keep almost one step ahead of time. In order to maintain the totalitarian character of their system, the leadership must constantly shuffle and reshuffle society according to an apparently ideologically formulated program. Totalitarian dictatorship cannot allow society to settle down completely to a stable existence and develop stable relationships. Thus with the increasing stability at the top of the totalitarian hierarchy comes an artificial instability on the lower levels—an instability, paradoxically enough, aimed at producing stability for the top. The lower echelons are not permitted to develop stable power relationships, and their personnel is kept in a mobile state. The society as a whole is perpetually given new goals to reach, new objectives to attain. Programs are restated and reformulated. Ideological orthodoxy is stressed at the same time that the grossest departures from such ideology occur. These twists and turns are frequently motivated by pure expediency. But just as frequently they are part of the general totalitarian process of constant internal movement and change. The leadership attempts to anticipate situations before they develop, and the purge is a part of the anticipatory technique. It cleanses the system even before there are clear indications that cleansing is necessary. It produces the necessary momentum and dynamism, fear and enthusiasm, without which efforts at great social changes are bound to fail. It is a rebirth of the initial struggle which gave to the totalitarian leadership its possession of power. The original revolution is thus reincarnated in the purge.

It would be erroneous, however, to imply that the revolutionary quality of totalitarianism is the only determinant of the purge. Totalitarianism is of course very much concerned with problems of stability and security. Instruments of power, seized by the totalitarian leaders and operating within the framework of a complex (or developing) industrialized society, have to be consolidated and sharpened. The totalitarian movement, having latched onto power and having maintained it through an internalized revolution, is not anxious to lose it through anarchy. The regime hence both promotes revolution and seeks security, both expands the purge and limits its scope. This conflict clearly must result in a certain tension: exigencies of administrative efficiency demand a curtailment of the revolution; exigencies of totalitarian dynamics and the sense of historical destiny demand its expansion. Oscillation between the extremes frequently results in the purging of those unable to escape the swinging pendulum.

These basic pressures for a purge which follow from the monopoly of power and the revolutionary nature of totalitarianism are further accentuated by certain stimuli which reach the leadership from the lower levels. These stimuli can hardly be described as causal; rather their significance lies in their contribution to the spread and intensification of the purge. And here the roots of pressure are to be found more in human nature than in governmental institutions. Totalitarianism, aptly called the closed society, is a system where personal advancement and security are often achieved at the expense of others. While trying to introduce rapid social changes, the regime almost simultaneously stratifies itself into a rigid power hierarchy. Individual careers come to depend to some extent on the ability to arrange for the removal of one's closest competitors or superiors. Totalitarianism is therefore a system of the most vicious in-fighting; the defeat of Nazi Germany has revealed to what an extent a superficially serene totalitarian surface can be torn by internal competition and maneuverings. And while generally these remain shrouded in mystery, they are revealed in their intensity through the purges, which bring out into the open all the pent-up animosity, fear, jealousy, and intrigue. Under these circumstances, it is relatively easy for the purge to pick up a momentum of its own. The more victims it swallows, the more denunciations it encourages. At its most acute stage, as during 1937 in the Soviet Union, one's chance for survival becomes a purely mathematical calculation made in terms of the number of denunciations handed in. Some people denounce willingly, others because they have to. A trickle of denunciations can swiftly become a flood.

It is, therefore, quite conceivable that a purging operation originally intended to be limited in scope may turn out to be much more extensive than the regime expected or desired. But here again, because of its tendency towards a state of relative isolation, the regime is not capable of distinguishing adequately between real and imaginary plots and dangers. It becomes safer, therefore, to eliminate all their potential sources. The purge thus may continue to embrace ever increasing circles, with each arrest leading to many more. It is symptomatic that one of the heroes of Soviet youth is Pavlik Morozov, noted for the fact that he did not hesitate to denounce his closest family, only to be murdered himself by his fellow villagers. The purge accordingly finds considerable support in three basic emotions of the totalitarian citizen: ambition, fear, and enthusiasm. These three give it a scope and magnitude which no secret police could supply on its own.

Certain institutional developments also tend to further the purge. The system cannot operate without a refined secret police. And although the secret police cannot be solely held responsible for the magnitude of the purge, it still is the most effective instrument of the totalitarian regime. It not only insures the leader's safety or position but is also the chief weapon of internal combat. Its *raison d'être* is to protect the existing regime. Consequently the actual value of the secret police to the regime is measured in terms of the dangers, real or imagined, that it succeeds in eliminating. The greater the alleged threats to the power of the dictatorship, the greater the role the secret police assumes. . . . There must be enemies to eliminate. Absence of enemies does not mean that the regime has none, but that the secret police has failed to uncover them. Hence the *agent provocateur,* hence the necessity of denunciations, hence all the imagined plots. And as the secret police realizes that its position within the system depends on the continuation of this continual combat, a tendency towards exaggeration of the opposition easily develops. The chiefs of the secret police, in their maneuvering for power within the totalitarian framework, are thus inclined to perpetuate or extend the terror. And the unreality of the totalitarian existence makes dangers easy to manufacture.

This tendency blends well with the general picture of the struggle for power which is constantly taking place on the upper levels of the totalitarian regime, always supplying added stimulus to the purge. The influence and security of any totalitarian leader or subleader are directly dependent on the power he is capable of wielding. All organizational changes and almost all appointments and dismissals are bound to affect the power relationships of the various rivals within the system. The problem of control over the cadres of the Communist Party of the Soviet Union, for instance, is closely related to personal maneuvers and competition. And documents now available on the Nazi regime paint a grim picture of the constant chess game played by Bormann, Goering, Goebbels, and their supporters for various "strategic" positions.

Much more dramatic is the combat for the position of the leader himself—the struggle for succession. So far, totalitarianism has had only one successful transition, and even that was not accomplished without extended struggles and bloodshed. The course of the struggles between Stalin and his opponents has been fully studied by Messrs. Deutscher, Souvarine, Besseches, and others. But it should be noted again that each struggle produced in its wake a purge of all the supporters of the vanquished erstwhile competitors. All protégés and many former appointees and sympathizers paid the price of defeat. The victor, in order to remain victor, had to make certain that the organization he now controlled was truly staffed with elements loyal to him. Thus an important aspect of all Soviet purges has been elimination of those minor figures whose fate was sealed by the defeat of their protectors.

The successful leader is also pushed towards a purge by his lieutenants, who in turn are under pressure from their own supporters, whose personal welfare depends on the solidification of their own positions. The accentuation of political conflicts thus is often caused by the very drive for stability of the lower echelons—a tendency which, it was pointed out, produces new dangers for the leadership and a need for periodic cleansings. It is on this lower level of the totalitarian regime that the least secure and most dependent elements are to be found. It is these that press for the spoils. The lieutenants of a totalitarian leader frequently have only one thing in common: their absolute loyalty to the leader. On all else they may be bitter enemies, constantly engaged in death duels for influence and position. And the lieutenants are themselves subjected to pressures from their supporters, demanding privileges and power.

This hostility among the immediate supporters of the totalitarian dictator seems to increase in direct ratio to the distance from the dictator. For while his immediate aides may have certain experiences in common which tend to bind them together, such as a joint struggle for power or even imprisonment and suffering, this is not likely to be the case with their own second and third lieutenants. The farther away these are from the center of power, the more they tend to view the situation through the prisms of their own organizations, their own interests, their own power. Each thus puts constant pressure on his sub-leader to improve the position of his given organization. Such improvement can frequently be effected at the expense of competing organizations. The struggles in Germany between the S.S., the Nazi Party, and the Wehrmacht, and between the supporters of Goering and Goebbels, were produced more by the animosity or insecurity of their underlings than by personal enmity between the principal participants. The same situation, with obvious modifications, probably prevails in the Soviet Union. Although regrettably little is known, it seems that the years following World War II witnessed bitter maneuverings between Zhdanov and Malenkov for influence and power. Zhdanov's death cut short the duel. Soon after Zhdanov's transfer to the catacombs of the Kremlin, his erstwhile supporters, including his own son (who, however, re-emerged from obscurity at the Nineteenth Party Congress), began to fade into the political background. The same is essentially true of the aftermath of Beria's elimination in the summer of 1953. . . . And an analysis of the new central Party bodies, as confirmed by the Nineteenth Congress, reveals that the principal lieutenants did make efforts to promote into these new bodies their own close collaborators. The totalitarian leader, of course, attempts to settle any exceptionally violent conflicts. His own position is dependent on keeping his supporters together, while, at the same time, preventing anyone from ascending too rapidly. But once an ambitious official has fallen, it would be difficult even for the dictator, should he be so inclined, to prevent the rapid elimination of the fallen lieutenants' supporters. The vacuum thus created is rapidly filled by a realignment of power, and the internal struggle continues between new alliances, new leaders, new pretenders. The purge, in the meantime, has swallowed more victims.

The purge is thus inherent in the totalitarian system. The position of the leadership of the system is one of relative isolation, which results in false conception of reality, the accentuation of violence, and the insistence on eliminating all possible challenges to the leadership's monopoly of power. This tendency is sharpened by the totalitarian emphasis on combat as the ultimate form of moral development, and by the necessity of preserving the original revolutionary fervor and ideological purity. Consequently the leadership continually demands new sacrifices for the sake of new goals, and the progress towards them constantly exacts a new toll of victims—even from the movement itself, as its members grow weary or satiated.

As the purge begins to penetrate the masses, they respond with mixed reactions of fear, ambition, or enthusiasm, and the purge may develop a dangerous momentum of its own, threatening to get out of hand. The police apparatus of the totalitarian state is particularly anxious to magnify the potentiality of subversion, as its own position in the power hierarchy is dependent on the regime's need of it for self-preservation. Finally, the struggles within the regime itself find external expression in the ruthless elimination of fallen idols and their supporters. The continual struggle for power among primary competitors and their second lieutenants results in the increased tendency to settle all conflicts through the total elimination of the losers. Totalitarianism is, accordingly, the system of the purge—bred both by the existential conditions of the system and by the subjective motivations of its leadership.

TOPICS FOR DISCUSSION AND WRITING

1. What does Brzezinski mean when he uses the term "constitutionalism"? How do constitutional forms of government resolve their power struggles?
2. What does the author mean by "totalitarian"? What is the first consequence of totalitarianism upon its leadership?
3. What effect does the isolation of the totalitarian leadership have upon the gathering and interpretation of information? What are some of the consequences of this handling of information? Is totalitarianism essentially secretive? Is totalitarianism incapable of evaluating its view of reality?
4. What is Brzezinski's thesis? What single sentence comes closest to stating it?
5. Do you consider the following enthymeme an adequate summary of his thesis and main supporting reason? Why?

   Totalitarianism must terrorize because of its nature.
6. How does Brzezinski demonstrate that it is the nature of totalitarianism to terrorize? Can this need to terrorize be removed without altering the essential nature of totalitarianism?
7. What are some of the characteristics of totalitarianism which reveal its nature to terrorize?
8. Do you think he has proven his thesis? What do you think is the weakest part of his proof? The strongest?
9. Write an essay showing how events inside of Russia during the last seven years have tended to confirm or weaken Brzezinski's thesis. Isn't there always a danger, in using arguments from the nature of people or governments, that people or governments might change?

Kenneth E. Boulding

Kenneth E. Boulding (1910–   ) received his A.B. (with honors, first class) at Oxford, taught at several American and British universities, and is now a member of the faculty of the University of Michigan. He has written extensively on both the theory and history of economics. The following essay was originally one of a group of studies stimulated by the Harvard Business Review *and later brought together under the editorship of Edward C. Bursk in a book entitled* Business and Religion.

The point of departure of this essay, which asserts that there is a close relationship between economic systems and the cultural background of which they are a part, is clearly stated in the opening paragraph. This relationship is then demonstrated by an examination of the connection between capitalism and Protestantism in modern times. This examination leads to a definition of the problems of modern capitalism and the statement that these problems cannot be resolved without the help of religious theory and practice.

Professor Boulding defends his thesis by defining capitalism and Protestantism and then analyzing the implications contained in his conception of their nature. His proof consists of showing how these two theories at first worked to support each other. He then goes on to show how they must continue to work together if the problems of modern capitalism are to be resolved. His proof is not based upon extensive inductive surveys but upon the juxtaposition of two ideas —modern capitalism and Protestantism—and an examination of their implications.

Religious Foundations of Economic Progress *

One of the most challenging—and most tantalizing—propositions of what may be called the "larger economics" is that the success of economic institutions depends to a large extent upon the nature of the whole culture in which they are embedded, and not on the nature of these institutions themselves. This proposition is of particular importance in two current fields of economic inquiry: (a) the study of the complex forces which underlie economic development, and (b) the study of the stability and survival power of the characteristic institutions of capitalism.

Indeed, it is only a slight exaggeration to say that the wealth of a nation is a by-product of certain elements in its culture, cumulated through the years. Over a broad range of human societies

* From *Business and Religion,* Edward C. Bursk, ed.

within the extremes of the Eskimo and the desert nomad, if one area is rich and another poor, it is not because of anything inherent in the natural resources or in the genetic make-up of the people, but because of the cumulative effect of certain familial, educational, and religious practices. Thus the forbidding soil and climate of New England provided a comfortable—if not opulent—homeland for the Puritan, while under the Turk, in his unspeakable days, the ancient cradles of civilization became barren and starving deserts.

Of all the elements of culture which shape economic institutions, religious practices particularly play a key role—a doubly important one because many other elements of the pattern of life, such as sex, child rearing, work habits, agricultural and industrial practices, are themselves profoundly affected by the prevailing religious beliefs. That religion plays such an important role is not, however, sufficiently recognized by most people, and it is my purpose here to throw more light on it. More specifically, I shall attempt to survey certain aspects of our own society in the light of the contribution which religious ideas, practices, and institutions have made to its economic development and to its power of survival.

ECONOMIC DEVELOPMENT

To appraise the role of religion in economic development, we must understand the process by which economic change takes place. All change may not be for the better, but it is clear that there can be no betterment without some change.

THE PROTESTANT ETHIC

The past three centuries have witnessed a rate of economic development in the Western world which, measured by any standard we choose, almost certainly exceeds the achievement of any other period of equal length in human history. We are so much acccustomed to this rapid progress, both in techniques and in general levels of income, that we are likely to take it for granted. Nevertheless, looking over the whole range of human history and prehistory, we can clearly see that these last three hundred years represent an episode in human development which has no parallel, except perhaps in that dim period when settled agriculture was invented and gave rise to the first civilizations.

The unique nature of the achievement makes it all the more important that we should not take it for granted, but should inquire very carefully into its sources in the culture of the Western world. The history of civilization reveals that it is perfectly possible, indeed easy, to dry up the springs of progress in a society, and that virtually all past civilizations have eventually done so. Therefore, unless we are aware of the nature of those elements in our total pattern of life which are responsible for this rapid rate of development, we may run into grave danger of changing that pattern, without knowing it, in a way that destroys those peculiar elements in the culture from which development springs.

Important among the elements in our complex culture having favorable influence on the rate of economic development are certain religious ideas and practices which comprise the so-called "Protestant ethic."

The thesis of Max Weber and his school that the Protestant ethic has influenced the development of capitalism is now well accepted; though one's estimate of the quantitative importance of this influence will depend to a great extent on the interpretation of history which one favors, the direction of the influence can hardly be in doubt.

What has not, I think, been pointed out with sufficient force is that the Protestant ethic has contributed to the *success* of capitalist institutions, particularly in regard to their fostering a high rate of economic progress. Economic sociologists like Weber, Sombart, and Tawney, who have emphasized the close connection between religious and economic ideas, have been on the whole unfriendly to capitalist institutions and have consequently tended to lay stress on their failures rather than their successes. This is perhaps because the ethical systems of these writers were conceived in fairly static terms—in terms, for instance, of the problem of justice in the distribution of a given total income, rather than in terms of the encouragement of a growing total income.

It has now become clear, however, that the consequence of even a small rate of economic progress, persistently raising average incomes, is so enormous over even a few decades that from the point of view of long-run human welfare the capacity of a system to generate economic development has come to overshadow all other criteria in judging it "good" or "bad." (Curiously enough, this has also become true of Communism; in the interest of inducing a rapid rate of economic development the rulers of Russia have thrown overboard practically every other idea of their ethical system and have developed degrees of inequality which even the most uncontrolled period of capitalist development could hardly rival.)

In other words, we see now that in practice the abolition of poverty can come only from development—not from redistribution, not from taking from the rich to give to the poor, but by making everybody richer. And it is on this score that the Protestant ethic, which was born with the Reformation, has been so influential.

Innovation in Religion

Innovation, imitation, and displacement in economic life have their counterparts in religious life. Thus the Reformation marked the beginning of a series of innovations in religion. Men like Martin Luther, John Calvin, Menno Simons, George Fox, John Wesley, General Booth, and even in our own day Frank Buchman, represent a disturbance of the previously established equilibrium, with a new form of religious enterprise and new arrangements of human time and spiritual energy. They are widely imitated, and the spread of the new technique forces profound adjustments even in those older institutions which do not go over completely to the new ideas.

It generally seems to be true that these innovations in religion have preceded and in some sense paved the way for innovations in economic life. Indeed, the most important innovation in any society is the *idea* of innovation itself, for this represents the Rubicon between the traditional stationary type of society, in which each generation repeats the pattern of its elders, and the "economic," dynamic society, in which innovation becomes an accepted and profitable role. A strong case can be made out for the claim that the principal historical agency bringing about this critical change is a reformation (or revolution) in religion, that this liberates the society from its previous equilibrium and exposes it to all the terrors and delights of dynamics. Once iconoclasm has succeeded in the most traditional and "sacred" area of life, once "free enterprise" has been successful in religion, the spirit of innovation seizes on all other areas of life.

What in our Western society we call *the* Reformation is of course only one among many. The period of rapid innovation which followed the rise of Mohammedanism is another and spectacular example. Within Christianity itself the monastic reformations—especially of the Benedictines and Cistercians—paved the way for the economic development of medieval Europe. Again—if only to remind us that Protestantism is not the whole story—the counter-reformation within the Catholic Church also represents a period of "innovation," though of a less dramatic and less iconoclastic nature.

Individual Responsibility

The fact remains that the Protestant Reformation has certain specific features of its own which have increased its importance for economic development. I am not referring to the sanctification of economic activity through the extension of the concept of "vocation," as emphasized by earlier writers. The concept of vocation is not peculiar to Protestantism, nor is it so important as what I have in mind.

First of all, there is the "unmediated" character of Protestant religion, that is, the emphasis on the individual's own responsibility for his religious life and salvation without the intermediary of priest or prescribed ritualistic "works." It is this unmediated quality of Protestant religion which underlies the sociological significance of the doctrine of justification by faith. Protestantism, that is to say, represents private enterprise in religion, as opposed to the great organized collectivism of the Catholic Church.

It is not surprising that private enterprise in religion carried over into the economic field. The full effect of this is seen in the eighteenth century, where the immense economic innovations which constituted the beginnings of the technical revolution in banking, trade, and industry were to an astonishing extent the work of British nonconformists, and especially of the Quakers, who had developed the most unmediated of all Protestant varieties of religion.

Perfectionism

Another aspect of Protestantism which relates closely to economic development is its perfectionism. Like the earlier monastic reformations, Protestantism reflects a discontent with compromise with the "world" and a serious attempt to return to the pristine revelation of perfection implied in the Christian vision of perfect love. Unlike the monastic reformation, however, the Protestant Reformation—because one of the things against which it was protesting was the corruption of the monastery and nunnery prevalent in the time of Luther—rejected the monastic solution and became an attempt to lead the life of Christian perfection in the workaday world rather than in cloistered separation.

Such an attempt, however, is almost doomed to fail, and the difficulty of practicing the major virtue of charity will lead to an insensible substitution of the "minor virtues" as attainable ends of the religious group. So the perfectionist subsides into the Puritan, and groups of people arise practicing, with some success, the minor virtues of thrift, hard work, sobriety, punctuality, honesty, fulfillment of promises, devotion to family, and so on. The minor virtues, however, lead almost inevitably to accumulation and increased productivity, and eventually therefore to an escape from poverty.

THE LOST ECONOMIC GOSPEL

This all adds up to what I call the "lost economic gospel" of Protestantism. Poverty is the result of "sin," sin being defined in terms of intemperance, loose living, prodigality, laziness, dishonesty, and so on (that is, in terms of violation of the "minor virtues"). On yielding to the power of Christ and the discipline of the congregation the individual is converted, gives up his evil ways, and becomes temperate, frugal, thrifty, hard working, honest, and so on; as a result of which he begins to accumulate skill and other capital and raises his standard of life. Thus he becomes respectable, and incidentally, but only incidentally, he may become rich by hitting on a successful innovation.

In the process of the individual's becoming richer, society also becomes richer. Indeed, the improvement of society is nothing more than the sum of the improvements of individuals. In a dynamic and improving society, therefore, the increase in riches of the individual is not thought of as a redistribution of wealth (one individual gaining at the expense of others) but rather as a creation of wealth (the gains of one individual representing net additions to the total and being taken from no man). Economic life is not a "zero sum" poker game in which a fixed volume of wealth is circulated among the players, but a "positive sum" enterprise in which the accumulation of each person represents something which he brings to the "pot" rather than something which he takes out.

Another doctrine which Protestantism shares with other forms of Christianity has combined with the "lost gospel" to contribute to the success of capitalist institutions: the doctrine of stewardship, of charity in the narrower sense of the word. Those whose virtue, energy, or plain good fortune have brought them material success are expected to regard their riches as in some sense a trust, to be used for the benefit of the less fortunate. Over the long pull, this aspect of Christian culture has proved of great importance in modifying the inequalities of capitalism. As in the Middle Ages, the establishment of monasteries was an important agency in the redistribution of wealth and income, so in the nineteenth and twentieth centuries the establishment of universities and foundations has provided a means whereby private accumulations have found their way into public uses.

The habit of mind engendered by the doctrine of stewardship has also been important in removing obstacles to legislative methods of correcting inequalities, such as progressive income and inheritance taxation. It is quite possible that this factor may have something to do with the different impact of capitalist institutions in the West and, say, in China, where the acquisitive opportunities have been less likely to be modified by the sense of responsibility for the welfare of those outside the circle of kinship.

It can hardly be doubted, then, that the "lost gospel"—the old gospel of individualism, of self-help—is in many respects a sound one. Indeed, the middle-class nature of Protestantism is a testimony to its long-run success. If Protestants are middle-class, it is largely because their Protestantism has made them so—has developed a culture in which hard work, thrift, family limitation, productivity, and frugality have been important values. There is hardly any better over-all recipe for economic development, whether for the individual or for a society.

Decline of Old Doctrines

Nevertheless, to a considerable degree the old doctrines are discredited in the churches today, especially, oddly enough, in the more prosperous ones. The old gospel of self-help flourishes among the little rising sects, the pentecostal people, and the store-front churches; it is actually the poor who seem to be least aware of the new "social gospel" and who cling to the old-time individual virtues. In the large Protestant denominations, as represented by the National Council of Churches, it is not perhaps unfair to say that there is more awareness of the weakness of the individualist gospel than of its strength, and that even where the older gospel is preached, it is often the result of the momentum of tradition rather than of any continuing spiritual insight.

There are significant reasons for the decline of the gospel of self-help and the rise of the "social gospel." Part of the cause lies in sheer misunderstanding, stemming from failure to appreciate the ethical significance of economic progress, and a resultant economic ethic based on static assumptions in which undue stress is laid on distributing a fixed sum of wealth fairly rather than on increasing the total to be distributed.

More fundamental is a certain inevitable tension between the ethic of the New Testament and the ethic of Samuel Smiles (the old Scottish biographer of industrialists and extoller of thrift and self-reliance). There is an antieconomic strain in the teaching of almost all the prophets and poets. The careful, calculating economizing way of life is neither prophetic nor poetic. It counts the cost; it asks for reward; it has no fine frenzies; it is humdrum, commonplace, even a little sordid. The stimulus to economic progress, therefore, is not in the ethic of the New Testament itself; rather it is in the "Puritan" substitute-ethic, the product of the impact of the ethic of love on the iron laws of the world.

The substitute-ethic, however, is itself somewhat unstable, because it is always subject to criticism by the pure ethic which generates it. Hybrids are vigorous but can generally only be reproduced from pure stock! Thus when the New Testament makes a fresh impact on a sensitive and vigorous mind—as it is likely to do at least once in a generation—the gospel of "be righteous and grow rich," for all its truth and practicality, looks cheap and pharisaical beside the poetic vision of "sell all thou hast and give to the poor"; and radical forms of Christianity tend to appear.

Weakness of Capitalism

Perhaps a more fundamental reason for the failure of capitalism to sustain the ethic which supports its most characteristic institutions is to be found in certain technical failures of these institutions themselves.

The ethic of capitalism is based firmly on the proposition that wealth is produced by saving and that saving is accomplished by producing much and consuming little. That is why the principal recipe for riches includes hard work and thrift and the other Protestant virtues. Under some circumstances, however, wealth is not produced by saving. Hard work works the worker out of a job, parsimony produces unemployment, and the fluctuations of the price system redistribute wealth without regard to any of the soberer virtues. The thrifty and hard working find their net worth disappearing in deflation and their hard-earned interest and pensions evaporating in inflation, while the speculator and the manipulator reap what others have sown.

In condition of general price and output instability, the poker-game aspects of capitalism come to the fore. Instead of wealth being accumulated by careful contributing to the physical stock more than one takes from it, it is accumulated by taking advantage of the shifting structure of relative values, by buying cheap and selling dear. Every economist will recognize, of course, that there is a legitimate function of speculation, and that some flexibility of the price structure is necessary to reflect changing structures of productivity and tastes. In fact, however, the characteristic institutions of capitalism—especially the organized commodity and security markets and the real estate market—have lent themselves to fluctuations far beyond what the flexibility of the system requires, and have therefore been the instrument of redistributions of wealth which have created a gap between economic virtue (in the sense of contribution to the progress of real wealth) and reward.

The phenomenon of depression has been particularly destructive to the capitalist ethic, because the misery which it has entailed has seemed to be so meaningless: why work and save when the end result is the foreclosure of a mortgage and selling apples in the street! The whole technical weakness of an ungoverned market economy can be summed up in two concepts: (a) speculative instability in price levels due to the dynamics of self-justified expectations, and (b) the limited or imperfect market resulting either from monopolistic imperfections in the market structure or from general deflation. Speculative instability leads to essentially meaningless redistributions of wealth. The limited market leads to an undue shift of emphasis away from production, to wasteful advertising and selling costs, to restrictions of output, to featherbedding, and to other familiar devices by which individuals or segments of the economy seek to protect themselves from the impact of general deflations or seek to enhance their own particular power position at the expense of others.

The all-important question is whether these defects are to be regarded as diseases of the free economy, potentially curable within the general framework of market institutions, or whether they are to be regarded as essential genetic characteristics of it, quite incurable without a radical overthrow of the whole market economy itself.

CHANCES OF SURVIVAL

It is in this connection that the contribution of Keynes to the survival of capitalism is so important, for it is the essence of the Keynesian view that the defects of capitalism are curable diseases rather than incurable deformities. While the actual cures may be a matter still in considerable dispute, it is the great virtue of the Keynesian analysis that it gives us a clearer picture than we have ever had before of the nature of the disease, and it has consequently engendered the hope that institutions can be devised within the general framework of a free market economy which will prevent deflation and unemployment, on the one hand, and inflation, on the other.

If such a "governor" can insure the over-all stability of the economy (it is not the purpose of this discussion to say how this should be done), most of the ethical objections to a market economy fall to the ground. Given a reasonable degree of stability of the over-all price and output system, the old-fashioned virtues of hard word, thrift, honesty, and so on come into their own.

Underdeveloped Areas

Perhaps the crucial test of the capitalist system will turn on its ability to solve what is by far the greatest single economic problem facing the world today: the development of the so-called underdeveloped areas—inhabited by about three-quarters of the world's population—to the point where at least the grim consequences of extreme poverty (malnutrition, early death, constant ill health, superstition, squalor, and misery) are mitigated.

There are, roughly speaking, two kinds of society in the world today. The "high-level" societies have low birth and death rates, an expectation of life at birth rising up toward 60 or 70 years, disease well under control, malnutrition rare, literacy universal, education widespread, a high status and much freedom for women, complex economic and political institutions, and so on. The "low-level" societies, on the other hand, have high birth and death rates, an expectation of life around 30 years, disease and malnutrition rampant, literacy and education confined to a small upper class, a low status for women among the mass of the people, burdensome and exploitative financial institutions, often a colonial status, and so on.

The crux of the problem is how to raise the three-quarters of the world that live on a low level to the high level of the other quarter, for it is precisely this wide disparity that makes our world so unstable. American-Russian relations, for instance, would not constitute the apparently insoluble problem which they now pose if the relationship were simply one of America and Russia; in that event they could perfectly well leave each other alone! The relationship is complicated almost unbearably by the fact that each power is competing for the support of the vast fringe of underdeveloped countries which divide them on the globe, from Poland to China. Many countries are dissatisfied with their present state and are hovering between the two cultures, wondering which offers them the best chance of shifting from their present low-level to a high-level economy.

In this whole difficult situation it is of vital importance to appreciate the relation of economic institutions and economic development to the *whole* culture pattern, and to realize that the success of any set of economic institutions depends on the total culture setting in which they are placed. The success, even of modern technology, therefore, may depend quite as much on the missionary as on the engineer. One of the tasks of human inquiry is to discover exactly what the elements are in any culture which perpetuate poverty—whether in family life, in religious life, in education, in politics, or in economic and financial institutions—and then to effect the *minimum* change in the culture which is necessary to eradicate these germs of poverty.

We do not want, of course, the kind of cultural imperialism that insists on giving the Fiji Islanders Coca-Cola and Christmas trees whether these things are meaningful extensions of their present culture or not. Cultural change and cultural impact, however, there must be. Such impact is immensely dangerous and may result in disaster to both cultures; yet with the collapse of isolation such impact is inevitable. If it is to be ultimately fruitful, it must be understood much better than we understand it now; the marriage of economics and cultural anthropology must be accomplished, even at the point of a shotgun!

Danger of Social Sciences

It must not be thought, however, that all that is needed for world salvation is a stiff dose of social science, no matter how well documented empirically and no matter how well integrated analytically. The rise of social science presents man with problems of an ethical and spiritual nature of which he is still for the most part not aware. The spectacular "success" of the physical sciences in expanding the power of man, both for good and for evil, is dramatically symbolized in the atom bomb. The worst that a physicist can do for anybody, however, is to cause pain and death. The social scientist, when he knows a little more, may be able to destroy the soul, that inner core of freedom and integrity which constitutes at once the humanity and the divinity of man.

The nightmare of the "manipulative society"—the brave new world of Aldous Huxley or George Orwell—is not too far from reality. We see it foreshadowed in the crudely manipulative society of Soviet Russia, and it is this aspect of Communism which rightly fills us with disgust and fear. In its very conflict with Communism, however, the West may find itself sliding imperceptibly into a manipulative society more horrible, because more efficient, than the Soviet counterpart.

A world of unseen dictatorship is conceivable, still using the forms of democratic government, in which education has been replaced by training, in which government creates artificially the public opinion which keeps it in power, in which "loyalty" investigations corrupt the whole system of communications, in which only "safe" ideas are expressed, in which love of country is corroded by conscription and integrity is swallowed up in expediency, and in which the springs of technical, as well as of moral, progress are eventually dried up. The cleverer we are and the more we know, the more thoroughly we may damn ourselves.

RELIGION AS GUIDE

When the final history of the human race comes to be written, therefore, the part played by religion and religious experience may be even more significant than I have suggested earlier. I have argued that religion is an important autonomous force in the development of the technical revolution. It may turn out to be even more important in the control of this revolution.

We do not yet realize, I believe, what a portentous watershed in human history we are now treading. Civilization is a product of the increase in human control over environment which resulted from the invention of settled agriculture. All past civilizations, however, have proved to be unstable; the "iron laws" of social dynamics have eventually caught up with them and destroyed them. It is by no means improbable that our own civilization will suffer the same fate.

Yet there is reason for hope. As our knowledge not only of nature but of man and society expands, we may get to the point where man comes not to be ruled by history but to rule it. He may be able to take the iron laws and fashion them into an instrument for his own purposes, to mold the unconscious dynamic which drives him to destroy his civilizations into a conscious dynamic which will empower him to perpetuate them indefinitely.

The possibility of permanent and universal civilization therefore rises before us, though the prospect is not necessarily one to be approached without fear. It might be the kingdom of heaven on earth, but it might also be an indestructible and universal tyranny, securely based on the power of both physical and social science. A world of refugees is bad enough, but a world in which there is no place of refuge would be worse.

An increase in human power, therefore, makes all the more urgent the question of the discipline of the human will. Economic development means an increase in our ability to get what we want. Religion, however, raises the question of whether we want the right things. As long as we are impotent, it does not perhaps matter so much in regard to externals whether we want the right things or the wrong things. We cannot get what we want in any case. But if we can get what we want, the question of whether we want the right things becomes acutely important.

There are those who think that as economic development comes to fruition in a humanistic heaven on earth where war, poverty, and disease are abolished, religion will wither away. In that millenium faith will be swallowed up in knowledge, hope in fulfillment, and love in psychoanalysis and group dynamics! Such a belief seems to be naive. As power and knowledge increase, the question of the *truth* of religion—of what is the "will of God," and how it is discovered and incorporated into the human will—becomes all-important. The feather of religious experience may then tip the great scales toward either heaven or hell on earth.

TOPICS FOR DISCUSSION AND WRITING

1. This is one of the most tantalizing theses of the study of modern economics. Paraphrase it in your own words. Why does the author consider this an important thesis?
2. Why does religion play such an important part in the success or failure of an economic system?
3. What, in the author's opinion, is the best criterion for determining the value of an economic system?
4. What has been the contribution of the Reformation to the development of an atmosphere sympathetic to innovation?

5. What are some of the aspects of modern Protestantism which have contributed to the development of modern capitalism?
6. What does he call the "lost economic gospel of Protestantism"?
7. Write an essay showing how contemporary capitalism differs from the capitalism Marx and Engels attacked in their *Manifesto*. Show how the differences between capitalism as they saw it and capitalism as it is has invalidated their arguments.
8. Does his explanation of the decline of old religious doctrines agree with Riesman's (in his explanation of the increase in other-directed behavior tendencies in the contemporary American citizen)?
9. Why has capitalism failed to support the ethic which sustains its most characteristic institutions? Are these defects diseases of the free economy or are they essential characteristics of the system?
10. Why may the success of modern technology in an undeveloped nation depend "quite as much on the missionary as on the engineer"?
11. What is, ultimately, Boulding's thesis? Does it have to do with the theory of capitalism? Has he proven it?

IV

Adapting Arguments to Audience and Circumstances

An argument can be logically correct but rhetorically ineffective. Few readers of William Shakespeare's *Julius Caesar* readily recall that Mark Antony's famous speech to the mob beginning, "Friends, Romans, countrymen, lend me your ears," was preceded by a speech of Brutus' to the same mob. Brutus' speech was brief, terse, completely logical, the utterance of a completely reasonable man speaking to supposedly reasonable people. Brutus' speech was completely ineffective because it was ill adapted to its audience (a mob) and the circumstances (a time of riot). To be effective, as well as correct, an argument must be presented in such a way that it will appeal to its intended audience. Mark Antony's speech was effective because he adapted what he had to say to the prejudices of a greedy, irrational mob.

Every failure of a logically correct argument to be persuasive is the result of a breakdown in communication between the writer and his intended audience. Failures in communication occur because an audience is unable to grasp the full significance of an argument either through prejudice or through lack of necessary background information. To communicate effectively, therefore, a writer must make his audience receptive to his ideas and provide them with the background necessary to grasp the full significance of what he is trying to say.

The selection included in this section from the book *The Universe and Doctor Einstein* illustrates how Lincoln Barnett tried to provide his intended audience with the background they would need to grasp the significance of some of Einstein's theories. What was originally but a few, short paragraphs in Einstein's own book, *Relativity, the Special and General Theory,* is expanded by the addition of illustrations and the expansion of definitions so that even a wide, popular audience could understand the basic concepts. In writing his own book, Einstein assumed that he was writing for a professional audience which had the technical preparation as well as the required motivation needed to grasp the implications of complex mathematical and physical equations. Lincoln Barnett was writing for a much wider audience which he assumed would have some interest in the implications of Einstein's widely discussed hypotheses but which he could not assume would be willing, or able, to follow any explanations requiring more than an elementary knowledge of physics or mathematics. A speaker or writer who is determined to communicate effectively must always remember that no matter how profound and logical his arguments may be, they will be ineffective unless his audience is willing and able to grasp their significance.

Carl Becker's essay, *Everyman His Own Historian,* is included as an illustration of a successful attempt to overcome anticipated prejudices in order to obtain a sympathetic hearing for a controversial thesis. The essay was originally an address to a professional society of historians, many of whom were still committed to a conception of history as a science dedicated to reconstructing the past with accuracy and certainty. Becker's thesis was that history "is a story that employs all the devices of literary art to present the succession of events in the life of man, and from the succession of events thus presented to derive a satisfactory meaning." If Becker had stated his thesis bluntly toward the beginning of his essay, he would have stirred prejudices and closed the minds of some of his hearers to all arguments, no matter how logical. He solved his problem in communication by explaining, in a very winning fashion, what he thought history, reduced to its lowest common denominator, was. Then he went on to show how Mr. Everyman in the conduct of his business affairs employed many of the techniques of the historian. After this anticipatory preparation he risked the explicit statement of his controversial position. An audience which had gone along with him this far would find it difficult not to agree with the rest of the essay.

The effectiveness of various arguments also depends upon circumstances of time and place. Judging from their frequent use in the *Federalist Papers,* arguments derived from the nature of the subject under discussion must have been considered effective during the latter part of the eighteenth century. Today arguments derived from expected effects and buttressed with many statistics seem to be more effective in politics. Television advertisements based upon the testimony of scientists, especially medical doctors, were for a time considered most effective. In the period immediately following the explosion of the first nuclear bombs, the testimony of atomic scientists on any subject was considered most compelling. The kind of argument a writer chooses may reflect not what he considers to be the most logical argument at his disposal, but the argument which he believes will be most effective at the time he is writing. Thus an effective argument must first be a correct argument, but it must then be adapted to the audience for which it is intended, as well as to the circumstances of time and place which may influence the receptivity of that audience.

Lincoln Barnett, The Universe and Dr. Einstein

The presentation of a complex idea in less complex terms is somewhat like a translation from one language into another; and the problem of "something being lost in the translation" is ever present. A noteworthy instance of how a "translation" can be made without unduly diluting the original, and thereby making available to many what hitherto had been accessible to only a few, is Lincoln Barnett's book, The Universe and Dr. Einstein. *Barnett presents, in terms understandable to the educated layman, Albert Einstein's theories of Special and General Relativity, and describes the processes through which Einstein formulated his theories.*

from THE UNIVERSE AND DR. EINSTEIN *

In the Special Theory of Relativity, Einstein studied the phenomenon of motion and showed that there appears to be no fixed standard in the universe by which man can judge the "absolute" motion of the earth or of any other moving system. Motion can be detected only as a change of position with respect to another body. We know for example that the earth is moving around the sun at the rate of twenty miles a second. The changing seasons suggest this fact. But until four hundred years ago men thought the shifting position of the sun in the sky revealed the sun's movement around the earth; and on this assumption ancient astronomers developed a perfectly practical system of celestial mechanics which enabled them to predict with great accuracy all the major phenomena of the heavens. Their supposition was a natural one, for we can't *feel* our motion through space; nor has any physical experiment ever proved that the earth actually is in motion. And though all the other planets, stars, galaxies, and moving systems in the universe are ceaselessly, restlessly changing position, their movements are observable only with respect to one another. If all the objects in the universe were removed save one, then no one could say whether that one remaining object was at rest or hurtling through the void at 100,000 miles a second. Motion is a relative state; unless there is some system of reference to which it may be compared, it is meaningless to speak of the motion of a single body.

Shortly after publishing the Special Theory of Relativity, however, Einstein began wondering if there is not indeed one kind of motion which may be considered "absolute" in that it can be detected by the physical effect it exerts on the moving system itself —without reference to any other system. For example, an observer in a *smoothly* running train is unable to tell by experiments performed inside the train whether he is in motion or at rest. But if the engineer of the train suddenly applies the brakes or jerks open the throttle, he will then be made aware, by the resulting jolt, of a change in his velocity. And if the train rounds a turn, he will know by the outward tug of his own body, resisting a change of direction, that the train's course has been altered in a certain way. Therefore, Einstein reasoned, if only one object existed in the entire universe —the earth, for example—and it suddenly began to gyrate irregularly, its inhabitants would be uncomfortably aware of their motion. This suggests that nonuniform motion, such as that produced by forces and accelerations, may be "absolute" after all. It also suggests that empty space can serve as a system of reference within which it is possible to distinguish absolute motion.

To Einstein, who held that space is emptiness and motion is relative, the apparently unique character of nonuniform motion was profoundy disturbing. In the Special Theory of Relativity he had taken as his premise the simple assertion that the laws of nature are the same for all systems moving *uniformly* relative to one another. And as a steadfast believer in the universal harmony of nature he refused to believe that any system in a state of nonuniform motion must be a uniquely distinguished system in which the laws of nature are different. Hence as the basic premise of his General Theory of Relativity, he stated: the laws of nature are the same for all systems regardless of their state of motion. In developing this thesis he worked out new laws of gravitation which upset most of the concepts that had shaped man's picture of the universe for three hundred years.

Einstein's springboard was Newton's Law of Inertia which, as every schoolboy knows, states that "every body continues in its state of rest, or of uniform motion in a straight line, unless it is compelled to change that state by forces impressed thereon." It is inertia, therefore, which produces our peculiar sensations when a railroad train suddenly slows down or speeds up or rounds a curve. Our body wants to continue moving uniformly in a straight line, and when the train impresses an opposing force upon us the property called inertia tends to resist that force. It is also inertia which causes a locomotive to wheeze and strain in order to accelerate a long train of freight cars.

But this leads to another consideration. If the cars are loaded the locomotive has to work harder and burn more coal than if the cars are empty. To his Law of Inertia Newton therefore added a second law stating that the amount of force necessary to accelerate a body depends on the mass of the body; and that if the same force is applied to two bodies of different masses, then it will produce a greater acceleration in the smaller body than in the bigger one. This principle holds true for the whole range of man's everyday experience—from pushing a baby carriage to firing a cannon. It simply generalizes the obvious fact that one can throw a baseball farther and faster than one can throw a cannonball.

There is, however, one peculiar situation in which there appears to be no connection between the acceleration of a moving body and its mass. The baseball and the cannonball attain exactly the same rate of acceleration when they are *falling*. This phenomenon was first discovered by Galileo, who proved by experiment that, discounting air resistance, bodies all fall at precisely the same rate regardless of their size or composition. A baseball and a handkerchief fall at different speeds only because the handkerchief offers a larger surface to air resistance. But objects of comparable shape, such as a marble, a baseball, and a cannonball, fall at virtually the same rate. (In a vacuum the handkerchief and the cannonball would fall side by side.) This phenomenon appears to violate Newton's Law of Inertia. For why should all objects travel vertically at the same velocity regardless of their size or mass, if those same objects, when projected horizontally by an equal force, move at velocities that are strictly determined by their mass? It would appear as though the factor of inertia operates only in a horizontal plane.

Newton's solution of this riddle is given in his Law of Gravitation, which states simply that the mysterious force by which a material body attracts another body increases with the mass of the object it attracts. The heavier the object, the stronger the call of gravity. If an object is small, its inertia or tendency to resist motion is small, but the force that gravity exerts upon it is also small. If an object of the same density is big, its inertia is great, but the force that gravity exerts upon it is also great. Hence gravity is always exerted in the precise degree necessary to overcome the inertia of any object. And that is why all objects fall at the same rate, regardless of their inertial mass.

This rather remarkable coincidence—the perfect balance of gravitation and inertia—was accepted on faith, but never understood or explained, for three centuries after Newton. All of modern mechanics and engineering grew out of Newtonian concepts, and the heavens appeared to operate in accordance with his laws. Einstein, however, whose discoveries have all sprung from an inherent distrust of dogma, disliked several of Newton's assumptions. He doubted that the balance of gravitation and inertia was merely an accident of nature. And he rejected the idea of gravitation being a force that can be exerted instantaneously over great distances. The notion that the earth can reach out into space and pull an object toward it with a force miraculous and invariably equal to the inertial resistance of that object seemed to Einstein highly improbable. So out of his objections he evolved a new theory of gravitation which, experience has shown, gives a more accurate picture of nature than Newton's classic law.

In accordance with his usual mode of creative thought Einstein set the stage with an imaginary situation. The details have doubtless been envisaged by many another dreamer in restless slumber or in moments of insomniac fancy. He pictured an immensely high building and inside it an elevator that had slipped from its cables and is falling freely. Within the elevator a group of physicists, undisturbed by any suspicion that their ride might end in disaster, are performing experiments. They take objects from their pockets, a fountain pen, a coin, a bunch of keys, and release them from their grasp. Nothing happens. The pen, the coin, the keys appear to the men in the elevator to remain poised in midair—because all of them are falling, along with the elevator and the men, at precisely the same rate in accordance with Newton's Law of Gravitation. Since the men in the elevator are unaware of their predicament, however, they may explain these peculiar happenings by a different assumption. They may believe they have been magically transported outside the gravitational field of the earth and are in fact poised somewhere in empty space. And they have good grounds for such a belief. If one of them jumps from the floor he floats smoothly toward the ceiling with a velocity just proportional to the vigor of his jump. If he pushes his pen or his keys in any direction, they continue to move uniformly in that direction until they hit the wall of the car. Everything apparently obeys Newton's Law of Inertia, and continues in its state of rest or of uniform motion in a straight line. The elevator has somehow become an inertial system, and there is no way for the men inside it to tell whether they are falling in a gravitational field or are simply floating in empty space, free from all external forces.

Einstein now shifts the scene. The physicists are still in the elevator, but this time they really *are* in empty space, far away from the attractive power of any celestial body. A cable is attached to the roof of the elevator; some supernatural force begins reeling in the cable; and the elevator travels "upward" with constant acceleration—i.e., progressively faster and faster. Again the men in the car have no idea where they are, and again they perform experiments to evaluate their situation. This time they notice that their feet press solidly against the floor. If they jump they do not float to the ceiling for the floor comes up beneath them. If they release objects from their hands the objects appear to "fall." If they toss objects in a horizontal direction they do not move uniformly in a straight line but describe a parabolic curve with respect to the floor. And so the scientists, who have no idea that their windowless car actually is climbing through interstellar space, conclude that they are situated in quite ordinary circumstances in a stationary room rigidly attached to the earth and affected in normal measure by the force of gravity. There is really no way for them to tell whether they are at rest in a gravitational field or ascending with constant acceleration through outer space where there is no gravity at all.

The same dilemma would confront them if their room were attached to the rim of a huge rotating merry-go-round set in outer space. They would feel a strange force trying to pull them away from the center of the merry-go-round, and a sophisticated outside observer would quickly identify this force as inertia (or, as it is termed in the case of rotating objects, centrifugal force). But the men inside the room, who as usual are unaware of their odd predicament, would once again attribute the force to gravity. For if the interior of their room is empty and unadorned, there will be nothing to tell them which is the floor and which is the ceiling except the force that pulls them toward one of its interior surfaces. So what a detached observer would call the "outside wall" of the rotating room becomes the "floor" of the room for the men inside. A moment's reflection shows that there is no "up" or "down" in empty space. What we on earth call "down" is simply the direction of gravity. To a man on the sun it would appear that the Australians, Africans, and Argentines are hanging by their heels from the southern hemisphere. By the same token Admiral Byrd's flight over the South Pole was a geometrical fiction; actually he flew *under* it—upside down. And so the men inside the room on the merry-go-round will find that all their experiments produce exactly the same results as the ones they performed when their room was being swept "upward" through space. Their feet stay firmly on the "floor." Solid objects "fall." And once again they attribute these phenomena to the force of gravity and believe themselves at rest in a gravitational field.

From these fanciful occurrences Einstein drew a conclusion of great theoretical importance. To physicists it is known as the Principle of Equivalence of Gravitation and Inertia. It simply states that there is no way to distinguish the motion produced by inertial forces (acceleration, recoil, centrifugal force, etc.) from motion produced by gravitational force. The validity of this principle will be evident to any aviator; for in an airplane it is impossible to separate the effects of inertia from those of gravitation. The physical sensation of pulling out of a dive is exactly the same as that produced by executing a steeply banked turn at high speed. In both cases the factor known to flyers as a "G-load" (Gravity load) appears, blood is drawn away from the head, and the body is pulled heavily down into the seat. To the pilot who is flying "blind" and without instruments, the identical nature of these effects can prove a serious and even fatal matter.

In this principle, which is the keystone of General Relativity, Einstein found an answer both to the riddle of gravitation and the problem of "absolute" motion. It showed that there is nothing unique or "absolute" about nonuniform motion after all; for the effects of nonuniform motion which can supposedly reveal the state of motion of a body, even if it exists alone in space, are indistinguishable from the effects of gravitation. Thus in the case of the merry-go-round, what one observer identified as the pull of inertia or centrifugal force and therefore an effect of motion, another observer identified as the familiar tug of gravitation. And any other inertial effect produced by a change of speed or a change of direction can equally well be ascribed to a changing or fluctuating gravitational field. So the basic premise of Relativity holds true; motion, both uniform and nonuniform, can only be judged with respect to some system of reference—absolute motion does not exist.

The sword with which Einstein slew the dragon of absolute motion was gravitation. But what *is* gravitation? The gravitation of Einstein is something entirely different from the gravitation of Newton. It is not a "force." The idea that bodies of matter can "attract" one another is, according to Einstein, an allusion that has grown out of erroneous mechanical concepts of nature. So long as one believes that the universe is a big machine, it is natural to think that its various parts can exert a force on one another. But the deeper science probes toward reality, the more clearly it appears that the universe is not like a machine at all. So Einstein's Law of Gravitation contains nothing about force. It describes the behavior of objects in a gravitational field—the planets, for example—not in terms of "attraction" but simply in terms of the paths they follow. To Einstein, gravitation is simply part of inertia; the movements of the stars and the planets stem from their inherent inertia; and the courses they follow are determined by the metric properties of space—or more properly speaking, the metric properties of the space-time continuum.

Although this sounds very abstract and even paradoxical, it becomes quite clear as soon as one dismisses the notion that bodies of matter can exert a physical force on each other across millions of miles of empty space. This concept of "action at a distance" has troubled scientists since Newton's day. It led to particular difficulty, for example, in understanding electric and magnetic phenomena. Today scientists no longer say that a magnet "attracts" a piece of iron by some kind of mysterious but instantaneous "action at a distance." They say rather that the magnet creates a certain physical condition in the space around it, which they term a magnetic field; and that this magnetic field then acts upon the iron and makes it behave in a certain predictable fashion. Students in any elementary

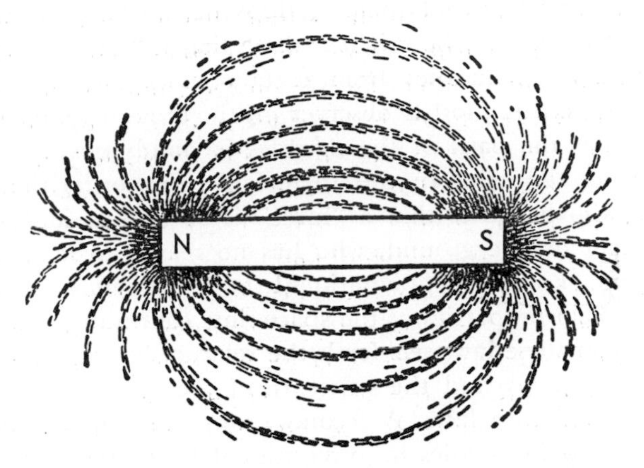

The field of a bar magnet

science course know what a magnetic field looks like, because it can be rendered visible by the simple process of shaking iron filings onto a piece of stiff paper held above a magnet. A magnetic field and an electrical field are physical realities. They have a definite structure, and their structure is described by the field equations of James Clerk Maxwell which pointed the way toward all the discoveries in electrical and radio engineering of the past century. A gravitational field is as much of a physical reality as an electromagnetic field, and its structure is defined by the field equations of Albert Einstein.

Just as Maxwell and Faraday assumed that a magnet creates certain properties in surrounding space, so Einstein concluded that stars, moons, and other celestial objects individually determine the properties of the space around them. And just as the movement of a piece of iron in a magnetic field is guided by the structure of the field, so the path of any body in a gravitational field is determined by the geometry of that field. The distinction between Newton's and Einstein's ideas about gravitation has sometimes been illustrated by picturing a little boy playing marbles in a city lot. The ground is very uneven, ridged with bumps and hollows. An observer in an office ten stories above the street would not be able to see these irregularities in the ground. Noticing that the marbles appear to avoid some sections of the ground and move toward other sections, he might assume that a "force" is operating which repels the marbles from certain spots and attracts them toward others. But another observer on the ground would instantly perceive that the path of the marbles is simply governed by the curvature of the field. In this little fable Newton is the upstairs observer who imagines that a "force" is at work, and Einstein is the observer on the ground, who has no reason to make such an assumption. Einstein's gravitational laws, therefore, merely describe the field properties of the space-time continuum. Specifically, one group of these laws sets forth the relation between the mass of a gravitating body and the structure of the field around it; they are called structure laws. A second group analyzes the paths described by moving bodies in gravitational fields; they are the laws of motion.

It should not be thought that Einstein's theory of gravitation is only a formal mathematical scheme. For it rests on assumptions of deep cosmic significance. And the most remarkable of these assumptions is that the universe is not a rigid and immutable edifice where independent matter is housed in independent space and time; it is on the contrary an amorphous continuum, without any fixed architecture, plastic and variable constantly subject to change and distortion. Wherever there is matter and motion, the continuum is disturbed. Just as a fish swimming in the sea agitates the water around it, so a star, a comet, or a galaxy distorts the geometry of the space-time through which it moves.

When applied to astronomical problems Einstein's gravitational laws yield results that are close to those given by Newton. If the results paralleled each other in every case, scientists might tend to retain the familiar concepts of Newtonian law and write off Einstein's theory as a weird if original fancy. But a number of strange new phenomena have been discovered, and at least one old puzzle solved, solely on the basis of General Relativity. The old puzzle stemmed from the eccentric behavior of the planet Mercury. Instead of revolving in its elliptical orbit with the regularity of the other planets, Mercury deviates from its course each year by a slight but exasperating degree. Astronomers explored every possible factor that might cause this perturbation but found no solution within the framework of Newtonian theory. It was not until Einstein evolved his laws of gravitation that the problem was solved. Of all the planets Mercury lies closest to the sun. It is small and travels with great speed. Under Newtonian law these factors should not in themselves account for the deviation; the

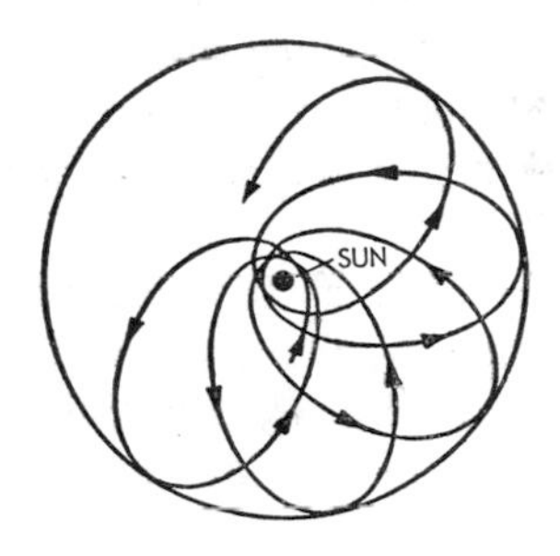

The rotation of Mercury's elliptical orbit, greatly exaggerated. Actually the ellipse advances only 43 seconds of an arc per century.

dynamics of Mercury's movement should be basically the same as those of any other planet. But under Einstein's laws, the intensity of the sun's gravitational field and Mercury's enormous speed make a difference, causing the whole ellipse of Mercury's orbit to execute a slow but inexorable swing around the sun at the rate of one revolution in 3,000,000 years. The calculation is in perfect agreement with actual measurements of the planet's course. Einstein's mathematics are thus more accurate than Newton's in dealing with high velocities and strong gravitational fields.

An achievement of far greater importance, however, than this solution of an old problem was Einstein's prediction of a new cosmic phenomenon of which no scientist had ever dreamed—namely the effect of gravitation on light.

The sequence of thought which led Einstein to prophesy this effect began with another imaginary situation. As before, the scene opens in an elevator ascending with constant acceleration through empty space, far from any gravitational field. This time some roving interstellar gunman impulsively fires a bullet at the elevator. The bullet hits the side of the car, passes clean through and emerges from the far wall at a point a little below the point at which it penetrated the first wall. The reason for this is evident to the marksman on the outside. He knows that the bullet flew in a straight line, obeying Newton's Law of Inertia; but while it traversed the distance between the two walls of the car, the whole elevator traveled "upward" a certain distance, causing the second bullet hole to appear not opposite the first one but slightly nearer the floor. However, the observers inside the elevator, having no idea where in the universe they are, interpret the situation differently. Aware that on earth any missile describes a parabolic curve toward the ground, they simply conclude that they are at rest in a gravitational field and that the bullet which passed through their car was describing a perfectly normal curve with respect to the floor.

A moment later as the car continues upward through space a beam of light is suddenly flashed through an aperture in the side of the car. Since the velocity of light is great the beam traverses the distance between its point of entrance and the opposite wall in a very small fraction of a second. Nevertheless the car travels upward a certain distance in that interval, so the beam strikes the far wall a tiny fraction of an inch below the point at which it entered. If the observers within the car are equipped with sufficiently delicate instruments of measurement they will be able to compute the curvature of the beam. But the question is, how will they explain it? They are still unaware of the motion of their car and believe themselves at rest in a gravitational field. If they cling to Newtonian principles they will be competely baffled because they will insist that light rays always travel in a straight line. But if they are familiar with the Special Theory of Relativity they will remember that energy has mass in accordance with the equation $m = E/c^2$. Since light is a form of energy they will deduce that light has mass and will therefore be affected by a gravitational field. Hence the curvature of the beam.

From these purely theoretical considerations Einstein concluded that light, like any material object, travels in a curve when passing through the gravitational field of a massive body. He suggested that his theory could be put to test by observing the path of starlight in the gravitational field of the sun. Since the stars are invisible by day, there is only one occasion when sun and stars can be seen together in the sky, and that is during an eclipse. Einstein proposed, therefore, that photographs be taken of the stars immediately bordering the darkened face of the sun during an eclipse and compared with photographs of those same stars made at another time. According to his theory the light from the stars surrounding the sun should be bent inward, toward the sun, in traversing the sun's gravitational field; hence the *images* of those stars should appear to observers on earth to be shifted outward from their usual positions in the sky. Einstein calculated the degree

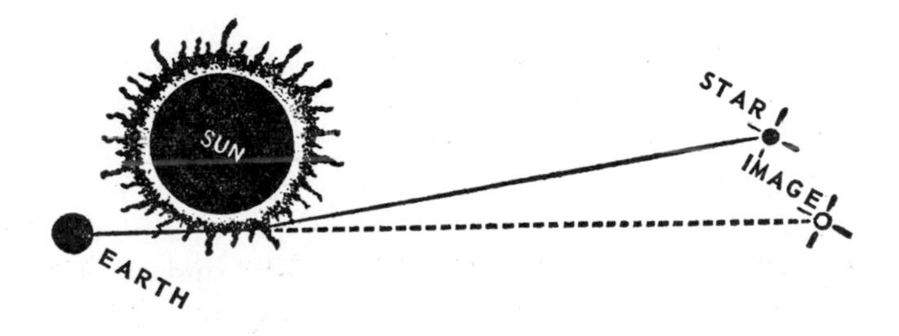

The deflection of starlight in the gravitational field of the sun. Since the light from a star in the neighborhood of the sun's disk is bent inward, toward the sun, as it passes through the sun's gravitational field, the image of the star appears to observers on earth to be shifted outward and away from the sun.

of deflection that should be observed and predicted that for the stars closest to the sun the deviation would be about 1.75 seconds of an arc. Since he staked his whole General Theory of Relativity on this test, men of science throughout the world anxiously awaited the findings of expeditions which journeyed to equatorial regions to photograph the eclipse of May 29, 1919. When their pictures were developed and examined, the deflection of the starlight in the gravitational field of the sun was found to average 1.64

seconds—a figure as close to perfect agreement with Einstein's prediction as the accuracy of instruments allowed.

Another prediction made by Einstein on the basis of General Relativity pertained to time. Having shown how the properties of space are affected by a gravitational field, Einstein reached the conclusion by analogous but somewhat more involved reasoning that time intervals also vary with the gravitational field. A clock transported to the sun should run at a slightly slower rhythm than on earth. And a radiating solar atom should emit light of slightly lower frequency than an atom of the same element on earth. The difference in wave length would in this case be immeasurably small. But there are in the universe gravitational fields stronger than the sun's. One of these surrounds the freak star known as the "companion of Sirius"—a white dwarf composed of matter in a state of such fantastic density that one cubic inch of it would weigh a ton on earth. Because of its great mass this extraordinary dwarf, which is only three times larger than the earth, has a gravitational field potent enough to perturb the movements of Sirius, seventy times its size. Its field is also powerful enough to slow down the frequency of its own radiation by a measurable degree, and spectroscopic observations have indeed proved that the frequency of light emitted by Sirius' companion is reduced by the exact amount predicted by Einstein. The shift of wave length in the spectrum of this star is known to astronomers as "the Einstein Effect" and constitutes an additional verification of General Relativity.

Up to this point the concepts of General Relativity have dealt with the phenomena of the individual gravitational field. But the universe is filled with incomputable bodies of matter—meteors, moons, comets, nebulae, and billions on billions of stars grouped by the interlocking geometry of their gravitational fields in clusters, clouds, galaxies, and supergalactic systems. One naturally asks, what then is the over-all geometry of the space-time continuum in which they drift? In cruder language, what is the shape and size of the universe? All modern replies to the question have been derived directly or indirectly from the principles of General Relativity.

Prior to Einstein the universe was most commonly pictured as an island of matter afloat in the center of an infinite sea of space. There were several reasons for this concept. The universe, most scientists agreed, had to be infinite; because as soon as they conceded that space might come to an end somewhere, they were faced with the embarrassing question: "And what lies beyond that?" Yet Newtonian law prohibited an infinite universe containing a uniform distribution of matter, for then the total gravitational force of all the masses of matter stretching away to infinity would be infinite. To man's feeble eye, moreover, it appeared that beyond the rim of our Milky Way the lamps of space became sparser and sparser, diffusing gradually in attenuated outposts like lonely lighthouses on the frontiers of the fathomless void. But the island universe presented difficulties too. The amount of matter it held was so small by contrast with an infinity of space that inevitably the dynamic laws governing the movements of the galaxies would cause them to disperse like the droplets of a cloud and the universe would become entirely empty.

To Einstein this picture of dissolution and disappearance seemed eminently unsatisfactory. The basic difficulty, he decided, derived from man's natural but unwarranted assumption that the geometry of the universe must be the same as that revealed by his senses here on earth. We confidently assume, for example, that two parallel beams of light will travel through space forever without meeting, because in the infinite plane of Euclidean geometry parallel lines never meet. We also feel certain that in outer space, as on a tennis court, a straight line is the shortest distance between two points. And yet Euclid never actually *proved* that a straight line is the shortest distance between two points; he simply arbitrarily *defined* a straight line as the shortest distance between two points.

Is it not then possible, Einstein asked, that man is being deceived by his limited perceptions when he pictures the universe in the garb of Euclidean geometry? There was a time when man thought the earth was flat. Now he accepts the fact that the earth is round, and he knows that on the surface of the earth the shortest distance between two such points as New York and London is not a straight compass course across the Atlantic but a "great circle" that veers northward past Nova Scotia, Newfoundland, and Iceland. So far as the surface of the earth is concerned Euclid's geometry is not valid. A giant triangle, drawn on the earth's surface from two points on the Equator to the North Pole, would not satisfy Euclid's theorem that the sum of the interior angles of a triangle is always equal to two right angles or 180 degrees. It would contain *more* than 180 degrees, as a glance at the globe will quickly show. And if someone should draw a giant circle on the earth's surface he would find that the ratio between its diameter and its circumference is less than the classic value *pi*. These departures from Euclid are due to the curvature of the earth. Although no one doubts today that the earth has a curvature, man did not discover this fact by getting off the earth and looking at

it. The curvature of the earth can be computed very comfortably on terra firma by a proper mathematical interpretation of easily observable facts. In the same way, by a synthesis of astronomical fact and deduction, Einstein concluded that the universe is neither infinite nor Euclidean, as most scientists supposed, but something hitherto unimagined.

It has already been shown that Euclidean geometry does not hold true in a gravitational field. Light rays do not travel in straight lines when passing through a gravitational field, for the geometry of the field is such that within it there are no straight lines; the shortest course that the light can describe is a curve or great circle which is rigorously determined by the geometrical structure of the field. Since the structure of a gravitational field is shaped by the mass and velocity of the gravitating body—star, moon, or planet—it follows that the geometrical structure of the universe as a whole must be shaped by the sum of its material content. For each concentration of matter in the universe there is a corresponding distortion of the space-time continuum. Each celestial body, each galaxy creates local irregularities in space-time, like eddies around islands in the sea. The greater the concentration of matter, the greater the resulting curvature of space-time. And the total effect is an over-all curvature of the whole space-time continuum: the combined distortions produced by all the incomputable masses of matter in the universe cause the continuum to bend back on itself in a great closed cosmic curve.

The Einstein universe therefore is non-Euclidean and finite. To earthbound man a light ray may appear to travel in a straight line to infinity, just as to an earthworm crawling "straight" ahead forever and ever the earth may seem both flat and infinite. But man's impression that the universe is Euclidean in character, like the earthworm's impression of the earth, is imparted by the limitations of his senses. In the Einstein universe there are no straight lines, there are only great circles. Space, though finite, is unbounded; a mathematician would describe its geometrical character as the four-dimensional analogue of the surface of a sphere. In the less abstract words of the late British physicist, Sir James Jeans:

> A soap-bubble with corrugations on its surface is perhaps the best representation, in terms of simple and familiar materials, of the new universe revealed to us by the Theory of Relativity. The universe is not the interior of the soap-bubble but its surface, and we must always remember that while the surface of the soap-bubble has only two dimensions, the universe bubble has four—three dimensions of space and one of time. And the substance out of which this bubble is blown, the soap-film, is empty space welded onto empty time.

Like most of the concepts of modern science, Einstein's finite, spherical universe cannot be visualized—any more than a photon or an electron can be visualized. But as in the case of the photon and the electron its properties can be described mathematically. By taking the best available values of modern astronomy and applying them to Einstein's field equations, it is possible to compute the *size* of the universe. In order to determine its radius, however, it is first necessary to ascertain its curvature. Since, as Einstein showed, the geometry or curvature of space is determined by its material content, the cosmological problem can be solved only by obtaining a figure for the average density of matter in the universe.

Fortunately this figure is available, for astronomer Edwin Hubble of the Mt. Wilson Observatory conscientiously studied sample areas of the heavens over a period of years and painstakingly computed the average amount of matter contained in them. The conclusion he reached was that in the universe as a whole there is .000000000000000000000000000001 gram of matter per cubic centimeter of space. Applied to Einstein's field equations this figure yields a positive value for the curvature of the universe, which in turn reveals that the radius of the universe is 35 billion light years or 210,000,000,000,000,000,000,000 miles. Einstein's universe, while not infinite, is nevertheless sufficiently enormous to encompass billions of galaxies, each containing hundreds of millions of flaming stars and incalculable quantities of rarefied gas, cold systems of iron and stone and cosmic dust. A sunbeam, setting out through space at the rate of 186,000 miles a second would, in this universe, describe a great cosmic circle and return to its source after a little more than 200 billion terrestrial years.

TOPICS FOR DISCUSSION AND WRITING

1. To meet the difficulty of translating abstruse mathematical reasoning into reasonably approximate layman's language, Barnett makes use of graphic examples and visual demonstrations. Why does Barnett draw his examples from such commonplace activities as riding on a train or in an elevator?
2. Barnett pictures Einstein as asking himself a specific question and then producing an answer. This is obviously an oversimplification. Why does Barnett proceed in this fashion?
3. Does Einstein's method of research, as described by Barnett, resemble the scientific method as outlined by John Rader Platt (p. 75)?
4. What special problem arises for Barnett in the fact that "Einstein's finite, spherical universe cannot be visualized"? How does Barnett overcome that problem?
5. How would you characterize the level of diction which Barnett uses? Is it appropriate to his purpose in writing? Show evidence that Barnett is mindful of his audience, and aware that he has a double responsibility—to subject and to reader.
6. Is Barnett's account of the universe a completely acceptable substitute for Dr. Einstein's account of it? If not, does this invalidate Barnett's work?

Carl Becker

Carl Becker (1873–1945) was a professor of history at Cornell University for over a quarter of a century. The author of many provocative essays, he stirred discussions not only of problems which preoccupied professional historians but also of political policies of his day. The following essay was originally presented as an address to the American Historical Association *in 1932; it was later reprinted in the* American Historical Review, *a professional historical journal.*

To grasp the full significance of Becker's thesis in this essay, it is important to realize that many of his first hearers and readers were committed to a nineteenth-century attitude which maintained that history was the certain and detailed record of the past. Becker wished to convince these historians that the counsels of perfection of the nineteenth-century theorists of history were really "counsels of futility," and that every age wrote history in keeping with its own image of the past and its hopes for the future. It is a tribute to the effectiveness of Becker's essay that his thesis, presented before a similar audience today, would be received not as a radical proposal but as a commonplace doctrine.

To try to secure the attention of his audience as long as possible before some of their prejudices began to shut him out, Becker divided his essay into three parts. In the first part, with ingratiating style and disarming anecdote, he set about to reduce the idea of history to its lowest common denominator. In the second part, he reviewed, again with skillfully narrated interesting detail, how Mr. Everyman keeps his records and organizes his memories of past events by using the same procedures as a professional historian. Then, in a third section, he brings his subject and predicate terms together in a provocative thesis. The rest of the essay continues to draw out the implications of the thesis. His audience could be counted on to agree with him through the first two sections of his speech or essay, for his manner of presentation, as well as his matter, made it difficult for them to disagree. By the time they realized what his purpose was in the third section they would be prepared to accept his controversial proposition.

EVERYMAN HIS OWN HISTORIAN *

Once upon a time, long long ago, I learned how to reduce a fraction to its lowest terms. Whether I could still perform that operation is uncertain; but the discipline involved in early training had its uses, since it taught me that in order to understand the essential nature of anything it is well to strip it of all superficial and irrelevant accretions—in short, to reduce it to its lowest terms. That operation I now venture, with some apprehension and all due apologies, to perform on the subject of history.

I ought first of all to explain that when I use the term "history" I mean knowledge of history. No doubt throughout all past time there actually occurred a series of events which, whether we know what it was or not, constitutes history in some ultimate sense. Nevertheless, much the greater part of these events we can know nothing about, not even that they occurred; many of them we can know only imperfectly; and even the few events that we think we know for sure we can never be absolutely certain of, since we can never revive them, never observe or test them directly. The event itself once occurred, but as an actual event it has disappeared; so that in dealing with it the only objective reality we can observe or test is some material trace which the event has left—usually a written document. With these traces of vanished events, these documents, we must be content since they are all we have; from them we infer what the event was, we affirm that it is a fact that the event was so and so. We do not say "Lincoln is assassinated"; we say "it is a fact that Lincoln was assassinated." The event *was,* but is no longer; it is only the affirmed fact about the event that *is,* that persists, and will persist until we discover that our affirmation is wrong or inadequate. Let us then admit that there are two histories: the actual series of events that once occurred; and the ideal series that we affirm and hold in memory. The first is absolute and unchanged—it was what it was whatever we do or say about it; the second is relative, always changing in response to the increase or refinement of knowledge. The two series correspond more or less; it is our aim to make the correspondence as exact as possible; but the actual series of events exists for us only in terms of the ideal series which we affirm and hold in memory. This is why I am forced to identify

* Reprinted with permission from the *American Historical Review* (January, 1932).

history with knowledge of history. For all practical purposes history is, for us and for the time being, what we know it to be.

It is history in this sense that I wish to reduce to its lowest terms. In order to do that I need a very simple definition. I once read that "History is the knowledge of events that have occurred in the past." This is a simple definition, but not simple enough. It contains three words that require examination. The first is knowledge. Knowledge is a formidable word. I always think of knowledge as something that is stored up in the *Encyclopaedia Britannica* or the *Summa Theologica;* something difficult to acquire, something at all events that I have not. Resenting a definition that denies me the title of historian, I therefore ask what is most essential to knowledge. Well, memory, I should think (and I mean memory in the broad sense, the memory of events inferred as well as the memory of events observed); other things are necessary too, but memory is fundamental: without memory, no knowledge. So our definition becomes, "History is the memory of events that have occurred in the past." But events—the word carries an implication of something grand, like the taking of the Bastille or the Spanish-American War. An occurrence need not be spectacular to be an event. If I drive a motor car down the crooked streets of Ithaca, that is an event—something done; if the traffic cop bawls me out, that is an event—something said; if I have evil thoughts of him for so doing, that is an event—something thought. In truth anything done, said, or thought is an event, important or not as may turn out. But since we do not ordinarily speak without thinking, at least in some rudimentary way, and since the psychologists tell us that we cannot think without speaking, or at least not without having anticipatory vibrations in the larynx, we may well combine thought events and speech events under one term; and so our definition becomes, "History is the memory of things said and done in the past." But the past—the word is both misleading and unnecessary: misleading, because the past, used in connection with history, seems to imply the distant past, as if history ceased before we were born; unnecessary, because after all everything said or done is already in the past as soon as it is said or done. Therefore I will omit that word, and our definition becomes, "History is the memory of things said and done." This is a definition that reduces history to its lowest terms, and yet includes everything that is essential to understanding what it really is.

If the essence of history is the memory of things said and done, then it is obvious that every normal person, Mr. Everyman, knows some history. Of course we do what we can to conceal this invidious truth. Assuming a professional manner, we say that so and so knows no history, when we mean no more than that he failed to pass the examinations set for a higher degree; and simple-minded persons, undergraduates, and others, taken in by academic classifications of knowledge, think they know no history because they have never taken a course in history in college, or have never read Gibbon's *Decline and Fall of the Roman Empire*. No doubt the academic convention has its uses, but it is one of the superficial accretions that must be stripped off if we would understand history reduced to its lowest terms. Mr. Everyman, as well as you and I, remembers things said and done, and must do so at every waking moment. Suppose Mr. Everyman to have awakened this morning unable to remember anything said or done. He would be a lost soul indeed. This has happened, this sudden loss of all historical knowledge. But normally it does not happen. Normally the memory of Mr. Everyman, when he awakens in the morning, reaches out into the country of the past and of distant places and instantaneously re-creates his little world of endeavor, pulls together as it were things said and done in his yesterdays, and coordinates them with his present perceptions and with things to be said and done in his tomorrows. Without this historical knowledge, this memory of things said and done, his today would be aimless and his tomorrow without significance.

Since we are concerned with history in its lowest terms, we will suppose that Mr. Everyman is not a professor of history, but just an ordinary citizen without excess knowledge. Not having a lecture to prepare, his memory of things said and done, when he awakened this morning, presumably did not drag into consciousness any events connected with the Liman von Sanders mission or the Pseudo-Isidorian Decretals; it presumably dragged into consciousness an image of things said and done yesterday in the office, the highly significant fact that General Motors has dropped three points, a conference arranged for ten o'clock in the morning, a promise to play nine holes at four-thirty in the afternoon, and other historical events of similar import. Mr. Everyman knows more history than this, but at the moment of awakening this is sufficient: memory of things said and done, history functioning, at seven-thirty in the morning, in its very lowest terms, has effectively oriented Mr. Everyman in his little world of endeavor.

Yet not quite effectively after all, perhaps; for unaided memory is notoriously fickle, and it may happen that Mr. Everyman, as he drinks his coffee, is uneasily aware of something said or done that he fails now to recall. A common enough occurrence, as we all know to our sorrow—this remembering, not the historical event, but only that there was an event which we ought to remember but cannot. This is Mr. Everyman's difficulty, a bit of history lies dead and inert in the sources, unable to do any work for Mr. Everyman because his memory refuses to bring it alive in consciousness. What then does Mr. Everyman do? He does what any historian would do: he does a bit of historical research in the sources. From his little Private Record Office (I mean his vest pocket) he takes a book in MS., volume XXXV, it may be, and turns to page 23, and there he reads: "December 29, pay Smith's coal bill, 20 tons, $1017.20." Instantaneously a series of historical events comes to life in Mr. Everyman's mind. He has an image of himself ordering twenty tons of coal from Smith last summer, of Smith's wagons driving up to his house, and of the precious coal sliding dustily through the cellar window. Historical events these are, not so important as the forging of the Isidorian Decretals, but still important to Mr. Everyman: historical events which he was not present to observe, but which, by an artificial extension of memory, he can form a clear picture of, because he has done a little original research in the manuscripts preserved in his Private Record Office.

The picture Mr. Everyman forms of Smith's wagons delivering the coal at his house is a picture of things said and done in the past. But it does not stand alone, it is not a pure antiquarian image to be enjoyed for its own sake; on the contrary, it is associated with a picture of things to be said and done in the future; so that throughout the day Mr. Everyman intermittently holds in mind, together with a picture of Smith's coal wagons, a picture of himself going at four o'clock in the afternoon to Smith's office in order to pay his bill. At four o'clock Mr. Everyman is accordingly at Smith's office. "I wish to pay that coal bill," he says. Smith looks dubious and disappointed, takes down a ledger (or a filing case), does a bit of original research in his Private Record Office, and announces: "You don't owe me any money, Mr. Everyman. You ordered the coal here all right, but I didn't have the kind you wanted, and so turned the order over to Brown. It was Brown delivered your coal: he's the man you owe." Whereupon Mr. Everyman goes to Brown's office; and Brown takes down a ledger, does a bit of original research in his Private Record Office, which happily confirms the researches of Smith; and Mr. Everyman pays his bill, and in the evening, after returning from the Country Club, makes a further search in another collection of documents, where, sure enough, he finds a bill from Brown, properly drawn, for twenty tons of stove coal, $1017.20. The research is now completed. Since his mind rests satisfied, Mr. Everyman has found the explanation of the series of events that concerned him.

Mr. Everyman would be astonished to learn that he is a historian, yet it is obvious, isn't it, that he has performed all the essential operations involved in historical research. Needing or wanting to do something (which happened to be, not to deliver a lecture or write a book, but to pay a bill; and this is what misleads him and us as to what he is really doing), the first step was to recall things said and done. Unaided memory proving inadequate, a further step was essential—the examination of certain documents in order to discover the necessary but as yet unknown facts. Unhappily the documents were found to give conflicting reports, so that a critical comparison of the texts had to be instituted in order to eliminate error. All this having been satisfactorily accomplished, Mr. Everyman is ready for the final operation—the formation in his mind, by an artificial extension of memory, of a picture, a definitive picture let us hope, of a selected series of historical events—of himself ordering coal from Smith, of Smith turning the order over to Brown, and of Brown delivering the coal at his house. In the light of this picture Mr. Everyman could, and did, pay his bill. If Mr. Everyman had undertaken these researches in order to write a book instead of to pay a bill, no one would think of denying that he was a historian.

I have tried to reduce history to its lowest terms, first by defining it as the memory of things said and done, second by showing concretely how the memory of things said and done is essential to the performance of the simplest acts of daily life. I wish now to note the more general implications of Mr. Everyman's activities. In the realm of affairs Mr. Everyman has been paying his coal bill; in the realm of consciousness he has been doing that fundamental thing which enables man alone to have, properly speaking, a history: he has been re-enforcing and enriching his immediate perceptions to the end that he may live in a world of semblance more spacious and satisfying than is to be found within the narrow confines of the fleeting present moment.

We are apt to think of the past as dead, the future as nonexistent, the present alone as real; and prematurely wise or disillusioned counselors have urged us to burn always with "a hard, gemlike flame" in order to give "the highest quality to the moments as they pass, and simply for those moments' sake." This no doubt is what the glowworm does; but I think that man, who alone is properly aware that the present moment passes, can for that very reason make no good use of the present moment simply for its own sake. Strictly speaking, the present doesn't exist for us, or is at best no more than an infinitesimal point in time, gone before we can note it as present. Nevertheless, we must have a present; and so we create one by robbing the past, by holding on to the most recent events and pretending that they all belong to our immediate perceptions. If, for example, I raise my arm, the total event is a series of occurrences of which the first are past before the last have taken place; and yet you perceive it as a single movement executed in one present instant. This telescoping of successive events into a single instant philosophers call the "specious present." Doubtless they would assign rather narrow limits to the specious present; but I will willfully make a free use of it, and say that we can extend the specious present as much as we like. In common speech we do so: we speak of the "present hour," the "present year," the "present generation." Perhaps all living creatures have a specious present; but man has this superiority, as Pascal says, that he is aware of himself and the universe, can as it were hold himself at arm's length and with some measure of objectivity watch himself and his fellows functioning in the world during a brief span of allotted years. Of all the creatures, man alone has a specious present that may be deliberately and purposefully enlarged and diversified and enriched.

The extent to which the specious present may thus be enlarged and enriched will depend upon knowledge, the artificial extension of memory, the memory of things said and done in the past and distant places. But not upon knowledge alone; rather upon knowledge directed by purpose. The specious present is an unstable pattern of thought, incessantly changing in response to our immediate perceptions and the purposes that arise therefrom. At any given moment each one of us (professional historian no less than Mr. Everyman) weaves into this unstable pattern such actual or artificial memories as may be necessary to orient us in our little world of endeavor. But to be oriented in our little world of endeavor we must be prepared for what is coming to us (the payment of a coal bill, the delivery of a presidential address, the establishment of a League of Nations, or whatever); and to be prepared for what is coming to us it is necessary, not only to recall certain past events, but to anticipate (note I do not say predict) the future. Thus from the specious present, which always includes more or less of the past, the future refuses to be excluded; and the more of the past we drag into the specious present, the more a hypothetical, patterned future is likely to crowd into it also. Which comes first, which is cause and which effect, whether our memories construct a pattern of past events at the behest of our desires and hopes, or whether our desires and hopes spring from a pattern of past events imposed upon us by experience and knowledge, I shall not attempt to say. What I suspect is that memory of past and anticipation of future events work together, go hand in hand as it were in a friendly way, without disputing over priority and leadership.

At all events they go together, so that in a very real sense it is impossible to divorce history from life: Mr. Everyman cannot do what he needs or desires to do without recalling past events; he cannot recall past events without in some subtle fashion relating them to needs or desires to do. This is the natural function of history, of history reduced to its lowest terms, of history conceived as the memory of things said and done: memory of things said and done (whether in our immediate yesterdays or in the long past of mankind), running hand in hand with the anticipation of things to be said and done, enables us, each to the extent of his knowledge and imagination, to be intelligent, to push back the narrow confines of the fleeting present moment so that what we are doing may be judged in the light of what we have done and what we hope to do. In this sense all *living* history, as Croce says, is contemporaneous: in so far as we think the past (and otherwise the past, however fully related in documents, is nothing to us) it becomes an integral and living part of our present world of semblance.

It must then be obvious that living history, the ideal series of events that we affirm and hold in memory, since it is so intimately associated with what we are doing and with what we hope to do, cannot be precisely the same for all at any given time, or the same for one generation as for another. History in this sense cannot be reduced to a verifiable set of statistics or formulated in terms of universally valid mathematical formulas. It is rather an imaginative creation, a personal possession which each one of us, Mr. Everyman, fashions out of his individual experience, adapts to his practical or emotional needs, and adorns as well as may be to suit his aesthetic tastes. In thus creating his own history, there are, nevertheless, limits which Mr. Everyman may not overstep without incurring penalties. The limits are set by his fellows. If Mr. Everyman lived quite alone in an unconditioned world, he would be free to affirm and hold in memory any ideal series of events that struck his fancy, and thus create a world of semblance quite in accord with the heart's desire. Unfortunately, Mr. Everyman has to live in a world of Browns and Smiths; a sad experience, which has taught him the expediency of recalling certain events with much exactness. In all the immediately practical affairs of life Mr. Everyman is a good historian, as expert, in conducting the researches necessary for paying his coal bill, as need be. His expertness comes partly from long practice, but chiefly from the circumstance that his researches are prescribed and guided by very definite and practical objects which concern him intimately. The problem of what documents to consult, what facts to select, troubles Mr. Everyman not at all. Since he is not writing a book on "Some Aspects of the Coal Industry Objectively Considered," it does not occur to him to collect all the facts and let them speak for themselves. Wishing merely to pay his coal bill, he selects only such facts as may be relevant; and not wishing to pay it twice, he is sufficiently aware, without ever having read Bernheim's *Lehrbuch,* that the relevant facts must be clearly established by the testimony of independent witnesses not self-deceived. He does not know, or need to know, that his personal interest in the performance is a disturbing bias which will prevent him from learning the whole truth or arriving at ultimate causes. Mr. Everyman does not wish to learn the whole truth or to arrive at ultimate causes. He wishes to pay his coal bill. That is to say, he wishes to adjust himself to a practical situation, and on that low pragmatic level he is a good historian precisely because he is not disinterested: he will solve his problems, if he does solve them, by virtue of his intelligence and not by virtue of his indifference.

Nevertheless, Mr. Everyman does not live by bread alone; and on all proper occasions his memory of things said and done, easily enlarging his specious present beyond the narrow circle of daily affairs, will, must inevitably, in mere compensation for the intolerable dullness and vexation of the fleeting present moment, fashion for him a more spacious world than that of the immediately practical. He can readily recall the days of his youth, the places he has lived in, the ventures he has made, the adventures he has had—all the crowded events of a lifetime; and beyond and around this central pattern of personally experienced events, there will be embroidered a more dimly seen pattern of artificial memories, memories of things reputed to have been said and done in past times which he has not known, in distant places which he has not seen. This outer pattern of remembered events that encloses and completes the central pattern of his personal experience, Mr. Everyman has woven, he could not tell you how, out of the most diverse threads of information, picked up in the most casual way, from the most unrelated sources—from things learned at home and in school, from knowledge gained in business or profession, from newspapers glanced at, from books (yes, even history books) read or heard of, from remembered scraps of newsreels or educational films of *ex cathedra* utterances of presidents and kings, from fifteen-minute discourses on the history of civilization broadcast by the courtesy (it may be) of Pepsodent, the Bulova Watch Company, or the Shepard Stores in Boston. Daily and hourly, from a thousand unnoted sources, there is lodged in Mr. Everyman's mind a mass of unrelated and related information and misinformation, of impressions and images, out of which he somehow manages, undeliberately for the most part, to fashion a history, a patterned picture of remembered things said and done in past times and distant places.

It is not possible, it is not essential, that this picture should be complete or completely true: it is essential that it should be useful to Mr. Everyman; and that it may be useful to him he will hold in memory, of all the things he might hold in memory, those things only which can be related with some reasonable degree of relevance and harmony to his idea of himself and of what he is doing in the world and what he hopes to do.

In constructing this more remote and far-flung pattern of remembered things, Mr. Everyman works with something of the freedom of a creative artist; the history which he imaginatively re-creates as an artificial extension of his personal experience will inevitably be an engaging blend of fact and fancy, a mythical adaptation of that which actually happened. In part it will be true, in part false; as a whole perhaps neither true nor false, but only the most convenient form of error. Not that Mr. Everyman wishes or intends to deceive himself or others. Mr. Everyman has a wholesome respect for cold, hard facts, never suspecting how malleable they are, how easy it is to coax and cajole them; but he necessarily takes the facts as they come to him, and is enamored of those that seem best suited to his interests or promise most in the way of emotional satisfaction. The exact truth of remembered events he has in any case no time, and no need, to curiously question or meticulously verify. No doubt he can, if he be an American, call up an image of the signing of the Declaration of Independence in 1776 as readily as he can call up an image of Smith's coal wagons creaking up the hill last summer. He suspects the one image no more than the other; but the signing of the Declaration, touching not his practical interests, calls for no careful historical research on his part. He may perhaps, without knowing why, affirm and hold in memory that the Declaration was signed by the members of the Continental Congress on the fourth of July. It is a vivid and sufficient image which Mr. Everyman may hold to the end of his days without incurring penalties. Neither Brown nor Smith has any interest in setting him right; nor will any court ever send him a summons for failing to recall that the Declaration, "being engrossed and compared at the table, was signed by the members" on the second of August. As an actual event, the signing of the Declaration was what it was; as a remembered event it will be, for Mr. Everyman, what Mr. Everyman contrives to make it: will have for him significance and magic, much or little or none at all, as it fits well or ill into his little world of interests and aspirations and emotional comforts.

What then of us, historians by profession? What have we to do with Mr. Everyman, or he with us? More, I venture to believe, than we are apt to think. For each of us is Mr. Everyman too. Each of us is subject to the limitations of time and place; and for each of us, no less than for the Browns and Smiths of the world, the pattern of remembered things said and done will be woven, safeguard the process how we may, at the behest of circumstance and purpose.

True it is that although each of us is Mr. Everyman, each is something more than his own historian. Mr. Everyman, being but an informal historian, is under no bond to remember what is irrelevant to his personal affairs. But we are historians by profession. Our profession, less intimately bound up with the practical activities, is to be directly concerned with the ideal series of events that is only of casual or occasional import to others; it is our business in life to be ever preoccupied with that far-flung pattern of artificial memories that encloses and completes the central pattern of individual experience. We are Mr. Everybody's historian as well as our own, since our histories serve the double purpose, which written histories have always served, of keeping alive the recollection of memorable men and events. We are thus of that ancient and honorable company of wise men of the tribe, of bards and storytellers and minstrels, of soothsayers and priests, to whom in successive ages has been entrusted the keeping of the useful myths. Let not the harmless, necessary word "myth" put us out of countenance. In the history of history a myth is a once valid but now discarded version of the human story, as our now valid versions will in due course be relegated to the category of discarded myths. With our predecessors, the bards and storytellers and priests, we have therefore this in common: that it is our function, as it was theirs, not to create, but to preserve and perpetuate the social tradition; to harmonize, as well as ignorance and prejudice permit, the actual and the remembered series of events; to enlarge and enrich the specious present common to us all to the end that "society" (the tribe, the nation, or all mankind) may judge of what it is doing in the light of what it has done and what it hopes to do.

History as the artificial extension of the social memory (and I willingly concede that there are other appropriate ways of apprehending human experience) is an art of long standing, necessarily so since it springs instinctively from the impulse to enlarge the range of immediate experience; and however camouflaged by the disfiguring jargon of science, it is still in essence what it has always been. History in this sense is story, in aim always a true story; a story that employs all the devices of literary art (statement and generalization, narration and description, comparison and comment and analogy) to present the succession of events in the life of man, and from the succession of events thus presented to derive a satisfactory meaning. The history written by historians, like the history informally fashioned by Mr. Everyman, is thus a convenient blend of truth and fancy, of what we commonly distinguish as "fact" and "interpretation." In primitive times, when tradition is orally transmitted, bards and storytellers frankly embroider or improvise the facts to heighten the dramatic import of the story. With the use of written records, history, gradually differentiated from fiction, is understood as the story of events that actually occurred; and with the increase and refinement of knowledge the historian recognizes that his first duty is to be sure of his facts, let their meaning be what it may. Nevertheless, in every age history is taken to be a story of actual events from which a significant meaning may be derived; and in every age the illusion is that the present version is valid because the related facts are true, whereas former versions are invalid because based upon inaccurate or inadequate facts.

Never was this conviction more impressively displayed than in our own time—that age of erudition in which we live, or from which we are perhaps just emerging. Finding the course of history littered with the *débris* of exploded philosophies, the historians of the last century, unwilling to be forever duped, turned away (as they fondly hoped) from "interpretation" to the rigorous examination of the factual event, just as it occurred. Perfecting the technique of investigation, they laboriously collected and edited the sources of information, and with incredible persistence and ingenuity ran illusive error to earth, letting the significance of the Middle Ages wait until it was certainly known "whether Charles the Fat was at Ingelheim or Lustnau on July 1, 887," shedding their "lifeblood," in many a hard-fought battle, "for the sublime truths of Sac and Soc." I have no quarrel with this so great concern with hoti's business. One of the first duties of man is not to be duped, to be aware of his world; and to derive the significance of human experience from events that never occurred is surely an enterprise of doubtful value. To establish the facts is always in order, and is indeed the first duty of the historian; but to suppose that the facts, once established in all their fullness, will "speak for themselves" is an illusion. It was perhaps peculiarly the illusion of those historians of the last century who found some special magic in the word "scientific." The scientific historian, it seems, was one who set forth the facts without injecting any extraneous meaning into them. He was the objective man whom Nietzsche described—"a mirror: accustomed to prostration before something that wants to be known, . . . he waits until something comes, and then expands himself sensitively, so that even the light footsteps and gliding past of spiritual things may not be lost in his surface and film." "It is not I who speak, but history which speaks through me," was Fustel's reproof to applauding students. "If a certain philosophy emerges from this scientific history, it must be permitted to emerge naturally, of its own accord, all but independently of the will of the historian." Thus the scientific historian deliberately renounced philosophy only to submit to it without being aware. His philosophy was just this, that by not taking thought a cubit would be added to his stature. With no other preconception than the will to know, the historian would reflect in his surface and film the "order of events throughout past times in all places"; so that, in the fullness of time, when innumerable patient expert scholars, by "exhausting the sources," should have reflected without refracting the truth of all the facts, the definitive and impregnable meaning of human experience would emerge of its own accord to enlighten and emancipate mankind. Hoping to find something without looking for it, expecting to obtain final answers to life's riddle by resolutely refusing to ask questions—it was surely the most romantic species of realism yet invented, the oddest attempt ever made to get something for nothing!

That mood is passing. The fullness of time is not yet, overmuch learning proves a weariness to the flesh, and a younger generation that knows not Von Ranke is eager to believe that Fustel's counsel, if one of perfection, is equally one of futility. Even the most disinterested historian has at least one preconception, which is the fixed idea that he has none. The facts of history are already set forth, implicitly, in the sources; and the historian who could restate without reshaping them would, by submerging and suffocating the mind in diffuse existence, accomplish the superfluous task of depriving human experience of all significance. Left to themselves, the facts do not speak; left to themselves they do not exist, not really, since for all practical purposes there is no fact until someone affirms it. The least the historian can do with any historical fact is to select and affirm it. To select and affirm even the simplest complex of facts is to give them a certain place in a certain pattern of ideas, and this alone is sufficient to give them a special meaning. However "hard" or "cold they may be, historical facts are after all not material substances which, like bricks or scantlings, possess definite shape and clear, persistent outline. To set forth historical facts is not comparable to dumping a barrow of bricks. A brick retains its form and pressure wherever placed; but the form and substance of historical facts, having a negotiable existence only in literary discourse, vary with the words employed to convey them. Since history is not part of the external material world, but an imaginative reconstruction of vanished events, its form and substance are inseparable: in the realm of literary discourse substance, being an idea, *is* form; and form, conveying the idea, *is* substance. It is thus not the undiscriminated fact, but the perceiving mind of the historian that speaks: the special meaning which the facts are made to convey emerges from the substance-form which the historian employs to re-create imaginatively a series of events not present to perception.

In constructing this substance-form of vanished events, the historian, like Mr. Everyman, like the bards and storytellers of an earlier time, will be conditioned by the specious present in which alone he can be aware of his world. Being neither omniscient nor omnipresent, the historian is not the same person always and everywhere; and for him, as for Mr. Everyman, the form and significance of remembered events, like the extension and velocity of physical objects, will vary with the time and place of the observer. After fifty years we can clearly see that it was not history which spoke through Fustel, but Fustel who spoke through history. We see less clearly perhaps that the voice of Fustel was the voice, amplified and freed from static as one may say, of Mr. Everyman; what the admiring students applauded on that famous occasion was neither history nor Fustel, but a deftly colored pattern of selected events which Fustel fashioned, all the more skillfully for not being aware of doing so, in the service of Mr. Everyman's emotional needs—the emotional satisfaction, so essential to Frenchmen at that time, of perceiving that French institutions were not of German origin. And so it must always be. Played upon by all the diverse, unnoted influences of his own time, the historian will elicit history out of documents by the same principle, however more consciously and expertly applied, that Mr. Everyman employs to breed legends out of remembered episodes and oral tradition.

Berate him as we will for not reading our books, Mr. Everyman is stronger than we are, and sooner or later we must adapt our knowledge to his necessities. Otherwise he will leave us to our own devices, leave us it may be to cultivate a species of dry professional arrogance growing out of the thin soil of antiquarian research. Such research, valuable not in itself but for some ulterior purpose, will be of little import except in so far as it is transmuted into common knowledge. The history that lies inert in unread books does no work in the world. The history that does work in the world, the history that influences the course of history, is living history, that pattern of remembered events, whether true or false, that enlarges and enriches the collective specious present, the specious present of Mr. Everyman. It is for this reason that the history of history is a record of the "new history" that in every age rises to confound and supplant the old. It should be a relief to us to renounce omniscience, to recognize that every generation, our own included, will, must inevitably, understand the past and anticipate the future in the light of its own restricted experience, must inevitably play on the dead whatever tricks it finds necessary for its own peace of mind. The appropriate trick for any age is not a malicious invention designed to take anyone in, but an unconscious and necessary effort on the part of "society" to understand what it is doing in the light of what it has done and what it hopes to do. We, historians by profession, share in this necessary effort. But we do not impose our version of the human story on Mr. Everyman; in the end it is rather Mr. Everyman who imposes his version on us—compelling us, in an age of political revolution, to see that history is past politics, in an age of social stress and conflict to search for the economic interpretation. If we remain too long recalcitrant Mr. Everyman will ignore us, shelving our recondite works behind glass doors rarely opened. Our proper function is not to repeat the past but to make use of it, to correct and rationalize for common use Mr. Everyman's mythological adaptation of what actually happened. We are surely under bond to be as honest and as intelligent as human frailty permits; but the secret of our success in the long run is in conforming to the temper of Mr. Everyman, which we seem to guide only because we are so sure, eventually, to follow it.

Neither the value nor the dignity of history need suffer by regarding it as a foreshortened and incomplete representation of the reality that once was, an unstable pattern of remembered things redesigned and newly colored to suit the convenience of those who make use of it. Nor need our labors be the less highly prized because our task is limited, our contributions of incidental and temporary significance. History is an indispensable even though not the highest form of intellectual endeavor, since it makes, as Santayana says, a gift of

> great interests . . . to the heart. A barbarian is not less subject to the past than is the civic man who knows what the past is and means to be loyal to it; but the barbarian, for want of a transpersonal memory, crawls among superstitions which he cannot understand or revoke and among people whom he may hate or love, but whom he can never think of raising to a higher plane, to the level of a purer happiness. The whole dignity of human endeavor is thus bound up with historic issues, and as conscience needs to be controlled by experience if it is to become rational, so personal experience itself needs to be enlarged ideally if the failures and successes it reports are to touch impersonal interests.

I do not present this view of history as one that is stable and must prevail. Whatever validity it may claim, it is certain, on its own premises, to be supplanted; for its premises, imposed upon us by the climate of opinion in which we live and think, predispose us to regard all things, and all principles of things, as no more than "inconstant modes or fashions," as but the "concurrence, renewed from moment to moment, of forces parting sooner or later on their way." It is the limitation of the genetic approach to human experience that it must be content to transform problems since it can never solve them. However accurately we may determine the "facts" of history, the facts themselves and our interpretations of them, and our interpretation of our own interpretations will be seen in a different perspective or a less vivid light as mankind moves into the unknown future. Regarded historically, as a process of becoming, man and his world can obviously be understood only tentatively, since it is by definition something still in the making, something as yet unfinished. Unfortunately for the "permanent contribution" and the universally valid philosophy, time passes; time, the enemy of man as the Greeks thought; tomorrow and tomorrow and tomorrow creeps in this petty pace, and all our yesterdays diminish and grow dim: so that, in the lengthening perspective of the centuries, even the most striking events (the Declaration of Independence, the French Revolution, the Great War itself; like the Diet of Worms before them, like the signing of the Magna Carta and the coronation of Charlemagne and the crossing of the Rubicon and the battle of Marathon) must inevitably, for posterity, fade away into pale replicas of the original picture, for each succeeding generation losing, as they recede into a more distant past, some significance that once was noted in them, some quality of enchantment that once was theirs.

TOPICS FOR DISCUSSION AND WRITING

1. Aristotle called the impact of a speaker's character on his audience an "ethical argument," an argument from the *ethos* or character of the speaker. How influential can the "ethical argument" be? Can it ever outweigh logical arguments? How important is the audience's impression of the speaker or writer (in this case, Becker) to the success of his argument?
2. What is Becker's "least common denominator" of history? Why does he simplify each of the three terms?
3. How does Becker manage his transition from a consideration of history to a consideration of the habits of Mr. Everyman? How does he disarm

any members of his audience who might have been momentarily disturbed by the implications of his transitional sentences?

4. How does he retain his audience's sympathy for his picture of Mr. Everyman? Are there any indications that his remarks, especially some parenthetical clauses, might have been more appealing to an audience of professional historians and college professors than they would be to a general audience?
5. Does he prove that Mr. Everyman uses the same techniques as professional historians? How?
6. Why did Becker first reduce history to its lowest common denominator and then go on to describe the activities of Mr. Everyman? Could the order of the first two parts be reversed?
7. What does he mean by the term "specious present"? Why did he not define this term closer to the beginning of his speech?
8. What is the thesis of this essay? When is it finally and completely revealed? What sentence comes closest to stating it most precisely?
9. What types of arguments does he use to prove his thesis?
10. When does he finally identify the conception of history against which he is arguing? Who was Fustel? What was his conception of history? Why does he delay the identification of the opposition until this point?
11. Is there any difference in tone between the first two sections and the third? Is there any difference in the way in which he argues? Account for any differences.
12. What do you think was most effective in winning his audience, what he had to say or the way in which he said it?
13. Write an essay demonstrating whether Spengler, De Riencourt, or Brinton would qualify as historians according to Becker's definition. How would they differ?

V

Adapting Language to Subject and Audience

During the late medieval period differences in dialect among English-speaking peoples living in various parts of the British Isles were quite pronounced. Dialect differences among Americans during the Colonial Period were much greater than those which have survived, but there are still some very noticeable differences between the speech of New Englanders and Southerners.

Much more noticeable than differences in dialect are the differences between the various levels of English which are considered appropriate to different subjects, audiences, and circumstances. The two extremes among the various levels of English usage are *vulgate* and *formal*. Vulgate English—not to be confused with vulgar English—is the level of English spoken by students in relaxed uninhibited conversation. It is characterized by the use of incomplete sentences, vague connections between nouns and their antecedents, hackneyed words, and slang. Though adequate for face-to-face communication where gestures can compensate for lack of clarity, it is utilized in writing only for the reproduction of conversations.

Formal English is the English used on ceremonial occasions. With its abstract, Latinate vocabulary, occasional periodic sentences, and measured movements, it is commonly used in orations and technical essays. Today's formal English is very close to yesterday's semiformal, and the essays by Matthew Arnold and Samuel Johnson included in this anthology can serve as illustrations of what would be, today, clearly formal usage.

Between the two extremes of formal and vulgate usage, there is a broad area which is known as *standard informal* English. Represented in this anthology by the essays of Robert Oppenheimer and Adlai Stevenson, it can be defined as the level of English used by educated speakers and writers of the language when on their best linguistic behavior. Toward the lower level of standard informal, where it borders on the vulgate, there is a level of usage which can be called *familiar.* Familiar English tolerates controversial and colloquial expressions like "It's me," permits colorful new coinages, and relies on the shared experiences of friends to provide a coherence which is not always as explicit as on the level of standard informal usage. Familiar English is represented by the selection from William Hazlitt's *My First Acquaintance with the Poets.* At the other extreme of standard informal, bordering on the formal, there is a level of usage which can be known as *scholarly and technical.* It is characterized by an abstract vocabulary, complex sentences, careful syntax, and precise coherence. The clearest example of this technical usage is to be found in Herman Kahn's *On Thermonuclear War.*

Our older surviving dialect differences can be called *horizontal dialects* because they are geographically distributed on the horizontal plane. The different levels of usage involve so many differences in the uses of the language that they also can be considered dialect differences. These differences can be considered vertical dialects—they result from differences in the educational level of speaker and writer and from differences in the level of complexity of the subject matter. Differences between the vertical dialects are clearly sensed by their users, as the *Fortune* editorial on "The Language of Business" makes clear. The writer who wants to establish an effective rapport with his intended audience must be very sensitive to these vertical dialects and be sure to choose the right one.

The use of formal English when the occasion or subject does not clearly call for it may convey the impression that the writer is stiff, pompous, and anxious to keep his audience at a distance. The use of familiar English in discussing a serious, complex subject at a crucial moment could give the impression that the writer is unaware of the seriousness of the problems with which he is supposedly concerned, or that he is attempting to substitute familiarity with his audience for competence in his subject. Standard informal English is a safe bet for most occasions and, when carefully and responsibly used, conveys the impression of a perceptive writer interested in his subject, respectful of his audience, and anxious to discuss his problems with them, not one who legislates an arbitrary conclusion.

Aristotle believed that the strongest arguments in favor of a thesis were the impressions made by the character of its proponents. Modern advertisers consider the image of a product the argument most likely to influence potential purchasers. The language a writer uses, like the impression made by the character of the speaker or the image of the product, is the single most important means at his disposal to convey to his readers a favorable impression of what he proposes. A writer can repeatedly protest that he is sincere; he can repeatedly call attention to the strength of the arguments he is using, yet the readers may remain unconvinced. However, if a writer, by the use of an English which his readers approve and with which they are familiar, conveys an impression of sincere concern for the truth as well as interest in his readers, his way of writing may prove much more effective than what he writes.

DENOTATIVE LANGUAGE

The meaning conveyed by most English words can be divided into two parts: the *denotation* and the *connotation* of the word. The denotation of a word is what the word specifically points to. A word's denotation is the core of its meaning. The word "house" denotes a shelter; the core of its meaning is a dwelling place.

The connotation of a word is what the word suggests. The connotation of a word is its aura, the overtones which are communicated along with the central core of meaning. The word "home" denotes the same thing as the word "house," but in addition, the word "home" communicates emotional overtones suggestive of familiarity, belonging, warmth, and friendliness.

Some words, like "house," have little connotation. Other words, like "exquisite," "awful," and "tremendous," have been so abused that they have lost most of their specific denotation and now do little more than connote emotional reactions of delight, fear, and wonder. Words which are neutral (or contain a balanced mixture of connotation and denotation) can become more or less connotative or denotative depending upon the context in which they are used. A fairly neutral word like "fear" can become highly connotative when used by President Roosevelt in his first inaugural address or highly emotional when used by Lady Macbeth goading her husband to murder the king.

The language of an essay whose purpose is to convince, not to excite, and which relies mainly on theoretical considerations to make its point will tend to be much more denotative than connotative. The language of Robert Oppenheimer's *Tradition and Discovery,* wherein he is trying to clarify the interrelationship of complex ideas, is chiefly Latinate, abstract, and colorless. The words were chosen for the sake of clarity and precision, to avoid imaginative and emotional overtones.

The selection from Jonathan Swift reflects his primary concern for clarity. Clarity demands the use of words with precise denotation and the avoidance of words which suggest atmosphere more than they point to specific things. Thus there is a singular absence in Swift of words which are colorful, evocative, or suggestive. If an idea made clear will compel assent, then denotative language is well adapted to convince an audience of the correctness of a thesis. If every failure to convince is a failure in communication, then the more a writer tends to use only language with clear denotation, the less likely is he ever to fail.

Essays which are concerned with specific, concrete situations and procedures also tend to use language which is more denotative than connotative. A writer who finds himself constantly referring to tangibles will find himself using words which have specific reference to these tangibles. Business is concerned with realities, and the language of business tends to be a "thing language," a language which is closely linked to the things it specifies. As the *Fortune* editorial points out, the language of business must be language which is bound to the concerns of the market place; these concerns are specific and real, and the less imagination and emotion which enters into the discussion the better the results will be.

J. Robert Oppenheimer

J. Robert Oppenheimer (1904–), Fermi prize winner for 1963, was director of the Los Alamos, New Mexico, laboratories from 1943 to 1945. Since 1947 he has been Professor of Physics and Director of the Institute for Advanced Study at Princeton. In many essays published since the Second World War, he has manifested a much greater concern for the moral and philosophical implications of contemporary scientific experimentation than for the development of increasingly powerful nuclear weapons.

Tradition and Discovery *was the main lecture delivered at the annual meeting of the American Council of Learned Societies in January of 1959. The audience consisted of representatives of many of the country's most respected professional and scientific societies. The address is interesting not only because it reflects the considered opinions of one of America's most distinguished scientists on a subject of continuing importance, but also because of the clarity of its style and structure. Since his audience consisted of some of the country's most learned scholars, Oppenheimer felt no need to translate complex ideas into more readily intelligible terms nor to provide illustrations and anecdotes to hold that audience's interest. The result is a sustained discussion of significant ideas on a high level of abstraction, in terms chosen because of their appropriateness to the subject—not watered down to cater to an unprepared and unsympathetic audience. The style is unremittingly denotative and informative. The connotative word is rare and, when it does occur, is controlled by the context.*

Tradition and Discovery *

When Columbus set sail on his first voyage of discovery, the evening of the first day he opened the page of what would later be the log of this voyage: on it he wrote, *Jesus cum Maria sit nobis in via*. Partly this was the terror of the voyage; but partly also it was some foreknowledge of the irreversible change that this *via* would make in human history, a change comparable to, perhaps greater than, the enrichment of European culture by the renewal and refreshment of the classic traditions.

In this middle of the Twentieth Century it has occurred to many that we are not in so dissimilar a fix: the sense of a voyage into a very unknown future, the sense of a tradition qualifying all our future but not exhausting it, the sense that in this immense,

* The ACLS Annual Lecture, delivered in connection with the Annual Meeting at the University of Rochester, Rochester, New York, on January 22, 1959. Reprinted by permission of the American Council of Learned Societies and the author.

almost thunderous impact of discovery upon tradition, we have come to a new phase of human history.

Terror attaches to new knowledge, and the unmooring, the unpreparedness that men have to deal with it. You may think of the two legends, of the story of the Tree of Knowledge, of the legend of Prometheus, which, though they are from different cultures and are different stories, have in common that they attest that when man gets too smart he gets into trouble. Indeed, even things which are not practical discoveries—not the discovery of America, or of fire—but are quite abstract, come with a sense of terror. I have found that among my colleagues in the sciences, when people know that they are making some deep finding, not a finding which has any threat in it to the security or comfort of man but some new insight into the order of the natural world, they measure its depth by the fear that comes over them. Niels Bohr once said to me, "When I am up to something important, I am touched with the thought of suicide."

This question of what discovery does to tradition and tradition for discovery, some parts of which I am to talk about tonight, of course touches on an ancient and inexhaustible theme: the struggle, the balance, and the lack of balance between the familiar and essentially timeless in human life, and the always manifest sense of change. Of tradition, I need not say what we mean by that word in a lecture under the auspices of a society of learned folk, whose whole effort is to preserve, to refresh, to transmit, and to increase our insight into what men have done as men, in their art, their learning, their poetry, their politics, their science, their philosophy. Tradition is no less than what makes it possible for us to deal as sentient and thinking beings with our experiences, to cope with our sorrows, to limit and ennoble our joys, to understand what happens to us, to talk to one another, to relate one thing to another, to find the themes which organize experience and give it meaning, to see the relevance of one thing to another. It is of course what makes us human, and what makes us civil. It is typically and decisively the common heritage, that which men do not have to explain to each other; that which in happier days they did explain to their children; that which they can rely on as being present, each in the other's head and heart. It has as such an assimilating quality; it points to the likenesses of things; it points to the connection of things; and of course it has also an oversimplifying quality, since things in fact really are not very alike. It finds the great human themes which run through everything, which we can come back to, which we can recognize, which we can communicate. This communication is often verbal, but it does not have to be.

In very primitive societies, as the anthropologists at least have told us about them, one even finds instances in which the meaning of tradition is to prevent any essential novelty, to assimilate one life to another, one generation to another, one season's cycle to another, so that everything has a place, so that everything is familiar. It has today a very different function. In the sense in which I shall be using the word, in a sense which is relevant to our time, tradition is also the matrix which makes discovery, in an important sense, possible. It is the organ of interpretation, of enrichment and understanding that, in the arts, and in the sciences, and even in our common ethical life, gives meaning to new discovery. It is of course the special mark, the *cachet specifique,* of the modern European tradition that it has catalyzed, for reasons that no one has really been quite clever enough to understand, an immense outpouring and an immense growth of discovery unlike anything which man has known, an unprecedented use of the past for the future; an unprecedented enrichment of the power to find new things by virtue of the extent to which we were in control of the old: unprecedented in volume, in weight, in wealth, in scope, and unprecedented in many ways in quality also, even if one thinks of the highest days of ancient cultures.

This discovery and this use of it is not precisely like the discovery of America; there is more of the element of invention and creation in it than in the discovery of America. There was, God knows, dedication, almost fanaticism, courage, and high skill in the discovery of America, but to an extent that is misleading; if we think of the contemporary world, America was really there; it was not in any sense an artifact of Columbus or of his time or of his voyage. If you think of some of the things which enrich the present time: atonality in music, or the structure of the genetic material which gives to all living things the qualities of life, or such a notion as parity, which has been prominent in discoveries in basic physics, these are not things which were quite so simply given and there to be found, simply, by anyone. It required a tradition, a culture, a background, even to come to these things, even to define them, even to know the means by which they can be found. It depends on where you are, what you are, how you talk; and the element of invention, the element of creation is very great in these. I need not talk about space travel, but it is worth noting that even in the primitive efforts so far, which will soon be much less primitive, to see how things are away from this earth, the one startling thing that has been found is something which would have been completely impossible for Columbus to have understood, or to have detected, though he might have died of it: a very intense zone of radiation whose presence was not expected. This is the kind of discovery that rests on an existing special tradition, in that we are used to looking for this order of experience; we know a great deal about the properties of the world, and did not simply send a piece of material up there, but sent up instruments which are themselves the outgrowths of centuries of study and of specialized skill.

I am not laboring this point because I want to argue either side of the ontological question, "Are the things which are discovered *there,* or are they improvised or invented?" I regard this as rather an empty question. Of course they are there, or they could not be discovered; but their discovery depends on an elaborate development of the human tradition without which they could not be discovered; and their discovery reminds us—and to this I must return later—that in the world there are countless wonders waiting to be discovered, were there in the human tradition the appropriate sophistication, the appropriate development. Discovery is neither wholly necessary, nor wholly free. We are not free to discover what is not there; and what is there is by no means necessarily discovered.

I think that it will add a little to the candor and clarity of what I have to say if I talk for a few minutes about the developments in this century in my own science, because, although I do not propose to lecture about them, and although I am convinced that the story I have to tell you is a story which does not depend for its telling on my having been a physicist, the way I tell it will be affected by that, and by one special episode in it; and perhaps rather than warn you at the end, I should warn you at the beginning, that there is a *parti pris*; there is an attitude in me which comes from the time of human history I have lived, from the kind of work I have seen and done and which, much as I might hope to persuade you to share it, you may not be free or able to share.

It has been a great half century of discovery in physics. Even if we leave out the subjects near physics, like cosmology, astrophysics, the wonders of biochemistry, even if we leave out practical things like nuclear power, just in the fundamental physics relating to our ideas of space, time, cause, and matter, there have been very profound changes, which, for those who have been blessed to live through them, have constituted an experience of deep wonder and excitement. The first of these was of course relativity, which started with the recognition that communication could not be instantaneous, that there was no such thing as an infinite velocity; and that, as a logical consequence, judgments, of simultaneity, of rates of clocks, and of distances would not appear the same to two observers moving with respect to each other. The logical outgrowth of this was the set of theories of relativity which are associated with Einstein's name.

The second great development is the one that I would like to come back to, the discovery and the understanding of what is called the quantum, the quantum of action, and its meaning. Its most primitive meaning is that, although in practical life, in large-scale affairs, we can legitimately think of an idealization, that idealization is not valid in the atomic domains. In ordinary experience, we can find out about a system—a physical system—without concern in principle about the way we inquire, which leaves the object that is being studied undisturbed, unconnected with us as observers. Thus the effects of an observation can be regarded as arbitrarily weak. This idealization is not valid in the atomic domain: there is a limit to the weakness of observation; and therefore the conditions of observation enter in a radical way into the kind of description that we must use for an atomic system. That is the root cause, and the quantum of action is itself simply the measure, of this granular or wholistic quality of observation. It is the barrier below which we cannot go in the gentleness with which we observe the system; and this barrier is itself the reason why, in the atomic domain, one cannot have a legitimate idealization of physical matter, as possessed of those properties which ordinary large-scale matter has, and why there is a logical contradiction in assuming, for instance, an object at a given place and moving with a certain speed—a logical contradiction in supposing that such an object can exist. I shall come back to why that has an effect on one's general outlook.

There have been other discoveries, some made, some in the making, some yet to be made, that probably will touch as deeply our notions of objectifiability and causality as these. One, for instance, has to do with the ancient theme of atoms. It has become very clear that there are in the world of nature no immutable atoms; that if there are immutable things—and there are—these are very abstract entities and structures, characterizing constellations of atoms; the changelessness which the philosophical atomists saw in the atoms themselves attaches not to the objects but to much more abstract quantities, which one is only beginning to sort out. We have at this time the feeling that we are wandering around in fog, somewhere near base camp number 1, for another great ascent, for a change in our view of matter, space, and time, which we hope we may live to see, which is clearly in the making, because of the critical contradictions in our knowledge as it is today.

These things, when I talk about them, may sound as though they should be intelligible and I do not believe they can be made honestly and deeply intelligible short of hard study, because they are not about ordinary experience, and they are not legitimately put in the vague words which I have used. I believe in trying, as I have tried, and will advocate that other people try, to explain them as well as possible; but I think that we must be aware of the fact that these are highly technical things, with their roots in a highly developed and very beautiful but by no means young tradition, and that we cannot short circuit that. To that I may return.

The point about atomic theory, quantum theory, is that we have made, largely because of the philosophic interest and insight of Niels Bohr, a parable of it, which is called "complementarity." I spoke of the fact that in atomic situations, one cannot make observation infinitely gentle; and that therefore one cannot logically attribute to objects on an atomic scale the full range of properties which are familiar in baseballs and planets, in Newtonian mechanics and all the rest of large-scale science.

The point now is that one can attribute some of these properties in a given context, and others in another context; the context is determined by the experimental arrangement, by the nature of the measuring equipment; the two contexts are not realizable in any single arrangement, and are called complementary. Such are, for instance, the context in which one may endeavor to find out where something is, and find indeed that it is localizable; and the other context in which one may make another kind of study, and find out what is the color of the wave associated with this object, and thus its momentum. One will not be able to find an experiment that reconciles these two, and which gives both pieces of information; one calls them complementary approaches to the study of the atomic system.

This indicates, in a way which is quite rigorous, that there is a place for many approaches to the study of a system, none of which completely exhausts the subject. You need to think of more than one approach, and you need to carry it out, in order to find out everything that you can find out. But if you do one, you lose the value of having done the other; you are doing a new study; you cannot apply what you have found in one experiment to a situation in which you set up another. Each is a whole chapter; and these chapters are not serial or cumulative; they have an individual quality, each of which partly erases what came before. One sees in this a very strong and useful analogy to the role of tradition in the varying cultures, in providing complementary bases for the organization of human experience. One cannot combine a primitive culture such as that of the Pueblo Indians, with a culture such as that of contemporary Japan, and have anything meaningful left. Yet it is clear that there are elements in the life of the Pueblo Indians which are lost in the life of the Japanese, and elements in the life of the Japanese which are completely unobtainable and unavailable to the life of the Pueblos. One is therefore prepared to find that the place and style and role of culture, of tradition, of our history, and of our role as observers does affect the nature of our discoveries and the nature of the organization of the world, and yet not to be misled by this to any view which would deprecate the objectivity, or, in the fancy philosophical word, the validity, of the discoveries that are made. This is perhaps helpful in coping with the immense problem of the impact of discovery on tradition.

I want to talk tonight about some of the consequences of this impact; some of the consequences of the growth of science. As I have said, I cannot help having my own science in mind, but I am thinking in terms of science as the word was used a few centuries ago, the sciences of man and of history as well as the sciences of nature. I would be very glad if I could talk to you about what has been happening and what seems likely to keep on happening, and to make it as serious as I think it really is, and then come up and present a course of action, a sort of therapy; but I am not in a position to do that. I do not have a complete therapy; and the suggestions I have are almost in the nature of footnotes. They are important, but they leave most unsaid. I regard our situation as grave, interesting, and radically novel, something which people have not quite had to face in man's history. It will put difficult choices to us; it is doing so today; and we can be judged, we will be judged, by our response. We can be judged by both in our conduct here, in what we make of this country of ours, and by the sort of example we set for the larger world, in which increasingly the troubles and the glories of which I must speak will become a larger part of the landscape.

It seems to me important that we know what it is that is happening, what it is that has struck us, and that we come with open eyes to face it. I think it may be not only that I do not have a cure, but that there is not a cure; that what is called for is a deep, rich acceptance.

Because science rests on, intersects with, alters, affects almost all of man's ethical life, the change in the world which its growth has made, both material and intellectual, is an unfathomably great one. I do not propose to talk about the material changes—they are too familiar to you—they are not unimportant. On the intellectual side I want to talk about three traits. One is the growth itself; one is the question of its structure; and one is a related question, the openness of knowledge—one could say its potential infiniteness and therefore of course, as far as man is concerned, its inevitable partialness.

It is by no means the first time that there has been such a great change in the intellectual scene. As recently as the sixteenth century, when in not much more than a hundred years, the closed, God-ordered world that was inherited from the earlier Renaissance suddenly changed into an open one, almost all man's ideas—that is, European man's ideas—the deep organizing ones about essence and final cause in nature and in the knowledge of nature, were changed. And a little later John Donne was to write of it, " 'Tis all in pieces, all cohaerence gone/All just supply, and all relation." Still that was a very different situation than we have today.

Two of the features—the third could hardly then have been guessed—two of the features which I want to illustrate and to elaborate a little lie in this: they are both a sort of imbalance. In saying imbalance, clearly, one has a norm of human life in mind; I think that one has in mind some earlier, typically simpler, and usually imaginedly happier time. There is imbalance between tradition, in its meaningful sense, what is intimate, familiar, relatively old and established in human knowledge, things that people have lived with for a long time, the contours and meanings of which they know, things that they know in terms of tradition, their own experience, their schooling; all of that on the one hand, and on the other, what is new and therefore known very superficially, or known in intimacy only to very few people. The other kind of imbalance is a related one. It is the imbalance between what is known to us as a community, what is common knowledge, what we can take for granted with each other, and in each other, what is known by man; and on the other hand, all the rest, that is known only by small special groups, by specialized communities, people who are interested and dedicated, who are involved in the work of increasing human knowledge and human understanding but are not able to put it into the common knowledge of man, not able to make it something of which we and our neighbors can be sure that we have been through together, not able to make of it someing which, rich and beautiful, is the very basis of civilized life.

I am one of those who in many ways think that education has improved, not only quantitatively but qualitatively, over this century that has just passed; but I think that, in spite of this, the center of man's knowledge, the common heritage and talk and world is very much less robust and very much less intimate, very much more vague and second-hand and insubstantial than it was a hundred years ago. Of course the core of our common life is many things: it is feeling, affection, common undertakings, and a way to communicate about them, a way to celebrate them together; but a large part of it is a cognitive core—what we know in common—and this part is not in very good shape. Because I believe that we are "knowers" among other things, and perhaps even first among other things, because what we know underlies what we value and what we do, I think we need to have this part of our house in better order.

The educational and cultural problem is vaster than it has ever been. In some ways this is trivial. Thus we deal with more people; we hope for more from a larger fraction; and this is one thing that I, myself, am fairly confident will spread, one American dream that is likely to be a practical dream for the whole world. We have ourselves that very loose, unhierarchical character in our society, that De Tocqueville noted. Our society is not ordered in the sense that we can look up its hierarchies in a book; we cannot find out anywhere who is the best composer or the best comic or the best physicist: I think it would be repugnant to us if we could; and when it is tried, as it sometimes is, we laugh at it.

The other side of the story is quite brutal. In the sixteenth century, much more even in the seventeenth, people began to express some anxiety about this trait of the European tradition. They were learning a great deal new, more than they had thought likely, and they thought that within half a century, perhaps a century, as much would be learned as had been known before. This frightened them. Now the sum of human knowledge is not a very clearly defined thing: if you think of the Gospel according to St. Matthew, or Oedipus, you cannot imagine saying that we are doing twice as much as that today; if you think of the Second Inaugural, you cannot think that there is any quantitative way to measure a change, but only some strong way to say how much it has come to mean in our life. But if we are talking of propositional knowledge, of statements that this and that are true, or that something follows from this, or that something is probable, then it is very different. Today, it can hardly be doubted—and I shall qualify this a little, but not much—that every ten years or so we know twice as much of such knowledge as we did ten years earlier. You can measure this in a number of rather stupid ways; but probably one way of measuring it is by volume of publication, because any society will protect itself against the redundant and the trivial. Things that ought not to be published more or less do not get published. Life is hard enough without that. And the physical weight of what is published in the natural sciences, just to take a narrow sample, the physical weight is a perfectly good measure of the growth of knowledge. It confirms this pattern of growth.

Dr. Price, at the Institute for Advanced Study, has made a study of another rather brutal thing, and that is the number of men occupied in the acquisition of knowledge. This is an exponential function of time, with a characteristic time of ten years, that goes back almost two centuries. It cannot go on, because some people will have to grow vegetables, though apparently not very many; some people will have to argue law cases, though I hope not very many; but it will go on, and the rate of knowedge will increase increasing, though it will not increase, increase, increase, increasing indefinitely. I think you may know the phrase, a very vivid one, that Professor Purcell of Harvard used. He said, "Over ninety percent of all scientists are alive." The results are not all funny. Some of them are very, very troublesome.

It makes a very new problem, because mature men today—and this is true of all of us, of all my hosts and me and all my hosts' guests—are really necessarily and deeply quite unaware of the greater part of what is known. They did not learn about it in school; they have no immediate practice in it; and it involves a way of talking and a tradition for which they are not prepared, because these too have grown out of what they learned when they last looked in on the subject, since they looked. Sometimes we are suddenly shocked into a recognition that big change has occurred. I think that may have been true of the sudden wartime development of atomic energy; but this is an accident, a mark of punctuation, and not of course in any way an encounter with the problem.

People do hear and read about new knowledge; they hear a little from friends, and over the radio. This would be better if it were more directly rooted in a living and commonly shared tradition; for most of new knowledge is specialized in character, not all equally so. Most new knowledge is something that you can understand with some kind of honest understanding if you know what has gone before, know the terms—for instance, know the instruments that are involved and know the abstract ideas that are involved. It is not something that you are likely to understand if you have spent all your previous life in a normal common-sense life. It involves the application of what was earlier acquired, it involves this tradition, words, experience, mathematics, logic; all these things rest on what went before; and that means that there is a certain danger, rather a grim one, in trying to pick up, without a good deal of skepticism and caution, a synopsis of modern genetics or cosmology just by reading about it. The words may sound familiar; and many of those I used in saying a few words about my own subject I think did sound familiar, like "time" for instance. They may suggest something that one has seen on the playing field or in human affairs. Sometimes that is true; but characteristically and much more often it is not true; the words have the characteristics of a bad pun; they sound the same, but the meaning has been redefined out of all similarity to the common meaning given by common experience.

If you think of the old questions about cosmology—what they meant in the fifteenth century and what they mean today—you will notice this. There was then the question, and there is today, of whether the universe is closed or open in space, whether it is closed in time, whether it had a beginning, whether it has an end, or neither one nor the other. These are questions that we are thinking about, and about which we are learning something, even questions for which a kind of qualified limited answer may well be forthcoming; but these are not the questions that the fifteenth-century men were asking, the ones we will answer. The words that we use, like "relativity," which I used, or "indeterminate" . . . do not mean what these words mean in ordinary human life; and I am afraid that if people without study began to get some indication of what they did mean, they would have been defined and refined out of all interest to primitive human curiosity. This will happen too in the sciences of man, and the sciences of life, which are just now taking such enormous steps toward fundamental discovery. When the biologists begin to answer the question, "What is life?" no layman will recognize that this is an answer to the question put as to what life was.

But this means that common sense and specialized knowledge are in a very special, unsymmetric relation to each other. All our knowledge, all our specialized knowledge, starts with common life: words which we know and do not have to argue about, that are in our experience. Then we begin to manipulate, intellectually and physically; and new things grow. I think always of this analogy of the fingers of the hand, separating in accordance with these manipulations, with these differences in technique, according to the plural ways with which one can question nature. What flows back from special knowledge, back into common knowledge, is rather a small part. I am not talking so much about the fact that we use difficult words. I am talking about the fact that behind the difficult words there is a difference in experience, in life and tradition, which is very hard to bridge. Anyone who tries to tell you what goes on in the specialized parts of the world of knowledge—and this is I believe not quite as true of the anthropologist as of the physicist, not quite as true of the philologist as of the biologist, but I think of it as true of everyone—has some of the same problems as a man who has been off to war for five years talking to people who stayed home, or a man who has been in prison; but in addition there is of course the intellectual problem, again varying in difficulty from subject to subject, particularly difficult where the abstractions of an explosively growing mathematics are involved. It is hard intellectual work, but it also involves this sense of remoteness and alienation.

This knowledge is, of course, not without order. It is essentially all about order; its purpose is to discover and create the order which relates things with one another and to reduce, though not quite eliminate, the arbitrary in human experience. Yet it is not orderly in the sense that there are a few general premises from which one can deduce everything else. It is not orderly in the sense that one can say, "But of course I don't really know about the world of nature and man, but I know the basic principles; and I could always pick up the rest," because, in a certain sense, there are no basic principles like that. The deep things in physics, and probably in mathematics, are not things you can tell about unless you are talking to someone who has lived a long time acquiring the tradition. You can say that the principle of sufficient reason is a basic principle, but it does not get you very far, and I am not all that sure that it is true.

One is faced here with a situation in which the practitioners of the specialized sciences have between them contacts, valuable, important; but there is no total relevance, no total mapping of one on the other; and between all these people—and as of now it is still a very small part of our society—between these and the people who do not live in this world, there is only such communication as is mediated by earlier or later education, by friendship, by patience, and by the best of good will. That is why the core of our cognitive life has this sense of emptiness. It is because we learn of learning as we learn of something remote, not concerning us, going on on a distant frontier; and things that are left to our common life are untouched, unstrengthened, and unilluminated by this enormous wonder about the world which is everywhere about us, which could flood us with light, yet which is only faintly, and I think rather sentimentally, perceived.

There is a lot of relation in this world of science. It has structure, and refers to a beautifully ordered world; it is rich; it is always astonishing; it is always different; it is always subtle. There is order so that things cohere, so that general things encompass special ones; and this means in fact that a great deal of what was in textbooks a long time ago does not have to be in them today. It means that there is a kind of sloughing off of knowledge, not because it was not true, but because we can learn a few larger truths from which we shall have more easy access to those which we may now, for the time being, forget. And that process gallops ahead. So, even more rapidly, does the diversification of what was found out, the increase and the strangeness and the variety, so that the balance on the whole is that it is much harder to get an education today, and it probably will be harder ten years from now. Arthur Ryder, my Sanskrit teacher in Berkeley, used to chide me, that if science were any good, it would be much easier to be an educated man than it ever was before. His view was that the world was closed; ours is that it is open.

There is another sense to this kind of unity, and it is important that we be aware of it. No part of science follows really from any other in any usable form. In principle, I suppose nothing happens in chemistry or in biology which is in any kind of contradiction with the laws of physics; but we cannot deduce anything of any interest about a living organism by knowing any amount of physics. It is a different order of nature. Now I think it is a great thing that the great synapses, the barriers which seem to break science down into noncommunicating parts, appear about to yield, not in the sense that any science is encompassed by any other, but in the sense that one sees no lack of logical compatibility, that one has a way of thinking without inconsistency. One sample is just that there have been good suggestions, and a bit of evidence, as to how, following known laws of physics, life could have originated in the state that the earth was in a long time ago. It is not a finished chapter; it has just begun. I do not think that it will go without some hitches; but is not now as though the world of the living and the world of the dead have a cleft between them. One can see how one could, and almost certainly did, grow from the other. You know of the really brilliant progress in understanding how, in living matter, there is information-bearing machinery, particularly in genetic material. We know a little of how it bears information, and something, not much, about how it transmits it. But the whole idea that a necessary cause, an efficient cause, could be consistent with purpose is illuminated by this, so that the characteristic features of life, which are that it has to be described in terms of ends and purposes, are not in conflict with the idea of necessity, the idea of efficient causation, the universal validity of the large and lovely laws of physics. One sees many other examples, perhaps just beginning, that elements of coding are present in the simplest psychic operations of cognition, perception, and recognition. We see really that in the whole of our knowledge of the natural world, including ourselves as natural objects, this whole arch that reaches from the earliest days of history, from the farthest our telescopes and imaginations can see, to the most subtle questions of human behavior, there are no signs of any unmanageable inconsistency. Of course that does not mean, and it never will, that from one part of our knowledge we can learn another. It means only that we will have compatible ways of understanding.

The receptacle of all this knowledge is, of course, not man in general; nor is it quite the individual specialist; rather it is the specialized communities of interlocking experts, men who may call themselves high energy physicists, or high polymer physicists, or radiobiologists. It comes to these groups of people who have very warm close professional relations, even if they do not know each other as friends, even if, alas, they are kept apart. We know each other; and we have this, to my mind, really remarkable characteristic, that we are grateful to each other for getting things straightened out. It is the hallmark of science in its largest sense that in it one finds this immediate and pervasive gratitude to others, who are smarter than we were. We notice this intimacy, this cordiality and warmth, notice it with great hope, and then sometimes with melancholy, partly because it does not in any real sense encompass the world; but even more when we think of its holding the world together, for the bonds really do not seem strong enough for that, for the times we live in. What we have is a modern version of the medieval guilds, a kind of cognitive syndicalism.

In addition to these two attributes, namely that knowledge increases, so that it is hard to keep up with, and to the fact that it is in specialized hands and not in man, there is one other feature about human learning to which I should turn. It is not new; and yet our understanding of its depth and omnipresence may be a little new. It is this: knowledge, understanding, even perception, involve the knower in a choice, an action, an exclusion. We have always known this. We know that education is a precondition for any kind of civilization; we know that history has made us; we know that it is responsible for what we can and cannot see, and that it is remaking us now individually and as a human society. But I have a more concrete and general trait in mind. It comes from the study of cognition. It is illustrated by some experiments of the French physiologist Rostand, who studied the impulses in the auditory nerves of dogs. When he rang a bell he found an electric current along these nerves, and if he rang the bell again he found the same current; but if he put a piece of meat in front of the dog, and rang the bell, he did not get the signal. The dog's sense organs have been instructed by efferent nerves running along, and almost invisible among the great afferent sensory nerves, by a coding system, not to respond, because the dog was out to lunch.

This example, for one thing, puts the British empiricists, with their fundamental sense datum, in place. The sense datum is a most complex artifact, in some ways much more complicated than what a mathematician talks about. But it also illustrates that in order for us to see or hear, in order for us to perceive or talk or communicate, we have to ignore. In order for us to undertand anything, we have to fail to perceive a great deal that is there. Knowledge is always purchased at the expense of what might have been seen and learned but was not. In all these matters the potential is enormously greater than what is really known; in terms of human knowledge the potential must transcend the real. This means that it is a condition of knowledge that we know a relatively small part of what is knowable. It is a condition of knowledge that somehow or other we pick the clues which give us insight into what we are to find out about the world. It is surely one of the great roles of the arts that they profoundly extend what and how people can see and perceive, and almost give new power to the organs of sense, and above all that they alter and extend what people can see, not only as individuals, but, even more, as a community, collectively, in common vision.

These three things, rapid growth, fragmentation, and the essentially infinite character of the knowable, characterize the cognitive house in which we now live. It seems to me clear, and historians of science and of ideas may often agree, that great discoveries in science, whatever they do for man's machines and man's mode of life, affect his thinking, not inherently because of what the ideas are, but almost by accident, for reasons that are essentially beyond human prediction: some sense of analogy between the scientific idea and a human or a political hope, some haunting word or image or reinforcement for what the mood of a society is, what men feel their future and their destiny to be. What we learn in science itself also has a great deal that is accidental, perhaps the beginnings more than the ends; but I speak of a much wider, more pervasive decoherence. I take a very loose, undoctrinaire view of the cognitive relation of what is learned in the sciences, and what the great ideas of a time are, the ways in which people organize and order their experience of life as a whole. I do not think that philosophy is grown from science, though it may be nourished by it, even philosophy in the unacademic, common sense of the word.

It must be clear then that one reason for an anxiety with regard to the firmness of tradition, one reason why we cannot help being somewhat anxious about the stability of values, derives just from the rapidity with which knowledge changes, and from the exclusion of individual men from any adequate sense of what it is. Values clearly mean a commitment to the future, what one will stand for, what one will do, what one cannot do, where one will not be. They involve an appreciation of the past, without which it is even hard to define what one could mean by such a word. Perhaps generally speaking, aesthetic values rest more heavily on an appreciation of the past, and ethical values on a commitment to the future; but if knowledge changes every few years, arching structures like values, which unite the past and the future through the present, will be put to it to retain their content, retain their factual practical meaning. It is easy to say that we believe in virtue; it is easy to say that there is a great deal of evil in the world; but it is not so easy to know in terms of common concrete experience in this changing scenery, all that these words should mean.

For this is a time when the specialized traditions flourish and the common one, binding all of us together, is eroded. It is eroded very much by the fact that the terms in which problems come to us are not familiar. It is eroded by the changing institutions and forms of our society, by the fact that the explosion in knowledge is coupled to and accompanied by an explosion in technology and by rapid change in every aspect of the way men live. I see with great misgivings the fact that faced, for instance, with the questions posed by the rapid development of superweapons, the resources of our traditional attitudes toward good and evil are hardly available. They seem hardly to bear on this problem, which nevertheless may involve the end or the survival of the human race, and which most certainly should not be taken out of the framework of man's ethical life.

These practical problems are one part of change; the other is the extraordinary change in the intellectual background of life, in the knowledge we have about nature, about man, in the increases which are now threatened and promised, but will, within the century, if we have some peace, entirely overshadow what we can now imagine as to the properties of living organisms and the characteristics of man himself.

One could, hearing of the consequences of change, ask whether it might not be a good idea to stop it. I do not think so: I think that the immense utility of knowledge, man's cupidity and curiosity, his sense of adventure, will probably put it wholly outside the probabilities of history that the quest for knowledge stop or that the success of the quest be impaired. I think that only religious or political tyranny, of a very total character, is likely to do that. It did happen when the Muslim Renaissance was extinguished; we live today with some of the consequent troubles. Yet that was a very different world. For myself, I think that the commitment to knowledge is so inherently a part of the human condition, and so inherently a human virtue, that one will not exorcise it, and yet leave man intact. It is not, I think, as some scientists have urged, the unique central principle for the organization of society; but it is a central part of human life.

It is of course true that the very growth of our knowledge has posed many kinds of practical problems. I hesitate to go into them. I have an enormous sense of inadequacy to it. I may mention two kinds. I have spoken of the troubles of communication, of the troubles of common understanding. From this I think it follows that you do not compound the troubles in any way that can be avoided. Thus I am disturbed, for instance, more than I otherwise would be, by habits which clutter, impede, or frustrate communication. What are they? What do I have in mind? For one thing, any source of information which has a monopoly of it, as a government often may, can be dogmatic. It can give so monolithic a view of what is going on, it can so oversimplify what it is doing, what the state of affairs is, that people cannot really learn the truth. Where we most manifestly do this, and perhaps with the best reasons, and the best conscience, is when we are deeply engaged in a great war. Yet when I think of the two World Wars of the century, I am not convinced that we have thus done any great service for ourselves, for our cause, for our country, or for peace by so grossly simplifying everything. For the evil of such dogmatism is not only that it limits the capacity of ordinary folk to understand something of the true complexity and the true variety of things; it does this also for the very functionaries of the government who have brought it about.

Secrecy is a terrible inhibition, obviously, to communication. This is the real agony about which technical people have been crying out: not so much that they could not do physics or biology; but that in a society dying of lack of communication, to do anything to make this disease worse was a very serious step to take, and should be taken only in the most grave and limited way.

Philistinism is a terrible trouble. One does not have to be a government to be philistine, philistine in believing that only those things which it requires no trouble to understand are important, that if something is complicated then it cannot be very important, that if something is recondite it cannot be very important, that if something is learned it cannot be very important. This is an easy view in a time when we know that we are unable to catch up with more than a minute fraction of the wonderful things that it is our duty, our privilege, to a certain extent our responsibility, to learn about. It is very, very nice to be able to say, "That is too complicated for me; and that cannot really go very deep"; it is very tempting to find reasons for closing our eyes and ears to things and saying, "No, no, this cannot be the reality; the reality must be easier." We need, I think, to fight against that in the air, in the climate, in our whole lives, to insist that what is difficult, what is recondite, what is obscure, what is specialized, is a great part of the human treasure; we must encourage people to learn it and not to leave it aside.

Another obvious practical point is that the goal of education, in a cognitive world as eclectic, as ignorant, as accidental, as disorganized as ours inevitably will be, needs very much to be rethought. We need, certainly in higher education, to be sure that some genuine experience of discovery and rediscovery is a part of the life of everyone who is educated; we need to be sure that some genuine appreciation of the gulf which separates knowledge and ignorance is also a part of it. I say this because only people who have been through these experiences are intellectually prepared to live in a world in which they are surrounded by knowledge of which they will largely remain ignorant, prepared not to take the vulgar and superficial account of knowledge for the reality.

These problems are not easy; these are not even in a sketch very easy; and they certainly provide no curriculum, neither a political program nor an educational curriculum. But I think in the end it is where we ourselves stand, and how we live in this, that may be the hardest.

In this vast world, with its unceasing change, its great novelty without precedent, not easy to grasp, its great alterations, its great nostalgia for a time when things were simple, more familiar, and easier to keep in place, there are yet present for us beautiful and growing perspectives of understanding and order, more than ever really in man's whole history. The great sciences offer in a most moving way an example of this harmonization, on the one hand of change and novelty and disorder, and on the other a great and overriding sense of harmony and order.

We have, I think, in dealing with this world, a double duty; a duty on the one hand to be constant and firm and faithful to what we really know, to what is close to us, to our art, our knowledge, our own community, our tradition, in the sense in which tradition has been the story of man's glory, where we live fully as men. To all the other traditions, to all the rest of the world with its wonders that we do not know very well, we need a sense of hospitality and openness, a willingness to make room for the strange, for the thing that does not fit. This is a hard double duty. If it is made possible at all, it is because it is moderated by things quite outside the cognitive order; by friendship, by the regard and love we bear one another, which soften the harshness of isolation, which bring us news and sympathy and understanding of what our fellows are doing, which bind a common human tie between us, and between the many, many branches of this growing tree of knowledge. These two parts of our duty make a picture of a common life and an ordered world very different from any that man has ever been content to accept, not very easy, not very tranquil, but with a hope of a common life touched and illuminated by community, and by knowledge of the world and of man.

TOPICS FOR DISCUSSION AND WRITING

1. What is the effect upon scientists of possibly making a new fundamental discovery? Is there any indication that this has been a common feeling since the dawn of history?
2. What does he understand by the term "tradition"? In what sense will he be using it through this essay?
3. Why does he begin his speech with a review of some of the scientific discoveries of the last generation? What kinds of scientific discoveries interest him?

4. What does he consider is the most important common aspect of all discoveries? Why does he refer to the impossibility of combining a primitive Pueblo culture with the contemporary Japanese culture? Is it an apt comparison?
5. What is his thesis about the growth of knowledge?
6. What thesis does he propose about the extent to which the existence of new knowledge is actually known to men who should know it?
7. What thesis does he defend about the unity or relatedness of the new knowledge? How does he try to prove this and the above theses?
8. What is the thesis of the entire speech? What is his primary subject, and how does he develop his argument?
9. What evidence can you find that he is using English which is more informal than formal? How would you classify an expression such as, "When man gets too smart he gets into trouble"? What evidence of informality do you find in the over-all tone of the speech? What kind of relationship does he seem to be trying to establish with his audience?
10. What evidence can you find that he is conscious of addressing a learned audience? Comment on his choice of words, his phrases, and his ideas.
11. Collect a list of some of the words which seem to you particularly representative examples of his usage. Are they mainly abstract, learned, Latinate, or all three? Give examples of denotative words.
12. How many analogies do you find him using? How many times does he use language in what is clearly a nonliteral sense? How many of his words would you consider clear examples of connotative words?
13. What aspect of his style do you think was mainly responsible for holding his audience's attention? What aspects of his style do you think most clearly reflect the qualities of his mind?
14. Write an essay explaining why you think Oppenheimer's ideas in this essay are in substantial agreement with Arnold's (p. 335). Does Oppenheimer maintain that science is more important than literature, or that literature must be studied as well as science?

Jonathan Swift

Jonathan Swift (1667–1745) is famous for his satirical prose style, displayed in such works as Gulliver's Travels, A Tale of a Tub, *and* A Modest Proposal, *but it is not widely known that Swift was a notable theorist of style, and that he paid particular attention to the problem of adapting language to subject and audience. His definition of a good style—"proper words in proper places"—is frequently quoted in discussions of adapting language. It is also one of the most frustrating remarks, for Swift did not expand on his phrase, and we would like to know what he meant by* proper. *We can infer his probable meaning from something he said in a sermon entitled "Upon Sleeping in Church." In that sermon Swift, speaking of the difficulty in reaching any audience, asked the question: "Do they [i.e., the clergymen] consider how mixed a thing is every audience, whose taste and judgment differ, perhaps every day, not only from each other, but themselves?" To answer his own question Swift wrote several essays advocating a concrete, clear, and largely denotative style—free of ambiguity, unnecessary ornateness, and affectation—as a way of making contact with subject and audience. One such essay is the following contribution to Sir Richard Steele's periodical* The Tatler, *in which Swift as a fictional correspondent attacks certain corruptions of style. His derision is apropos not only to his own time, but to ours as well.*

On Corruptions of Style

FROM MY OWN APARTMENT, SEPTEMBER 27

The following letter has laid before me many great and manifest evils in the world of letters which I had overlooked; but they open to me a very busy scene, and it will require no small care and application to amend errors which are become so universal. The affectation of politeness is exposed in this epistle with a great deal of wit and discernment; so that whatever discourses I may fall into hereafter upon the subjects the writer treats of, I shall at present lay the matter before the world without the least alteration from the words of my correspondent.

To Isaac Bickerstaff, *Esq;*

Sir,

There are some abuses among us of great consequence, the reformation of which is properly your province, tho', as far as I have been conversant in your papers, you have not yet considered them. These are, the deplorable ignorance that for some years hath reigned among our English writers, the great depravity of our taste, and the continual corruption of our style. I say nothing here of those who handle particular sciences, divinity, law, physick, and the like; I mean, the traders in history and politicks, and the belles-lettres; together with those by whom books are not translated, but (as the common expressions are) done out of French, Latin, or other language, and made English. I cannot but observe to you, that till of late years a grub-street book was always bound in sheepskin, with suitable print and paper, the price never above a shilling, and taken off wholly by common tradesmen or country pedlars. But now they appear in all sizes and shapes, and in all places. They are handed about from lapfulls in every coffeehouse to persons of quality, are shewn in Westminster-Hall and the Court of Requests. You may see them gilt, and in royal paper, of five or six hundred pages, and rated accordingly. I would engage to furnish you with a catalogue of English books published within the compass of seven years past, which at the first hand would cost you a hundred pounds, wherein you shall not be able to find ten lines together of common grammar or common sense.

These two evils, ignorance and want of taste, have produced a third; I mean, the continual corruption of our English tongue, which, without some timely remedy, will suffer more by the false refinements of twenty years past, than it hath been improved in the foregoing hundred: And this is what I design chiefly to enlarge upon, leaving the former evils to your animadversion.

But instead of giving you a list of the late refinements crept into our language, I here send you the copy of a letter I received some time ago from a most accomplished person in this way of writing, upon which I shall make some remarks. It is in these terms:

Sir,

I *cou'dn't* get the things you sent for all *about town*. . . . I *thot* to *ha'* come down my self, and then *I'd ha' brot 'um;* but *I han't don't,* and I believe I *can't do't,* that's *pozz.* . . . *Tom* begins to *gi'mself airs* because *he's* going with the *Plenipo's.* . . . 'Tis said, the *French* king will *bamboozl' us agen,* which *causes many speculations.* The *Jacks,* and others of that *kidney,* are very *uppish,* and *alert upon't,* as you may see by their *phizz's.* . . . *Will Hazzard* has got the *hipps,* having lost *to the tune of* five hundr'd pound, *tho* he understands play very well, *no body better.* He has promis't me upon *rep,* to leave off play; but you know 'tis a weakness *he's* to apt *to give into, tho* he has as much wit as any man, *no body more.* He has lain *incog* ever since. . . . The *mobb's* very quiet with us now. . . . I believe you *thot* I *banter'd* you in my last like a *country put.* . . . I *sha'n't* leave town this month, &c.

This letter is in every point an admirable pattern of the present polite way of writing; nor is it of less authority for being an epistle. You may gather every flower in it, with a thousand more of equal sweetness, from the books, pamphlets, and single papers offered us every day in the coffeehouses: and these are the beauties introduced to supply the want of wit, sense, humour, and learning, which formerly were looked upon as qualifications for a writer. If a man of wit who died forty years ago were to rise from the grave on purpose, how would he be able to read this letter? And after he had got through that difficulty, how would he be able to understand it? The first thing that strikes your eye is the breaks at the end of almost every sentence; of which I know not the use, only that it is a refinement, and very frequently practised. Then you will observe the abbreviations and elisions, by which consonants of most obdurate sound are joined together, without one softening vowel to intervene; and all this only to make one syllable of two, directly contrary to the example of the Greeks and Romans; altogether of the Gothick strain, and a natural tendency towards relapsing into barbarity, which delights in monosyllables and uniting of mute consonants, as it is observable in all the northern languages. And this is still more visible in the next refinement, which consists in pronouncing the first syllable in a word that has many, and dismissing the rest; such as *phizz, hipps, mobb, poz, rep,* and many more; when we are already overloaded with monosyllables, which are the disgrace of our language. Thus we cram one syllable and cut off the rest, as the owel fatten'd her mice after she had bit off their legs to prevent their running away; and if ours be the same reason for maiming our words, it will certainly answer the end, for I am sure no other nation will desire to borrow them. Some words are hitherto but fairly split, and therefore only in their way to perfection, as *incog* and *Plenipo*; but in a short time 'tis to be hoped they will be further dock'd to *inc* and *Plen.* This reflexion has made me of late years very impatient for a peace, which I believe would save the lives of many brave words, as well as men. The war has introduced abundance of polysyllables, which will never be able to live many more campagnes: *speculations, operations, preliminaries, ambassadors, pallisadoes, communication, circumvallation, battalions,* as numerous as they are, if they attack us too frequently in our coffeehouses, we shall certainly put them to flight, and cut off the rear.

The third refinement observable in the letter I send you consists in the choice of certain words invented by some pretty fellows; such as *banter, bamboozle, country put,* and *kidney,* as it is there applied; some of which are now struggling for the vogue, and others are in possession of it. I have done my utmost for some years past to stop the progress of *mobb* and *banter,* but have been plainly borne down by numbers, and betrayed by those who promised to assist me.

In the last place, you are to take notice of certain choice phrases scattered through the letter; some of them tolerable enough, till they were worn to rags by servile imitators. You might easily find them, though they were not in a different print, and therefore I need not disturb them.

These are the false refinements in our style which you ought to correct, first by argument and fair means; but if those fail, I think you are to make use of your authority as censor, and by an annual *Index Expurgatorius* expunge all words and phrases that are offensive to good sense, and condemn those barbarous mutilations of vowels and syllables. In this last point the usual pretence is that they spell as they speak, a noble standard for language!—to depend upon the caprice of every coxcomb who, because words are the cloathing of our thoughts, cuts them out, and shapes them oftner than his dress. I believe all reasonable people would be content that such refiners were more sparing in their words, and liberal in their syllables: and upon this head I should be glad you would bestow some advice upon several young readers in our churches who, coming up from the University full fraught with admiration of our town politeness, will needs correct the style of their prayer books. In reading the absolution, they are very careful to say *pardons* and *absolves;* and in the prayer for the royal family, it must be, *endue 'um, enrich 'um, prosper 'um,* and *bring 'um.* Then in their sermons they use all the modern terms of art, *sham, banter, mobb, bubble, bully, cutting, shuffling,* and *palming,* all which, and many more of the like stamp, as I have heard them often in the pulpit from such young sophisters, so I have read them in some of those sermons that have made most noise of late. The design, it seems, is to avoid the dreadful imputation of pedantry, to shew us that they know the town, understand men and manners, and have not been poring upon old unfashionable books in the university.

I should be glad to see you the instrument of introducing into our style that simplicity which is the best and truest ornament of most things in life, which the politer ages always aimed at in their building and dress (*simplex munditiis*) as well as their productions of wit. 'Tis manifest that all new, affected modes of speech, whether borrowed from the court, the town, or the theatre, are the first perishing parts in any language and, as I could prove by many hundred instances, have been so in ours. The writings of Hooker, who was a country clergyman, and of Parsons the Jesuit, both in the reign of Queen Elizabeth, are in a style that, with very few allowances, would not offend any present reader; much more clear and intelligible than those of Sir H. Wotton, Sir Robert Naunton, Osborn, Daniel the historian, and several others who writ later; but being men of the court, and affecting the phrases then in fashion, they are often either not to be understood, or appear perfectly ridiculous.

What remedies are to be applied to these evils I have not room to consider, having, I fear, already taken up most of your paper. Besides, I think it is our office only to represent abuses, and yours to redress them. I am, with great respect,

Sir,

Yours, &c.

TOPICS FOR DISCUSSION AND WRITING

1. What does Swift see as the basic reason for corruption in style?
2. Are there any such "corruptions" which, despite Swift's ridicule of them, have become acceptable?
3. What are the four classes of corruptions?
4. Could these same classes be discovered in contemporary writing? Which examples might you cite to demonstrate that some or all of these classes are still operative?
5. Swift forbears to offer any solutions to the problem of corrupted style. What steps might be taken to "remedy these evils"?
6. Compare Swift's essay with the editorial from *Fortune* magazine which follows. Is there any agreement between the two?

7. Write an essay demonstrating why you think that Swift would, or would not, have approved of the style of Oppenheimer's essay (p. 452). Is Oppenheimer guilty of any of Swift's "corruptions"?
8. Why does Swift think speakers tend to use the latest fashionable words? Do they do so out of concern for either subject or audience? Is such use of fashionable words—slang—ever effective? Might a particular writing situation call for the use of slang?
9. Dr. Samuel Johnson once complained that Swift could "never be caught using a metaphor." Is this passage from Swift's writing entirely denotative?

from *Fortune:* The Language of Business *

Not so long ago, the businessman used to take his language pretty much for granted. He could afford to. His place was respected and his authority unquestioned. And so he bought, he sold, he collected his bills, made an occasional speech perhaps—and if the public, the workers, or the government didn't quite understand what he was up to, well, so much the better for all concerned.

But no longer. Acknowledging the fact—and the necessity—of others' scrutiny, he has made the interchange of facts and ideas with them one of his principal jobs. The house organ, the interoffice memo, the press release, the press conference, the annual report—the range of his efforts has grown enormous. So widespread, indeed, that business has become almost as extensive a publisher as the government itself.

Is the language of business up to the job? The news—and refreshing news it is—is that the American businessman himself has begun to conclude that it is not. Some, in fact, have gone so far as to assert that the pomposity of management prose is the "root ill of our communication troubles." While that may be an overexcited judgment, management's surveys have demonstrated that a large amount of its language has been not only incomprehensible to the people it is trying to reach, but enormously expensive in money, time, and misunderstanding as well. "It is high time the American businessman discovered the English language." "It would be very

* Reprinted from the November, 1950 issue of *Fortune Magazine* by special permission of the editors.

useful to him." . . . "We've turned our offices into paper mills." . . . "We love curt clear correspondence—but damned few of us know how to write it." Everywhere the chorus of self-criticism is growing.

The positive results of this self-examination have been impressive. In company after company, executives have been setting up "writing clinics" to scour management copy, staging correspondence improvement courses, holding school in conference and public speaking techniques, and, at the very least, peppering subordinates with "For God's sake won't you people learn to use English around here" memos. All of which is clearly to the good. At the same time —and not so clearly to the good—a school of experts has come forward to help the businessman by redesigning the language of industry. To accomplish this, the experts have developed a scientific method that, as we shall see later, has some disturbing implications. Meanwhile, a look at the anatomy of the language that is to be redesigned.

First, the written variety—and that infamous jargon, which, for want of a better term, we'll call businesese. Its signal characteristic, as the reader and all other critics of businesese will recognize, is its uniformity. Almost invariably, businesese is marked by the heavy use of the passive construction. Nobody ever *does* anything. Things *happen*—and the author of the actions is only barely implied. Thus, one does not refer to something, reference is made to. Similarly, while prices may rise, nobody *raises* them. To be sure, in businesese there is not quite the same anonymity as is found in federal prose, for "I" and "we" do appear often. Except when the news to be relayed is good, however, there is no mistaking that the "I" and "we" are merely a convenient fiction and that the real author isn't a person at all but that great mystic force known as the corporation.

Except for a few special expressions, its vocabulary is everywhere quite the same. Midwesterners are likely to dispute the latter point, but a reading of approximately 500,000 words of business prose indicates no striking difference—in the Midwest or anywhere else. Moreover, in sounding out a hundred executives on the subject, *Fortune* found that their views coincided remarkably, particularly so in the matter of pet peeves (principally: "please be advised," "in reference to yours of. . . ." "We wish to draw attention," "to acknowledge your letter"). The phrases of businesese are everywhere so uniform, in fact, that stenographers have a full set of shorthand symbols for them.

Because of this uniformity, defenders of businesese can argue that it doesn't make for misunderstanding. After all, everybody knows the symbols, and furthermore, wouldn't a lot of people be offended by the terseness of more concise wording? There is something to this theory. Since businesese generally is twice as wordy as plain English, however, the theory is rather expensive to uphold. By the use of regular English the cost of the average letter—commonly estimated at 75 cents to $1—can be cut by about 20 cents. For a firm emitting a million letters a year, this could mean an annual saving of $200,000. Probably it would be even greater; for, by the calculations of correspondence specialist Richard Morris, roughly 15 per cent of the letters currently being written wouldn't be necessary at all if the preceding correspondence had been in regular English in the first place.

Where do the terms of businesese come from? Most, of course, are hand-me-downs from former generations of businessmen, but many are the fruit of crossfertilization with other jargons. A businessman who castigates government bureaucrats, for example, is at the same time apt to be activating, expediting, implementing, effectuating, optimizing, minimizing, and maximizing—and at all levels and echelons within the framework of broad policy areas. Similarly, though he is amused by the longhairs and the social scientists, he is beginning to speak knowingly of projective techniques, social dynamics, depth interviewing, and sometime soon, if he keeps up at this rate, he will probably appropriate that hallmark of the sound sociological paper, "insightful." Businesese, in fact, has very nearly become the great common meeting ground of the jargons.

Why do people who in private talk so pungently often write so pompously? There are many reasons: tradition, the demands of time, carelessness, the conservative influence of the secretary. Above all is the simple matter of status. Theorem: the less established the status of a person, the more his dependence on jargon. Examine the man who has just graduated from pecking out his own letters to declaiming them to a secretary and you are likely to have a man hopelessly intoxicated with the rhythm of businesese. Conversely, if you come across a blunt yes or no in a letter, you don't need to glance further to grasp that the author feels pretty firm in his chair.

The application of euphemism, a favored device of businesese, further illustrates this status principle. Take the field of selling. At the top of the ladder you will find a great many people in it: *sales* managers, vice presidents for *sales*, etc. As you go down the ranks, however, it becomes difficult to find people in this line of work. Field underwriters, estate planners, merchandising apprentices, social engineers, distribution analysts, and representatives of one kind or another, yes. But *sales*men? Rarely.

Not only does businesese confer status, it protects it as well, by its magnificent usefulness for buck passing and hedging. "All you have to remember," one executive says, "is the one basis which characterizes all such intracommunication: let the language be ambiguous enough that if the text be successfully carried out, all credit may be claimed, but if the text be unsuccessfully carried out, a technical alibi can be set up out of the text itself."

For this purpose there is a regular subglossary of businesese. Most notable terms: "in the process of," "at this time," "under consideration," "in the not-too-distant future," "company policy," and, when one is unable to explain something properly, "obviously." People who have to submit periodic reports to their superiors are particularly dependent on such terms—salesmen, for example, would have a hard time if they couldn't report of some prospects that they were "very impressed." ("I am allergic to that word," says one sales manager. "It results in so few orders.")

The full application of businesese to hedging occurs when more than two heads are put to work on a problem. As the members of top management sit around the table, a relatively simple policy statement is introduced for discussion. This is kicked around a bit, as the saying goes, for though it certainly is a fine statement, couldn't agree with it more, there are just a few little angles and suggestions that maybe ought to be noted. Thereupon each executive, much as a baseball captain grasps a bat in choosing up sides, adds his qualification, until finally the original statement has been at once pointed up, toned down, given more dignity, made more forceful, altered to anticipate possible objections, concretized, amended, and resolved. Now no longer a mere statement but a philosophy, or collection of philosophies, it is turned over to the Public Relations Department to give to the waiting public. There is nothing, as so many people say, quite like what you get when everybody on the team works together.

Besides written businesese, there is another and far more influential category of business English. Generally, it is found in the spoken language of business—in particular, that brand to be heard at the banquet table, the convention, and the conference table.

It might best be called *reverse* gobbledegook, for in almost every outward respect it is the opposite of written jargon. Where written jargon is multisyllabic, the other is filled with short terse words; its sentences are short and their construction so much more active than passive that exclamation marks occur almost as frequently as periods. It is English that is on the beam. English with its feet on the ground, in short, *shirt-sleeve* English.

Thanks to reverse gobbledegook, the less you have to say, the more emphatically you can say it. All one has to do is use certain hard-hitting expressions, and refer as frequently as possible to the fact that these expressions are being used. A sure forewarning of its onrush, accordingly, is a prefatory announcement by the speaker that he is not going to beat around the bush, pull any punches, pussyfoot, use two-dollar words, or the like. The rest is inevitable; so standardized are the expressions of reverse gobbledegook that an audience would be stunned to attention were a single one of them altered by so much as a word. (One of these days a clever speaker is going to capitalize on this. "Gentlemen," he will say, "I offer a panacea.")

As a result, reverse gobbledegook can be self-defeating; that is, since its whole effect lies in the dynamic quality the words convey, their constant use tends to neutralize them. This can be overcome, however, by adding strengtheners—so that, in a very real sense of the word, it cannot be overemphasized that you sincerely, and unquestionably, meant what you said in the first place.

Like written businesese, reverse gobbledegook also confers status. For this purpose, its provides a sort of slang that, skillfully applied —particularly at the conference table—will impart to the user an appearance of savviness, cooniness, and general know-how. Want to mark yourself as a comer in the advertising field? Speak, then, of fun stories, sweet guys, the hard sell, straw men you set up to back into, and points you can hang your hat on.[1] For each field you will find a subglossary, and, common to all of them, such universal terms as "play it by ear," "the pitch," "the deal," and the many expressions built on the suffix "wise." ("Budget-wise, Al, the pitch shapes up like this. . . .")

Another characteristic of reverse gobbledegook is its dependence on analogy and metaphor. During a single banquet you may find business problems equated with an airplane, a broad highway, a boat being rocked, a river, a riverbank, a stream, a bridge, a train, a three-legged stool, and, sometimes, three or four of these things at once in which case the passage is generally summed up with something like "It's as simple as that," or "That's all there is to the problem." (From a recent speech: "So business enterprise of America is trying to hone a sales force into the cutting edge of an economy and there is a virus running rampant in the flock. Security-mindedness is a log across the stream when it comes to developing the optimistic salesman outlook.")

Outstanding is the great American football analogy. No figure of speech is a tenth as seductive to the businessman. Just why this should be so—baseball, curiously, is much less used—is generally explained by its adaptability to all sorts of situations. Furthermore, the football analogy is *satisfying*. It is bounded by two goal lines and is thus finite. There is always a solution. And that is what makes it so often treacherous.

For analogy and metaphor can be insidiously attractive substitutes for thought. They are not, of course, when fleetingly used, when, as H. W. Fowler puts it (in *Modern English Usage*), they "flash out for the length of a line or so and are gone," but this is

[1] Other current advertising favorites: "let's pull all the stops out on this one"; "let's noodle this one"; "let's sneak the message across"; "we'll touch all bases on this one"; "means absolutely nothing to the lay mind"; "we'll get a plus value on this one"; "it was quite a hassle"; "let's not hassle over this."

Journalists laugh and laugh at this sort of thing. Just why, it is difficult to say, except possibly that being less inventive, they prefer to hang on to the old expressions rather than coin new ones. Terms now nearing the end of the run (including some of *Fortune's*): ambivalence, dichotomy, schizophrenic, "two hours and four martinis (beers, etc.) later"; "it's as difficult (easy, etc.) as it is complex (difficult, etc.)"; "their profits (feelings, etc.) are showing."

rarely the case in reverse gobbledegook. The user starts innocuously enough, his policy is *like* a thingamajig in one respect. But only the stanchest mind can resist the analogy further. Before long he is entwined, and unconsciously operating on the premise that his policy *is* a thingamajig. The language, in short, has molded thinking, and the results can be a good bit more serious than a poor speech.

The mishaps of one consumer-goods corporation illustrate this hazard. Not so long ago, the men who owned the company were casting about for a Goal. Up to then it had been money. But now they had acquired a lot of it, they were getting on in years, and anyway it didn't sound good. And so, on this enlightened-goal problem, the Chief fell to pondering at the conference table. When you get right down to it, the company was just like a big football team. You don't win unless you have a good team, do you? You could say that again. Well, before he gets a good team, what does the coach have to do? Very simple. He has to go out and find good players. Just thinking out loud, mind you, but wasn't the big job then to get the right recruits?

Almost automatically, this was mimeographed as the company's rationale—"The Touchdown Play" it was called—and before long executives were spending almost as much time on the new trainees as they were on their regular jobs, and when they weren't doing this, they were scouring the colleges for more. Everything went swimmingly; the policy was soon the wonder of the merchandising world; the top executives were suffused with a sense of enlightenment—and the place was jammed with eager young men.

In only one respect did the analogy break down. A year later practically all of the competition came out with a new product embodying a notable technical advance. Our company didn't. It was still getting the team ready.

Now with almost every use of the cliché and stereotype mentioned so far, a better case could be made out for the use of simple, unhackneyed English. It is a mistake, however, to be too rigorously critical on the score. Since the symbols of language convey emotion as well as communicate facts and ideas, many a prefabricated phrase has become inextricably tied with certain emotional responses. This infuriates the semanticists—"intensional thinking" is their cuss word for it—but a good part of business has been built on it.

The American sales meeting, certainly, would be quite impossible otherwise.

Furthermore business, like many another occupation, is governed by a ritual as rigid as the steps of ballet, and while the efficient executive makes fun of all this, he has the good sense to know when to put it to use himself. The dinner for the retiring employee, for example; for years this has been prime fodder for short-story writers. But what if the toastmaster were to dispense with the timeworn expressions and thus tacitly concede what everyone knows to be nothing less than the truth: that old Charlie has been getting in everybody's hair for the last fifteen years and it'll be wonderful to see him go. Everyone, Charlie's worst enemies included, would be shocked, morale would suffer, and the usefulness of the executive to the organization would be lessened.

So with the interoffice memo about the man being horizontally promoted to some branch office. Again the ceremonial is unvarying: pillar of strength . . . larger responsibilities . . . Ed's invaluable experience in this field makes him the logical . . . know the whole staff will join me in wishing Ed good luck in his new job. . . . Nobody is fooled in the slightest, of course, but what could have been a disagreeable, and for Ed a shattering, experience is smoothed over by the blessed analgesic of businesese. There is *something* of a case for time-worn expressions. But it is a case that needs no further making.

For all its faults, business language is the subject of plenty of good news. Over a third of top U.S. corporations, a *Fortune* sampling indicates, have set up some sort of program to improve it. Monsanto Chemical and Glidden Co. are working on both letters and interoffice memos. "In our campaign to simplify communications," reports Glidden's President Dwight Joyce, "we encourage 'Yes' and 'No' answers, which in turn makes for briefer, clearer questions." Montgomery Ward uses slide films to show its people how to write good-will building letters. Numerous banks, insurance companies, and department stores have engaged experts to simplify and personalize their letters. And over the past two years the "Cy" Frailey business-correspondence courses sponsored by the Dartnell Corp. in major cities of the U.S. have attracted 25,000 executives.

Public-speaking courses are provided by such companies as SKF,

Jones & Laughlin, and Johnson & Johnson. In the last two years General Motors has encouraged 2,000 of its management and supervisory people to express themselves better by taking Dale Carnegie speech courses. Business and management associations (e.g., National Association of Manufacturers, American Management Association, American Institute of Banking, National Association of Foremen) publish material on speech training. In one notable instance, at Bridgeport, Connecticut, an informal group of businessmen became so absorbed in the problem that they chipped in and hired a Yale professor to teach them how to address groups and conduct meetings. And evidently the crusade is more than a nine-to-five concern of businessmen. To judge from recent book sales, they are reading more "practical English" and vocabulary-building books than ever before.

Paralleling these better-business-English efforts has been a movement of even greater significance. It has been called the "plain talk" movement, but it is, in fact, a sort of prose-engineering program, for its core is the use of some newly refined scientific techniques to achieve readability. In only four years it has already produced a measurable effect on the English of business and, if it continues to thrive, it will have a profound effect not only on the English of business but on the English of advertising, journalism, and literature as well.

How did it happen? Such phenomena are usually hard to account for. This one, however, is not.

"My own contribution . . . has been quite modest," readability expert Dr. Rudolf Flesch recently told a convention of P.R. men, "but I think I can truthfully say that it has already had some effect." Dr. Flesch was unduly modest. Rarely have the man and the moment collided so effectively. Almost from the moment in 1946 when he turned his Columbia Ph.D. thesis on readability into the best-selling *The Art of Plain Talk,* Flesch's impact has been tremendous.

The scientific basis was not new; it was evolved by psychologists in the 1920's for the grading and writing of children's textbooks. But as developed by Flesch it gave a new form—and justification—to a movement that had been overtaking American prose. "It was as if," recalls one enthusiast, "we had just been waiting for someone to break the ice."

What Flesch teaches, briefly, is a scientific method of achieving plain, understandable prose. To this end we should write as we talk; eschew irony, rhythm, rhetorical sentences; substitute concrete for abstract words. Equally important, we should surcharge our prose with as much human interest as possible. Then, to measure how we are succeeding, we can apply two formulas. One, based on syllable and sentence count per 100 words, measures the "reading ease" of our writing. The other, based on the percentage of "personal" words and sentences, measures its "human interest." The reading-ease index is tied to the different levels of the U.S. adult population. Thus we can scientifically make sure that we are writing to the level of our particular audience—or better yet, as Flesch advises, somewhat below it.[2]

The first impact of this doctrine was on newspaper writing, but soon it was making itself felt in another field. For years industrial psychologists had been champing to apply scientific methods to employee-management communication material, but, what with cultural-lag troubles, they hadn't been able to get very far. And now here at last was the ideal wedge; "the effectiveness . . . [of] the Flesch formula," as one put it, "forces the issue." Enthusiastically they fell to work measuring house-organ prose, reconstructing information bulletins, and in general showing business just how terrible its stuff was and how much better it could be.

Before long another readability expert, Robert Gunning, was making studies for Borden's, the B. & O. Railroad, and other large companies. John McElroy (formerly head of Gunning's industrial division) set up Readability Associates, and was soon holding seminars on his "fog-count" system for such firms as Ford, Detroit Edison, and American Airlines. General Motors, making a broad attack on the readability problem, has at times employed all three

[2] The reading-ease formula—statisticians call it "regression equation"—is 206,835 minus (1.015 times the average number of words per sentence) plus (.846 times the number of syllables per 100 words). Using this (simplified in chart form for quick use), we find that the reading-ease score of the two preceding text paragraphs is 53. This puts them on the "fairly difficult"—i.e., high school—reading level, and thus readable by 54 per cent of the adult population. Human-interest score: 30 ("interesting").

experts, Gunning, McElroy, and Flesch.[3] The Psychological Corp. began four-day worshops, where, at $500 a head, company representatives could be instructed in the readability techniques so that they in turn could go back and teach them to others. Even the military joined in; in the most notable of such efforts the Air Material Command got out an official—and highly readable—manual on the Flesch approach and put psychologist A. O. England to work indoctrinating all hands in it.

What's been the effect of all this? The readability formulas have dramatized, as no subjective critique ever could, the needless obscurity and pomposity of much everyday language. Furthermore, the readibility texts have been full of so much good sense on such matters as grammar and punctuation that they have served to encourage the timid away from outworn do's and dont's of writing. Where the readability doctrines have been taught, there has been not only a decrease in the use of jargons, but a new enthusiasm and respect for the rhythm of colloquial speech.

So far, so good. But how much further, and then how good? The implications of the readability approach warrant careful thought. For if American "functional" English is to be homogenized more and more along these new lines, we should at least, before it all becomes official, have a hard look at what it is leading us to. In purest businesese, is there a danger that we'll jump out of a Pandora's box into a fire?

First, a look at some of the new rules. Most important, the advice that is the core of the movement: to write as we talk. Part of the "secret" of readable writing, we are told, lies in repetition and loosely built sentences—because that is the way we talk. Well, at least that's the way some people talk—haltings, back-trackings, and that sort of thing—they talk on forever sometimes—a lot of excelsior, that's what it adds up to—and it's not difficult at all, because it's certainly easier than the old-fashioned way of organizing your thoughts. In fact,. there is only one real question to be raised. Are talking and writing the same thing? They are not—and to say

[3] G.M. has devised a "Reading-Ease Calculator"—a kind of wheel by which, with a minimum of mathematics, the prose in its twenty-seven employee publications can be measured. Also it has Purdue psychologists compiling a list of the words most frequently used by G.M. personnel, and is measuring the reading ability levels of some of its employee groups.

that they should be allows and encourages us to rationalize sloppiness and faulty thinking.

In this colloquializing we are also adjured to make everything into a human-interest story. (Flesch: "There's nothing on earth that cannot be told through a hero or heroine who's trying to solve a problem in spite of a series of obstacles.") It is true, of course, that one who describes a problem in terms of the simple love of a man for his dog, a tale as old as time, will have a more *readable* piece than one who tends to somewhat more abstract treatment. But there are quite a number of things that *cannot* be explained by a human-interest tale, and to treat them as if they could be is to mislead the reader by oversimplifying.

Emphasis on the short word, naturally enough, is another feature of the plain-talk movement, and while the readability experts themselves caution people against applying this prescription too rigidly, it has reached a rather extreme point of veneration. Short words, certainly, need no defense. But there are times when the longer one is the *right* word, and if it were not used the writer would have to take up more space saying it another way. And even if the long word were unknown to such and such a percentage of the audience, it might be perfectly clear—or stimulating—to them in a context of sound, lucid English. The Elizabethans knew this well—and so, for that matter, do the pulp writers (e.g., the gibbous moon, the lambent rays, diaphanous dresses, etc.).

By now, if we have followed the above rules, our style should be understandable enough. Just to make sure, however, Flesch has a few more rules:

Do not use rhythm (maybe your reader won't catch on).
Do not use periodic sentences.
Do not use rhetorical questions.
Do not use metaphors without an explanation.
Do not use contrast without an explanation.
Do not use irony (half the people won't get it).

Now we are not to forswear these devices because they are bad; we are to discard them because somebody *might* possibly misunderstand us. The blood-toil-tears-and-sweat metaphor of Churchill, for example: "The reader gets a vague notion," says Flesch, "that Churchill used a little word picture of three wet things instead of saying *war*; and that's that." Flesch goes on to ask a rhetorical question: would "you must expect great suffering and hard work" have been a better way to put it? "Nobody, of course," he says, "can answer such a question." Nobody? We'll take a crack at it. NO!

If we have followed these rules, we are now able to talk the level of language the audience will be able to understand "without effort." But even this is not enough. *We must go one step below that level.* We must "shoot beneath the target"; we must "translate down the scale." And for this we don't even need the formulas, for, as Flesch correctly points out, this writing down should by now have become instinctive to us.

Let us imagine that over the next hundred years everyone followed this advice and deliberately wrote beneath the capabilities of his audience. What would happen? Theoretically, we would get ourselves into a sort of ever decreasing circle, and, as layer after layer of our language atrophied, eventually spiral our way back to the schoolbook level that got the whole readability doctrine under way in the first place. The "regression" equation would be complete.

And haven't we gone quite far enough as it is? Already we have turned the man in the street into a Frankenstein. We hand him an electric recorder to edit our movies; we watch his radio dial to predetermine what we will put on the air—and now we are to ape him to learn how to write.

We should long since have delivered ourselves of this oaf, for in reality he does not even exist. He is a self-perpetuating stereotype, the reflection of the lowest common denominators we have been looking for. In creating him we have done not only ourselves but our audiences a disservice, for though they will respond to the tawdry, they will also respond—as many a book, speech, ad, and movie has demonstrated—to the best we give them. But they cannot if we abdicate our moral obligation to give the best that is in us.

So what of the formulas? What do they really measure? Understandability? (And, if so, of what?) Simplicity? Or merely the number of things they are supposed to measure? For a practical experiment, *Fortune* selected thirteen out of a collection of 100 business speeches. The eight most fatuous of the speeches were put in one group; the five most lucid were put in another. Each speech was then evaluated by means of the two formulas to find its reading-ease and human-interest scores. The result: there was practically no *significant difference* between the average scores of the two groups. (Average reading-ease score: 61—eighth- and ninth-grade reading level; average human interest score: 40—"very interesting.") All, then, represented good "plain talk"—and there was nothing in the scores to indicate the tremendous disparity between the two types.

In thus ignoring the relationship between style and content, the formulas have ignored the fundamentals of language. Language is not something we can disembody; it is an ethical as well as mechanical matter, inextricably bound up in ourselves, our positions, and our relations with those about us. When a businessman double-talks, for example, it is often for reasons deeper than mishandled prose—hypersensitivity to criticism, fear of the competition, fear of getting out of line with trade-association policy, fear of a government suit, a serious split in corporation policy—or, as is occasionally the case, the lack of any policy to begin with. Is "plain talk" the answer here? It is not. It is a fraud on the listener.

For it is only the illusion of simplicity that the manipulation of language can win for us. Simplicity is an elusive, almost complex thing. It comes from discipline and organization of thought, intellectual courage—and many other attributes more hard won than by short words and short sentences. For plain talk—honest plain talk—is the reward of simplicity, not the means to it. The distinction may seem slight, but it is tremendously important.

In a sense, this whole prose-engineering movement is a measure of the growing specialization of our society—for it is an attempt to provide a sort of pidgin English by which we can intercommunicate over the gaps. So let us give the readability people their due. At least they have tried to bridge the gaps and, perhaps more important, they have called our attention to the necessity for doing so. We owe them, then, a debt—and if their solution falls short in many respects, the very avidity with which people have seized on it is proof enough that there is a void to fill.

Thus the readability movement is also the measure of the failure of our schools and colleges. Patently, something is very wrong with the teaching of English when graduates so fail to grasp the fundamentals of good English that they feel they must learn a separate kind for everyday life—and a rather bobtail one at that. The fault may be, as some have claimed, that our academic English courses are still set up on the implicit assumption that their function is to provide a schooling for those who are to be novelists, poets, and scholars. Perhaps it is for this reason that the word "literary" is increasingly used as a term of opprobrium.

Meanwhile the teaching of English in the non-liberal-arts courses has been geared more and more to the "functional" kind of writing the graduate will perform. "In my opinion," says Professor Edward Kilduff of N.Y.U.'s School of Commerce, "the most effective kind of English composition being taught today . . . is the realistic, practical nonliterary American type that we find in such courses as business writing, engineering writing, newspaper writing, publicity writing, and advertising writing."

True or not, is a further extension of this trend necessarily the answer? Specialization in our colleges has already gone so far that it is hard to see how a further breakdown of the humanities would be anything but harmful. We do not need more "applied" English courses; what we need, first of all, is better basic ones. How this is to be achieved in our schools and colleges is a difficult problem, but it is time we were about it.

For somewhere, certainly, between the extremes of the "functional" and the "literary" there is a happy middle ground. Those firms who have pioneered in improving the language of their people seem to have reached the same conclusion. The great majority of their courses, seminars, and "clinics" have been concentrated not on supplying rules to be slavishly followed—but on provoking an *awareness* of good English. Their example is one that all of U.S. business can follow with great profit.

In the meantime let us not forswear all the richness of our language. Its misuse is not the root ill of our communication problem; it is only the signal of it. And if we make a real effort to win mutual understanding, we need have no fear of the infinite variety of our language—or the ability of our listeners to respond to it. All of which applies to businessmen no less than to everyone else in our society. When businessmen have something to say, and mean it, and feel it, their audience will understand.

TOPICS FOR DISCUSSION AND WRITING

1. What was the occasion for this editorial?
2. What is the thesis here expressed?
3. What are the characteristics of "businesese"? How did they develop?
4. What are the characteristics of "shirt-sleeve English"? How did they develop?
5. Evaluate the "plain talk" style advocated by Dr. Rudolf Flesch? What are the dangers of this kind of writing?
6. Does the editorial itself illustrate the use of the kind of English it advocates?
7. Which of the selections you have recently read seems to illustrate the use of the kind of English which the editorial has in mind? Would the essay have to be on a "business" subject for it to illustrate what the editorial advocates?
8. Compile a list of "businesese" and "reverse gobbledegook" expressions. What characteristics have they in common? Translate them into lucid English.
9. Does this article have the same purpose as Swift's essay? Compare the different methods of approach. Which is more effective? Why?

TROPICAL LANGUAGE

Though a word may have many meanings, all meanings can be classified under the headings of literal and nonliteral. The literal meaning of a word is the natural, usual sense of the word. The nonliteral meaning of a word is to be found in those instances when it is used in an unusual manner, in a transferred sense. The literal sense of the word *icy,* for example, pertains to ice (frozen, brittle, cold) and only liquids which can freeze into a brittle and cold state can be called *icy* in the literal sense. When *icy* is used to modify nouns like *silence* or *stare,* it is not being used in its literal sense for a silence or a stare cannot assume a state of matter which is possible only to liquids. When a silence is qualified as icy, the word *icy* is being used in a transferred sense; the quality which it properly denominates has been taken from the substance to which it can only apply properly and it has been transferred to something else to which it cannot strictly apply.

One label which is very commonly used to identify the uses of words in their nonliteral sense is "figurative." This is a confusing label for words used in their nonliteral senses, for words can be used in their literal sense in patterns which can be called "figured." There are many rhetorical patterns such as alliteration, assonance, anaphora, epistrophe, wherein words are used in their literal senses but which are sometimes referred to as "figures of speech." A much-quoted report during the Second World War which made dramatic use of alliteration, "Sighted sub; sank same," was often referred to as "a figure of speech."

A less confusing way of referring to the nonliteral uses of language is employed by classical rhetoricians. All nonliteral uses of words are considered examples of *tropes.* The word *trope* is derived from a Greek word which means, basically, a turning, or shifting. The best known kinds of tropes are metaphor and simile. All uses of language which involve a turning or twisting of words from their commonly accepted sense, all nonliteral uses of words, are tropes. Language so used can be called *tropical language* and it is at the very opposite pole of language usage from denotative language.

Since tropical language is language which is used in its uncommon sense, all tropical language tends to be imaginative and (when the tropes are fresh and unhackneyed) startling. All uses of tropes involve a transfer of meaning, and all transfers of meaning from the proper sense to an unfamiliar sense involve some risk that the novel usage will be understood. It is for this reason that Samuel Johnson called attention to the habit Jonathan Swift had of avoiding all tropical uses of language by saying that Swift never "hazarded" a metaphor. Swift, as we saw in the preceding section, labored first to be perfectly clear, and this requires the avoidance of language which might be misunderstood. John Donne, on the other hand, was always gambling, taking a chance that a new use of language might stir a fresh reaction, a new insight into an old truth. Thus in the selection from his *Devotions* we find him striving to illuminate old truths with repeated use of tropical language.

Words which have tropical meanings can be arranged in patterns so that they communicate on two levels: the literal and the tropical. In many of Shakespeare's plays a constant use of imagery from one source results in the creation of an undercurrent of identification of a character with a favorable or unfavorable object, as Richard III with rodents. In the Joyce selection included herein, there is a second level of meaning which may be called a metaphorical level of meaning. Metaphorical meaning is never explicitly stated, but is repeatedly suggested by a constant use of words in their nonliteral but tropical sense. This second level of meaning, communicated by the use of words in a tropical sense, is fully as important and perhaps even more powerfully suggestive than the first level of meaning which is directly communicated by the use of words in their literal sense.

In this section we will be concerned with analyzing the various senses in which words can be used and the different effects which can be achieved by a concentrated use of one kind of word in preference to another. We shall see that an author like Robert Oppenheimer, who is aware of the differences between audiences and between subjects, can vary his language to achieve entirely different effects.

J. Robert Oppenheimer

J. Robert Oppenheimer is already familiar (see p. 451) as the author of an address to the American Council of Learned Societies entitled Tradition and Discovery. *The following essay is included to show how the same writer, addressing himself to different audiences on a similar subject, must vary his use of language if he is to achieve his purpose. The audience for* Tradition and Discovery *was learned, well informed, and highly motivated. There was no need to adapt ideas to make meaning more readily intelligible. The audience for which this essay was intended was much broader, much less specialized, not as well informed, and not as well motivated to listen.*

Tradition and Discovery *might be said to employ a rhetoric of information. The words are denotative, the sentences declarative, and there is little interruption of forward movement by illustrations. The style of the whole essay gives the impression that the writer is anxious to inform an audience of the implications of recent scientific advances. But the following essay might be said to employ a rhetoric of eloquence. The language is much more tropical, the sentence movement is much more varied, and there are many illustrations and analogies used. The whole reflects a desire to reach a popular audience, to interest them in something which scientists have known for some time, to give the common reader a greater sympathy for the problem of science and scientists. The language used here is consequently much more colorful, imaginative, and emotional.*

Prospects in the Arts and Sciences *

The words "prospects in the arts and sciences" mean two quite different things to me. One is prophecy: What will the scientists discover and the painters paint, what new forms will alter music, what parts of experience will newly yield to objective description? The other meaning is that of a view: What do we see when we look at the world today and compare it with the past? I am not a prophet; and I cannot very well speak to the first subject, though in many ways I should like to. I shall try to speak to the second, because there are some features of this view which seem to me so remarkable, so new and so arresting, that it may be worth turning our eyes to them; it may even help us to create and shape the future better, though we cannot foretell it.

In the arts and in the sciences, it would be good to be a prophet. It would be a delight to know the future. I had thought for a while of my own field of physics and of those nearest to it in the natural sciences. It would not be too hard to outline the questions which natural scientists today are asking themselves and trying to answer. What, we ask in physics, is matter, what is it made of, how does it behave when it is more and more violently atomized, when we try to pound out of the stuff around us the ingredients which only violence creates and makes manifest? What, the chemists ask, are those special features of nucleic acids and proteins which make life possible and give it its characteristic endurance and mutability? What subtle chemistry, what arrangements, what reactions and control make the cells of living organisms differentiate so that they may perform functions as oddly diverse as transmitting information throughout our nervous systems or covering our heads with hair? What happens to the brain to make a record of the past, to hide it from consciousness, to make it accessible to recall? What are the physical features which make consciousness possible?

All history teaches us that these questions that we think the pressing ones will be transmuted before they are answered, that they will be replaced by others, and that the very process of discovery will shatter the concepts that we today use to describe our puzzlement.

It is true that there are some who profess to see in matters of culture, in matters precisely of the arts and sciences, a certain macrohistorical pattern, a grand system of laws which determines the course of civilization and gives a kind of inevitable quality to the unfolding of the future. They would, for instance, see the radical, formal experimentation which characterized the music of the last half-century as an inevitable consequence of the immense flowering and enrichment of natural science; they would see a necessary order in the fact that innovation in music precedes that in painting and that in turn in poetry, and point to this sequence in older cultures. They would attribute the formal experimentation of the arts to the dissolution, in an industrial and technical society, of authority, of secular, political authority, and of the catholic authority of the church. They are thus armed to predict the future. But this, I fear, is not my dish.

If a prospect is not a prophecy, it is a view. What does the world of the arts and sciences look like? There are two ways of looking at it: One is the view of the traveler, going by horse or foot, from village to village to town, staying in each to talk with those who live there and to gather something of the quality of its life. This is the intimate view, partial, somewhat accidental, limited by the limited life and strength and curiosity of the traveler, but intimate and human, in a human compass. The other is the vast view, showing the earth with its fields and towns and valleys as they appear to a camera carried in a high-altitude rocket. In one sense this prospect will be more complete; one will see all branches of knowledge, one will see all the arts, one will see them as part of the vastness and complication of the whole of human life on earth. But one will miss a great deal; the beauty and warmth of human life will largely be gone from that prospect.

It is in this vast high-altitude survey that one sees the general surprising quantitative features that distinguish our time. This is where the listings of science and endowments and laboratories and books published show up; this is where we learn that more people are engaged in scientific research today than ever before, that the Soviet world and the free world are running neck and neck in the training of scientists, that more books are published per capita in England than in the United States, that the social sciences are pursued actively in America, Scandinavia, and England, that there are more people who hear the great music of the past, and more music composed and more paintings painted. This is where we learn that the arts and sciences are flourishing. This great map, showing the world from afar and almost as to a stranger, would show more: It would show the immense diversity of culture and life, diversity in place and tradition for the first time clearly manifest on a world-wide scale, diversity in technique and language, separating science from science and art from art, and all of one from all of the other. This great map, world-wide, culture-wide, remote, has some odd features. There are innumerable villages. Between the villages there appear to be almost no paths discernible from this high altitude. Here and there passing near a village, sometimes through its heart, there will be a superhighway, along which windy traffic moves at enormous speed. The superhighways seem to have little connection with villages, starting anywhere, ending anywhere, and sometimes appearing almost by design to disrupt the quiet of the village. This view gives us no sense of order or of unity. To find these we must visit the villages, the quiet, busy places, the laboratories and studies and studios. We must see the paths that are barely discernible; we must understand the superhighways, and their dangers.

In the natural sciences these are and have been and are likely to continue to be heroic days. Discovery follows discovery, each both raising and answering questions, each ending a long search, and each providing the new instruments for a new search. There are radical ways of thinking unfamiliar to common sense and connected with it by decades or centuries of increasingly specialized and unfamiliar experience. There are lessons of how limited, for all its variety, the common experience of man has been with regard to natural phenomena, and hints and analogies as to how limited may be his experience with man. Every new finding is a part of the instrument kit of the sciences for further investigation and for penetrating into new fields. Discoveries of knowledge fructify technology and the practical arts, and these in turn pay back refined techniques, new possibilities of observation and experiment.

In any science there is harmony between practitioners. A man may work as an individual, learning of what his colleagues do through reading or conversation; he may be working as a member of a group on problems whose technical equipment is too massive for individual effort. But whether he is a part of a team or solitary in his own study, he, as a professional, is a member of a community. His colleagues in his own branch of science will be grateful to him for the inventive or creative thoughts he has, will welcome his criticism. His world and work will be objectively communicable; and he will be quite sure that if there is error in it, that error will not long be undetected. In his own line of work he lives in a community where common understanding combines with common purposes and interest to bind men together both in freedom and in cooperation.

This experience will make him acutely aware of how limited, how inadequate, how precious is this condition of his life; for in his relations with a wider society, there will be neither the sense of community nor of objective understanding. He will sometimes find, in returning to practical undertakings, some sense of community with men who are not expert in his science, with other scientists whose work is remote from his, and with men of action and men of art. The frontiers of science are separated now by long years of study, by specialized vocabularies, arts, techniques, and knowledge from the common heritage even of a most civilized society; and anyone working at the frontier of such science is in that sense a very long way from home, a long way too from the practical arts that were its matrix and origin, as indeed they were of what we today call art.

The specialization of science is an inevitable accompaniment of progress; yet it is full of dangers, and it is cruelly wasteful, since so much that is beautiful and enlightening is cut off from most of the world. Thus it is proper to the role of the scientist that he not merely find new truth and communicate it to his fellows, but that he teach, that he try to bring the most honest and intelligible account of new knowledge to all who will try to learn. This is one reason—it is the decisive organic reason—why scientists belong in universities. It is one reason why the patronage of science by and through universities is its most proper form; for it is here, in teaching, in the association of scholars, and in the friendships of teachers and taught, of men who by profession must themselves be both teachers and taught, that the narrowness of scientific life can best be moderated, and that the analogies, insights, and harmonies of scientific discovery can find their way into the wider life of man.

In the situation of the artist today there are both analogies to and differences from that of the scientist; but it is the differences which are the most striking, and which raise the problems that touch most on the evil of our day. For the artist it is not enough that he communicate with others who are expert in his own art. Their fellowship, their understanding, and their appreciation may encourage him; but that is not the end of his work, nor its nature. The artist depends on a common sensibility and culture, on a common meaning of symbols, on a community of experience and common ways of describing and interpreting it. He need not write for everyone or paint or play for everyone. But his audience must be man; it must be man, and not a specialized set of experts among his fellows. Today that is very difficult. Often the artist has an aching sense of great loneliness, for the community to which he addresses himself is largely not there; the traditions and the culture, the symbols and the history, the myths and the common experience, which it is his function to illuminate, to harmonize, and to portray, have been dissolved in a changing world.

There is, it is true, an artificial audience maintained to moderate between the artist and the world for which he works: the audience of the professional critics, popularizers, and advertisers of art. But though, as does the popularizer and promoter of science, the critic fulfills a necessary present function and introduces some order and some communication between the artist and the world, he cannot add to the intimacy and the directness and the depth with which the artist addresses his fellow men.

To the artists' loneliness there is a complementary great and terrible barrenness in the lives of men. They are deprived of the illumination, the light and tenderness and insight of an intelligible interpretation, in contemporary terms, of the sorrows and wonders and gaieties and follies of man's life. This may be in part offset, and is, by the great growth of technical means for making the art of the past available. But these provide a record of past intimacies between art and life; even when they are applied to the writing and painting and composing of the day, they do not bridge the gulf between a society, too vast and too disordered, and the artist trying to give meaning and beauty to its parts.

In an important sense this world of ours is a new world, in which the unity of knowledge, the nature of human communities, the order of society, the order of ideas, the very notions of society and culture have changed and will not return to what they have been in the past. What is new is new not because it has never been there before, but because it has changed in quality. One thing that is new is the prevalence of newness, the changing scale and scope of change itself, so that the world alters as we walk in it, so that the years of man's life measure not some small growth or rearrangement or moderation of what he learned in childhood, but a great upheaval. What is new is that in one generation our knowledge of the natural world engulfs, upsets, and complements all knowledge of the natural world before. The techniques, among which and by which we live, multiply and ramify, so that the whole world is bound together by communication, blocked here and there by the immense synapses of political tyranny. The global quality of the world is new: our knowledge of and sympathy with remote and diverse peoples, our involvement with them in practical terms, and our commitment to them in terms of brotherhood. What is new in the world is the massive character of the dissolution and corruption of authority, in belief, in ritual, and in temporal order. Yet this is the world that we have come to live in. The very difficulties which it presents derive from growth in understanding, in skill, in power. To assail the changes that have unmoored us from the past is futile, and in a deep sense, I think, it is wicked. We need to recognize the change and learn what resources we have.

Again I will turn to the schools and, as their end and as their center, the universities. For the problem of the scientist is in this respect not different from that of the artist or of the historian. He needs to be a part of the community, and the community can only with loss and peril be without him. Thus it is with a sense of interest and hope that we see a growing recognition that the creative artist is a proper charge on the university, and the university a proper home for him; that a composer or a poet or a playwright or painter needs the toleration, understanding, the rather local and parochial patronage that a university can give; and that this will protect him from the tyranny of man's communication and professional promotion. For here there is an honest chance that what the artist has of insight and of beauty will take root in the community, and that some intimacy and some human bonds can mark his relations with his patrons. For a university rightly and inherently is a place where the individual man can form new syntheses, where the accidents of friendship and association can open a man's eyes to a part of science or art which he had not known before, where parts of human life, remote and perhaps superficially incompatible, can find in men their harmony and their synthesis.

These then, in rough and far too general words, are some of the things we see as we walk through the villages of the arts and of the sciences and notice how thin are the paths that lead from one to another, and how little in terms of human understanding and pleasure the work of the villages comes to be shared outside.

The superhighways do not help. They are the mass media—from the loudspeakers in the deserts of Asia Minor and the cities of Communist China to the organized professional theatre of Broadway. They are the purveyors of art and science and culture for the millions upon millions—the promoters who represent the arts and sciences to humanity and who represent humanity to the arts and sciences; they are the means by which we are reminded of the famine in remote places or of war or trouble or change; they are the means by which this great earth and its peoples have become one to one another, the means by which the news of discovery or honor and the stories and songs of today travel and resound throughout the world. But they are also the means by which the true human community, the man knowing man, the neighbor understanding neighbor, the school boy learning a poem, the women dancing, the individual curiosity, the individual sense of beauty are being blown dry and issueless, the means by which the passivity of the disengaged spectator presents to the man of art and science the bleak face of inhumanity.

For the truth is that this is indeed, inevitably and increasingly, an open and, inevitably and increasingly, an eclectic world. We know too much for one man to know much, we live too variously to live as one. Our histories and traditions—the very means of interpreting life—are both bonds and barriers among us. Our knowledge separates as well as it unites; our orders disintegrate as well as bind; our art brings us together and sets us apart. The artist's loneliness, the scholar despairing, because no one will any longer trouble to learn what he can teach, the narrowness of the scientist—these are not unnatural insignia in this great time of change.

For what is asked of us is not easy. The openness of this world derives its character from the irreversibility of learning; what is once learned is part of human life. We cannot close our minds to discovery, we cannot stop our ears so that the voices of far-off and strange people can no longer reach them. The great cultures of the East cannot be walled off from ours by impassible seas and defects of understanding based on ignorance and unfamiliarity. Neither our integrity as men of learning nor our humanity allows that. In this open world, what is there any man may try to learn?

This is no new problem. There has always been more to know than one man could know; there have always been modes of feeling that could not move the same heart; there have always been deeply held beliefs that could not be composed into a synthetic union. Yet never before today has the diversity, the complexity, the richness so clearly defied hierarchical order and simplification, never before have we had to understand the complementary, mutually not compatible ways of life and recognize choice between them as the only course of freedom. Never before today has the integrity of the intimate, the detailed, the true art, the integrity of craftsmanship and the preservation of the familiar, of the humorous and the beautiful stood in more massive contrast to the vastness of life, the greatness of the globe, the otherness of people, the otherness of ways, and the all-encompassing dark.

This is a world in which each of us, knowing his limitations, knowing the evils of superficiality and the terrors of fatigue, will have to cling to what is close to him, to what he knows, to what he can do, to his friends and his tradition and his love, lest he be dissolved in a universal confusion and know nothing and love nothing. It is at the same time a world in which none of us can find hieratic prescription or general sanction for any ignorance, any insensitivity, any indifference. When a friend tells us of a new discovery we may not understand, we may not be able to listen without jeopardizing the work that is ours and closer to us: but we cannot find in a book or cannon—and we should not seek—grounds for hallowing our ignorance. If a man tells us that he sees differently than we or that he finds beautiful what we find ugly, we may have to leave the room, from fatigue or trouble; but that is our weakness and our default. If we must live with a perpetual sense that the world and the men in it are greater than we and too much for us, let it be the measure of our virtue that we know this and seek no comfort. Above all let us not proclaim that the limits of our powers correspond to some special wisdom in our choice of life, of learning, or of beauty.

This balance, this perpetual, precarious, impossible balance between the infinitely open and the intimate, this time—our twentieth century—has been long in coming; but it has come. It is, I think, for us and our children, our only way.

This is for all men. For the artist and for the scientist there is a special problem and a special hope, for in their extraordinarily different ways, in their lives that have increasingly divergent character, there is still a sensed bond, a sensed analogy. Both the man of science and the man of art live always at the edge of mystery, surrounded by it; both always, as the measure of their creation, have had to do with the harmonization of what is new with what is familiar, with the balance between novelty and synthesis, with the struggle to make partial order in total chaos. They can, in their work and in their lives, help themselves, help one another, and help all men. They can make the paths that connect the villages of arts and sciences with each other and with the world at large the multiple, varied, precious bonds of a true and world-wide community.

This cannot be an easy life. We shall have a rugged time of it to keep our minds open and to keep them deep, to keep our sense of beauty and our ability to make it, and our occasional ability to see it in places remote and strange and unfamiliar; we shall have a rugged time of it, all of us, in keeping these gardens in our villages, in keeping open the manifold, intricate, casual paths, to keep these flourishing in a great, open, windy world; but this, as I see it, is the condition of man; and in this condition we can help, because we can love one another.

TOPICS FOR DISCUSSION AND WRITING

1. Why does Oppenheimer open his essay with a distinction? What is the distinction that he is trying to make?
2. What are some of the questions which physicists of today are asking?
3. What is the relationship some think they see between the arts and sciences on the one hand and cultural dvelopment on the other?
4. What are the two ways of looking at the world of arts and sciences? What are the advantages and disadvantages of each?
5. How detailed is his comparison of the view of the arts and sciences with the view of the world from a high-altitude rocket? Is it a good analogy or comparison? Why does he carry it out in such detail? Why does he not develop analogy to any similar extent in *Tradition and Discovery?*
6. What use does he make of the familiar comparison of life on the frontier?
7. Make a list of the most noticeably connotative words in the paragraph which begins with the sentence: "To the artist's loneliness there is a complementary great and terrible barrenness in the lives of men." Compare this use of language with his other essay.
8. What examples are there of the use of tropical language in the paragraph which begins: "These then, in rough and far too general words, are some of the things we see as we walk through the villages of the arts and of the sciences"? In the paragraph beginning: "The superhighways do not help"? In the paragraph beginning: "For what is asked of us is not easy"?
9. What is the metaphor which underlies most of the essay? Does it help to achieve the purpose of the essay? How?

John Donne

John Donne (1571–1631), whose name has become synonymous with "metaphysical poetry," has also bequeathed an impressive and important body of prose writing. Although his popular reputation rests on his Songs and Sonnets *(written probably between 1589 and 1610, but not published until after his death), and his* Holy Sonnets *(written between 1609 and 1615, also published posthumously), more and more attention is now being given to his prose works. These include* The Pseudo-Martyr *and* Ignatius His Conclave, *Donne's contribution to the religious controversy between Anglican and Catholic in his time; the* Biathanatos, *a discussion of the legitimacy of suicide which probably reveals Donne's attitudes at a depressing period of his life; the* Essays in Divinity, *Donne's consideration of reasons for and against his entering the ministry; a total of 160 (possibly more) sermons, which won him the reputation of being the most eloquent preacher of his day; and finally, the* Devotions Upon Emergent Occasions, *composed during a serious illness in 1623. Though we may distinguish his poetry from his prose, Donne was a poet in all that he wrote, and the symbolic and metaphorical consideration of ideas is as evident in his* Devotions *as it is in his* Songs. *Donne believed that any idea is fully realized only when it is seen in correspondence with other ideas and other themes. Tropical or symbolic language was not a device but an instinct, a natural and necessary way of revealing the nuances and implications of any subject. In the following meditation, occasioned by the sending for the physician, we observe how a single fact develops, through symbol, an important dimension which a literal statement would have overlooked.*

from Devotions Upon Emergent Occasions

It is too little to call man a little world; except God, man is a diminutive to nothing. Man consists of more pieces, more parts, than the world; than the world doth, nay, than the world is. And if those pieces were extended, and stretched out in man as they are in the world, man would be the giant, and the world the dwarf; the world but the map, and the man the world. If all veins in our bodies were extended to rivers, and all the sinews to veins of mines, and all the muscles that lie upon one another, to hills, and all the bones to quarries of stones, and all the other pieces to the proportion of those which correspond to them in the world, the air would be too little for this orb of man to move in, the firmament would be but enough for this star; for, as the whole world hath nothing, to which something in man doth not answer, so hath man many pieces of which the whole world hath no representation. Enlarge this meditation upon this great world, man, so far as to consider the immensity of the creatures this world produces; our creatures are our thoughts, creatures that are born giants; that reach from east to west, from earth to heaven; that do not only bestride all the sea and land, but span the sun and firmament at once; my thoughts reach all, comprehend all. Inexplicable mystery; I their creator am in a close prison, in a sick bed, any where, and any one of my creatures, my thoughts, is with the sun, and beyond the sun, overtakes the sun, and overgoes the sun in one pace, one step, everywhere. And then, as the other world produces serpents and vipers, malignant and venomous creatures, and worms and caterpillars, that endeavour to devour that world which produces them, and monsters compiled and complicated of divers parents and kinds; so this world, ourselves, produces all these in us, in producing diseases, and sicknesses of all those sorts: venomous and infectious diseases, feeding and consuming diseases, and manifold and entangled diseases made up of many several ones. And can the other world name so many venomous, so many consuming, so many monstrous creatures, as we can diseases of all these kinds? O miserable abundance, O beggarly riches! how much do we lack of having remedies for every disease, when as yet we have not names for them? But we have a Hercules against these giants, these monsters; that is, the physician; he musters up all the forces of the other world to succour this, all nature to relieve man. We have the physician, but we are not the physician. Here we shrink in our proportion, sink in our dignity, in respect of very mean creatures, who are physicians to themselves. The hart that is pursued and wounded, they say, knows an herb, which being eaten throws off the arrow: a strange kind of vomit. The dog that pursues it, though he be subject to sickness, even proverbially, knows his grass that recovers him. And it may be true, that the drugger is as near to man as to other creatures; it may be that obvious and present simples, easy to be had, would cure him; but the apothecary is not so near him, nor the physician so near him, as they two are to other creatures; man hath not that innate instinct, to apply those natural medicines to his present danger, as those inferior creatures have; he is not his own apothecary, his own physician, as they are. Call back therefore thy meditation again, and bring it down: what's become of man's great extent and proportion, when himself shrinks himself and consumes himself to a handful of dust; what's become of his soaring thoughts, his compassing thoughts, when himself brings himself to the ignorance, to the thoughtlessness of the grave? His diseases are his own, but the physician is not; he hath them at home, but he must send for the physician.

TOPICS FOR DISCUSSION AND WRITING

1. The basic metaphor which Donne employs in this meditation was a familiar one in his age: it is the idea of the microcosm (the little world of man) reflecting the macrocosm (the external universe). How, in the first four sentences, does Donne develop and make explicit this basic metaphor?
2. How does Donne amplify his basic metaphor in the fifth sentence and apply it to his own situation? Does this amplification shed any light on how he considers his situation?
3. What new direction does the metaphor take after the sixth sentence? How, thus far, is the metaphor being used to define and illustrate the literal idea of Donne's illness?
4. Why, from the tenth sentence to the end of the meditation, does Donne apparently reverse his metaphor?
5. Is the metaphor in this passage merely an added element, or is it an essential element? Could Donne have expressed the same idea without metaphor?
6. Compare Donne's use of metaphor with Robert Oppenheimer's. What are the similarities and differences in their use of metaphoric language?

James Joyce

James Joyce (1882–1941) dealt always profoundly and sometimes puzzlingly with the problems of art, the artist, and society in his major works: Dubliners *(1914), a collection of short stories;* A Portrait of the Artist as a Young Man *(1916), a largely autobiographic novel;* Ulysses *(1922), a retelling of the Odysseus legend in contemporary terms; and* Finnegan's Wake *(1939), an experimental novel based on Jungian psychology. He was concerned with the recognition of the subsurface activity of the human mind, with the alienation of the artist from an impersonal world, with the search for values, and with the need for myth in the modern world. To express these themes, Joyce developed an instinctively analogical habit of mind to the point where every word, idea, scene, or image was intended to carry symbolic overtones, to express something beyond itself. The passage printed here exemplifies the way in which Joyce achieves a maximum of connotative effect through simile, metaphor, and selective description, whereby each detail retains its literal or denotative value, and at the same time becomes a symbol. Prior to this particular moment in the novel* (A Portrait of the Artist as a Young Man) *Joyce's protagonist, Stephen Dedalus, has passed through early childhood, early schooling, and has reached late adolescence. Through all his maturer experiences Stephen has been engaged, in terms of John Keats's* Ode to a Grecian Urn, *in the search for Truth and Beauty. This episode in Stephen's life is a turning point: what he witnesses becomes, symbolically, a vision of Truth and Beauty.*

from A PORTRAIT OF THE ARTIST AS A YOUNG MAN *

A girl stood before him in midstream: alone and still, gazing out to sea. She seemed like one whom magic had changed into the likeness of a strange and beautiful seabird. Her long slender bare legs were delicate as a crane's and pure save where an emerald trail of seaweed had fashioned itself as a sign upon the flesh. Her thighs, fuller and softhued as ivory, were bared almost to the hips where the white fringes of her drawers were like feathering of soft white down. Her slate-blue skirts were kilted boldly about her waist and dovetailed behind her. Her bosom was as a bird's, soft and slight, slight and soft as the breast of some dark-plumaged dove. But her long fair hair was girlish: and girlish, and touched with the wonder of mortal beauty, her face.

She was alone and still, gazing out to sea; and when she felt his presence and the worship of his eyes her eyes turned to him in quiet sufferance of his gaze, without shame or wantonness. Long, long she suffered his gaze and then quietly withdrew her eyes from his and bent them towards the stream, gently stirring the water with her foot hither and thither. The first faint noise of gently moving water broke the silence, low and faint and whispering, faint as the bells of sleep; hither and thither, hither and thither: and a faint flame trembled on her cheek.

TOPICS FOR DISCUSSION AND WRITING

1. What is the single image which the descriptive details help create? For instance, why does Joyce use the words "feathering," "dovetailed," "dark-plumaged"? What other descriptive details unite with these to create an image?
2. What is the meaning of Stephen's last name, *Dedalus?* What relation exists between Stephen's name and the image of this passage?
3. What is there in this episode which would account for its being a major point in Stephen's life?
4. Why does Joyce use simile and metaphor in this passage? Would a literal, denotative description achieve the same effect?
5. How does Joyce's use of the tropes of metaphor and simile differ from Oppenheimer's and Donne's?

VI Style and the Forms of Thought

THE KINDS OF STYLE

"The style is the man" is a remark that usually appears in any discussion of style. What is commonly implied by the remark is that a man will reveal himself by his expression: a judicially grave man will be attracted to a solemn, balanced style; an impetuous man will be tempted to use a staccato, truncated sentence structure; a meditative man might find his most natural expression in a digressive, highly parenthetical style; a disorganized personality will be revealed by a disorganized syntax or sentence pattern.

This is true, and we can all verify it from our own experience. But no one is ordinarily *bound* to use a single style; anyone can choose to use a style which is appropriate to a particular occasion (excepting, of course, those rare instances where there can be no choice, as when a schizoid personality creates a schizoid style). Style is an option, not a determined factor. Since a particular style may reveal a personality, a writer may wish to create an *image* of himself which will help win the assent he seeks from his audience. The attitude we have toward the writer is often an important element in our acceptance of what he has to say; the writer, therefore, must do what he can to create a favorable impression, an acceptable "image." One of the ways of creating such an image is style. A style which announces "Here is a determined man," "Here is a learned man," "Here is a practical man" may re-enforce the idea being presented and insure its persuasiveness.

More than revealing a true personality or a persuasive image, style may help determine what reaction is to be given an idea. Anyone who takes the trouble to write in the first place clearly considers his ideas as something important. He can reveal his own emotional or intellectual reaction to his idea through his style—for style can suggest anxiety, urgency, thoughtfulness, resignation, most of the emotions or attitudes of which man is capable. He can express, in other words, the way he responds to an idea. In the act of reading, the audience temporarily adopts the writer's style, and so momentarily adopts his response and reaction. If the impression created by style is emphatic enough and skillful enough, that reaction may be more than momentary, and may continue long enough to have been *persuasive*.

Which image to create, which reaction to first project and then transfer to the audience so that it becomes *their* reaction, depends on several circumstances: the idea itself, the kind of audience being addressed, the purpose of the writing. Which style to use will depend on a writer's knowledge of what styles are available to him and what effects the various styles are intended to produce. There are four basic styles, each calculated to help determine a different form of reaction to what is written: the curt, loose, balanced, and informal styles. Only rarely will any one of these styles be used in isolation; manifold combinations are always possible, depending on the writer's purpose. But each is a distinctive style and each deserves to be analyzed.

The curt style relies on an accumulation of short sentence elements for its effect. The simple sentence or the accumulation of short phrases and clauses within a complex sentence are its chief tools. The curt style is characterized by a minimum of introductory or interrupting phrases, a limited use of such devices as parallelism or balance, and a striving for an aphoristic or epigrammatic quality. The impression such a style produces is one of directness, importance, and memorableness. It is a style particularly useful at the end of an exposition, where the writer wishes to summarize his major arguments and to impress on his audience the importance of his ideas.

The loose style, on the other hand, aims at different effects. Longer sentence elements, such as modifying clauses or phrases; compound sentences held together by commas or unemphatic (*and, but, so, then*) rather than emphatic (*therefore, thus, consequently*) conjunctions; general absence of noticeable stylistic elements such as balanced or periodic form; digressiveness and extended parentheses—these are the identifying marks of the loose style. It creates the impression of a mind still exploring an idea, not yet having reached any final conclusions. It is a style which invites the reader to join the writer in an investigation of an idea, but does not present the reader with the results of an investigation.

The balanced style gives the impression of gravity, of judicial seriousness, of decisions having been reached after long consideration. Not as terse or abbreviated as the curt style, it is more sculptured than the loose style. Sentence elements will balance one another in length and importance; parallel structure will be evident, as when independent clause will balance independent clause, or dependent clause will be formally repeated in the same sentence; periodic sentence structure, in which the major clause or predicate will appear as the climax to introductory elements, will be a recurring pattern. The effect is one of authority, prudence, and solemnity. This style is best suited to occasions on which the appeal to authority is likely to be an important factor in persuasion.

The familiar style is an apparently style-less expression of ideas. The sentence structure is modeled on the patterns of ordinary speech; it carefully avoids any of the artifices of the curt or balanced style but is reminiscent of the loose style, avoiding, however, the proliferation of sentence elements usually found in the loose style. The familiar style creates the impression of a straightforward, inartificial statement of ideas. It encourages the audience to think of itself as being part of a dialogue, or as an active participant in the discussion of an idea. It is a style which capitalizes on the accepted idea of democracy in action, egalitarianism, and individualism.

None of these styles is the "right" style. A writer is free to use any or all in the course of his writing, singly or in combination. If a particular style is appropriate to the occasion, the idea, or the audience, if it re-enforces the argument and intention of the writer, only then is it "right." Only then can it be part of the persuasion inherent in good writing.

THE ANALYSIS OF STYLE

In any writing, the analysis of style is a first step. It must be followed by our asking ourselves the question: "Does this style announce the intention of the author, cooperate with the intention of the author, or in any way relate to or re-enforce the object the author is pursuing?" Seeing what a style *is* must be followed by seeing what a style *does*. The style must be related to the work as a whole, and any stylistic analysis, no matter how complete, is useless until such relation takes place. Henry James' style is unique and distinguished—does it also reveal him, or his subject, or the attitude he attempts to create in the mind of the reader? Bacon's style is not Johnson's style, and neither is it Hazlitt's style. What do the different styles have to do with each author's intention? This is the ultimate task of the analyst, and any analysis which stops short of asking this question is of little or no value. The proposed questions at the end of the selections in this group of essays are intended to lead you to asking and answering that question.

The formal analysis itself cannot be content with vague or impressionistic remarks, such as "Note the sinuous movement of this sentence," or "Notice the colorful placement of the adverbial phrases," or "The clause has a haunting melancholy." Such subjective commentary on any style may reveal a great deal about the analyst, but it tells us nothing about the style itself. Before each of the following sections, we offer sample analyses of the various styles, as exemplified by Sir Francis Bacon (the curt style), Sir Thomas Browne (the loose style), Samuel Johnson (the balanced style), and William Hazlitt (the familiar style). We hope that the reader will exercise the same objectivity in his analysis of style, and will move from this analysis to a consideration of the relation of style to meaning.

THE CURT STYLE

The style of the essay *Of Simulation and Dissimulation* is characterized by its heavy reliance on brief sentence elements. The third, fifth, and seventh paragraphs each begin with a brief simple sentence. The final summarizing paragraph contains five simple sentences. Even in those instances where Bacon uses an involved compound-complex sentence, as in the last sentence of the second paragraph, each of the phrases and clauses are briefly set forth and clearly marked off by strong punctuation from what precedes and follows: in this particular sentence, there are four independent clauses, three dependent clauses, six additive phrases (*and frankness of dealing, and veracity, well managed, or turn, spread abroad of their good faith, and clearness of dealing*) which amplify the basic content of the clauses to which they are attached. The longest of these units follows the colon, which precedes a clause of thirty-nine words; but even here, that clause is sharply divided into nine separate units, the longest of which (*spread abroad of their good faith*) is but six words. The entire sentence is composed of twenty separate sections, with lines of demarcation set out thus—three commas followed by a semicolon; comma, semicolon; comma, semicolon; comma, comma, colon; and finally eight commas. None of these separate elements is allowed to develop beyond the strictest of boundaries.

Though Bacon does make use of balanced sentence structure, the balanced elements themselves are noticeably brief: "*expressly feigns,* and *pretends to be,* that he is not"; "while men rather *discharge their minds,* than *impart their minds*"; "*openness in fame and opinion; secrecy in habit; dissimulation in seasonable use.*" As compared with the ornate and extended balances of Dr. Johnson, Bacon's are remarkably terse.

The direction of Bacon's argument is as economical as possible; he often announces his general thesis at the beginning of a paragraph so that there will be no mistaking his argument, and then lists his proofs or demonstrations. Thus, "There be three degrees of this hiding," "For the first of these, secrecy," "For the second, which is dissimulation," "But for the third degree, which is simulation," "The great advantages of simulation and dissimulation are three."

The brevity and independence of most of the sentence elements in Bacon's style result in a precise, economical, clinical style, a form of address entirely suited to the scientific attitude which underlies his commentary.

Francis Bacon

Lord Chancellor of England, lawyer, scientist, and philosopher, Francis Bacon (1561–1626) is best remembered in his role of buccinator novi temporis, *"the herald of a new time." Man's consideration of his world was being dramatically revised during the late sixteenth and seventeenth centuries. What we now think of as "the scientific outlook" was being formulated and established. Bacon saw his responsibility of setting forth the guidelines along which the new science and the new philosophy were to be conducted. He was never able to complete his great work, entitled the* Magna Instauratio; *but it remains one of the most ambitious projects ever attempted by one man. He hoped to accomplish several things in his "great revival of true learning": to review all the sciences, rejecting what was false and misleading; to create a new inductive method of analysis; to gather together all the significant theses which resulted from such induction; to achieve a massive synthesis of all such theses and thereby to advance learning on all fronts.*

His Essays, *which he wrote in 1597 and greatly expanded in 1612 and 1625, were probably intended to be a part of the* Magna Instauratio. *They are a reasonable, primarily inductive examination of certain facts of human behavior, divorced from the traditional or time-honored generalities which, Bacon believed, often obscured the real truth of things. His* Essays *present us with what he considered practical, necessary, and scientifically valid observations in place of outworn antique notions no longer important in the new age of fact and discovery.*

Of Simulation and Dissimulation

Dissimulation is but a faint kind of policy, or wisdom; for it asketh a strong wit, and a strong heart, to know, when to tell truth, and to do it. Therefore it is the weaker sort of politics, that are the great dissemblers.

Tacitus saith; Livia sorted well, with the arts of her husband, and dissimulation of her son: attributing arts or policy to Augustus, and dissimulation to Tiberius. And again, when Mucianus encourageth Vespasian, to take arms against Vitellius, he saith: We rise not, against the piercing judgment of Augustus, nor the extreme caution or closeness of Tiberius. These properties of arts or policy, and dissimulation or closeness, are indeed habits and faculties, several, and to be distinguished. For if a man, have that penetration of judgment, as he can discern, what things are to be laid open, and what to be secreted, and what to be showed at half lights, and to whom, and when (which indeed are arts of state, and arts of life, as Tacitus well calleth them), to him, a habit of dissimulation, is a hinderance, and a poorness. But if a man cannot obtain to that judgment, then it is left to him, generally, to be close, and a dissembler. For where a man cannot choose, or vary in particulars, there it is good to take the safest and wariest way in general; like the going softly by one that cannot well see. Certainly the ablest men, that ever were, have had all an openness, and frankness of dealing; and a name of certainty, and veracity; but then they were like horses, well managed; for they could tell passing well, when to stop, or turn: and at such times, when they thought the case indeed, required dissimilation, if then they used it, it came to pass, that the former opinion, spread abroad of their good faith, and clearness of dealing, made them almost invisible.

There be three degrees of this hiding, and veiling of a man's self. The first closeness, reservation, and secrecy; when a man leaveth himself without observation, or without hold to be taken, what he is. The second dissimulation, in the negative; when a man lets fall signs, and arguments, that he is not, that he is. And the third simulation, in the affirmative; when a man industriously, and expressly feigns, and pretends to be, that he is not.

For the first of these, secrecy: it is indeed, the virtue of a confessor; and assuredly, the secret man, heareth many confessions; for who will open himself, to a blab or babbler? But if a man be thought secret, it inviteth discovery; as the more close air, sucketh in the more open: and as in confession, the revealing is not for world use, but for the ease of a man's heart, so secret men come to the knowledge of many things, in that kind; while men rather discharge their minds, than impart their minds. In few words, mysteries are due to secrecy. Besides (to say truth) nakedness is uncomely, as well in mind, as body; and it addeth no small reverence to men's manners, and actions, if they be not altogether open. As for talkers and futile persons, they are commonly vain, and credulous withal. For he that talketh, what he knoweth, will also talk, what he knoweth not. Therefore set it down: that an habit of secrecy, is both politic, and moral. And in this part, it is good, that a man's face, give his tongue, leave to speak. For the discovery, of a man's self, by the traits of his countenance, is a great weakness, and betraying; by how much, it is many times, more marked and believed, than a man's words.

For the second, which is dissimulation. It followeth many times upon secrecy, by a necessity: so that, he that will be secret, must be a dissembler, in some degree. For men are too cunning, to suffer a man, to keep an indifferent carriage, between both, and to be secret, without swaying the balance, on either side. They will so beset a man, with questions, and draw him on, and pick it out of him, that without an absurd silence, he must show an inclination, one way; or if he do not, they will gather as much by his silence, as by his speech. As for equivocations, or oraculous speeches, they cannot hold out long. So that no man can be secret, except he give himself a little scope of dissimulation; which is, as it were, but the skirts or train of secrecy.

But for the third degree, which is simulation, and false profession; that I hold more culpable, and less politic; except it be in great and rare matters. And therefore a general custom of simulation (which is this last degree) is a vice, rising either out of a natural falseness, or fearfulness; or of a mind, that hath some main faults;

which because a man must needs disguise, it maketh him practice simulation, in other things, lest his hand should be out of use.

The great advantages of simulation and dissimulation are three. First to lay asleep opposition, and to surprise. For where a man's intentions, are published, it is an alarm, to call up, all that are against them. The second is, to reserve to a man's self, a fair retreat: for if a man engage himself, by a manifest declaration, he must go through, or take a fall. The third is, the better to discover the mind of another. For to him that opens himself, men will hardly show themselves adverse; but will fair let him go on, and turn their freedom of speech, to freedom of thought. And therefore, it is a good shrewd proverb of the Spaniard: tell a lie, and find a truth. As if there were no way of discovery, but by simulation. There be also three disadvantages, to set it even. The first, that simulation and dissimulation, commonly carry with them, a show of fearfulness, which in any business, doth spoil the feathers, of round flying to the mark. The second, that it puzzleth and perplexeth the conceits of many; that perhaps would otherwise cooperate with him; and makes a man walk, almost alone, to his own ends. The third, and greatest is, that it depriveth a man, of one, of the most principal instruments for action; which is trust and belief. The best composition, and temperature is, to have openness in fame and opinion; secrecy in habit; dissimulation in seasonable use; and a power to feign, if there be no remedy.

TOPICS FOR DISCUSSION AND WRITING

1. It is reasonably certain that Bacon considered his essays as a part of his program for the reform of science, and that the essays are an empirical examination of certain ethical questions, conducted in the spirit of objective, scientific search for the truth, regardless of what preconceptions might have to be shattered. Are there any conservative or idealistic notions of human conduct that are disturbed by this essay?
2. Bacon obviously has in mind the political uses of simulation and dissimulation. He is interested in practicality, not speculation. Why would the loose style have been inappropriate in this context?
3. In the fourth paragraph, Bacon straightforwardly gives directions: "Therefore set it down." How does this help define his intention in writing? How does the curt style adapt itself to his intention?

4. Are Bacon's remarks on the values and defects of simulation and dissimulation relevant today?
5. Write an essay in the curt style using material from the *Fortune* editorial (p. 479) and the Swift essay (p. 474) to argue for the use of the curt style in contemporary journalism.

William H. Whyte, Jr.

William H. Whyte, Jr. (1917–) was born in Pennsylvania, educated at Princeton, and took part in the invasion of Guadalcanal. After the war, as an editor of Fortune *magazine, he became interested in the manners and mores of people who worked for large organizations. In 1956, after three years of research, he published* The Organization Man, *which immediately became a best seller and generated many discussions, both pro and con.*

In The Organization Man, *Whyte maintained the general thesis that the large American corporation discouraged individualism and encouraged conformity. He saw in this aspect of organization life a symptom of the mounting pressures of our time. The selection which follows is part of a larger section which was intended to demonstrate how scientists working for large corporations felt the pressures toward conformity, how they were bureaucratized, discouraged from pursuing research which seemed only of theoretical interest and encouraged to concentrate on those leads which seemed to promise to yield immediate practical results.*

The style of the selection is characterized by an almost exclusive use of simple sentences (or of compound sentences made up of two relatively simple, independent clauses). The diction is that of the business world—factual and denotative, not colorful and metaphorical. Details are plentiful, and the essay persuades by its no-nonsense tone and its quick, forward rush of conviction.

THE FIGHT AGAINST GENIUS *

Of the $4 billion currently being spent on research and development by government, industry, and the universities, only about $150 million—or less than 4 per cent—is for creative research.

The overwhelming majority of people engaged in research, furthermore, must now work as supervised team players, and only a tiny fraction are in a position to do independent work. Of the 600,000 people engaged in scientific work, it has been estimated that probably no more than 5,000 are free to pick their own problems.

And this is because people think it should be so. In the current orgy of self-congratulation over American technical progress, it is the increasing collectivization of research that is saluted. Occasionally the individual greats of the past are saluted, but it is with a subtle twist that manages to make them seem team researchers before their time. In the popular ideology, science means applying ideas; knowing *how*, not asking *why*.

We have indeed been very good at applying basic ideas. It is our natural bent to be good at exploitation. It is also our natural bent to recognize too late the necessity for replenishing that which we exploit. We have never had a strong tradition of basic science in this country and now, even less than before, we do not seem to care about creating new ideas—the ideas which thirty or forty years from now would nourish the technological advances we so confidently expect.

So far only a few people have had the nerve to come out flatly against the independent researcher, but the whole tenor of organization thinking is unmistakably in that direction. Among Americans there is today a widespread conviction that science has evolved to a point where the lone man engaged in fundamental inquiry is anachronistic, if not fundamental inquiry itself. Look, we are told, how the atom bomb was brought into being by the teamwork of huge corporations of scientists and technicians. Occasionally somebody mentions in passing that what an eccentric old man with a head of white hair did back in his study forty years ago had something to do with it. But people who concede this point are likely to say that this merely proves that basic ideas aren't the problem any more. It's nice to have ideas and all that, sure, but it's American know-how that does something with them, and anyway there are plenty of ideas lying fallow. We don't really need any more ivory-tower theorizing; what we need is more funds, more laboratory facilities, more organization.

The case for more fundamental inquiry has been argued so

eloquently by scientists that there is little the layman can contribute in this respect. My purpose . . . however, is not to add an amen, though this is in order, but to demonstrate the relationship between the scientist and the management trends I have been discussing in other contexts. The parallels between the organization man and the scientist should not be drawn too closely; their functions are not alike and between the managerial outlook and the scientific there is a basic conflict in goals that is not to be smothered by optimism.

I do not say this in qualification of my argument. It is my argument. For the fact is that the parallels are being drawn too closely, and in a profoundly mistaken analogy The Organization is trying to mold the scientist to its own image; indeed, it sees the accomplishment of this metamorphosis as the main task in the management of research. It may succeed.

Let us look first at the corporation's laboratories. On the surface the corporation would seem to be on the verge of becoming one of the most enlightened of patrons. $1.6 billion of America's total research budget is now concentrated in the great laboratories that corporations have been building up, and proportionately as well as in absolute dollars this is a greater investment in research than industry has ever made before. As industry points out, one result is going to be a speeding up of the production of tangibly better things for more people. But the price may be steep. If corporations continue to mold scientists the way they are now doing, it is entirely possible that in the long run this huge apparatus may actually slow down the rate of basic discovery it feeds on.

Let us ask a brutal question. How good are the corporations' scientists? In the past industry has had many brilliant ones—Langmuir, Steinmetz, Carothers, and many others. But does it have them now? My colleague Francis Bello did a study of young scientists which yielded some very surprising figures. To get a representative group of young scientists, he set out to get nominations of the men under forty in both industry and universities who were thought to be among the most promising. He went first to the foundations and such government agencies as the Office of Naval Research and the Atomic Energy Commission, for it is their business to know who the top men are.

When the many duplications in the names nominated were eliminated, Bello found he had the names of 225 young scientists. He had expected that the nominations would probably split between industry and the universities about half and half. To his amazement, however, he found that only four of the 225 names were of men in industry.

Fearing that the sample was too biased, Bello went directly to the directors of leading corporation laboratories and asked them for nominations. He also asked the top academic scientists to think of scientists in industry and name any they thought top rank.

After all this effort, only thirty-five were forthcoming. Outside of some of their own subordinates, corporation research directors were hard put to it to think of anybody else in their field of industry worth naming—and so were the university people. Most industrial scientists, Bello had to conclude, don't know one another, nor are they known by anybody else.

Two laboratories stood out. In all, there were only seven in which at least two men were nominated as outstanding and in which one man had at least two votes. Of these, General Electric and Bell Laboratories had almost as many men nominated as the other five put together. (The other five: Merck, I.B.M., Lederle, Eastman Kodak, and Shell Development Corporation.)

The chemical industry—the industry that has spent more money on research than any other—fared particularly badly. No scientist in Du Pont was named more than once, and except for American Cyanamid, no one in the other leading chemical firms was named at all. As for discovery, Bello found that chemists could think of only one new chemical reaction discovered by an American chemical company during the last fifteen years.

It is to be expected that industry should spend far less of its time on fundamental research than the universities, and for the same reason it is to be expected that the most outstanding men would tend to stay in the universities. But when all this is said and done, the fact remains that industry has a disproportionately small share of top men.

Why? The failure to recognize the virtue of purposelessness is the starting point of industry's problem. To the managers and engineers who set the dominant tone in industry, purposelessness is anathema, and all their impulses incline them to highly planned, systematized development in which the problem is clearly defined. This has its values. If researchers want to make a practical application of previous discovery—if a group at GM's Technical Center want a better oil for a high-compression engine, for example—they do best by addressing themselves to the stipulated task. In pure research, however, half the trick is in find out *that there is a problem*—that there is something to explain. The culture dish remained sterile when it shouldn't have. The two chemicals reacted differently this time than before. Something has happened and you don't know why it happened—or if you did, what earthly use it would be?

By its very nature, discovery has an accidental quality. Methodical as one can be in following up a question, the all-important question itself is likely to be a sort of chance distraction of the work at hand. At this moment you neither know what practical use the question could lead to nor should you worry the point. There will be time enough later for that; and in retrospect, it will be easy to show how well planned and systematized the discovery was all along.

Rationalize curiosity too early, however, and you kill it. In the case of the scientist it is not merely that he finds it difficult to foresee what it will prove at the cash register; the sheer act of having to address himself to this or, as management would put it, the $64 question, dampens his original curiosity—and the expectation that the company will ask him to do it is just as dampening as the actual demand. The result is a net loss, not postponement, for if the scientist is inhibited from seizing the idle question at the time, it is not easily recaptured later. Like the nice gestures we so often think of and so often forget to do, many a question that would have led to great discoveries has died as quickly as it was born; the man was too busy to pause for it.

If ever there were proof of the virtues of free research, General Electric and Bell Labs provide it. Consider three facts about them: (1) Of all corporation research groups these two have been the two outstandingly profitable ones; (2) Of all corporation research groups these two have consistently attracted the most brilliant men. Why? The third fact explains the other two. *Of all corporation research groups these two are precisely the two that believe in "idle curiosity."* In them the usual chronology is often reversed; instead of demanding of the scientists that they apply themselves to a practical problem, they let the scientists follow the basic problems they want to follow. If the scientists come up with something they then look around to see what practical problem the finding might apply to. The patience is rewarded. The work of GE's Irving Langmuir in heated solids, for example, eventually led to a new kind of incandescent lamp; similarly, the recent, and highly abstract, work of Bell Labs' Claude Shannon in communication theory is already proving to be a mine of highly practical applications.

The few notable successes elsewhere follow the same pattern. The succession of synthetic fibers that have made so much money for the Du Pont Company sprang from the curiosity of one man—Wallace Hume Carothers. Carothers did not start out to make nylon. When Du Pont ran across him he was working on molecular structure at Harvard. While the result was eminently practical for Du Pont, for Carothers it was essentially a by-product of the experimental work he had started at Harvard rather than an end in itself. The company's interest was the final product, but it got it only because Carothers had the freedom to pursue what would today seem to many mere scientific boondoggling.

These successes are disheartening. There is nothing at all new in the research philosophy that led to them; both GE and Bell Labs established their basic procedures several generations ago, and their pre-eminence has been commercially apparent for as long. Yet with these models before them, U.S. industry has not only failed to draw any lessons, it has been moving further and further in the opposite direction.

By their own statements of policy the majority of corporations make it plain that they wish to keep their researchers' eyes focused closely on the cash register. Unlike GE or Bell Labs, they discourage their scientists, sometimes forbid them, from publishing the results of their work in the learned journals or communicating them in any way to scientists outside the company preserve. More inhibiting, most corporations do not let their scientists devote more than a fraction of their time following up problems of their own choosing, and this fraction is treated more as a sort of indulgence than an activity worthwhile in its own right. "It is our policy," one research director says, "to permit our men to have *as much as* 5 to 10 per cent of their time to work on anything they feel would be of interest." (Italics are mine.)

Even this pitiably small fraction is begrudged. Lest scientists interpret "free" work too freely, company directives imply strongly that it would be very fine if what the scientist is curious about during this recess coincides with what the organization is curious about. In "Research: The Long View," Standard Oil of New Jersey explains its policy thus:

> The researchers, as a matter of long-range policy, are encouraged, when circumstances permit, to give something like 10 per cent of their time to "free research"—that is, work not currently part of a formal project. [The company] finds, however, that when its research people are kept well informed about the broad areas in which the company's needs and interests lie, a man's independent as well as his closely directed work both tend to have the same objectives (*The Lamp,* June 1954.)

To some management people the desire to do "free" work is a downright defect—a symptom of maladjustment that demands cure, not coddling. When a man wants to follow his own hunch, they believe, this is a warning that he is not "company oriented." The solution? Indoctrination. In "Personnel Practices in Industrial Laboratories" (*Personnel,* May 1953) Lowell Steele puts the issue squarely. "Unless the firm wants to subsidize idle curiosity on the part of its scientists," he says, "it must aid them in becoming 'company-conscious.'" Company loyalty, in other words, is not only more important than idle curiosity; it helps *prevent* idle curiosity.

The administrators are perfectly correct. If they get scientists to be good company men like other normal people, they won't be bothered much by scientists' following their curiosity. The policy will keep out that kind of scientist. For what is the dominant characteristic of the outstanding scientist? Every study has shown that it is a fierce independence.

In her study of eminent scientists, psychologist Anne Roe found that what decided them on their careers almost invariably was a college project in which they were given free rein to find things out for themselves, without direction, and once the joys of freedom were tasted, they never lost the appetite. The most important single factor in the making of a scientist, she concludes, is "the need and ability to develop personal independence to a high degree. The independence factor is emphasized by many other findings: the subjects' preference for teachers who let them alone, their attitudes toward religion . . . their satisfaction in a career in which, for the most part, they follow their own interests without direction or interference" (*Scientific American,* Nov. 1952).

In the outstanding scientist, in short, we have almost the direct antithesis of the company-oriented man. If the company wants a first-rate man it must recognize that his allegiance must always be to his work. For him, organization can be only a vehicle. What he asks of it is not big money—significantly, Bell Labs and GE have not had to pay higher salaries than other research organizations to attract talent. Nor is it companionship, or belongingness. What he asks is the freedom to do what he wants to do.

For its part, The Organization can ask only so much in return. The Organization and he have come together because its long-range interests happen to run parallel with what he wants to do. It is in this, his work, that The Organization's equity in him lies. Only one *quid pro quo* can it properly ask for the money that it gives him. It can ask that he work magnificently. It cannot ask that he love The Organization as well.

And what difference would it make if he did? The management man is confusing his own role with that of the scientist. To the management man such things as The Organization and human relations are at the heart of his job, and in unconscious analogy he assumes that the same thing applies to the scientist, if perhaps in lesser degree. These things are irrelevant to the scientist—he works *in* an organization rather than for it. But this the administrator cannot conceive; he cannot understand that a man can dislike the company—perhaps even leave in disgust after several years—and still have made a net contribution to the company cash register infinitely greater than all of his better-adjusted colleagues put together.

Thus, searching for their own image, management men look for the "well-rounded" scientists. They don't expect them to be quite as "well-rounded" as junior-executive trainees; they generally note that scientists are "different." They do it, however, in a patronizing way that implies that the difference is nothing that a good indoctrination program won't fix up. Customarily, whenever the word *brilliant* is used, it either precedes the word *but* (cf. "We are all for brilliance, but . . .") or is coupled with such words as *erratic, eccentric, introvert, screwball,* etc. To quote Mr. Steele again,

> While industry does not ignore the brilliant but erratic genius, in general it prefers its men to have "normal" personalities. As one research executive explained, "These fellows will be having contact with other people in the organization and it helps if they make a good impression. They participate in the task of 'selling' research."

By insisting on this definition of well-roundedness, management makes two serious errors. For one thing, it seems to assume that the pool of brilliant scientists is so large that it can afford to consider only those in the pool who are well-rounded. There is, of course, no such oversupply; even if there were, furthermore, no such pat division could be made. For brilliance and the kind of well-roundedness management asks are a contradiction in terms. Some brilliant scientists are gregarious, to be sure, and some are not—but gregariousness is incidental to the harmony management is so intent upon. A brilliant scientist can enjoy playing on the company bowling team and still do brilliant and satisfying work. But there is no causal relationship. If the company makes him drop what he wants to do for something he doesn't, he may still enjoy playing on the company softball team, may even lead it to victory in the interurban championships. But at the same time he is doing it he may be pondering how exactly to word his resignation. The extracurricular will not have sublimated his frustration; and for all his natural amiability, in the place where it counts—the laboratory—his behavior will very quickly show it. Quite truly, he has become maladjusted.

He couldn't do otherwise. Management has tried to adjust the scientist to The Organization rather than The Organization to the scientist. It can do this with the mediocre and still have a harmonious group. It cannot do it with the brilliant; only freedom will make them harmonious. Most corporations sense this, but, unfortunately, the moral they draw from it is something else again. A well-known corporation recently passed up the opportunity to hire one of the most brilliant chemists in the country. They wanted his brilliance, but they were afraid that he might "disrupt our organization." Commenting on this, a fellow scientist said, "He certainly would disrupt the organization. He is a man who would want to follow his own inclinations. In a laboratory which understood fundamental research, he wouldn't disrupt the organization because they would want him to follow his inclinations. But not in this one."

Even when companies recognize that they are making a choice between brilliance and mediocrity, it is remarkable how excruciating they find the choice. Several years ago my colleagues and I listened to the management of an electronics company hold a post-mortem on a difficult decision they had just made. The company had been infiltrated by genius. Into their laboratory three years before had come a very young, brilliant man. He did magnificent work and the company looked for even greater things in the future. But, though he was a likable fellow, he was imaginative and he had begun to chafe at the supervision of the research director. The director, the management said, was a rather run-of-the-mill sort, though he had worked loyally and congenially for the company. Who would have to be sacrificed? Reluctantly, the company made its decision. The brilliant man would have to go. The management was unhappy about the decision but they argued that harmonious group thinking (this was the actual word they used) was the company's prime aim, and if they had promoted the brilliant man it would have upset the whole chain of company interpersonal relationships. What else, they asked plaintively, could they have done?

Listening to some of industry's pronouncements, one would gather that it is doing everything possible to ward off the kind of brilliant people who would force such a choice. Here, in this excerpt from a Socony-Vacuum Oil Company booklet on broad company policy, is a typical warning:

NO ROOM FOR VIRTUOSOS

> Except in certain research assignments, few specialists in a large company ever work alone. There is little room for virtuoso performances. Business is so complex, even in its nontechnical aspects, that no one man can master all of it; to do his job, therefore, he must be able to work with other people.

The thought is put even more forcibly in a documentary film made for the Monsanto Chemical Company. The film, which was made to inspire young men to go into chemistry, starts off in the old vein. You see young boys dreaming of adventure in faraway places as they stand by the station in a small town and watch the trains roll by. Eventually the film takes us to Monsanto's laboratories. We see three young men in white coats talking to one another. The voice on the sound track rings out: "No geniuses here; just a bunch of average Americans working together."

This was no mere slip of the script writer's pencil. I had a chance later to ask a Monsanto executive why the company felt impelled to claim to the world that its brainwork was carried on by just average Americans. The executive explained that Monsanto had thought about the point and wanted to deter young men from the idea that industrial chemistry was for genius types.

At the very moment when genius types couldn't agree more, the timing hardly seems felicitous. It could be argued, of course, that since the most brilliant stay in the universities anyway, management's barriers against genius would be at worst unnecessary. But it is not this clear-cut; whether or not they have geniuses, companies like Monsanto do not have their research work carried on by just average Americans, and if they did the stockholders would do well to complain. As Bell Labs and General Electric prove, there are many brilliant men who will, given the right circumstances, find industrial research highly absorbing. For company self-interest, let alone society's, a management policy that repels the few is a highly questionable one.

Society would not be the loser if the only effect on management policy were to make the most brilliant stay in the university. This screening effect, however, is only one consequence of management's policy. What concerns all of us, just as much as industry, is the fact that management also has a very powerful molding effect on the people it does get. They may not all be geniuses, but many are highly capable men, and in the right climate they could make great contributions.

That management is not only repelling talent but smothering it as well is told by management's own complaints. Privately, many of the same companies which stress team play criticize their young Ph.D.s for not being interested enough in creative work—or, to put it in another way, are a bunch of just good average Americans working together. "Practically all who are now Ph.D.s want to be told what to do," one research leader has complained. "They seem to be scared to death to think up problems of their own." Another research leader said that when his firm decided to let its chemists spend up to 25 per cent of their time on "free" work, to the company's surprise hardly any of the men took up the offer.

But it shouldn't be surprising. A company cannot bring in young men and spend several years trying to make them into one kind of person, and then expect them, on signal, to be another kind. Cram courses in "brainstorming" and applied creativity won't change them. If the company indoctrinates them in the bureaucratic skills and asks them to keep their minds on the practical, it cannot suddenly stage a sort of creative play period and then, on signal, expect them to be like somebody else.

In any person a native ability cannot remain very long dormant without atrophying, but this is particularly true in the case of the scientist. Compared to people in other fields, scientists characteristically reach their peak very early in their careers. If the climate is stultifying the young scientist will rarely be vouchsafed a chance later to make up for the sterility of his early years. "It is the effect on the few first-rate men you find in industrial labs that is noticeable," says Burleigh Gardiner, of Social Research. Inc. "The most able men generally rise to the top. But how high up the top is depends so much on the environment you put them in. In the average kind of corporation laboratory we have studied, the force of the majority opinion makes them divert their energies to a critical degree. I doubt if any of them could ever break through the group pressures to get up to the blue sky, where the great discoveries are made."

In a perverse way there is one small advantage to society in the big corporation's research policy. If corporation policy inhibits the scientist, it inhibits the flow of really good ideas that will aggrandize the corporation, and this lack may eventually prove a deterrent to overcentralization.

Those who see the growing concentration of technology in Big Business as irrevocable argue that advances are no longer possible except with the huge laboratories and equipment which only the big corporations can afford. But this is not true. For some scientific ends elaborate facilities—cyclotrons for physicists, ships for oceanographers—are necessary means. But this is only part of the picture; historically, almost every great advance has been made by one man with a minimum of equipment—sometimes just paper and pencil —and though this is more true of fundamental research, it is true of applied research as well. Go down the list of commercial inventions over the last thirty years: *with very few exceptions the advances did not come from a corporation laboratory.* Kodachrome, for example, was perfected in Eastman's huge laboratories but was invented by two musicians in a bathroom. The jet engine is an even clearer case in point. As Launcelot Law Whyte points out, none of the five earliest turbojet developments of Germany, Britain, and the United States was initiated within an established aircraft firm. "It is usually the relatively isolated outsider," Whyte says, "who produces the greatest novelties. It is a platitude, but it is often neglected."

Because it is small, the small firm has one potential advantage over the big one. It can't afford big research teams to administrate or interlocking committees to work up programs, and it doesn't have a crystallized company "family" to adjust to. Because it hasn't caught up yet with modern management, to put it another way, it provides an absence of the controls that make the scientist restive. Few small corporations have seized the opportunity, and at this writing there is no sign they ever will. But the opportunity is there.

TOPICS FOR DISCUSSION AND WRITING

1. What does Whyte try to demonstrate in his first paragraph? What is his method of argument? Show how this paragraph embodies characteristics of the curt style as discussed earlier. Keep your answers in mind as you read and reread the entire essay to see if what he does in this first paragraph is characteristic of his style throughout.
2. What distinction does he make between applying scientific ideas and creating new scientific ideas? What tendency does he think has characterized American science in the past?

3. What is Whyte's thesis? What sentence comes closest to stating it?
4. What is his characteristic way of proving his thesis: By arguments derived from the nature of the subject? Deductively? Inductively? Statistically?
5. What is the organization's conception of the right-thinking scientist?
6. Describe Whyte's characteristic sentence form. Do many of his sentences follow or deviate from the pattern of subject-verb-object? When the subject does not appear first in the sentence, how frequently is it replaced with a short modifying phrase?
7. How many of his sentences are compound constructions? Does he use periodic sentences or rhetorical questions?
8. Does his language usage conform with the standards advocated in the *Fortune* editorial? Does he make frequent use of connotative words? Does he use words tropically?
9. How would you characterize his style? What was the basis of the book's appeal? The music of its sentences? The color of his words? The inherent interest of the details he chose to use as the bases of his arguments?
10. Write an essay in the curt style arguing for greater freedom in scientific investigation. Use material from the Oppenheimer (p. 498) and Kahn essays (p. 304) to strengthen your case.

THE LOOSE STYLE

Whereas the curt style relies on brevity, short sentence units, and economy of expression, the loose style is deliberately digressive, extended, and parenthetical. In this particular section from Sir Thomas Browne's *Religio Medici,* there is but one simple sentence, and that one has an abundance of verb-objects: " 'Tis my solitary recreation to pose my apprehension with those involved enigmas and riddles of the Trinity, with Incarnation and Resurrection." Every other sentence is compound, complex, or compound-complex. Whereas Bacon reduced even his most complex sentences to a series of brief elements, Browne is not concerned with reducing or contracting: The sentence in the second paragraph beginning "That allegorical description of Hermes" contains eleven clauses, six of them independent and loosely joined together. Single clauses are extended by the use of multiple objects—" 'tis good to set down with a *description, periphrasis,* or *adumbration*"—or by multiple modifiers—"*humble* and *submissive* unto the subtleties of faith," "*haggard* and *unreclaimed* reason." A sentence movement which advances and then retreats is common: "to credit ordinary and visible objects is not faith, but reason"; "with an easy metaphor we may say the sword of faith; but in these obscurities I rather use it [as] a buckler." Parenthetical observations which prevent the sentence from moving in the economical subject-verb-object march are frequent: "Now contrarily I bless myself, *and am thankful that I lived not in the days of miracles,* that I never saw Christ nor his disciples"; "I believe that the Serpent (*if we shall literally understand it*) from his proper form and figure, made his motion on his belly before the curse." Clauses and phrases which contain clearly separable ideas are added to more often than they are subordinated to the initial clause: "Without this the world is still as though it had not been, *or* as it was before the sixth day when as yet there was not a creature that could conceive, *or* say there was a world." Balanced constructions are allowed to become lax so that the formality usually associated with balance and parallelism is reduced; in the final sentence, *vulgar heads* balances with *judicious inquiry, gross rusticity* with *deliberate research, receives small honor* with *return the duty:* but it is not an insistent or obtrusive balance and, indeed, may escape detection.

The loose style pursues ideas rather than reduces them to patterns. The very laxness of the style permits the writer to turn aside from a predetermined sentence movement and to develop an idea in a semi-extemporaneous way. It is a style which reveals the process of thought rather than the results of thought.

Sir Thomas Browne

Sir Thomas Browne (1605–1682) was a late contemporary of Francis Bacon; and as scientist and medical man, he was in sympathy with much of Bacon's program for the new science. But as a man of strong faith and imagination, he refused to let the methods of science dictate all of his responses to the world around him. At a time when scientific induction, laboratory experimentation, and factual observation of external nature were the primary concerns of many intellectuals, Browne reserved the right to explore the inexplicable, to contemplate the mysterious, and to speculate on the intangible. "As for those wingy mysteries in Divinity," he wrote in his Religio Medici, *"and ayery subtleties in religion, which have unhing'd the brains of better heads, they never stretched the* Pia Mater *of mine; methinks there be not impossibilities enough in religion for an active faith; the deepest mysteries ours contains, have not only been illustrated, but maintained by syllogism, and the rule of reason: I love to lose myself in a mystery, to pursue my reason to an* O altitudo." *His* Religio Medici *("Religion of a Doctor") is a per-*

sonal account of his speculative absorption into mystery and imaginative subtleties.

from RELIGIO MEDICI

As for those wingy mysteries in divinity, and ayery subtleties in religion, which have unhing'd the brains of better heads, they never stretched the *Pia Mater* of mine; methinks there be not impossibilities enough in religion for an active faith; the deepest mysteries ours contains, have not only been illustrated, but maintained by syllogism, and the rule of reason: I love to lose myself in a mystery, to pursue my reason to an *O altitudo*. 'Tis my solitary recreation to pose my apprehension with those involved enigmas and riddles of the Trinity, with Incarnation and Resurrection. I can answer all the objections of Satan, and my rebellious reason, with that odd resolution I learned of Tertullian, *Certum est quia impossibile est* [it is certain because it is impossible]. I desire to exercise my faith in the difficultest point, for to credit ordinary and visible objects is not faith, but persuasion. Some believe the better for seeing Christ's sepulchre, and when they have seen the Red Sea, doubt not of the miracle. Now contrarily I bless myself, and am thankful that I lived not in the days of miracles, that I never saw Christ nor his disciples; I would not have been one of those Israelites that passed the Red Sea, nor one of Christ's patients, on whom he wrought his wonders; then had my faith been thrust upon me, nor should I enjoy that greater blessing pronounced to all that believe and saw not. 'Tis an easy and necessary belief to credit what our eye and sense hath examined: I believe he was dead, and buried, and rose again; and desire to see him in his glory, rather than to contemplate him in his cenotaph, or sepulchre. Nor is this much to believe, as we have reason, we owe this faith unto history: they only had the advantage of a bold and noble faith, who lived before his coming, who upon obscure prophecies and mystical types could raise a belief, and expect apparent impossibilities.

'Tis true, there is an edge in all firm belief, and with an easy metaphor we may say the sword of faith; but in these obscurities I rather use it, in the adjunct the Apostle gives it, a buckler; under which I perceive a wary combatant may lie invulnerable. Since I was of understanding to know we knew nothing, my reason hath been more pliable to the will of faith; I am now content to understand a mystery without a rigid definition in an easy and Platonic description. That allegorical description of Hermes, pleaseth me beyond all the metaphysical definitions of divines; where I cannot satisfy my reason, I love to humour my fancy; I had as lief you tell me that "the soul is the angel of man and the body of God" as "the soul is *actual being*"; "light is the shadow of God" as "the act of seeing": where there is any obscurity too deep for our reason, 'tis good to set down with a description, periphrasis, or adumbration; for by acquainting our reason how unable it is to display the visible and obvious effect of nature, it becomes more humble and submissive unto the subtleties of faith: and thus I teach my haggard and unreclaimed reason to stoop unto the lure of faith. I believe there was already a tree whose fruit our unhappy parents tasted, though in the same chapter, when God forbids it, 'tis positively said, the plants of the field were not yet grown; for God had not caused it to rain upon the earth. I believe that the Serpent (if we shall literally understand it) from his proper form and figure, made his motion on his belly before the curse. I find the trial of the Pucellage and virginity of women, which God ordained in the Jews, is very fallible. Experience and history inform me that not only have many particular women, but likewise whole nations have escaped the curse of childbirth, which God seems to pronounce upon the whole sex: yet do I believe that all this is true, which indeed my reason would persuade me to be false; and this I think is no vulgar part of faith to believe a thing not only above, but contrary to reason, and against the arguments of our proper senses.

In my solitary and retired imagination, I remember I am not alone, and therefore forget not to contemplate him and his attributes who is ever with me, especially those two mighty ones, his wisdom and eternity; with the one I re-create, with the other I confound my understanding: for who can speak of eternity without a solecism, or think thereof without an ecstasy? Time we may comprehend, 'tis but five days elder than ourselves, and hath the same horoscope with the world; but to retire so far back as to apprehend a beginning, to give such an infinite start forward, as to conceive an end in an essence that we affirm hath neither the one nor the other; it puts my reason to Saint Paul's sanctuary; my philosophy dares not say the angels can do it; God hath not made a creature that can comprehend him, 'tis the privilege of his own nature. . . . The world was made to be inhabited by beasts, but studied and contemplated by man: 'tis the debt of our reason we owe unto God, and the homage we pay for not being beasts; without this the world is still as though it had not been, or as it was before the sixth day when as yet there was not a creature that could conceive, or say there was a world. The wisdom of God receives small honour from those vulgar heads, that rudely stare about, and with a gross rusticity admire his works; those highly magnify him whose judicious inquiry into his acts, and deliberate research unto his creatures, return the duty of a devout and learned admiration.

TOPICS FOR DISCUSSION AND WRITING

1. Browne apparently did not intend, at first, to publish his *Religio Medici,* but thought of it as a personal meditation on certain aspects of religion. Does this have anything to do with the style in which he wrote it?
2. In the first paragraph, Browne speaks of his "pursuit" of "mystery" and "impossibilities," and disclaims the reasonable and logically ordered approach to religion. Why would the balanced style have been inappropriate in this context?
3. How does Browne's statement that he desires to exercise his faith in the "difficultest" point account for the various subjects which he considers in the passage?
4. What is the meaning of the metaphors of faith as a buckler (paragraph 2) and the horoscope of time (paragraph 3)? Is there any particular reason why Browne should use metaphors in abundance while Francis Bacon is much more restrained in his use of metaphors?
5. How does the emphasis on *inquiry* and *research* in the last sentence identify Browne's intention in writing?
6. Write an essay in the loose style reflecting on the relevance of Browne's view of reason to some of today's problems.

Henry James

Henry James (1843–1916) left America, his native country, in protest against what he felt to be a raw, valueless, and tradition-poor culture. In Europe he sought what his own land seemed to withhold. His early novels, Roderick Hudson *(1875) and* The American *(1877), deal with the clash between American provincialism and European wisdom; but later, in* The Portrait of a Lady *(1881), James raised the possibility that the* naïveté *of his American heroine is really a form of innocence, while the cultured accomplishments of the European may be a mask for decadence. By the time he came to write* The Golden Bowl *in 1905, James seemed to have repudiated his early notions of the faults of American culture.*

Although it would be an oversimplification to say that James' writings constitute a continuous search for meaning—a definition that would apply to most literature—it is a simplification which helps explain not only his major literary themes but his prose style as well. The digressiveness, the probing and retreating, the modification and refining, conform to that inquisitive, experiential, and tenuous process which any genuine search must always involve. A close study of the style of Henry James reveals the attitude which underlies the "loose style": The reader is invited to observe the search, *whereas the other styles invite him to observe the* results *of the search.*

The End of the Civil War *

Wherever I dip, again, I pull out a plum from under the tooth of time—this at least so to my own rapt sense that had I more space I might pull both freely and at a venture. The strongest savour of the feast—with the fumes of a feast it comes back—was, I need scarce once more insist, the very taste of the War as ending and ended; through which blessing, more and more, the quantity of military life or at least the images of military experience seemed all about us, quite paradoxically, to grow greater. This I take to have been a result, first of the impending, and then of the effective, break-up of the vast veteran army, swamping much of the scene as with the flow of a monster tide and bringing literally home to us, in bronzed, matured faces and even more in bronzed, matured

* Reprinted by permission of Charles Scribner's Sons from *Notes of a Son and Brother* by Henry James. Copyright 1914 by Charles Scribner's Sons; renewal copyright 1942 by Henry James.

characters, above all in the absolutely acquired and stored resource of overwhelming reference, reference usually of most substance the less it was immediately explicit, the more in fact it was faded and jaded to indifference, what was meant by having patiently served. The very smell of having so served was somehow, at least to my supersensitive nostrils, in the larger and cooler air, where it might have been an emanation, the most masculine, the most communicative as to associated far-off things (according to the nature, ever, of elements vaguely exhaled), from the operation of the general huge gesture of relief—from worn toggery put off, from old army cloth and other fittings at a discount, from swordbelts and buckles, from a myriad saturated articles now not even lying about but brushed away with an effect upon the passing breeze and all relegated to the dim state of some mere theoretic commemorative panoply that was never in the event to be objectively disposed. The generalization grew richly or, as it were, quite adorably familiar, that life was ever so handsomely reinforced, and manners, not to say manner at large, refreshed, and personal aspects and types accented, and categories multiplied (no category, for the dreaming painter of things, could our scene afford not to grab at on the chance), just by the fact of the discharge upon society of such an amount of out-of-the-way experience, as it might roughly be termed—such a quantity and variety of possession and assimilation of unprecedented history. It had been unprecedented at least among ourselves, as had had it in our own highly original conditions—or "they," to be more exact, had had it admirably in theirs; and I think I was never to know a case in which his having been directly touched by it, or, in a word, having consistently "soldiered," learnt all about it and exhausted it, wasn't to count all the while on behalf of the happy man for one's own individual impression or attention; call it again, as everything came back to that, one's own need to interpret. The discharge upon "society" is moreover what I especially mean; it being the sense of how society in *our* image of the word was taking it all in that I was most concerned with; plenty of other images figured, of course, for other entertainers of such. The world immediately roundabout us at any rate bristled with more of the young, or the younger, cases I speak of, cases of "things seen," and felt, and a delectable difference in the man thereby made imputable, than I could begin here to name even had I kept the record. I think I fairly cultivated the perceiving of it all, so that nothing of it, under some face or other, shouldn't brush my sense and add to my impression; yet my point is more particularly that the body social itself was for the time so permeated, in the light I glance at, that it became to its own consciousness more interesting. As so many existent parts of it, however unstoried yet, to their minor credit, various thrilled persons could inhale the interest to their fullest capacity and feel that they too had been pushed forward—and were even to find themselves by so much the more pushable yet.

I resort thus to the lift and the push as the most expressive figures for that immensely *remonté* state which coincided for us all with the great disconcerting irony of the hour, the unforgettable death of Lincoln. I think of the springtime of '65 as it breathed through Boston streets—my rememberance of all those days is a matter, strangely enough, of the out-of-door vision, of one's constantly dropping down from Beacon Hill, to the brave edge of which we clung, for appreciation of those premonitory gusts of April that one felt most perhaps where Park Street Church stood dominant, where the mouth of the Common itself uttered promises, more signs and portents than one could count, more prodigies than one could keep apart, and where further strange matters seemed to charge up out of the lower districts and of the "business world," generative as never before of news. The streets were restless, the meeting of the seasons couldn't but be inordinately so, and one's own poor pulses matched—at the supreme pitch of that fusion, for instance, which condensed itself to blackness roundabout the dawn of April 15th: I was fairly to go in shame of its being my birthday. These would have been the hours of the streets if none others had been—when the huge general gasp filled them like a great earth-shudder and people's eyes met people's eyes without the vulgarity of speech. Even this was, all so strangely, part of the lift and the swell, as tragedy has but to be of a pure enough strain and a high enough connection to sow with its dark hand the seed of greater life. The collective sense of what had occurred was of a sadness too noble not somehow to inspire, and it was truly in the air that, whatever we had as a nation produced or failed to produce, we could at least gather round this perfection of a classic woe. True enough, as we were to see, the immediate harvest of our loss was almost too ugly to be borne—for nothing more sharply comes back to me than the tune to which the "aesthetic sense," if one glanced but from *that* high window (which was after all one of many too), recoiled in dismay from the sight of Mr. Andrew Johnson perched on the stricken scene. We had given ourselves a figurehead, and we were to have it in our eyes for three or four years and to ask ourselves in horror what monstrous thing we had done. I speak but of aspects, those aspects which, under a certain turn of them, may be all but everything: gathered together they become a symbol of what is behind, and it was open to use to waver at shop windows exposing the new photograph, exposing, that is, *the* photograph, and ask ourselves what we had been guilty of as a people, when all was said, to deserve the infliction of that form. It was vain to say that we had deliberately invoked the "common" in authority and must drink the wine we had drawn. No countenance, no salience of aspect nor composed symbol, could superficially have referred itself less than Lincoln's mould-smashing face to any mere matter-of-course type of propriety; but his admirable unrelated head had itself revealed a type—as if by the very fact that what made in it for roughness of kind looked out only less than what made in it for splendid final stamp, in other words for commanding style. The result thus determined had been precious for representation, and above all for fine suggestional function, in a degree that left behind every medal we had ever played at striking; whereas before the image now substituted representation veiled her head in silence and the element of the suggested was exactly the direst. What, however, on the further view, was to be more refreshing than to find that there were excesses of native habit which truly we couldn't bear? So that it was for the next two or three years fairly sustaining to consider that, let the reasons publicly given for the impeachment of the official in question be any that would serve, the grand inward logic or mystic law had been that we really couldn't go on offering each other before the nations the consciousness of such a presence. That was at any rate the style of the reflection to which the humiliating case reduced me; just this withal now especially working. I feel, into that image of our generally quickened activity of spirit, our having by the turn of events more ideas to apply and even to play with, that I have tried to throw off. Everything I recover, I again risk repeating, fits into the vast miscellany—the detail of which I may well seem, however, too poorly to have handled.

TOPICS FOR DISCUSSION AND WRITING

1. Henry James comments on two different experiences, but each evokes a similar mood and creates a similar problem. The first experience is the sudden national relaxation following the end of a terrible war: Society has been running on nerve, and has not had time to pause and ask such questions as: "What does it mean?" "What are we doing?" "Where are we going?" Now there is time, and some meaning has to be discovered for what has happened. The second experience is the recollection of Lincoln's death and the inauguration of the ineffective and uninspiring Johnson. Neither of these experiences was fully understood at the time, and now the passage of time has dulled their meaning even further. What problem arises for the writer who wishes to re-create not only the experiences themselves but the mood of incompleteness and nonunderstanding surrounding the experiences? How well does James solve the problem?
2. At the beginning and again at the end, James implies that his search for meaning has been incomplete and fragmentary. Is this an admission of defeat, or does it help to define the attitude he has toward his subject?
3. How many interrupting elements—parentheses, modifying words and phrases—occur in the first paragraph? Why does James not use a curt or a balanced style in the paragraph or the essay? Is his style appropriate to the experience he describes?
4. The first paragraph is general, dealing with the end of war and the confusion which followed in its wake. The second paragraph is more specific, dealing with the death of Lincoln and the national discomposure at having to tolerate Johnson as President. What theme holds the two paragraphs together?
5. Would the same meaning emerge from this passage if it were written in a different style? Would the curt or balanced style be appropriate? Rewrite James' essay in another style and compare the result of that rewriting with the original version.

THE BALANCED STYLE

If the loose style often creates the impression of extemporaneity, the balanced style never does. Instead, the effect is that of a mind having thoroughly digested an experience and molded the experience into artistic patterns. If the loose style suggests immediacy, the balanced style suggests stability. Furthermore, the balanced style is to be distinguished from the curt style by its use of longer sentence elements as opposed to terseness, and by a repetition of fairly involved sentence structures as opposed to the aggregation of shorter structures. *Balanced* is a completely adequate description of the style; it also describes the "image" of the writer who uses such a style.

The components of the balanced style can be noticed in every paragraph of the selection from Dr. Johnson's essay on Shakespeare. The first sentence of the essay begins with two noun clauses which are nearly identical in structure: subject, predicate, prepositional phrase, gerund, prepositional phrase—balanced after the comma by subject, predicate, prepositional phrase, verb, prepositional phrase. This balanced structure, which operates as the subject of the entire first sentence, is succeeded by a second and briefer balanced construction following the predicate *is a complaint:* "those who, being able to add nothing to truth" balances with "those who, being forced by disappointment."

An important feature is the full use of interrupting modifiers not (as in the loose style) as parentheses but as qualifications of the initial sentence element: "Antiquity, *like every other quality that attracts the notice of mankind,* has undoubtedly votaries that reverence it, *not from reason,* but from prejudice." Periodic structure, wherein the thought of the sentence is left suspended until the very end of the whole unit, is frequent: "To works, however, of which the excellence is not absolute and definite, but gradual and comparative, to works not raised upon principles demonstrative and scientific, but appealing wholly to observation and experience, *no other test can be applied than length of duration and continuance of esteem.*"

A slight variation on the technique of the balanced structure is the advancing of one judgment, and then countering it with a second and opposed judgment. The first sentence of the fifth paragraph is a case in point, as is "his works support no opinion with arguments, nor supply any faction with invectives; they can neither indulge vanity nor gratify malignity; but are read without any other reason than the desire of pleasure"; or "The irregular combinations of fanciful invention may delight a while, by that novelty of which the common satiety of life sends us all in quest; but the pleasures of sudden wonder are soon exhausted, and the mind can only repose on the stability of truth"; or "In the writings of other poets a character is too often an individual: in those of Shakespeare it is commonly a species." The reader reaction to such a technique is commonly an admission that the writer is aware of alternatives and that he has made a considered judgment of a matter.

The final impression created by such a style is, in the majority of instances, that of a grave, informed mind having weighed several factors and reduced matters to an intellectual and civilized pattern.

Samuel Johnson

Samuel Johnson (1709–1784) was undoubtedly the most authoritative (and probably the most authoritarian) critic of his generation. His production of important critical documents was prodigious: two major periodicals, A Dictionary of the English Language, *a collection of the biographies of notable English poets* (Lives of the Poets), *and an edition of Shakespeare, as well as a large body of creative work in poetry, a drama, and a novel. As a critic, Johnson was (and still is) noted for his sensible and definitive application of generally accepted literary principles to particular works. He was not a highly original critic, nor did he intend to be; he saw himself as the guardian of a respected treasure-trove of valid generalities which had been accumulated and tested over the centuries, and his function as critic was to judge literature as it conformed to or disregarded these great principles. He was a preserver, not an innovator. As T. S. Eliot once remarked, it is always dangerous to disagree with Dr. Johnson; his critical estimate of Shakespeare may have to be refined in part, but on the whole it remains one of the most lucid and valuable commentaries in the language.*

from PREFACE TO SHAKESPEARE

That praises are without reason lavished on the dead, and that the honours due only to excellence are paid to antiquity, is a complaint likely to be always continued by those who, being able to add nothing to truth, hope for eminence from the heresies of paradox; or those who, being forced by disappointment upon consolatory expedients, are willing to hope from posterity what the present age refuses, and flatter themselves that the regard which is yet denied by envy will be at last bestowed by time.

Antiquity, like every other quality that attracts the notice of mankind, has undoubtedly votaries that reverence it, not from reason, but from prejudice. Some seem to admire indiscriminately whatever has been long preserved, without considering that time has sometimes cooperated with chance; all perhaps are more willing to honour past than present excellence; and the mind contemplates genius through the shades of age, as the eye surveys the sun through artificial opacity. The great contention of criticism is to find the faults of the moderns and the beauties of the ancients. While an author is yet living, we estimate his powers by his worst performance; and when he is dead, we rate them by his best.

To works, however, of which the excellence is not absolute and definite, but gradual and comparative, to works not raised upon principles demonstrative and scientific, but appealing wholly to observation and experience, no other test can be applied than length of duration and continuance of esteem. What mankind have long possessed they have often examined and compared; and if they persist to value the possession, it is because frequent comparisons have confirmed opinion in its favour. As among the works of nature no man can properly call a river deep, or a mountain high, without the knowledge of many mountains and many rivers, so in the production of genius, nothing can be styled excellent till it has been compared with other works of the same kind. Demonstration immediately displays its power, and has nothing to hope or fear from the flux of the years; but works tentative and experimental must be estimated by their proportion to the general and collective ability of man, as it is discovered in a long succession of endeavours. Of the first building that was raised, it might be with certainty determined that it was round or square; but whether it was spacious or lofty must have been referred to time. The Pythagorean scale of numbers was at once discovered to be perfect; but the poems of Homer we yet know not to transcend the common limits of human intelligence but by remarking that nation after nation, and century after century, has been able to do little more than transpose his incidents, new-name his characters, and paraphrase his sentiments.

The reverence due to writings that have long subsisted arises therefore not from any credulous confidence in the superior wisdom of past ages, or gloomy persuasion of the degeneracy of mankind, but is the consequence of acknowledged and indubitable positions, that what has been longest known has been most considered, and what is most considered is best understood.

The poet of whose works I have undertaken the revision may now begin to assume the dignity of an ancient and claim the privilege of established fame and prescriptive veneration. He has long outlived his century, the term commonly fixed as the test of literary merit. Whatever advantages he might once derive from personal allusions, local customs, or temporary opinions, have for many years been lost; and every topic of merriment or motive of sorrow which the modes of artificial life afforded him now only obscure the scenes which they once illuminated. The effects of favour and competition are at an end; the tradition of his friendships and his enmities has perished; his works support no opinion with arguments, nor supply any faction with invectives; they can neither indulge vanity nor gratify malignity; but are read without any other reason than the desire of pleasure, and are therefore praised only as pleasure is obtained; yet, thus unassisted by interest or passion, they have passed through variations of taste and changes of manners, and, as they devolved from one generation to another, have received new honours at every transmission.

But because human judgment, though it be gradually gaining upon certainty, never becomes infallible; and approbation, though long continued, may yet be only the approbation of prejudice or fashion; it is proper to inquire by what peculiarities of excellence Shakespeare has gained and kept the favour of his countrymen.

Nothing can please many, and please long, but just representations of general nature. Particular manners can be known to few, and therefore few only can judge how nearly they are copied. The irregular combinations of fanciful invention may delight a while, by that novelty of which the common satiety of life sends us all in quest; but the pleasures of sudden wonder are soon exhausted, and the mind can only repose on the stability of truth.

Shakespeare is, above all writers, at least above all modern writers, the poet of nature, the poet that holds up to his readers a faithful mirror of manners and of life. His characters are not modified by the customs of particular places, unpracticed by the rest of the world; by the peculiarities of studies or professions, which can operate but upon small numbers; or by the accidents of transient fashions or temporary opinions; they are the genuine progeny of common humanity, such as the world will always supply, and observation will always find. His persons act and speak by the influence of those general passions and principles by which all minds are agitated and the whole system of life is continued in motion. In the writings of other poets a character is too often an individual: in those of Shakespeare it is commonly a species.

TOPICS FOR DISCUSSION AND WRITING

1. What is the subject matter of the first four paragraphs of Johnson's essay? Why does he not begin immediately with a discussion of Shakespeare?

2. In his second paragraph, Dr. Johnson notes the merits of a comparative approach in criticism, whereby the qualities of one author are balanced against the qualities of another author. How is this idea of Johnson's reflected in his style? Although there is nothing inevitable in a writer's choice of style, is Johnson's style pertinent to his approach?
3. Why does Johnson place so much emphasis on the "endurance" of a literary work? How does he refer the principle of "endurance" to the works of Shakespeare?
4. Johnson carried great weight as a critic, and he was regarded as a man who spoke with authority. How does his style create the impression of authority?
5. Would Johnson's essay and the evaluation he makes of Shakespeare have been as effective if he had written in the familiar style?

Adlai Stevenson

Adlai Stevenson, currently United States Ambassador to the United Nations, was elected Governor of Illinois in 1948; he was the Democratic candidate for the Presidency in the 1952 and 1956 campaigns, and made an exciting bid for the Democratic nomination at the 1960 Presidential convention. As titular head of the Democratic party from 1952 to 1960, his widespread appeal was fortified by his reputation for discretion and intellect, a reputation which continues to develop at the U.N. The essay which follows may be considered one of the earliest and perhaps one of the most effective of the "dialogue between business and statesmen" which the present administration has decided to conduct.

My Faith in Democratic Capitalism *

I am invited by the editors of *Fortune* to look forward with them toward 1980 and to join in the suggestion of goals for American achievement during the next quarter-century. The ultimate goals are, of course, very clear: peace, freedom for ourselves as individuals, and a realization of man's place in a meaningful scheme of things. But it is to a narrower focus that I am asked to address myself: namely, the future of the relationship between two great forces in America's structure—the force of business and indus-

* Reprinted from the October, 1955 issue of *Fortune Magazine* by special permission.

try on the one hand, and on the other, the force of government, particularly the federal government.

If it is expected that comment on this subject by one sometimes close to government—particularly a Democrat!—must inevitably be antagonistic and critical, and slanted against "Big Business," I promise disappointment. I think of this relationship between business and government as essentially one of cooperation between two institutional forces wholly dependent upon each other. If there were but one twenty-five-year goal to fix upon in this area it would be, for me, to stop the talk about a basic antagonism between American business and government, and replace such nonsense with a recognition of the common purposes and obligations of these two cornerstones of democratic capitalism.

We all make the mistake of thinking about institutions, such as business and government, as ends in themselves. Most of the friction between businessmen and bureaucrats in this country has arisen from their constantly having to remind each other that neither government nor business is an end in itself, that they both are only institutional means to the ends of individual purpose; and that whether the relationship between them is "good or bad" is measurable solely in terms of how the relationship pays off in the lives and satisfactions of 165 million people, or, more broadly, of all humanity.

I find the measure of the strength of this relationship in the fact that the past quarter-century has seen in America the most extraordinary growth any nation or civilization has ever experienced. Our rise in population has been largely a function of our increased prosperity and productivity; our millions of new mouths to feed are better fed than fewer mouths were only twenty-five years ago. The possessions of a modest family today exceed those of a "prosperous" one in 1930. While the population of some unhappy countries rises against the most dreadful counterpressures and in spite of wishes that it could be restrained, our numbers increase out of a sense that we can well afford such increase. An important part of the example we show the world is the fact that we are the nation of the most powerful consumers on earth.

It was not always so. It was not so twenty-five years ago. It is a curious thing that the two institutional forces in the democratic capitalistic society that contributed most directly to this emergence of the powerful consumer during this quarter-century seemed to snarl at each other every step of their common way. The bounding prosperity of postwar America has been due in large measure to processes in which government and business have in effect played complementary and cooperative roles. The New Deal legislation of the thirties helped to provide a "built-in" consumer demand that business could then work to satisfy, and the increase of 70 per cent in the scale of the American economy between 1939 and 1944 was achieved by the closest cooperation between government and industry in America's war effort.

Yet, in spite of this practical realization of common interests and common goals, it became part of the ritual of New Deal politics to castigate a business system that has always been recognized by Americans as the only permanent source of the jobs and consumer purchasing power which "the government" was trying to restore. And in the meantime the businessmen, who rose from prostration to record-breaking prosperity through satisfying a multibillion consumer demand that was stimulated and buttressed by New Deal legislation, became the bitterest critics of this New Deal legislation.

I know the arguments that business *might* have recovered even faster in the later thirties if it hadn't been for government "regimentation" (also referred to as "drift") and "exercise of arbitrary power" (also referred to as "indecisiveness"). If those arguments ever needed answer they have it in the decision of the present "businessman's government" in Washington not to curtail the federal programs that underwrite consumer purchasing power but to enlarge them. Nor in current talk of "getting government out of business" does there appear to be much recognition that government is in business to the tune of about $15 billion worth of military orders each year and is therefore playing, whatever the theory of the matter, a decisive part in keeping demand steady through the whole economy.

One of the future goals for American government and American business must surely be a fuller recognition that the maintenance of demand in the interests of the consumer—which is one of the few things everybody in this country is—is basic to both.

A broader aspect of the common purpose of business and government in America emerges from recognition of the new and tremendous sense of commonality that has come over this nation in the past twenty-five years. The individual no longer stands alone. His smallest community is larger, and more diverse in its services. His light and power come no longer from his own windmill or from some small local utility company, but usually from a vast network. His bank is strongly interconnected with its fellows, and his deposits are insured. The same news reaches him and his neighbors, and faster than it ever did before. An incredible linkage of wires and roads and cooperative enterprises, public and private, has taken isolation (and now isolationism) from all but the remotest homes in America.

In ways we hardly realize, this commonality brings inevitable interweavings of the functions of business and government. When the services of even two people are joined there are decisions of "governing" to be made; and when thousands and then millions invest or work together in a common business enterprise, their dealings together become more and more like the relationships we call government. What we used to think of as the "decentralized decision-making of the market place" has given way to various processes of large-scale private institutional decision-making remarkably like that of government in both its methods and its results. We constantly see in such things as labor unions, corporations, and trade associations, and in the "bargaining" that goes on between them, a reflection of the private institutional needs for "government."

As a people we are doing world-shaking and history-making things today—partly as the result of individual genius, but perhaps even more because we have learned of the powers of individuals working together. A brilliant professor turned businessman, Beardsley Ruml (who reformed the nation's thinking on how to collect the income tax and has more recently been trying to perform an equal miracle on our notion of the federal budget), has declared that the greatest economic discovery of the twentieth century so far is the realization that the wisely directed actions of all of us, *as a whole,* can compensate for the aberrations or misfortunes of a few. A. J. Toynbee suggests that three hundred years from now the twentieth century will be remembered, not for its wars, not for its conquests of distance and disease, not even for the splitting of the atom—but for "having been the first age, since the dawn of civilization, some five or six thousand years back, in which people dared to think it practicable to make the benefits of civilization available for the whole human race." I hope the judgment of this great historian comes true. My instincts tell me it will.

It was in America that the first practical stirrings of this great idea began. We must bring the idea to such a perfection that it will save the very civilization it has awakened. Another goal, then, for 1980 America—so that we may disprove George Orwell's terrifying prediction for 1984—is that this process of our growing commonality must and will be everywhere recognized and acknowledged, *not so that it can be senselessly accelerated, but so that it can be wisely guided and controlled.* I hold no belief in economic determinism; I bow to Shakespeare, not Marx, when I declare that there is a tide in the affairs of men, and that we had better acknowledge it.

This new sense of commonality is not without its dangers. Security, whether economic, political, or social, has become an individual and national obsession. I wonder if we fully realize the relationship between this yearning for security and the problem of maintaining our civil liberties. Security doesn't come free. Sometimes its price—or the price some would charge for it—is conformity and groupthink, and so it becomes part of the future joint obligation of the forces of business and government to respect, yes and protect, those elements of individuality that commonality threatens.

It is not true that the individual rolls around today like a kernel of grain between the upper and nether millstones of Big Government and Big Business—but there is a danger here that is great enough to warrant our keeping such a picture always in mind. Even as we become increasingly vigilant in our battle against the debilitating force of Communism we must be aware of another enemy that creeps upon us even more quietly and insidiously: the army of mass mediocrity, with banners flying.

Democracy's literature is full of warnings against the overpowering of the individual by the agencies of government and business. A hundred years ago John Stuart Mill deplored society's encroachments on the individual. John Ruskin prophesied the destruction of aesthetics by the Industrial Revolution. Lord Acton used some of his careful, rationed counsel to warn that democracy's flaw might prove to be—despite its protestations of the state's sublimation to the individual—a lack of moral criteria. Learned, sensitive, eloquent, these eminent Victorians voiced their concern that progress in the arts of statecraft and industry might make its intended beneficiaries its victims. Perhaps our survival in the face of these unhappy prophecies shows how wrong they were. Surely the individual is still today not *wholly* fenced in, except by the Kremlin, of which Mill did not happen to be thinking. As for the destruction of aesthetics, it turns out that in some ways—in modern design, in support of artistic efforts—industry is one of the best friends aesthetics has in the modern world.

Yet we know, from warnings that are more sensed than seen or heard, that all is not well with our status as individuals. Consciously or unconsciously, we are erecting battlements against our own accomplishments. Man in the individual sense today is not man's only adversary. We are concerned, too, about a strange, not wholly definable force in which there are at least the identifiable elements of "government" and "technology" and "massiveness" in this age of mass population, mass education, mass communications—yes, and mass manipulation. Indeed it seems that at mid-twentieth century, mass manipulation is a greater danger to the individual than was economic exploitation in the nineteenth century; that we are in greater danger of becoming robots than slaves. Surely it is part of the challenge of this next quarter-century that industry and government and the society they both support must find new and better ways of restoring scope to that strange eccentric, the individual.

Nostalgia won't help. We shall never dis-invent the airplane, which sets down the evil of Communism in our back yard instead of leaving it to fester outside our notice five thousand miles away. We shall never recover the quiet privacy the individual had before the telephone, the hand camera, and the microphone. We shall not relock the atom. A small fraction of our citizens have already come out flatly for government by lie-detector. Some businesses maintain, in the name of security, "blacklists" that in effect can deprive a man of the right to work without inquiry, due process, or even hope of ultimate redress. I can't help suspecting that some social scientists and even psychiatrists would love to find a combination of electronic devices by which every citizen could be measured for the slightest personal or social aberrations from some assigned "norm," and I suspect they will get it from our onrushing technologists. On this kind of assault on the individual I stand precisely where Calvin Coolidge stood on sin: I am agin it. I propose to keep on being agin it.

But we shall have to learn the art of coexistence with many strange things in the future, some of them perhaps even stranger than Communism. Technology, while adding daily to our physical ease, throws daily another loop of fine wire around our souls. It contributes hugely to our mobility, which we must not confuse with freedom. The extensions of our senses, which we find so fascinating, are not adding to the discrimination of our minds, since we need increasingly to take the reading of a needle on a dial to discover whether we think something is good or bad, right or wrong.

Deepest pride in the accomplishments of America's inventive genius is no warrant for congratulating ourselves on any best-of-all-possible-worlds. Materially we can—and will—do better still. But spiritually, morally, and politically, I don't think we are doing so well. Both industry and government are contributing enormously to the almost unbelievable advance of technology in America—but both must become increasingly aware of their moral and spiritual responsibilities. The representative of a great manufacturing concern, speaking about the phenomenon we call automation, concluded: "I don't think it is the part, nor can it be the part, of industry to try to plan the social aspects of this thing." It seems to me, to the contrary, that industry is eventually, with government, going to have to do its full share of thinking about the sociology as well as the economics of such things as automation and the split atom. The more realistic and broad-gauge view is suggested by David Sarnoff's comment, in an earlier article in this *Fortune* series, that "if freedom is lost, if the dignity of man is destroyed, advances on the material plane will not be 'progress' but a foundation for a new savagery."

There is increasing realization that one of the biggest problems of these next twenty-five years will be what we are going to do with "the new leisure" which it appears will develop as one of the fruits of the new technology. As people learn how to live longer after their service in the regular work force is done, as machines and "feedbacks" and push buttons take on more and more of the job of production, as the inevitably shortened work week materializes —with these things there comes a whole host of new adjustments to be made. No one need fear the long-range effects of machines replacing men, but the adjustment is going to require responsible and thoughtful administration, and the new leisure will mean new happiness only if care is taken not to confuse leisure with just plain having nothing to do.

It is inevitable that government in America will be called upon during this next quarter-century to meet the social implications of these ever more rapid technological advances, and I see no reason why American industry should not participate fully and freely in this enterprise. There seems to me no escape from this obligation. It just will not do to leave all worrying about our souls to the educators, the clergy, and the philosophers. The men to whom mass-America tunes its ear today are businessmen—indeed, they seem to have more influence on youth than the schools, more influence on the devout than the clergy, more influence on the wicked than the thought of perdition. With this prestige goes a responsibility that can be given no artificial boundaries.

I shall not attempt to suggest a particular role for industry in the transforming of technology's dark threats into bright promises. Part of this role will undoubtedly lie in an increased laying aside of great funds to foster education in all fields, not confining such funds to the sciences or to what is of immediate or "practical" significance. The day of the great individual philanthropist is nearly over, and industry must step into this breach. Even as I write this there comes to my desk a list of fifty research memoranda being prepared as part of a joint project of a large private corporation and a branch of the federal government. Would that just one of the fifty memoranda related to the heart of industrial progress—instead of all of them to its hands and feet and muscle! Adolf A. Berle, Jr., suggests in his recent book a broader emergent concept of the corporation as an instrument of social leadership and responsibility, chargeable with a stewardship as broad as all the implications of its economic effects. This, it seems to me, must be the direction of our progress.

It could be hoped that one of the dividends of a "businessman's government" might be a merging of the thinking *both* in business and in government about economic and human affairs. And yet there has been quite a lot of talk from high government spokesmen about being "conservative" in economic affairs and "liberal" in human affairs. I don't know how this works where something like unemployment or social security is involved. Are those "economic" or "human" affairs?

If there is value in a definition of "conservatism" that would cross economic human and business-government lines (and even Republican-Democratic lines), may I reiterate what Thomas Carlyle said a hundred years ago: the conservatism that *really* conserves is that which lops off the dead branch to have the living tree. Our American economy has fewer dead branches than that of any other nation, I am sure; but that we shall need pruning and spraying and the application of new fertilizers and growth regulators in the future as in the past, I have no doubt. Should it perhaps be part of our purpose in these years ahead to recognize that the process of conservation must be a joint government and business responsibility, and that division of function between "human" and "economic" is unrealistic in today's complex society?

I hope this quarter-century will see a frank recognition that every new frontier in American progress has been, and will always be, opened up by the *joint* enterprise of business and government. Great respect for the concept of the "rugged individualist" (usually incorporated) is no warrant for the illusion that modern America was *created* by businessmen—any more than it was by Senators or the Founding Fathers. Before colonial America could emerge from its colonialism, and a few cities could become interconnected with a subsistence agriculture and the tinkering sheds of a few ingenious Yankees, the federal government had to assert its power. Before America could become a great industrial nation the federal government had to assert its power over territory in terms of a U.S. Army that would explore and protect; in terms of a federal treasury that would regulate and expand the national credit;

and in many other terms of a state that would hold title to the whole public domain until private entrepreneurs could slowly, on terms adjudged to be for the public benefit, take over vital business and industrial procedures. There were very few businessmen (and no government officials) in the Conestoga wagons that toiled across the West only a little more than a century ago; their time and place and function came later.

No; business did not create America or the American way. The American way was created in a complex collaboration whereby the federal government offered to individuals the best soil and nurture for enlightened capitalism ever devised—and the individuals took it on the generous terms offered.

Nor is this interdependence of government and business reflected only in historical vignettes. We accept today as one of our great principles that operation of industry is a properly private function. Yet so long as technology burgeons, the interrelationships between government and industry will continue to grow more complex, not less. Where technology disemploys workers, government will be asked to help. It must help. Where it creates surpluses, government will be asked to help. It must help.

There is no reason to be afraid of growing complexity; indeed our option is to deal cheerfully and courageously with growing complexity—or to go over the authoritarian abyss. I see no reason why the need to confront complexity is more ominous merely because it may require new formulas of private-public cooperation.

A fascinating future relationship between government and business, for example, will occur when Alaska is truly "opened." Before business and industry can begin to pour Alaska's resources into the mainstream of the world's commercial life, millions of dollars worth of trunk and access roads will have to be built, and someone will have to complete the geological mapping of 586,400 square miles of territory so that private mining companies will have some notion of what, where, and how great the mineral treasure of Alaska really is—facts unknown today. Shall we organize a purely private Alaskan Corporation of America to take all these risks? Or may it be necessary to accept some subvention from the federal government to get things going? Regardless of our preachments we may be sure it will be the latter, as in large part it already has been.

In spite of resounding keynote speeches and business-convention oratory, it is an obvious fact that this pattern of cooperation between government and private enterprise runs through our economy from end to end. One of the most pervasive of all influences is without doubt the tariff—that massive governmental intervention that is generally left off the standard anathema list of many businessmen. Much of the work of the Atomic Energy Commission is undertaken through the agency of private corporations. Business in the Northwest has certainly not been retarded by cheap public power. And just how much of the newspaper and magazine industry is carried by the taxpayer through the government's massive subsidy of second-class mail?

There will be a testing of a good deal of unthinking talk when it comes time to consider translating into action the Hoover Commission's recommendations for liquidating the structure of government lending agencies. It seems a conservative prognosis that these recommendations will be loudly honored for their expression of the sacrosanct and sound principle of the least-government-possible and that it will then be more quietly decided that most of these agencies (with perhaps a little exterior redecoration) come within the least-possible limits.

I am not suggesting that American business and industry owe either an unpaid debt or any attitude of servile gratitude to the federal government. The creative record of American capitalism is altogether too strong and dignified in its own right to call for subservience to any other force. What I am suggesting, however, is that there could be a good deal more realism and quite a lot less nonsense in the recognition by the business community of the interdependence, if you will, of the two essential democratic capitalistic institutions of business and government. We are past the point of adolescence in a relationship where it once was perhaps understandable that those who profited in largest sum from the operation of our system of things might still clamor about the federal government as a childishly operated nuisance, which hampers business, which intrudes, which confiscates or expropriates profits, and in a thousand ways spoils all the fun and is constantly threatening to "socialize" all America by creeping. It seems to me an essential element of our present maturity to recognize that the relationships between the two institutions do not consist exclusively of government's recourseless taxation or browbeating of business.

We too rarely realize how very great and needless a strain is placed on this relationship just by the verbal violence that is indulged in in describing its elements. "Economic royalists" was an unfair and unfortunate epithet. To call the TVA "Communism," or rural electrification "Socialism"—the list of such clichés is long—is a kind of nonsense that insults the facts and serves only evil. It is an important goal for America-1980 that what is publicly said or reported regarding such things be better adjusted to what is generally true. This will require, among other things, an enormous improvement in the standards and practices of American journalism.

Before leaving the subject of the interaction of government and industry, I should speak of a vital area in which failure to formulate joint and consistent policies can have the effect not simply of weakening the domestic economy but of imperiling America's position of leadership in the free world. I refer, of course, to those tariff, trade, and custom practices that hamper and addle world commerce to the disadvantage of the whole Western world, ourselves included. As a goal for the future, to be achieved many years sooner than distant 1980, I would certainly hope for relaxed restrictions on world commerce—a relaxation not just on tariffs—to the end of freer and freer trade among the nations. Policies that were appropriate only in the day when it was accurate to speak of "our infant industries" can lead to social, political, and economic misfortune in our industrial manhood. And insofar as the need for capital and technical assistance in the less developed areas has become perhaps the greatest limiting factor on expanding world trade, I would hope, too, for new and courageous action by public and private agencies in this field as well. On tariff reductions the government (under Democratic administrations, at least) has led the way since 1934 and earlier. In providing capital and technical "know-how" for world development, it is the government that has made the start. Business must educate its members to follow.

But perhaps the most urgent problem that will be set before government and business alike by pressures generated beyond America's frontier will prove to be the issue of disarmament. We cannot deny that the overwhelming desire of our own people and of all the world's peoples is to be rid of the nightmare of atomic war. There are some signs that the Communists are feeling this enormous pressure of popular longing for peace. It is not inconceivable that in the next decade we shall be required to take the lead in dismantling a part of our vast military structure of preparedness. The impact upon the national economy of falling expenditures for arms will be profound and it will take the best efforts and the concerted efforts of government and business to see that the transition from a large measure of military spending to an overwhelmingly civilian economy is accomplished without a downward spiral and grave dislocation in the whole economic system. Neither government nor business can manage that alone. It would be well if its implications were examined jointly—and soon.

Perhaps most of what I have mentioned here comes together in a suggestion that we might profitably think in terms of a doctrine of "separation of powers" in this area of business and government relations—a separation resembling the constitutional differentiation between the executive, the legislative, and the judicial in government itself. This is a formula for "checks and balances," and yet essentially for coordination and cooperative functioning toward common goals. The future of government and business does not consist in *either one* having ambitions to take over the functions of the other. It is an essential goal for the future to keep their separation jealously guarded.

Government in America has *always* regarded the operation of industry as a purely private function. To return to an earlier example, even the newest-biggest of all governmental agencies, born in the early days of the Atomic Age and the Fair Deal—the AEC—operates its vast, complex, "monopolistic," and largely secret domain through private industrial contractors. But business has yet to show a comparably broad and tolerant understanding of the legitimate domain of government. In fact, some sections of the business community could not do better than follow, in this regard, Dr. Johnson's advice, and clear their minds of cant and prejudiced misinformation, not to say the downright nonsense about "governmental dictatorship," and, of course, "creeping Socialism" that all too often, as a species of businessmen's groupthink, takes the place of responsible consideration of the proper functions of government in free society.

This idea of a different kind of "separation of powers" does not require being against "businessmen in government." Not at all. But it does suggest that when businessmen, like anyone else, are being selected for government posts, it should be because of their talents for the job of government and for no other reason. To the extent that "businessmen in government" means the introduction into government of the ideals and practices of efficiency for which American business is justly famous—and to the degree that it also means adding to government councils an intimate understanding of industry and commerce—to that extent and degree this is all to the good and none should object. The case is very different, though, wherever a businessman brings with him to government any ideas other than a completely objective and independent concept of the public good.

An intelligent businessman, now a member of the current administration, said before he reached his present public eminence: "Commercial interests are not the same as national interests." How right he was, and is. Although commercial interests and national interests can and usually do walk a certain distance hand in hand, no full identity between them can ever be forced, and any attempt to force it would be apt to end in misery, or disaster, or both—and for both.

Over the years, the federal government, in Republican and Democratic administrations, enacted the Sherman and the Clayton acts to prevent concentrations of power in plutocratic hands, and no wiser or more beneficial legislation has ever been enacted in America—for business. In Europe, where these laws are incomprehensible, and a cozy hand-in-glove-ism between governments and industries has its expression in the cartel system, we see many brilliant accomplishments. But we do *not* see any properly significant diffusion downward of the profits and benefits of the industrial system, which, in this country, constitutes our most effective safeguard against radical infection in any large masses of our public.

It was governmental intervention, beginning about fifty years ago, that broke up the trusts. If American business had remained in the image of the "oil trust," the "steel trust," the "sugar trust," the "whiskey trust," America as we know it today would never have come into existence, and the leadership of the modern world would almost certainly reside elsewhere—doubtless in a totally Prussianized or Communized Europe, with the British Isles reduced to the status of a tourist resort, and America still a giant agricultural bumpkin among the nations.

Events took a very different turn. We are not yet fully grown up to our responsibilities of world leadership, and we groan understandably under the burdens placed upon us. But despite two hideous wars, the history of the twentieth century is by no means so tragic—yet—as it might be, and the vast area of hope still alive in the world lies squarely here, with us. The past interactions between American government and American business, brawling and ill natured though they were, have been a major determinant of the shape and course of the modern Western world. Given an improved respect and understanding between these properly separated forces in America, I can look forward to the next twenty-five years with confidence, and think of all the Western world, potentially, as a land of hope and glory, Mother of the Free.

"What is past," says the inscription in front of the National Archives Building in Washington, "is prologue." To this I say amen.

TOPICS FOR DISCUSSION AND WRITING

1. What "image" of Stevenson emerges from the essay? By what means does Stevenson create that image? Does it contribute in any way to the arguments and judgments which he presents?
2. Are the characteristics of the balanced style as evident in this essay as they are in Johnson's essay on Shakespeare? What other style does Stevenson have recourse to, besides the balanced? How would you account for his use of the different styles?
3. Where are there clear examples of the balanced style? Why do they appear at these points?
4. Stevenson's acceptance and campaign speeches reveal a much wider use of the balanced style than does this essay in a widely-circulated magazine. Why would the extensive use of the balanced style be appropriate in campaign speeches?
5. Reread the editorial from *Fortune* on "The Language of Business." Do you see any agreement between that editorial and Stevenson's essay?

THE FAMILIAR STYLE

The familiar style, as we have said, is an *apparently* style-less expression of ideas. But the absence of artifice is only an appearance and not a reality. Familiar style, when used properly, is an art which conceals art. It should certainly not be confused with haphazard, uncontrolled, or random utterance. For reasons that any number of circumstances may force on him, the writer may wish to avoid the images of clinical detachment, of thinking-in-process, or of intellectual superiority which the curt, loose, or balanced styles are likely to create. Any one of those attitudes might conflict with his own personality, with the experience he is describing, or with the audience he is addressing. Should the writer wish to speak directly to his audience—to convince them of the immediacy of the idea or experience which he is discussing, to involve them on an equal basis in his own judgments, and to keep his discourse at the level of common understanding—his strategy would be to use the familiar style.

And such a style does involve strategy. It demands closest attention to clarity, emphasis, and variety, all in the spirit of "man speaking directly to man," carefully avoiding the oracular, the pompous, or the aloof. It is a style achieved by the modified and very tempered use of the characteristics of the other styles.

Thus Hazlitt utilizes the terse, aphoristic quality of the curt style—"Poetry and philosophy had met together"; "I had a light before me, it was the face of Poetry"; "The one still lingers there, the other had not quitted my side"—but these are widely spaced and not congregated, as in the case of Bacon's style. Again, Hazlitt accumulates a series of many brief units, as in the second sentence of the selection printed below; but in comparison with Bacon's series, Hazlitt's is minimal.

Traces of the loose style are seen in Hazlitt's use of the parenthetical and interrupting phrase: "Never, the longest day I have to live, shall I have such another walk"; "the sermon was on peace and war; upon church and state—not their alliance, but their separation—on the spirit of the world and the spirit of Christianity"; "It might seem that the genius of his face as from a height surveyed and projected him (with sufficient capacity and huge aspiration into) the world unknown of thought and imagination." But as with the characteristics of the curt style, these stylistic devices are used sparingly.

A cautious and limited use of a balanced structure is evident throughout Hazlitt's essay: "the rudder of the face, the index of the will"; "this delay did not damp, but rather increased my ardour"; "it sprung out of the ground like a flower, or unfolded itself from a green spray." Unlike Dr. Johnson's balanced structures, however, Hazlitt's are brief, depending on a balance between words or phrases rather than balances between entire clauses. Conspicuously absent from Hazlitt's style is the periodic structure, which would demand an inversion of normal sentence movement and is therefore alien to the "naturalness" of the familiar style.

The familiar style is an epitome of the other styles, but with all their most noticeable characteristics carefully muted. It is a style which hesitates to announce itself or call attention to itself as being unique; but underlying its unremarkable surface is a sure knowledge of stylistic technique.

William Hazlitt

If such a broad label as "neoclassic" has any meaning at all, it is applicable to Samuel Johnson; if the label "romantic" means anything, it is applicable to William Hazlitt (1778–1830). Although Hazlitt views literature in an entirely different spirit from Johnson, he has the same unyielding conviction that his principles are the correct ones. A liberal (even a revolutionist) in politics, his taste in literature was for the innovative, the daring, the original. Criticism was not a preservative of old values and ideals, but an exposition of new attitudes and different responses. Literature was not something to be weighed and judged, but something to be experienced and felt. As essayist and critic he aimed not at judicial decisions, but at re-creating his own excitement of discovery and sharing that excitement with the reader. It was no accident that Hazlitt became generally acknowledged as one of the founders of the informal essay, for it was only through such a form that he could communicate his own response to literature and ideas and involve the reader in such a way that his own enthusiasms might become those of the reader.

from MY FIRST ACQUAINTANCE WITH POETS

My father lived ten miles from Shrewsbury, and was in the habit of exchanging visits with Mr. Rowe, and with Mr. Jenkins of Whitechurch (nine miles farther on) according to the custom of dissenting ministers in each other's neighbourhood. A line of communication is thus established, by which the flame of civil and religious liberty is kept alive, and nourishes its smouldering fire unquenchable, like the fires in the *Agamemnon* of Aeschylus, placed at different stations, that waited for ten long years to announce with their blazing pyramids the destruction of Troy. Coleridge had agreed to come over to see my father, according to the courtesy of the country, as Mr. Rowe's probable successor; but in the meantime I had gone to hear him preach the Sunday after his arrival. A poet and philosopher getting up into a Unitarian pulpit to preach the Gospel, was a romance in these degenerate days, a sort of revival of the primitive spirit of Christianity, which was not to be resisted.

It was in January, 1798, that I rose one morning before daylight, to walk ten miles in the mud, and went to hear this celebrated person preach. Never, the longest day I have to live, shall I have such another walk as this cold, raw, comfortless one, in the winter of the year 1798. *Il y a des impressions que ni le tems ni les circonstances peuvent effacer. Dussee-je des siècles entiers, le doux tems de ma jeunesse ne peut renaitre pour moi, ni s'effacer jamais dans ma mémoire.* [There are impressions which neither time nor circumstances can erase. If I should live for entire centuries, the sweet time of youth cannot return for me, nor erase itself from my memory.] When I got there, the organ was playing the 100th psalm, and, when it was done, Mr. Coleridge rose and gave out his text, "And he went up into the mountain to pray, himself, alone." As he gave out this text, his voice "rose like a steam of rich distilled perfumes," and when he came to the two last words, which he pronounced loud, deep, and distinct, it seemed to me, who was then young, as if the sounds had echoed from the bottom of the human heart, and as if that prayer might have floated in solemn silence through the universe. The idea of St. John came into mind, "of one crying in the wilderness, who had his loins girt about, and whose food was locusts and wild honey." The preacher then launched into his subject, like an eagle dallying with the wind. The sermon was upon peace and war; upon church and state—not their alliance, but their separation—on the spirit of the world and the spirit of Christianity, not as the same, but as opposed to one another. He talked of those who had "inscribed the cross of Christ on banners dripping with human gore." He made a poetical and pastoral excursion, and to show the fatal effects of war, drew a striking contrast between the simple shepherd boy, driving his team afield, or sitting under the hawthorn, piping to his flock, "as though he should never be old," and the same poor country lad, crimped, kidnapper, brought into town, made drunk at an alehouse, turned into a wretched drummer boy, with his hair sticking on end with powder and pomatum, a long cue at his back, and tricked out in the loathsome finery of the profession of blood.

"Such were the notes our once-loved poet sung." And for myself, I could not have been more delighted if I had heard the music of the spheres. Poetry and philosophy had met together, truth and genius had embraced, under the eye and with the sanction of religion. This was even beyond my hopes. I returned home well satisfied. The sun that was still labouring pale and wan through the sky, obscured by thick mists, seemed an emblem of the *good cause*; and the cold dank drops of dew that hung half melted on the beard of the thistle, had something genial and refreshing in them; for there was a spirit of hope and youth in all nature, that turned every thing into good. The face of nature had not then the brand of *Jus Divinum* on it:

> Like to that sanguine flower incribed with woe.

On the Tuesday following, the half-inspired speaker came. I was called down into the room where he was, and went half-hoping, half-afraid. He received me very graciously, and I listened for a long time without uttering a word. I did not suffer in his opinion by my silence. "For those two hours," he afterwards was pleased to say, "he was conversing with W.H.'s forehead!" His appearance was different from what I had anticipated from seeing him before. At a distance, and in the dim light of the chapel, there was to me a strange wildness in his aspect, a dusty obscurity, and I thought him pitted with the smallpox. His complexion was at that time clear, and even bright—

> As are the children of yon azure sheen.

His forehead was broad and high, light as if built of ivory, with large projecting eyebrows, and his eyes rolling beneath them like a sea with darkened lustre. "A certain tender bloom his face o'erspread," a purple tinge as we see it in the pale thoughtful complexions of the Spanish portrait painters, Murillo and Velasquez. His mouth was gross, voluptuous, open, eloquent; his chin good-humoured and round; but his nose, the rudder of the face, the index of the will, was small, feeble, nothing—like what he has done. It might seem that the genius of his face as from a height surveyed and projected him (with sufficient capacity and huge aspiration) into the world unknown of thought and imagination, with nothing to support or guide his veering purpose, as if Columbus had launched his adventurous course for the New World in a scallop, without oars or compass. So at least I comment on it after the event. Coleridge in his person was rather above the common size, inclining to the corpulent, or like Lord Hamlet, "somewhat fat and pursy." His hair (now, alas! grey) was then black and glossy as the raven's, and fell in smooth masses over his forehead. This long pendulous hair is peculiar to enthusiasts, to those whose minds tend heavenward; and is traditionally inseparable (though of a different colour) from the pictures of Christ. . . .

On my way back, I had a sound in my ears, it was the voice of

Fancy: I had a light before me, it was the face of Poetry. The one still lingers there, the other had not quitted my side! Coleridge in truth met me half-way on the ground of philosophy, or I should not have been won over to his imaginative creed. I had an uneasy, pleasurable sensation all the time, till I was to visit him. During those months the chill breath of winter gave me a welcoming; the vernal air was balm and inspiration to me. The golden sunsets, the silver star of evening, lighted me on my way to new hopes and prospects. *I was to visit Coleridge in the spring.* This circumstance was never absent from my thoughts, and mingled with all my feelings. I wrote to him at the time proposed, and received an answer postponing my intended visit for a week or two, but very cordially urging me to complete my promise then. This delay did not damp, but rather increased my ardour. In the meantime I went to Llangollen Vale, by way of initiating myself in the mysteries of natural scenery; and I must say I was enchanted with it. I had been reading Coleridge's description of England, in his fine *Ode on the Departing Year,* and I applied it, *con amore,* to the objects before me. That valley was to me (in a manner) the cradle of a new existence: in the river that winds through it, my spirit was baptized in the waters of Helicon! . . .

That morning, as soon as breakfast was over, we strolled out into the park, and seating ourselves on the trunk of an old ash tree that stretched along the ground, Coleridge read aloud with a sonorous and musical voice the ballad of *Betty Foy.* I was not critically or sceptically inclined. I saw touches of truth and nature, and took the rest for granted. But in the *Thorn,* the *Mad Mother,* and the *Complaint of a Poor Indian Woman,* I felt that deeper power and pathos which have since been acknowledged,

> In spite of pride, in erring reason's spite,

as the characteristics of this author; and the sense of a new style and a new spirit in poetry came over me. It had to be something of the effect that arises from the turning up of the fresh soil, or of the first welcome breath of spring:

> While yet the trembling year is unconfirmed.

Coleridge and myself walked back to Stowey that evening, and his voice sounded high

> Of Providence, foreknowledge, will, and fate,
> Fixed fate, free will, foreknowledge absolute,

as we passed through echoing grove, by fairy stream or waterfall, gleaming in the summer moonlight! He lamented that Wordsworth was not prone enough to believe in the traditional superstitions of the place, and that there was something corporeal, a *matter-of-the-factness,* a clinging to the palpable, or often to the petty, in his poetry, in consequence. His genius was not a spirit that descended to him through the air; it sprung out of the ground like a flower, or unfolded itself from a green spray, on which the goldfinch sang. He said, however (if I remember right), that this objection must be confined to his descriptive pieces, that his philosophic poetry had a grand and comprehensive spirit in it, so that his soul seemed to inhabit the universe like a palace, and to discover truth by intuition, rather than by deduction. The next day Wordsworth arrived from Bristol at Coleridge's cottage. I think I see him now. He answered in some degree to his friend's description of him, but was more gaunt and Don-Quixote-like. He was quaintly dressed (according to the costume of that unconstrained period) in a brown fustian jacket and striped pantaloons. There was something of a roll, a lounge in his gait, not unlike his own Peter Bell. There was a severe, worn pressure of thought about his temples, a fire in his eye (as if he saw something in objects more than the outward appearance), an intense high narrow forehead, a Roman nose, cheeks furrowed by strong purpose and feeling, and a convulsive inclination to laughter about the mouth, a good deal at variance with the solemn, stately expression of the rest of his face. Chantry's bust wants the marking traits; but he was teased into making it regular and heavy; Haydon's head of him, introduced into the *Entrance of Christ into Jerusalem,* is the most like his drooping weight of thought and expression. He sat down and talked very naturally and freely, with a mixture of clear gushing accents in his voice, a deep guttural intonation, and a strong tincture of the northern *burr,* like the crust on wine. He instantly began to make havoc of the half of a Cheshire cheese on the table, and said triumphantly that "his marriage with experience had not been so unproductive as Mr. Southey's in teaching him a knowledge of the good things of this life." He had been to see the

Castle Spectre, by Monk Lewis, while at Bristol, and described it very well. He said "it fitted the taste of the audience like a glove." This *ad captandum* merit was however by no means a recommendation of it, according to the severe principles of the new school, which reject rather than court popular effect. Wordsworth, looking out of the low, latticed window, said "How beautifully the sun sets on that yellow bank!" I thought within myself, "With what eyes these poets see nature!" and ever after, when I saw the sunset stream upon the objects facing it, conceived I had made a discovery, or thanked Mr. Wordsworth for having made one for me! We went over to All-Foxden again the day following, and Wordsworth read us the story of Peter Bell in the open air; and the comment made upon it by his face and voice was very different from that of some later critics! Whatever might be thought of the poem, "his face was a book where men might read strange matters," and he announced the fate of his hero in prophetic tones. There is a *chaunt* in the recitation both of Coleridge and Wordsworth, which acts as a spell upon the hearer, and disarms the judgment. Perhaps they have deceived themselves by making habitual use of this ambiguous accompaniment. Coleridge's manner is more full, animated, and varied; Wordsworth's more equable, sustained, and internal. The one might be termed more *dramatic,* the other more *lyrical.* Coleridge has told me that he himself liked to compose in walking over uneven ground, or breaking through the straggling branches of a copse wood; whereas Wordsworth always wrote (if he could) walking up and down a straight gravel walk, or in some spot where the continuity of his verse met with no collateral interruptions. . . .

TOPICS FOR DISCUSSION AND WRITING

1. The setting of Hazlitt's essay is rural and middle-class, while the political and religious persuasion he describes is what we now refer to as "democratic" and "liberal." The poems of Coleridge to which he pays particular attention are the ballads. He notes Coleridge's judgment of the *matter-of-factness* of Wordsworth's poetry, and the simplicity of both poets in their manners, dress, and appearance. Do such items as these have anything to do with Hazlitt's use of the familiar style?
2. How is Hazlitt's reaction to poetry different from Dr. Johnson's reaction? What has taken the place of the "endurance" principle?

3. Hazlitt quotes from both poetry and Scripture in the course of his essay. Does this strike you as merely an accidental association, or is it a deliberate juxtaposition? What does such a juxtaposition imply about the nature of poetry?
4. Hazlitt concentrates on Coleridge's dramatic poetry, Wordsworth's lyrical poetry. Does Hazlitt's style relate to the dramatic or lyrical qualities in the writings of his two subjects? Would he have been likely to adopt a different style if he had been describing the work of the epic poet?
5. Dr. Johnson's style seems to locate the reader as an audience listening to a lecture by a competent authority, whereas Hazlitt's style encourages the reader to think of himself as a participant in the discovery of the two poets. How is this effect related to Hazlitt's opinions on the value of poetry?

William James

William James (1842–1910) was the spokesman if not the founder of American pragmatism, a philosophy which argues that the meaning and value of an idea resides in its practicality. If an idea "works," or has an effect, it is a valid idea; to discuss the value of an ineffective idea is irrelevant and immaterial. His emphasis in philosophy was on experience *rather than* theory; *and while his idea of "workability" as the criterion of truth has offended many, even his attackers have had to admit that there is a flexibility, an open-mindedness, underlying his philosophy. One of the most eloquent of philosophers, James' persuasiveness in writing*—Principles of Psychology *(1890),* The Will to Believe and Other Essays *(1897),* Varieties of Religious Experience *(1902),* Pragmatism *(1907), and* The Meaning of Truth *(1909)—has prompted the remark that he wrote psychology like a novelist while his brother, Henry James, wrote the novel like a psychologist. The essay printed here is from the 1897 collection.*

WHAT MAKES A LIFE SIGNIFICANT *

In my previous talk, "On a Certain Blindness," I tried to make you feel how soaked and shot-through life is with values and meanings which we fail to realize because of our external and

* Reprinted by permission of Paul R. Reynolds & Son.

insensible point of view. The meanings are there for the others, but they are not there for us. There lies more than a mere interest of curious speculation in understanding this. It has the most tremendous practical importance. I wish that I could convince you of it as I feel it myself. It is the basis of all our tolerance, social, religious, and political. The forgetting of it lies in the root of every stupid and sanguinary mistake that rulers over subject peoples make. The first thing to learn in intercourse with others is non-interference with their own peculiar ways of being happy, provided those ways do not assume to interfere by violence with ours. No one has an insight into all the ideals. No one should presume to judge them offhand. The pretension to dogmatize about them in each other is the root of most human injustices and cruelties, and the trait in human character most likely to make the angels weep.

Every Jack sees in his own particular Jill charms and perfections to the enchantment of which we stolid onlookers are stone-cold. And which has the superior view of the absolute truth, he or we? Which has the more vital insight into the nature of Jill's existence, as a fact? Is he in excess, being in this matter a maniac? Or are we in defect, being victims of a pathological anaesthesia as regards Jill's magical importance? Surely the latter; surely to Jack are the profounder truths revealed; surely poor Jill's palpitating little life-throbs are among the wonders of creation, are worthy of this sympathetic interest, and it is to our shame that the rest of us cannot feel like Jack. For Jack realizes Jill concretely, and we do not. He struggles toward a union with her inner life, divining her feelings, anticipating her desires, understanding her limits as manfully as he can, and yet inadequately, too; for he is also afflicted with some blindness, even here. Whilst we, dead clods that we are, do not even seek after these things, but are contented that that portion of eternal fact named Jill should be for us as if it were not. Jill, who knows her inner life, knows that Jack's way of taking it—so importantly—is the true and serious way; and she responds to the truth in him by taking him truly and seriously, too. May the ancient blindness never wrap its clouds about either of them again! Where would any of us be, were there no one willing to know us as we really are or ready to repay us for our insight by making recognizant return? We ought, all of us, to realize each other in this intense, pathetic, and important way.

If you say that this is absurd, and that we cannot be in love with everyone at once, I merely point out to you that, as a matter of fact, certain persons do exist with an enormous capacity for friendship and for taking delight in other people's lives; and that such persons know more of truth than if their hearts were not so big. The vice of ordinary Jack and Jill affection is not its intensity, but its exclusions and its jealousies. Leave those out, and you see that the ideal I am holding up before you, however impractical today, yet contains nothing intrinsically absurd.

We have unquestionably a great cloud-band of ancestral blindness weighing down upon us, only transiently riven here and there by fitful revelations of the truth. It is vain to hope for this state of things to alter much. Our inner secrets must remain for the most part impenetrable by others, for beings as essentially practical as we are are necessarily short of sight. But, if we cannot gain much positive insight into one another, cannot we at least use our sense of our own blindness to make us more cautious in going over the dark places? Cannot we escape some of those hideous ancestral intolerances and cruelties, and positive reversals of the truth?

For the remainder of this hour I invite you to see with me some principle to make our tolerance less chaotic. And, as I began my previous lecture by a personal reminiscence, I am going to ask your indulgence for a similar bit of egotism now.

A few summers ago I spent a happy week at the famous Assembly Grounds on the borders of Chautauqua Lake. The moment one treads that sacred enclosure, one feels one's self in an atmosphere of success. Sobriety and industry, intelligence and goodness, orderliness and ideality, prosperity and cheerfulness, pervade the air. It is a serious and studious picnic on a gigantic scale. Here you have a town of many thousands of inhabitants, beautifully laid out in the forest and drained, and equipped with means for satisfying all the necessary lower and most of the superfluous wants of man. You have a first-class college in full blast. You have magnificent music—a chorus of seven hundred voices, with possibly the most perfect open-air auditorium in the world. You have every sort of athletic exercise from sailing, rowing, swimming, bicycling, to the ball field and the more artificial doings which the gymnasium affords. You have kindergartens and model secondary schools. You have general religious services and special clubhouses for the several sects. You have perpetually running soda-water fountains, and daily popular lectures by distinguished men. You have the best company, and yet no effort. You have no zymotic diseases, no poverty, no drunkenness, no crime, no police. You have culture, you have kindness, you have cheapness, you have equality, you have the best fruits of what mankind has fought and bled and striven for under the name of civilization for centuries. You have, in short, a foretaste of what human society might be, were it all in the light, with no suffering and no dark corners.

I went in curiosity for a day. I stayed for a week, held spellbound by the charm and ease of everything, by the middle-class paradise, without a victim, without a blot, without a tear.

And yet what was my own astonishment, on emerging into the dark and wicked world again, to catch myself quite unexpectedly and involuntarily saying: "Out! what a relief! Now for something primordial and savage, even though it were as bad as an Armenian massacre, to set the balance straight again. This order is too tame, this culture too second-rate, this goodness too uninspiring. This human drama without a villain or a pang; this community so refined that ice-cream and soda-water is the utmost offering it can make to the brute animal in man; this city simmering in the tepid lakeside sun; this atrocious harmlessness of all things—I cannot abide with them. Let me take my chances again in the big outside worldly wilderness with all its sins and sufferings. There are the heights and depths, the precipices and the steep ideals, the gleams of the awful and the infinite; and there is more hope and help a thousand times than in this dead level and quintessence of every mediocrity."

Such was the sudden right-about-face performed for me by my lawless fancy! There had been spread before me the realization—on a small, sample scale of course—of all the ideals for which our civilization has been striving: security, intelligence, humanity, and order; and here was the instinctive hostile reaction, not of the natural man, but of a so-called cultivated man upon such a Utopia. There seemed thus to be a self-contradiction and paradox somewhere, which I, as a professor drawing a full salary, was in duty bound to unravel and explain, if I could.

So I meditated. And, first of all, I asked myself what the thing was that was so lacking in this Sabbatical city, and the lack of which kept one forever falling short of the higher sort of contentment. And I soon recognized that it was the element that gives to the wicked outer world all its moral style, expressiveness and picturesqueness—the element of precipitousness, so to call it, of strength and strenuousness, intensity and danger. What excites and interests the looker-on at life, what the romances and the statues celebrate and the grim civic monuments remind us of, is the everlasting battle of the powers of light with those of darkness; with heroism, reduced to its bare chance, yet ever and anon snatching victory from the jaws of death. But in this unspeakable Chautauqua there was no potentiality of death in sight anywhere, and no point of the compass visible from which danger might possibly appear. The ideal was so completely victorious already that no sign of any previous battle remained, the place just resting on its oars. But what our human emotions seem to require is the sight of the struggle going on. The moment the fruits are being merely eaten, things become ignoble. Sweat and effort, human nature strained to its uttermost and on the rack, yet getting through alive, and then turning its back on its success to pursue another more rare and arduous still—this is the sort of thing the presence of which inspires us, and the reality of which it seems to be the function of all the higher forms of literature and fine art to bring home to us and suggest. At Chautauqua there were no racks, even in the place's historical museum; and no sweat, except possibly the gentle moisture on the brow of some lecturer, or on the sides of some player in the ball field.

Such absence of human nature *in extremis* anywhere seemed, then, a sufficient explanation for Chautauqua's flatness and lack of zest.

But was not this a paradox well calculated to fill one with dismay? It looks indeed, thought I, as if the romantic idealists with their pessimism about our civilization were, after all, quite right. Bourgeoisie and mediocrity, church sociables and teachers' conventions, are taking the place of the old heights and depths and romantic chiaroscuro. And, to get human life in its wild intensity, we must in future turn more and more away from the actual, and forget it, if we can, in the romancer's or the poet's pages. The whole world, delightful and sinful as it may still appear for a moment to one just escaped from the Chautauqua enclosure, is nevertheless obeying more and more just those ideals that are sure to make of it in the end a mere Chautauqua Assembly on an enormous scale. *Was im Gesang soll leben muss im Leben unterghen.* Even now, in our own country, correctness, fairness, and compromise for every small advantage are crowding out all other qualities. The higher heroisms and the old rare flavors are passing out of life.

With these thoughts in my mind, I was speeding with the train toward Buffalo, when, near that city, the sight of a workman doing something on the dizzy edge of a sky-scaling iron construction brought me to my senses very suddenly. And now I perceived, by a flash of insight, that I had been steeping myself in pure ancestral blindness, and looking at life with the eyes of a remote spectator. Wishing for heroism and the spectacle of human nature on the rack, I had never noticed the great fields of heroism lying around about me, I had failed to see it present and alive. I could only think of it as dead and embalmed, labelled and costumed, as it is in the pages of romance. And yet there it was before me in the daily lives of the laboring classes. Not in clanging fights and desperate marches only is heroism to be looked for, but on every railway bridge and fireproof building that is going up today. On freight trains, on the decks of vessels, the cattle yards and mines, on lumber rafts, among the firemen and the policemen, the demand for courage is incessant; and the supply never fails. There, every day of the year somewhere, is human nature *in extremis* for you. And wherever a scythe, an axe, a pick, or a shovel is wielded, you have it sweating and aching and with its powers of patient endurance racked to the utmost under the length of hours of the strain.

As I awoke to all this unidealized heroic life around me, the scales seemed to fall from my eyes; and a wave of sympathy greater than anything I had ever before felt with the common life of common men began to fill my soul. It began to seem as if virtue with horny hands and dirty skin were the only virtue genuine and vital enough to take account of. Every other virtue poses; none is absolutely unconscious and simple, and unexpectant of decoration or recognition, like this. These are our soldiers, thought I, these our sustainers, these the very parents of our life.

Many years ago, when in Vienna, I had had a similar feeling of awe and reverence in looking at the peasant women, in from the country on their business at the market for the day. Old hags many of them were, dried and brown and wrinkled, kerchiefed and short-petticoated, with thick wool stockings on their bony shanks, stumping through the glittering thoroughfares, looking neither to the right nor the left, bent on duty, envying nothing, humble-hearted, remote—and yet at bottom, when you came to think of it, bearing the whole fabric of the splendors and corruptions of that city on their laborious backs. For where would any of it have been without their unremitting, unrewarded labor in the fields? And so with us; not to our generals and poets, I thought, but to the Italian and Hungarian laborers in the subway, rather, ought the monuments of gratitude and reverence of a city like Boston to be reared.

If any of you have been readers of Tolstoi, you will see that I passed into a vein of feeling similar to his, with its abhorrence of all that conventionally passes for distinguished, and its exclusive deification of the bravery, patience, kindliness, and dumbness of the unconscious natural man.

Where now is *our* Tolstoi, I said, to bring the truth of all this home to our American bosoms, fill us with a better insight, and wean us away from that spurious literary romanticism on which our wretched culture—as it calls itself—is fed? Divinity lies all about us, and culture is too hide-bound to even suspect the fact. Could a Howells or a Kipling be enlisted in this mission? Or are they still too deep in the ancestral blindness, and not humane enough for the inner joy and meaning of the laborer's existence to be really revealed? Must we wait for some one born and bred and living as a laborer himself, but who, by grace of Heaven, shall also find a literary voice?

And there I rested on that day, with a sense of widening of vision, and with what is surely fair to call an increase of religious insight into life. In God's eyes the differences of social position, of intellect, of culture, of cleanliness, of dress, which different men exhibit, and all the other rarities and exceptions on which they so fantastically pin their pride, must be so small as practically quite to vanish; and all that should remain is the common fact that here we are, a countless multitude of vessels of life, each of us pent in to peculiar difficulties, with which we must severally struggle by using whatever of fortitude and goodness we can summon up. The exercise of the courage, patience, and kindness, must be the significant portion of the whole business; and the distinction of position can only be a manner of diversifying the phenomenal surface upon which these underground virtues may manifest their effects. At this rate, the deepest human life is everywhere, is eternal. And, if any human attributes exist only in particular individuals, they must belong to the mere trapping and decoration of the surface show.

Thus are men's lives leveled up as well as leveled down—leveled up in their common inner meaning, leveled down in their outer gloriousness and show. Yet always, we must confess, this leveling insight tends to be obscured again; and always the ancestral blindness returns and wraps us up, so that we end once more by thinking that creation can be for no other purpose than to develop remarkable situations and conventional distinctions and merits. And then always some new leveler in the shape of a religious prophet has to arise—the Buddha, the Christ, or some Saint Francis, some Rousseau or Tolstoi—to redispel our blindness. Yet, little by little, there comes some stable gain; for the world does get more humane, and the religion of democracy tends toward permanent increase.

This, as I said, became for a time my conviction, and gave me great content. I have put the matter into the form of a personal reminiscence, so that I might lead you into it more directly and completely, and so save time. But now I am going to discuss the rest of it with you in a more impersonal way.

Tolstoi's leveling philosophy began long before he had the crisis of melancholy commemorated in that wonderful document of his entitled *My Confession,* which led the way to his more specifically religious works. In his masterpiece *War and Peace*—assuredly the greatest of human novels—the role of the spiritual hero is given to a poor little soldier named Karataïeff, so helpful, so cheerful, and so devout that, in spite of his ignorance and filthiness, the sight of him opens the heavens, which have been closed, to the mind of the principal character of the book; and his example evidently is meant by Tolstoi to let God into the world again for the reader. Poor little Karataïeff is taken prisoner by the French; and, when too exhausted by hardship and fever to march, is shot as other prisoners were in the famous retreat from Moscow. The last view one gets of him is his little figure leaning against a white birch tree, and uncomplainingly awaiting the end.

"The more," writes Tolstoi in the work, *My Confession,*

> the more I examined the life of these laboring folks, the more persuaded I became that they veritably have faith, and get from it alone the sense and the possibility of life. . . . Contrariwise to those of our own class, who protest against destiny and grow indignant at its rigor, these people receive maladies and misfortunes without revolt, without opposition, and with a firm and tranquil confidence that all had to be like that, could not be otherwise, and that it is all right so. . . . The more we live by our intellect, the less we understand the meaning of life. We see only a cruel jest in suffering and death, whereas these people live, suffer, and draw near to death with tranquillity, and oftener than not with joy. . . . There are enormous multitudes of them happy with the most perfect happiness, although deprived of what for us is the sole good of life. Those who understand life's meaning, and know how to live and die thus, are to be counted not by twos, threes, tens, but by hundreds, thousands, millions. They labor quietly, endure privations and pains, live and die, and throughout everything see the good without seeing the vanity. I had to love these people. The more I entered into their life, the more I loved them; and the more it became possible for me to live, too. It came about not only that the life of our society, of the learned and of the rich, disgusted me—more than that, it lost all semblance of meaning in my eyes. All our actions, our deliberations, our sciences, our arts, all appeared to me with a new significance. I understood that these things might be charming pastimes, but that one need seek in them no depth, whereas the life of the hardworking populace, of that multitude of human beings who really contribute to existence, appeared to me in its true light. I understood that there veritably is life, that the meaning which life there receives is the truth; and I accepted it.

In a similar way does Stevenson appeal to our piety toward the elemental virtue of mankind.

> What a wonderful thing [he writes] is this Man! How surprising are his attributes! Poor soul, here for so little, cast among so many hardships, savagely surrounded, savagely descended, irremediably condemned to prey upon his fellow lives—who should have blamed him, had he been of a piece with his destiny and a being merely barbarous? . . . [Yet] it matters not where we look, under what climate we observe him, in what stage of society, in what depth of ignorance, burdened with what erroneous morality; in ships at sea, a man inured to hardship and vile pleasures, his brightest hope a

> fiddle in a tavern, and a bedizened trull who sells herself to rob him, and he, for all that, simple, innocent, cheerful, kindly like a child, constant to toil, brave to drown, for others; . . . in the slums of cities, moving among indifferent millions to mechanical employments, without hope of change in the future, with scarce a pleasure in the present, and yet true to his virtues, honest up to his lights, kind to his neighbors, tempted perhaps in vain by the bright gin-palace, . . . often repaying the world's scorn with service often standing firm upon a scruple; . . . everywhere some virtue cherished or affected, everywhere some decency of thought and courage, everywhere the ensign of man's ineffectual goodness—ah! if I could show you this! If I could show you these men and women all the world over, in every stage of history, under every abuse of error, under every circumstance of failure, without hope, without help, without thanks, still obscurely fighting the lost fight of virtue, still clinging to some rag of honor, the poor jewel of their souls.

All this is as true as it is splendid, and terribly do we need our Tolstois and Stevensons to keep our sense for it alive. Yet you remember the Irishman who, when asked, "Is not one man as good as another?" replied, "Yes; and a great deal better, too!" Similarly (it seems to me) does Tolstoi overcorrect our social prejudices, when he makes his love of the peasant so exclusive, and hardens his heart toward the educated man as absolutely as he does. Grant that at Chautauqua there was little moral effort, little sweat or muscular strain in view. Still, deep down in the souls of the participants we may be sure that something of the sort was hid, some inner stress, some vital virtue not found wanting when required. And, after all, the question recurs, and forces itself upon us: Is it so certain that the surroundings and circumstances of the virtue do make so little difference in the importance of the result? Is the functional utility, the worth to the universe of a certain definite amount of courage, kindliness, and patience, no greater if the possessor of these virtues is in an educated situation, working out far-reaching tasks, than if he be an illiterate nobody, hewing wood and drawing water just to keep himself alive? Tolstoi's philosophy, deeply enlightening though it certainly is, remains a false abstraction. It savors too much of that Oriental pessimism and nihilism of his, which declares the whole phenomenal world and its facts and their distinctions to be a cunning fraud.

A mere bare fraud is just what our Western common sense will never believe the phenomenal world to be. It admits fully that the inner joys and virtues are the *essential* part of life's business, but it is sure that *some* positive part is also played by the adjuncts of the show. If it is idiotic in romanticism to recognize the heroic only when it sees it labeled and dressed-up in books, it is really just as idiotic to see it only in the dirty boots and sweaty shirt of some one in the fields. It is with us really under every disguise: at Chautauqua; here in your college; in the stockyards and on the freight trains; and in the Czar of Russia's court. But, instinctively, we must make a combination of two things in judging the total significance of a human being. We feel it to be some sort of a product (if such a product only could be calculated) of his inner virtue *and* his outer place—neither singly taken, but both conjoined. If the outer differences had no meaning for life, why indeed should all this immense variety of them exist? They *must* be significant elements of the world as well.

Just test Tolstoi's deification of the mere manual laborer by the facts. This is what Mr. Walter Wyckoff, after working as an unskilled laborer in the demolition of some buildings at West Point, writes of the spiritual condition of the class of men to which he temporarily chose to belong:

> The salient features of our condition are plain enough. We are grown men, and are without a trade. In the labor market we stand ready to sell to the highest bidder our mere muscular strength for so many hours each day. We are thus in the lowest grade of labor. And, selling our muscular strength in the open market for what it will bring, we sell it under peculiar conditions. It is all the capital that we have. We have no reserve means of subsistence, and cannot, therefore, stand off for a "reserve price." We sell under the necessity of satisfying imminent hunger. Broadly speaking, we must sell our labor or starve; and, as hunger is a matter of a few hours, and we have no other way of meeting this need, we must sell at once for what the market offers for our labor.
>
> Our employer is buying labor in a dear market, and he will certainly get from us as much work as he can at the price. The gang-boss is secured for this purpose, and thoroughly does he know his business. He has sole command of us. He never saw us before, and he will discharge us all when the débris is cleared away. In the meantime he must get from us, if he can, the utmost physical labor which we, individually and collectively, are capable of. If he should drive some of us to exhaustion, and we should not be able to con-

> tinue at work, he would not be the loser; for the market would soon supply him with others to take our places.
>
> We are ignorant men, but so much we clearly see—that we have sold our labor where we could sell it dearest, and our employer has bought it where he could buy it cheapest. He has paid high, and he must get all the labor that he can; and, by a strong instinct which possesses us, we shall part with as little as we can. From work like ours there seems to us to have been eliminated every element which constitutes the nobility of labor. We feel no personal pride in its progress, and no community of interest with our employer. There is none of the joy of responsibility, none of the sense of achievement, only the dull monotony of grinding toil, with the longing for the signal to quit work, and for our wages at the end.
>
> And being what we are, the dregs of the labor market, and having no certainty of permanent employment, and no organization among ourselves, we must expect to work under the watchful eye of a gang-boss, and be driven, like the wage slaves that we are, through our task.
>
> All this is to tell us, in effect, that our lives are hard, barren, hopeless lives.

And such hard, barren, hopeless lives, surely, are not lives in which one ought to be willing permanently to remain. And why is this so? Is it because they are so dirty? Well, Nansen grew a great deal dirtier on his polar expedition; and we think none the worse of his life for that. Is it the insensibility? Our soldiers have to grow vastly more insensible, and we extol them to the skies. Is it the poverty? Poverty has been reckoned the crowning beauty of many a heroic career. Is it the slavery to a task, the loss of finer pleasures? Such slavery and loss are of the very essence of the higher fortitude, and are always counted to its credit—read the records of missionary devotion all over the world. It is not any one of these things, then, taken by itself—no, nor all of them together—that makes such a life undesirable. A man might in truth live like an unskilled laborer, and do the work of one, and yet count as one of the noblest of God's creatures. Quite possibly there were some such persons in the gang that our author describes; but the current of their souls ran underground; and he was too steeped in the ancestral blindness to discern it.

If there *were* any such morally exceptional individuals, however, what made them different from the rest? It can only have been this—that their souls worked and endured in obedience to some inner *ideal,* while their comrades were not actuated by anything worthy of that name. These ideals of other lives are among those secrets that we can almost never penetrate, although something about the man may often tell us when they are there. In Mr. Wyckoff's own case we know exactly what the self-imposed ideal was. Partly he had stumped himself, as the boys say, to carry through a strenuous achievement; but mainly he wished to enlarge his sympathetic insight into fellow lives. For this his sweat and toil acquire a certain heroic significance, and make us accord to him exceptional esteem. But it is easy to imagine his fellows with various other ideals. To say nothing of wives and babies, one may have been a convert of the Salvation Army, and had a nightingale singing of expiation and forgiveness in his heart all the while he labored. Or there might have been an apostle like Tolstoi himself, or his compatriot Bondareff, in the gang, voluntarily embracing labor as their religious mission. Class loyalty was undoubtedly an ideal with many. And who knows how much of that higher manliness of poverty, of which Phillips Brooks has spoken so penetratingly, was or was not present in that gang?

"A rugged, barren land," says Phillips Brooks,

> is poverty to live in—a land where I am thankful very often if I can get a berry or a root to eat. But living in it really, letting it bear witness to me of itself, not dishonoring it all the time by judging it after the standard of the other lands, gradually there come out its qualities. Behold! no land like this barren and naked land of poverty could show the moral geology of the world. See how the hard ribs . . . stand out strong and solid. No life like poverty could so get one to the heart of the things and make men know their meaning, could let us feel life and the world with all the soft cushions stripped off and thrown away. . . . Poverty makes men come very near each other, and recognize each other's human hearts; and poverty, highest and best of all, demands and cries out for faith in God. . . . I know how superficial and unfeeling, how like mere mockery, words in praise of poverty may seem. . . . But I am sure that the poor man's dignity and freedom, his self-respect and energy, depend upon his cordial knowledge that his poverty is a true region and kind of life, with its own chances of character, its own springs of happiness and revelations of God. Let him resist the characterlessness which often goes with being poor. Let him insist on respecting the condition where he lives. Let him learn to love it, so that by and by (if) he grows rich, he shall go out of the low door of the old familiar poverty with a true pang of regret, and with a true honor for the narrow home in which he has lived so long.

The barrenness and ignobleness of the more usual laborer's life consist in the fact that it is moved by no such ideal inner springs. The backache, the long hours, the danger, are patiently endured—for what? To gain a quid of tobacco, a glass of beer, a cup of coffee, a meal, and a bed, and to begin again the next day and shirk as much as one can. This really is why we raise no monument to the laborers in the subway, even though they be our conscripts, and even though after a fashion our city is indeed based upon their patient hearts and enduring backs and shoulders. And this is why we do raise monuments to our soldiers, whose outward conditions were even brutaler still. The soldiers are supposed to have followed an ideal, and the laborers are supposed to have followed none.

You see, my friends, how the plot now thickens; and how strangely the complexities of this wonderful human nature of ours begin to develop under our hands. We have seen the blindness and deafness to each other which are our natural inheritance; and, in spite of them, we have been led to acknowledge an inner meaning which passeth show, and which may be present in the lives of others where we least descry it. And now we are led to say that such inner meaning can be *complete* and *valid for us also,* only when the inner joy, courage, and endurance are joined with an ideal.

But what, exactly, do we mean by an ideal? Can we give no definite account of such a word?

To a certain extent we can. An ideal, for instance, must be something intellectually conceived, something of which we are not unconscious, if we have it; and it must carry with it that sort of outlook, uplift, and brightness that go with all intellectual facts. Secondly, there must be *novelty* in an ideal—novelty at least for him whom the ideal grasps. Sodden routine is incompatible with ideality, although what is sodden routine for one person may be ideal novelty for another. This shows that there is nothing absolutely ideal: ideals are relative to the lives that entertain them. To keep out of the gutter is for us here no part of consciousness at all, yet for many of our brethren it is the most legitimately engrossing of ideals.

Now, taken nakedly, abstractly, and immediately, you see that mere ideals are the cheapest things in life. Every body has them in some shape or other, personal or general, sound or mistaken, low or high; and the most worthless sentimentalists and dreamers, drunkards, shirks and verse-makers, who never show a grain of effort, courage, or endurance, possibly have them on the most copious scale. Education, enlarging as it does our horizon and perspective, is a means of multiplying our ideals, of bringing new ones into view. And your college professor, with a starched shirt and spectacles, would, if a stock of ideals were all alone by itself enough to render a life significant, be the most absolutely and deeply significant of men. Tolstoi would be completely blind in despising him for a prig, a pedant and a parody; and all our new insight into the divinity of muscular labor would be altogether off the track of truth.

But such consequences as this, you instinctively feel, are erroneous. The more ideals a man has, the more contemptible, on the whole, do you continue to deem him, if the matter ends there for him, and if none of the laboring man's virtues are called into action on his part—no courage shown, no privations undergone, no dirt or scars contracted in the attempt to get them realized. It is quite obvious that something more than the mere possession of ideals is required to make a life significant in any sense that claims the spectator's admiration. Inner joy, to be sure, it may *have,* with our own ideals; but that is its own private sentimental matter. To extort from us, outsiders as we are, with our own ideals to look after, the tribute of our grudging recognition, it must back its ideal visions with what the laborers have, the sterner stuff of manly virtue; it must multiply their sentimental surface by the dimension of the active will, if we are to have *depth,* if we are to have anything cubical and solid in the way of character.

The significance of a human life for communicable and publicly recognizable purposes is thus the offspring of a marriage of two different parents, either of whom alone is barren. The ideals taken by themselves give no reality, the virtues by themselves no novelty. And let the orientalists and pessimists say what they will, the thing of deepest—or, at any rate, of comparatively deepest—significance in life does seem to be its character of *progress,* or that strange union of reality with ideal novelty which it continues from one moment to another to present. To recognize ideal novelty is the task of what we call intelligence. Not every one's intelligence can tell which novelties are ideal. For many the ideal thing will always seem to cling still to the older more familiar good. In this case character, though not significant totally, may be still significant pathetically. So, if we are to choose which is the more essential factor of human character, the fighting virtue or the intellectual breadth, we must side with Tolstoi and choose that simple faithfulness to his light or darkness which any common unintellectual man can show.

But, with all this beating and tacking on my part, I fear you take me to be reaching a confused result. I seem to be just taking things up and dropping them again. First I took up Chautauqua, and dropped that; then Tolstoi and the heroism of common toil, and dropped them; finally, I took up ideals, and seem now almost dropping those. But please observe in what sense it is that I drop them. It is when they pretend *singly* to redeem life from insignificance. Culture and refinement all alone are not enough to do so. Ideal aspirations are not enough, when uncombined with pluck and will. But neither are pluck and will, dogged endurance and insensibility to danger enough, when taken all alone. There must be some sort of fusion, some chemical combination among these principles, for a life objectively and thoroughly significant to result.

Of course, this is a somewhat vague conclusion. But in a question of significance, of worth, like this, conclusions can never be precise. The answer of appreciation, of sentiment, is always a more or a less, a balance struck by sympathy, insight, and good will. But it is an answer, all the same, a real conclusion. And, in the course of getting it, it seems to me that our eyes have been opened to many important things. Some of you are, perhaps, more livingly aware than you were an hour ago of the depths of worth that lie around you, hid in alien lives. And, when you ask how much sympathy you ought to bestow, although the amount is, truly enough, a matter of ideal on your own part, yet in this notion of the combination of ideals with active virtues you have a rough standard for shaping your decision. In any case, your imagination is extended. You divine in the world about you matter for a little more humility on your own part, and tolerance, reverence, and love for others; and you gain a certain inner joyfulness at the increased importance of our common life. Such joyfulness is a religious inspiration and an element of spiritual health, and worth more than large amounts of that sort of technical and accurate information which we professors are supposed to be able to impart.

To show the sort of thing I mean by these words, I will just make one brief practical illustration, and then close.

We are suffering today in America from what is called the labor question; and, when you go out into the world, you will each and all of you be caught up in its perplexities. I use the brief term labor question to cover all sorts of anarchistic discontents and socialistic projects, and the conservative resistances which they provoke. So far as this conflict is unhealthy and regrettable—and I think it is so only to a limited extent—the unhealthiness consists solely in the fact that one-half of our fellow-countrymen remain entirely blind to the internal significance of the lives of the other half. They miss the joys and sorrows, they fail to feel the moral virtue, and they do not guess the presence of the intellectual ideals. They are at cross-purposes all along the line, regarding each other as they might regard a set of dangerously gesticulating automata, or, if they seek to get at the inner motivation, making the most horrible mistakes. Often all that the poor man can think of in the rich man is a cowardly greediness for safety, luxury, and effeminacy, and a boundless affectation. What he is, is not a human being, but a pocketbook, a bank account. And a similar greediness, turned by disappointment into envy, is all that many rich men can see in the state of mind of the dissatisfied poor. And, if the rich man begins to do the sentimental act over the poor man, what senseless blunders does he make, pitying him for just those very duties and those very immunities which, rightly taken, are the condition of his most abiding and characteristic joys! Each, in short, ignores the fact that happiness and unhappiness and significance are a vital mystery; each pins them absolutely on some ridiculous feature of the external situation; and everybody remains outside of everybody else's right.

Society has, with all this, undoubtedly got to pass toward some newer and better equilibrium, and the distribution of wealth has doubtless slowly got to change: such changes have always happened, and will happen to the end of time. But if, after all that I have said, any of you expect that they will make any *genuine vital difference* on a large scale, to the lives of our descendants, you will have missed the significance of my entire lecture. The solid meaning of life is always the same eternal thing—the marriage, namely, of some unhabitual ideal, however special, with some fidelity, courage, and endurance; with some man's or woman's pains. And, whatever or wherever life may be, there will always be the chance for that marriage to take place.

Fitz-James Stephen wrote many years ago to this effect more eloquent than any I can speak: "The 'Great Eastern,' or some of her successors," he said,

> will perhaps defy the roll of the Atlantic, and cross the seas without allowing their passengers to feel that they have left the firm land. The voyage from the cradle to the grave may come to be performed with similar facility. Progress and science may perhaps enable untold millions to live and die without a care, without a pang, without an anxiety. They will have a pleasant passage and plenty of brilliant conversation. They will wonder that men ever believed at all in clanging fights and blazing towns and sinking ships and praying hands; and, when they come to the end of their course, they will go their way, and the place thereof will know them no more. But it seems unlikely that they will have such a knowledge of the great ocean on which they sail, with its storms and wrecks, its currents and icebergs, its huge waves and mighty winds, as those who battled with it for years together in the little craft, which, if they had few other merits, brought those who navigated them full into the presence of time and eternity, their maker and themselves, and forced them to have some definite view of their relations to them and to each other.

In this solid and tridimensional sense, so to call it, those philosophers are right who contend that the world is a standing thing, with no progress, no real history. The changing conditions of history touch only the surface of the show. The altered equilibriums and redistributions only diversify our opportunities and open new chances for us for new ideals. But, with each new ideal that comes into life, the chance for a life based on some old ideal will vanish; and he would needs be a presumptuous calculator who should with confidence say that the total sum of significances is positively and absolutely greater at any one epoch than at any other of the world.

I am speaking broadly, I know, and omitting to consider certain qualifications in which I myself believe. But one can only make one point in one lecture, and I shall be well content if I have brought my point home to you this evening in even a slight degree. *There are compensations:* and no outward changes in condition in life can keep the nightingale of its eternal meaning from singing in all sorts of different men's hearts. That is the main fact to remember. If we could not only admit it with our lips, but really and truly believe it, how our convulsive insistencies, how our antipathies and dreads of each other, would soften down! If the poor and the rich could look at each other in this way, *sub specie aeternatis,* how gentle would grow their disputes! What tolerance and good humor, what willingness to live and let live, would come into the world!

TOPICS FOR DISCUSSION AND WRITING

1. James attacks dogmatism, argues for universal concern for the affairs of others, criticizes disengagement and aloofness, and extols the "unconscious natural man." Why is his familiar style particularly apt in such a context? Is his style appropriate to subject or audience or both?
2. Why does James reject the kind of life he found at Chautauqua Lake? How would he react to contemporary American society if he were able to observe it at this moment?
3. Why does James, after first praising Tolstoi, go on to refer to his philosophy as "a false abstraction"? What is the balance which should be struck between Chautauqua and Tolstoi?
4. What does James mean when he says: "The significance of a human life for communicable and publicly recognizable purposes is thus the offspring of a marriage of two different parents, either of whom alone is barren"?
5. Do you find that James's idea of what makes a life significant has anything in common with the attitudes of any other authors in this collection?
6. Write an essay in which you make a close stylistic analysis of the essays by Hazlitt and William James, pointing out the unique use which each makes of the characteristic features of the familiar style.